AIR POLLUTION
LAW AND REGULATION

AIR POLLUTION
LAW AND REGULATION

David Hughes
Professor of Housing and Planning Law
De Montfort University

Neil Parpworth
Lecturer in Law
De Montfort University

Joan Upson
Senior Lecturer in Law
De Montfort University

JORDANS
1998

Published by
Jordan Publishing Limited
21 St Thomas Street
Bristol BS1 6JS

British Library Cataloguing-in-Publication Data

A catalogue record for this book is available from the British Library.

ISBN 0 85308 489 0

Photoset by Mendip Communications Ltd, Frome
Printed in Great Britain by MPG Books Ltd, Bodmin, Cornwall

ACKNOWLEDGEMENTS

In Chapter 9, SI 1986/1078, reg 61, Table II (amended) and SI 1992/3107, reg 13 are reproduced with the permission of the controller of The Stationery Office Limited.

PREFACE

Much has been written in the last 15 years or so by way of general – indeed even encyclopaedic – works on environmental law, and the time is now ripe for the emergence of monographic works on particular issues in environmental protection. We have focused on an area which has, perhaps, not been so well researched and commented on as others in the environmental sphere. Water, land, plants, animals and buildings are tangible and they excite the sympathies of people concerned to ensure that they are conserved. The atmosphere, on the other hand, is intangible, easily ignored – yet equally easily damaged. Our hope is that this book gives its readers a sound theoretical understanding of the legal measures which are belatedly being put in place to protect the precious asset of the air, and also sound practical advice on the use and implementation of those measures.

With such a rapidly developing area of legal activity, new developments occurred in Europe, at Westminster and Whitehall and in the courts all the way through this work's gestation. We are therefore most grateful to our publishers not only for giving us the chance to undertake this book, but also for their kindness in allowing us to incorporate new material bringing our statement of law and practice up to date to July 1998.

David Hughes
Neil Parpworth
Joan Upson
September 1998

CONTENTS

			Page
Acknowledgements			v
Preface			vii
Table of Cases			xxi
Table of Statutes			xxxiii
Table of Statutory Instruments			xxxix
Table of Codes, Guidance Notes etc			xlv
Table of EC Material			xlvii
Table of International Law Materials and Conventions			li
Table of Abbreviations			liii
Chapter 1	**THE EC DIMENSION – LEGISLATION AND INSTITUTIONS**		1
	1.1	INTRODUCTION	1
		1.1.1 Post-war Europe	1
		1.1.2 The Treaty of Rome	2
		1.1.3 The coming of an environmental agenda	3
	1.2	EC ENVIRONMENTAL POLICY	5
	1.3	EUROPEAN ENVIRONMENT AGENCY	7
	1.4	SOURCES OF EC LAW	8
		1.4.1 The Treaty	8
		1.4.2 Title XVI – Environment	9
		1.4.3 *Danish Bottles* case	10
		1.4.4 *Wallonian Waste* case	12
	1.5	SECONDARY LEGISLATION	13
		1.5.1 Regulations	14
		1.5.2 Directives	15
		1.5.3 Decisions	16
		1.5.4 Recommendations and opinions	17
	1.6	GENERAL PRINCIPLES	17
		1.6.1 Sustainable development	19
		1.6.2 The 'polluter pays' principle	20
		1.6.3 The precautionary principle	20
		1.6.4 Rectification at source	21
		1.6.5 Subsidiarity	21
		1.6.6 Proportionality	23
	1.7	JUDICIAL REVIEW	23
		1.7.1 Locus standi	25

1.8	THE INSTITUTIONS		25
	1.8.1	The Commission	26
	1.8.2	The Council of the European Union	27
		The function of the Council	28
		Decision-making	29
	1.8.3	The European Council	29
	1.8.4	COREPER – Comité des Représentants Permanents	29
	1.8.5	The European Parliament	30
1.9	THE EUROPEAN COURT OF JUSTICE		30
	1.9.1	The Court of First Instance	32
	1.9.2	Article 177 references	32
1.10	DIRECT EFFECT		35
	1.10.1	*Van Gend en Loos*	36
	1.10.1	The *Marshall* case	38
1.11	DUTY OF INTERPRETATION – *VON COLSON*		39
1.12	STATE LIABILITY		41

Chapter 2	**THE EC DIMENSION – SPECIFIC PROTECTION**			43
	2.1	ENFORCEMENT		43
		2.1.1	Background	43
		2.1.2	The reasoned opinion	44
	2.2	SUBSTANTIVE PROVISIONS		46
	2.3	AIR POLLUTION FROM INDUSTRIAL PLANT		47
		2.3.1	Directive 88/609/EEC	49
	2.4	MUNICIPAL WASTE INCINERATORS		50
		2.4.1	Directive 89/429/EEC	51
		2.4.2	Directive 94/67/EC: Hazardous waste incineration	51
	2.5	AIR QUALITY LIMIT VALUES/GUIDE LEVELS FOR SULPHUR DIOXIDE AND SMOKE		52
		2.5.1	Directive 93/12: Sulphur content of fuels	53
		2.5.2	Directive 85/203	53
	2.6	NEW AIR QUALITY FRAMEWORK DIRECTIVE 96/62		54
	2.7	LEAD		54
		2.7.1	Directive 82/884: Lead in air	55
		2.7.2	Directive 85/210: Lead content of petrol	55
	2.8	INFORMATION AND RESEARCH		56
		2.8.1	Regulation 3528/86: Forest damage	57
		2.8.2	Decision 97/101: Reciprocal exchange of information	58
		2.8.3	Directive 92/72: Ozone pollution	58
	2.9	INTERNATIONAL OBLIGATIONS		59
		2.9.1	Regulation 3093/94: Ozone depletion	59

		2.9.2	Directive 94/63/EC: Volatile organic compounds	61
	2.10	A NEW AGE OF EC CONTROL		62
Chapter 3	**INTERNATIONAL LAW**			67
	3.1	INTRODUCTION		67
	3.2	SOURCES		68
		3.2.1	Introduction	68
		3.2.2	Treaty	69
		3.2.3	Custom	71
		3.2.4	General principles	73
			Sustainable development	74
			Preventative/precautionary principle	74
		3.2.5	'The teachings of the most highly qualified publicists of the various nations'	76
		3.2.6	Judicial/arbitral tribunals	76
	3.3	EC POSITION IN THE INTERNATIONAL ARENA		77
	3.4	TRANSBOUNDARY POLLUTION		78
		3.4.1	Geneva Convention on Long-Range Transboundary Air Pollution 1979	80
		3.4.2	Protocols	81
	3.5	GLOBAL CONCERNS		82
		3.5.1	Customary law	83
		3.5.2	Vienna Convention for the Protection of the Ozone Layer 1985	83
		3.5.3	Montreal Protocol 1987	84
	3.6	CLIMATE CHANGE		86
		3.6.1	Global Climate Change Convention 1994	87
	3.7	BEYOND RIO		89
	3.8	KYOTO PROTOCOL		91
		3.8.1	Emission trading	92
			'Bubble' concept	92
			'Banking' concept	93
		3.8.2	Carbon mitigation schemes	94
Chapter 4	**COMMON LAW REMEDIES**			97
	4.1	INTRODUCTION		97
	4.2	PUBLIC NUISANCE		97
	4.3	PRIVATE NUISANCE		99
		4.3.1	For what is a remedy available?	99
		4.3.2	'Give and take'	99
		4.3.3	State of mind	100
		4.3.4	Proving the nuisance	101
		4.3.5	Who may sue?	103
		4.3.6	Who can be sued?	104
		4.3.7	Position of landlords	105
		4.3.8	For what damage is the defendant liable?	105

4.4 DEFENCES 107
4.4.1 Prescription 107
4.4.2 Statutory authority 108
4.4.3 Effect of a grant of planning permission 109
4.4.4 Ineffectual defences 109
4.5 REMEDIES 110
4.5.1 Damages 110
4.5.2 Injunctions 111
4.5.3 Self-help 113
4.6 STRICT LIABILITY 114
4.6.1 The rule in *Rylands v Fletcher* 114
4.6.2 Damage suffered is not of a type contemplated by the rule 116
4.6.3 Consent 118
4.6.4 Common benefit 118
4.6.5 Act of a stranger 118
4.6.6 Act of God 119
4.6.7 Statutory authority 119
4.6.8 Damage too remote 119
4.7 STATUTORY LIABILITY 119
4.8 NEGLIGENCE LIABILITY 120
4.8.1 Duty of care 121
4.8.2 Breach of duty 122

Chapter 5 **STATUTORY NUISANCES AND STUBBLE BURNING** 127
5.1 INTRODUCTION 127
5.2 THE CURRENT LAW 128
5.2.1 Exclusions 128
5.2.2 The realm of statutory nuisances 129
5.3 PROCEDURE 131
5.3.1 Local authority procedures: Environmental Protection Act 1990 131
5.3.2 Local authority procedures: Abatement notices 132
5.3.3 Local authority procedures: grounds for appeal 133
5.3.4 Defences and offences 134
'Best practicable means' 135
'Reasonable excuse' 136
No lawful requirement? 136
5.3.5 Supplementary provisions 137
5.3.6 Proceedings in the High Court 138
5.3.7 Procedures available to private citizens 140
5.3.8 'Person aggrieved' 142
5.3.9 Content of magistrates' orders 143
5.4 STUBBLE BURNING 143
5.4.1 The current law 144

Chapter 6 **INTEGRATED POLLUTION CONTROL** 147
6.1 INTRODUCTION 147
6.1.1 Environmental Protection Act 1990 149
6.2 PRESCRIBED PROCESSES AND PRESCRIBED SUBSTANCES 150
6.2.1 Part 'A' list processes 150
6.2.2 Interpretation of Sch 1 to the Environmental Protection (Prescribed Processes and Substances) Regulations 1991 153
6.2.3 Exemptions 153
6.2.4 Prescribed substances 154
6.3 AUTHORISATIONS 155
6.3.1 Applying for an authorisation 155
6.3.2 Granting an authorisation 158
6.4 BATNEEC 159
6.4.1 New processes 160
6.4.2 Existing processes 160
6.5 BPEO 161
6.5.1 Origins and background 161
6.5.2 Meaning 162
6.5.3 Determining BPEO 163
6.5.4 Defining the objective of BPEO 164
6.5.5 Generating options for achieving the objective of BPEO 165
6.5.6 Assessing the options of BPEO 166
6.5.7 Summarising and presenting the assessment of BPEO 167
6.5.8 Identifying BPEO 167
6.5.9 Reviewing BPEO 168
6.5.10 BATNEEC and BPEO in practice 169
6.6 GUIDANCE 170
6.6.1 Industry sector guidance notes 170
6.6.2 Process-specific guidance notes 170
6.6.3 Technical guidance notes 171
6.7 MONITORING 171
6.8 AUTHORISATION APPLICATION FEES 172
6.9 TRANSFER OF AUTHORISATIONS 174
6.10 VARIATION NOTICES 175
6.11 REVOCATION NOTICES 177
6.12 ENFORCEMENT NOTICES 177
6.12.1 Questioning the validity of an enforcement notice 179
6.13 PROHIBITION NOTICES 181
6.14 GENERAL ENFORCEMENT ISSUES 183
6.15 APPEALS 184
6.15.1 Status of an appealed decision 187
6.15.2 The appeal process 187

	6.15.3	Written representations	188
	6.15.4	Hearings	188
	6.15.5	Determination of an appeal	189
	6.15.6	Appeals: a critique	191
6.16	GENERAL POWERS OF ENTRY		192
	6.16.1	Limitations to powers of entry	193
	6.16.2	Powers of seizure	194
6.17	OBTAINING INFORMATION		194
6.18	ENVIRONMENTAL INFORMATION – PUBLICITY		195
6.19	PUBLIC REGISTERS OF INFORMATION		196
	6.19.1	Type of information to be recorded on register	196
	6.19.2	Removal of information	198
	6.19.3	Public accessibility	199
6.20	INFORMATION EXCLUDED FROM REGISTERS		199
	6.20.1	Information affecting national security	199
	6.20.2	Commercially confidential information	200
6.21	CHEMICAL RELEASE INVENTORY		202
6.22	ENFORCEMENT BY THE HIGH COURT AND OTHER COURTS		204
6.23	POWER OF THE AGENCY TO REMEDY HARM		205
6.24	IPC/PLANNING INTERFACE		205
6.25	IPC IN PRACTICE		208
6.26	THE FUTURE OF IPC		210
	6.26.1	Scope of the IPPC Directive	210
	6.26.2	Meaning of a 'permit'	211
	6.26.3	Obtaining a permit	211
	6.26.4	Conclusions	212

Chapter 7	**LOCAL AUTHORITY AIR POLLUTION CONTROL**		215
7.1	INTRODUCTION		215
	7.1.1	Royal Commission on Environmental Pollution	215
7.2	PRESCRIBED PROCESSES AND PRESCRIBED SUBSTANCES		218
	7.2.1	Part 'B' list processes	218
	7.2.2	Interpretation of Sch 1 to the Environmental Protection (Prescribed Processes and Substances) Regulations 1991	221
	7.2.3	Exceptions	221
7.3	DEREGULATION		222
	7.3.1	Prescribed substances	222

7.4 AUTHORISATIONS 222
7.4.1 Applications for authorisation: the local authority decision 225
7.4.2 The *Compton* decision 225
7.4.3 Recent developments 228
7.5 BATNEC AND BPEO 230
7.6 FEES AND CHARGES FOR LAAPC AUTHORISATIONS 230
7.7 GUIDANCE 233
7.7.1 Process guidance notes 233
7.7.2 General guidance notes 234
7.7.3 Upgrading guidance notes 235
7.7.4 Additional guidance notes 235
7.8 TRANSFER OF AUTHORISATIONS 236
7.9 VARIATION NOTICES 236
7.10 REVOCATION NOTICES 236
7.11 ENFORCEMENT NOTICES 237
7.12 PROHIBITION NOTICES 238
7.13 APPEALS 238
7.14 GENERAL POWERS OF ENTRY 240
7.15 OBTAINING INFORMATION 241
7.16 PUBLIC REGISTERS OF INFORMATION 241
7.17 JUDICIAL ENFORCEMENT 242
7.18 LAAPC IN PRACTICE 243
7.19 LAAPC/PLANNING INTERFACE 244
7.20 THE FUTURE FOR LAAPC 244
7.20.1 NAQS and LAAPC 245
7.20.2 IPC and LAAPC 245
7.20.3 CPC and LAAPC 246
7.20.4 The consultation paper 246

Chapter 8 **CLEAN AIR LEGISLATION** 249
8.1 HISTORY 249
8.1.1 The great smog and its aftermath 249
8.2 PROHIBITION OF DARK SMOKE EMISSIONS 250
8.2.1 Definitions 251
8.2.2 Trade premises 252
8.3 SMOKE, GRIT, DUST AND FUMES 254
8.3.1 Installation of furnaces 254
8.3.2 Grit and dust controls 255
8.3.3 Arrestment plant for non-domestic furnaces over specified sizes 256
8.3.4 Arrestment plant for specified types of domestic furnace 257
8.3.5 Appeals 257
8.3.6 Measurement of grit and dust 257
8.3.7 Information on furnaces 258

8.4	HEIGHT OF CHIMNEYS		259
	8.4.1	Furnace chimneys	259
	8.4.2	Obtaining approval	259
	8.4.3	Other chimneys	261
8.5	SMOKE CONTROL AREAS		262
	8.5.1	Declaration by local authorities	262
	8.5.2	Prohibitions in smoke control areas	264
	8.5.3	Unauthorised fuel	265
	8.5.4	Adapting fireplaces	265
8.6	ASSESSMENT OF THE EFFECTS OF THE CLEAN AIR ACT PROVISIONS		266
8.7	SPECIAL CASES		267
	8.7.1	Relationship of the 1993 Act powers with those under the Environmental Protection Act 1990	267
	8.7.2	Colliery spoil banks	267
	8.7.3	Railway engines	267
	8.7.4	Vessels	268
	8.7.5	Crown premises and ships	269
	8.7.6	Exemptions	269
	8.7.7	Fumes and gases	270
8.8	ADMINISTRATION AND ENFORCEMENT		270
	8.8.1	Cumulative penalties	270
	8.8.2	Notification to occupiers	271
	8.8.3	Offences by companies	271
	8.8.4	Authorisation of works	271
	8.8.5	General enforcement functions	272
8.9	FUNCTIONS OF THE SECRETARY OF STATE – DEFAULT AND OTHER POWERS		273
8.10	CLEAN AIR LEGISLATION AND UK EUROPEAN OBLIGATIONS		274

Chapter 9	**ATMOSPHERIC POLLUTION AND MOTOR VEHICLES**		277
9.1	INTRODUCTION		277
9.2	THE PROBLEM AND ITS CAUSES		278
9.3	FUEL COMPOSITION STANDARDS		279
9.4	REGULATIONS		280
	9.4.1	Sulphur content of gas oil	282
9.5	VEHICLE CONSTRUCTION STANDARDS		282
9.6	DEVELOPMENT OF EC REQUIREMENTS		283
9.7	VOLATILE ORGANIC COMPOUNDS		286
9.8	STATUTORY BASIS FOR VEHICLE EMISSION CONTROL		287
	9.8.1	Regular testing of vehicles	288
	9.8.2	Provisions with regard to goods vehicles	289
	9.8.3	Type approval	289

9.8.4 Other supplementary provisions 290
9.8.5 Vehicle examination 291
9.8.6 Miscellaneous 292
9.9 THE DETAILED REGULATORY FRAMEWORK 293
9.9.1 Type approval regulations 298
9.9.2 Stopping engines of stationary vehicles 300

Chapter 10 **AIR QUALITY** 303
10.1 INTRODUTION 303
10.1.1 The air we breathe and our health 303
10.1.2 The legislative basis for a National Air Quality Strategy 304
10.1.3 Road traffic reduction legislation 306
10.2 EUROPEAN AIR QUALITY ISSUES 306
10.3 EUROPE – THE FUTURE 309
10.4 INFORMATION ON AIR POLLUTION 311
10.4.1 The general research and publicity power 311
10.4.2 Supplementary powers 312
10.4.3 Requiring information 312
10.4.4 Appeals 313
10.4.5 Further powers and duties of the Secretary of State 314
10.5 MISCELLANEOUS ISSUES 316
10.6 INFORMATION ABOUT AIR POLLUTION – THE PRACTICE 316
10.6.1 Emissions inventories 317
10.6.2 Pollution forecasts 317
10.7 THE NATIONAL AIR QUALITY STRATEGY 318
10.7.1 EPAQS and COMEAP recommendations 319
10.7.2 The Government's response 320
10.8 THE LEGISLATIVE SKELETON OF THE NATIONAL AIR QUALITY STRATEGY 322
10.8.1 Duties of the Secretary of State, the Environmental Agencies and Scottish Environmental Protection Agency 322
10.8.2 Obligations of local authorities 323
10.8.3 Local authority functions – supplementary provisions 324
10.8.4 Supplementary powers of the Secretary of State 325
10.8.5 Powers to make regulations 326
10.8.6 Fixed penalty offences 327
10.8.7 Supplementary development of air quality policy in practice 328
10.8.8 Responses to the draft NAQS 329
10.8.9 Existing legislation 330

	10.8.10	Approaches to local implementation	332
		A phased approach	332
		A step-by-step approach	332
		A timed approach	333
		A flexible approach	333
	10.8.11	Duties once the AQMA is designated	333
	10.8.12	The special role of county councils	335
	10.8.13	The draft air quality regulations	335
		'The relevant period'	336
		Air quality objectives	336
10.9	AN INTERIM ASSESSMENT		337
	10.9.1	Subsequent developments	337
10.10	RELEASE OF THE NAQS		339
	10.10.1	Features of the NAQS	339
	10.10.2	Policy background	340
	10.10.3	Standards and objectives	341
	10.10.4	Further explanation	343
	10.10.5	A controversial issue	343
	10.10.6	Possible future standards	343
10.11	ACHIEVING THE OBJECTIVES: THE NATIONAL PATTERN		343
	10.11.1	Nitrogen dioxide and other nitrogen oxides	344
	10.11.2	Ozone	344
	10.11.3	Particles	345
	10.11.4	Sulphur dioxide	345
10.12	ACHIEVING THE NAQS: SECTORAL CONTRIBUTIONS		346
	10.12.1	Contribution of business and industry	346
	10.12.2	Contribution of transport	349
	10.12.3	Achieving policy	349
	10.12.4	Other transport sectors	350
	10.12.5	Contribution of local authorities	351
	10.12.6	Two inescapable principles for authorities	352
	10.12.7	Relating local air quality powers to other functions	352
		Planning	352
		Smoke controls	353
		Transport planning	353
		Urban environmental management	353
	10.12.8	The role of individuals, commerce and industry	353
10.13	AFTER THE NAQS		354
	10.13.1	The Labour Government and the NAQS	354
	10.13.2	Green transport initiatives	355
	10.13.3	Reiteration of the air quality objectives	357
	10.13.4	Emission Factor Database	357

10.14 GENERAL GUIDANCE 358
10.14.1 The first stage – compilation of information 359
10.14.2 The second stage – further screening 360
10.14.3 The third stage – the detailed review 361
10.14.4 Designating an AQMA 361
10.14.5 The action plan 362
10.14.6 Consultative requirements 362
Consultation with county councils 363
10.15 DEVELOPING LOCAL AIR QUALITY ACTION PLANS AND STRATEGIES 364
10.15.1 Local air quality strategies 364
10.15.2 Action plans for AQMAs 364
10.16 AIR QUALITY AND TRAFFIC MANAGEMENT 365
10.16.1 Aims and objectives 366
10.16.2 Considerations and principal features 366
10.17 AIR QUALITY AND LAND USE PLANNING 367
10.18 FURTHER DEVELOPMENTS IN LATE 1997 368
10.18.1 Fixed penalties offences 368
10.18.2 Further likely developments 370
10.19 THE PROBLEMS 371

Index 373

TABLE OF CASES

References are to paragraph numbers.

Table of common sources: AC (Appeal Cases); All ER (All England Reports); All ER Rep (All England Law Reports (Reprint)); App Cas (Appeal Cases); BCC (British Company Law Reports); BLR (Business Law Review); Ch (Chancery Law Reports); Ch App (Chancery Appeals); ChD (Chancery Division); CMLR (Common Market Law Reports); CML Rev (Common Market Law Review); COD (Crown Office Digest); Const LJ (Construction Law Journal); Co Rep (Coke's Reports); CP (Comon Pleas); Crim LR (Criminal Law Review); DeG & Sm (De Gex & Smithson); DLR (Dominion Law Reports); ECR (European Court Reports); EG (Estates Gazette); EGCS (Estates Gazettes Case Summaries); EHLR (Environmental Health Law Reports); EHRR (European Human Rights Reports); ELM (Environmental Law and Management); ENDS Report (Environmental News Data Services Report); Env LR (Environmental Law Reports); ER (English Reports); Exch (Exchequer); ExD (Exchequer Division); H&C (Hurlestone & Coltman); HL Cas (House of Lords Cases); HLR (Housing Law Reports); ICR (Industrial Cases Reports); IRLR (Industrial Relations Law Reports); JC (Judiciary Cases); JEL (Journal of Environmental Law); JP (Justice of the Peace Reports); JPL (Journal of Planning and Environmental Law); JPN (Justice of the Peace Journal); KB (King's Bench); LGR (Local Government Reports); LG Rev (Local Government Review); LJ (Law Journal Newspaper); LJCh (Law Journal Chancery); LJKB (Law Journal King's Bench); LJPC (Law Journal Privy Council); LJQB (Law Journal Queen's Bench); LJR (Law Journal Reports); LMELR (Land Management and Environmental Law Report); LR (Law Reports); LS Gaz (Law Society's Gazette); LT (Law Times); M&W (Meeson & Welsby); NLJ (New Law Journal); NPC (New Property Cases); NZLR (New Zealand Law Reports); P&CR (Property and Compensation Reports); PIQR (Personal Injuries and Quantum Reports); PLCR (Planning Law Case Reports); QB (Queen's Bench); RRC (Ryde's Rating Cases); RTR (Road Traffic Reports); SCCR (Scottish Criminal Cases Reports); SJ (Solicitors Journal); SLT (Scots Law Times); TLR (Times Law Reports); Ves Sen (Vesey Senior); WLR (Weekly Law Reports); WN (Weekly Notes (Law Reports)).

AMEC Building Ltd v London Borough of Camden [1997] Env LR 330 5.3.1, 5.3.2
Adams v Ursell [1913] ChD 269 4.4.4
Administrazioni delle Finanze dello Stato v Essevi and Salongo (Cases 142, 143/80) [1981] ECR 1413, ECJ 2.1.2
Aldred's Case (1610) 9 Co Rep 576, 58a, 77 ER 816, [1558–1774] All ER Rep 622 4.3.3
Allen v Gulf Oil Refining Co Ltd [1981] AC 101, [1981] 2 WLR 188, [1981] 1 All ER 353, HL 4.4.2
Alphacell v Woodward [1972] AC 824, [1972] 2 WLR 1320, [1972] 2 All ER 475, HL 8.2.2
American Cyanamid Co v Ethicon Ltd [1975] AC 396, [1975] 2 WLR 316, [1975] 1 All ER 504, HL 4.5.2
Andrews v HE Kershaw [1922] 1 KB 70 9.8
Arbitration between the Mayor, Aldermen, and Burgesses of the Borough of Willesden and Municipal Mutual Insurance [1944] 2 All ER 600 8.3.1
Armitage Ltd v Nicholson (1913) 108 LT 993, 11 LGR 547, 77 JP 239 5.3.4
Atkinson v Newcastle Waterworks Co (1877) 2 ExD 441 4.7
Attorney General v Cory Brothers and Co Ltd [1921] 1 AC 521, 19 LGR 145, 90 LJ Ch 221, HL 4.6.3

Attorney General v Doughty (1752) 2 Ves Sen 453 4.3.3
Attorney General v Gastonia Coaches [1977] RTR 219 4.5.2
Attorney General v Keyner Brick and Tile Co Ltd (1903) 67 JP 434, 1 LGR 654 4.2
Attorney General v PYA Quarries Ltd [1957] 2 QB 169, [1957] 2 WLR 770; *sub nom* Attorney General (on the relation of Glamorgan County Council and Pontardawe RDC) v PYA Quarries Ltd [1957] 1 All ER 894, CA 4.2, 5.1
Attorney General (Gambia) v N'Jie [1961] AC 617, [1961] 2 WLR 845, [1961] 2 All ER 504, PC 5.3.8
Aviation and Shipping Co v Murray [1961] 1 WLR 974, [1961] 2 All ER 805, 105 SJ 441, CA 5.2.2

Bacup Corporation v Smith (1890) 44 ChD 395 5.3.2
Bainbridge v Chertsey Urban District Council (1914) LJ Ch 626, 13 LGR 935, 79 JP 134 4.3.3
Barnes v Irwell Water Board [1939] 1 KB 21 4.8.1
Bass v Boynton [1960] Crim LR 497, DC 9.8.1
Birmingham District Council v McMahon (1987) 19 HLR 452, (1987) 151 JP 709, (1988) 86 LGR 63 5.3.8
Bishop Auckland Local Board v Bishop Auckland Iron and Steel Co (1882) 1 QBD 138, 47 JP 389, 31 WR 288, DC 5.2.2
Blackburn v ARC (1998) 276 *ENDS Report* 51 4.5.2
Blackburn Corporation v Micklethwaite (1886) 54 LT 539 5.3.2
Bland v Mosely (1587). *See* Aldred's Case 4.3.3
Bone v Seale [1975] 1 WLR 797, [1975] 1 All ER 787, (1974) 119 SJ 137, CA 4.3.1, 4.5.1
Boomer v Atlantic Cement 257 NE 2d 870 (1970) 4.5.2
Bottross v Hammersmith and Fulham London Borough Council (1994) 27 HLR 179, (1995) 93 LGR 269, [1995] Env LR 217, QBD 5.3.7
Bower v Peate (1876) 1 QB 321, 40 JP 789, [1874–80] All ER Rep 905 4.3.6
Box v Jubb (1879) 4 ExD 76, 48 LJQB 417, [1874–80] All ER Rep 741 4.6.5
Brew Brothers Ltd v Snax (Ross) Ltd [1970] 1 QB 612, [1969] 3 WLR 657, [1970] 1 All ER 587, CA 4.3.7
Bridlington Relay Ltd v Yorkshire Electricity Board [1965] Ch 436, [1965] 2 WLR 349, [1965] 1 All ER 264 4.3.2
Bristol Corporation v Sinnott [1918] 1 Ch 52 5.3.1
British Celanese Ltd v AH Hunt (Capacitors) Ltd [1969] 1 WLR 959, [1969] 2 All ER 1252; *sub nom* British Celanese Ltd v AM Hunt (Capacitors) Ltd (1969) 113 SJ 368 4.3, 4.6.1
British Steel Corporation v Pittock (1970) 16 RRC 374 8.3.1
Brown v Burns Tractors Ltd 1986 SCCR 146 9.8
Bryan v United Kingdom (1996) 21 EHRR 342 6.15.6
Budden v BP Oil and Shell Oil; Albery-Speyer v BP Oil and Shell Oil [1980] JPL 586, (1980) 124 SJ 376, CA 4.8.2
Bugg v DPP; DPP v Percy [1993] QB 473, [1993] 2 WLR 628, [1993] 2 All ER 815, DC 6.12.1
Burton v Winters [1993] 1 WLR 1077, [1993] 3 All ER 847, CA 4.5.3
Bussone v Italian Ministry for Agriculture and Forestry (No 31/78) [1978] ECR 2429, [1978] 3 CMLR 18, ECJ 1.5.1

CILFIT v Ministro della Sanita (Case 283/81) [1982] ECR 3415, [1983] 1 CMLR 472, ECJ 1.9.2
Cambridge Water Co v Eastern Counties Leather plc; Same v Hutchings and Harding [1994] 2 AC 264, [1994] 2 WLR 53, [1994] 1 All ER 53, HL 4.3.8, 4.6.1, 4.6.2, 4.6.8
Camden London Borough Council v Alpenoak Ltd (1985) 135 NLJ 1209, (1985) *Surveyor*, 5 December, 17 5.3.6
Canterbury City Council v Ferris (1996) *The Independent*, November 11 5.3.4
Cartwright v Post Office [1968] 2 QB 439, [1968] 3 WLR 63, [1968] 2 All ER 646 10.1.2
Cassidy v Ministry of Health [1951] 2 KB 343, [1951] 1 All ER 574, 95 SJ 253, CA 4.3.6
Castle v St Augustines Links Ltd (1922) 38 TLR 615 4.2
Chappell & Co Ltd v Nestle Co Ltd [1958] Ch 529, [1958] 2 WLR 657, [1958] 2 All ER 155, CA 8.5.3
Charing Cross West End and City Electricity Supply Co v London Hydraulic Power Ltd [1914] 3 KB 772, 12 LGR 807, [1914–15] All ER Rep 85, CA 4.6.1, 4.6.2
Chastey v Ackland [1895] 2 Ch 389 4.3.3
Cheshire County Council v Woodward [1962] 2 QB 126, [1962] 2 WLR 636, [1962] 1 All ER 517, DC 8.2.1
City of London Corporation v Bovis Construction Ltd (1988) 86 LGR 600 5.3.6
City of London Corporation v Bovis Construction Ltd [1992] 3 All ER 697, 84 LGR 660, [1989] JPL 263, CA 4.2, 6.22
Clarke v Newsam (1847) 1 Exch 131 4.3.8
Clayton v Sale Urban District Council [1926] 1 KB 415 5.3.2
Colls v Home and Colonial Stores Ltd [1904] AC 179, 73 LJ Ch 484, [1904–7] All ER Rep 5, HL 4.3.2
Commission of the European Communities v Belgium (C-2/90) [1993] JEL 133, (1992) *The Times*, July 23, ECJ 1.4.3, 1.4.4
Commission of European Communities v Denmark (Case 211/81) [1982] ECR 4547, [1984] 1 CMLR 278, ECJ 2.1.2
Commission of the European Communities v European Council [1991] 3 LMELR, ECJ 1.1.3
Commission of the European Communities v European Council (Generalised Tariff Preferences) (Case 45/86) [1987] ECR 1493, [1988] 2 CMLR 131, ECJ 1.7
Commission of the European Communities v European Council [1993] ECR 1-939, ECJ 1.1.3
Commission of the European Communities v Italian Republic (C-22/87) [1989] ECR 143, ECJ 1.12
Costa v Ente Nazionale per l'Energia Elettrica (ENEL) (Case 6/64) [1964] ECR 585, [1964] CMLR 425, ECJ 1.9, 1.9.2
Council of the Civil Service Unions v Minister for the Civil Service [1985] AC 374, [1984] 1 WLR 1174, [1984] 3 All ER 935, HL 6.20.1
Coventry City Council v Cartwright [1975] 1 WLR 845, [1975] 2 All ER 99, 73 LGR 218, DC 5.2.2, 5.3.8
Coventry City Council v Doyle [1981] 1 WLR 1325, [1981] 2 All ER 184, [1981] JPL 666, DC 5.3.9
Coventry City Council v Finnie (1996) 29 HLR 658 5.3.6
Crump v Lambert (1867) LR 3 Eq 409, 31 JP 485, 15 LT 600 4.3.3, 5.2.2
Cutler v Wandsworth Stadium Ltd [1949] AC 398, [1949] 1 All ER 544, [1949] LJR 824, HL 4.7

Da Costa en Schaake v Nederlandse Belastingadministratie (Cases 28-30/62) [1963] ECR 31, [1963] CMLR 224, 1 CML Rev 213, ECJ 1.9.2
Dalton v Angus (1881) 6 App Cas 740; *sub nom* Public Works Commrs v Angus & Co, Dalton v Angus & Co 50 LJQB 689, [1881–85] All ER Rep 1, HL 4.3.3
Danish Bottles case. *See* Disposable Beer Cans, Re; Commission of European Communities v Denmark
Davenport v Walsall Metropolitan Borough Council (1995) 28 HLR 754 5.3.7
Dear v Thames Water [1993] 33 Con LR 43, [1993] 4 W LAW 116 4.8.1
Department of Transport v North West Water Authority [1984] AC 336, [1983] 3 WLR 707, [1983] 3 All ER 273, HL 4.4.2
Disposable Beer Cans, Re; Commission of European Communities v Denmark (Case 302/86) [1989] 1 CMLR 619, (1988) *The Times*, October 3, ECJ 1.4.3
Donoghue v Stevenson [1932] AC 562 4.8.1
Drummond and Sons Ltd v Nicholson (1915) 84 LJKB 2190 5.3.4
Dunne v North Western Gas Board; Lambert v Same; Doyle v Same [1964] 2 QB 806, [1964] 2 WLR 164, [1963] 3 All ER 916, CA 4.6.2, 4.6.4

East Northamptonshire District Council v Foster [1994] Env LR 388, QBD 5.2.2
Eastern & South African Telegraph Co Ltd v Cape Town Tramways Companies Ltd [1902] AC 381, 71 LJPC 122, 50 WR 657, PC 4.6.3
Elliot v Islington London Borough Council [1991] 10 EG 145, (1990) *The Times*, July 6, CA 4.5.2
Emanuel (H & N) Ltd v Greater London Council [1971] 2 All ER 835, [1971] 2 Lloyd's Rep 36, 115 SJ 226, CA 4.6.5
Empress Car Company (Abertillery) Ltd v National Rivers Authority [1998] 1 All ER 481, [1998] EHLR 3, (1998) *The Times*, February 9 8.2.2

Federation Charbonniere de Belgique v High Authority (Case 8/55) [1954–56] ECR 245, ECJ 1.6
Fishmonger's Co v East India Co (1752) 1 Dick 163, [1558–1774] All ER Rep 614 4.3.3
Foster v British Gas (Case C-188/89) [1991] 1 QB 405, [1991] 2 WLR 258, [1990] 3 All ER 897, ECJ 1.10.2
Foster v Warblington Urban District Council [1906] 1 KB 648, 4 LGR 735, 70 JP 233, CA 4.3.5
France (EC Commission intervening) v UK, Re Fishing Net Mesh Sizes (Case 141/78) [1979] ECR 2923, [1980] 1 CMLR 6, ECJ 2.1.2
Francovich v Italy (Joined cases C-6/90 and C-9/90) [1992] IRLR 84, [1995] ICR 722, (1991) *The Times*, November 20, ECJ 1.12, 2.1.2

Gateshead Metropolitan Borough Council v Secretary of State for the Environment [1995] JPL 432, CA 6.24
Gibbons v South West Water Services [1995] 5 LMELR 6 4.2
Giles v Walker (1890) 24 QBD 656, 54 JP 599, [1886–90] All ER Rep 501, DC 4.6.1
Gillingham Borough Council v Medway (Chatham) Dockyard Co Ltd [1993] QB 343, [1992] 3 WLR 449, [1992] 3 All ER 923 4.3.2, 4.4.3
Goldman (Allan William) v Hargrave (Rupert William Edeson) [1967] 1 AC 645, [1966] 3 WLR 513, [1966] 2 All ER 989, PC 4.4.4

Graham and Graham v Rechem International [1995] 7 ELM 175 4.3.4, 4.8.2
Great Western Railway Co v Bishop (1872) LR 7 QB 550 5.2.2
Green Environmental Industries Ltd and Another, Re (1997) *The Times*, October 9, CA 6.16.1, 6.17
Griffin, Re, ex parte Board of Trade (1890) 60 LJQB 235 5.2.2
Griffin v South West Water Services [1995] IRLR 15, ChD 1.10.2
Grimaldi v Fonds des Maladie Professionelles (C-322/88) [1989] ECR 4407, [1990] IRLR 400, [1991] 2 CMLR 265, ECJ 1.5.4
Gunn v Wallsend Slipway and Engineering Co Ltd (1989) *The Times*, January 23 4.8.1

Hale v Jennings Brothers [1938] 1 All ER 579, 82 SJ 193, CA 4.6.1, 4.6.2
Halliday v Wakefield Corporation (1887) 57 LT 559 8.3.6
Halsey v Esso Petroleum Co Ltd [1961] 1 WLR 683, [1961] 2 All ER 145, 105 SJ 209 4.2, 4.3.3, 4.3.5, 4.3.8, 4.5.1, 4.5.2, 4.6.2
Hammersmith London Borough Council v Magnum Automated Forecourts [1978] 1 WLR 50, [1977] 1 All ER 401, [1978] JPL 106, CA 5.3.6
Hammond v St Pancras Vestry (1874) LR 9 CP 316, 38 JP 456, [1874–80] All ER Rep 153 4.4.2
Harrison v Hall 1932 JC 13 9.8.1
Hancock v JW Roberts Ltd, Margereson v The Same [1996] 8 ELM 8 4.8.1
Hedley Byrne & Co v Heller & Partners [1964] AC 465, [1963] 3 WLR 101, [1963] 2 All ER 575, HL 4.8.1
Herbert v Lambeth London Borough Council (1991) 24 HLR 299, 90 LGR 310, (1992) 156 LG Rev 421, DC 5.3.7
Hesketh v Birmingham Corporation [1924] 1 KB 260 4.7
Hewett v Alf Brown's Transport [1992] ICR 530, [1992] PIQR P199, (1992) *The Times*, February 4, CA 4.8.1
Holliday v National Telephone Co [1899] 2 QB 392 4.3.6
Hollis v Dudley Metropolitan Borough Council (1997) *The Times*, December 12, *sub nom* R v Dudley Magistrates' Court, ex parte Hollis [1998] EHLR 42 5.3.7
Hollywood Silver Fox Farm Ltd v Emmett [1936] 2 KB 468, [1936] 1 All ER 825, 105 LJKB 829 4.3.3
Hope v BNFL plc [1993] 5 ELM 178 4.8.2
Hope Butuyuyu v London Borough of Hammersmith and Fulham [1997] Env LR D13 5.3.4
Howard v Walker [1947] KB 860, [1947] 2 All ER 197, [1947] LJR 1366 4.3
Howton v Buchanan [1940] 2 All ER 179 9.8
Huckerby v Elliot [1970] 1 All ER 189, (1969) 113 SJ 1001, DC 8.8.3
Hunter v Canary Wharf Ltd; Hunter v London Docklands Development Corporation [1997] 2 WLR 684, HL; [1996] 1 All ER 482, CA 4.3.2, 4.3.5, 4.4.3, 4.5.1, 4.6.2

Invercargill County Council v Hamlyn [1991] 3 NZLR 513 4.8.1

JB and M Motor Haulage Ltd v London Waste Regulation Authority [1993] Env LR 243, DC 6.17

James and Son Ltd v Smee; Green v Burnett [1955] 1 QB 78, [1954] 3 WLR 631, [1954] 3 All ER 273, DC 8.3.7
Johnson News of London v Ealing Borough Council (1990) 154 JP 33, [1990] COD 135, (1989) 153 JPN 765 5.3.4

Kennaway v Thompson [1981] QB 88, [1980] 3 WLR 361, [1980] 3 All ER 329, CA 4.3.2, 4.5.2
King v Liverpool City Council [1986] 1 WLR 890, [1986] 3 All ER 544, (1986) 18 HLR 307, CA 4.3.6
Kirklees Metropolitan Borough Council v Wickes Building Supplies Ltd; Mendip District Council v B&Q [1993] AC 227, [1992] 3 WLR 170, [1992] 3 All ER 717, HL 4.2, 5.3.6
Kirklees Metropolitan Borough Council v Field (1997) *The Times*, November 26 5.3.1

Lagan Navigation Co v Lambeg Bleaching, Dyeing and Finishing Co Ltd [1927] AC 226, 25 LGR 1, [1926] All ER Rep 230, HL 4.5.3
Lambert (A) Flat Management v Lomas [1981] 1 WLR 898, [1981] 2 All ER 280, (1980) 125 SJ 218, DC 5.3.4
Lambeth London Borough Council v Stubbs [1980] JPL 517, (1980) 78 LGR 650, (1980) 255 EG 789, DC 5.3.4
Lambton v Mellish [1894] 3 Ch 163, 58 JP 835, 63 LJ Ch 929 4.3.8, 4.4.4
Landcatch Ltd v Gilbert Gillies 1990 SLT 688 4.8.1
Laws v Florinplace Ltd [1981] 1 All ER 659 4.5.2
Leakey v National Trust for Places of Historic Interest and Natural Beauty [1978] QB 849, [1978] 2 WLR 774, [1978] 3 All ER 234, CA 4.3.6, 4.4.4
Lemmon v Webb [1895] AC 1, 59 JP 564, [1891–94] All ER Rep 749, HL 4.5.3
Lewisham London Borough Council v Fenner (1995) 248 *ENDS Report* 44, Crown Ct 5.3.4
London, Brighton and South Coast Railway Co v Truman (1886) 11 App Cas 45, 50 JP 388, 55 LJ Ch 354, HL 4.4.2
Lonrho Ltd v Shell Petroleum Co Ltd [1981] 3 WLR 33, [1981] 2 All ER 456, (1981) 125 SJ 429, HL 4.7
Lowe v South Somerset District Council [1997] EGCS 113 5.3.1, 5.3.3

McGillivray v Stephenson [1950] 1 All ER 942, [1950] WN 209, 48 LGR 409, DC 5.3.1
McKinnon Industries Ltd v Walker (1951) 3 DLR 577 4.3.2
McLeod v Buchanan [1940] 2 All ER 179 8.2.2
McMullin v ICI Australia Operations Pty Ltd (1997) 24 June (unreported), Fed Ct of Australia 4.6.2, 4.8.1
McNair v Baker [1904] 1 KB 208 8.5.4
Maddison v Ducktown Sulphur, Copper and Iron Co 83 SW 658 (1904) 4.5.2
Malone v Laskey [1907] 2 KB 141, 76 LJKB 1134, [1904–07] All ER Rep 304, CA 4.3.5
Malton Board of Health v Malton Manure Co (1879) 4 ExD 302, 44 JP 155, 27 WR 802 5.2.2
Manchester Corporation v Farnworth [1930] AC 171, 94 JP 62, [1929] All ER Rep 90, HL 4.3.3, 4.4.2, 4.5.2

Margereson v JW Roberts Ltd, Hancock v The Same [1996] 8 ELM 118 4.8.1
Marleasing SA v La Comercial Internacional de Alimentacion SA (Case C-106/89) [1992] 1 CMLR 305, [1993] BCC 421, ECJ 1.11
Marshall v Southampton and South West Hampshire Area Health Authority (Teaching) (Case 152/84) [1986] QB 401, [1986] 2 WLR 780, [1986] 2 All ER 584, ECJ 1.10.2
Mason v Levy Auto Parts of England Ltd [1967] 2 QB 530, [1967] 2 WLR 1384, [1967] 2 All ER 62 4.6.1
Masters v Brent London Borough Council [1978] 1 QB 841, [1978] 2 WLR 768, [1978] 2 All ER 664 4.3.5
Matania v National Provincial Bank Ltd and Elevenist Syndicate Ltd [1936] 2 All ER 633, 106 LJKB 113, 80 SJ 532, CA 4.3.6
Metropolitan Asylum District v Hill (1881) 6 App Cas 193, 45 JP 664, 50 LJQB 353, HL 4.4.2
Mickleborough v BRS (Contracts) [1977] RTR 389, [1977] Crim LR 568, DC 9.8
Midland Bank plc v Bardgrove Property Services Ltd and John Willmott (WB) (1992) 65 P&CR 153, [1992] NPC 83, (1992) 37 EG 126, CA 4.5.2
Midwood & Co v Manchester Corporation [1905] 2 KB 597, 3 LGR 1136, 69 JP 348, CA 4.4.2
Miles v Forest Rock Granite Co (Leicestershire) Ltd (1918) 34 TLR 500, 62 SJ 634, CA 4.6.1
Millard v Wastell [1898] 1 QB 342 5.3.1
Miller-Mead v Minister of Housing and Local Government [1963] 2 QB 196, [1963] 2 WLR 225, [1963] 1 All ER 459, CA 6.12
Mint v Good [1951] 1 KB 517, [1950] 2 All ER 1159, 94 SJ 822, CA 4.4.4
Moir v Williams [1892] 1 QB 264 8.2.1
Moss v Christchurch Rural District Council [1925] 2 KB 750, 23 LGR 331, 95 LJKB 81 4.5.1
Murphy v Brentwood District Council [1991] 1 AC 398, [1990] 3 WLR 414, [1990] 2 All ER 908, HL 4.8.1
Myatt (Patricia) v Teignbridge District Council [1994] Env LR D18, QBD 5.3.1

NV Algemene Transport-en Expeditie Onderneming Van Gend en Loos v Nederlandse Belastingadministratie (Case 26/62) [1963] ECR 1, [1963] CMLR 105, ECJ 1.1.2, 1.9, 1.9.2, 1.10.1
National Coal Board v Neath Borough Council [1976] 2 All ER 478, DC 5.2.2
National Rivers Authority v Alfred McAlpine Homes South Ltd [1994] 4 All ER 286, [1994] Env LR D5, [1994] NPC 6, QBD 8.8.3
National Rivers Authority v Wright Engineering Co Ltd [1994] 4 All ER 281, [1994] Env LR 186, [1994] Crim LR 453, DC 4.6.5
Netherlands Government v ECSS High Authority (Case 6/54) [1954–56] ECR 103, ECJ 1.6
Network Housing Association v Westminster City Council (1994) 27 HLR 189, 93 LGR 280, [1994] EGCS 173, DC 5.3.1
Newcastle under Lyme Corporation v Wolstanton Ltd [1947] Ch 427, [1947] 1 All ER 218, [1947] LJR 1311, CA 4.3.5
Newport Borough Council v Khan (Sabz Ali) [1990] 1 WLR 1185, [1991] COD 157, (1992) 156 LG Rev 4, CA 4.2
North Western Utilities Ltd v London Guarantee & Accident Co Ltd [1926] AC 108, 105 LJPC 18, [1935] All ER Rep 196, PC 4.6.5

Northern Ireland Trailers Ltd v Preston Corporation [1972] 1 WLR 203, (1971) 116 SJ 100; *sub nom* Northern Ireland Trailers Ltd v County Borough of Preston [1972] 1 All ER 260, DC 5.3.4
Nottingham City District Council v Newton; Nottingham Friendship Housing Association v Newton [1974] 1 WLR 923, 118 SJ 462; *sub nom* Nottingham Corporation v Newton; Nottingham Friendship Housing Association v Newton [1974] 2 All ER 760, DC 5.3.1, 5.3.9

O'Fee v Copeland Borough Council [1995] 7 ELM 129, (1995) 159 JPN 860, (1995) *The Times*, April 22, QBD 8.2.2
Overseas Tankships (UK) Ltd v Miller SS Co Pty, The Wagon Mound (No 2) [1967] 1 AC 617, [1966] 3 WLR 498, [1966] 2 All ER 709, PC 4.3.8
Overseas Tankships (UK) Ltd v Morts Dock & Engineering Co, The Wagon Mound (No 1) [1961] AC 388, [1961] 2 WLR 126, [1961] 1 All ER 404, PC 4.3.8

Page Motors Ltd v Epsom and Ewell Borough Council (1982) 80 LGR 337, [1982] JPL 572, (1981) 125 SJ 590, CA 4.3.6
Patel v Mehtab (1989) 5 HLR 78 5.2.2
Paterson v Humberside County Council (1996) 12 Const LJ 64 4.3.8
Pearson v North Western Gas Board [1968] 2 All ER 669 4.7, 4.8.2
Pennington v Brinsop Hall Coal Co (1877) 5 ChD 589, 46 LJ Ch 773, 37 LT 149 4.5.2
Perry v Kendricks Transport Ltd [1956] 1 WLR 85, [1956] 1 All ER 154, 100 SJ 52, CA 4.6.1, 4.6.4, 4.6.5
Peters v Prince of Wales Theatre (Birmingham) Ltd [1943] KB 73, [1942] 2 All ER 533, 112 LJKB 433, CA 4.6.3
Phillips v Britannia Hygienic Laundry Co Ltd [1923] 2 KB 832 9.8
Polychronakis v Richards and Jerrom Ltd (1997) *The Times*, November 19 5.3.4
Pontardawe Rural District Council v Moore-Gwyn [1929] 1 Ch 656, 27 LGR 493, 98 LJ Ch 242 4.6.1
Price v Cromack [1975] 1 WLR 988, [1978] 2 All ER 113, 119 SJ 458, DC 8.2.2
Price's Patent Candle Co v LCC [1908] 2 Ch 526 4.5.2
Pride of Derby and Derbyshire Angling Association v British Celanese Ltd [1953] Ch 149, [1953] 2 WLR 58, [1953] 1 All ER 179, CA; affirming [1952] 1 All ER 1326, [1952] WN 227, 96 SJ 263 4.3.8, 4.4.2
Public Works Commrs v Angus & Co, Dalton v Angus & Co. *See* Dalton v Angus
Pwllbach Colliery Co Ltd v Woodman [1915] AC 634, 84 LJKB 874, [1914–15] All ER Rep 124, HL 4.3.3, 4.3.7

R v Birmingham Justices ex parte Guppy (1988) 152 JP 159, (1988) 86 LGR 264, (1988) 152 LG Rev 713, DC 5.3.1
R v Boal (Francis) [1992] QB 591, [1992] 2 WLR 890, [1992] 3 All ER 177, CA 8.8.3
R v Breeze [1973] 1 WLR 994, [1973] 2 All ER 1141, [1973] Crim LR 458, CA 5.2.2
R v Bristol City Council ex parte Everett (1998) *The Times*, May 27 5.2.2
R v Carrick District Council ex parte Shelley (1996) *The Times*, April 15 5.3.1

R v Crown Court at Inner London ex parte Bentham [1989] 1 WLR 408, (1989) 21 HLR 171, [1989] COD 293, DC 5.3.7
R v Exeter City Council ex parte JL Thomas & Co Ltd [1991] 1 QB 471, [1990] 3 WLR 100, [1990] 1 All ER 413 4.4.3
R v Greenwich London Borough ex parte Jack Williams (1995) 253 *ENDS Report* 49 10.1.2
R v Horseferry Road Magistrates ex parte Prophet [1995] Env LR 104 5.3.7
R v Hudson [1966] 1 QB 448, [1965] 2 WLR 604, [1965] 1 All ER 721, CCA 8.2
R v Kerrier District Council ex parte Guppy's (Bridport) Ltd (1975) 30 P&CR 194, 74 LGR 55, (1975) 119 SJ 577, DC 5.3.1
R v Lam and Brennan (t/a Namesakes of Torbay) and Torbay Borough Council [1998] PLCR 30, *sub nom* R v Lam [1998] EHLR 111 4.8.1
R v Liverpool Crown Court ex parte Cooke (1997) 29 HLR 249 5.3.7
R v North West Suffolk (Mildenhall) Magistrates' Court ex parte Forest Heath District Council [1998] Env LR 9, CA 5.3.3
R v Oxted JJ ex parte Franklin [1976] 1 WLR 420 5.3.4
R v Secretary of State for the Environment and NC Compton T/A RJ Compton and Sons ex parte West Wiltshire District Council [1996] Env LR 312, HC 7.4.2, 7.4.3
R v Secretary of State for the Environment and Peninsular Proteins Ltd ex parte Torridge District Council [1997] Env LR 557, HC 7.4.3
R v Secretary of State for the Environment ex parte Watney Mann (Midlands) Ltd [1976] JPL 368, DC 5.3.1
R v Secretary of State for the Home Department ex parte Ruddock [1987] 1 WLR 1482, [1987] 2 All ER 518, (1987) 131 SJ 1550 6.20.1
R v Secretary of State for Trade and Industry ex parte Duddridge [1996] Env LR 325 1.6.3
R v Secretary of State for Transport, ex parte Factortame (No 2) (C-213/89) [1991] 1 AC 603, [1990] 3 WLR 818, [1991] 1 All ER 70, HL 1.12
R v Southend Stipendiary Magistrates ex parte Rochford District Council [1995] Env LR 1 5.3.3
R v The Environment Agency and Redland Aggregates Ltd, ex parte Gibson, R v The Environment Agency and Redland Aggregates Ltd, ex parte Leam, R v The Environment Agency, ex parte Sellers and Petty (1998) CO/3598/96, CO/2104/96, CO/3796/97, QBD 6.5.10
R v Tunbridge Wells JJ ex parte Tunbridge Wells Borough Council [1996] Env LR 88 5.3.1
R v Turner [1910] KB 346 8.5.1
R v Wheatley (1885) 16 QB 34 5.3.1
R v Wicks [1997] 2 All ER 801, HL 6.12.1
Read v J Lyons and Co Ltd [1947] AC 156, [1946] 2 All ER 471, [1947] LJR 39, HL 4.6.1, 4.6.2
Reay v BNFL plc [1992] 4 LMELR 195 4.8.2
Redland Bricks Ltd v Morris [1970] AC 652, [1969] 2 WLR 1437, [1969] 2 All ER 576, HL 4.5.2
Rickards v Lothian [1913] AC 263, 82 LJPC 42, [1911–13] All ER Rep 71, PC 4.6.1, 4.6.5
Rigby v Chief Constable of Northamptonshire [1985] 1 WLR 1242, [1985] 2 All ER 985, (1986) 83 LS Gaz 46 4.6.1
Robinson v DPP [1991] RTR 315 9.8
Robinson v Kilvert (1889) 41 ChD 88, 58 LJ Ch 392, 37 WR 545, CA 4.3.2
Rolls v Miller (1894) 27 ChD 71 5.2.2

Runnymede Borough Council v Ball [1986] 1 WLR 353, [1986] 1 All ER 629, (1985) 135 NLJ 889, CA 5.3.6
Rust v Victoria Graving Dock Co and London and St Katherine Dock Co (1887) 36 ChD 113, 35 WR 673, 56 LT 216, CA 4.3.5
Ruxley Electronics and Construction Ltd v Forsyth; Laddingford Enclosures Ltd v Forsyth [1996] AC 344, [1995] 3 WLR 118, [1995] 3 All ER 268, HL 4.5.1
Ryeford Homes Ltd v Sevenoaks District Council (1989) 46 BLR 34, (1989) 2 EGLR 281, [1990] JPL 36 4.8.1
Rylands v Fletcher (1866) LR 1 Ex 265, 30 JP 436, 4 H&C 263 4.1, 4.6.1, 4.6.2, 4.6.7, 4.6.8

Saddleworth Urban District Council v Aggregate and Sand (1970) 114 SJ 931, 69 LGR 103, DC 5.3.4
St Anne's Well Brewery Co v Roberts (1928) 140 LT 1, 26 LGR 638, [1928] All ER Rep 28, CA 4.3.6
St Helen's Corporation v Kirkham (1885) 16 QBD 403 5.3.2
St Helens Smelting Co v Tipping (1865) 11 HL Cas 642, (1865) 29 JP 579, 11 ER 1483 4.3.1, 4.3.3, 4.5.2, 8.1
Salford City Council v McNally [1976] AC 379, [1975] 3 WLR 87, [1975] 2 All ER 860, HL 5.3.9
Salvin v North Brancepeth Coal Co (1874) LR 9 Ch 705, 44 LJ Ch 149, 31 LT 154 8.1
Sandford Motor Sales Ltd v Habgood [1962] Crim LR 487, DC 9.8.6
Sandwell Metropolitan Borough Council v Bujok [1990] 1 WLR 1350, [1990] 3 All ER 385, (1991) 23 HLR 48, HL 5.3.8
Scott-Whitehead v National Coal Board (1985) 53 P&CR 263, [1987] 2 EGLR 227 4.4.1, 4.8.1
Sedleigh-Denfield v O'Callaghan [1940] AC 880, [1940] 3 All ER 349, 84 SJ 657, HL 4.3.6
Sheffield City Council v ADH Demolition Ltd (1983) 82 LGR 177, (1984) JPL 658, DC 8.2.2
Shelfer v City of London Electric Lighting Co [1895] 1 Ch 287, 64 LJ Ch 216, [1891–94] All ER Rep 838, CA 4.5.2
Shiffman v Venerable Order of the Hospital of St John of Jerusalem [1936] 1 All ER 557, 80 SJ 346 4.6.1, 4.6.2
Shoreham-by-Sea Urban District Council v Dolphin Canadian Proteins Ltd (1972) 71 LGR 261, Vacation Ct 4.2, 4.4.1
Smeaton v Ilford Corporation [1954] Ch 450, [1954] 2 WLR 668, [1954] 1 All ER 923 4.6.1
Smith v Giddy [1904] 2 KB 448, 73 LJKB 894, [1904–07] All ER Rep 289 4.5.3
Smith v Miller [1894] 1 QB 192 8.3.1
Southern Water Authority v Pegrum [1989] 2 All ER 357, [1989] Crim LR 442, (1989) 153 LG Rev 672, DC 4.6.6, 8.2.2
Southport Corporation v Esso Petroleum Co Ltd [1953] 3 WLR 773, [1952] 2 All ER 1204, 52 LGR 22 4.3.6
Spicer v Smee [1946] 1 All ER 498, 175 LT 163 4.3.6
Stagecoach Ltd v McPhail 1988 SCCR 289 5.3.4
Sterling Homes (Midlands) Ltd v Birmingham City Council [1996] Env LR 121 5.3.1, 5.3.4

Stevens v Bromley London Borough Council [1972] Ch 400, [1972] 2 WLR 605; *sub nom* Stevens v London Borough of Bromley [1972] 1 All ER 712, CA 8.2.1
Stoke-on-Trent City Council v B&Q Retail Ltd [1984] Ch 1, [1983] 3 WLR 78, [1983] 2 All ER 787, CA 5.3.6
Stollmeyer v Petroleum Development Co Ltd [1918] AC 498, 87 LJPC 83, 118 LT 518, PC 4.5.2
Stovin v Wise [1996] 3 All ER 801, [1997] 9 ELM 8 4.8.1
Strathclyde Regional Council v Tudhope [1983] JPL 536, High Ct of Justiciary 5.3.1
Stretton's Derby Brewery Co v Derby Corporation [1894] 1 Ch 431, 63 LJ Ch 135, [1891–94] All ER Rep 731 4.4.2
Stringer v Minister of Housing and Local Government [1970] 1 WLR 1281, [1971] 1 All ER 65, [1971] JPL 114 4.4.3
Sturgess v Bridgman (1879) 11 ChD 852, 43 JP 716, 48 LJ Ch 785, CA 4.4.4
Sullivan v Creed [1904] 21 R 317 4.6.1
Surrey Free Inns plc v Gosport Borough Council [1998] EHLR 23, (1998) *The Times*, January 13, DC 5.3.4
Swindon Waterworks Co Ltd v Wilts and Berks Canal Navigation Co (1875) LR 7 HL 697, 40 JP 117, 45 LJ Ch 638, HL 4.3

Tan Chye Choo v Chong Kew Moi [1970] 1 WLR 147, [1970] 1 All ER 266, 113 SJ 1000, PC 9.8
Tandridge District Council v P & S Civil Engineering Ltd [1995] Env LR 67 6.2.3
Tate & Lyle Food and Distribution Ltd v Greater London Council [1983] 2 AC 509, [1983] 2 WLR 649, [1983] 1 All ER 1159, HL 4.4.2
Taylor v Walsall and District Property and Investment Co Ltd (1998) *The Times*, February 5 5.3.7
Taylor's Central Garages (Exeter) Ltd v Roper [1951] WN 383, (1951) 115 JP 445; *sub nom* Roper v Taylor's Central Garages (Exeter) [1951] 2 TLR 284 8.3.7
Tetley v Chitty [1986] 1 All ER 663, (1985) 135 NLJ 1009 4.3.7, 4.5.2
Thomas v Lewis [1937] 1 All ER 137, 81 SJ 98 4.6.3
Thompson v Gibson (1841) 7 M & W 456, 151 ER 845, [1835–42] All ER Rep 623 4.3.6
Thorpe v Brumfitt (1873) LR 8 Ch App 650, 37 JP 742 4.3.8, 4.4.4
Town Investments v Department of the Environment [1976] 3 All ER 147 5.2.2
Trecarrell, The [1973] 1 Lloyd's Rep 402 4.3.8
Tyne Boiler Works Co v Overseers of Long Benton (1886) 18 QBD 81 8.3.1

UK v European Council (Case 56/88) [1989] ECR 1615, [1989] 2 CMLR 789, ECJ 1.7

Vacwell Engineering Co Ltd v BDH Chemicals Ltd [1971] 1 QB 88, [1969] 3 WLR 927; *sub nom* Vacwell Engineering Co Ltd v BDH Chemicals Ltd (formerly British Drug Houses) 4.3.8
Vale of White Horse District Council v DC and RJ Allen (1997) 264 *ENDS Report* 43 4.2, 5.3.6
Von Colson and Kamann v Land Nordrhein-Westfahlen (Case 14/83) [1984] ECR 1891, [1986] 2 CMLR 430, ECJ 1.11

Wallonian Waste case. See Commission of the European Communities v Belgium
Walter v Selfe (1851) 4 DeG & Sm 315, 20 LJ Ch 433, 15 Jur 416 4.3.3
Warner v Lambeth Borough Council (1984) 15 HLR 42, DC 5.3.8
Warwick Rural District Council v Miller-Mead; Miller-Mead v Warwick Rural District Council [1961] Ch 590, [1961] 3 WLR 737, [1961] 3 All ER 542 5.3.6
Wellingborough Borough Council v Gordon [1991] JPL 874, [1991] COD 154, (1991) 155 JP 494, DC 5.3.4
Weller & Co v Foot and Mouth Disease Research Institute [1966] 1 QB 569, [1965] 3 WLR 1082, [1965] 3 All ER 560 4.6.2
Welton v North Cornwall District Council [1997] 1 WLR 570, [1997] 9 ELM 7 4.8.1
West v Bristol Tramway Co [1908] 2 KB 14, 6 LGR 609, [1908–10] All ER Rep 215, CA 4.6.1
Whalley v Lancashire and Yorkshire Railway Co (1884) 13 QBD 131, 48 JP 500, 32 WR 711, CA 4.6.1
Wheeler v JJ Saunders Ltd [1995] 3 WLR 446, [1995] 2 All ER 697, [1995] Env LR 286, CA 4.3.2, 4.4.3
White v Jameson (1874) LR 18 Eq 303, 38 JP 694, 22 WR 761 4.3.6
Wilson v Bird [1963] Crim LR 57, 106 SJ 880, DC 9.8
Wiltshire Construction (London) Ltd v Westminster City Council [1997] Env LR 321 5.3.3
Wivenhoe Port v Colchester Borough Council [1985] JPL 175 5.2.2, 5.3.1, 5.3.4
Woodhouse v Walsall Metropolitan Borough Council [1994] Env LR 30 8.8.3
Wrothwell (FJH) Ltd v Yorkshire Water Authority Services Ltd [1984] Crim LR 43, CA 8.2.2

Zamora, The [1918] 2 AC 77 6.20.1

TABLE OF STATUTES

References are to paragraph numbers.

Agriculture Act 1947
- s 109(3) 8.4.1
- s 109(5) 8.3.3

Alkali etc Works Regulations Act 1906 2.5, 5.2.1, 6.5.2

Alkali etc Works Regulations Act 1909 2.3, 6.5.2

Building Act 1984
- s 16(6) 8.4.3
- s 73 8.4.3

Clean Air Act 1956 8.1, 8.1.1, 10.7

Clean Air Act 1958 3.4

Clean Air Act 1968 3.4, 8.1, 8.3.3
- s 2 6.3.2

Clean Air Act 1993 5.2.1, 8.1, 8.3.3, 8.4.3, 8.6, 8.7.1, 9.4, 10.1.3, 10.6, 10.7.1, 10.10, 10.10.1, 10.11.4, 10.12.7
- Pts I–III 8.7.2, 8.7.3, 8.7.4, 8.8.5
- Pt V 10.4.1, 10.5
- Pt VI 8.8.5
- ss 1–29 8.8.5
- s 1 8.2.2, 8.3.1, 8.7.6, 8.8.2
  - (1) 8.2, 8.2.1
  - (2) 8.2
  - (3) 8.2.1
  - (4), (5) 8.2
- s 2 8.2.2, 8.7.6, 8.8.2
  - (1) 8.2.2
  - (3)–(6) 8.2.2
- s 3(1) 8.2
  - (2) 8.2, 8.2.2
  - (3) 8.2.2
- s 4 8.3.1, 8.7.7
  - (1) 8.3.1
  - (2) 8.3.1, 8.7.6
- ss 5–13 8.3.7
- s 5 8.3.2, 8.7.6, 8.7.7
- s 6 8.3.3, 8.3.5, 8.7.6, 8.7.7
- s 6(1) 8.3.3
  - (3) 8.3.3, 8.9
- s 7 8.3.3, 8.7.7
  - (2), (3) 8.3.3
- s 8 8.3.4, 8.3.5, 8.7.6
- s 9 8.3.5
- ss 10–13 10.5
- s 10 8.3.6, 8.7.6
  - (5) 8.3.6, 8.9
- s 11 8.7.7
  - (1)–(3) 8.3.6
- s 14 8.4.2
  - (1), (2) 8.4.1
  - (4), (5) 8.4.1
  - (7) 8.4.1
- s 15 8.4.2
  - (2) 8.4.2
  - (4) 8.4.2
- s 16 8.4.3
  - (6) 8.4.2
- s 18 8.5.1, 8.5.2, 8.9
  - (6) 8.5.1
- s 19 8.5.1
  - (1) 8.9
  - (4) 8.9
- s 20 8.5.2, 8.5.3, 8.5.4, 8.7.6, 8.8.2
  - (4) 8.5.2
- s 21 8.5.2, 8.9
- s 22 8.5.2, 8.5.3, 8.9
- s 23 8.7.6
  - (1) 8.5.3
  - (4) 8.5.3
- s 24 8.5.4
  - (1) 8.5.4
- s 25 8.5.4
  - (5) 8.5.3
- s 26 8.5.4
- s 27 8.5.4
  - (3) 8.5.4
- s 28 8.5.4
- s 30 9.3, 9.4.1
  - (4) 9.3
- s 32 9.3

Clean Air Act 1993 – *cont*
s 33 8.7.1, 8.8.5
s 34 10.4.2
(1) 10.4.1, 10.4.2, 10.4.5
(1)(b) 8.8, 10.5
(2)–(4) 10.4.1
s 35 10.4.2, 10.4.5
(1) 10.4.5
(2) 10.4.2, 10.4.3
(3)–(6) 10.4.2
s 36 10.4.2, 10.4.3, 10.4.4, 10.4.5
(1)–(8) 10.4.3
s 37 10.4.4, 10.4.5
(1)–(4) 10.4.4
s 38(1), (2) 10.4.5
s 39 10.4.5
s 40 10.5
ss 41–46 8.8.5
s 41 8.3, 8.7.1
s 42 5.2.1, 8.3, 8.7.2
(4) 8.7.7
s 43 8.7.6
(1) 8.7.3
(5) 8.3, 8.7.7
s 44 8.7.4, 8.7.5
(6) 8.3, 8.7.4, 8.7.7
s 45 5.2.1, 8.7.6
(2) 8.7.6
(3) 8.7.4
s 46 8.7.5
(1) 8.7.7
(4) 8.3, 8.7.4, 8.7.5
(5) 8.7.5
s 47 8.7.7
(2) 8.9
s 49 8.8, 10.5
s 50 8.7.2, 8.8.1
(3) 8.8.1
s 51 8.2, 8.2.2, 8.5.2, 8.8.2
(1) 8.2.2
s 52 8.8.3
s 53 8.8.3
s 54 8.8.4
ss 56–58 10.4.3
s 56 8.8.5, 10.4.2
(1) 8.8.5
(3) 8.8.5
s 57(1) 8.8.5
(3) 8.8.5
(5)–(7) 8.8.5
s 58 10.5
(1), (2) 10.5
s 59 8.9
s 60 8.9
(2), (3) 8.9
(4)(a), (b) 8.9
(5) 8.9
(7) 8.9
s 61 8.8.5
s 62 8.8.5
s 63 8.9
(3) 8.9
s 64 8.7.3
(1) 8.2, 8.2.1, 8.3, 8.3.2, 8.3.4
(5) 8.5.4
Sch 1 8.5.1
Sch 2 8.5.4
para 1(2) 8.5.4
(5) 8.5.4
Sch 3, para 3 8.9
Sch 5, Pt III 8.5.1

Comprehensive Environmental Response Compensation Liability Act 1980 (USA) 4.6

Control of Pollution Act 1974 2.5, 2.5.1, 2.7.1, 8.1
Pts II–IV 6.3.2
s 3 6.17
s 60 6.22
ss 75–77 9.4.1
s 75 9.4
s 93 6.17

Deregulation and Contracting Out Act 1994 8.6

Environment Act 1995 2.6, 10.1.2, 10.3, 10.6.2, 10.7.2, 10.8.6, 10.8.7, 10.8.8, 10.8.9, 10.8.10, 10.9, 10.10, 10.10.1, 10.10.2, 10.10.3, 10.11.3, 10.12.1, 10.12.5, 10.12.6, 10.12.7, 10.13, 10.13.4, 10.14.3, 10.15.2, 10.18
Pt IV 7.20.1, 10.7, 10.8, 10.8.2, 10.14.3
s 4(1) 10.8.11
s 41 6.8, 6.10, 7.6, 7.9
(2)(a) 6.8
(6) 6.8
s 51 6.17
s 56 6.8
(1) 6.8
s 80 10.8
(1)–(7) 10.8.1

Environment Act 1995 – *cont*
s 81 10.8, 10.8.1
s 82 10.8.2, 10.8.3, 10.8.13
(1)–(3) 10.8.2
s 83 7.20.1, 10.8.2, 10.8.3, 10.8.4, 10.8.5
s 84 10.8.2, 10.8.3, 10.8.11
(1) 10.8.2, 10.14.4, 10.14.5, 10.14.6
(2)–(5) 10.8.2
s 85 10.8.2
(2)–(5) 10.8.4
(7) 10.8.4
s 86 10.8.2
(2) 10.8.2, 10.8.12, 10.14.6
(3) 10.8.2, 10.8.3, 10.8.12, 10.8.13, 10.13.3, 10.14.6
(4) 10.8.2, 10.8.3
(5)–(9) 10.8.2
ss 87–89 10.8
s 87 6.3.2, 10.8.5, 10.8.6
(1), (2) 10.17.1
(3), (4) 10.8.5
(5) 10.8.5, 10.18.1
(6), (7) 10.8.5
(8) 10.8.5, 10.18.1
s 88 10.8.6
s 90 10.8
s 91 10.8.2
s 108 6.16, 6.16.1, 6.16.2, 7.1.1, 7.14
(4) 6.16, 6.16.2
(12), (13) 6.16.1
(15) 6.16
s 109 6.16, 6.16.2, 7.1.1, 7.14
s 110 6.16.2, 7.14
(3) 6.16.2
s 120(3) 6.16
Sch 11 10.8, 10.8.6, 10.8.11, 10.14.6, 10.18.1
para 1 10.8.3
para 1(2)(e) 10.8.13
paras 2–4 10.8.3
Sch 18 6.16.1, 6.16.2
Sch 22, para 48 6.8
para 50 7.6
Sch 24 6.16
Environmental Protection Act 1990 2.3, 2.3.1, 2.4.2, 2.5, 2.7.1, 2.10, 5.2.1, 5.3.1, 5.3.2, 5.3.4, 6.1.1, 6.3.1, 6.4, 6.5.2, 6.9, 6.10, 6.12, 6.12.1, 6.13, 6.15.1, 6.16, 6.20.2, 6.24, 6.25, 7.4.1, 7.4.2, 7.6, 7.20.2, 8.7.1, 8.7.7, 10.1, 10.2, 10.4.3, 10.7.1, 10.8.6, 10.8.7, 10.8.9, 10.10, 10.10.1, 10.10.2, 10.10.3, 10.12.1, 10.13, 10.13.1, 10.14.1
Pt I 5.2.1, 6.1, 6.2, 6.2.4, 6.3.2, 6.4, 6.6, 6.7, 6.8, 6.9, 6.10, 6.11, 6.12.1, 6.13, 6.14, 6.15, 6.15.6, 6.16, 6.19, 6.19.1, 6.20, 6.20.2, 6.24, 7.1.1, 7.3.1, 7.4, 7.4.1, 7.5, 7.7, 7.7.1, 7.7.2, 7.13, 7.14, 7.15, 7.16, 7.18, 7.20.1, 7.20.2, 7.20.4, 8.3, 8.7.1, 8.10, 10.4.2, 10.4.3
Pt II 6.8
Pt III 5.1, 8.7.2, 8.7.6
s 1 6.26.1, 7.1.1
(3) 6.2, 6.13
(4) 6.13
(5) 6.2
(13) 7.3.1
s 2 6.2, 6.24, 7.2
(1) 6.2, 6.3, 7.4
(5), (6) 6.2
s 3 6.3.2
(5) 2.3.1, 6.3.2
ss 6–12 6.3
s 6 2.3.1, 6.2.4, 6.5.10, 6.24, 7.3.1
(1) 6.3, 6.14, 6.15.1, 6.19.1, 7.4, 7.10
(2) 6.8, 7.6
(3) 6.24, 7.4.1, 7.6
(4) 7.4.1, 7.4.2, 7.4.3
(6) 6.3.2, 6.25, 6.26.3, 7.9
s 7 2.3.1, 2.4.1, 6.2.4, 6.3.2, 6.5.8, 6.5.10, 6.10, 7.1.1, 7.3.1, 7.4.1, 7.4.3
(1) 7.5, 10.8.9
(2) 6.3.1, 6.3.2, 6.5, 6.5.8, 7.4.2, 7.5, 7.20.1
(2)(a) 2.3.1
(2)(c) 10.8.9, 10.13.1
(4) 6.3.1, 6.3.2, 6.4.1
(4)(a), (b) 7.5
(7) 6.3.1, 6.5, 6.5.2, 6.5.8, 7.5
(10) 6.4
(11) 6.6.1, 7.7, 7.7.2, 7.13
(12)(g) 10.12.1
s 8 6.8, 7.1.1, 7.6, 7.9
(2)–(4) 7.6
(5)(a) 7.6
(6) 7.6
(8) 6.8, 7.6, 7.10
s 9 6.9, 7.1.1
(1) 7.8
(2) 6.9, 6.19.1, 7.8
(3) 6.9, 7.8
s 10 6.10, 7.9

Environmental Protection Act 1990 – *cont*
s 10(3A) 6.10
(4) 6.10
(5) 6.10, 6.19.1
(6) 6.10
(8) 6.10
s 11 6.5.10, 6.10, 7.1.1, 7.9
(2), (3) 6.10
(6) 6.10
(11) 6.10
s 12 6.9, 6.11, 6.15.1, 7.10
(2) 6.11, 7.10
(4) 6.11
(5) 7.10
s 13 6.9, 6.12, 6.12.1, 6.13, 7.1.1, 7.11
(1), (2) 6.12
s 14 6.13, 7.1.1, 7.12
(1)–(5) 6.13
s 15 6.10, 6.12, 6.15, 6.15.1, 6.15.4, 6.15.5, 6.15.6, 6.19.1, 6.24, 7.4.2, 7.13
(1)(a), (b) 6.15
(1)(c) 6.10, 6.15
(1)(d) 6.11, 6.15, 7.10
(2) 6.9, 6.13, 6.15
(5)(a), (b) 6.15.2
(8), (9) 6.15.1
ss 16–18 6.16
s 19 6.17, 7.15
(2) 6.19.1, 6.20.2, 7.15
s 20 6.19.1, 6.19.2, 6.19.3, 6.20, 6.20.1, 6.20.2, 7.1.1, 7.16
(2) 7.16
(6) 6.19.2
(7) 6.19.3
s 21 6.19.2, 6.20.1, 6.20.2, 7.1.1, 7.16
(2) 6.19.1
(4)(b) 6.20.1
s 22 6.19.1, 6.19.2, 6.20.2, 7.1.1, 7.13, 7.16
(2)–(5) 6.20.2
(7)–(10) 6.20.2
s 23 6.15.6, 6.23, 7.4, 7.11, 7.15, 7.17
(1) 6.19.1, 7.4.3
(1)(a) 6.3, 6.4.1, 6.7, 6.9, 6.15.1, 7.4, 7.10, 7.11
(1)(b) 6.9
(1)(c) 6.12, 6.12.1, 6.13, 6.15.1, 7.11
(1)(g) 6.17, 7.15
(1)(l) 6.22, 7.17
s 24 6.12, 6.22, 7.17
s 25 6.4.1
s 26 6.22, 6.23, 7.17
(3) 6.22
s 27 6.23
s 33(1) 4.7
s 64 6.19
s 69(8) 6.16.1
s 71 6.17
s 73(6)–(9) 4.7
s 79(1) 5.2
(1)(b)–(d) 5.2.2
(3)–(5) 5.2.1
(7) 5.2, 5.2.1, 5.2.2, 5.3.2
(9) 5.3.4
(10) 5.2.1
s 80 5.3.1, 5.3.4, 5.3.5
(2) 5.3.2, 5.3.4
(3) 5.3.1, 5.3.3, 5.3.4
(4)–(8) 5.3.4
s 81(1)–(4) 5.3.5
(5) 5.3.6
s 81A 5.3.5
(3) 5.3.5
(6) 5.3.5
(8) 5.3.5
s 81B 5.3.5
s 82 5.3.7, 5.3.8
(1), (2) 5.3.7
(4), (5) 5.3.7
(6) 5.3.7, 5.3.8
(7), (8) 5.3.8
(9), (10) 5.3.7
(11) 5.3.8
(12) 5.3.7, 5.3.8
(13) 5.3.8
s 152 5.4
s 157 6.14
s 160 5.3.2
Sch 1 7.1.1
Sch 1, Pt I 6.3.1, 7.4
para 1(3) 6.3.1, 6.19.1
para 3 6.3.1
para 5(1) 7.4
(3) 7.4
Sch I, Pt II 6.10
para 7 6.10
para 8 6.3.1
Sch 3, para 6 5.3.1
European Communities Act 1972 1.5.1
s 2 6.3.2
(4) 1.9
Explosives Act 1975 8.2.2

Fatal Accidents Act 1976 4.7
Finance Act 1997
 s 7 9.4.1

Gas Act 1965
 s 14 4.7

Health and Safety at Work Act 1974 2.3, 2.7.1, 10.12.4
 Pt I 6.3.2
 s 5 5.2.1
Highways Act 1980
 s 161(2) 5.4
 s 161A 5.4
Highways Amendment Act 1986 5.4

Interpretation Act 1978
 s 7 9.9.1

Law of Property Act 1925 5.3.5
Law Reform (Contributory Negligence) Act 1945 4.6.3
Local Government Act 1972
 s 201 9.3
 s 222 4.2, 5.3.6
 s 233 5.3.1, 5.3.2
 s 250(2)–(5) 6.3.1, 8.5.1, 8.9
Local Government etc (Scotland) Act 1994
 s 2 10.8.2

Magistrates' Courts Act 1980
 s 34 5.3.4
 s 64 5.3.3
 s 101 6.2.3
Merchant Shipping Act 1995 8.7.4
Military Lands Act 1892 6.12.1
Mines and Quarries Act 1954 5.2.1

Petroleum Spirit (Consolidation) Act 1928
 s 23 9.4
Powers of Criminal Courts Act 1973
 s 35 5.3.7
Public Health Act 1848 5.1
Public Health Act 1875 5.1, 8.1
Public Health Act 1936 2.7.1, 5.1, 5.3.2, 5.3.4
 Pt XII 8.5.4
 s 100 5.3.6
 ss 275, 276 8.8.5
 s 278 8.8.5
 ss 283–285 8.8.5
 s 289 8.8.5
 s 291 8.8.5
 ss 293, 294 8.8.5
 s 299 8.8.5
 s 305 8.8.5
Public Health Act 1961 5.1
Public Health (Recurring Nuisances) Act 1969 5.1
Public Health (Smoke Abatement) Act 1926 8.1.1

Radioactive Substances Act 1993 6.12
Railways Act 1993 10.12.4
Road Traffic Act 1988 9.6
 s 40(7) 9.8.3
 s 41 9.8, 9.8.5, 9.8.6
  (1), (2) 9.8
  (6) 9.8
 s 42 9.8
 s 45 9.8.5
  (1), (2) 9.8.1
 s 46 9.8.1
 s 47(1) 9.8.1
 s 49 9.8.2, 9.8.5
 s 50 9.8.2
 s 51 9.8.2
 ss 54–61 9.8.3, 9.8.4
 s 54 9.8.3
 s 55(1), (2) 9.8.3
 s 58(1) 9.9.1
 s 61 9.8.5
 s 62 9.8.4
 s 63(1) 9.8.4
  (1(A)) 9.8.4
 s 65 9.8.4
  (2) 9.8.4
 s 66A 9.8.5
 s 67 9.8.5
  (1) 9.8.5
  (4), (5) 9.8.5
  (9) 9.8.5
 s 68 9.8.5
  (1) 9.8.5
  (3), (4) 9.8.5

Road Traffic Act 1988 – *cont*
s 69 9.8.5
(1) 9.8.5
(3)–(6) 9.8.5
(8) 9.8.5
s 69A 9.8.5
s 71 9.8.5
s 72 9.8.5
(1) 9.8.5
s 72A 9.8.5
s 74(1) 9.8.6
s 75(1) 9.8.6
(3)–(5) 9.8.6
s 76(1) 9.8.6
s 77 9.8.5
s 85 9.8.4
s 192(1) 9.8.1, 9.8.2
Road Traffic Offences Act 1988
s 51 9.8
Sch 3 9.8
Road Traffic Reduction Act 1997 10.1.3
s 2(1), (2) 10.1.3
(4)–(8) 10.1.3
Road Traffic Reduction (National Targets) Act 1998 10.1.3
Road Traffic Regulation Act 1984 10.1.2, 10.12.7
s 1 10.1.2
s 6 10.1.2
s 122 10.1.2
Roads Act 1920 9.8.1

Sanitary Act 1866 8.1
Supreme Court Act 1981
s 50 4.5.2

Town and Country Planning Act 1971
s 87 6.12.1
Town and Country Planning Act 1990 6.15.6, 6.24
Pt VII 6.12.1
s 70(1) 7.4.1
s 172 6.12.1
s 177 6.3.1
s 179(1) 6.12.1
s 288 6.24
Trade Descriptions Act 1968 9.3
Transport Act 1980
s 64(3) 9.8.1
Tribunals and Inquiries Act 1992 8.9

Vehicle (Excise) Act 1949 9.8.1
Vehicle (Excise) Act 1962 9.8.1
Vehicle (Excise) Act 1971 9.8.1

Water Industry Act 1991
s 196 6.19
Water Resources Act 1991 6.3.2, 6.21
s 190 6.19

TABLE OF STATUTORY INSTRUMENTS

References are to paragraph numbers.

SI 1992/2137 9.6
SI 1993/2199 9.6
SI 1997/1544 9.6
SI 1997/1960 9.4.1

Air Quality Regulations 1997, SI 1997/3043 10.10.3, 10.13.3
Air Quality Standards Regulations 1989, SI 1989/317 2.5, 2.5.2, 2.7.1, 8.10, 10.2
reg 4 10.2
reg 6 10.2
Air Quality Standards (Amendment) Regulations 1995, SI 1995/3146 10.2

Building Regulations 1991, SI 1991/2768 8.4.3

Clean Air (Arrestment Plant) (Exemption) Regulations 1969, SI 1969/1262 8.3.3
Schs 1–3 8.3.3
Clean Air (Emission of Dark Smoke) (Exemption) Regulations 1969, SI 1969/1263 8.2.2
Clean Air (Emission of Grit and Dust from Furnaces) Regulations 1971, SI 1971/162 8.3, 8.3.2
reg 4(2) 8.3.2
reg 5 8.3.2
Sch 1 8.3.2
Sch 2 8.3.2
Clean Air (Height of Chimneys) (Exemption) Regulations 1969, SI 1969/411 8.4.1
Clean Air (Measurement of Grit and Dust from Furnaces) Regulations 1971, SI 1971/161 8.3.6
Control of Atmospheric Pollution (Appeals) Regulations 1977, SI 1977/17 10.4.4
Control of Atmospheric Pollution (Research and Publicity) Regulations 1977, SI 1977/19 10.4.4
reg 3 10.4.5
reg 4 10.4.5
(2) 10.4.5
Control of Industrial Air Pollution (Registration of Works) Regulations 1989, SI 1989/318 2.3
Crop Residues (Burning) Regulations 1993, SI 1993/1366 5.4.1
Crop Residues (Restrictions on Burning) (No 2) Regulations 1991, SI 1991/1590 5.4

Dark Smoke (Permitted Periods) Regulations 1958, SI 1958/498 8.2.1
Dark Smoke (Permitted Periods) (Vessels) Regulations 1958, SI 1958/878 8.7.4
Deregulation (Model Appeal Provisions) Order 1996, SI 1996/1678 6.12
Ch II 6.12, 6.13

Enforcement of Road Traffic Debts Order 1993, SI 1993/2073
Art 2(1)(a) 10.18.1
Environment Act (Commencement No 5) Order 1996, SI 1996/186 10.8
Environmental Information Regulations 1992, SI 1992/3240 2.8, 6.18, 10.8.12, 10.14.6
Environmental Protection (Amendment of Regulations) Regulations 1991, SI 1991/836 6.2
Environmental Protection (Applications, Appeals and Registers) Regulations 1991, SI 1991/507 6.3.1, 6.8, 6.15, 6.19.1, 7.4, 7.13
reg 2 6.3.1, 6.15
(3) 7.4
reg 5 6.19.1
reg 9 6.15, 6.15.2, 6.20.2
(2) 6.15
(a) 6.19.1
(d), (e) 6.19.1
reg 10 6.15
(1)(d) 6.15
reg 11 6.15
reg 12 6.15.3
reg 13 6.15.4
(2) 6.15.4
(6) 6.15.4
reg 15 6.19.1, 6.19.2
reg 17 6.19.2
Environmental Protection (Applications, Appeals and Registers) (Amendment) Regulations 1996, SI 1996/667 6.15, 7.13
Environmental Protection (Authorisation of Processes) (Determination Periods) Order 1991, SI 1991/513 7.4
Environmental Protection (Controls on Substances that Deplete the Ozone Layer) Regulations 1996, SI 1996/506 2.9.1
Environmental Protection (Non-Refillable Refrigerant Containers) Regulations 1994, SI 1994/199 2.9.1
Environmental Protection (Prescribed Processes and Substances) Regulations 1991, SI 1991/472 2.3, 6.2, 6.25, 7.1.1, 7.2, 7.3, 8.7.1
reg 4 6.2.3, 7.2.3
Sch 1 6.2.1, 6.2.2, 6.24, 7.2.1, 7.2.2
ch 1
s 1.1 6.2.1, 7.2.1
s 1.2 6.2.1
s 1.3 6.2.1, 7.2.1
s 1.4 6.2.1, 7.2.1
ch 2 7.7.1
s 2.1 6.2.1, 7.2.1, 7.2.2
s 2.2 6.2.1, 7.2.1, 7.2.2
ch 3

Environmental Protection (Prescribed Processes and Substances) Regulations 1991 – *cont*
s 3.1 6.2.1, 7.2.1
s 3.2 6.2.1, 7.2.1
s 3.3 6.2.1
s 3.4 7.2.1
s 3.5 6.2.1, 7.2.1
s 3.6 6.2.1, 7.2.1
ch 4
s 4.1 6.2.1, 7.2.1
s 4.2 6.2.1, 7.2.1
s 4.3 6.2.1, 7.2.1
s 4.4 6.2.1
s 4.5 6.2.1
s 4.6 6.2.1
s 4.7 6.2.1
s 4.8 6.2.1
s 4.9 7.2.1
ch 5
s 5.1 6.2.1, 7.2.1
s 5.2 6.2.1
s 5.3 6.2.1
ch 6
s 6.1 6.2.1
s 6.2 6.2.1, 7.2.1
s 6.3 6.2.1, 7.2.1
s 6.5 6.2.1, 7.2.1
s 6.6 6.2.1, 7.2.1
s 6.7 6.2.1, 7.2.1
s 6.8 7.2.1
s 6.9 6.2.1, 7.2.1
Sch 2 6.2.2, 7.2.1, 7.2.2
rule 2 6.2.2
rule 2C 7.2.2
rule 3 6.2.2, 7.2.2
rule 4 6.2.2
rule 7(1) 7.2.2
Sch 3, Pt II 7.4
Sch 4 6.2.3, 6.2.4, 7.2.3, 7.3.1, 7.5
Sch 5 6.2.1, 6.2.3, 6.2.4
Sch 6 6.2.3, 6.2.4
Environmental Protection (Prescribed Processes and Substances) (Amendment) Regulations 1992, SI 1992/614 6.2
Environmental Protection (Prescribed Processes and Substances) (Amendment) Regulations 1993, SI 1993/1749 6.2
Environmental Protection (Prescribed Processes and Substances) (Amendment) (No 2) Regulations 1993, SI 1993/2405 6.2
Environmental Protection (Prescribed Processes and Substances) (Amendment) Regulations 1994, SI 1994/1271 6.2, 7.3, 7.4
Environmental Protection (Prescribed Processes and Substances etc) (Amendment) (No 2) Regulations 1994, SI 1994/1329 6.2

Environmental Protection (Prescribed Processes and Substances etc) (Amendment) (Petrol Vapour Recovery) Regulations 1996, SI 1996/2678 2.9.2, 6.2, 9.7

Goods Vehicles (Plating and Testing) Regulations 1988, SI 1988/1478 9.8.2

Health and Safety (Emissions to the Atmosphere) (Amendment) Regulations 1989, SI 1989/319 2.3

Large Combustion Plant (New Plant) Directions 1995 6.3.2

Marketing of Gas Oil (Sulphur Content) Regulations 1994, SI 1994/2249 2.5.1, 9.4.1
Motor Fuel (Composition and Content) Regulations 1994, SI 1994/2295 2.5.1, 9.4, 9.4.1
Motor Fuel (Lead Content of Petrol) Regulations 1976, SI 1976/1866 9.4
Motor Fuel (Lead Content of Petrol) Regulations 1981, SI 1981/1523 9.4
Motor Fuel (Lead Content of Petrol) (Amendment) Regulations 1979, SI 1979/1 9.4
Motor Fuel (Lead Content of Petrol) (Amendment) Regulations 1985, SI 1985/1728 2.7.2
Motor Vehicle (Test) Regulations 1981, SI 1981/1694 9.8.1
Motor Vehicles (EC Type Approval) Regulations 1992, SI 1992/3107 9.8.3, 9.9, 9.9.1
Pt III 9.9.1
reg 3(1)–(4) 9.9.1
(10) 9.9.1
reg 4 9.8.4
(2) 9.9.1
regs 5–7 9.9.1
reg 8(2)–(4) 9.9.1
(6), (7) 9.9.1
reg 9 9.9.1
reg 10(10) 9.9.1
reg 11 9.9.1
reg 12 9.9.1
(1) 9.9.1
reg 13 9.9.1
(1)–(3) 9.9.1
reg 14(1)–(3) 9.9.1
reg 15 9.9.1
Motor Vehicles (Type Approval and Approved Marks) (Fees) Regulations 1996, SI 1996/958 9.8.3
Motor Vehicles (Type Approval for Goods Vehicles) (Great Britain) Regulations 1982, SI 1982/1271 9.8.3, 9.9
Motor Vehicles (Type Approval) (EEC Manufacturers) Regulations 1981, SI 1981/493 9.8.4
Motor Vehicles (Type Approval) (Great Britain) Regulations 1984, SI 1984/981 9.8.3, 9.9
Municipal Waste Incineration Directions 1991 2.4.1, 6.3.2

Ozone Monitoring and Information Regulations 1994, SI 1994/440 2.8.3, 10.2

Road Traffic (Vehicle Emissions) (Fixed Penalty) Regulations 1997, SI 1997/3058 10.18.1
regs 2, 3 10.18.1
reg 5 10.18.1
regs 7–12 10.18.1
Road Vehicles (Construction and Use) Regulations 1982
reg 98 9.9.2
Road Vehicles (Construction and Use) Regulations 1986, SI 1986/1078 9.6, 9.8, 9.8.6, 9.9, 10.18.1
reg 61 10.18.1
(1) 9.9
(3B) 9.9
(4)–(7) 9.9
Table II 9.9
reg 98 10.18.1
Road Vehicles (Construction and Use) (Amendment) (No 2) Regulations 1990, SI 1990/1131 9.6
Road Vehicles (Construction and Use) (Amendment) (No 5) Regulations 1995, SI 1995/2210 9.6
Road Vehicles (Construction and Use) (Amendment) (No 5) Regulations 1996, SI 1996/2329 9.6
Road Vehicles (Prohibition) Regulations 1992, SI 1992/1285 9.8.5
Rules of the Supreme Court 1965, SI 1965/1776 4.3.4
Ord 53 6.15.6

Smoke Control Areas (Authorised Fuels) Regulations 1991, SI 1991/1282 8.5.2
Smoke Control Areas (Authorised Fuels) (Amendment) Regulations 1997, SI 1997/2658 8.5.2
Smoke Control Areas (Exempted Fireplaces) Order 1970/615 8.5.2
Smoke Control Areas (Exempted Fireplaces) Order 1971, SI 1971/1265 8.5.2
Smoke Control Areas (Exempted Fireplaces) Order 1972, SI 1972/438 8.5.2
Smoke Control Areas (Exempted Fireplaces) Order 1973, SI 1973/2166 8.5.2
Smoke Control Areas (Exempted Fireplaces) Order 1978, SI 1978/1609 8.5.2
Smoke Control Areas (Exempted Fireplaces) Order 1982, SI 1982/1615 8.5.2
Smoke Control Areas (Exempted Fireplaces) Order 1983, SI 1983/277 8.5.2
Smoke Control Areas (Exempted Fireplaces) Order 1984, SI 1984/1649 8.5.2
Smoke Control Areas (Exempted Fireplaces) Order 1986, SI 1986/638 8.5.2
Smoke Control Areas (Exempted Fireplaces) Order 1988, SI 1988/2282 8.5.2
Smoke Control Areas (Exempted Fireplaces) Order 1989, SI 1989/1769 8.5.2
Smoke Control Areas (Exempted Fireplaces) Order 1990, SI 1990/345 8.5.2
Smoke Control Areas (Exempted Fireplaces) Order 1991, SI 1991/2892 8.5.2
Smoke Control Areas (Exempted Fireplaces) Order 1992, SI 1992/2811 8.5.2
Smoke Control Areas (Exempted Fireplaces) Order 1993, SI 1993/2277 8.5.2
Smoke Control Areas (Exempted Fireplaces) Order 1997, SI 1997/3009 8.5.2
Smoke Control Areas (Exempted Fireplaces) (No 2) Order 1970, SI 1970/1667 8.5.2
Smoke Control Areas (Exempted Fireplaces) (No 2) Order 1972, SI 1972/955 8.5.2
Smoke Control Areas (Exempted Fireplaces) (No 2) Order 1975, SI 1975/1001 8.5.2
Smoke Control Areas (Exempted Fireplaces) (No 2) Order 1983, SI 1983/426 8.5.2

Smoke Control Areas (Exempted Fireplaces) (No 2) Order 1990, SI 1990/2457 8.5.2
Smoke Control Areas (Exempted Fireplaces) (No 3) Order 1975, SI 1975/1111 8.5.2
Smoke Control Areas (Exempted Fireplaces) (No 3) Order 1983, SI 1983/1018 8.5.2
Smoke Control Areas (Exempted Fireplaces) Order 1982, SI 1982/448 8.5.2
Smoke Control Areas (Exempted Fireplaces) Order 1984, SI 1984/1805 8.5.2
Smoke Control Areas (Exempted Fireplaces) Order 1985, SI 1985/315 8.5.2
Smoke Control Areas (Exempted Fireplaces) Order 1987, SI 1987/383 8.5.2
Statutory Nuisance (Appeals) Regulations 1995, SI 1995/2644 5.3.3

Town and Country Planning (Inquiries Procedure) Rules 1988, SI 1988/944 7.13

TABLE OF CODES, GUIDANCE NOTES ETC

References are to paragraph numbers.

DoE Circular 25/81 Third Memorandum on Chimney Heights (1981) 8.4.2
DoE General Guidance Notes GG1(91)–GG4(91) 7.7.2
DoE General Guidance Notes GG5(91) 7.7.2, 7.13
DoE Guidance GG5(91) 6.15.4
DoE Guidance PPG 23, Planning and Pollution Control 6.24

Environment Agency Technical Guidance Note D1 Guidelines on Discharge Stack Heights for Polluting Emissions, June 1993 6.5.5, 6.6.3
Environment Agency Technical Guidance Note (Environmental) E1 Best Practicable Environmental Option Assessments for Integrated Pollution Control 1997 6.5.2, 6.5.3, 6.6.3
Environment Circular 15/97 10.13.4

General Guidance Note 1 7.6
Guidance Note No 1: section 15 Appeals 6.15
Annex A 6.15.5
Guidance Note PG2/5(96) Hot and Cold Blast Cupolas 7.7.1
Guidance Note PG6/1(91) Animal by–product rendering 7.4.3

HMIP Guidance Notes IPR1–IPR5 6.6, 6.6.1

IPC Guidance Notes IPR 1/1, 2/1, 3/1, 4/1 6.6
IPC Guidance Note IPR 1/11 6.6.2
IPC Guidance Note S2 1.08 6.6.2

LAQMG1(97) The framework for review and assessment of air quality 10.14
LAQMG2(97) The framework for review and assessment of air quality 10.15
LAQMG3(97) The framework for review and assessment of air quality 10.16
LAQMG4(97) The framework for review and assessment of air quality 10.17
LAQM.TG1(98) Monitoring for air quality reviews and assessment 10.14
LAQM.TG2(98) Preparation and use of atmospheric emissions inventories 10.14
LAQM.TG3(98) Selection and use of dispersion models 10.14

National Farmers' Union Code on stubble burning 5.4

Welsh Office Circular 63/97 10.13.4

TABLE OF EC MATERIAL

References are to paragraph numbers and to figures in text.

Convention on Certain Institutions Common to the European Communities 1957 1.8

Decision 89/367 OJ 1989 L165/4, on the setting up of a standing forestry committee 2.8.1
Decision 93/731 OJ 1993 L340/43, on public access to Council documents 2.8
Decision 94/90 OJ 1994 L46/58, on public access to Commission documents 2.8
Decision 97/101 on information and research 2.2, 2.8.2

Directive 70/156/EEC OJ 1970 L42/1, on light passenger vehicle type approvals 9.8.4
Directive 70/220/EEC, OJ 1970 L76/1, on air pollution from positive-ignition engines of motor vehicles 9.6
Directive 74/290/EEC, OJ 1974 L159/61, amending Directive 70/220/EEC 9.6
Directive 75/442/EEC OJ 1975 L194/39, on waste 2.4.2
Directive 75/716/EEC OJ 1975 L307/22, on the sulphur content of certain liquid fuels 2.5.1, 9.4.1
Directive 76/207/EEC OJ 1976 L39/40, on equal treatment 1.11
Directive 76/464/EEC, OJ 1976 L129/23, on pollution caused by certain dangerous substances discharged into the aquatic environment of the Community 2.10
Directive 77/102/EEC OJ 1977 L32/32, amending Directive 70/220/EEC 9.6
Directive 78/611/EEC OJ 1978 L197/19, on the lead content of petrol 2.7.2, 9.4
Directive 78/665/EEC OJ 1978 L223/48, amending Directive 70/220/EEC 9.6, Fig 1
  Annex I, paras 3, 5, 8, 11 Fig 1
Directive 79/409/EEC OJ 1979 L103/1, wild birds Directive 1.1.3
Directive 80/778/EEC OJ 1980 L229/11, on drinking water 4.3.8
Directive 80/779/EEC OJ 1980 L229/30, on air quality limit values and guide values for sulphur dioxide and suspended particulates 2.5, 8.10, 10.2
  Annex II 8.10
Directive 80/1987 1.12
Directive 82/884/EEC OJ L378/15, on a limit value for lead in air 2.2, 2.7, 2.7.1, 10.2
Directive 83/351/EEC OJ 1983 L197/1, amending Directive 70/220/EEC 9.6
  Annex I, paras 5, 7, 8, 12 Fig 1
Directive 84/360/EEC OJ 1984 L188/20, Air Framework Directive 2.2, 2.3, 2.4, 2.4.2, 2.5.2, 2.10, 6.2.4, 6.4
  Art 8 2.3
  Annexes I, II 2.3
Directive 84/631/EEC OJ 1984 L326/31, on the transfrontier shipment of hazardous waste 1.4.4
Directive 84/860 2.3
Directive 85/203/EEC OJ 1985 L87/1, on nitrogen dioxide 2.2, 2.5.2, 10.2
Directive 85/210/EEC OJ 1985 L96/25, on the lead content of petrol 2.2, 2.7, 2.7.2, 9.4

Directive 85/337/EEC OJ 1985 L175/40, on the assessment of the effects of certain public and private projects on the environment 2.10
Directive 87/219/EEC OJ 1987 L91/19, amending Directive 75/716/EEC 9.4.1
Directive 87/416/EEC OJ 1987 L225/33, amending Directive 85/210/EEC 9.4
Directive 88/76/EEC, on air pollution by gases from the engines of motor vehicles; amending Directive 70/220/EEC 9.6
Annex I, paras 5, 7, 8, 13 Fig 1
Directive 88/77/EEC OJ 1988 L36/33, on pollutants from diesel engines 9.6
Art 1 Fig 1
Annex I, paras 6, 7, 8 Fig 1
Directive 88/436/EEC OJ 1988 L214/1, amending Directive 70/220/EEC 9.6
Annex I, paras 5, 7, 8 Fig 1
Directive 88/609/EEC OJ 1988 L336/1, on large combustion plants 2.2, 2.3, 2.3.1, 6.3.2, 10.7.1
Annex IX 2.3.1
Directive 89/369/EEC OJ 1989 L163/32, on new municipal waste incineration plants 2.2, 2.3, 2.4, 2.4.2, 6.3.2
Directive 89/429/EEC OJ 1989 L203/50, on existing municipal waste incineration plants 2.4, 2.4.1, 2.4.2, 6.3.2
Directive 89/458/EEC OJ 1989 L226/1, on European emission standards for cars below 1.4 litres; amending Directive 70/220/EEC 9.6
Annex I, paras 5, 7, 8, 13 Fig 1
Directive 90/313/EEC OJ 1990 L158/56, on freedom of access to information on the environment 2.8, 2.10, 6.18
Art 2A 2.8
Directive 91/441/EEC OJ 1991 L242/1, amending Directive 70/220/EEC 9.6
Annex I, paras 5, 7, 8, 13 Fig 1
Directive 91/542/EEC OJ 1991 L295/1, amending Directive 88/77/EEC 9.6
Annex I, paras 5, 6, 7, 8 Fig 1
Directive 92/13/EEC OJ 1992 L76/14, on procurement procedures 9.4.1
Directive 92/53/EEC OJ 1992 L225/1, amending Directive 70/156/EEC 9.9.1
Directive 92/72/EEC OJ 1992 L297/1, on ozone pollution 2.2, 2.8.3, 10.2, 10.3
Directive 20.92/55/EEC 2.7.2
Directive 93/12/EEC OJ 1993 L74/81, on the sulphur content of fuels 2.2, 2.5.1, 9.4, 9.4.1
Directive 93/59/EEC OJ 1993 L186/21, amending Directive 70/220/EEC 9.6
Annex I, paras 5, 7, 8 Fig 1
Directive 21.93/116/EEC 2.7.2
Directive 94/12/EEC OJ 1994 L100/42, on air pollution by emissions from motor vehicles; amending Directive 70/220/EEC 9.6
Annex I, paras 5, 7, 8 Fig 1
Directive 94/63/EC, on volatile organic compounds 2.2, 2.9.2, 9.7
Annex II 2.9.2
Directive 94/66/EEC, on large combustion plant 6.3.2
Directive 94/67/EC, on hazardous waste incineration 2.2, 2.3, 2.4.2
Directive 96/1/EC 9.6
Directive 96/61/EC Integrated Pollution Prevention and Control (IPPC) Directive 2.2, 2.10, 6.26, 6.26.1, 6.26.2, 6.26.3, 6.26.4, 7.4.3, 7.20.2, 7.20.3, 7.20.4
Art 3 6.26.2
Art 7 7.20.2
Art 9 6.26.3
Annex I 6.26

Annex III 6.26.3
Directive 96/62/EC, on ambient air quality assessment and management 2.2, 2.3, 2.5, 2.5.2, 2.6, 2.7.1, 2.8.2, 2.8.3, 10.3, 10.7.1, 10.10.2
Annex I 2.8.2
Directive 96/64/EC 2.10
Directive 96/69/EC 9.6
Arts 3, 4 9.6
Annex I, paras 5, 7, 8 Fig 1
Directive 96/97
Annex I, paras 5, 7, 8 Fig 1

EC Auto Oil Agreement of June 1997 10.13.1
EC Auto/Oil Programme 1996 9.4
Environmental Action Programme (First) 1973 OJ 1973 C112/1 1.2, 1.6.2, 3.2.4, 3.3
Environmental Action Programme (Second) 1977 OJ 1977 C139/1 1.2
Environmental Action Programme (Third) 1983 OJ 1983 C46 1.2
Environmental Action Programme (Fourth) 1987 OJ 1987 C328/1 1.2, 2.8, 2.8.3, 6.1.1
Environmental Action Programme (Fifth) 1993 OJ 1993 C138 1.2, 1.6.1, 1.6.4, 2.8, 2.8.2, 2.9.2, 3.2.4, 9.7
European Atomic Energy Community Treaty 1957 (Euratom)
Art 1 1.8

Merger Treaty 1965 1.8

Regulation 17/62, OJ 1959–1962/87, implementing EEC treaty, arts 85, 86 2.1.1
Regulation 3528/86/EEC OJ 1986 L326/2, on the protection of EC forests against atmospheric pollution 2.2, 2.8.1
Regulation 1210/90 OJ 1990 L120/1, on the establishment of the European Environment Agency and the European environment information and observation network 1.3
Art 1(2) 1.3
Art 6 2.8
Art 20 1.3
Regulation 2157/92 OJ 1992 L217/1, amending Regulation 3258/86/EEC 2.8.1
Regulation 3093/94/EC, on ozone depletion international obligations 2.2, 2.9.1

Single European Act 1986 1.1.3, 1.4.1, 1.7, 1.8.5, 1.9.1, 9.6
Title VII 1.4.1
Art 2 1.8.3

Treaty of European Union (Treaty of Maastricht) 1.1.3, 1.2, 1.4.1, 1.4.2, 1.4.3, 1.5.2, 1.5.3, 1.6.5, 1.7, 1.8.2, 1.9.2
Title I 1.4.1
Art B 1.4.1
Art G 1.4.1
Art G(64) 1.10.1

Treaty of Rome 1957 (EC Treaty)	1.1.2, 1.4, 1.4.1, 1.5, 1.6, 1.6.4, 1.7, 1.8.1, 1.9, 1.10, 1.10.1, 2.1.1
Pt III, Title VII, Environment	1.1.3
Ch 3, Title XVI	1.4.1, 1.4.2
Art 1	1.1.2
Art 2	1.1.2
Art 3	1.1.2
Art 3B	1.6.5, 1.6.6
Art 5	1.4.1, 1.8.1, 1.9, 1.11, 1.12, 2.1.2
Art 12	1.9.2, 1.10.1
Art 30	1.1.2, 1.4.3
Art 36	1.1.2, 1.4.3
Arts 92–95	1.8.1
Art 100	1.1.2, 1.1.3, 2.3
Art 100A	1.1.3, 1.4.3, 2.5.1
Art 130	1.1.3, 1.4.3, 1.6
Arts 130R–130T	1.9.2
Art 130R	1.1.3, 1.2, 1.4.4, 1.6.5
(1)	1.4.2
(2)	1.1.3, 1.4.1, 1.4.2, 1.4.3, 1.4.4, 1.6.2, 1.6.3, 1.9.2
(3)	1.4.4
(4)	1.4.2, 3.3
Art 130S	1.1.3, 1.2, 1.4.4, 6.26
(2)	1.8.2
(5)	1.4.4, 1.5.2
Art 130T	1.1.3
Arts 145–154	1.8.2
Art 151	1.8.4
Arts 155–163	1.8.1
Art 155	1.10
Art 158 EC	1.8.1
(2) EC	1.8.1
Art 164	1.6, 1.9
Art 169	1.4.1, 1.5.2, 1.8.1, 1.10.1, 1.12, 2.1.1, 2.1.2, 10.2
Art 170	1.4.1, 1.10.1, 2.1.2
Art 171	1.4.1, 1.9, 1.10.1, 2.1.1
Art 173	1.6, 1.6.5, 1.7, 1.7.1, 1.9.1, 2.8
Arts 173–175	1.9
Art 175	1.7, 1.7.1, 1.9.1
Art 177	1.5.4, 1.9, 1.9.2, 1.10, 1.12
Art 184	1.7.1
Art 189	1.5, 1.5.1, 1.5.2, 1.5.3, 1.5.4, 1.10.1, 1.10.2
(3)	1.11
(b)	1.5.3
Art 189B	1.2
Art 189C	1.8.2
Art 190	1.7
Art 191	1.5.3, 1.10.1
(2)	1.5.2
Art 215	1.6
Art 228	3.3
Art 235	1.1.2, 1.1.3, 1.7, 2.3

TABLE OF INTERNATIONAL LAW MATERIALS AND CONVENTIONS

References are to paragraph numbers.

Cases

Barcelona Traction case (1970) ICJ Reports 3; (1970) 46 ILR 178, ICJ 3.2.4

Nicaragua 1986 ICJ Reports 14; p 76 ILR 349, ICJ 3.2.3

North Sea Continental Shelf case, ICJ 3.2.2, 3.2.3

Serbian Loans case (1929) PCIJ Series A, No 20; 5 ILR 466 3.2.4

Temple case (1962) ICJ Reports; (1962) 33 ILR, ICJ 3.2.4

Trail Smelter arbitration (1939) 33 AJIL 182, (1941) 35 AJIL 684 3.4, 3.4.1

Conventions etc

Convention on Civil Liability for Oil Pollution Damage (1969) 3.2.4

Convention on the Establishment of an International Fund for the Compensation of Oil Pollution Damage (1992) 3.2.4

Council of Europe's Convention on Civil Liability 1993 4.6

European Convention on Human Rights and Fundamental Freedoms
- Art 6(1) 6.15.6

Geneva Convention on Long-range Transboundary Air Pollution 1979 2.3.1, 2.9.2, 3.4.1, 3.5.1, 3.5.2, 3.5.3, 9.7
- Art 1(a), (b) 3.4.1
- Art 2 3.4.1
- Art 6 3.4.1
- Art 8(b) 3.4.1
- Protocol of 1984 3.4.2
- Protocol of 1985 3.4.2
- Protocol of 1988 3.4.2
- Protocol of 1991 3.4.2
- Protocol of 1994 3.4.2
- Protocol of 1998 3.4.2

Global Climate Change Convention 1994 3.6.1, 3.7, 3.8
Art 1(8) 3.6.1
Art 3 3.8
(3) 3.6.1
Art 7 3.6.1
Art 14 3.6.1
Kyoto Protocol 1997 3.6, 3.6.1, 3.8, 3.8.1, 3.8.2

New York Earth Summit June 1997 3.7

Paris Convention for the Protection of the Marine Environment of the North Atlantic 3.2.4
Art 2 3.2.4

Statute of the International Court of Justice (1946)
Art 38 3.2.4, 3.2.6
(1) 3.2.1, 3.2.2
Art 59 3.2.1, 3.2.6
Stockholm Declaration on the Human Environment 1972 1.1.3
Principle 21 3.4, 3.5.1, 3.5.2

United Nations Charter
Art 2(6) 3.2.2
Art 51 3.2.2
United Nations Conference on Environment and Development (UNCED) Global 1992 (Rio Declaration) 3.7
Principle 15 3.2.4
Principle 16 3.2.4
United Nations Economic Commission for Europe (UNECE) Convention on Environmental Impact Assessment 1991 3.4.1

Vienna Convention for the Protection of the Ozone Layer 1985 3.5.1, 3.5.2, 3.6, 3.6.1
Art 1(2) 3.5.2
Art 2 3.5.2
Art 4 3.5.2
Art 10(b) 3.5.2
Art 11 3.5.2
Montreal Protocol 1987 2.9.1, 3.5.2, 3.5.3
Art 2(9) 3.5.3
Montreal Protocol London amendments 1990 3.5.3
Montreal Protocol Copenhagen amendments 1992 3.5.3

TABLE OF ABBREVIATIONS

AQLVs	air quality limit values
AQMA	air quality management area
BAT	best available techniques
BATNEEC	best available techniques not entailing excessive cost
BPEO	best practicable environmental option
BTU	British thermal units
CAA 1993	Clean Air Act 1993
CFCs	chlorofluorocarbons
CFI	Court of First Instance
CO	carbon monoxide
CO_2	carbon dioxide
COMEAP	Committee on the Medical Aspects of Air Pollution
COREPER	Comité des Représentants Permanents
CPC	co-ordinated pollution control
CRI	Chemical Release Inventory
DETR	Department of the Environment, Transport and the Regions (from 1997)
DoE	Department of the Environment (to 1997)
DoH	Department of Health
EAL	environmental assessment level
EAP	Environmental Action Programmes
EC	European Community
ECB	European Central Bank
ECJ	European Court of Justice
ECSC	European Coal and Steel Community
EEA	European Environment Agency
EEMIN	European Environmental Monitoring and Information Network
EFD	Emission Factor Database
EHO	environmental health officer
EIA	environmental impact assessment
EIC	Environmental Industries Commission
EMEP	European Monitoring and Evaluation Programme
EMMA	environmental monitoring in metropolitan areas
ENDS	Environmental Data Service
EPA 1990	Environmental Protection Act 1990
EPAQS	Expert Panel on Air Quality Standards
EQ	environmental quotient
EQOs	environment quality objectives
EQS	environmental quality standard
EU	European Union

HBFCs	hydrobromofluorocarbons
HC	hydrocarbons
HCFCs	hydrochlorofluorocarbons
HFCs	hydrofluorocarbons
HMIP	Her Majesty's Inspectorate of Pollution
HMPI	Her Majesty's Pollution Inspectorate
ICAO	International Civil Aviation Organisation
ICJ	International Court of Justice
IEI	integrated environmental index
IPC	integrated pollution control
IPPC	integrated pollution prevention and control
LAAPC	local authority air pollution control
MEP	Member of the European Parliament
NAQS	National Air Quality Strategy
NO_2	nitrogen dioxide
N_2O	nitrous oxide
NO_x	nitrogen oxide (NO_x is a generic term covering nitric oxide, nitrous oxide and nitrogen dioxide)
NPV	net present value
NWG	Northumbrian Water Group plc
ODTs	odour detection thresholds
OECD	Organisation for Economic Co-operation and Development
OPRA	operator and pollution risk appraisal
ORTs	odour recognition thresholds
O_3	ozone
PAHs	polycyclic aromatic hydrocarbons
PC	process contribution
PFCs	perfluorocarbons
PCP	photochemical ozone creation potential
PM_{10}	particulate matter of less than 10 microns diameter
POCP	photochemical ozone creation potential
SACTRA	Standing Advisory Committee on Trunk Road Assessment
SEA 1986	Single European Act 1986
SEPA	Scottish Environmental Protection Agency
SO_2	sulphur dioxide
SF_6	sulphur hexafluoride
TEQ	Toxic Equivalent
TEU	Treaty of European Union
TRI	Toxics Release Inventory
TRO	traffic regulation order
UNCED	United Nations Conference on Environment and Development
UNECE	United Nations Economic Commission for Europe
UNEP	United Nations Environment Programme
VLS	very low sulphur
VOCs	volatile organic compounds
WHO	World Health Organisation
YHPAC	Yorkshire and Humberside Pollution Advisory Council

CHAPTER 1

THE EC DIMENSION – LEGISLATION AND INSTITUTIONS

1.1 INTRODUCTION

As we enter the twenty-first century, it is generally recognised that pollution, and environmental issues in general, go way beyond national concerns. Pollution, particularly atmospheric pollution, presents problems at global level which dictate that solutions must also be dealt with globally.

The European Community (EC) was not originally designed to have any authority over the environment. Indeed, in the immediate post-war years, when the idea of a European Economic Community (EEC) was first considered, the environment, as a concept, did not really exist. None the less, as we can see, the boundaries of EC influence have extended to encompass it. Formerly, as a tangential influence on its primary economic and market task, and, latterly, as a legitimate interest in its own right.

The aim of this chapter is to outline some of the fundamental principles of EC law; to identify the roots of EC influence in the environment; to explain the status of the EC as a player in the legal arena; to examine the approach of EC policy to the environment in general with the specific measures in relation to air quality and atmospheric pollution control being addressed in Chapter 2.

1.1.1 Post-war Europe

The EEC was essentially a product of post-war necessity. The end of the Second World War saw the nations of mainland Europe devastated, and the emergence of a new global power balance. The old powers which had entered the conflict had given way to the new global duopoly. In the west lay the USA, whose power had been enhanced not only by its relative geographical isolation from the field of war, but also by the technological innovation which necessity brings. To the east lay the emerging Soviet Union, which, although it had made huge sacrifices, maintained large reserves in terms of both raw materials and manpower. This polarisation of power highlighted the tactical and political significance of Central Europe, where the new world order dictated a need for stability. Such stability could only be wrought from devastation by sound investment.

The price of resurgence exhorted from the European nations was not simply political stability, but co-operation. US investment came primarily in the Marshall Plan, named after the then US Secretary of State. The Marshall Plan led to the establishment of the Council of Europe in 1949, and eventually the Organisation for Economic Co-operation and Development (OECD) in 1961.

The themes of integration and co-operation were quickly adopted by the forefathers of the EC, particularly in the efforts of Jean Monnet and Robert Schumann, although economic integration was not their initial plan.

The first concrete development came in 1952 when the original six Member States – France, Germany, Italy, Belgium, The Netherlands and Luxembourg – came together to form the European Coal and Steel Community (ECSC). Not only was this a prime example of co-operation and integration, but it had the additional benefit of ensuring that none of its members could rearm without their actions quickly becoming obvious to the others.

1.1.2 The Treaty of Rome

The ECSC set itself above traditional international co-operative arrangements, establishing its own institutional framework independent of the Member States. Both the model of integration and some of the institutions were later adopted by the EEC and Euratom by the Treaties of Rome 1957.

Like the ECSC, the EEC established its own intra-national institutions whose independence from the Member States has played a key role in the development of what has long been identified as 'a new legal order'.[1]

Reference to Article 1 of the original Treaty of Rome 1957 indicates the intention of the Member States to 'establish among themselves a European Economic Community'. The aim, according to Article 2 of the Treaty of Rome 1957, was:

> '... by establishing a common market and progressively approximating the economic policies of Member States, to promote throughout the Community a harmonious development of economic activities, a continuous and balanced expansion, an increase in stability, an accelerated raising of the standard of living and closer relations between the States belonging to it.'

It is to be noted that neither protection nor enhancement of environmental quality is mentioned in these aims. The statement of objectives contained in Article 3 of the Treaty of Rome is similarly silent on that point. Further, reference to the main body of the Treaty itself gives little evidence of an anticipated environmental role. Certainly, Article 36 refers to 'the protection of health and life of humans, animals or plants', but this is clearly to be interpreted within the restrictive context of Article 36, of derogation from the prohibition enshrined in Article 30. It is certainly not to be read as a general presumption in favour of environmental quality.

The rationale behind such an omission is simple. Not only would the introduction of environmental issues have been seen as something of a luxury in the immediate post-war Europe, but identification of an environmental

---

1 *NV Algemene Transport-en Expeditie Onderneming Van Gend en Loos v Nederlandse Belastingadministratie* [1963] ECR 1, [1963] CMLR 105.

agenda at that time would have been rather over-sophisticated and somewhat premature in terms of the development of the environment as a recognised agenda. Whilst this may be an acceptable position for the 1950s, it represented an omission in the Community interest in later years.

However, although the original Treaty makes no reference to the environment, it does contain certain general powers to facilitate its broadest aims. In particular, Article 100:

> 'The Council shall, acting unanimously on a proposal from the Commission, issue directives for the approximation of such provisions laid down by law, regulation or administrative action in Member States as directly affect the establishment or functioning of the common market ...'[1]

Article 235 states:

> If action by the Community should prove necessary to attain, in the course of the operation of the common market, one of the objectives of the Community and this Treaty has not provided the necessary powers, the Council shall, acting unanimously on a proposal from the Commission and after consulting the European Parliament, take the appropriate measures.'[2]

It is in reliance upon these general powers that the EEC made its first incursions into environmental protection.

1.1.3 The coming of an environmental agenda

At its simplest, it may be argued that the single market and the aim of a 'level playing field' for economic activity might be difficult to ensure when the players find themselves under differing economic conditions because of differing levels of environmental control. A simple translation of environmental standards into economic terms for producers would indicate a logical interest in environmental issues, if for no other reason than a wish to harmonise externalities of production. On this basis, there seems to be no problem in achieving what might be a dual purpose under the powers of Articles 100 and 235. However, extending these general provisions to the specific protection of environmental quality is of more questionable vires.

Since the birth of the EC, not only has its membership grown from the original six to fifteen Member States, but it has found itself operating in a very different context. Recognition of the environment as a concept worthy, not only of our protection, but promotion, leads the EC to take an active role. Before the Single European Act 1986 (SEA 1986) amended the Treaty to include environmental competence, the Community had already produced more than 100 environmental provisions ranging from measures to protect water and air, to flora and fauna, and waste management. All these provisions were based upon the general authority of Articles 100 and 235.

Whilst a sympathetic interpretation may lead one to accept that standards in relation to water and air may impact upon economic costs, as might waste

1 Article 100, Treaty of Rome.

2 Article 235, Treaty of Rome.

control, it is difficult to see how the European Court of Justice (ECJ) could have accepted provisions such as the Birds Directive,[1] under this authority, if its vires had been subject to challenge.

The formal interest of the Community in the environment dates from the Paris Summit of 1972. At this forum, the Community Heads of State took the opportunity to acknowledge that economic success should be reflected in the improvement of environmental quality and the level of protection accorded to it. The Paris Summit had been prompted by the Stockholm Declaration on the Human Environment of the same year, which is generally acknowledged as the starting point for the globalisation of environmental concern.

The environment did not, however, become officially recognised in the Treaty until the amendment of Article 130 under the SEA 1986. Earlier incursions into the area of environmental control can therefore be explained largely by reference to the will of the Member States rather than the strict authority of the Community. Competency developed on the flimsiest of foundations yet remained unchallenged.

Since the SEA 1986, the competency of the Community is beyond question. The SEA 1986 added Title VII, Environment (Articles 130R–130T) to Part III of the Treaty. This has since been subject to further development in the Treaty of European Union (TEU or Maastricht), which brings into line the voting arrangements in relation to Articles 130S and 100A. The former, giving specific environmental authority, had previously been subject to the requirement of a 'unanimous' vote, in contrast to the general power for facilitating the completion of the single market under Article 100A, where a qualified majority operated. This is a significant change, not only because it frees the environment from the yoke of unanimity which must pull the standards towards the lowest possible denominator, but because it resolves the temptation to take the increasingly litigious route of basing environmental provisions once more on the general authority of Article 100A.

The issue of appropriate authority has been before the ECJ. In the case of *Commission of the European Communities v European Council*,[2] the Commission sought a review of the acts of the Council in founding the programme aimed at reducing titanium dioxide pollution on Article 100A rather than Article 130S. Such a manoeuvre on the part of the Council would, if successful, have benefited from the difference in voting regimes. The ECJ concluded that the legal basis should not be vulnerable to the subjective wish of the institutions, but should be made objectively in consideration of the purpose of the measure. In the instant case, the measure actually played a dual function: the harmonisation of the internal market on the one hand, and the protection of the environment on the other. In such cases, the ECJ was of the view that the existence of the environmental perspective should not, however, force it into the constraints of Article 130S where the application of Article 100A could be justified.

1 EEC Directive 79/409.

2 [1991] 3 LMELR.

Subsequent case-law indicates that the 'primary objective' of the measure should dictate the authoritative basis, which represents a rather less flexible approach. See *Commission of the European Communities v European Council.*[1] The impetus, however, may have been lost by the developments which the TEU brought to Article 130S where the application of Article 100A could be justified.

The basis of authority for environmental policy and action is now firmly established in the EC Treaty. Its influence upon the development of the internal market continues to be recognised. Indeed, Article 130R(2) states that:

> '... Environmental protection requirements must be integrated into the definition and implementation of other Community policies.'

This not only gives the EC the vires to enter into the environmental debate, but provides enduring authority for influence in all spheres of Community activity. The Treaty is, however, quick to point out that measures taken in furtherance of Articles 130R–130T should not limit Member States who wish to adopt more stringent standards. It might, therefore, be argued that this allows Member States to treat EC provisions rather as a minimum standard.

1.2 EC ENVIRONMENTAL POLICY

EC environmental policy, in its broadest sense, is contained in the Environmental Action Programmes (EAP). The first of these programmes developed from the Paris Summit of 1972. At this time, as has been noted, an environmental policy could not gain its authority from the Treaty. The will of the Member States, therefore, seems an important factor in securing the initial environmental role for the EC. Since 1972, there has been a series of five Environmental Action Programmes: 1973 (OJC112); 1977 (OJ139); 1983 (OJC46); 1987 (OJC328/1); 1993 (OJC138), the most recent covering the period to the year 2000.

Amendments to Article 130S of the Treaty now provide an authoritative base for the EAP in the following terms:

> 'In other areas, general action programmes setting out priority objectives to be attained shall be adopted by the Council, acting in accordance with the procedure referred to in Article 189B and after consulting the Economic and Social Committee.'[2]

The Environmental Action Programmes are designed to guide environmental policy and development for a period of approximately five years. Although their existence now gains authority from Article 130S of the EC Treaty, their status remains at a policy level. The provisions of any Environmental Action Programme may govern the thoughts of the EC on the environment, but there are no penalties for failure to implement or activate its contents within the five-

1 [1993] ECR 1-939.
2 Article 130S(3).

year period. The Member States may be influenced in their approach to environmental protection by the EAP irrespective of any elements which may have been translated into legislation, and may adopt equivalent provisions in their domestic policy, but they will not be penalised for failing to do so.

The First Environmental Action Programme of 1973 was, understandably, reactive in its approach. The recognition of an environmental agenda at all levels calls initially for the legacy of past pollution to be addressed. The first programme was, therefore, reactive and structural in nature, establishing a framework of principles for guidance, many of which remain authoritative today, the chief of which are: the expectation that pollution should be tackled at source and that the polluter should pay either in relation to prevention, clean-up or disposal.

It is understandable that the first incursion into the environment should concentrate largely, as the EAP did, on the need to redress historical pollution. The approach of the second and third programmes is, by comparison, rather more sophisticated, placing the emphasis on long-term solutions/protection. Their approach is somewhat more proactive, reflecting a need for prevention and the improvement of environmental quality, whilst recognising the continuing need to uphold the principles of the first programme.

The character of the fourth and fifth programmes in particular indicates an increasing sophistry, with, once more, a shift in emphasis. These programmes take a more integrative stance in relation to environmental control, rather than the strictly media-based approach of earlier programmes. The current programme seeks to promote involvement in environmental policy at all levels, from the individual citizen, through to the institutional framework of the EC itself. It aims to increase awareness of a shared responsibility in the environment through the dissemination of information, education, and co-operation. This will be emphasised by the increased use of economic and fiscal techniques, which reflect back to the original principles enshrined in the first EAP, reminding us that, in many instances, we, the consumers, are the polluter.

In addition, the Fifth Environmental Action Programme identifies five sectors of the economy as a particular focus of attention: industry, energy, transport, agriculture and tourism. The central theme running through the approach to each sector is the internalisation of environmental protection. Industry is encouraged to incorporate the environment into strategic planning, management and production, encouraging self-regulation and the minimum of environmental impact through design. In the field of energy, the prime aim is the reduction of sulphur dioxide (SO_2), carbon dioxide (CO_2) and nitrous oxide (N_2O), with the emphasis on improving efficiency and the development of alternative, less environmentally costly energy sources. The guiding principle is, therefore, the internalisation of the environment, encouraging reduction in damage and consumption through research and design.

Atmospheric concerns are clearly at the heart of the latest EAP through the identification of energy as a focal point, and through the general emphasis of the programme, even though it has left the media specific approach behind.

The integrative approach is confirmed by the amendments made to Article 130R of the EC Treaty by the TEU (Maastricht), which confirms the need for the integration of the environment into Community policies in general.

1.3 EUROPEAN ENVIRONMENT AGENCY

The idea of a European Environment Agency (EEA) was the subject of long debate between the Member States. Its emergence was delayed by the Member States' own inability to reconcile themselves as to where the Agency would be based, with several States vying for the honour. The Agency finally opened its doors in Copenhagen in October 1993. Because environmental issues are no longer merely of domestic interest, the Agency's constituency extends beyond EC borders.

Whilst the enforcement function of the Commission entails a certain amount of monitoring, it has neither the staff nor the remit to undertake the detailed investigations to be performed by the European Environment Agency, assisted in this function by the European Environmental Monitoring and Information Network (EEMIN), established by Regulation 1210/90/EEC.[1] Their purpose is rather narrower than Directorate-General XI, being restricted to the monitoring and collection of information. Article 1(2) of Regulation 1210/90 establishes the aim of the Agency as being an information source providing the EC institutions and Member States with 'objective, reliable and comparable' information, to facilitate both environmental protection and 'to assess the results'. The Agency and EEMIN are therefore mandated to collect data across Europe in a form which is readily comparable; to establish systems for the dissemination of information; to develop environmental forecasting and ensure a healthy exchange of information on 'best available technology'.

To this end, the Agency is required to issue a report on the state of the environment across the EC every three years. It also encourages dialogue between the various levels – EC, domestic and regional – to facilitate information retrieval and dissemination, and to encourage the cross-fertilisation of methodology and data collection within the EC.

The work of the Agency is at present complemented by the continuing function of its predecessor. By providing a fuller knowledge base, the work of the Agency should facilitate a more accurate view of the environment across Europe and a better informed Commission, thereby leading to better informed policy and proposals for legislation.

The remit of the Agency is, however, currently strictly limited. It has no policing function. That remains largely with the Commission. The founding regulation does, however, provide authority to increase the powers and function of the Agency in the future, in the light of operative experience. Article 20, Regulation 1210/90 indicates that the work of the Agency will

1 OJ 1990 L120.

eventually extend beyond data collection to the monitoring and implementation of EC environmental legislation, assessment of environmental impact, and eco labelling. These developments should lead to significant improvements in overall compliance and enforcement.

1.4 SOURCES OF EC LAW

Having its roots in the civil law systems of the original six Member States, the primary sources of law upon which the EC is based are relatively accessible. In order to understand EC law, it is essential to have a working knowledge of the various sources of law which contribute to its jurisprudence.

The key source is the Treaty itself, which establishes both the parameters of Community competence, and the operational framework. A glance at the Treaty will give some indication of its skeletal nature. It seems impossible in the literalist tradition, that so few pages can provide the blueprint for such a large and intricate Community and its accompanying legal system. The simple reason for this is that the Treaty document itself provides authority for further binding legislation, in the form of Regulations, Directives and policy; the whole corpus of law being subject to the teleological interpretative techniques of the ECJ.

Our understanding of the law of the EC is reliant not only in its words, but upon its spirit. Similarly, the sum of EC law is not only to be found in the legislation, but also the general principles which have developed to govern operations.

1.4.1 The Treaty

Although the Treaty has been subject to amendment over the years, both in the SEA 1986 and the TEU (Maastricht), much of the substance of the Treaty of Rome remains. In particular, the general obligation of membership contained in Article 5 establishes the duty of Member States, not only to act in accordance with the Community interest, but also not to act in any way contrary to that interest. This basic obligation is fundamental to Community membership and the basis upon which specific compliance is achieved through the enforcement mechanisms contained in Articles 169–171.

The most significant development in the Treaty for our purpose has been the express inclusion of the Environment as a policy heading under Chapter 3, Title XVI (formerly Title VII, SEA 1986). It is not simply the undeniable authority to develop policy and regulate the environment which Title XVI brings, but also the express incorporation of major policy principles (Article 130R(2)).[1]

---

1 It is appropriate to refer to the Treaty as the EC Treaty. The title, Treaty of Rome, remains of historical significance and the Treaty of European Union refers to an over-arching document of which the content of the EC Treaty is just a part.

The TEU was the result of a full year of negotiations between the Member States. Article G introduces substantial amendments to the original Treaty, not least in changing the nomenclature from EEC to EC, in recognition of the wider aspirations since the original Treaty of Rome. The TEU also makes amendments to the institutional framework, with particular reference to the power and operative functions of the Parliament (of which more at **1.8.5**).

A major function of Article G, however, was to facilitate the movement towards monetary union scheduled for completion by 1 January 1999. Further significant developments were made in the introduction of the concept of 'citizenship of the European Union' and the completion of the rights of free movement of workers, and non-discrimination born out of the original Treaty.

The remainder of the TEU comprises the political intentions and aspirations for the future, particularly in relation to foreign policy, security, defence and the foundations for the development of Commission policies in justice and home affairs. It is this second political pillar of the TEU which has proved most controversial, and yet, as history indicates, such proposals would be no surprise to Jean Monnet and Robert Schumann whose original ideas encompassed both a political and defence Community.

Title I of the TEU, Common Provisions, establishes the aims and objectives of the document. These provisions are of significance, both in relation to their content and the extent to which they are indicative of the 'spirit' of the Treaty. As such, they have a role to play in the interpretations of the European Court of Justice. Whilst no express reference is made to the environment, it is implicit in the objectives of the Union under Article B of the TEU which states, inter alia:

> 'The union shall set itself the following objectives: ... to promote economic and social progress which is balanced and sustainable ...'

1.4.2 Title XVI – Environment

Title XVI not only provides the authoritative basis for EC legal provision on the environment, but it establishes its status relative to other EC interests/policies, the general principles which will govern EC environmental control, legislative models and the relationship between EC and domestic policies.

Article 130R(1) sets out the EC objectives for the environment in the following terms:

> '[Policy] shall contribute to pursuit of the following objectives:
>
> - preserving, protecting and improving the quality of the environment;
> - protecting human health;
> - prudent and rational utilisation of natural resources;
> - promoting measures at international level to deal with regional or worldwide environmental problems.'

It is interesting to note from Article 130R(1) and (4) that the EC clearly recognises a role for itself at the international level. This objective will be given further consideration in Chapter 2.

It is clear from Article 130R(2) of the Treaty that EC policy recognises the differing needs across the Community. This is reflected in differential standards which apply in some substantive provisions where the burden of reducing emissions to the atmosphere may be greater on the more developed Member States. It is recognised that some overall EC standards have only been achieved by the burden being shared unequally. Indeed, this point was made in Kyoto in response to criticisms of the US stance on emissions trading and 'offset'.

The governing principles of EC environmental law are laid down in Article 130R(2), namely:

- the precautionary principle and the presumption that preventive action is to be preferred
- that environmental damage should be rectified at source
- the polluter should pay
- preference for an integrative approach in relation to other EC policies.

The integration of the environment into all EC policies has raised issues of primacy of policy. If issues of environmental protection are to be integrated, should the principles of, for example, free movement be subjugated in their favour, or is such integration limited to the extent that it remains compatible with the principal objectives?

Several actions had been brought before the ECJ before the Maastricht amendments, the result indicating that perhaps the court anticipated, if somewhat timidly, the further enhancement of environmental protection.

1.4.3 *Danish Bottles* case

Such a discussion was central to the *Danish Bottles* case.[1] As has been noted, the ECJ's original stance in relation to Article 36 and the principles of derogation in relation to Article 30 has been restrictive. Article 30 protects the free movement of goods by prohibiting 'quantitative restrictions' and 'measures having equivalent effect'. As a major objective of the Customs Union and Single Market, a broad interpretative stance is to be expected on the part of the ECJ. The corollary of this position is that a narrow interpretation is to be expected in relation to the derogation contained in Article 36. Clearly, this is dictated not only by the letter, but also the spirit of the Treaty. The pervasive status of the environment as provided by Article 130R(2) now infers that the protection of the environment is a justifiable reason to derogate from Article 30, along with 'the protection of health and life of humans, animals or plants' as provided by Article 36. The case highlights the enhanced status of the environment in the eyes of the ECJ, notwithstanding the later express developments.

---

1 *Re Disposable Beer Cans, Commission of European Communities v Denmark* [1989] 1 CMLR 619.

The ECJ concluded that, as a 'mandatory requirement', environmental protection could take primacy over the general principles of operation of the single market, although subject to the assumption of proportionality, and the limitation that such derogation would not extend to action under Article 100A in relation to the approximation of laws for the promotion of the internal market.

The Commission had brought an action against the Danish authorities, in response to the introduction of a law requiring that drinks only be marketed in returnable bottles. Indeed, the Danish authorities went further, seeking to regulate the shape and size of containers. The stated rationale behind the provision was to enforce recycling; in particular, the more environmentally efficient option of recycling the container itself by returning it to the product manufacturer rather than simply relying on the recycling of the raw material. The Commission saw the measure as discriminatory in relation to the importers, and, as such, an infringement of Article 30, the prohibition of 'quantitative restrictions' and 'measures having equivalent effect'.

In the final analysis, the ECJ considered that environmental considerations could justifiably excuse a discriminatory measure. None the less, such a measure must be proportionate to the result to be achieved. In this case, it was recognised that the requirement of 'returnability' was indeed more environmentally friendly than simple recycling. However, the additional element prescribing permissible shapes of containers was not warranted, offending against the principle of proportionality.

The case illustrates three important points:

(i) it confirms that the Member States retain the power to legislate in stricter terms than the EC itself, except in such circumstances as the measure is contrary to a specific measure of EC law;

(ii) it enhances the thematic status of environment protection as later confirmed in the amendments to Article 130. Environmental protection requirements must be integrated into the definition and implementation of other Community policies;

(iii) it supports the position of the original principles, ie the preference that environmental damage should be rectified at source with costs lying with the polluter.

It is clear that both the *Danish Bottles* and *Wallonian Waste*[1] cases have had considerable impact on the status of the environment and have, to a certain extent, found immortality in the TEU. Article 130R(2) provides that the status of environmental issues is secure, not only to the extent that they *may* be taken into account in the exercise of wider policies, but that they *must* be so honoured.

1 *Commission of the European Communities v Belgium* C–2/90 [1993] JEL 133.

1.4.4 *Wallonian Waste* case

In the *Wallonian Waste* case, the extent to which environmental issues should be taken into consideration to the exclusion of other general policies is further highlighted. However, the parameters of such integration are clearly evident where the general aim of environmental protection is faced with a specific legislative provision to the contrary, even though, as in this case, it may lead to a rather odd legal conclusion.

The Belgian regional authorities had moved to prevent the importation of waste for disposal, contrary to the free movement of goods. The ECJ confirmed that 'waste' fell within the definition of goods, but none the less considered that the environmental issues weighed in favour of justification. The presumption in Article 130R(2) that waste should be dealt with as locally as possible ('rectified at source'), favoured the ban on importation and thus overturned the general presumption of free movement of goods. However, such a ban resting upon Article 130R(2) could only be lawful in relation to ordinary, non-hazardous waste. Absurdly, the exercise of the presumption embodied in Article 130R(2) could not extend to 'hazardous waste', by virtue of the fact that specific EC legislation, Directive 84/631, existed to regulate and control the transshipment of such material. A ban on the importation of this more noxious material would therefore be contrary to the Directive, and thereby unlawful, even though it might satisfy the more general terms of Article 130R(2). The Court was therefore prepared to support the general aim of environmental protection over other guiding policies, but only to the extent that it was not in conflict with express environmental provisions.

The response of the ECJ is an interesting one. Whilst it might appear that, by analogy, the Court would recognise the quality of direct effect in relation to Article 130R(2), as Ludwig Kramer points out,[1] the words of the Treaty fail to convince the reader that it possesses the characteristics normally expected in a provision capable of direct effect (see below). The wording in relation to 'integration' appears mandatory, but, by its nature, it cannot identify what 'environmental protection' actually entails, and thereby would appear to fail to provide the necessary 'certainty'.

Provision is also made for 'a safeguard clause allowing Member States to take provisional measures, for non-economic environmental reasons, subject to a Community Inspector's proceedings', indicating recognition of Member States' activities in relation to environmental control which go beyond that of the EC itself. This is further acknowledged in Article 130R which confirms that the provisions contained in Article 130S would not prevent the Member States from implementing 'more stringent protective measures' independently, subject only to compatibility with the Treaty as a whole and notification to the Commission.

1 Kramer *Direct Effect of EC Environmental Law Protecting the European Environment: Enforcing Environmental Law* Somsen (ed), (Blackstone Press Ltd, 1996).

Article 130R(3) provides a statement of a range of factors which will be taken into consideration when formulating EC environmental policy. These factors represent objective considerations beyond the principles of Article 130R(2). Account shall be taken of:

> ' – available scientific and technical data;
> – environmental conditions in the various regions of the Community;
> – the potential benefits and costs of action or lack of action;
> – the economic and social development of the Community as a whole and the balanced development of its regions.'

In contrast to Article 130R, Article 130S is more concerned with 'housekeeping matters', providing, inter alia, authority for the Environmental Action Programmes. Article 130S emphasises that the cost of implementation of environmental policy will lie with the Member States, except in such circumstances that costs impose a 'disproportionate' burden on the Member State. In such a case, Article 130S(5) indicates that it is within the power of the Council to indicate a stay of execution, by way of temporary derogation and/or financial support from the Cohesion Fund.

This clause is of real practical utility to some Member States. In the case of the former, an extension of the time-limit for compliance will save a Member State from the inevitable failure to implement, although that does not divert from the fact that the reality of the environment, and rights of enjoyment will, as a result, be less than those in other Member States for an extended period.

In relation to the latter, there is no doubt that the southern nations have found this invaluable in relation to their environmental response. The complication which might arise in the future is, as with any other 'aid' type situation, that any further enlargement would be likely to feature environmental remediation problems, against which those who currently enjoy the support of the Cohesion Fund pale into insignificance.

1.5 SECONDARY LEGISLATION

Although this section is headed 'secondary legislation', there remains some debate as to whether the body of EC legislation should correctly be viewed as primary or secondary in nature. The legislation which flows from the EC must root its authority in the Treaty itself. Some fulfils the function of adding detail to the skeleton of the Treaty itself but, in other respects, EC legislation is more appropriately viewed as primary in nature. None the less, it remains useful to think of it in terms of secondary legislation in the context that it is not beyond challenge in the Court.

There are several forms of legislative, and other less binding, instruments available to the EC institutions. The choice of mechanism will depend not only upon the content of the provision but the nature of the task. The categories are identified and subject to definition in Article 189 of the Treaty in the following terms:

> 'In order to carry out their task and in accordance with the provisions of this Treaty, the European Parliament acting jointly with the Council, the Council and the Commission shall make regulations and issue directives, take decisions, make recommendations or deliver opinions.'

1.5.1 Regulations

Article 189 of the EC Treaty states:

> 'A regulation shall have general application. It shall be binding in its entirety and directly applicable in all Member States.'

The Regulation is generally accepted as the most powerful legislative form, providing legislation in a single homogenous form across all the Member States. It is defined as 'directly applicable' and leaves no room for local cultural or structural differences. Direct applicability means that it is complete and needs no further action on the part of the Member States. Indeed, the Member States are prevented from any action which may purport to implement or authorise the Regulation.[1] This is essential because the Regulation becomes incorporated into domestic law as a Community measure. To allow Member States to appear to adopt the measure would not only compromise necessary uniformity but endanger the 'duty of solidarity'. 'Implementation' will, therefore, only be permitted to the extent to which the Regulation itself indicates.

All Member States have in fact given their prior authorisation to the direct applicability of Regulations by the constitutional measures undertaken pursuant to their original membership. Thus, in the case of the UK, authority for the acceptance of Article 189 and the status of Regulations flows from the European Communities Act 1972.

The characteristic of 'directly applicable' distinguishes the Regulation from other legislative forms, for example Directives. It infers a uniform and synchronised application, removing all power from the Member State to moderate its content, or voice an objection, but it does not, of itself, encompass any greater rights than those which may, or may not, be implicit in its substantive content. This is to be contrasted with 'direct effect' (see para **1.10**).

The use of a Regulation may be dictated by the Treaty, but more frequently the Treaty will leave the choice of legislative forms to the institutions. There is no strict formula which will indicate the appropriate choice of legislative form, although the form itself may indicate certain circumstances. As Steiner[2] observes, 'A Regulation is normative rather than an individual act, designed to apply to situations in the abstract'. Its use is therefore more likely to be in situations where the EC wishes to create a presumption beyond the Treaty; to pre-empt action in order to keep the Member States from their own devices and designs; or to pass on the burden of an international obligation.

1 *Bussone v Italian Ministry for Agriculture and Forestry* (No 31/78) [1978] ECR 2429.

2 Steiner and Woods *Textbook on EC Law* 5th edn (Blackstone, 1996).

1.5.2 Directives

Article 189 of the EC Treaty states:

> 'A directive shall be binding, as to the result to be achieved, upon each Member State to which it is addressed, but shall leave to the national authorities the choice of form and methods.'

The Directive is the most used legislative form. It is certainly the predominant form in relation to environmental legislation. Unlike the Regulation, it is not described as 'directly applicable'. The very fact that it prescribes the end, but not the means, gives it the flexibility to achieve a level of regulatory provision, whilst continuing to respect not only the distinct cultural and legal traditions of the individual Member States but also the fact that some Member States may have already reached a certain level of regulatory maturity and will require far less to reach the given goal of the Directive. Therefore, the Directive may be the preferred instrument where the object is to seek a move towards harmonisation, rather than a position of uniformity. By its nature the Directive also recognises the idiosyncrasies of the Member State. Even before the principle of subsidiarity rose to prominence, the Directive recognised that, whilst it might be appropriate to provide the 'what' at EC level, the 'how' is frequently better left to the individual Member State.

The Directive does not take effect immediately and will generally be accompanied by an implementation date, frequently around 18 months to 2 years in the future. Article 191(2) provides that a Directive will generally be required to be implemented by the date specified, or failing that, where no date is specified, 20 days after publication. The length of the implementation period will very much depend upon how complex or onerous the task proves to be. Unlike the Regulation, which had 'general application', the Directive is only binding 'upon each Member State to which it is addressed'. Whilst it is unlikely that a Regular distinction would be made, applying Directives to some Member States and not others, the power exists. Perhaps, more importantly, this and the terms of Article 130S(5) can permit the extension of implementation periods in relation to Member States which face particularly intransigent problems. This may be preferred to a position where it is clear from the outset that a Member State cannot achieve implementation even under the threat of an enforcement action.

A further distinguishing feature between Regulations and Directives has traditionally been the requirement for publication. The Regulation has always been subject to publication in the Official Journal, as befits a directly applicable measure. The Directive, on the other hand, was originally only required to be notified to those Member States to whom it was directed and not published for general notice. The significance of this difference has always been greater in theory than in practice because Directives, although not required to be published generally, have been, since TEU amendments to Article 191(2), required to be published in the same way as Regulations. Whilst this may appear unimportant, its significance will become apparent when we consider the question of direct effect.

Although the 'choice' of form and methods of implementation is left in the hands of the Member States, the ECJ has made it clear that implementation will not be satisfied by the use of purely administrative measures.

Although it may seem that the obligation contained in a Directive is 'sprung' on Member States with only the lead-in time for implementation as notice, the reality is that, by virtue of the legislative process itself (see **1.8**), the Member States will have considerably more warning in relation to their pending obligations. This is frequently contrary to the picture portrayed in the media, who are often keen to suggest that 'Brussels' has crept up on us without warning.

None the less, Member States do regularly find that they have failed to meet the requirements of the Directive by the date of implementation. The result is that the question of failed obligations frequently features in enforcement actions under Article 169 (see **2.1** for detail). The issue of non-compliance, however, may be magnified in the case of environmental Directives. Each day of non-compliance which passes after the date of implementation may in reality be measured in an increased need for remediation.

A mixed record of compliance exists across the Member States. Whilst the UK is relatively compliant, some Members, such as Greece and Portugal, are regular miscreants. None the less, as Weatherill and Beaumont report,[1] 'Even the States with the poorest record have managed to implement more than four-fifths of the Directives applicable to them'. The problem with the remaining one-fifth is that non-compliance is frequently measurable in years rather than months.

1.5.3 Decisions

Article 189 of the EC Treaty states:

> 'A decision shall be binding in its entirety upon those to whom it is addressed.'[2]

Like Directives, the decision, will come into force on the date specified or, where no such date is specified, on the 20th day after publication (Article 191). Otherwise, decisions will take effect upon notification. Traditionally, some of the most important decisions have found themselves appearing in the Official Journal, but now, since the TEU decisions, which have been adopted under the Article 189B procedure, are required to be published, publication of the remainder continues to be discretionary.

As with Regulations and Directives the use of the decision format may be directed by the terms of the Treaty itself. On other occasions, it may be the instrument of choice. Decisions are, by their definition, not intended to be of general application. Indeed, unlike Regulations and Directives, they may, in fact, be addressed to undertakings in addition to Member States, although this is likely to be in relation to competition law rather than the environment.

1 Weatherill and Beaumont, *EC Law*, 2nd edn (Penguin, 1995).
2 Article 191, EC Treaty.

1.5.4 Recommendations and opinions

'Recommendations and opinions shall have no binding force.'[1]

There are occasions when the Treaty will indicate the use of recommendations or opinions. The clarity with which Article 189 removes any potential for recommendations and opinions to be binding raises the question, what is their status? The domestic courts may not rely on them in the way that they might a Regulation or Directive (see Direct Effect at **1.10**), but they remain significant in the persuasive sense,[2] and may be the subject of an Article 177 reference in order to elicit an interpretation from the ECJ.

1.6 GENERAL PRINCIPLES

Reference has already been made to the general principles of EC law. This body of law emanates from the deliberations of the ECJ and is, in many respects, judge-made. In fact, many of the principles adopted have their roots in the domestic jurisdictions of the Member States. These principles are therefore, on the whole, tried and tested. On adoption by the ECJ they may, however, take on characteristics of their own as 'Community concepts' and should not be expected to remain unchanged.

Some principles may be regarded as having been founded in the Treaty, but this is generally not the case. Others have latterly been incorporated in the Treaty. Indeed, as has been noted, there are those who would consider that certainty, if not justice, would be better served if all of the general principles were transcribed into the Treaty so that we would all be aware of their nature, content and implications. It might also be argued, however, that the law retains a certain flexibility and the capacity to develop and respond to need if left to the ECJ.

It is appropriate to give some consideration at this point to the historical development, and indeed authority supporting the incorporation, of these extra-Treaty principles. Although the ECJ serviced the European Coal and Steel Community before the EEC was established, its legal history remains very limited. The parameters of its authority are established by the 'letter' and the 'spirit' of the Treaty. Whilst the spirit of the Treaty may allow the flesh to be placed on the bones of the basic Treaty provisions, none the less the task of adjudication within such a vacuum would be tedious without more. Reliance upon general principles might at an operational level be viewed as an essential assumption.

It was clear from the early stages of the ECSC that the Treaty did not, and could not, anticipate all the problems which would arise. Nor could it, in its skeletal form, portray such a full picture of its operation and assumed values that would lead to all the answers. In order to function, the interpretative role

1 Article 189, EC Treaty.

2 *Grimaldi v Fonds des Maladie Professionelles* (C–322/88) [1989] ECR 4407.

of the ECJ must rest upon certain held values or principles, in addition to the spirit of the Treaty. Operating in an otherwise sterile environment, it is faced with two options: either it reinvents the wheel, without the benefit of its own cultural, political, or economic heritage; or it rests upon the experience of its founding States. Presented with the rich heritage of the Member States, the obvious move is to select from the range of legal systems before it. Indeed, in the early ECSC case of *Netherlands v ECSS High Authority* (Case 6/54)[1] the Advocate-General took the initiative, stating that, in order to carry out its interpretative function, the Court would have to take note of the laws of the Member States. The significance of domestic law was further highlighted in *Federation Charbonnière de Belgique v High Authority* (Case 8/55),[2] in which the Advocate-General stated that the Court was not in a position to deny authority simply because it was faced with a gap in ECSC law. If it cannot deny authority then logically it must gain the means of breaching the gap by reference to some other source of law, that source being the domestic jurisdictions.

The Treaty provides no direct authority to permit the ECJ to look to these sources. There are, however, arguably certain presumptions within the Treaty itself, for example the role of the ECJ is outlined in Article 164 which states that it is obliged to ensure that the 'law is observed' in carrying out its function:

> 'The Court of Justice shall ensure that in the interpretation and application of this Treaty the law is observed.'

Such a statement must rest upon an assumption that there exists a body of inalienable law outside of this Treaty, which all must observe.

This is further supported by the wording of Article 173 which provides for judicial review in relation to the acts of the institutions. Judicial review is available in relation to an:

> '... infringement of this Treaty or of any rule of law relating to its application.'

The wording assumes that an infringement of 'any rule of law' must be something beyond that which is contained in the Treaty itself, or the phrase would add nothing.

Finally, Article 215 expressly refers to the laws of the Member States in identifying the non-contractual liability of the Community itself:

> 'In the case of non-contractual liability, the Community shall, in accordance with the general principles common to the laws of the Member States, make good any damage caused ...'

In Article 215, there is no question as to where this other law comes from; in this instance, it is expressly stated to be the domestic law of the constituent Member States.

1 [1954] ECR 103.
2 [1956] ECR 245.

Having recognised that the ECJ has a justifiable interest in the laws of the Member States, the jurisprudence of the EC is open to accelerated development. However, even in the early days, there were six distinct legal systems to choose from, and although there may be some legal themes which are so fundamental that they make an appearance in most, if not all legal systems, they do not necessarily do so in the same form. It is therefore not particularly helpful for Article 215 to refer to:

> '... the general principles common to the laws of the Member States.'

This is even more poignant since the EC has grown to incorporate not only civil law systems, which at least have some common root, but common law and, latterly, Scandinavian jurisdictions.

The position of the ECJ is more akin to the child in the sweet shop who is told that he can 'pick and mix'. The whole jurisprudence of the Member States is open to them to take an appropriate range of domestic principles and create from them 'Community principles' which no longer have any reliance on the jurisprudence of their birth. It would be absurd for the ECJ to be required to formulate its own principles from scratch when it has such a fertile range of tried and tested formulas before it.

The general policy assumptions of EC law to be found in the Treaty, for example free movement, environment, etc, are therefore supplemented not only by those principles which have been specifically incorporated into the Treaty but are further bolstered by the principles adopted from the domestic context by the ECJ. These include human rights, proportionality, equality, legal certainty (including legitimate expectation and non-retroactivity), and the right to a hearing (inclusive of the right to information to make representations and to be given reasons). These themes will generally feel familiar although they may have been operative as EC concepts before our own influence came to bear. The English system none the less has influenced the continually developing principles, particularly by reference to principles of natural justice.

The Treaty itself is a useful source of general principles. Some of these principles may have been assumed within the Treaty from its inception, others have been introduced at a later date. The additions made to Article 130 in particular establish both the protection of the environment as a general presumption, and indicate the principles by which the interests of the environment will be advanced, namely: the polluter pays, the precautionary principle, prevention rather than remediation and rectification at source. Further, in relation to the establishment of general principles of environmental law, the Environmental Action Programmes should not be overlooked.

1.6.1 Sustainable development

Founded in the *Brundtland Report* of 1987, this global principle has infiltrated environmental regulation at all levels. It does not represent a scale against which environmental measures can be compared, but an approach which should govern the whole rationale behind environmental regulation, encompassing the legal, political and economic dimensions with equal verve.

The adoption of the principle of sustainable development in the field of EC environmental policy is best seen in the approach and terms of the Fifth Environmental Action Programme, which, taking to itself the very essence of the principle expounded in Brundtland, sets out its aims as being to achieve:

> '... "sustainable development" which is defined as "a policy and strategy for continued economic and social development without detriment to the environment and the natural resources on the quality of which continued activity and further development depend".'

The approach of the Fifth Programme focuses on the actions and actors which cause damage to the environment and use natural resources, seeking a strategic rather than reactive approach, initiating rather than lamenting change. Having divided its task into five sectors significant for their effect on the environment, the EAP then calls for strategic programmes in each area, with the aim of redirecting current consumption in the direction of sustainable consumption.

1.6.2 The 'polluter pays' principle

Influenced by the OECD, one of the founding principles of the First Environmental Action Programme, the 'polluter pays' principle, is now enshrined in Article 130R(2) of the EC Treaty. The principle pays service to moral logic, but the polluter is not always easy to select: we may identify a producer who is in control of the manufacturing process, but should we ignore the role of the consumer, without whom there would be no production? Further, the principle has been used flexibly to justify anything from a simple administrative charge to full clean-up costs, although some would argue that only the latter represents true adherence to the principle.

The extent to which 'polluter pays' has been taken on board in the UK is represented in the White Paper *This Common Inheritance*,[1] para 3.16 which states that where:

> '... production processes threaten or cause damage to the environment the cost of necessary environmental measures should be borne by the producer and not by society at large ...'

1.6.3 The precautionary principle

Incorporated into Article 130R(2) of the EC Treaty, the precautionary principle is particularly difficult to measure in practice, not least because of the frequent uncertainty of the relationship between 'action' and 'reaction'.

The problem is compounded by the fact that, as Smith J considered in the recent case of *Duddridge*,[2] there is 'no comprehensive and authoritative definition of the precautionary principle'. Arguably, without a definition, no practical formula exists indicating the level of risk acceptance for a given benefit. The threat is, therefore, that, in practice, any application of the principle will amount to lip service.

1 Cm 2426.

2 *R v Secretary of State for Trade and Industry ex parte Duddridge* [1996] Env LR 325.

Further, even if some measure of acceptable outcome were ascertained, the data necessary to make an informed decision minimising future environmental impact may not be available. The concern is then that, as a result, no action will be taken. In such circumstances, the precautionary principle calls for anticipation of future data, if necessary to minimise the detrimental effect of the time lag between the acknowledgement of risk through positive scientific data and the practical effect of measures taken.

On a practical note, the EC has given support to the principle through measures like the need for environmental impact assessment. In addition, the emphasis on information and prevention of harm in later Environmental Action Programmes reinforces the principle. This is further supported by the present and future remit of the EEA, which will assist the extent to which the precautionary principle can be turned into practice.

1.6.4 Rectification at source

The inclusion of this principle at Treaty level places emphasis on an emission standards approach. Emission standards have been set in relation to BATNEEC (best available technology not entailing excessive cost) and, latterly, BAT (best available techniques). The advantages of an emission standards approach is the relative ease of implementation and monitoring. The equal status of players also ensures that distortions of competition can be largely avoided.

The emission standards approach has not always enjoyed universal acclaim, with major opposition being found in the UK camp. Relatively isolated by our island status and enjoying fast flowing rivers, etc, the UK's historic approach has rested upon the capacity of the environment to absorb pollution without adverse effect. Initially, the UK Government resisted movement away from this position, primarily because of the economic benefit to producers which this model conferred.

Whilst the Fifth Environmental Action Programme calls for an integrated approach to emissions standards and environmental quality standards, the principle of rectification at source perhaps benefits the former approach where appropriate.

1.6.5 Subsidiarity

The principle of subsidiarity has raised much interest in the Member States, particularly in the area of the environment, and, indeed, was, until Maastricht, specifically part of Article 130R rather than being of general application. The notion rests upon the assumption that regulation should occur at the level most appropriate for the task in hand. If there is a need for a unified or co-ordinated EC approach, then the regulatory framework should be put in place at EC level. If, on the other hand, the problem is localised, it is more appropriately dealt with at that level. Resting upon this assumption, there is, from time to time, argument from the Member States that some of the EC's intervention in the environment could happily be left to the Member States. The question does not arise in relation to those matters which are the sole competence of the EC, or the Member States, but is central to the large range of issues for which there is joint or overlapping competence.

The major problem in relation to subsidiarity is that, like the principles remaining in Article 130R, it lacks precise definition, and therefore, as between the various levels of operation, it lacks certainty.

The question of appropriate competence has been expressly addressed in the TEU, which incorporates the general principle of subsidiarity into EC law by virtue of the new Article 3B. Reference to subsidiarity is now made in the all-important preamble which identifies that EC decisions will be taken as closely as possible to the people, in accordance with the principle of subsidiarity.

Article 3B states:

> 'In areas which do not fall within its exclusive competence, the Community shall take action in accordance with the principle of subsidiarity, only if and in so far as the objectives of the proposed action cannot be sufficiently achieved by the Member States and can therefore, by reason of the scale or effects of the proposed action, be better achieved by the Community.'

The new wording of the preamble has the additional significance that it may be relied upon as an indication of the 'spirit' of the Treaty, so fundamental is it to the interpretations of the ECJ. Of course, the wording of the preamble may indicate that, in some instances, decisions are not appropriately made by the EC or Member State but by some regional or local authority. This is, no doubt, an option which was not necessarily foremost in the mind of the Member States in making the amendments to the Treaty at Maastricht.

The principle of subsidiarity requires that the legislature, in particular, assess the appropriateness of their actions. The Commission, as the proposer, will review its draft legislation in the light of subsidiarity and indicate its view in the preamble to that legislation. The Commission has developed guidelines which point to the need to consider a variety of factors, including transnational implications, potential conflict with the Treaty and proven benefit in scale or effect, before concluding that an EC-wide approach is appropriate.

On the question of whether or not subsidiarity is having any effect on the level at which decisions are made, Weatherill and Beaumont[1] voice the opinion that 'the Commission is taking fewer but ... better targeted initiatives', and point, as evidence, to the decline in legislative proposals from over 180 in 1990 to a little over 70 in 1993. They suggest that the need to question the appropriate level at which regulation occurs is also leading the Commission to consider the very need for regulation. They are also of the view that, whilst all the institutions involved in the legislative process are called to make similar assessments, to the credit of the Commission, there is none the less some evidence to suggest that it may be more stringent in its assessment. The fact that the Commission had withdrawn 11 proposals up to the end of 1994 and

1 *EC Law*, 2nd edn (Penguin, 1995).

had simplified others, lends some support to this view. Parliament, on the other hand, opposed the Commission's stance on most counts. The Commission has indicated its disappointment with both the Parliament and the Council on this issue.

The requirement for self-scrutiny indicated in Article 3B should be taken seriously by all parties, not least because it is open to review by the ECJ under Article 173. The major difficulty for the ECJ is, however, that whilst it may be relatively straightforward to assess the approach to subsidiarity on a procedural basis, any review which touches upon the substance delves into the realms of the political, and is, as such, beyond its authority.

1.6.6 Proportionality

The EC principle of proportionality has its roots in German law, although the EC principle is now recognised as a subtly different concept. It refers to the idea that the steps taken to resolve an issue, or to punish, or to control, should be no more than are necessary and justifiable in response to the severity of the problem. There are clear overtones of our own doctrine of 'unreasonableness' in the extremities, but proportionality is, it seems, a much more precisely calibrated principle.

Proportionality was originally adopted by the ECJ, but is now enshrined in the third paragraph of Article 3B, '... Any action by the Community shall not go beyond what is necessary to achieve the objectives of this Treaty'.

Clearly, this provision may operate as a hold on actions within the sole authority of the EC, but it may also support the principle of subsidiarity in helping to regulate the 'relative' interest in areas of joint authority. In relation to the environment, the incorporation of the principle of proportionality goes some way to suggest that, in the setting of standards, the minimum level of intervention is to be preferred, although individual Member States might make their own domestic arrangements at a higher level. Whilst this might please Member States, and allow for a flexibility of approach, it could be argued that the environment is the loser where a lower than preferred standard is legislated on the basis of proportionality. It might also be suggested that this could lead to an uneven playing field in relation to production costs for industry resulting in differing environmental standards across the EC where Member States have chosen to adopt more stringent standards than absolutely necessary as a proportionate response. This argument would, of course, take us back full circle to the justification for EC involvement in the environmental arena in the first place!

1.7 JUDICIAL REVIEW

Articles 173 and 175 are the general measures concerning judicial review, although they are not the only mechanisms. Article 173 refers to the 'acts' of the institutions, whilst Article 175 concerns their omissions.

Unlike the UK position, EC legislation is open to review before the ECJ. Where challenged, the ECJ will consider whether the legislation satisfies procedural requirements, and can be justified substantively on the basis of the Treaty and not an abuse thereof. In addition, the legislation will be judged in relation to the general principles of EC law. Whilst some of the general principles are now enshrined in the Treaty, for example subsidiarity, others depend upon the application of the ECJ. This has been criticised by some as an unsatisfactory state of affairs which operates against certainty itself. Indeed, Weatherill and Beaumont[1] have suggested that all general principles should be incorporated into the Treaty itself, which would satisfy certainty. They consider that: 'it is not good for legal certainty nor the respect due to legislation passed by the appropriate Political Institutions that a Court can strike it down on the basis of a principle that it has just developed'. Such a concrete expression as incorporating the general principles into the Treaty would also support wider notions of natural justice.

Whilst the appeal for certainty is strong, and some would welcome some strictures on the activities of the ECJ, there must be concern that the rigidity arrived at could stifle the continuous growth and shaping of what remains a relatively youthful jurisprudence, even if it is one which effectively enjoys the advice of 15 elders.

The difficulties encountered in relation to judicial review are not confined to the realm of general principles. Procedural difficulties can arise as a result of the differing legislative templates. The legislative process is dictated by the authority relied upon. This should be simple as we have already identified the significance of Article 190 which requires that the legislation itself 'shall state the reasons on which they are based'.

The case of *Commission for the European Communities v European Council* (*Generalised Tariff Preferences*) (Case 45/86)[2] indicates that failure to provide indicative authority within the preamble of the legislation would not necessarily amount to 'an infringement of an essential procedure requirement' if such information could be ascertained within the body of the document. The Court considered that: 'such explicit reference is indispensable where, in its absence, the parties concerned and the Court are left uncertain as to the precise legal basis'.

None the less, where the legislation may arguably be based on more than one authoritative provision, it may be tempting to try to categorise it in such a way as to avoid the hurdle of unanimity (Case 56/88) *UK v European Council.*[3] The significance of 'emphasis' of authority cannot be overstated. The means by which the authority is arrived at must therefore be open to the review of the Court.

1 *EC Law*, 2nd edn (Penguin, 1995).

2 [1987] ECR 1493.

3 [1989] ECR 1615, [1989] 2 CMLR 789.

The increase in specific authority provided under the SEA 1986 and TEU go some way to resolve the problems of authority. Environmental legislation no longer needs to scour the Treaty looking for tangential authority, or rely so heavily upon the general powers of Article 235. Legislation which seeks to serve more than one master must ensure that the basis of its duty is objectively justifiable. The role of Article 235 becomes residual, and no doubt the requirement for unanimity will guard against the attempted use of such a general power where a specific power is available (*Generalised Tariff Preferences* case).[1]

1.7.1 Locus standi

The general authority by which a challenge may be mounted by way of judicial review stems from Articles 173, 175 and 184. Article 173 provides an essential mechanism of 'quality control' in relation to legislation, but it has the wider function, along with Article 175 of providing for the monitoring of the major institutions. Article 173 provides:

> 'The Court of Justice shall review the legality of acts adopted jointly by the European Parliament and the Council, of acts of the Council, of the Commission and of the ECB, other than recommendations and opinions, and of acts of the European Parliament intended to produce legal effects vis-à-vis third parties.'

Full locus standi for such challenge extends to the institutions themselves, the Council, and Commission. In the case of the Parliament and the European Central Bank, standing is enjoyed to the extent necessary for 'protecting their prerogatives'. A more limited standing extends to individuals in relation to 'decisions addressed' to them or 'against a decision which, although in the form of a regulation or a decision addressed to another person, is of direct and individual concern to the former'.

Generally, a challenge to legislation under Article 173 will be brought by a Member State, and might frequently be prompted by their status as a minority dissenting view. Any successful challenge questioning the choice of Treaty authority might clearly be beneficial in these circumstances.

The opportunities for natural or legal persons to challenge are restricted, and governed by the requirement to show 'direct and individual concern'.

The narrowness of the approach of the ECJ to 'direct and individual concern' has been subject to criticism, not least because it contrasts starkly with the opportunities for the individual to challenge the Member State in relation to their failings through direct effect, indirect effect, etc.

1.8 THE INSTITUTIONS

The institutional framework of the EC represents a division of power along the lines that might be expected as between organs of State, ie legislature, executive

1 [1987] ECR 1493.

and judicature. The power wielded by the major institutions also represents a balance between the interests of Member States, EC and the citizen.

The original framework of the EEC was largely influenced by the established European Coal and Steel Community. The EEC in fact adopted part of that existing framework sharing both a Court and an Assembly with ECSC and Euratom under the Convention on Certain Institutions Common to the European Communities 1957. Euratom was founded with the EEC in 1957, for the purpose of creating the conditions necessary for the speedy establishment and growth of nuclear industries (European Atomic Energy Community Treaty 1957, Article 1).

The three Communities originally enjoyed independence in relation to their Commission (in the case of the ECSC known as the High Authority) and Council, until rationalised under the Merger Treaty of 1965.

1.8.1 The Commission

The Commission undertakes the executive function of the Community and is, as such, its servant, and guardian of the Treaty. Its role in the legislative function is largely preparatory. It develops ideas based upon EC policy and presents draft legislation for the consideration of the legislature (this will consist of the Council and Parliament, although the detail of their respective roles will depend upon the source of Treaty authority which the legislation in question is based upon). The detail of the powers and constitution of the Commission are contained in Articles 155–163 of the EEC Treaty. Its wide powers and duties are laid down in Article 155 in the following terms:

> 'In order to ensure the proper functioning and development of the common market, the Commission shall:
>
> - ensure that the provisions of this Treaty and the measures taken by the institutions pursuant thereto are applied;
> - formulate recommendations or deliver opinions on matters dealt with in this Treaty, if it expressly so provides or if the Commission considers it necessary;
> - have its own power of decision and participate in the shaping of measures taken by the Council and by the European Parliament in the manner provided for in this Treaty;
> - exercise the powers conferred on it by the Council for the implementation of the rules laid down by the latter.'

The first element of Article 155 outlines the function of the Commission as 'guardian of the Treaty', and indeed of the obligations flowing from the Treaty and subsequent legislation. It is the Commission which observes the Member States as they fulfil their obligations of membership. The obligation contained in Article 5 of the EC Treaty in particular calls upon Member States to take:

> 'all appropriate measures, whether general or particular, to ensure fulfilment of the obligations arising out of this Treaty or resulting from action taken by the institutions of the Community. They shall facilitate the achievement of the Community's tasks.

They shall abstain from any measure which could jeopardise the attainment of the objectives of this Treaty.'

If Member States are found wanting in respect of this general obligation, it is the Commission's function to instigate the enforcement process under Article 169 (detailed discussion at **2.1**). This may arise either because a Member State is acting in some way contrary to a specific Treaty measure, or in relation to the exercise or implementation of EC legislation. A similar specific power lies in relation to the monitoring and control of State aid under Articles 92–95. Under these provisions, the Commission has the authority to permit activities at its discretion, or enforce against infringements.

As the executive limb of the EC, the Commission undertakes the detailed implementation of Council policy, which may include legislation under the delegated power of the Council. Such powers, however, are not enjoyed without regulation, the Commission being subject to the scrutiny of the complex committee structures or 'comitology'.

The Commission is comprised of 20 members appointed by the 'common accord' of the governments of the Member States (Article 158(2) EC). The 'Big Four' nations (UK, Germany, Italy and France) and Spain nominate two Commissioners each, with the remaining 10 Member States nominating one each. Appointment is for a five-year period, but is renewable (Article 158 EC).

The Commission is headed by a President who takes the appointment for a two-year renewable period. The selection of President is subject to the approval of both Member States and the Parliament.

The Commission is divided into 23 specialist 'Directorates General', of which DGXI (Environment, Nuclear Safety and Civil Protection) is of particular importance in environmental matters. Commissioners appointed as Director-General are given responsibility for areas of EC policy.

1.8.2 The Council of the European Union

The constitution and operations of the Council are governed by Articles 145–154 of the EC Treaty. Article 145 establishes its function in the following terms:

'To ensure that the objectives set out in this Treaty are attained, the Council shall, in accordance with the provisions of this Treaty:

- ensure co-ordination of the general economic policies of the Member States;
- have power to take decisions;
- confer on the Commission, in the acts which the Council adopts, powers for the implementation of the rules which the Council lays down. The Council may impose certain requirements in respect of the exercise of these powers. The Council may also reserve the right, in specific cases, to exercise directly implementing powers itself. The procedures referred to above must be consonant with principles and rules to be laid down in advance by the Council, acting unanimously on a proposal from the Commission and after obtaining the opinion of the European Parliament.'

Although the Council is a permanent body, its membership is not fixed. Each Member State is represented by a single delegate of ministerial level. However, the personality of the Council in any given instance may be dictated by the subject in hand (eg Minister of Agriculture, Chancellor, etc). This flexibility provides the Council with the automatic expertise required and thereby takes advantage of the efforts of the domestic ministries.

Whilst the membership of the Council may vary, the status of representation does not. Representative must emanate from ministerial level and carry with them the authority of their Government (Article 146). This ensures that, in addition to the interests of the EC, those of the Member States are central to the decision-making and legislative process. It does not, however, ensure Member State compliance with the decisions taken or measures adopted.

The Council is headed by a President chosen from its number, who holds office for a period of six months only. The decision-making process gives due recognition to the fact that, although members are equal, the weight that their voices carry is not. Therefore, as will be seen, weighting gives more credence to the views of the larger Member States. Critics are correct to point to the ever-increasing danger of coalitions of smaller nations acting together to defeat the will of the dominant membership.

The function of the Council

Article 145 provides the basis for the function and authority of the Council. This breaks down into three strands:

- the co-ordination of economic policy
- the power to take decisions
- the authority to confer power on the Commission in relation to the implementation of rules laid down by the Council.

The Council is a principal player in the legislative process. Historically, we might have summed up the legislative process simply with the words, 'the Commission proposes, the Council disposes'. The legislative process has, however, become rather more complex over recent years, particularly in response to the expanding power of the Parliament. This is represented by the co-decision-making procedures introduced under the TEU. This development places the Council and Parliament on an equal footing for the purpose of some legislation. The range of legislative models and the varied electoral weightings operated by the Council – simple majority, qualified majority, unanimity – may present an incentive in some instances to attempt to justify the substance of legislation according to the preferred legislative model, rather than the obvious source of authority.

The gradual increase in the influence of the Parliament must be viewed as a reduction in the power of the Council, and with it, of course, the direct influence of the Member States themselves. This change in the balance of power as between Member States, EC and citizens is further reflected in the extension of the voting models beyond unanimity.

Decision-making

Meetings of the Council are largely behind closed doors. The decision-making process is necessarily a secret affair. The Council needs the freedom to discuss issues in the broadest sense without each representative being tied blindly to their own particular national interest. Further, the posturing and negotiation which is essential to decision-making within a political arena would not always be viewed sympathetically by the outside world. The unfortunate consequence of this freedom is, however, that there is little or no direct scrutiny of the Council's operations.

In relation to the development of environmental regulation, under the process enshrined in Article 189C, the Council is only required to act upon a qualified majority. However, Article 130S(2) states that by derogation in the case of provisions of a fiscal nature; measures concerning Town and Country Planning, land use with the exception of waste management and measures of a general nature, and management of water resources; or measures significantly affecting a Member State's choice between different energy sources and the general structure of its energy supply, the Council will act unanimously.

1.8.3 The European Council

For some purposes, the Council will quite rightly be comprised of the Heads of Government, although for practical purposes it is more likely to be the minister with responsibility in relation to the subject-matter under discussion. The importance of regular meetings at the highest possible level is, however, well recognised. The European Council, established in 1974, is made up of the various heads of State or Government, and supported by their Foreign Ministers and the President of the Commission, who meet for discussions on a six-monthly basis.[1] This body provides an arena for wider discussion in relation to legal and political issues and operates in addition to the deliberations of the Council.

1.8.4 COREPER – Comité des Représentants Permanents

As the members of the Council retain their domestic ministerial responsibilities and only meet on a few days each month for Council business, COREPER represents an essential back-up. The Comité des Représentants Permanents is, as the title indicates, a permanent committee comprising of representatives of the Member States at the highest ambassadorial level. Their function is authorised by Article 151 of the EC Treaty in simple terms, to be:

> '... responsible for preparing the work of the Council and for carrying out the tasks assigned to it by the Council.'

Without this support, the pace of Council operations would be very slow indeed. In addition, the criticisms levelled at the coordination of policy are at least minimised by the provision of the permanent committee, who provide

1 Article 2 of SEA 1986.

coherency and prevent the Council's function from disintegrating into a series of ad hoc responses by the diverse ministries.

1.8.5 The European Parliament

Originally operating under the title of 'Assembly', the European Parliament (as it is now called) was little more than a talking shop. Its membership consisted of persons nominated from the Member States' own parliaments. In accordance with developments anticipated by the Treaty, the Assembly became directly elected in 1979. Under the SEA 1986, its nomenclature changed to Parliament and, in recognition of this and its new-found democratic credentials, its status and functions have changed quite dramatically. Although it does not have power to initiate EC legislation, it has power to withhold the Community budget and, in extremis, to force the resignation of the Commission.

Since the 1979 elections, the Members of the European Parliament (MEPs) have become responsible to their electorate, rather than simply representing further influence of the Member States as nominees. This change has altered the balance of influence within the institutions, reducing that of the Member States to the Council, and adding the voice of the citizens of Europe. Since the latest extension in EC membership, the European Parliament has 626 members. The constituencies are spread across the Member States, being established roughly along demographic lines. This means that constituencies are much larger than for their domestic counterparts.

The 'Big Four' enjoy the representation of 87 members; Spain 64; The Netherlands 31; Belgium, Greece and Portugal 25; Sweden 21; Austria 20; Denmark and Finland 16; Ireland 15; and Luxembourg 6.

1.9 THE EUROPEAN COURT OF JUSTICE

The function of the ECJ, according to Article 164 of the EC Treaty is to:

> '... ensure that in the interpretation and application of this Treaty the law is observed.'

It operates as a supreme source of knowledge in relation to both the Treaty and subsidiary legislation, as well as presenting a forum for the enforcement of obligations and review of the acts/omissions of the institutions. The functions of the ECJ can loosely be divided into two categories:

(i) the general function of interpretation at the request of the domestic courts under Article 177, to which the development of EC law is heavily indebted;

(ii) substantive authority provided elsewhere in the Treaty, for example enforcement of Member States' obligations – Article 171 (judicial review), Articles 173–175, etc.

The relationship between the ECJ and the domestic courts is one of equals. The ECJ only stands superior to the domestic courts in the sense that it alone is provided with the authority to interpret EC law. The domestic courts must turn to it for this service, but, once provided, the ECJ has no authority to become involved in the domestic context. The relationship is not hierarchical, but co-operative. The interpretative function is central to the EC legal system.

For example, no reference is made within the wording of the Treaty itself to the relative status of domestic and EC law. No doubt, left to their own devices and designs, the Member States may have preferred to rest upon the assumption of their own sovereign status. But where would this have left the EEC and indeed the obligations of membership? Without attributing some primacy to the Treaty and the laws of the EC, its existence would have been of short duration indeed, quickly degenerating into six divergent versions.

This truth highlights the importance of the ECJ's work in cases such as *Costa v ENEL* (Case 6/64)[1] and, indeed, *Van Gend en Loos* (Case 26/62).[2] Resting upon the spirit and words of the Treaty, in these cases the interpretation of the ECJ spelled out the essential imperatives of the relationship between EC and national law. In the case of *Costa*, the Italian electricity industry tried to rely upon a piece of Italian legislation which was later in time than the Treaty of Rome and in contrary terms. Ordinarily, as within our own system, it might be expected that a statute of a newer vintage would impliedly repeal anything to the contrary, even if the time had not been taken to indicate thus by express repeal. The ECJ confirmed the essential status of EEC law in the following terms:

> 'The reception, within the laws of each Member State, of provisions having a community source, and more particularly of the terms and of the spirit of the Treaty, has as a corollary the impossibility, for the Member State, to give preference to a unilateral and subsequent measure against a legal order accepted by them on a basis of reciprocity.'

The status and force of EC law cannot vary within the domestic jurisdictions, except by endangering the uniformity of the EC, and causing the objectives of the Treaty to fail.

The response of the ECJ to the particular dilemma in *Costa* reflects the spirit not only of the Treaty, but of the Court itself in the constitutional landmark of *Van Gend en Loos*, where it stated:

> '... the community constitutes a new legal order of international law for the benefit of which States have limited their sovereign rights, albeit within limited fields, and the subjects of which comprise not only Member States but also their nationals. Independently of the legislation of Member States, Community law therefore not only imposes obligations on individuals but is also intended to confer upon them rights which become part of their legal heritage.'[3]

---

1 *Costa v Ente Nazionale per l'Energia Elettrica (ENEL)* [1964] CMLR 425, [1964] ECR 585.

2 *NV Algemene Transport-en Expeditie Onderneming Van Gend en Loos v Nederlandse Administratie der Belastingen* [1963] ECR 1, [1963] CMLR 105.

3 1 [1963] ECR 1, para 4.

Whilst there is no binding precedent in the ECJ, that of course does not mean that there is no certainty. The ECJ would be loath to alter a previous opinion, although that is not to say that it would never do so where the weight of evidence supported such a move. Even though the Court of First Instance now operates in support of the ECJ, for many purposes it remains a single-tier jurisdiction, where legal development would in any case be clearly fettered by any notion of binding precedent.

The domestic courts of the Member States are none the less obliged to follow the ECJ, applying its interpretation in their own jurisdictions. This obligation arises from the notion of primacy of EC law enunciated in *Costa*, the general obligation of membership enshrined in Article 5 of the EC Treaty and, in our own case, in the terms of s 2(4) of the European Communities Act 1972 by which the obligations of EC membership were recognised domestically.

1.9.1 The Court of First Instance

Authorised by the SEA 1986, the Court of First Instance (CFI) was approved by Council in 1988 and opened for business in 1989. Like the ECJ, it comprises 15 judges selected from the highest calibre of legal representatives of the Member States. There are no Advocates-General attached to the CFI but, where needed, the role is fulfilled by one of the judges. The CFI was established to ease the load of the ECJ. Although the size of the ECJ has increased over the years, the increase in personnel has been offset by the increase in Member States and the consequent case-load.

The CFI's jurisdiction extends to disputes between the EC and its employees, and Articles 173 and 175 cases brought by natural and legal persons. Whilst the former releases the ECJ from the domestic burden of staff cases, the latter set the CFI up as something of a specialist court. The judicial review cases can cover the ranges of complaints against the institutions, but a very large number arise in relation to the powers of the Commission particularly in the area of competition law.

The existence of the CFI means that for the first time a right of appeal exists to a higher court. The only possibility of appeal from the ECJ itself arises in very limited circumstances where additional facts may be brought to light after a decision such as to render reconsideration appropriate.

1.9.2 Article 177 references

Article 177 states:

> 'The Court of Justice shall have jurisdiction to give preliminary rulings concerning:
>
> (a) the interpretation of this Treaty;
> (b) the validity and interpretation of acts of the institutions of the Community and of the ECB
> (c) the interpretation of the statutes of bodies established by an act of the Council, where those statutes so provide.'

By far the bulk of the work of the ECJ falls into the category of Article 177 references. It is through the vehicle of Article 177 that EC law is interpreted by the ECJ in order to facilitate the adjudication of the domestic courts. Article 177 establishes the co-operative and equal relationship between the domestic courts and the ECJ and provides the means for the development of EC law through the judicial activism of the ECJ.

An Article 177 reference does not represent an appeal, but rather identifies in clear terms the respective authority and function of the domestic and European courts. The domestic court has sole jurisdiction until, and unless, a matter of European law requires interpretation. The reference to the ECJ concerns the matter of interpretation and nothing more. The ECJ has no authority to draw any conclusions in the light of that interpretation, no matter how obvious the ultimate outcome at domestic level may be. The 'interpretation of law' is then returned to the domestic court, where it will facilitate the final decision on the facts.

As has been noted, the ECJ makes its interpretation according to 'teleological' techniques applying not only the letter, but the spirit of the law. This is of particular importance in relation to environmental matters, since the wording of Articles 130R–T has been extended by the TEU to recognise the need for its integration into the definition and implementation of other Community policies (Article 130R(2)).

The wording of Article 177 recognises two types of domestic court. Those courts which have a discretion in relation to making a reference, and those which are under a mandatory duty to make such a reference. This is couched in the following terms:

> 'Where such a question is raised before any court or tribunal of a Member State, that court or tribunal *may*, if it considers that a decision on the question is necessary to enable it to give judgment, request the Court of Justice to give a ruling thereon.
>
> When any such question is raised in a case pending before a court or tribunal of a Member State against whose decisions there is no judicial remedy under national law, that court or tribunal *shall* bring the matter before the Court of Justice.' (emphasis added)

As early as *Costa*,[1] it was recognised that the category of court depended not on the hierarchical position of the court, but on the question before the court in any given instance. In *Costa*, the financial sum at the centre of the debate was of such insignificance that there was in fact no appeal available, even though the forum for adjudication was not the highest, but the lowest court in the land. In accordance with the spirit of the Treaty, this is the only possible outcome if Article 177 is to fulfil its wider function of according the means of developing a single coherent body of EC law applicable equally in all Member States.

1 [1964] CMLR 425, [1964] ECR 585.

If a Member State fails to make a reference either through belligerence or oversight, there is nothing that the ECJ can do about it. There is no 'call in' power.

The ECJ has given guidance on the question of when a reference should be made. Shortly after the landmark interpretation given to Article 12 in *Van Gend en Loos*, the ECJ was subject to a further Article 177 reference on the same point in the case of *Da Costa en Schaake v Nederlandse Belastingadministratie* (Cases 28–30/62).[1] Whilst the Court was quick to point out that it retained the legal authority to readjudicate, in order to ensure that it had not in fact erred in its previous position, it none the less considered that ordinarily, where the domestic courts had raised before them a question which had already been subject to the interpretation of the ECJ, they should not be obliged to make a further reference even if the Court itself fell within the latter category operating under the duty to refer.

The position of the 'court of final jurisdiction' was revisited in the case of *CILFIT v Ministro della Sanita* (Case 283/81),[2] where the ECJ came up with a formula indicating three positions where even the 'court of final jurisdiction' may exercise a certain discretion against making an Article 177 reference:

(1) where the question of EC law is not relevant to the case;
(2) where the question has already been subject to interpretation by the ECJ;
(3) where the meaning is so obvious as to leave no reasonable doubt.

The essence of the approach in *CILFIT* is not to attack the duty and obligation addressed to the court of final jurisdiction, but rather to give close consideration to the question of when a reference is actually necessary. This is the same question whether it leads to the exercise of a discretion or a mandatory duty. What *CILFIT* does avoid, however, is the implicit invitation to the domestic courts to try to artificially 'shoe horn' themselves into the discretionary category.

The most onerous burden of the *CILFIT* judgment falls in the third category, ie that the meaning is 'so obvious as to leave no reasonable doubt'.[3]

This approach is an adaptation of the French doctrine of 'act claire'. Whilst it appears to grant the domestic courts a considerable freedom with the one hand, it takes it back with the other. It is a brave court indeed that is prepared to say that its own interpretation would not only be universal to all other courts, including the ECJ, but that it would be universal to all other language and methods of interpretation.

An interpretation of the ECJ given in response to an Article 177 reference becomes binding upon all domestic courts. The purpose of this mechanism is to ensure, inter alia, a single unified legal system. Any other conclusion would therefore be inappropriate. The corollary of this position must therefore be

1 [1963] ECR 31.
2 [1982] ECR 3415.
3 [1982] ECR 3415 at 3430.

that the interpretation given stands for all purposes, and is not simply to be relied upon by the litigants themselves.

1.10 DIRECT EFFECT

The object of the Article 177 reference is not solely to ensure the development of a single coherent body of European law. It also acts as a vehicle through which that body of law develops and grows to meet new challenges. The Treaty of Rome, and now the EC Treaty, represents the basis of European law. They are skeletal in nature, and consequently rely heavily on the interpretations of the ECJ, not only to give them full force, but to ensure their organic development. This function is recognised in civil law circles even if it sometimes appears to our own eyes to be blatant judicial legislation. Not only would it have been impossible for the original Treaty to have been large enough to cover all the details on which to base a legal system, but it would have been very difficult to establish in advance the true needs of a unique intra-national relationship. The task of interpretation, by reference to the words and spirit of the Treaty (Article 155) provides the ECJ with the tools to ensure the organic development of this legal system.

Amongst the major developments by the ECJ is the recognition of the primacy of EC law. This relationship between domestic and EC law is not provided for in the Treaty, but was arrived at by reference to its words and spirit. The benefit of hindsight of course ensures both the necessity of such a position and the obviousness of its existence. This was not, of course, the case at the time.

By establishing the notion of primacy of EC law, the doors are open to a whole range of developments to ensure recognition of that fact, and of the reality of the burden of membership. The most obvious example is the development of the principle of 'direct effect'. The development of 'direct effect' can be viewed as both a consequence of primacy and as a case study in the same.

At its simplest, direct effect means that a natural or legal person may go to their own domestic court, relying on an EC law measure even if that measure has been ignored by their own jurisdiction, and even if their own jurisdiction has deliberately acted contrary to the EC obligation. That this can be the case is testament to the primacy of EC law. Authority for this position is not based in the express wording of the Treaty (if it had been, it is questionable as to whether the sovereignty of the original Member States would have allowed them to sign up!), but is necessitated by pure logic. It is a creation of the 'spirit' of the Treaty, and, without it, the development of the intra-national relationship which it represents would have proved much the poorer.

1.10.1 *Van Gend en Loos*

The ECJ first acknowledged the idea that natural and legal persons might enjoy rights emanating from EC law, exercisable in their own courts, in the case of *NV Algemene Transport-en Expeditie Onderneming Van Gend en Loos v Nederlandse Administratie der Belastingen*,[1] otherwise known as *Van Gend en Loos*.

Notwithstanding the customs duty standstill provisions of Article 12, the records of Van Gend en Loos showed that the total duties paid by them for a set amount of trade had increased during the period of EC membership. This, they argued, could only be explained by an increase in customs duties contrary to Article 12 of the Treaty of Rome.

The complaint raised two distinct issues. First, had the Dutch authorities in fact increased the levels of duty payable contrary to their obligation under Article 12? Secondly, could a natural or legal person enjoy any right arising from the quasi-contractual relationship between nations represented by the Treaty in international law? It would certainly not normally be expected that rights could extend to individuals, effectively third parties. This position was supported by the fact that the Treaty itself contains specially designed enforcement procedures (Articles 169–171) which exist to ensure that Member States fulfil their obligations and thereby guarantee that natural and legal persons suffer no such loss as a result of a Member State's failure to comply with its Treaty obligations. None the less the ECJ concluded:

> '... this treaty is more than an agreement creating only mutual obligations between the contracting parties ... community law ... not only imposes obligations on individuals, but also confers on them legal rights.'

The ECJ was clearly of the opinion that natural or legal persons had the right to ask questions in the courts, notwithstanding the legal relationship represented by the Treaty, or the specific enforcement measures therein.

The approach to direct effect since *Van Gend* has been on a 'piecemeal' basis. This would seem indicative of the fact that not all EC law is capable of having direct effect. In the case of *Van Gend*, it was acknowledged that, in order to claim direct effect, a provision must be capable of satisfying certain criteria. The provision must be:

(i) clear and precise;
(ii) unconditional; and
(iii) leave no discretion to the Member State (also referred to as requiring no further implementation on the part of the Member State).

Whilst the three criteria are essential hurdles for establishing direct effect, it may be that, in reality, clarity can be achieved only through the interpretation of the ECJ. This will not necessarily be a barrier to direct effect.

1 [1963] ECR 1, [1963] CMLR 105.

There has been much debate over the years as to the relationship between 'direct effect' and 'directly applicable'. From time to time the phrases have been considered to have the same meaning, and thus be effectively interchangeable. Alternatively, a finding of direct effect relies upon the court first accepting as a prerequisite direct applicability. Neither position is in fact true. However, the two principles are clearly related. Confusion arises because in the early days the question of direct effect would not arise except in relation to a provision which already professed the quality of direct applicability, for example, Regulations.

Direct applicability is understood to mean that a provision is 'automatically' part of domestic law, without any further action on the part of the Member State. It is a characteristic of the Regulation because it is defined as such in Article 189:

> 'A regulation shall have general application. It shall be binding in its entirety and *directly applicable* in all Member States.' (emphasis added)

The fact that both Treaty and Regulations may be described as directly applicable, and that the ECJ indicated that they might also be capable of direct effect led to the initial confusion. As no other provision was being considered at this time, it seemed safe for commentators to assume that either direct effect and direct applicability were the same thing, or at least that one was dependent upon the other.

However, problems arose in extending the principle to the Directive. The Directive is not directly applicable. We know this because it is not described as such by Article 189, and because its very characteristics indicate that it is not capable of 'automatic' effect. Member States have to adopt it within their own jurisdiction through the process of implementation.

The domestic courts also showed their alarm for those who would be required to shoulder the duties of their Member State if Directives were directly effective, a duty which should, from the wording of Article 189, clearly rest upon the Member State. To add insult to injury, the domestic courts highlighted the fact that, as there was no legal requirement to publish the Directive in the Official Journal, such a person might wake up to discover that they were being held responsible for the failure of their Member State in relation to an obligation which they could have no knowledge of, or means of discovering.

The argument that a Directive may not come to the wider knowledge because of there being no obligation to publish is now history. Article 191 of the EC Treaty (as amended by Article G (64) of TEU) requires that Regulations, Directives and decisions, be published in the Official Journal. In fact, it has long been the practice to publish Directives in this way irrespective of any obligation.

1.10.2 The *Marshall* case

The idea of natural and legal persons sharing the obligations of State remains abhorrent. This feature, known as horizontal effect, presents the last remaining barrier to the direct effect of Directives. The question arose, inter alia, in the case of *Marshall v Southampton and South West Hampshire Area Health Authority (Teaching)* (No 152/84).[1] If Directives were capable of direct effect, did this Directive satisfy the criteria, and could it be exercised against the Health Authority, a public body, in its capacity as employer?

Advocate-General Slynn considered that the fact that the Directive creates an obligation on the State to act, rather than on natural or legal persons (Article 189), should suffice to justify the limitation of direct effect as it applies to Directives. The fact that the obligation extends to the Member State should, on the other hand, prevent it from denying responsibility, and thereby hiding behind its own failure. He took the view, however, that the definition of the State should be broad, extending beyond legislature and executive, to include even the State as an employer. This view was confirmed by the ECJ and is recognised as supporting the direct effect of Directives on a vertical plane only, ie against the body actually in default.

The *Marshall* case represents something of a compromise. Direct effect of Directives is confirmed, but limited to situations where the litigant wishes to challenge the Member State, however widely defined, thus effectively leaving those who have perhaps suffered in the same way, but at the hands of a private party, without a remedy. Whilst the ECJ recognises that this situation might lead to some perceived injustice, it rightly points out that this is in fact down to the failure of the Member State rather than the ECJ. If the Member State had undertaken its obligation to implement, everyone would enjoy the same conditions.

The important question which remains is how should 'Member State' be defined for this purpose? The trend to privatisation in recent years appears to make it a crucial question. The fact that in *Marshall* the Health Authority fell within the definition of Member State indicates the breadth of the view. However, if the definition extends to include bodies such as the Health Authority where should the boundaries of the State lie, and on what rational basis?

The question was particularly poignant in the case of *Foster v British Gas* (No C-188/89),[2] as the defendant company had moved from the public to the private sector between the time of the facts complained of and the case reaching the Court. Advocate-General Van Gervan gave careful consideration to this question rejecting both the notions of simple 'public control' and 'the classic duties of the State', before concluding that the appropriate questions to ask should be whether there is exercise of a 'public function', and whether

---

1 [1986] QB 401.
2 [1991] 1 QB 405.

there can be said to be any 'real control' on the part of the State. The Court concurred in the following terms:

> '... a body, whatever its legal form, which has been made responsible, pursuant to a measure adopted by the State, for providing a public service under the control of the State and has for that purpose special powers beyond those which result from the normal rules applicable in relations between individuals.'

This definition may therefore exclude some bodies which merely exercise a function for the public, and include others who, although they may be in the private sector, none the less enjoy such 'special powers'. Thus, even a commercial body may be viewed as an emanation of the State where it carries out a public service which is under State control, as seen in *Griffin v South West Water Services.*[1]

The direct effect of Directives represents an important arena, if for no other reason than the popularity of the legislative form. This is particularly the case in the field of environmental control and well illustrated by the ratio of atmospheric Directives and Regulations. Further, the programme of privatisation over recent years has moved many of the would-be defendants out of the public sector, at a crucial point in time in relation to the enforcement or lack of enforcement of many environmental provisions.

The potential of direct effect should therefore be fully appreciated. It represents an essential tool in relation to the fullest enforcement of EC obligations.

1.11 DUTY OF INTERPRETATION – *VON COLSON*

None the less, the restrictions applying to the direct effect of Directives does mean that there are would-be litigants who are robbed of a remedy, simply because they have suffered at the hands of a body which does not qualify as 'public' for this purpose, rather than on any objective view of their suffering. An alternative approach was considered by the ECJ in the case of *Von Colson and Kamann v Land Nordrhein-Westfahlen* (No 14/83).[2]

It was clear, in this case, that the Directive was incapable of satisfying the 'three criteria', and therefore could not be considered to be directly effective. The effect of this conclusion would have been to leave the litigant without a remedy, and to allow the State to gain a benefit from its own failings. None the less, direct effect could offer no resolution.

The ECJ resolved the issue by reference to the general obligation contained in Article 5 of the EC Treaty. The duty to 'take all appropriate measures ... to ensure fulfilment of the obligations arising out of this Treaty ...' applies to Member States. In *Von Colson*, the ECJ considered, further, that this obligation must extend to all organs of the State, including the judicature.

---

1 [1995] IRLR 15.
2 [1984] ECR 1891, [1986] 2 CMLR 430.

Assuming the legislature to have intended to implement a Directive, the obligations of Article 5, and the principle of effectiveness, dictate a sympathetic interpretation. In the view of the ECJ:

> '...in applying the national law specifically introduced in order to implement Directive 76/207, national courts are required to interpret their national law in the light of the wording and purpose of the Directive in order to achieve the result referred to in Article 189(3).'[1]

None the less, the obligation to interpret may present difficulties for the courts. This may be highlighted for those from a literalist tradition. *Von Colson* does at least expect the legislation to have been adopted for the purpose of implementation, and it does not require the domestic courts to go further than they are able by national law. Whilst this seems to temper the effect, it is the case that the differing national traditions may allow the courts in some jurisdictions to go a lot further than in others.

Since *Von Colson* the ECJ has indicated that the obligation to interpret should extend beyond the scenario anticipated by that case. This was confirmed in the case of *Marleasing SA v La Comercial Internacional de Alimentacion SA* (C-106/89).[2] In that case, the ECJ considered that:

> '... in applying national law, whether the provisions in question were adopted before or after the Directive, the national court called upon to interpret it is required to do so, so far as possible, in the light of the wording and purpose of the Directive in order to achieve the result pursued by the latter.'

Unlike *Von Colson*, *Marleasing* extends the obligation of interpretation even where there has been no attempt to implement. If there is any legislative provision on point, *Marleasing* suggests the need for a sympathetic interpretation. The factual background to *Marleasing* itself was such that not only did the legislation in question predate the obligation, but it actually predated (by some time) the accession of the Member State.

It could be suggested that, taken to its extreme, *Marleasing* might seriously damage legal certainty, by resurrecting legislation and giving it new meaning in the name of Article 5. However, the general principles of EC law, which include certainty and non-retroactivity, should offer sufficient protection against this threat.

In practical terms, the potential of indirect effect might be harnessed in relation to situations where the Member State believes itself to have complied. In such circumstances, interpretation sympathetic with the obligation itself will be less controversial than the *Marleasing* model.

1 See **1.10.1**.

2 [1992] 1 CMLR 305.

1.12 STATE LIABILITY

The third major vehicle by which the obligations of EC law may be indirectly impressed upon the Member States is through compensation. Simplistically, if a Member State fails to implement a provision which would otherwise have inferred a financial benefit, the person who has been penalised may seek redress in the courts.

This is an interesting development because, unlike direct effect, it is available to all, irrespective of who should have conferred the benefit, if the Member State has failed to honour its obligations. Further, it presents none of the problems of linguistic acrobatics which may face the domestic courts in relation to 'indirect effect'. As a means of indirect enforcement, it ensures that a Member State may neither hide behind its own failure nor enjoy a financial bonus from that failure.

The recognition of State liability is a major leap of imagination on the part of the ECJ. Previously, the ECJ had been of the opinion that the potential for such liability could only arise in national law. Whilst the original position might protect the fragile sovereignty of Member States, it allowed them the protection of their own failure. In addition, the policy of leaving such matters to national law could never ensure a 'level playing field' and equality before the law.

The imposition of State liability by the ECJ rests upon the recognised primacy of EC law. The logical necessity of this position has been tested in the ECJ over the years giving rise to direct and indirect effect and culminating in the case of *Factortame.*[1] *Factortame* required the English courts to disapply a measure of domestic law and grant 'interim relief' pending the conclusion of an Article 177 reference. In doing so, it supported the notion that the ECJ should be called upon to establish a remedy where the existing law fails so to do. This theme was also central to the case of *Francovich v Italy* (joined cases C-6/90 and C-9/90).[2] The plaintiffs, Francovich and Boniface, had lost their jobs due to their employers becoming insolvent. Directive 80/1987, if implemented, would have entitled them to compensation. The two could not rely upon direct effect because, although the Directive required Member States to set up appropriate compensation schemes, it did not provide sufficient detail to satisfy the three criteria. Neither could the parties rely on indirect effect. They were therefore ostensibly without a remedy. In this case, there was no question as to the failings of the Italian State because this had already been established before the ECJ at the suit of the Commission (Article 169).[3] Against this background the losses of the litigants seems even more poignant. Without the intervention of the ECJ, the State would have successfully hidden behind its own proven failure.

1 *R v Secretary of State for Transport ex parte Factortame (No 2)* (C-213/89) [1991] 1 AC 603.

2 [1992] IRLR 84.

3 *Commission of the European Communities v Italian Republic* (C-22/87) [1989] ECR 143.

Relying jointly on the obligation of Article 5 of the EC Treaty and the principle of 'effectiveness', so important to previous developments, the ECJ established the new remedy. This new remedy will however, only be available in very specific circumstances. It is essential for the would-be litigants to prove the following:

(i) a right which is traceable to the Directive;
(ii) an ascertainable or quantifiable loss;
(iii) a causal link between the failure of the Member State and the loss.

Although showing some similarity to the logic on which direct effect is established, the fact that direct effect was not available in these circumstances should indicate a broader approach. None the less, the question remains as to how broad that approach will be. Presumably there would be no reason to prevent damages being obtained in relation to an obligation which is directly effective. A claim based upon both might be particularly useful to compensate for past losses and future enjoyment of a right. Further, because the State is compensating for loss due to its failure, it would seem that a remedy may even be available in a situation which might otherwise be defined as 'horizontal direct effect'. The subject matter of the provision may indicate that the monies are payable by a private party, but that does not prevent blame for the fact that the obligation has never been activated, from resting on the Member State.

By emphasising State liability as inherent in the Treaty, some authors have postulated the extension of *Francovich*-type liability, to provide a remedy in relation to a general rather than specific breach of EC obligations.[1] The question as to how the criteria would be satisfied in such cases, however, remains to be seen.

None the less, the practical implications of *Francovich* are immense, not purely in terms of the satisfaction of the individual litigants, but of the informal enforcement of EC obligations. As with direct and indirect effect, hindsight shows us the inescapable logic of this development. Similarly, the full effect of *Francovich* may be appreciated only with further use.

1 Ross, 'Beyond *Francovich*' (1993) 56 MLR 55.

CHAPTER 2

THE EC DIMENSION – SPECIFIC PROTECTION

2.1 ENFORCEMENT

2.1.1 Background

In a perfect world the question of enforcement would not arise. Debate at EC level leading to legislation would invoke an instant response in the Member States, who would exercise or implement their obligations perfectly and without question. This is not a perfect world. That is not to say that failure on the part of Member States is necessarily due to deliberate objection or recalcitrance. As has been noted, support through the legislative process cannot assume a trouble-free route to application in the domestic arena.

It is possible, because of the skeletal nature of the Treaty, and the importance of the interpretative role of the ECJ, that a Member State may believe that it has satisfied its obligation, only to find that it has not. As Regulations are directly applicable, no implementation is required, and the question of enforcement is therefore confined to operative points, ie that the Member State is failing to apply or exercise the law according to the Regulations in some way.

The Directive presents a number of opportunities for enforcement:

- the Member State may have failed to implement the Directive into domestic law by the due date;
- implementation itself may be found to be defective in some way. Either the Member State has misinterpreted the obligation, or the implementation has been partial only;
- (as with Regulations) the obligation may have been translated into domestic law, but is not being applied or exercised in practice.

Enforcement is one of the principal functions of the Commission. It is an onerous task and one which the Commission arguably lacks the staff and information base to carry out efficiently. In some policy areas, competition law in particular, additional powers are provided to facilitate efficient enforcement. In relation to competition law, wide supplementary powers provide authorising investigations of premises with or without notice, allowing inspection of documentation, etc. Whilst such powers would no doubt be useful in facilitating the enforcement of environmental obligations, the difference in approach may have as much to do with the identity of the parties as the relative status of the policy. In competition, case investigation is generally into the actions of companies whereas, more generally, it is the failings or otherwise of

Member States which is in question. In these circumstances, the Draconian powers of Regulation 17/62 would be inappropriate.

In relation to the enforcement of environmental obligations, the role of the Commission should, however, be assisted in the future by the information provided by the European Environmental Agency.

The Commission is not under a duty to enforce, but rather enjoys a discretion to consider the actions of the Member States (Article 169). This is an important stage in the process, as informal discussions may ease the mind of the Commission. If the Member State is in the process of compliance, or finds itself facing severe domestic problems which prevent compliance, the Commission may tailor its response accordingly. Whilst it is important that enforcement is efficient, in reality it is a waste of resources if the Member State cannot comply. Domestic problems do not provide a defence, but logic dictates that an enforcement action brought prematurely will simply result in further failures: failure to comply with the original obligation; failure to comply with the reasoned opinion; failure to comply with the order of the court.

Historically, the Commission invested a great deal of time in the informal stages, delaying the reasoned opinion and/or subsequent action before the ECJ, in some instances for years. By the time the Member State was brought before the ECJ, the original failure had subsisted for many years. However, the number of cases which required further action on the part of the Commission was relatively few. This being the case, the approach could be viewed as a success, with few Member States failing to comply with the order of the ECJ. Nevertheless, we must consider at what cost, when the time taken from the date of the original failure to compliance was likely to be measured in years; in environmental matters delay is, of course, crucial.

In response to vociferous complaints, the Commission has altered its approach, entering into the enforcement process more readily. At the same time, however, it must be noted that the number of actions requiring a second or even a third visit to the ECJ has increased dramatically, such as to lead to amendments in Article 171 of the Treaty, providing for the imposition of financial penalties for non-compliance. It will be interesting to see how frequently this new power will be used, but as is generally the case with environmental matters the financial penalty is not likely to equate to the full environmental cost of non-compliance, nor is it likely to be applied to remediate the damage caused.

2.1.2 The reasoned opinion

If the Commission is of the view that the Member State has failed in its obligation, it is duty-bound to deliver a 'reasoned opinion'. The reasoned opinion issued to the Member State indicates the nature of the infringement, and the steps which should be taken to achieve full compliance. It effectively identifies the failure of the Member State and makes submissions which the Commission will rely upon in the ECJ. Although the Commission is under a duty to issue a reasoned opinion, it takes the form of a request rather than a demand, inviting the observations of the Member State. This means that no action is available to prompt a Member State where it fails to respond. This position was confirmed by the ECJ in the case of *EC Commission v Denmark* (Case 211/81).[1]

This is in contrast to the obligations imposed on the Commission, which in the same case were considered to be: 'an essential formal requirement under Article 169'. The logic of this position rests upon the fact that the notification of the reasoned opinion establishes the infringement, putting the Member State on notice, and providing the opportunity of preparing a defence or response. Whilst there is no duty to respond on the part of the Member State, failure to assist the Commission may well lead to a breach of the general obligation of membership under Article 5 of the EC Treaty, in addition to the original infringement.

The response of the Member State is requested within a 'reasonable period'. The reasonable period is not defined, but response is generally required within 30 days.

Traditionally, it has been accepted that the majority of cases will be satisfactorily resolved either by informal negotiations, or by the reasoned opinion. This may be for a variety of reasons: a reminder may be all that is necessary; in other cases, the interest of the Commission may indicate misinterpretation of the obligation on the part of the Member State which it may be happy to correct.

There is some evidence, however,[2] that an increasing number of cases will go beyond the informal stage to reasoned opinion. This is a logical parallel to the increase in cases which fail to be resolved by their first visit to the ECJ and may similarly be affected by the change in the approach of the Commission, as well as an increase in recalcitrance.

A positive response to the reasoned opinion will be to the satisfaction of the Commission, although it should be remembered that questions of interpretation are for the ECJ alone. It will therefore be no defence for a Member State to claim compliance with the reasoned opinion of the Commission, if its actions are later found wanting before the ECJ. This point is illustrated in the joint cases of *Administrazioni delle Finanze dello Stato v Essevi and Salongo* (Cases 142, 143/80).[3]

Where the Member State fails to comply with the reasoned opinion, the Commission, in the words of Article 169, 'may' refer the matter to the ECJ. The use of the discretionary 'may' is in contrast to the mandatory 'shall' in relation to the reasoned opinion.

1 [1982] ECR 4547.

2 Seventh and Eighth Annual Reports to the European Parliament on Commission Monitoring of the Application of Community Law, 1989 (OJ 1990 C232/1) and 1990 (OJ 1991 338/1).

3 [1981] ECR 1413.

The Member State may of course act to comply with the obligation at any time but, even where compliance occurs before the case arrives at the ECJ, it will not necessarily prevent the case from being heard. This is because the deliberations of the ECJ are not simply aimed at enforcement; they are also an important means of establishing the meaning of an obligation, and thereby providing certainty for all.

Whilst the Member State may, in some instances, face real domestic problems effectively precluding compliance, these will rarely amount to a defence in the eyes of the ECJ. Weatherill and Beaumont[1] report that fewer than 10 per cent of cases before the ECJ are resolved in favour of the Member State. The opportunities offered by the prolonged pre-court stages should cause this to be no surprise.

In addition to the enforcement actions brought by the Commission, Article 170 provides for enforcement actions to be brought by a fellow Member State. Although this action allows the Member States to act in lieu of the Commission, there are good political reasons to suggest that it will never be a regular form of action. The single example of such a case is *France v UK Re Fishing Net Mesh Sizes* (Case 141/78).[2] In reality, any complaint which a Member State may have is likely to lead it to lobby the Commission to act.

There is no equivalent power allowing natural or legal persons to bring an enforcement action. An individual or company complaining may lobby the Commission, or alternatively seek to rely upon the informal methods before the domestic courts with the hope of a reference to the ECJ where appropriate. The informal mechanisms of direct effect, indirect effect or *Francovich* may, however, be available.

2.2 SUBSTANTIVE PROVISIONS

The EC was not as quick to respond to the degradation of air and atmospheric quality as it was to other pollution problems. Air pollution is less visible, and, therefore, perhaps presented a less urgent agenda. However, when problems of air quality manifest themselves in damage to land, it becomes a focal point for attention, particularly if that damage crosses international boundaries. Damage to the European forests therefore rendered the problem not only visible, but urgent.

The EC became involved in the regulation and control of air quality and atmospheric pollution for the dual purpose of ameliorating physical damage, and ensuring that intervention was not at the cost of a level commercial playing field.

The major Directives relating to the atmosphere to be dealt with here can be categorised in the following terms:

---

1 *EC Law*, 2nd edn (Penguin, 1995).
2 [1979] ECR 2923.

The Air Framework Directive 84/360, and its daughter provisions:
88/609/EEC;
89/369/EEC;
94/67/EC.
The new Air Quality Framework Directive, 96/62/EC.

The Fuel and the Vehicular Emissions Directives:
93/12/EEC;
85/203/EEC;
82/884/EEC;
85/210/EEC.

Information and Research Decision 97/101
Directive 92/72/EEC
Regulation 3528/86/EEC

International Obligations Regulation 3093/94/EC
Directive 94/63/EC

A New Age of EC Control Directive 96/61/EC

2.3 AIR POLLUTION FROM INDUSTRIAL PLANT

The Air Framework Directive, 84/360/EEC, represents an early response to the problems of acid rain and associated forest damage. The apparent damage to forests prompted pressure, in particular from the German Government, leading the matter to be discussed at the Environment Council's meeting in 1982, and later the same year at the Stockholm Ministerial Conference. German concern was also raised before the European Council in 1983, identifying the need for immediate action. The design of the Directive rests upon an assumption of later detailed provisions identifying emission limits. The so-called 'daughter' Directives have included the limitation of SO_2, NO_x and dust from large combustion plants (88/609/EEC); Municipal Waste Incineration (89/369/EEC) and Hazardous Waste Incineration (94/67/EC).

The early vintage of the Air Framework Directive explains its reliance upon the authority of Articles 100 and 235 of the Treaty, relying therefore on the harmonisation provision and the general 'catch-all' of Article 235, which provides authority for provisions 'necessary to attain ... one of the objectives of the Community ...'. The relationship between emissions to the air and commercial costs places industry and the environment in close proximity, enabling this authority to be claimed in this instance without question.

The Directive requires prior emissions authorisation to be obtained for certain new plant and major alterations to plant specified in the annex to the Directive. The approach is based upon the BATNEEC principle (best available techniques not entailing excessive cost). Approval will only be given in relation to plant design which includes all appropriate measures for the reduction of air pollution based upon BATNEEC. The proposal should not envisage significant air pollution particularly in relation to plant identified in

Annex II, with the design criteria acknowledging emission limit values and air quality limits.

The obligation of BATNEEC applies not only to design, but also to operational standards. In the case of older plant, the Member State is expected to ensure the operation of BATNEEC by attaching conditions and calling for operational changes where necessary. Provision is made in the Directive for 'emissions limits' to be established by the Council. These will also be established by reference to BATNEEC. Where an area is identified for special protection or suffers excessive pollution levels, the emission limit values set may reflect the need for greater protection in their stringency.

There is an expectation in the Directive that the approval process will take place in the public arena. Both the original applications and the final decision are therefore open to public scrutiny. Furthermore, Member States are required to inform the Commission and their counterparts of information obtained which relates to the prevention or reduction of pollution levels.

Although the UK was at pains to point to similarities between the proposal and domestic practice, formal compliance was not achieved until two years after the date of implementation. Until then the Government had sought to rely upon the pre-existing regulatory framework principally provided by the Alkali etc Works Regulation Act 1909 and the Health and Safety at Work Act 1974, notwithstanding the fact that these provisions did not extend control across the whole range of plant specified.

The compliance measures were implemented formally in the Health and Safety (Emissions to the Atmosphere) (Amendment) Regulations 1989, SI 1989/319, and Control of Industrial Air Pollution (Registration of Works) Regulations 1989, SI 1989/318, which were to bridge the gap until the passing of the Environmental Protection Act 1990 (EPA 1990). The EPA now extends control to plant and processes specified in Directive 84/360 through the Environmental Protection (Prescribed Processes and Substances) Regulations 1991, SI 1991/472, as amended. The Act itself replaces the original standard of 'best practicable means' with BATNEEC and empowers the Secretary of State for the Environment in relation to emissions/quality objectives. The Act responds to the Directive's requirement for public scrutiny by providing for the availability of information to the public by way of registers.

The design of EPA 1990 is considered to satisfy the basic requirement of the Framework Directive, but it is assumed to do more, with the non-media specific response of integrated pollution control largely anticipating the Integrated Pollution Prevention and Control (IPPC) Directive, 96/62, being designed to replace Directive 84/360 in due course.

As noted, Article 8 of Directive 84/360 provides authority for a series of subsequent 'daughter' Directives. These Directives establish emission limit values in relation to a wider range of processes than 84/360 itself. The most prominent of the so-called 'daughter' Directives is Directive 88/609/EEC, limiting emissions from large combustion plants. Indeed, the impact of this Directive has almost overshadowed the original parent Directive.

2.3.1 Directive 88/609/EEC

The specific aim of Directive 88/609/EEC is to address the problem of acid rain by setting emission limits for sulphur dioxide (SO_2) and nitrogen oxide (NOx) from certain power stations (50 megawatts or above) and other large combustion plants. The Directive applies separate standards to new and pre-existing sources. Like the parent Directive, it recognises the wider powers of control which exist from the design stage. Power stations fuelled by diesel, petrol or gas are excluded from these limit controls.

The emissions of pre-existing power stations and plant must comply with new national emission totals, although emission levels will not necessarily be uniform across the Member States. This has benefited the UK, whose emissions total was arrived at on the basis of traditional use of high-sulphur-content domestic coal supplies. Since these standards were set, however, the pattern of fuel consumption of power stations in the UK has altered significantly, moving towards increased reliance upon gas and lower-sulphur-content imported coals. Compliance with emission levels has therefore proved a relatively painless process so far, as these structural changes have generally effected a sufficient reduction in emissions.

The overall projected reduction in SO_2 emissions across the EC is a 58 per cent reduction on 1980 levels, equating to a reduction of some six million tonnes per year by 1998. This, however, masks a wide difference in the task before the Member States. Germany, Belgium, France, and The Netherlands on the one hand are faced with the total of a 70 per cent reduction, whilst Portugal, on the other hand, is permitted a 79 per cent increase. Portugal, Greece and Ireland are each scheduled for an overall increase on 1980 levels on the basis of their initially low levels of power production and the desire to offer some protection to further structural development.

NOx emissions are similarly scheduled for reduction. In relation to existing plant, the requirement is for emission levels to be reduced by 20 per cent by 1993, and 36 per cent by 1998. In comparison, the approach to new facilities is more stringent, with the expectation that new plant will achieve emission levels of 80 per cent and 50 per cent respectively of the SO_2 and NOx levels of existing plant.

The Directive requires Member States to design and implement appropriate reduction programmes. Progress reports are to be made to the Commission at the midway point, and after the conclusion of each stage.

Limit levels were established by reference to both 'the state of technology and environmental requirements'. Although this may arguably lead to a very fixed scheme, the Directive does contain a proviso enabling it to deal with unforeseen changes in demand or necessitated changes in fuel sources.

Monitoring of emission levels falls into two distinct regimes. New power stations and plant with a capacity in excess of 300 megawatts are subject to continuous monitoring, whilst all other power stations and plant require 'regular' periodical monitoring only, in compliance with Annex IX of the

Directive. This is in addition to the provision of an 'annual emission inventory' in relation to SO_2 and NOx emissions of existing refinery and power station/plant in excess of 300 megawatts, with reportage 'en masse' for the rest of the industry.

The Directive did not enjoy a smooth ride in the development stage. The UK was particularly vociferous in its opposition, largely because of the high sulphur content of domestic coal. As noted, however, the final compromise position gave the UK an advantage which compensated for this characteristic.

Compliance with Directive 88/609/EEC in the UK has largely been satisfied by the provisions of EPA 1990. Section 6 establishes the requirement for authorisations, with s 7 providing for the attachment of conditions, and s 7(2)(a) incorporating BATNEEC.

The 'reduction schedule' is incorporated into the national plan of emission levels for large combustion plants and authorised by s 3(5) of EPA 1990. The plan itself is complemented by the integrated pollution control (IPC) process, and allows plant emissions to be reviewed downwards on an annual basis.

UK compliance with the Directive appears to be well on schedule.[1] However, whilst this achievement is laudable, it should not be forgotten that it has been arrived at largely through structural changes within the industry, and a progressive movement away from power stations powered by high sulphur domestic coal suppliers, rather than investment in technology. This move itself is not without wider cost.

It is unlikely that future obligations imposed by the Convention on Long-Range Transboundary Air Pollution (see **3.4.1**) will be as easily satisfied. Further, debate remains as to the extent to which BATNEEC, and the establishment of a public arena in which assessments are to be made, have been satisfied.[2]

2.4 MUNICIPAL WASTE INCINERATORS

Directives 89/369/EEC and 89/429/EEC are categorised as 'daughter Directives of the Air Framework Directive 84/360'. They concern the prevention/reduction of air pollution from new and pre-existing municipal waste incineration plants respectively. The definition of 'municipal waste' excludes such matter as sewage, chemical waste, toxic and dangerous waste, as well as hospital waste. In the case of new plant, Directive 89/369 establishes emission limit values and conditions to be attached to authorisations under the parent Directive (84/360) both in relation to operation and monitoring.

Emission limit values apply to dust, heavy metals, hydrochloric and hydrofluoric acid, and sulphur dioxide, although authority is provided to

1 (1995) *ENDS Reports* 248, September.
2 (1996) *END Reports*, March.

extend these limits to include other pollutants. The Directive also seeks to reduce to a minimum the conditions which lead to the production of dioxins.

Three categories of emission limit values apply according to plant size:

- three tonnes per hour;
- one to three tonnes per hour;
- under three tonnes per hour.

As may be expected, the most stringent limits attach in relation to plant which produces three tonnes or more per hour. In common with the other Directives in the family, monitoring is required and defined according to plant size. If a plant is found to have emissions exceeding the prescribed limits, it will be required to undertake remedial action as a matter of urgency, to bring it back within these limits. Failure to do so may result in closure.

Limited provision exists within the Directive for derogation in the case of plant specifically designed to operate using 'waste derived fuels', assuming satisfaction of the BATNEEC principle.

2.4.1 Directive 89/429/EEC

Directive 89/429/EEC aims to bring the emission limit values of existing plant in line with those set for new plant. It is recognised, however, that a sympathetic timetable is necessary to facilitate the investment programme required to achieve the ultimate goal. Plant operating above six tonnes per hour output are required to comply by December 1996 (or on renewal of furnace equipment where the obligation presents major technical difficulties). Plant operating at an output below six tonnes per hour have until December 2000 to comply.

Full compliance with the Waste Incineration Directives was achieved in the UK with the Municipal Waste Incineration Directions 1991, established under s 7 of EPA 1990.

2.4.2 Directive 94/67/EC: Hazardous waste incineration

Born of Directives 84/360 and 75/442, Directive 94/67 applies a similar regime to hazardous waste incineration.

The term 'hazardous waste' covers solid or liquid waste to the exclusion of certain combustible liquid waste; hazardous waste from offshore gas and oil production; non-hazardous sewage; animal carcasses; certain clinical waste and those wastes dealt with by the sister Directives 89/369/EEC and 89/429/EEC above.

As with the rest of the family of Directives, authorisation is required and incineration will only be permitted on approval of both the plant itself, and the operational process. Approval will not be granted unless it can be seen that all appropriate measures have been taken to reduce pollution to a minimum. The approval permit will indicate both the type and quantity of waste permitted, as well as recording and monitoring the practices to be adopted.

Although the Directive has much in common with 89/369 and 89/429, in this case the standard imposed goes beyond BATNEEC, requiring the incineration to be 'as complete as possible'. The obligation of 94/67/EC does not therefore simply require authorisation and the setting of emission limit levels. Standards are also set in relation to the operation of the plant itself, dictating temperatures, oxygen content, and maximum carbon monoxide in combustion, etc.

If permitted emission levels are exceeded, the plant is required to notify the relevant authority immediately. Limited flexibility may be available in relation to some emissions, but the limits set for dust amount to an absolute.

As with the other Directives, existing plant are given longer to achieve full compliance than new plant. In addition, plant which is scheduled to close within a five-year period will be given dispensation on the understanding that it will not be operative for more than 20,000 hours during that period.

The Commission is required to give ongoing consideration to the emission levels set in the light of technical development. It is, in any event, required to report to the Council by the turn of the century indicating progress and appropriate amendments.

In terms of implementation, it is thought that the IPC and local authority air pollution control (LAAPC) provisions of EPA 1990 will satisfy compliance, although some standards may require adjustment.

2.5 AIR QUALITY LIMIT VALUES/GUIDE LEVELS FOR SULPHUR DIOXIDE AND SMOKE

Directive 80/779 takes a pioneering stance in establishing, for the first time, mandatory air quality standards across the Community. Quality standards are set in relation to smoke and sulphur dioxide on the understanding that the Member States might take on board a stricter regime, where necessary, for the protection of the environment.

The Directive was some four years in the making, largely because some Member States (including the UK) had difficulty with the concept of 'air quality standards' and all that such a system entailed. In addition, there was some debate in scientific circles as to the utility of a system which sought to link sulphur dioxide and smoke in setting quality standards.

The UK sought to rely on a whole basket of legislative provisions which it claimed satisfied the Directive, including the Clean Air Acts, Alkali Works Regulations Act 1906 and the Control of Pollution Act 1974. None the less, the Commission questioned the reality of implementation, and a reasoned opinion was issued before final compliance was achieved in the Air Quality Standards Regulations 1989, SI 1989/317, and eventually EPA 1990.

Compliance has finally lead to the establishment of mandatory air quality standards and the protection of a monitoring system which might otherwise have become marginalised. Having proved its purpose, Directive 80/779 will also be replaced by the new family of Directives under framework Directive 96/62.

2.5.1 Directive 93/12: Sulphur content of fuels

Based upon the authority of Article 100A of the Treaty, Directive 93/12 has a dual purpose. The harmonisation of sulphur content levels effects a unified standard across the single market and removes barriers to trade in addition to presenting the vehicle by which damaging sulphur levels may be reduced.

Directive 93/12 replaces an earlier series of Directives and amendments setting the sulphur content of 'gas oils' (diesel included) at 0.2 per cent for 'gas oils' in general and 0.05 per cent for diesel in particular. Further reductions in sulphur levels are anticipated. Member States are expected to monitor these limits by reference to 'all necessary measures' and to check by sampling.

Initial compliance by the UK to the earlier levels (Directive 75/716) was anticipated in the terms of the Control of Pollution Act 1974, which authorises the Secretary of State to regulate the contents of fuels. The amendments to the original compliance were facilitated by further regulatory provisions, in particular the Marketing of Gas Oil Regulations 1994, SI 1994/2249, and the Motor Fuel Regulations 1994, SI 1994/2295.

The Departments of Environment and Transport indicate that the limits set by the Directive have presented few problems to the UK where sulphur levels were generally within the parameters set.

2.5.2 Directive 85/203

Directive 85/203/EEC is worthy of mention at this point, not necessarily because of its relationship with the old Air Framework Directive but because it is to be replaced by Directive 96/62, a daughter Directive of 84/360 which will also have wide implications for the rest of the family of Directives.

The Directive establishes air quality standards for nitrogen dioxide (NO_2) for the protection of health and the environment. In addition to direct emissions from vehicles, nitrogen dioxide pollution is often the result of the synergistic effects of other environmental pollutants, specifically nitric oxide, ozone and other oxidants. It therefore represents both a local and a transboundary problem.

The directive establishes a general NO_2 limit of 200 micrograms per cubic metre in relation to ambient air quality. Member States are, however, in a position to set more stringent levels which they may use for the protection or improvement of specific zones where a particular need is identified. If any such zones are located within the proximity of the national border, the Member State is required to notify the Commission, who may then wish to have some input. The Commission may also become involved if it appears that limit values are in jeopardy as a result of transboundary pollutants. As may be expected, monitoring and reporting requirements are specified.

UK compliance can be identified in the Air Quality Standards Regulations 1989, SI 1989/317, which empowers the Secretary of State to 'take any necessary measures' to ensure that limit values are not exceeded.

2.6 NEW AIR QUALITY FRAMEWORK DIRECTIVE 96/62

The whole area of air quality regulation will be affected by the new Air Quality Framework Directive 96/62. The Directive represents an overhaul of the regulatory framework for the protection of air quality, establishing new quality standards and objectives for ambient air. The approach of the Directive is to establish a pattern for monitoring and management, with specific limit values and new 'alert thresholds' being left once more to subsequent daughter Directives. These standards will be set by reference to population exposure, flora, fauna, and buildings etc, in addition to economic and technical factors. Once in place, the new network of Directives will require Member States to monitor and assess ambient air quality. Monitoring will be mandatory in highly populated areas and areas where the pollution levels are above a given percentage of the limit level.

The Directive envisages three categories of area:

- risk of occasional exceedance where action plans are required;
- general exceedance, requiring the preparation of plans to achieve general compliance with the limit values within the timetable set;
- lower limit values to 'endeavour to preserve the best ambient air quality compatible with sustainable development'.

A new feature present in Directive 96/62 is the requirement to notify the public if pollution levels should exceed 'alert thresholds', in addition to the requirement to notify the Commission. The Directive also breaks new ground in establishing a Committee comprising representatives of the Member States and Commission, to assist the Commission itself.

In this instance, the UK may congratulate itself in anticipating the obligation imposed under Directive 96/62 in the terms of the Environment Act 1995.

2.7 LEAD

In addition to the family of associated Directives discussed above, the EC legislative programme has directed its attention to a whole series of Directives concerned with vehicle emissions. Directive 82/884 establishes limit values for lead in air, whilst Directive 85/210 establishes the lead content of petrol, with some 21 further Directives tailored to various aspects of vehicular emissions. It is the intention here to deal only briefly with these provisions as further reference will be made below in relation to vehicular emissions.

2.7.1 Directive 82/884: Lead in air

The Directive sets limit value levels for lead concentrations in air at a maximum of two micrograms per cubic metre, although Member States are not prevented from setting more stringent standards, the purpose of the Directive being the protection of human health.

The Directive requires Member States to establish plans for the improvement of air quality for those areas where emissions exceed set levels and should include details of measures to be taken to reduce lead pollution, these highly polluted areas to be brought into line with the general limit levels by December 1989.

Monitoring should take place by reference to sampling stations based at points where people may be at risk from lead levels, and in particular, in those areas which have been made subject to improvement plans. Exceedance must be reported to the Commission on an annual basis with details of concentrations and measures to ensure future compliance.

The UK originally relied upon a variety of legislative provisions which they claimed fulfilled the requirements of the Directive. These included the Control of Pollution Act 1974, the Health and Safety at Work Act 1974 and the Public Health Act 1936, to be supplemented by an explanatory departmental circular which would indicate just how the bundle of pre-existing legislation would satisfy the obligation. The circular, however, never materialised and it was not until the Air Quality Standards Regulations 1989, SI 1989/317, which directed a duty to the Secretary of State to establish sampling stations, that the obligation of the Directive was met. The EPA 1990 further rationalised this obligation.

Directive 82/884 will also be replaced by the new generation of daughter Directives under Directive 96/62.

2.7.2 Directive 85/210: Lead content of petrol

The involvement of the EC in the regulation of petrol lead levels predates the 1985 Directive. Directive 78/611 established uniform lead levels at a maximum level between 0.15 and 0.40 grams per litre. This was on the basis of a need to ensure that environmental regulation did not inhibit intra-Community trade in petrol and vehicles.

Directive 85/210 encourages Member States to reduce lead to the lower limit levels of 0.15 grams per litre, and promotes the availability of lead-free petrol. Benzene levels of both leaded and unleaded petrol are also set at a maximum of 5 per cent from October 1989. The Directive requires Member States to report the effect of the Directive to the Commission, both in terms of sales of lead-free petrol and the effect on environmental quality.

UK compliance with the original Directive 78/611 was achieved by powers granted to the Government under provisions relating to the composition of petrol in general. This has been supplemented by a series of statutory instruments effecting a gradual reduction in levels to 0.15 grams per litre. The

1985 regulations, SI 1985/1728, approve the sale of unleaded petrol and establish a British Standard. Sales of unleaded petrol have been further encouraged by the operation of a differential tax regime in relation to leaded and unleaded petrol.

Specific attention has been given to vehicular emissions, identifying three main categories of vehicle: passenger cabs; commercial vehicles; and diesel engines for tractors. There are detailed sub-categories identified in each. In addition, specific provision is made for vehicle emission testing in Directives 20.92/55/EEC and 21.93/116/EEC.

2.8 INFORMATION AND RESEARCH

The need for access to environmental information was recognised as a priority by the Fourth Environmental Action Programme. The public need access to information on the environment as a necessity if they are to play a meaningful role in the promotion of sustainable development. The Directive on Freedom of Access to Information on the Environment, 90/313/EEC, requires the Member States to ensure that public authorities make information available on request.

For this purpose, the term 'public authority' is defined to include public administration at all levels: national, regional, and local (judicial and legislative bodies excepted).

Under the terms of Article 2A of the Directive, 'information relating to the environment' is broadly defined to include information on water, air, soil, fauna, flora, land and natural sites and activities which may adversely affect, or be likely to adversely affect, natural resources, or activities or measures for their protection. Such information should be available, be it in written, aural, visual or database form.

The Directive does, however, recognise the need for exceptions in relation to commercial and industrial confidentiality as well as public security. Nevertheless, such exceptions will rarely be available without evidence.

The Directive has been implemented in the UK through the Environmental Information Regulations 1992, SI 1992/3240. The regulations have not been without their critics to the extent to which they embrace the spirit of the Directive. Against this background, it is useful to note, as Rose points out,[1] at least some of the provisions of the Directive are considered likely to be capable of direct effect.

Interestingly, the impact of the Directive does not extend to the Community institutions themselves. Some attempt at openness is made in a range of

1 Rose, 'Industry and Access to Information on the Environment', *Protecting the European Environment*, (ed Somsen) (Blackstone, 1996).

alternative sources but these ad hoc provisions do not match the comprehensive approach of the Directive.

Article 6 of Regulation 1210/90, which establishes the European Environment Agency, lays it open to public scrutiny in the following terms:

> 'Environmental data supplied or emanating from the Agency may be published and shall be accessible to the public subject to compliance with the rules of the Commission and the Member States on the dissemination of information, particularly as regards confidentiality.'

Similarly, Decisions 93/731 and 94/90 concern the question of public access to the work of the Council and the Commission respectively. Whilst the decisions give the appearance of transparency, the accompanying caveats question the reality of openness. Decision 93/731 in particular states: 'the public will have the widest possible access to the documents held by the Commission and Council . . .' but is swift to qualify, stating that access 'may be refused in order to protect the confidentiality of the Council's proceedings'. Recognising the political importance of the Council's 'confidentiality', one is tempted to muse as to which is likely to be the practical norm, access granted or denied.

This distinction between the rights of the public in relation to domestic and EC matters is not, however, unique, and comparisons might be made with the broad provision of challenges to Member States through direct effect, etc and the narrow access to challenge the EC institutions through Article 173.

General public access to information is as important in relation to the protection of the atmosphere as it is in relation to any other media. The EC has, however, highlighted not only the need for access to information in this area, but the need for more research to further our understanding of the nature and extent of atmospheric degradation and its impact on other media. This need is central to the philosophy behind the Fifth Environmental Action Programme.

2.8.1 Regulation 3528/86: Forest damage

The Regulation on the protection of EC forests against atmospheric pollution, Regulation 3528/86 (as amended), with its subsidiary Commission Regulations, is designed to establish a 'common methodology' by which damage levels may be ascertained and monitored.

Member States are required: first, to draw up an 'inventory' of forest damage, with supporting health reports; and secondly, to develop 'pilot projects', and undertake research and field experiments in order to further understanding of the relationship between atmospheric quality and the health of forests. This is to be facilitated by the creation of a grid of monitoring stations set at 16 kilometre intervals. Each station will allow detailed observation of the trees in the immediate locality.

The Regulation is supported by financial aid (50 per cent) to the Member States to assist in underwriting the costs of this research. It was originally only intended to run for five years, but this has since been extended to 10 years (Regulation 2157/92).

The Regulation provided for the establishment of a 'Committee on Forest Protection' to assist with the task of formulating detailed regulation. This group has since been superseded by the Standing Forestry Committee (Decision 89/367).

In response to this 'directly applicable' obligation, the Forestry Commission in the UK has introduced new regimes, as its existing practices did not meet with the stringency of the observation network under the EC Regulation.

2.8.2 Decision 97/101: Reciprocal exchange of information

Decision 97/101 concerns the reciprocal exchange of information/data. It is the latest in a series of decisions which have been time-limited. Decision 97/101 presents a permanent regime to facilitate the exchange of information over a wider range of pollutants than previously provided for. The decision contains the list of substances in Annex I of the new Framework Directive 96/62 and more.

Member States are required to submit data to the Commission, which will then be represented in a technical report to be submitted to the European Environment Agency, and open to the public. This openness reflects the character, not only of the new Framework Directive 96/62, but of the Fifth Environmental Action Programme, which highlights 'freedom of environmental information' as a key policy into the next century.

2.8.3 Directive 92/72: Ozone pollution

Unlike the major substantive provisions discussed thus far, Directive 92/72 does not set emission limit level for ozone. The Directive, prompted by the Fourth Environmental Action Programme seeks information on this complicated product of the synergistic effect between volatile organic compounds (VOCs), NO*x* and sunlight, in the hope that future Directives under Framework Directive 96/62 will be able to establish effective limits.

Ozone is both complex and threatening. The Directive establishes an information monitoring/collection regime prompted by geographical and climatic factors. The Directive also adopts the categories of the World Health Organisation in relation to threshold guidelines, including health protection, vegetation, population information, and population warning, Member States being obliged to inform the public if the 'population information' and 'population warning' thresholds are exceeded. The method of communication in these instances must be such as to allow the people to take appropriate action to protect themselves. Any such incidences must also be referred to the Commission.

UK compliance is achieved by way of the Ozone Monitoring and Information Regulations 1994, SI 1994/440.

2.9 INTERNATIONAL OBLIGATIONS

By far the larger part of EC environmental legislation is in the form of Directives, thereby allowing the Member States some input into how to achieve the standards set. There are some instances, however, where controls more appropriately take the form of a unified obligation across the EC. Such may be the case where the subject matter is in the nature of an international obligation. In such circumstances, the Regulation is clearly the more appropriate legislative form.

2.9.1 Regulation 3093/94: Ozone depletion

Concern about the effects of chlorofluorocarbons (CFCs) on the environment date from the mid-1970s. Such concern led the USA to impose restrictions on the use of non-essential CFCs in aerosols from 1976. International concern can be seen in the Montreal Protocol to the Vienna Convention for the Protection of the Ozone Layer 1985. Regulation 3093/94 aims to satisfy the EC's obligation in relation to the Montreal Protocol by imposing a ban on CFCs and other substances viewed as a danger to the ozone layer. In fact, the EC response goes beyond the initial requirements of the Protocol, although further provisions will be necessary in response to developments in relation to methyl bromide, in order to ensure continued compliance.

Protection is achieved by the control of production, import, export, supply and use of certain 'controlled' substances. These substances are detailed in Annex I and include CFCs, halons, carbon tetrachloride, trichloroethane, methyl bromide, hydrobromofluorocarbons (HBFCs) and hydrochlorofluorocarbons (HCFCs). Control levels are set by reference to the dangers which each substance presents to the ozone layer. Some of the listed substances are subject to a total ban, whilst the production of others is limited in the short term and subject to a more gradual eradication in the long term, on the basis of the following timetable:

1 January 1994	Ban on production of halons
1 January 1995	Ban on production of CFCs and carbontetrachloride
1 January 1996	Ban on production of 1,1,1-trichloroethane and HBFCs
	Methyl bromide production to be stabilised at 1991 levels
	Supply of HCFCs frozen in relation to 1989 levels with further reductions planned until supply ceases in 2015
1 January 1998	Methyl bromide production to be reduced by 25 per cent on 1991 levels

In addition, the Regulation controls imports and exports and requires producers, importers and exporters to make annual returns, on a confidential basis, to both the domestic authorities and the Commission regarding quantities produced, destroyed, recycled, held in stock and exported. The

Commission may also approach the domestic authorities for information, or request that they gain further information on their behalf.

Unlike the Directives, the Regulations are of course 'directly applicable', thereby dispensing of the need for any implementation measures. None the less, the Regulation does require that the obligations addressed to producers are administered. These matters are dealt with by way of the Environmental Protection (Controls on Substances that Deplete the Ozone Layer) Regulations 1996, SI 1996/506. The Regulation identifies the Secretary of State for the Environment as the 'competent authority' for this purpose; provides for enforcement powers and fines (in addition to powers to require the disposal of unauthorised imports) and recovery of used substances and leakage procedures; details restrictions on importation, landing etc and confers appropriate powers on customs authorities. Further support is gained from the Environmental Protection (Non-Refillable Refrigerant Containers) Regulations 1994, SI 1994/199.

Although the consumption of CFCs in the UK had fallen considerably by the late 1980s, this was largely due to consumer reaction to the newly discovered dangers. Reductions did not gain the support of Government until late 1988, following the publication of the second report of the Stratospheric Ozone Review Group. Since then, the UK Government has been firmly behind the call for reductions. Facilitating the administration of the Regulation has therefore presented few problems.

Department of the Environment evidence shows a reduction in consumption of CFCs from 58,000 tonnes in 1986 to a mere 1,700 tonnes in 1995[1] although it has to be noted that HCFC consumption grew threefold over the same period.

In addition, the dangers of HFCs have been recognised. These gases have been used as a safer alternative to CFCs because they do not have the same ozone-depleting properties. However, they have been identified as a not insignificant greenhouse gas, and, as such, seem to present an 'out of the frying pan into the fire' scenario. A year after the dangers were noted by the Governmental Panel on Sustainable Development, the Government entered into voluntary agreements with users to encourage the use of less harmful alternatives where possible.

Whilst the framework has proved effective, it has not prevented the development of black-market operations in banned substances. In summer 1997, the Commission and customs authorities across the EC uncovered a smuggling racket involving at least 1,000 tonnes of CFC covertly imported from China. The chemicals had been imported into the EC bearing false identity labels. They had then received counterfeit documentation, which claimed them to be part of a residual, lawful, market in recycled CFCs. The incident marks the continued need for vigilance on the part of customs and the

1 *UK Use and Emissions of Selected Halocarbons* (HMSO, 1996).

Commission, as well as the nominated competent authorities, if the spirit of the Regulation is to be achieved.

2.9.2 Directive 94/63/EC: Volatile organic compounds

Although, as has been noted, the Regulation generally provides the ideal model by which the EC will seek to comply with its international obligations, this does not preclude the use of Directives. In this instance, the Directive has been adopted as the appropriate method of satisfying the Convention on Long-Range Transboundary Air Pollution and the Fifth Environmental Action Programme, which incorporates the expectations of the Convention into EC policy.

The obvious benefit of the Directive in this instance is that it leaves the Member States free to decide how best to reach the targets set. In this case, they are also free to set more stringent targets generally, with the exception of limits applying to 'mobile containers'. The reason for this exception has less to do with the emissions, and more to do with the free movement of goods: to allow differing standards in relation to mobile containers might help the atmosphere, but it would not facilitate the single market in relation to petrol products.

The significance of market factors is illustrated by the authoritative base of the Directive, which is founded in Article 100A. By relying on Article 100A rather than Article 130, significant differences between the levels set in Member States could be addressed by reference to the single market and the principle of free movement.

The drawback to the Directive is, however, that it relies upon Member States to implement appropriate measures for compliance. Indeed, this is one area where the UK cannot claim the moral high ground, with formal compliance only being achieved one year after the date of implementation in the shape of the Environmental Protection (Prescribed Processes and Substances etc) (Amendment) (Petrol Vapour Recovery) Regulations 1996, SI 1996/2678.

The release of volatile organic compounds (VOCs) is very much a symptom of the way of life of the developed world. These compounds are released through evaporation from petrol at each stage in transit, ie storage on importation, transport to point of sale, delivery. This form of pollution is even more unfortunate than most, as it occurs without benefit or product.

Directive 94/63 was envisaged as stage one of a regime to minimise all petrol vapour emissions. However, it now seems that emissions from the final stages of delivery to the consumer will be regulated along with other vehicular emissions.

The operation of the petrol industry causes the release of some 500,000 tonnes of VOCs into the EC atmosphere per year, without any benefit accruing. The aim of this Directive is to reduce emissions to 10 per cent below 1990 levels by 1996, and 30 per cent by 1999.

The regime applies to each stage of the marketing of petrol until it reaches the forecourt:

- storage at terminals;
- loading/unloading of 'mobile containers';
- mobile containers themselves;
- loading/unloading at service stations.

At each stage, the design and operation of facilities is required to comply with 'target reference values'. In the case of existing storage terminals, reduction in VOC emissions is to be achieved by the use of reflective paints to reduce evaporation where vapour recovery units are in place. Attention is drawn to seals where tanks are of a 'floating roof' design.

Standards are imposed in relation to the loading and unloading of 'mobile containers' in Annex II of the Directive. Emphasis is on vapour recovery and the method of loading, which is advised to be 'bottom up', reducing the escape of vapours to a minimum. Limited derogation is permitted in relation to loading facilities which predate 1 January 1993, where compliance with the general emission standard and loading facilities (gantries) is extended until 2004.

The design of 'mobile containers' must be such as to ensure retention of vapours after the transfer of fuel to service stations. They must also be capable of retaining vapours displaced from the petrol station storage tanks when transfer occurs. The design of the petrol station storage tanks is required to complement that of mobile containers, to ensure retention of gases.

Whilst the VOC regime appears comprehensive, controlling emissions almost on a 'cradle to grave' basis, the extension of controls to final sale is yet to be achieved. Further, certain anomalies exist, the most obvious being shipping. This would seem an obvious source of emissions and its exclusion seems down to the political and economic strength of the oil industry lobby.

Of less significance is the exception negotiated by the UK and others, on behalf of small rural petrol stations. In this instance, it was argued that these small small petrol stations should be protected from the adverse effect on their business on the basis of social utility.

2.10 A NEW AGE OF EC CONTROL

The Integrated Pollution Prevention and Control (IPPC) Directive, 96/61/EC, represents a new approach to environmental regulation on the part of the EC. The idea of a holistic approach is not, however, new to the UK, and is reminiscent of integrated pollution control under the Environmental Protection Act 1990.

The new way forward is to direct control at emissions per se, rather than concentrating on a media-specific approach. Industry is thereby encouraged to develop clean technology by design, which is an improvement on the traditional 'end of pipe' approach where reduction in one form of emission seems inevitably at the expense of others.

The Directive also operates according to an enlightened definition of 'pollution', including within its ambit vibration, heat and noise in addition to the traditional media emissions.

Like the Air Framework Directive, the IPPC Directive assumes further legislative provision to establish, inter alia, standard EC emissions. The Directive itself provides a framework for new and certain pre-existing legislation. Although implementation of the Directive is required by October 1999, the new regime will not be operative overnight. Pre-existing legislation such as that establishing emission levels for 'dangerous substances to water' (76/464/EEC) and emissions to the air from industrial plant (84/360/EEC), for example, will continue to be relevant until such time as they are brought under the auspices of Directive 96/61/EC. They will, however, cease to be law 11 years after the Directive comes into force, except to the extent that 76/464/EEC in particular extends beyond the purpose of 96/61/EC. Other existing Directives may be subject to amendment in the light of 96/64/EC.

The IPPC Directive extends to a range of industrial processes: energy; metal processing and production; minerals; chemicals; waste management; and a miscellaneous category which includes processes such as paper production, textiles, tanning, food production and intensive pig and poultry rearing. The range of activities falling into this last category gives recognition to the environmental risks presented rather than any historic classification of processes.

Each category is further subdivided according to the specific detail and scale of the process.

New processes within the ambit of the Directive will require prior authorisation. Existing processes will be brought within the scheme within eight years of the date of implementation (October 1999). Authorisation will be by way of a 'permit'. The permit itself may approve the process as submitted, or be subject to conditions to ensure compliance with the detail and spirit of the Directive. The permit should not be granted unless the subject operation satisfies the Directive. Any permit granted must specify arrangements in relation to air, water and land emissions. The permit must also ensure minimisation of transboundary pollution.

Further, any significant change in the process must be communicated to the 'competent authority' in the Member State, and be subject to an application to amend the permit. In exceptional circumstances, however, an operator may exceed the permit on the basis that compliance is ensured within a period of six months.

The 'competent authority' must also keep an overview of the wider picture and be prepared to step in to amend permits, and consequent production practices, where necessary for the protection of the environment in the light of excessive pollution. The permit itself should identify monitoring processes and recognise the need for the provision of necessary data.

Applications for permits are required to provide a full picture, describing the installation and details of the site, processes, materials, emissions and significant environmental effects, which may include information provided for the purpose of environmental impact assessment (EIA) under Directive 85/337; measures/techniques taken to reduce pollution prevention and recovery of waste, monitoring, etc.

The presumption is that permits will be approved by reference to BAT (best available techniques). Although a cursory comparison between BAT and BATNEEC (best available techniques not entailing excessive cost) highlights the absence of an overt reference to economic considerations in the former, social and environmental costs are implied in 'available'. In particular, the annex to the Directive identifies certain factors for consideration. The list includes: recovery and recycling, energy efficiency, low waste technology, use of less hazardous substances, consumption of raw materials and water. Operators are, therefore, required to adhere to basic principles, including the need to take preventative measures against pollution. They are expected to undertake production methods which will minimise the production of waste, facilitate recovery of materials, or ensure safe disposal thereof, with waste management systems being specified at the application stage. The operator is further obliged to ensure maximum energy efficiency, take steps to avoid all accidents and pledge responsibility to the site after production has come to an end.

It is clear that certain factors will vary across the EC, and it is therefore recognised that variances will arise in emission limits. This feature emphasises the need for an exchange of information between Member States. Without this movement towards Community, emission limits would not even be a possibility. Community limits are, none the less, some way off as Member States are not required to make their first submissions until 18 months after the Directive has taken effect. In the interim, limit values contained in related pre-existing Directives will continue to represent EC standards.

The Directive imposes an obligation upon Member States to ensure practical compliance through their 'competent authority'. Operators are obliged to provide general data and details of any accident promptly. They are also expected to facilitate inspections as requested by the competent authority.

The permit process very much represents the new 'public' approach of the EC. Applications are open to public scrutiny before any decision is taken. The same transparency will be required of the monitoring process, although this is subject to the general requirements of Directive 90/313/EEC, which provides the caveat of commercial confidentiality.

In relation to the question of compliance or implementation, the UK has benefited from the experience of integrated pollution control (IPC) under EPA 1990. This is no coincidence, as the IPPC Directive was largely based upon the UK IPC regime. The distinctions between the two systems will, however, call for some amendments. In particular, the aims of IPPC are rather wider than IPC, both in concept and application. IPPC does not confine itself to pollution, but extends its remit to resource conservation and the minimisation of waste production. To this end, the requirements to specify waste management systems under IPPC present a major development in the holistic approach.

In practical terms the IPPC approach is also wider, with some processes which would, under the UK regime, be subject to media-specific scrutiny by LAAPC, and others which would be outside control altogether, falling under IPPC.

Other differences between the two systems have already been referred to, namely the guiding principle of BAT, the greater depth of information called for in relation to IPPC, and the link between IPPC and EIA. These changes should, however, be easily integrated into the IPC system which, none the less, provides a basic foundation.

CHAPTER 3

INTERNATIONAL LAW

3.1 INTRODUCTION

The system of public international law is increasingly important as world interaction becomes more sophisticated. The disagreements which arise between neighbours in the microscale are mirrored in world affairs. The extent of rights needs to be assessed, and competing rights placed in order. These relative rights of nations need to be established within an equitable context which prevents the strong from abusing the weak. In addition, the environment raises interests which are increasingly seen as global irrespective of who or where an action takes place.

However, in the environmental context, nations cling to their sovereignty promoting their own self-interest before the interest of the many. While international law in general represents a relatively mature forum for the regulation of inter-State activity, its weaknesses are evident in environmental regulation. Perhaps it is the difficulty to see an instant and personal benefit which leads nations to act against the global interest, or the lack of any real sanctions which allows complacency in the application of accepted measures. None the less, it is to be hoped that in airing truly global issues, such as ozone and climate changes, States will become attuned to the wider community interest rather than personal benefit. It should be acknowledged that the global atmospheric conventions illustrate a more mature approach, recognising the inequity of all paying for the past pleasures of the few and that those who have long enjoyed polluting activities should not seek to prevent next generation development in the developing world, but should help to ease these nations past earlier mistakes whilst not denying the benefit to others.

International environmental law is to be found in a variety of sources. Much of it derives from customary law and general principles of law recognised by civilised nations. This represents a body of law which generally develops without the intervention of international agreement. That said, customary law may be reflected in formal legal instruments. Decisions of the international Court or arbitrators represent a further important source. Such decisions may also act to discern the status or content of a custom or general principle. Decisions may also be arrived at by reference to the use of international jurists whose views represent a valid source of international law in their own right.

In this context, however, the most important source is represented by Treaty law which is the result of international agreement. Unlike custom law, Treaty law is particularly appropriate to establishing proactive measures which may alter the approach of the international community. Treaty law provides general guidance in relation to international interaction in addition to specific measures tailored for environmental regulation.

The purpose of this chapter is to give consideration to the sources of international law and their influence upon the environment; the role of the European Community in relation to the international arena; problems of transboundary air pollution; and international protections for the atmosphere. Further detailed discussion can be found in general texts such as Shaw, *International Law* 3rd edn (Grotius, 1995) and Shearer *Starkes Introduction to International Law* 11th edn (Butterworths, 1994). Specific reference to environment issues can be found in particular in Birnie and Boyle, *International Law and the Environment* (Clarendon, 1993) and in the primary texts of the international documents themselves. The importance of these texts is acknowledged in both general and personal terms.

3.2 SOURCES

3.2.1 Introduction

Unlike domestic law, the law of the international community cannot be established by reference to a limited and concrete set of sources. This deprives international law of some of the certainties enjoyed by individual States. The principles and substance of international law can be ascertained only by reference to a range of sources and materials. These sources are identified by Article 38(1) of the Statute of the International Court of Justice which states:

> 'the court whose function is to decide in accordance with international law such disputes as are submitted to it, shall apply;
>
> (a) internationtal conventions, whether general or particular, establishing rules expressly recognised by the contesting States;
> (b) international custom, as evidence of a general practice accepted as law;
> (c) the general principles of law recognised by civilised nations;
> (d) subject to the provisions of article 59, judicial decisions and the teachings of the most highly qualified publicists of the various nations, as subsidiary means for the determination of rules of law.'

From these sources, international obligations and standards, policies, and the expected conduct within the international community may be identified. As with any community, it may be necessary from time to time to temper or restrict the rights of one player in favour of another. The complicating factor in this context is the ever-present issue of sovereignty.

In order to appreciate the impact of international law within the domestic arena, it is necessary to consider the nature and implications of these sources further. In addition, the influence of 'soft law' should be noted. The need for 'agreement' between nations means that, on occasion, it will be easier to gain approval for non-binding instruments. States may approve a principle but be unwilling to bind themselves, and this compromise position enables them to underline the principle without having to refuse to sign or to ratify a binding instrument. In the long term, the instrument may, none the less, prove to be influential. This type of provision includes codes of practice, guideline resolutions, declarations etc and are generally termed 'soft law', recognising their status as non-binding but influential.

3.2.2 Treaty

Treaty law is generally recognised as the second most important source of international law behind customary law. It has, however, become more important during the course of the nineteenth and twentieth centuries. Further, in relation to more recent matters of international concern, such as the environment, it is of prime significance.

Although Article 38(1) of the Statute of the International Court of Justice refers to 'Conventions', this is understood as an 'umbrella' term which includes not only Conventions but also International Agreements, Pacts, General Acts, Charters, Statutes, Declarations and Covenants. These are in fact all terms which may be applied to the Treaty. Shaw[1] defines the characteristics of the Treaty as the: 'creation of written agreements whereby the States participating bind themselves legally to act in a particular way or to set up particular relations between themselves'.

Treaties are viewed as falling into two categories: those described as law-making Treaties are intended to be of general relevance and universal in nature; those known as 'Treaty contracts' are of a more limited nature, governing the relationship between only a very small number of States.

The Treaty, whichever camp it falls into, does have overtones of the contractual relationship which may bind individuals by their own agreement. The States themselves define the content or terms of the Treaty and freely undertake to be bound by those terms. However, unlike the simple contractual model, the State is not tied to the obligation simply by signing up to it. Without ratification, the Treaty may exert no holds on the State. Further, without the ratification of a large number of States, the Treaty may be without real influence. It is frequently the case that the Treaty will require a set number of States to ratify it before it becomes operational. Achieving the magic number for ratification does not ensure the success of the Treaty's aims. In this instance, it is true to say that: 'all are equal, but some are more equal than others'. A Treaty enjoying the support of a small number of dominant States is more likely to be influential in achieving its goal than a Treaty which gains wider but less weighty support. Hence, the anxiety in relation to the US position in the days before Rio.[2] It may be worth some compromise to gain the support of a major player such as the US.

A State which does not sign and ratify a Treaty will ordinarily not be bound by it. However, there are exceptions to this position. Major Treaties which create

---

1 *International Law* 3rd edn (Grotius, 1995).

2 Hajost 'The Role of the United States' *The Environment after Rio* eds Campiglio, Pinescti, Siniscakon and Treves (Kluwer, 1994).

a system for the regulation of international affairs may be couched in terms to include non-signatories, for example Article 2(6) of the UN Charter.

In some instances, a Treaty will, in effect, be a re-statement of customary law. In such a case, even non-parties may be bound by the principle. Any differences between the Treaty and the principle of customary law will, however, be reflected in the extent to which signatories and non-parties may be bound (see Article 51 of the UN Charter). Treaty provisions may also, in certain circumstances, lead to the creation of new customary law. The International Court of Justice (ICJ) has, however, ruled that this will be the case only in relation to provisions: 'of a fundamentally norm creating character'.[1]

Some writers have opined that, where a Treaty is of a general nature, it should normally be capable of binding signatories and non-signatories alike.[2] While this might seem particularly useful in relation to Treaties on the environment, it would lead to the many being governed by the few. Not only would this be politically inappropriate, but the practical reality would be non-compliance with both the Treaty and any subsequent action before the ICJ.

Law-making Treaties are generally divided into two broad categories:

(1) those which are a statement of universal international rules (eg the UN Charter), whose practical application has been averred to above;
(2) those establishing more general rules, which might either dictate policy or substance.

In this instance, Treaties fall into those broader statements of environmental concern and response, for example Rio, and those which, perhaps following on from the broad response, establish specific standards and programmes or timetables by which signatories may seek to achieve those standards, ie framework conventions followed by detailed substantive protocols.

The Treaty contract, on the other hand, is perhaps of less significance to the wider ambit of international law, as it dictates the obligations only of the parties, which is necessarily a limited number. Although regulating behaviour only as between the parties, it may have wider implications for environmental quality by representing a regional agreement. It will become of general interest only if it:

- represents the foundations of a measure of customary law;
- provides some evidence of the exceedance of a wider rule;
- at some time in the future is accepted or intimated by a wider range of States.

---

1 *North Sea Continental Shelf.*
2 D'Amato *The Concept of Custom in International Law* (Cornell University Press, 1971).

3.2.3 Custom

Customary rules comprise the oldest and largest part of international law. Although they have lost out over the last century to the Treaty, there are many reasons for this. In a time when the possibilities of instant communication have made the world a smaller place, new rules are needed to regulate new relationships and modes of interaction. The traditional age-long process of developing customary law can no longer keep up with the needs of the law. Further, the work undertaken by the International Law Commission into the codification of international law means that in some instances customary law has been superseded by Treaty.

Customary law develops from usage, but it is more than a simple habit of nations. It has been used and relied upon in such a way, over such a period of years, that the assumption develops that it must be relied upon. Nations then act in a certain way because they assume that they are bound to do so by law. Shearer[1] points to two tests as a working rule in identifying the customary law: the material; and the psychological.

The material test has been satisfied when there is evidence of recurrence or repetition. A single act will not generally be evidence of a customary rule. Some writers are, none the less, of the view that, in the right circumstances, customary law may be created instantly and without the need for repetition, assuming that the act or omission is guided by the *opinio jurisor* belief that it is law.[2] Time is accepted as being reliant upon context. The psychological test may be satisfied where there is an indication of general acceptance or adoption of a practice within the international community.

A customary rule must, in the words of the ICJ, be: 'Seen in accordance with a constant and uniform usage practised by the States in question'.[3] Evidence of alternative practices might, therefore, defeat a claim of customary law, although it is generally accepted that evidence of some difference in practice will not necessarily defeat the claim where the deviation is minimal. As Shaw points out: 'The threshold that needs to be attained before a legally binding custom can be created will depend both upon the nature of the alleged rule and the opposition it arouses'.[4]

Evidence that a practice is widespread (if not universal) is important to ensure that customary law is not seen as a unilateral product; otherwise, it may be difficult to assess silence. If a State makes its opposition to a would-be rule clear by its actions, then its view can be registered as such. Mere silence, on the other hand, could be acquiescence, ignorance or idleness. Silence may be even more important when it emanates from a major player. A continued protest on the part of a single State might eventually lead to a recognised exception

1 Shearer *Starkes International Law* 11th edn (Butterworths, 1994).

2 Bin Cheng 'UN Resolutions on Outer Space: Instant International Customary Law?' (1965) 5 *Indian Journal of International Law*.

3 (1950) Asylum ICJ Reports.

4 *International Law* 3rd edn (Grotius, 1995).

applying to that State. A similar protest by a large number of States, on the other hand, must deny the rule its qualifying characteristics and/or establish a competing rule. If this position is maintained consistently over a duration then it must be seen as a negative position in relation to the practice, although the inherent dangers in such an assumption are recognised, as noted by Shaw.

Customary law may be founded in domestic laws or by international legal bodies themselves. Where the domestic legal stance of one nation has been adopted or imitated by others, customary law may develop as though by contagion.

In relation to the psychological (or *opinio juris sive necessitatis*) test, repetition may occur as a matter of habit or convenience. This will not suffice to establish customary law. The repetition must occur because the State believes that it is obliged to act as it does by law. As stated by Judge Negulesco of the Permanent Court of International Justice:[1] 'it is the mutual conviction that the recurrence ... is the result of a compulsory rule', or, as the ICJ stated more recently:[2]

> 'For a new customary rule to be formed, not only must the acts concerned "amount to a settled practice", but they must be accompanied by the *opinio juris sive necessitatis*. Either the States taking such an action or other States in a position to react to it, must have behaved so that their conduct is "evidence of a belief" that this practice is rendered obligatory by the existence of a rule of law requiring it. The need for such a belief, ie the existence of a subjective element, is implicit in the very notion of the *opinio juris sive necessitatis*.'

However, in the same case, the ICJ went on to consider that if a State were to rely on a 'modified' view of the customary position, and that view gained the support of other States, it might lead to a general modification of the rule.

All this would indicate that, whilst the usual view of customary law is that it is slow to develop and ill-suited to the speed of change in the modern world, it may prove to be more flexible in practice. There is some support in judicial opinion to suggest that the material action of the State should be viewed as evidence of *opinio juris*. This would enhance the reputation of customary law in relation to flexibility.[3] None the less, the dangers of making such an assumption are evident. The material act must be the result of *opinio juris* rather than any lesser motivation.

The assumption thus far has rested upon the notion of a customary rule of general application (individual protest exceptions notwithstanding). Customary rules may also develop on a purely localised basis. In these cases, although the general qualifying characteristics will be applied according to the scale and context of the locality, it is understood that acceptance of the rule will be necessary by both/all the parties involved.

---

1 PCIJ 1927, Series B, No 14, p 105.

2 Nicaragua 1986 ICJ Reports 14; p 76 ILR 349.

3 See the *Continental Shelf* cases.

3.2.4 General principles

The futility of ignoring principles which already exist in domestic law was recognised in Chapter 1 in relation to the ECJ. As was noted, it is pointless for a court to struggle in a legal vacuum, trying to invent the wheel when it already exists elsewhere. Article 38 of the Statute of the International Court of Justice acknowledges this when it refers to, 'the general principles of law recognised by civilised nations' as a source of law. The Statute recognises the problem for the ICJ operating, as it does, with a relatively light case-load in an as yet underdeveloped system. However, what are these principles and how are they chosen?

Shaw*International Law* 3rd edn (Grotius, 1995).[1] highlights the polarisation of approach. On the one hand, there are those who view the acceptance of 'general principles' as 'an affirmation of Natural Law concepts, which are deemed to underlie the system of international law'; while, on the other hand, there are those who believe that general principles can offer nothing that is not already contained in either Treaty or customary law, as principles cannot be adopted unless by consensus. There is a certain logic to both positions. Understandably, a middle way, recognising the existence of a separate, if rather limited source, represents a popular stance. This is certainly the approach of the ICJ.

Whether or not a general principle is adopted into international law lies in the hands of the ICJ. Where neither Treaty nor customary law offer answers, the Court may look to principle evident in municipal law. The danger of ignoring this source of law was pointed out in the *Barcelona Traction* case.[2]

The problem in the *Barcelona Traction* case hinged upon the domestic notion of the limited liability company. The ICJ conceded that if:

> 'The courts were to decide the case in disregard of the relevant institutions of municipal law it would, without justification, invite serious legal difficulties. It would lose touch with reality for there are no corresponding institutions of international law to which the court could resort'.

To the extent that these broad principles may be evident over a range of legal systems indicates a close relationship with customary law. The importation into international law relies upon the 'need' of the ICJ, and, as such, development is piecemeal. Their continued relevance to international law is dependent upon the continued approval of the ICJ. While the Court may adopt a concept for the adjudication of one case, it may reject it thereafter.[3]

In the present context, it is now generally accepted that the development of international law, both through the Court and Treaty, will rest upon certain accepted principles, namely: sustainable development; the polluter pays principle; the precautionary principle; the acceptance of the notion, in some

---

1 *International Law* 3rd edn (Grotius, 1995).

2 (1970) ICJ Reports 3; (1970) 46 ILR 178.

3 See the cases of Temple (1962) ICJ Reports; (1962) 33 ILR; and the *Serbian Loans* case (1929) PCIJ Series A, No 20; 5 ILR 466.

instances, of a 'common but differentiated responsibility'; and, in the case of transboundary pollution (see below), the notion of 'non-discrimination', which dictates that a polluter whose actions are felt beyond its own borders is treated no less severely than where a similar offence takes place within its own borders.

Sustainable development

The World Commission on the Environment and Development stated in the *Brundtland Report* (1987), that sustainable development is: 'development that meets the needs of the present without compromising the ability of future generations to meet their own needs'. The principle of sustainable development, therefore, indicates a legal, political and economic response to the environmental challenge of enjoying today only that sum of right and benefits which is compatible with maximum future benefit. As such, it has been cited as 'the first and greatest principle'.[1] Certainly, it would seem to be an overarching aim, within which other principles are akin to matters of housekeeping.

It is suggested that the principle should, more accurately, be viewed as the sum of four constituent assumptions:[2]

(1) the conservation of natural resources for future generations, or 'intergenerational equity';
(2) the sustainable use of natural resources;
(3) equitable use – with the assumption that use by one State should take account of the needs of others;
(4) the need for integration of the environment into other fields of activity.

What the principle of sustainable development does not provide is an objective measure by which nations may compare their actions. It appears that sustainable development, as a principle, is not capable of such precise calibration; nor, it seems, is it capable of forming the basis of legal obligations as between States in the international community. This should not, however, cause us to discard the principle or question its validity.

The principle has been adopted at all levels, and is widely evident in the approach to environmental regulation internationally, and at EC and domestic level. A prime example is found in the terms and approach of the Fifth Environmental Action Programme of the European Community, which acknowledges the definition given by the *Brundtland Report* (above), and shapes its policy accordingly, anticipating rather than reacting, and initiating change through knowledge and information.

Preventative/precautionary principle

The preventative principle is a well-established principle of international law which seeks to keep environmental damage to the minimum by pre-empting that damage through early action or by prohibiting the damaging action. The

1 Hughes, *Environmental Law* (Butterworths, 1996).
2 Birnie and Boyle *International Law and The Environment* (Oxford, 1994).

precautionary principle is of newer vintage, although it has featured in international provisions.

The danger with the precautionary principle is that, without careful direction, this approach may be hijacked into protecting the polluter where evidence of long-term effect is weak. The true force of the principle can, however, be appreciated in Principle 15 of the Rio Declaration[1] which states:

> 'Where there are threats of serious irreversible damage lack of full scientific certainty shall not be used as a reason for postponing cost-effective measures to prevent environmental degradation.'

None the less, problems exist elsewhere where the preventative principle is linked with the presumption of a need for 'reasonable grounds for concern' (eg Article 2 of the Paris Convention for the Protection of the Marine Environment of the North Atlantic).

In the application of these principles, it is to be hoped that the Rio approach will prevail, although evidence suggests that the approach taken in the Paris Convention is not a lone stance.

Polluter pays

The polluter pays principle emerged from the work of the OECD in the early 1970s, which viewed the principle as meaning that the polluter should pay for any measures considered necessary to ameliorate such damage or environmental degradation which resulted from the polluter's action. This principle is evident in provisions regulating civil and State liability, for example the Convention on Civil Liability for Oil Pollution Damage (1969) and the Convention on the Establishment of an International Fund for the Compensation of Oil Pollution Damage (1992).

The essence of the polluter pays principle does not, however, merely concern itself with questions of compensation. Polluter pays is a more invasive principle directing that all economic activity which touches upon the environment should incorporate any cost the environment may have incurred fully. This position is recognised in the Rio Declaration, Principle 16, which states:

> 'National authorities should endeavour to promote the internalisation of environmental costs and the use of economic instrument, taking into account the approach that the polluter should, in principle bear the cost of pollution, with due regard to the public interest and without distorting international trade and investment'.

Although there is broad evidence of the adoption of the polluter pays principle, Sands questions whether it has achieved a sufficiently widespread acceptance to qualify for recognition as a 'general principle' of international law. He considers[2] that: 'it is doubtful whether it has achieved the status of a generally applicable rule of customary international law, except perhaps in relation to

1 United Nations Conference on Environment and Development (UNCED) 1992.

2 Sands (1995).

states in the EC, the UN/ECE and the OECD'. Certainly, the principle has been operative in the European Community since the First Environmental Action Programme. Its status in the UK is evident from publications such as *This Common Inheritance*, *Sustainable Development: The UK Strategy* (Cm 2426 (1990), in addition to the obvious influence on legislative provision.

3.2.5 'The teachings of the most highly qualified publicists of the various nations'[1]

Traditionally, the opinions of international jurists have been fundamental in shaping international law, and only the development of Treaty and customary sources has pushed the works of these publicists to the margins. Whether consequent upon, or causal, the change in emphasis of sources of law represents a movement to the States themselves. Treaty and custom place the development of international law very much in the hands of sovereign States rather than philosophers and jurists, but that is not to say that the publicists have become redundant.

The largely piecemeal nature of international law ensures a continuing role for writers whose interpretations and commentaries may assist in holding the patchwork of law together. Certainly, the ICJ, and litigants before it, continue to make reference to any authoritative sources available in order to bring full cogency to their arguments. More generally, however, in contrast to their historical role, the work of publicists is seen as a repository, rather than a primary source, of international law.

3.2.6 Judicial/arbitral tribunals

The ICJ (created by the Statute of 1946), and its predecessor, the Permanent Court of International Justice, have played an essential role in the adjudication and development of international law. However, the decisions of these courts are not, and have never been, legally binding. This is clear from the terms of Article 59 of the Statute which declares decisions to have 'no binding force except between the parties and in respect of that particular case'. The influence of judicial decisions is, however, recognised by Article 38, albeit as a 'subsidiary means for the determination of rules of law'.

Both courts have operated on the assumption that they are not bound by their previous decisions, but have recourse to those decisions by way of guidance. The ICJ has, however, tried to follow its own decisions and thereby import some certainty into the international arena. It seems logical that if, while adjudicating within the set parameters of customary and Treaty law, a set of facts leads to a certain outcome on one occasion, it will lead to a similar or the same outcome if those facts present themselves again. If it was a good decision the first time, then it will be a good decision the second time. The difference between this, and the common law position of *stare decisis*, is that the latter offers no choice on the basis of certainty

1 Statute of the International Court of Justice, Article 38.

The status accorded to the judicial pronouncements of the ICJ (and its predecessor) by Articles 38 and 59 of the Statute means that it cannot be taken for granted that such pronouncements will gain a wider acceptance. The reputation and respect accorded the Court ensures that it has an essential role in the development of international law. As Shearer observes:[1]

> 'the judgements and advisory opinions delivered by them are considered by international lawyers generally as elucidating the law, as being the expression of what the most authoritative international judicial body holds to be the international law on a given point, having regard to a given set of circumstances.'

The expression 'judicial decision' is not generally given a restrictive definition here, but may extend to cover domestic courts and the decisions or findings of international arbitrators. In the case of the former, while decisions may not provide a source of international law as such, they may present evidence of the current practice of States. In addition to illustrating the material fact of law, the reasoning of the courts may shed light upon the 'psychological' element. In this way, reference to the domestic courts may be an important means of discovering customary law.

There has been some debate as to the role of arbitration. Some argue that it lacks the procedural stringency of the courts, and that the outcome may present an effective compromise rather than triumphs of law. The evidence, however, supports the view that arbitration cases have contributed to the development of law.

3.3 EC POSITION IN THE INTERNATIONAL ARENA

In addition to the obligations arising from any international instrument to which the UK may be a party, obligations of international law may be imposed by the EC. This can occur either because the EC is keeping its policies in line with the international agenda (eg the First Environmental Action Programme), or because the EC is itself a party to an international agreement.

Authority for the EC to enter into international agreements in the field of environmental law derives from Article 130R(4) of the EC Treaty, which states that:

> 'Within their respective spheres of competence, the Community and the Member States shall co-operate with third countries and with the competent international organisations. The arrangements for Community co-operation may be the subject of agreements between the Community and the third parties concerned, which shall be negotiated and concluded in accordance with Article 228.'

The ability of the EC to enter into negotiations is dependent upon its 'competence' in the subject-matter, and may be affected by the assumption of subsidiarity. The approach of the ECJ is, however, broad: 'competence' will be recognised where it is specifically founded in the EC Treaty, and wherever the

1 Shearer *Starkes International Law*, 11th edn (Butterworths, 1994) p42.

subject has been found within EC competence in relation to internal regulation.

The EC Treaty confirms that this is without prejudice to the competence of Member States to enter into their own agreements. It does, none the less, affect the extent to which Member States may regulate their own obligations under international law. For example, where a Member State does not sign, or signs but chooses not to ratify, a Treaty, it would ordinarily remain free of its obligations. However, where the EC is itself a party to the agreement, the international obligation may be passed on to the Member State through EC law. The same problem may arise in relation to a protocol. The Member State may find itself subject to the obligation via EC law, and in the final analysis to the rigours of the EC enforcement process.

This position would seem to compromise the very freedoms to which Article 130R(4) expressly refers, ie the continued competence of Member States 'to negotiate in international bodies and to conclude international agreements'. Some protection is offered by the involvement of the Council whose permission will be sought before EC negotiations take place. As ratification is by way of Council decision, this at least provides the opportunity of Member State representatives to make their position clear before any EC obligation arises. In practice, this is unlikely to present too many problems for the UK as experience indicates that a Member State and the EC will generally be *ad idem* on the acceptability of conventions and any subsequent protocols.

The bonus for the international community is that any obligation adopted by EC law will become subject to the scrutiny of the Commission. Enforcement action may arise subsequently in response to a failure to comply with the obligation.

3.4 TRANSBOUNDARY POLLUTION

Although regulation of transboundary pollution presents difficulties, such regulation can be approached using the range of legal tools available. While these tools may need some refining, they have facilitated the development of a framework for regulation based upon current knowledge of the air.

Air is ever-moving. The currents circulating in the atmosphere cause air to move from one part of the globe to another, taking with it pollutants picked up along the way. Simplistic controls on the pollution of air date back to medieval days, but these have traditionally been local in nature. Unfortunately, some local solutions seem to have been the distinct causes of pollution incidents further afield. The Clean Air Acts 1958 and 1968, for example, have received considerable acclaim for their success in cleaning up urban air in the UK, largely through tackling domestic sources. By encouraging domestic households to cease using coal fires in favour of 'cleaner' heating systems the smogs of the 1950s became a thing of the past. However, alternative sources of heat at that time led to increasing demand on other power sources, notably electricity.

The increased production of power stations may have solved the local problem, but it has also shunted the problem further afield.

The regulation of transboundary pollution calls on States to restrict their sovereign rights in favour of their neighbour. It has developed in reliance on principles of self-interest and neighbourly co-existence rather than any more sophisticated stance. The customary position is reiterated in Principle 21 of the Stockholm Declaration, which reaffirms the sovereign rights of States subject to the obligation: 'to ensure that activities within their jurisdiction or control do not cause damage to the environment of other States or the areas beyond the limits of national jurisdiction'. International arbitration services were called upon to consider this position early in the development of environmental concerns to establish the relative rights and obligations arising from transboundary incidents. The *Trail Smelter* arbitration of 1939[1] is an important landmark in international law and the only international adjudication thus far on air pollution. In that case the tribunal of arbitration was convened to consider the relative rights and obligations of Canada, the producing State, and the USA, the receiving State. The smelter was in operation on Canadian territory some seven miles from the US border. Scientific evidence showed that the emissions from the smelter were responsible for damage across the border in the US State of Washington. The tribunal concluded importantly that:

> 'No State has the right to use or permit the use of territory in such a manner as to cause injury by fumes, in or to the territory of another or the properties or persons therein, when the case is of serious consequence and the injury is established by clear and convincing evidence.'

The tribunal went on to consider both the question of compensation for damage and any restrictions which might be placed upon the operation of the smelter in the future. The approach taken was reminiscent of the regulation of the activity of neighbours under the common law. The result of the case provided some protection for the environment, but, like the tort of nuisance, did so only tangentially. The principal aim of the action was to compensate for physical damage done and to limit such damage for the future. However, the case did establish some restriction on emissions, but only as a result of the physical damage caused and the 'clear and convincing' evidence of causation.

In *Trail Smelter*, it proved relatively easy to satisfy the evidential requirements of the tribunal, there being only one, obvious, single source of pollution. The utility of the model presented here becomes more questionable in the case of multiple sources, or the more complex synergistic effects of a range of emissions. In practice, the resolution of disputes of this nature are more generally undertaken through tortious models in the domestic courts through reliance on customary principles of 'equal access'. In reality, however, these actions are likely to face similar difficulties to those caused by the *Trail Smelter* model.

---

1 (1939) 33 AJIL 182, (1941) 35 AJIL 684.

Further, while it may be suggested[1] that the *Trail Smelter* approach may not be limited to actions which can be shown to be 'unreasonable', this does not necessarily impose a higher standard of duty on States than that of 'due diligence'. Once a sophistry of approach is required which goes beyond the reactive or the compensatory model, the planned intervention of international agreements is necessary.

The range of negotiated instruments for the regulation of transboundary air pollution includes bilateral, regional and multilateral agreements establishing both standards of emission and behaviour. None the less, as Birnie and Boyle conclude, the approach of these generally regional responses to transboundary air pollution also fail to attribute to customary law an international standard of due diligence. They further point to the fact that in relation to the setting of standards, States are instructed to 'take account' rather than adopt or apply set levels. This reiterates the 'generality' of approach of customary law in this area, as illustrated both by international adjudication and negotiated instruments.

It would be inappropriate to give consideration to transboundary pollution without making reference to the OECD, the contribution of which is evident in both policy and practice, and which introduced a programme for monitoring emissions across Europe as early as 1972.

3.4.1 Geneva Convention on Long-Range Transboundary Air Pollution 1979

A 'planned' approach to pollution can be found in the Geneva Convention on Long-Range Transboundary Air Pollution. The Convention was completed in 1979 and is supported by a series of subsequent protocols. The Convention is a regional agreement, with interest being concentrated in the northern hemisphere. This is not surprising since the problem of acid rain, which it seeks to address, is largely a northern hemisphere problem.

The Convention is not an attempt merely to reiterate the contents of customary law, but rather it responds to the problems of transboundary pollution which are beyond the competence of custom. The *Trail Smelter* case (above) represents an ideal model for dealing with an identifiable cause, but offers little assistance in tackling distance pollution from divergent sources. As the Convention itself identifies (Article 1(b)), in relation to longer-distance pollution: 'it is not generally possible to distinguish the contributions of individual emission sources'. This also dictates a difference in approach. The Convention (and protocols) aim to provide a framework and flexible programme for tackling the problem of acid rain rather than simply allocating blame and compensating for past damage.

The Convention takes a broad-ranging and sophisticated view of pollution beyond merely harm to health and property. The operative definition, contained in Article 1(a), includes 'harm of living resources', ecosystems, interference with amenities and legitimate uses of the environment. This

1 See Birnie and Boyle, *International Law and the Environment* (Oxford, 1994).

characterises the objectives of the Convention in establishing the framework to tackle the wide range of environmental measures necessary to achieve its aim.

The number of States which have become party to the Treaty is a measure of its success. However, as with all international instruments, to maximise its attraction is to pander to the lowest common denominator. Thus, some parties, notably those which are net importers of pollution, would criticise the Convention for its weakness. Indeed, it has been referred to by some commentators as a 'symbolic victory' only.[1] This criticism is not wholly fair. It could be argued (as is often the case with international agreements) that a broad acceptance of lesser controls is better than nothing, as, indeed, are the self-imposed rigours of a minority of high-minded States amid the quagmire of general non-regulation.

The Convention sets up a framework only. The supporting protocols contain details in relation to emission levels. It might be argued that by achieving healthy participation at the framework stage the Convention is more likely to carry its signatories to consider or accept positions which they might otherwise have found untenable. None the less, the language of the Convention is somewhat apologetic in places. Article 2, for example, imposes the obligation to 'endeavour to limit ... as far as possible, gradually reduce and prevent' pollution. It also encourages the development of a strategy approach by the parties. Article 6 continues the bond between that which is technologically attainable and that which is economically feasible.

A major feature of the Convention is its commitment to research and the exchange of information. This extends to information and consultation in relation to development. Article 8(b) establishes a duty on a State to notify relevant States of any major industrial development which is likely to have a significant polluting effect. Further, consultation may be required at the request of the receiving State. While these provisions do not establish as stringent a regime as the UN Economic Commission for Europe (UNECE) Convention on Environmental Impact Assessment 1991, the former are, of course, enhanced by the requirements of the latter.

The operation of the Convention and its protocols are subject to the scrutiny of an Executive, which is, comprised of the environmental advisers to the UNECE governments. Progress is reviewed by reference to implementation at domestic level.

The powers of the Executive and Secretariat are few, but the success of their function in negotiating the detail of subsequent protocols is evident.

3.4.2 Protocols

The protocols to the Convention cover a range of issues, from the funding of the European Monitoring and Evaluation Programme (EMEP) (1984), to establishing reduction programmes for sodium dioxide (1985 and 1994),

1 Wetstone and Rosencranz, *Acid Rain in Europe and North America* (Washington DC, 1985).

nitrogen oxide (1998) and volatile organic compounds (1991). By placing the substantive elements in individual protocols, the Convention provides the parties with something of a 'pick-and-mix' opportunity. Acceptance of the Convention framework does not necessarily guarantee that party States will actually take the next step and accept the various obligations to reduce emissions. Further, the argument remains that, like the Convention itself, the substance of the protocols represents not that which is necessary, but the result of compromise.

This reality should also inform the way in which outcomes are viewed. It is arguable that the Convention is something of a success story, with many signatories moving towards compliance levels. As the product of compromise, however, compliance levels represent achievable goals. In addition, commentators such as Sands remind us that compliance has been assisted by the natural reductions of emissions connected with the recent global economic and industrial downturn.

While it has been recognised that 'something is better than nothing', the reality remains that even perfect compliance would fail to achieve the goal of neutralising the problem of acid rain.

Protocols under the Convention on Long-Range Transboundary Air Pollution

1984	Funding for the EMEP
1985	Helsinki: Reduction in transboundary SO_2 by 30 per cent by 1993 (the EC, the UK, the USA and Poland did not sign)
1988	Sofia: Freezing of emissions of NO*x* at 1987 levels by 1994
1991	Geneva: Reduction in transboundary VOCs on 1988 levels by 1999 Requirement for the introduction of national strategies
1994	Oslo: Further reduction in transboundary SO_2. Target to vary from State to State based upon 'critical loads'. UK: 50 per cent reduction of 1980 levels by 2000 70 per cent reduction by 2005 80 per cent reduction by 2010

3.5 GLOBAL CONCERNS

It is recognised that transboundary pollution is largely a regional affair. The emissions giving rise to the problems of acid rain are generally the product of the developed world. The northern hemisphere is both responsible for acid rain and is its victim. While the rest of the world might voice its concern for the environmental destruction in this part of the globe, it is aware that the nature of the pollution and wind patterns mean that it will remain largely in the north.

Other problems are not so conveniently contained. The higher atmosphere is particularly vulnerable to the effects of certain pollutants, which vulnerability presents a threat to the whole globe. Unlike transboundary pollution, this is not the transportation of particulates which may react with other chemicals and/or rain water, producing a damaging effect to the planet's surface; the atmosphere itself is attacked by a range of pollutants. The damage caused represents, on the one hand, a weakening of the earth's defences against the harmful rays of the sun, and, on the other hand, destruction of the insulatory properties of the atmosphere, leaving the climate vulnerable to upward pressures.

The reasons for these global problems lie not only in current industrial patterns, but also in the industrial heritage of centuries. The cause lies largely with the same polluting States responsible for transboundary pollution, but, in this case, the effects are not isolated and any hope of redress rests upon the whole of the global community.

3.5.1 Customary law

As with transboundary pollution control, it appears that customary law has a role to play, but that role is both limited and uncertain. An extension of the 'no harm' principle to the atmosphere seems logical; indeed, the adoption by the Geneva Convention of Principle 21 of the Stockholm Declaration gives some credence to this. However, transboundary pollutants can clearly be seen to 'cause damage to the environment of other States or to areas beyond the limits of national jurisdiction' (Principle 21). The status of the high atmosphere is less clear in these terms. Principle 21 was, none the less, adopted by the Vienna Convention for the Protection of the Ozone Layer 1985.

If it can be addressed by Treaty without difficulty, it might be suggested that any problem as to whether the atmosphere satisfied the jurisdictional question is merely semantic. The recurrent difficulty with customary law is that it is generalistic in nature, providing no means of establishing emission standards beyond 'due diligence' and, therefore, providing no means of reducing such emissions in order to halt damage to the atmosphere. Any realistic attempts to slow down or reverse the damage to the global atmosphere must rely upon the negotiation of planned instruments by which nations may seek to regulate their behaviour for the common good.

3.5.2 Vienna Convention for the Protection of the Ozone Layer 1985

The principal 'planned instrument' for the protection of the atmosphere is the Vienna Convention for the Protection of the Ozone Layer 1985, which represents four years' work on the part of United Nations Environment Programme (UNEP), and a whole series of drafts, before an acceptable programme could be found. The time and effort leading up to the Convention is representative of the range of opposing interests involved. The fact that a compromise position could be found at all is worthy of high praise and regard. While some of the weighty players on the world stage had already embraced both the theory and practice of reducing ozone-threatening substances, calls for global reduction presented a burden on the developing nations.

The developed world enjoys both the technology and capital to look towards replacement products to CFCs and HCFCs: the developing world possesses neither. Global restrictions of these compounds therefore impose on developing nations the need effectively to 'leapfrog' a stage in their industrial development. It also caps their emerging consumer markets by effectively restricting the goods in circulation and increasing their price. Further reluctance of other players, including the EC, was not based simply upon self-interest, but on a divergence of opinions in scientific fraternities as to the reality of the risks faced.

Like the Geneva Convention, the Vienna Convention represents a framework. The obligation of Principle 21 of the Stockholm Declaration is embraced, but few other real obligations are imposed. The Convention does, however, provide a means of dispute resolution (Article 11). The parties are called upon to take appropriate measures for the protection of the environment 'against adverse effects resulting or likely to result from human activities which modify or are likely to modify the ozone layer' (Article 2). What form these 'measures' should take is not indicated. The instrument does not even identify in the main document the substances concerned, but instead leaves this to annexes. However, the definition of 'adverse effects' is very broad, being defined as: 'changes in the physical environment or biota, including changes in climate, which have significant deleterious effects on human health or on the composition, resilience and productivity of natural and managed ecosystems, or on materials useful to mankind' (Article 1(2)). The Convention dictates the need for continued co-operation to establish the detail in terms of 'agreed measures, procedures and standards'. It raises an expectation that the parties will apply themselves to the cause and effect of damage to the ozone layer, establishing appropriate monitoring and research programmes. The exchange of information and technology, particularly between the developed and developing world, is a central theme. The criticism of the developing world is that the obligation contained in Article 4 is couched in such terms as to leave the practical reality of exchange entirely in the hands of the developed world. The 1990 revisions to the Montreal Protocol (see below) strengthens this obligation to require that 'every practical step' is taken towards 'fair and most favourable conditions' of transfer to developing states (Article 10(a)).

As with the Geneva Convention, critics point to the lack of firm regulation. The Vienna Convention has, however, gained wide support amongst nations with widely divergent views. It marks an important step in international law reaching out to protect the whole atmosphere for the benefit of all, rather than any individual self-interest.

Furthermore, the progressive approach taken in defining the 'global environment' in terms which recognise its value beyond our own needs, along with the precautionary stance taken, represents a milestone in our approach to the environment.

3.5.3 Montreal Protocol 1987

As with the Geneva Convention, the detail of planned reductions in ozone-depleting substances is to be found in the protocol to the Vienna Convention. The Montreal Protocol establishes a programme intended to lead to the reduction and final elimination of ozone depleters. The Protocol, like the Convention itself, has gained strong support from the USA, which had already set in motion reduction programmes. While the USA has anticipated reductions, it has not sought a unilateral position, but instead seeks a 'level playing field' and the avoidance of potential economic inequality. None the less, it is right to stress the need for care, particularly in the pursuit of intergenerational equity.

The levels set in 1987 have been subject to greater stringency in the light of:

(1) improved scientific understanding of the problem; and
(2) technological developments in relation to alternative substances.

Amendments have therefore been made to the Protocol in 1990 (London) and 1992 (Copenhagen), which effect an overall acceleration of the programmes.

Controls apply to both the consumption and manufacture of substances.

In order for the Protocol to attract the interest of the developing world it was necessary to recognise the fact that the contribution of these nations to the overall problem was minimal in comparison to that of the developed world. The current provisions take the dual approach of an extended timetable, and financial and technical benefits. The cost of providing this assistance is met by the 'non-qualifying' States, and is supported by the means of access to the 'meeting of parties' if the measures prove ineffective. The original provisions had attracted approximately 50 parties by 1993, with the added attractions raising interest in China, India and beyond.

Contrary to the general understanding of international instruments, the Protocol takes an embracing approach to non-parties. The way in which it is constructed – banning both the trade in substances and the manufacturing technology – effectively overrules the will of non-parties, except in relation to manufacture for home consumption. This ensures that the effect of the Protocol is felt globally. The approach is mirrored as between the parties, where the institutional decision-making process is designed in such a way as to allow binding decisions to be taken by a two-thirds' majority when a unanimous position proves impossible (Article 2(9)). To ensure equity, the majority position will be assessed by reference to developed and developing nations independently. Further, the scheme, as amended, provides a compliance procedure through the operation of its 'implementation Committee', although, as Birnie and Boyle comment, clarification is needed as to the extent to which its decisions are binding upon the parties.

As with the Geneva Convention, the Vienna Convention may also be judged as something of a success by reference to the number of States which have become party to it. The developed world has not only embraced its obligations, but, in many instances, has gone further. If this enthusiasm can be extended to the task of facilitating the objectives of the developing world, the Convention and its protocols must indeed be measured as a success.

The difficulties which remain are chiefly in relation to the time-span for effective control of ozone-depleting substances. Even after amendment to the protocols, levels are likely to rise until at least the turn of the century. Further, while the obligation to reduce these substances has led to technological innovations and the development of alternatives, the scientific community may not yet have the full measure of each or all of the substances. None the less, the measures taken are likely to be sufficient to reverse damage to the ozone layer, and seal the breach, by the year 2060, assuming, of course, that the promised measures become practice.

Proof of breach of the Montreal Protocol through black market operations came to light in 1997. Governments and industry had suspected a covert and illegal international trade in CFCs for some time, evidenced, perhaps, by the relatively stable market price in the decreasing legal trade. A lawful trade remains in chemicals already stockpiled at the time of the 1995 standstill, and for the recycled product. Understandably, this is a finite and ever-shrinking stock, and yet prices remain low. An illegal trade has been identified between China and companies in Europe.[1] The EC Commission, working with customs authorities across Europe, uncovered a black market operation which is thought to have led to the importation of some 1,000 tonnes of ozone-depleting substances banned under the Montreal Protocol. The scheme relied upon falsely labelled imports from China provided with counterfeit paperwork before being passed off as legally tradable, recycled CFCs. The risk of black market trade from developing nations such as China will continue until 2010 when they are required to cease production. The interim period calls for vigilance from the customs authorities and honesty from industry itself, if the protection offered by the Montreal Protocol is to be achieved. Further, it might be argued that this vigilance should continue after 2010.

3.6 CLIMATE CHANGE

As with ozone depletion, much of the threat to the global climate from excessive CO_2 emissions comes from the developed world. The task of negotiating agreement from the multitude of interest groups is onerous. However, unlike the Vienna Convention, and supporting Protocols, calls for a reduction in CO_2 levels have attracted a varying level of support from the major polluters. The USA alone accounts for some 25 per cent of CO_2 emissions. CO_2 emissions are endemic to the American lifestyle. However, although the USA is keen to throw its support behind a reduction in ozone-depleting substances, it seems unprepared to shoulder the burden of CO_2 reduction. Further, as seems clear from the US domestic response to the Kyoto Protocol (see below), even where negotiators have voiced agreement, the political support at Senate level cannot be relied upon. The opinion of commentators suggests that, at best, the Kyoto Protocol will have a long and tortuous road to ratification in the USA, and that it will never achieve ratification, either because it cannot hope to find favour with the Republican majority in the Senate, or because it will inevitably be caught up in the

1 See (1997) *The Independent*, 1 August.

domestic timetable for Presidential elections. Either result will suit the oil lobby, which has invested a fortune in denigrating the entire exercise as measures to destroy industry and employment. This is an important factor – not only is it essential that reductions are achieved overall, including the 25 per cent of emissions controlled by the USA, but it is important for the viability of any agreement that the major players are seen to be supportive.

3.6.1 Global Climate Change Convention 1994

The Global Climate Change Convention was presented at the United Nations Conference on Environment and Development (UNCED) in Rio in 1992, and came into force two years later. It establishes a framework for progress toward the reduction in climate-threatening emissions, with the detail being left to Kyoto (see below) and beyond.

The fact that the burden on the atmosphere varies greatly between nations is recognised in the Convention. In this context the approach to global control operates not on the assumption of a universal restriction, but on the fact that internationally negotiated limits may differ from State to State, on the basis of the threat posed, and on the difficulties presented. The principle of 'differentiated responsibility' ensures that the greater burden will rest upon those States which pose the greatest threat. This approach means that the needs of the developing nations can be offset against more stringent restrictions on the developed world. In this way, some protection may be offered to the developing world without making it dependent on the technological 'alms' of their industrialised neighbours, as might be the case with the Vienna Convention. Indeed, the needs of the developing world are essential to the approach of the Convention, which takes the view that it should not share responsibility for past and present emissions created by the developed world. As the general text of the Convention states, the parties to the Convention are:

> '... affirming that responses to climate change should be co-ordinated with social and economic development in an integrated manner with a view to avoiding adverse impacts on the latter, taking into full account the legitimate priority needs of developing countries for the achievement of sustained economic growth and eradication of poverty.'

The Convention further states that:

> '... all countries, especially developing countries, need access to resources required to achieve sustainable social and economic development and that, in order for developing countries to progress towards their goal, their energy consumption will need to grow taking into account the possibilities for achieving greater energy efficiency and for controlling greenhouse gas emissions in general, including through the application of new technologies on terms which make such an application economically and socially beneficial.'

This approach provides the basis for a co-operative response, while indicating that the burden of emissions reduction will lie primarily on the shoulders of the developed nations. Compliance itself might offer opportunities for co-operative development.

The Convention recognises the status of the atmosphere as being of 'common concern'. Raising it above the self-interest of nations, the Convention acknowledges the 'responsibility of all countries to make efforts at the national, regional and global levels to limit or reduce greenhouse gas emissions and prevent activities which could adversely affect the climate'. This approach to atmospheric protection represents a leap forward for environmental regulation and, in this sentiment, it is not surprising that the Convention does not permit reservations.

Although the Convention is merely a framework, the detail of which will be filled in at a later date, its importance can be measured by the interest it has attracted in the international community, with some 160 nations being represented at Kyoto in December 1997. This must be some measure of success. However, as with ozone regulation, success can only truly be measured by reference to the level at which negotiations peg future protection and the enthusiasm displayed in compliance.

Like the Vienna Convention, emphasis is placed upon knowledge. The importance of environmental impact assessment, the need for consultation and information exchange are all stressed. This form of proactive intervention is further supported by the encouragement of practical measures which may be taken in order to minimise or neutralise the actual effect of remaining emissions. Article 3(3) calls on the parties to: 'take precautionary measures to anticipate, prevent or minimise the causes of climate change and mitigate its adverse effect'. It directs the attention of the parties to the utility of 'sinks', and co-operative measures. 'Sink' is defined as: 'any process, activity or mechanism which removes a greenhouse gas, an aerosol or a precursor of a greenhouse gas from the atmosphere' (Article 1(8)), thus highlighting a potential 'double effect' to be achieved by the co-ordination of emissions and positive measures, such as afforestation.

The Convention also provides the basis for an institutional framework. The 'Conference of the Parties' is the supreme functioning body. Article 7 provides that the aim of the 'Conference' is to: 'keep under regular review the implementation of the Convention and any related legal instruments'. As the 'supreme body', its function will be achieved through, inter alia:

- a periodical examination of the obligations of the parties;
- the promotion and facilitation of information exchange;
- at the request of two or more parties, co-ordinating measures adopted by them;
- promoting and guiding the development and periodic refinement of methodology for the provision of information;
- assessing the implementation of the Convention;
- giving consideration to regular reports;
- making recommendations;
- 'mobilising financial resources'; and
- establishing subsidiary bodies.

The Conference is authorised to establish its own operative rules. However, the Convention itself establishes the frequency of meetings, which will generally be on an annual basis, although provision exists for further 'extraordinary sessions'. The Convention further provides that a Secretariat be established for the support and guidance of the Conference, in addition to subsidiary bodies 'for scientific and technological advice and implementation'. One of the first jobs identified for the Conference is to give thought to the establishment of a 'multilateral consultative process' to facilitate the resolution of questions of implementation.

Finally, the Convention identifies measures for the resolution of disputes. In the event of a dispute, Article 14 states that: 'the parties concerned shall seek a settlement of the dispute through negotiation or any other peaceful means of their own choice'. The parties are, none the less, advised that they may make written dispositions to the effect that they will submit to the adjudication of the ICJ and/or arbitration. Authority is also provided for a 'Conciliation Commission' to be established at the request of a disputing party. The Commission would comprise an equal number of appointees chosen by each party, and a chairperson chosen by mutual agreement. By giving such ranging attention to the question of dispute-resolution, the Convention anticipates any argument between the parties and, it is hoped, provides for peaceful resolution.

The Convention has, as has been noted, many similarities to its counterpart, the Vienna Convention. Both represent what is now a successful model for international co-operation and the governance of issues of 'common concern'. Like the Vienna Convention, any detailed measures are left to future conferences of the parties. In this case the first substantive provisions are to be found in the results of the Kyoto Conference of December 1997. Without such detail, it is relatively painless for States to pledge themselves to the protection of the atmosphere. The 'proof of the pudding' is not only in the ease, or otherwise, by which substantive agreements are reached, but by reference to the reality of future compliance.

3.7 BEYOND RIO

Promises are easily made. The promises made at Rio are measurable only by reference to the action taken by the participant nations since that auspicious occasion. Five years after Rio, its success, or otherwise, was the subject of close international scrutiny on three occasions within just a few short months.

The New York Earth Summit in June 1997, and the Denver meeting of the G8 nations which preceded it, suggest that the enthusiastic will for change, so apparent in Rio, has largely evaporated. As in Rio, the US stance indicated a less than whole-hearted support for the international goal. When the Earth Summit opened in New York, President Clinton chose to be on the West Coast addressing a convention of mayors, an event which he could not even argue was an earlier commitment.

The success story of Rio has been the EC, where greenhouse gases have been reduced by 10 per cent overall. The USA has, in the past, been prompt in highlighting the fact that this aggregate figure has been achieved largely by sizeable reductions in the UK and Germany. Targets have, however, been set by the Southern European nations, with Spain playing a leading role. This 'moral high ground' has given Europe the strength with which to challenge the US position.

The consistency of the US position is not representative of ignorance or lack of compassion for our future. The USA does recognise the problem of global warming, and has for some time berated those who suggest that it is not real. The problem lies rather in the power of the oil lobby and the industrial interests of the Senate. US industry in general, and the oil industry in particular, continue to lobby against the cuts necessary in emission levels. They argue that such cuts would lead to inevitable economic decline and high unemployment. This is not a fear that they have kept to themselves – successful lobbying has ensured that large sections of the US public and Senate are behind them.

However, the global oil industry no longer speaks with one voice. Hope for the future may be found in the European-based companies, perhaps because these companies have first-hand experience of life after emissions reductions. Such companies recognise that global warming should be taken seriously, although they do not go so far as to suggest a reduction in oil consumption.

The UK showed the way at the Earth Summit, with experts outlining how promised cuts of 20 per cent emissions of greenhouse gases on 1990 levels would be achieved as follows:

- a reduction in car use, encouraged through a variety of means, from improvements in public transport to increased taxes on fuel, parking charges and restrictions on the use of private vehicles within cities. This would be complemented by encouraging improvements in fuel efficiency, with differential road taxes benefiting the fuel efficient;
- this would be supported by improvements in energy efficiency in homes, encouraged by grants funded from levies on the gas and electricity industries:
- similar increased efficiency in energy production through greater use of combined heat and power systems – currently 3,500 megawatts, rising to 10,000 megawatts by the year 2010;
- an increased reliance on renewable energy sources – currently two per cent of energy needs, projected at 10 per cent by 2010;
- business energy tax to reduce energy use and encourage technological development.

It is claimed that this will not only *not* lead to industrial demise, but also encourage the development of new goods and services, and, with them, jobs.

Generally, the achievements of the global community in the five years since Rio do not read well.

- Forest covering an area five times the size of England has been lost to loggers or land clearance.
- Amazonian deforestation has risen from 11,000 to 15,000 square kilometres.
- As a result of these statistics, it is estimated that plant/animal extinction is running at between one and three species per hour.
- Third World debt has increased from $1,662 billion to $2,000 billion.
- Aid levels have fallen from 0.34 per cent to 0.27 per cent of gross national product, a long way from the 0.7 per cent promised. Furthermore, the evidence suggests that a larger proportion of aid is being applied to emergency relief than to long-term projects.
- Although private sector investment has increased, the benefit is concentrated in only a handful of emerging nations.

In relation to the Climate Convention in particular, the carbon dioxide particulate ratio in the atmosphere has risen from 356/million to 364/million. Only the UK, Germany and Russia remain on schedule to achieve promised reductions.

The New York Summit itself proved similarly disappointing, the initial absence of President Clinton seeming indicative of the US approach. While not denying the problem of global warming, no clear commitment was forthcoming from the USA at this point. The seeming lack of commitment is significant, not only because of the sheer size of US emissions, but because of the signals it transmits to the global community.

3.8 KYOTO PROTOCOL

The deliberations of the Kyoto Conference of December 1997 led to the first substantive detail under the Climate Convention. Approximately 160 nations took part in intensive negotiations over a period of 10 days (and nights!). The result was an agreement which received a mixed response, but which, no doubt, represents a starting-point.

Representing the UK at the negotiating table were Deputy Prime Minister, John Prescott, and the Environment Minister, Michael Meacher. In addition, the UK contingency played a supporting role to the EC team. Although the UK Presidency did not commence until January 1998, representations had been made by Luxembourg for the UK to lend assistance to their team of negotiators representing the EU interest. As a result, UK negotiators are considered to have played an important part in securing the eventual agreement.

Although some parties would have wished for more stringent cuts (the UK and EU in particular), the resulting agreement is no doubt a near miracle in diplomacy – the original negotiating positions being as far apart as the UK calling for a 20 per cent reduction in certain gases, to Australia calling for an 18 per cent increase. The USA, on the other hand, sought to minimise the impact of any final agreement on its own lifestyle, calling for 'tradable permits' by which it might 'fund' continually increasing emissions. The fact that any agreement was reached, even if less than some might have hoped for, is impressive.

The Protocol sets legally binding agreements. The outcome for most of the developed nations is a mandatory reduction of 5.2 per cent on 1990 levels of six main greenhouse gases between the years 2008 and 2012. Some nations, including the UK, had argued for limits to be set in relation to three major gases only. A strong argument, however, was made by the USA and reductions were extended over a range of six gases: carbon dioxide; methane; nitrous oxide; hydrofluorocarbons (HFCs); perfluorocarbons (PFCs); and sulphur hexafluoride (SF_6). The 5.2 per cent reduction does not apply across the board. In reliance upon the principle of 'differentiated responsibility' contained in the Climate Convention, some parties are required to make greater cuts, while the particular difficulties of others have been recognised in the form of lower reductions. In particular, the EU, the USA and Japan have been singled out as subject to greater reductions, while Australia, Iceland and Norway are subject to smaller than average cuts.

The EU is called upon to reduce its emissions by eight per cent. This might be thought of as ironic, because the negotiating stance adopted by the EU called for substantially greater reductions (15 per cent). The required reduction should not, however, cause too much difficulty as the EU has already adopted a framework to enable it to achieve the reduction. In addition, some Member States have pledged to continue to aim for greater reductions than called for by the Protocol. The greater than average burden upon the USA seems both inevitable and morally justifiable in the light of its 25 per cent share of total global emissions. For Japan, the required reduction may prove more difficult because it already claims to be emission efficient. As Japan is wholly reliant upon imported fuels, it has been in its own interest to make their use as efficient as possible.

The Protocol introduces novel measures, based upon the principles contained in Article 3 of the Convention, to the global arena, aimed at spreading the burden of emission reduction, namely:

- trading in carbon emission permits; and
- undertaking projects abroad to achieve carbon mitigation

(although the supporting detail is still to be set).

3.8.1 Emission trading

The introduction of 'emission permit trading' to the international arena came at the insistence of the USA. Although the detail is yet to be established, it is anticipated that it will include the concepts of 'bubble' and 'banking'.

'Bubble' concept

The 'bubble' concept anticipates a group of emission sources, in this case States, operating together to ensure that aggregate emissions are below the required level. Any given, individual nation may, in fact, be above the level set, but this is offset by the remaining nations, whose emissions are below the given level. In the USA, where emission permit trading has been legislated for some time, this concept may be adopted in relation to undertakings which have more than one emission source. These emission sources will be more, or less, efficient. Permission may be granted for the emission sites to be aggregated as though they were a single source.

There may be many appropriate applications for this type of arrangement. Indeed, the EC operates largely upon this assumption through 'burden sharing'. Member States which are able to improve their emissions beyond the average do so, with a beneficial effect on the overall target. The danger in the current international arena is that it has been suggested that the USA may wish to enter into a 'bubble' arrangement with Canada, Japan and Russia. Canada has relatively low emissions, and Russia is likely to enjoy instant popularity in relation to the obligations of Kyoto because its recent industrial collapse means that current emissions are some 30 per cent below 1990 levels. This arrangement could therefore facilitate a continued increase in US emissions, and cancel any benefit to be gained from the reductions.

'Banking' concept

'Banking' allows the emission source to stockpile permissions for the future. In this way, current Russian emission savings might equip it for some future expansion well beyond its 1990 levels. The increase would be justified by past savings, which could facilitate domestic industrial re-emergence, or the relocation of plant from other States. In this way, as considered by Nicholas Schoon:[1] 'Not only would there be a market in permits, but a futures or options market too – in which the players would be gambling on the future price of permits' – a market in which any small atmospheric benefits achieved might be wiped out.

Permit trading has been tried and tested under US legislation. The system operates on the basis that permits are required to cover proposed emissions. Any undertaking/State wishing to exceed limits set can only do so if it first obtains sufficient permits to cover those emissions. Permits may be purchased on the open market from those undertakings/States which have reduced emission levels below their permit holdings. The system operates on the assumption that the free market will lead to the most efficient regulation. Those in a position to reduce their emission levels easily and cheaply will be motivated to do so by the profits which can be made in selling their excess emission permits.

In many ways, control of climate-changing emissions lends itself to a system of permit trading. As geographical factors have no relevance in relation to these emissions: there is no fear of 'hotspots'. Domestic applications of permit trading regimes to pollutants of the lower atmosphere can lead to over-heavy concentration of pollutants in the air at given locations. Minimisation of this problem requires complex consideration to be given to the assessment of

1 See (1997) *The Independent*, 9 December.

'airsheds', but may not always resolve the problem. In contrast, the global atmosphere does not suffer to any greater extent by a geographical concentration of emissions. Therefore, if the USA wished to continue to enjoy its current emission levels into the future, it could do so by purchasing sufficient permits to cover those emissions which were in excess of 1990 levels, less seven per cent. This could be done without any net increase in the level of greenhouse gases in the atmosphere and, because the location of emissions is irrelevant, no further climate damage.

Such a system would encourage the most efficient to reduce their emission levels to the optimum. The price of permits traded would be governed by supply and demand. In addition, it would be possible for permits to be bought up by the Conference of Parties, in order to reduce emissions further. An increase in the price of permits which this would effect may eventually encourage those with inefficient technology to invest in new, cleaner plant. It may also lead the State to impose reductions. Theoretically, the open market in permits could also attract environmental groups whose purchases could reduce the permits in circulation. However, the cost implications mean that this would be unlikely in practice.

As with the 'bubble' model, the danger is that the overall benefit of reductions could be nullified if those with high emissions sought to continue that tradition by purchasing sufficient permits to cushion themselves from the international obligation to reduce emissions. The suggestion is that in demanding the inclusion of emission trading in the Kyoto Protocol, the USA seeks to rely on the permit market for just such a purpose.

3.8.2 Carbon mitigation schemes

The inclusion in the Kyoto Protocol of an option allowing nations to offset their emissions by undertaking projects abroad is a novel extension of the now traditional expectation of co-operation between the developed and developing nations. While the restrictions contained in the Kyoto Protocol do not extend to the developing world, the pace of their development does have ramifications for the global environment. Indeed, the USA drew attention to this and sought to have some 'intermediate' nations, such as India and China, included because of their potential. In allowing the developed nations to offset their own emission obligations by investment in cleaner technologies elsewhere, both the environment and the recipient State benefit.

While this creates potential benefit, it would be naïve to accept it at face value without asking why a State would wish to embark upon such a project. Presumably, in some instances, it may simply be a question of cost. The labour costs of building an emission-saving power station in a developing country would represent a considerable saving on a similar domestic enterprise. In addition, it may be possible to make emission savings by building a not quite 'state of the art' model overseas, which would not be suitable at home; alternatively, it may simply avoid the anger of the home fuel lobby.

Further, laudable though benefits of this scheme may be, the cynic rests on the hope that there is sufficient monitoring to ensure that these projects are actually needed.

Although the agreement reached at Kyoto represents a valued way forward, it cannot, of itself, solve the problem of climate change. Unlike the position in relation to ozone depletion, even perfect compliance will be nowhere near enough to resolve the threat of climate change. What it does offer is a hope that on future occasions the Conference of Parties can increase the rigour of its approach to meet the challenge which our polluting tradition has set.

CHAPTER 4

COMMON LAW REMEDIES

4.1 INTRODUCTION

The common law offers remedies in public and private nuisance and, additionally, although perhaps theoretically in the case of atmospheric emissions, under the rule in *Rylands v Fletcher*.[1] It may further be possible to ground an action in negligence and, possibly, for breach of a particular statutory duty. Statute may also, however, in an appropriate case create a defence for what would otherwise be a tortious act. Each of these matters must be considered in turn.

4.2 PUBLIC NUISANCE

A public nuisance is an act or omission materially affecting the reasonable comfort and convenience of a class of Her Majesty's subjects: but what is such a class? It appears that it must be a definable section of the public in the area affected by the alleged nuisance, and it would seem to follow from remarks in *Attorney-General v PYA Quarries Ltd*[2] that a sufficient number of persons to form a class will be affected where the nuisance is so widespread in its range or indiscriminate in effect that it is reasonable for action to be taken on behalf of the community as opposed to any given individual. Public nuisance actions are criminal proceedings usually dealt with on indictment. The Attorney-General may, however, seek an injunction to restrain the activity – a relator action – brought on the information of a member of the public where the Attorney-General considers it is appropriate to act.

Similarly, a local authority may take action in respect of a public nuisance under s 222 of the Local Government Act 1972 where they consider it 'expedient for the promotion or protection of the interests of the inhabitants of [their] area'. In *Shoreham-by-Sea Urban District Council v Dolphin Canadian Proteins Ltd*,[3] it was considered appropriate to utilise this power to deal with the smell emanating from a particular factory, as it generally appears proper to resort to such proceedings in relation to matters where an authority is: (a) under an obligation to protect the environment; and (b) the alleged nuisance constitutes an infringement of those environmental responsibilities. Only exceptionally, however, will an authority resort to their powers under s 222.

1 (1866) LR 1 Ex 265.
2 [1957] 2 QB 169.
3 (1972) 71 LGR 261.

The remedy usually sought will be an injunction, and these are not granted to restrain mere routine infringements of the criminal law. What has to be shown is that an unlawful activity is happening that will continue unless restrained by an injunction.[1] Certainly, an authority does not have to show that the respondent would have no defence to a criminal prosecution before injunctive relief can be granted.[2] Furthermore, where interim relief is sought by way of an interlocutory injunction, a local authority does not have to give a cross-undertaking to pay damages to the respondent should the substantive issue be decided against the authority, for, like the Crown, an authority seeking such relief is acting in its capacity as an enforcer of the law.[3] What does have to be shown, however, is that before proceedings were instituted the authority considered the interests of all the inhabitants of its district, not merely those of one section of the community. (On injunctive relief under s 222, see also *Vale of White Horse District Council v DC and RJ Allen*[4] and **5.3.6** et seq.)

In tort, action may be taken for damages in respect of a public nuisance where an individual suffers damage over and above that suffered by others, ie something substantial, directly affecting the plaintiff and appreciably different from the affectation of other people in general.[5] It is not, however, necessary to show that health has been harmed by the nuisance in question; no more is needed than material interference with the comfort and convenience of life.[6] However, the damage suffered must be substantial and must directly affect the plaintiff – mere personal inconvenience is not enough to satisfy this requirement, although, arguably, personal injuries and particular property damage will indicate that a plaintiff has indeed suffered 'over and above' that suffered by other persons. An example of such an action relating to an atmospheric nuisance is *Halsey v Esso Petroleum Co Ltd*[7] where action was taken in respect of smuts and smells allegedly being emitted from the premises of the defendant and then, inter alia, affecting the goods and chattels of a number of persons in the locality. There can, of course, be a number of people deleteriously affected by a public nuisance who can show that they have suffered damage over and above that suffered by the public at large. It does not appear possible, however, to recover either aggravated or exemplary damages in such a claim. In *Gibbons v South West Water Services*,[8] the litigation arising out of the Camelford Water incident where aluminium sulphate was introduced into the drinking water supply, although aggravated and exemplary damages were not awarded, substantial amounts of up to £10,000 were accepted by way of out-of-court settlements.

1 *City of London Corporation v Bovis Construction Ltd* [1989] JPL 263.
2 *Newport Borough Council v Khan* [1990] 1 WLR 1185.
3 *Kirklees Borough Council v Wickes Building Supplies Ltd* [1993] AC 227.
4 (1997) 264 *ENDS Report* 43.
5 *Castle v St Augustines Links Ltd* (1922) 38 TLR 615.
6 *Attorney-General v Keyner Brick and Tile Co Ltd* (1903) 67 JP 434.
7 [1961] 2 All ER 145.
8 [1993] 5 LMELR 6.

4.3 PRIVATE NUISANCE

A private nuisance occurs when one person unlawfully interferes with another person's use or enjoyment of land, or of some right over or in connection with it.[1] The basic situation will generally be that one person interferes, usually for some substantial length of time, with another's use and enjoyment of his property, or with that property's physical nature. The basis for action is the unreasonable use of the defendant's land, although certain conditions must be satisfied before such a situation is actionable. First, the alleged nuisance must affect land other than that in the occupation of the defendant. Secondly, a nuisance will generally be a continuing wrong, ie a long-standing, unreasonable use of land, although a single deleterious incident may be evidence of a continuing 'state of affairs'. However, a serious and grave single incident may amount in itself to a nuisance where the consequences to the plaintiff are serious (see *British Celanese Ltd v AH Hunt (Capacitors) Ltd*,[2] where a high wind blew the defendant's metallic strips about an industrial estate so that the plaintiff's electrical equipment was short-circuited). Finally, the plaintiff must show that the damage suffered is 'real' or 'sensible' in that it is measurable in some way.[3]

4.3.1 For what is a remedy available?

What is remediable by way of an action for nuisance will be *either* interference with the use and enjoyment of land, for example where a right to pure air is infringed by unpleasant smells invading land from a neighbouring pig farm,[4] *or* physical interference with the land, which may be hard to prove where a nuisance affects the atmosphere only. The remedy may, however, extend to the incidental loss of enjoyment of land consequent on personal affectation of a landholder or occupier by the nuisance, as where, for example, an occupier is forced to abandon the use of a garden because to go there would expose him to coughing and retching brought on by fumes emitted by a neighbouring factory. However, the distinction between what may be called 'use and enjoyment' cases and 'physical damage' cases is important, because in the former the burden of proving that there has been an unreasonable activity is generally greater than in the latter, while the influence of location also plays a part.[5]

4.3.2 'Give and take'

An interference with the use and enjoyment of land is measured, in part at least, by reference to the locality of that land. As nuisance is a tort based essentially on the notion of 'mutual give and take' where activities are subject

1 *Howard v Walker* [1947] KB 860.
2 [1969] 1 WLR 959.
3 *Swindon Waterworks Co Ltd v Wilts and Berks Canal Navigation Co* (1875) LR 7 HL 697.
4 *Bone v Seale* [1975] 1 WLR 797.
5 *St Helens Smelting Co v Tipping* (1865) 11 HL Cas 642 at 650, per Lord Westbury, a case where fumes from the defendants' works led to physical deterioration in the state of the plaintiffs' land.

to restraint only where they transgress notions of 'reasonable', ie generally acceptable, behaviour, it follows that those who live in the centres of towns and cities may have to put up with more by way of smells, for example, than those living in suburban areas.[1] Furthermore, as land uses change consequent on development permitted under planning law, the character of an area may alter so that what was unacceptable in the context of an area at one time may become acceptable over time and part of the normal pattern of 'give and take within an area'.[2]

Whether in any given case the bounds of 'mutual give and take' have been exceeded will depend on a weighing of many factors – including locality. Others include the actual pattern of the defendant's use of land – everyday uses are unlikely to attract liability provided they are carried out conveniently and with reasonable care and skill. The burden of taking preventive action will also be considered, as will the practicability of prevention. On the other hand, the seriousness and extent of the interference with the plaintiff will also be taken into account, and the extent and nature of the harm suffered. The social value of both the damaged interest and the defendant's activity will be weighed in the balance.[3] A plaintiff will not, however, be able to recover if the damage suffered is only to some abnormally sensitive operation, ie a use of land which requires exceptional freedom from damaging circumstances.[4] However, damages for injury to a sensitive operation can be granted where other substantial interference with land or its use and enjoyment is otherwise proved. In *McKinnon Industries Ltd v Walker*[5] atmospheric emissions from the defendant's factory deleteriously affected the plaintiff's greenhouses, plants and shrubs, and also his orchids, the growing of which is a very sensitive operation.

4.3.3 State of mind

The defendant's state of mind, ie whether he acted intentionally or negligently, is not always a factor to be considered, because it will not always be a defence to argue that 'all reasonable care and skill were used'. In some cases the defendant's state of mind will 'tip the balance' in determining whether a particular activity exceeds what is mutually acceptable 'give and take', as in *Hollywood Silver Fox Farm Ltd v Emmett*[6] where the defendant maliciously instigated the firing of guns on his own land but close to that of the plaintiff so that the plaintiff's breeding foxes miscarried. The noise itself was on the

1 *Colls v Home and Colonial Stores Ltd* [1904] AC 179 at 185, per Lord Halsbury.
2 *Gillingham Borough Council v Medway (Chatham) Dockyard Co Ltd* [1993] QB 343; *Wheeler v JJ Saunders Ltd* [1995] 2 All ER 697; and *Hunter v Canary Wharf Ltd, Hunter v London Docklands Development Corporation* [1996] 1 All ER 482 (CA).
3 *Kennaway v Thompson* [1981] QB 88.
4 *Robinson v Kilvert* (1889) 41 ChD 88; *Bridlington Relay Ltd v Yorkshire Electricity Board* [1965] Ch 436; and *Hunter v Canary Wharf Ltd, Hunter v London Docklands Development Corporation* [1996] 1 All ER 482 (CA), [1997] 2 WLR 684 (HL).
5 (1951) 3 DLR 577.
6 [1936] 2 KB 468.

boundary of acceptability, but the malice in creating it was enough to make it actionable.

The following atmospheric affectations have been held to be actionable as nuisances in the past: creating stenches;[1] causing fumes or noxious smoke to pass over another's land;[2] raising clouds of coal dust;[3] and emitting large black smuts and other fumes.[4] In contrast, the following are not actionable: spoiling a view;[5] restricting the flow of air onto a neighbour's land;[6] and taking away light from a neighbour's windows.[7] In the latter two instances, there may, however, be an easement; for example a right of light in respect of interference with which an action may be taken. In general, it may be argued that, at least as far as 'use and enjoyment' cases are concerned, a landowner is entitled to have the air over his land untainted and unpolluted by the acts of neighbours, ie air not incompatible with a physically comfortable existence, although such air may not always be as pure as, for example, it was when the landowner first erected a dwelling on the land. It should be noted that the burden of proving an interference with the use and enjoyment of property is generally considered to be heavier than in a case of physical damage to property.[8]

Before liability in nuisance can be established, there are a number of issues to be dealt with, such as:

- proving the nuisance;
- determining who may sue;
- determining who may be sued;
- deciding for what damage a defendant is liable;
- considering whether any defences are available;
- determining the appropriate remedy.

4.3.4 Proving the nuisance

Proving the existence of a nuisance is not easy as a question of fact and causation. As has already been stated, most nuisances arise out of 'state of affairs', ie they are continuing matters. An affectation of someone's property may not be initially noticed. Once damage is apparent, of course, the plaintiff will wish to obtain a private remedy and must amass sufficient technical evidence to satisfy the court that on the balance of probabilities it was the

1 *Walter v Selfe* (1851) 4 DeG & Sm 315; *Bainbridge v Chertsey Urban District Council* (1914) LJ Ch 626.

2 *Crump v Lambert* (1867) LR 3 Eq 409; *St Helens Smelting Co v Tipping* (1865) 11 HL Cas 642.

3 *Pwllbach Colliery Co Ltd v Woodman* [1915] AC 634.

4 *Halsey v Esso Petroleum Co Ltd* [1961] 1 WLR 683; *Manchester Corporation v Farnworth* [1930] AC 171.

5 *Attorney-General v Doughty* (1752) 2 Ves Sen 453; *Fishmonger's Co v East India Co* (1752) 1 Dick 163.

6 *Bland v Mosely* (1587), cited in *Aldred's* case (1610) 9 Co Rep 576, 58a, and *Chastey v Ackland* [1895] 2 Ch 389.

7 *Dalton v Angus* (1881) 6 App Cas 740.

8 *St Helens Smelting Co v Tipping* (1865) 11 HL Cas 642.

defendant's activities that caused the loss suffered. Thus, in a case where it is alleged that particular substances have been emitted from a plant and that these are toxic to animals and humans, it is not necessary to show that the defendant knew the exact physico-chemical details of the process that led to the emissions. Foreseeability is satisfied if the defendant knows generally that a particular operation or activity can result in the production of particular pollutants. What has to be shown is knowledge that the plant can and does emit such toxic substances, *and* that these substances were actually emitted and that they were transmitted to the plaintiff's land where, for example, they were ingested by the plaintiff's animals which, in consequence thereof, suffered the injury complained of.[1] To amass such a body of proof it will be necessary to have:

- 'times and events' records detailing pollution incidents, their duration, persistence, and recurrence;
- expert evidence able to show the causal link between the actual emissions and the injuries complained of;
- other technical and monitoring evidence to confirm flow rates and quantities of pollutants passing from the defendant's to the plaintiff's land;
- soil and plant analysis samples to show the degree of affectation of the land – which is not easy to show where an area has been subject historically to past pollution;
- the assistance of local environmental health officers to confirm pollution details and also to confirm past warnings given under pollution regulation regimes;
- photographic evidence showing the 'before and after' state of affected property, together with other sample evidence verified as indicating the occurrence and extent of a particular pollution incident, for example clothes from a washing line ruined by smuts.

None of the above is easily obtained, and many claims for nuisance are never brought because potential plaintiffs cannot or do not undertake a systematic and regular approach to evidence-gathering. Furthermore, the cost element involved in gathering evidence and taking an action all the way through its initial phases, followed by yet further costs in actually fighting the case in court, may prove to be prohibitive – particularly where complex scientific issues are involved. For example, in *Graham and Graham v Rechem International*,[2] the total cost of the action (which at the time was the longest-running single civil action in English legal history, taking some 14 months in court) was approximately £7 million. For the plaintiffs the cost was borne by the legal aid fund, while the defendants recouped some of their costs from their insurers. However, other features of the case need to be noted.

- The writ in respect of the alleged damage was issued some six years after the occurrence, and was not served until 12 months later, which was in compliance with the then in force Rules of the Supreme Court.

---

1 *Graham and Graham v Rechem International* [1995] 7 ELM 175.
2 [1995] 7 ELM 175.

- In the meantime, the plant alleged to be the source of the nuisance had closed, its workforce had been dispersed, and documentation had been stowed in a variety of places. This inevitably placed a strain on the memories of witnesses when they came to court almost 10 years after the events in question.
- The preliminary proceedings were contentious in themselves, with the initially broad claim by the plaintiffs being met with requests for further and better particulars from the defendants, which the plaintiffs claimed were oppressive and would not be answered until the defendants released certain documents. The defendants then counter-argued that they could not determine what documentation would be relevant until the details requested were specified, and that the plaintiffs were engaging in a 'fishing expedition'. The defendants further served interrogatories on the plaintiffs about the alleged damage in order to establish the factual issues involved – another lengthy, time-consuming and expensive process, but one found to be essential.
- By the end of the case, some 7,000 documents had been disclosed; the best way of digesting these was to schedule them so that the various items of information could be collated to enable the trial judge to appreciate the pattern of events.
- There were, additionally, 55 expert reports exchanged, and it was found early on in the proceedings to be essential to identify relevant scientific disciplines and appropriate technical experts. The disciplines included incineration, meteorology, veterinary science, toxicology, monitoring of the environment, plume-dispersion modelling, metallurgy, agricultural valuation and accountancy.
- To keep down the cost of expert witnesses, resort was had to witness statements and the strict timetabling of the case so that experts were not kept waiting with their costs mounting, especially where they had come from abroad.[1]

4.3.5 Who may sue?

The traditional view has long been that a person with no interest in the land in question cannot sue in nuisance.[2] Thus, a freeholder, a leaseholder, a licensee with a right of exclusive occupation may sue,[3] as may a person with de facto possession of the land.[4] Even a person with a merely reversionary interest in land can sue if permanent damage to the reversion can be shown to exist. More recently, however, it was argued that possession of land is not needed to ground an action; it is enough to be able to show a substantial link between

1 See, further, Nicole Paradise, '*Graham and Graham v Rechem International Ltd*: Some Problems in Environmental Litigation' [1996] 8 ELM 141.
2 *Malone v Laskey* [1907] 2 KB 141.
3 *Newcastle under Lyme Corporation v Wolstanton Ltd* [1947] Ch 427.
4 *Foster v Warblington Urban District Council* [1906] 1 KB 648.

land and its enjoyment, as, for example, where someone, such as the freeholder's child, occupies land as his home.[1] However, the House of Lords rejected that argument by a majority verdict in *Hunter v Canary Wharf Ltd*[2] and reasserted the traditional understanding. The House of Lords was clear that where a nuisance affects a property, each member of that property's occupying family does not have a separate course of action.[3] Equally, their Lordships were insistent that, as in *Malone v Laskey*[4] someone with a 'mere licence' to occupy a property, for example as the spouse or child of its owner or tenant, has no right to sue, although the position is different where the injured party's licence grants him an exclusive right to possession.

A person may sue in respect of damage caused either before or after acquisition of the land, provided there is a continuing nuisance,[5] but (and, of course, this is a general rule) only in respect of damage recognised by law. In this context, it must be remembered that the law does not recognise mere aesthetic nuisances, such as the obscuring of a view by atmospheric pollution. Furthermore, the burden of proof is on the plaintiff, as already stated, and in relation to damage, alleged to have resulted as a consequence of the release of fumes or smell, there must be proof of actual damage as opposed to a mere 'sensible alteration' in the quality of the air.[6]

4.3.6 Who can be sued?

Clearly, the perpetrator of a nuisance can be sued for it, assuming that that person can be found and the necessary causal link established.[7] Interestingly, it appears that the perpetrator remains liable even where he has no power to abate the nuisance. However, what of the situation where the perpetrator is not the occupier of the land whence the nuisance emanates? The occupier of land is liable for the acts of his servants and others under his control, for example members of his family or licensees on his land.[8] Likewise, there will be liability for the 'non-delegable' acts of an independent contractor. In *Cassidy v Minister of Health*,[9] Lord Denning said that in situations where the occupier 'is himself under a duty to use care, he cannot get rid of his responsibility by delegating the performance of it to someone else, no matter whether the delegation be to a servant under a contract of service or to an independent contractor under a contract for services'. The cases appear to establish that such 'non-delegable' duties arise where the activities in question lead to special dangers for

---

1 *Hunter v Canary Wharf Ltd* [1996] 1 All ER 482 (CA).
2 [1997] 2 WLR 684.
3 *Rust v Victoria Graving Dock Co and London and St Katharine Dock Co* (1887) 36 ChD 113.
4 [1907] 2 KB 141.
5 *Masters v Brent London Borough Council* [1978] 1 QB 841.
6 *Halsey v Esso Petroleum Co Ltd* [1961] 1 WLR 683.
7 *Thompson v Gibson* (1841) 7 M & W 456; *Southport Corporation v Esso Petroleum Co Ltd* [1953] 3 WLR 773; *Sedleigh Denfield v O'Callaghan* [1940] AC 880.
8 *White v Jameson* (1874) LR 18 Eq 303.
9 [1951] 2 KB 343 at 363.

neighbours such as: interferences with rights of support;[1] the making of noise and dust;[2] creating fire hazards;[3] and creating nuisances on a highway.[4]

Occupiers are not, however, generally liable for nuisances caused by the actions of their predecessors in title, unless they have actual or constructive knowledge of the state of affairs which amounts to continuing or 'adopting' the nuisance.[5] Similarly, liability does not generally arise for the activities of trespassers unless the nuisance is continued or 'adopted', ie an occupier knows of the nuisance *and* appreciates the risk it poses *and* does nothing to bring it to an end. Knowledge alone, however, is not enough; there must also be a failure to take reasonable abatement action, bearing in mind the occupier's means and abilities.[6] Liability will be even clearer where an occupier actually utilises the deleterious situation to add to harm caused.[7] Where a nuisance arises from 'an act of nature', such as a latent defect in property, there will be no liability; but there will be liability where such a nuisance is adopted, or where an occupier with actual or constructive knowledge of the situation fails to take reasonably early and effective abatement action.[8]

4.3.7 Position of landlords

Landlords out of possession are generally not liable for nuisances committed by their tenants unless a landlord has authorised the nuisance in advance,[9] although 'authorisation' may be taken to be given if the nuisance is the natural and necessary consequence of the purpose of the letting.[10] Where such a nuisance is the 'inevitable consequence', the fact that the tenant has covenanted not to commit a nuisance or to abate a nuisance existing at the time of the lease will not avail the landlord as a defence.[11]

4.3.8 For what damage is the defendant liable?

A defendant may be liable to a plaintiff for the totality of the loss suffered, even where the defendant is only one of a number of tortfeasors who have together caused the harm, in circumstances both where there is another tortfeasor whose acts alone would have been enough to cause the harm complained of, and where the deleterious consequence is the product of cumulative acts by a number of persons.[12] Liability will also arise in the case of a 'cumulative

1 *Bower v Peate* (1876) 1 QB 0321.
2 *Matania v National Provincial Bank Ltd and Elevenist Syndicate Ltd* [1936] 2 All ER 633.
3 *Spicer v Smee* [1946] 1 All ER 489.
4 *Holliday v National Telephone Co* [1899] 2 QB 392.
5 *St Anne's Well Brewery Co v Roberts* (1928) 140 LT 1.
6 *King v Liverpool City Council* [1986] 1 WLR 890; *Page Motors Ltd v Epsom and Ewell Borough Council* (1982) 80 LGR 337.
7 *Sedleigh-Denfield v O'Callaghan* [1940] AC 880.
8 *Leakey v National Trust for Places of Historic Interest or Natural Beauty* [1978] QB 849.
9 *Pwllbach Colliery Co v Woodman* [1915] AC 634.
10 *Tetley v Chitty* [1986] 1 All ER 663.
11 *Brew Brothers Ltd v Snax (Ross) Ltd* [1970] 1 QB 612.
12 *Pride of Derby and Derbyshire Angling Association v British Celanese Ltd* [1952] 1 All ER 1326.

nuisance' where the actions of the individuals concerned would not, taken in isolation, be actionable,[1] although in all such cases it appears necessary for each 'contributor' to have an awareness of the activities of the others.[2] It is, of course, also essential for the necessary causal link to be established.[3]

A limit is, nevertheless, set to a defendant's liability in that damages can be claimed only for foreseeable losses. This, of course, has long been the rule in negligence, and it made an incursion into the realms of nuisance in *Overseas Tankships (UK) Ltd v Miller SS Co Pty, The Wagon Mound (No 2)*.[4] The issue has been put beyond question – in principle at least – by the decision in *Cambridge Water Co v Eastern Counties Leather plc*.[5] There, a water source was discovered to be unusable for drinking purposes because it did not comply with standards laid down by EC Directive 80/778/EEC (Drinking Water), even though the polluting chemicals had entered the water table long before the Directive was promulgated. Those who had spilled the material in the past could not have foreseen the development of the EC standards, and the House of Lords determined that foreseeability of the *type* of damage which has eventuated is a precondition of liability in nuisance. In the instant case the damage, ie that the water source could not be commercially used because of its failure to reach EC standards, was not foreseeable by those responsible for the spillages, and, hence, there could be no liability.

What is it that the defendant must foresee? Clearly, any release of a polluting substance into an environmental medium will cause 'harm' in a very broad, general sense. However, it appears that this is not enough to ground liability; instead there must be a *type* of harm that is foreseeable. By analogy with the tort of negligence it is clear that 'type' is not to be confused with 'extent' of damage, nor with the exact way in which it comes about. Negligence cases have, moreover, tended to take a 'broad' view of what is meant by 'type'. Thus, damage by impact, damage by fire (including explosion) and damage by fouling are three broad 'types' of damage.[6] In *The Trecarrell*,[7] a drum of inflammable material was dropped across an electric cable which was severed, and which short-circuited, giving off sparks. These sparks inflated the material escaping from the drum, and the spread of fire ignited other drums of similar material already in the hold of the ship. Extensive damage was done to the ship and the quay where it was moored, and it was considered that the 'type' of damage, ie by burning, was foreseeable. It is not, however, easy to reconcile the negligence cases with the actual outcome in the *Cambridge Water* case (above) where, on the facts, the 'type' of damage which must be foreseen would appear to be specific. Anyone who spills chemicals should surely foresee that the receiving

1 *Thorpe v Brumfitt* (1873) LR 8 Ch App 650.
2 *Lambton v Mellish* [1894] 3 Ch 163.
3 *Clarke v Newsam* (1847) 1 Exch 131.
4 [1967] 1 AC 617.
5 [1994] 2 AC 264.
6 *Overseas Tankship (UK) Ltd v Morts Dock & Engineering Co, The Wagon Mound (No 1)* [1961] AC 388; *Vacwell Engineering Co Ltd v BDH Chemicals Ltd* [1971] 1 QB 88.
7 [1973] 1 Lloyd's Rep 402.

medium will be, to an extent, contaminated by them; but that would not appear to be enough to ground liability. Instead, it appears that there must be foresight of a particular type of pollution, ie that the receiving medium will become harmful in itself or will be put into an unlawful condition for a particular purpose. On this basis liability is not likely to arise in cases of cumulative spillages of material not considered harmful at the time of spilling. On the other hand, much may depend on the facts of individual cases. Thus, in *Paterson v Humberside County Council*,[1] liability arose when a tree's roots dried out the soil around a house and damaged it on the basis that the soil conditions in the area were well known and the outcome was foreseeable. Some releases into the atmosphere likely to result in harm will result in foreseeable types of damage, for example the releases of smuts in *Halsey v Esso Petroleum Co Ltd*.[2] On the other hand, there could be a slow, insidious release of chemicals which could apparently disperse in the air, although they could actually be accumulating slowly inside some other medium, such as a tree or a building, only to become apparent as damage later on. It may be that what will sway the court in such cases in nuisance in determining what 'type' of damage must be foreseen will be the known characteristics of the material at the time of its release, coupled with the character and nature of the property damaged, and whether that damage is of an open and obvious kind or is simply 'technical' damage because the property is no longer fit for a purpose determined by reference to legislation made after the release in question. From a practical point of view, however, the difficulties of determining what is or is not foreseeable will probably pale into insignificance compared with the issue of showing factual causation as discussed above, and it could well be that proving causation in relation to a particular item of damage may be enough by itself to convince a court that the damage suffered was also foreseeable.

4.4 DEFENCES

4.4.1 Prescription

'Prescription', ie the patent continuance of an actionable *private* nuisance (as opposed to a mere activity) for 20 years without permission, and without the use of force, on one piece of land, as against another piece of land (the servient tenement), will be a defence to an action in nuisance. In practice, prescription is rarely used because the defendant must prove all the elements above while also showing that the damage was unknown and unsuspected by the owner of the servient tenement.[3] Furthermore, abuse of a prescriptive right is unacceptable and, therefore, once established, the activity must be carried on in a way causing the least annoyance according to prevailing contemporary standards.[4]

1 (1996) 12 Const LJ 64.
2 [1961] 1 WLR 683.
3 *Scott-Whitehead v National Coal Board* (1985) 53 P & CR 263.
4 *Shoreham Urban District Council v Dolphin Canadian Proteins Ltd* (1972) 71 LGR 261.

4.4.2 Statutory authority

Statutory authority is a more likely defence, but here everything will depend upon the wording of the relevant legislation, and the courts tend to interpret legislation so as to reduce the ambit of statutory exemptions.[1] Thus, where a statute commands the doing of an act, and that act necessarily results in a nuisance or other injury, there will generally be no liability either for the nuisance or any other consequence proved to be a necessary consequence of the activity by the defendant. On the other hand, if a statute is merely permissive, the general rule is that authority is given only to do the act without causing a nuisance or other injurious act. However, over these simple concepts the individual wording of statutes (particularly local legislation) has woven an elaborate filigree of situations.

The initial starting point is to see whether the statute in question has specifically preserved civil liability in respect of the offending activity.[2] In such a case, statutory authority will not be an issue. At the other end of the scale, the existence of a special statutory scheme of compensation, taken with other appropriate exclusionary words and phrases, may be conclusive of the exemption of the authorised activity from common law liability.

The next question is to determine the nature of the function authorised by the statute. Where the statute is imperative, ie where it lays a duty on a body to achieve an object, clear words may exempt the body from any liability at all; otherwise there will usually be liability only where it can be shown there was 'negligence' in carrying out the activity. Where a statute is permissive (ie grants powers), in the absence of negligence there will usually be no liability for any consequential nuisances, although a statute may make the empowered body liable even in the absence of negligence.[3]

Much clearly depends on whether the statute exempts the activity in question from liability in the absence of 'negligence', which has a particular meaning in this situation. Where a defendant seeks to show that a nuisance was either the necessary consequence of what was authorised by statute, or that the operation in question was carried on with all the reasonable care and skill required by the statute, it is necessary for him to show 'due diligence', ie the exercise of all reasonable scientific care and skill. In deciding the issue the court will then consider what the costs of avoiding the nuisance would have been,[4] whether the activity would properly have been carried on elsewhere,[5] and the actual nature of the authorised activity itself. In *Allen v Gulf Oil Refining Ltd*,[6] it was

1 *Tate & Lyle Food and Distribution Ltd v GLC* [1983] 1 All ER 1159.

2 *Pride of Derby and Derbyshire Angling Association v British Celanese Ltd* [1953] Ch 149.

3 See, generally, *Department of Transport v North West Water* [1984] AC 336; *Hammond v St Pancras Vestry* (1874) LR 9 CP 316; and *Stretton's Derby Brewery v Derby Corporation* [1894] 1 Ch 431 (liability in 'duty'); *Midwood & Co v Manchester Corporation* [1905] 2 KB 597 (liability in 'power').

4 *Manchester Corporation v Farnworth* [1930] AC 171.

5 *Metropolitan Asylum District v Hill* (1881) 6 App Cas 193; *London, Brighton and South Coast Railway Co v Truman* (1886) 11 App Cas 45.

6 [1981] AC 1001.

accepted that where an oil refinery is authorised by statute, Parliament must have accepted that some amount of odour nuisance would be inescapable. Thus:

- where a defendant is acting under a duty, and liability for nuisance is imposed, actual liability will be dependent on proof of 'negligence', as outlined above;
- where a defendant is acting under a power, and no liability for nuisance is imposed, actual liability will depend on proof of 'negligence';
- where a defendant is acting under a power, and liability for nuisance is imposed, actual liability will not depend on proof of 'negligence'.

4.4.3 Effect of a grant of planning permission

Following the decision in *Gillingham Borough Council v Medway (Chatham) Dock Co Ltd*[1] and certain remarks therein by Buckley J, it was fashionable to argue that a grant of planning permission could be analogous to statutory authority in granting exemption from liability in nuisance. However, the better view of the law, following *Wheeler v JJ Saunders Ltd*,[2] is that the core issue is whether a grant of permission has led to such changes in the character of an area that what might at one time have been a nuisance is no longer such. This approach was confirmed in *Hunter v Canary Wharf Ltd, Hunter v London Docklands Development Corporation*.[3] The contrary is also apparently true, as there appears to be no prohibition on a local planning authority pursuing planning policies which have the effect of bringing together incompatible land uses, so that what was once non-actionable in nuisance may become so.[4] Thus, old industrial uses of land may be forced to quit an area because new residential uses are being introduced which will lead to complaints about the industrial activities, odours and emissions etc, and this can be a perfectly acceptable planning policy provided it is not pursued solely to advance the interests of particular known individuals.[5]

4.4.4 Ineffectual defences

It is no defence to show that a nuisance existed in an area before the plaintiff's arrival, arguing that the plaintiff 'came to the nuisance',[6] which, of course, can be related back to the point made above that planning policy may bring together incompatible land uses so that incomers to an area can complain about nuisances created by those already there. On the other hand, it appears that consent may be a defence in an appropriate case. If a person knows of a nuisance and its risks to property, but, nevertheless, has shown in word and/or deed a willingness to accept the risk, there may be no liability.[7]

---

1 [1992] 3 WLR 449.
2 [1995] 2 All ER 697.
3 [1996] 1 All ER 482 (CA).
4 *R v Exeter City Council ex parte Thomas & Co Ltd* [1991] 1 QB 471.
5 *Stringer v Minister of Housing and Local Government* [1971] 1 All ER 65.
6 *Sturgess v Bridgman* (1879) 11 ChD 852.
7 *Leakey v National Trust for Places of Historic Interest and Natural Beauty* [1980] QB 485.

Similarly, where the act bringing about the nuisance is that of a third party, to plead *novus actus interveniens* will be no defence if the act in question is what the defendant ought to have foreseen when the situation with the potential to result in a nuisance was created. Neither is it a defence to argue that the defendant was acting for 'the public benefit' – as in *Adams v Ursell*[1] where the defendant set up a smelly chip shop in a 'select' residential area – or that the locality was particularly suited to the defendant's activities, or that others in the same area were carrying on the same activity, or even that the injury was the result of the separate actions of a number of persons.[2]

It will not always be a defence to argue that the nuisance arose from the natural state of the land. In *Leakey v National Trust for Places of Historic Interest and Natural Beauty*,[3] the Court of Appeal argued that no distinction in principle should be drawn between hazards arising out of misfeasance and those otherwise arising, for example by non-feasance or in consequence of the geological or biological state of the land. However, in such cases what is required of a landowner to prevent nuisance will depend, in part at least, on particular factors such as personal capabilities, or resources of individual landowners. Those able to do more to deal with nuisances on their land may be expected to do so. Certainly, in such circumstances it will not be a defence to plead ignorance of the existence of the nuisance – the law imposes liability for what is known or ought to be known.[4] However, in such circumstances where the defendant has not created the physical situation in question, liability will be dependent on showing that the defendant was guilty of some negligence and was thus at fault in that he should have taken action to deal with the situation but failed to do so; the situation is similar where a landlord fails to carry out repairs on property for which he is responsible so that injury eventuates.[5]

4.5 REMEDIES

4.5.1 Damages

In most cases, an award of damages will be the award granted in respect of a proven nuisance. Past loss can easily be compensated by common law damages where physical harm has been suffered because the loss will generally be easy to quantify on the normal basis of calculation for all damages, and thus will reflect the diminished market value of the damaged property.[6] In *Hunter v Canary Wharf Ltd*,[7] Lord Lloyd classified nuisance actions into three types: (1) encroaching on a neighbour's land; (2) directly physically injuring a neighbour's land; and (3) interfering with a neighbour's quiet use and

1 [1913] ChD 269.
2 *Lambton v Mellish* [1894] 3 Ch 163; *Thorpe v Brumfitt* (1873) LR 8 Ch App 650.
3 [1980] QB 485.
4 *Goldman v Hargrave* [1967] 1 AC 645.
5 *Mint v Good* [1951] 1 KB 517, per Lord Denning.
6 *Moss v Christchurch Rural District Council* [1925] 2 KB 750.
7 [1997] 2 WLR 684.

enjoyment of his land. He argued that in all cases the principle underlying awards of damages should be the same, ie that damages should reflect the diminution in value of the land. Even in the case of a 'class 3' nuisance, Lord Lloyd argued, although there may be no loss of market value there will still be damages for a loss of amenity value, which, even though they cannot be assessed mathematically, are still awardable.[1] Lord Hoffmann, in *Hunter*, however, disapproved *dicta* in *Bone v Seale*[2] which indicated that in such cases damages should be calculated by analogy with damage for loss of amenity in personal injury cases. Diminution in capital value will be the main test, but in a case where no such diminution can be shown a value has to be placed on the intangible diminution in the pleasantness of a property during its affectation by the nuisance in question. Lord Hoffmann pointed out that estate agents place valuations on the intangible aspects of properties 'all the time', and, so it is not impossible for courts also to do this. Other relevant issues to the calculation of damages in amenity cases include the size and commodiousness of the property involved, although not the number of the persons in occupation, nor the legal nature of their particular interests in the property. An affected person is also entitled to consequential loss where a nuisance is proved, for example for loss of profits consequent on an inability to use land for the purpose of its occupier's business, or where chattels or livestock are damaged by an invading nuisance. Where future loss is anticipated, equitable damages can, but will rarely, be awarded because, effectively, they allow a defendant to 'pay' for the 'right' to inflict damage. In respect of damage to the use and enjoyment of land the cases appear to make a distinction between transient or minor interference on the one hand, and long-standing or more offensive interferences on the other. Thus, for example, in *Bone v Seale*,[3] where odours from a pig farm had been endured for 12 years, only £1,000 damages were awarded on appeal.[4]

4.5.2 Injunctions

The abatement of a nuisance may also be secured by an injunction. This is technically a discretionary, equitable remedy, although in practice it is nearly always granted where a nuisance is a continuing one.[5] Of course, the plaintiff still has to establish that the nuisance is a substantial interference with rights, and the discretion will not be exercised in favour of someone whose interests have been only marginally or slightly affected.[6] However, once a substantial interference has been established an injunction will usually be issued irrespective of the claimed economic burdens imposed on the defendant, for example that there will be a loss of jobs consequent on compliance.[7] In this connection UK courts could take a leaf from North American practice where courts have refused injunctive relief in cases where the economic cost to the

1 *Ruxley Electronics Ltd v Forsyth* [1996] AC 344.
2 [1975] 1 WLR 797.
3 [1975] 1 All ER 787.
4 See also *Halsey v Esso Petroleum Co Ltd* [1961] 1 WLR 683.
5 *Redland Bricks Ltd v Morris* [1970] AC 652.
6 *Elliot v Islington London Borough Council* [1991] 10 EG 145.
7 *Pennington v Brinsop Hall Coal Co* (1877) 5 ChD 589.

defendant would far outweigh any benefit to the plaintiff. In *Boomer v Atlantic Cement*,[1] and *Maddison v Ducktown Sulphur, Copper and Iron Co*[2] relief was refused because the consequential loss to the community in terms of unemployment was unacceptable. The most recent *dicta* from UK courts suggest, however, that the primary focus of the law remains the vindication of the invaded private rights of the plaintiff.[3]

The inherent flexibility of injunctive relief can be used to ensure that the order is suspended on terms allowing the defendant time for compliance while, on the other hand, a heavy award of damages could have the effect of forcing a small business into liquidation as, it appears happened following *St Helens Smelting Company v Tipping*.[4] Thus, once granted, an injunction may be suspended – an option which may be coupled with an award of damages in respect of losses suffered until implementation. This practice may be followed where immediate, crushing burdens on the defendant could vastly outweigh any immediate benefit to the plaintiff, but it should be noted that suspension rather than refusal is the issue, as opposed to the US practice considered above.[5] A suspended injunction may also be granted, so that an injuncted utility may continue to supply essential services.[6]

Injunctive relief may, of course, take many forms. Examples are:

- a perpetual injunction, which is issued at the final end of proceedings;
- a mandatory order, which requires the defendant to take positive steps to abate a nuisance;
- an interlocutory order, which can be issued pending the outcome of proceedings without prejudging the issue.

Interlocutory injunctions are granted only where the plaintiff establishes that there is a serious issue for trial.[7] It is then for the court to decide whether the balance of convenience lies in favour of granting injunctive relief.[8] Such an interlocutory injunction can be granted even before the occurrence of actual damage, but the plaintiff must be able to show that, if unchecked, the defendant's conduct will almost certainly result in substantial damage.[9]

Mandatory orders are generally awarded only where it is shown that there is a very strong probability of grave future damage, for which damages will not be an adequate remedy. Otherwise, injunctions normally require the defendant

1 257 NE 2d 870 (1970).

2 83 SW 658 (1904).

3 *Kennaway v Thompson* [1981] QB 88; *Elliott v Islington London Borough Council* [1991] 10 EG 145.

4 (1865) 11 HL Cas 642.

5 *Stollmeyer v Petroleum Development Co Ltd* [1918] AC 498; *Halsey v Esso Petroleum Co Ltd* [1961] 2 All ER 145; *Attorney-General v Gastonia Coaches* [1977] RTR 219.

6 *Prices Patent Candle Co v LCC* [1908] 2 Ch 526; *Manchester Corporation v Farnworth* [1930] AC 171.

7 *Laws v Florinplace Ltd* [1981] 1 All ER 659.

8 *American Cyanamid Co v Ethicon Ltd* [1975] AC 396.

9 See *Midland Bank plc v Bardgrove Property Services Ltd* (1992) 37 EG 126 for an example of such a *quia timet* injunction.

only to desist from a particular activity or practice. The amount to be expended by the defendant to ensure compliance will be considered before a mandatory order is made, and it appears that the court will be more inclined to make such an award in the case of a wanton wrongdoer whose activities have already caused harm. A mandatory order must make it clear what is required by way of compliance.[1] It is, of course, possible to obtain both damages and an injunction.[2]

Damages may be awarded in lieu of an injunction under s 50 of the Supreme Court Act 1981, but only exceptionally where the plaintiff's injury is: (a) small; (b) capable of monetary estimation; and (c) adequately compensatable by a small money payment. It must also be considered oppressive to the defendant to issue an injunction.[3]

Injunctive relief may be refused on grounds other than those outlined above, for example where a plaintiff has been guilty of serious misconduct adding to the damage to himself or to others, or where it would be impossible for the court to oversee and enforce any order made. In both cases, injunctions may be refused on the basis that 'he who comes to equity must come with clean hands' and 'equity does nothing in vain'.

4.5.3 Self-help

Self-help will be an appropriate course of action only where there is a patent and simple nuisance, and where going to court for a remedy would not be justifiable in terms of cost. Self-help will also be appropriate in circumstances of emergency where the nuisance threatens to cause immediate harm.[4] Notice should be given to the person responsible for the nuisance before self-help is resorted to, save where the action can be taken without entering that person's land, or where there is the threat of immediate harm, or where the tortfeasor is in actual occupation of the land which is the 'seat of the nuisance'.[5] The consequence of resorting to self-help is the loss of the right to take further legal action in respect of the nuisance, although a right to damages for past loss may remain. Furthermore, in exercising the remedy the plaintiff must not cause unnecessary damage. However, such damage is justifiable if it is necessary to interfere with a wrongdoer's property in order to avoid damage to the property of an innocent third party.[6] The right to abate a nuisance by self-help arises even before actual damage is suffered; but, where injunctive relief in respect of a nuisance is sought and refused, the right to self-help is lost.[7]

1 *Redland Bricks Ltd v Morris* [1970] AC 652.
2 *Tetley v Chitty* [1986] 1 All ER 663.
3 *Shelfer v City of London Electric Lighting Co* [1895] 1 Ch 287; *Kennaway v Thompson* [1981] QB 88; *Blackburn v ARC* (1998) 276 *ENDS Report* 51.
4 *Burton v Winters* [1993] 1 WLR 1077.
5 *Lemmon v Webb* [1895] AC 1.
6 *Lagan Navigation Co v Lambeg Bleaching, Dyeing and Finishing Co Ltd* [1927] AC 226.
7 *Smith v Giddy* [1904] 2 KB 448; *Burton v Winters* [1993] 1 WLR 1077.

4.6 STRICT LIABILITY

As has been argued above, the tort of nuisance can be committed without any fault (ie want of reasonable care) on the part of the defendant. Historically, private nuisance could be categorised as a 'strict liability' tort, ie as one where, at least in some cases, it is no defence to allege that 'all reasonable precautions were taken'. However, as liability in nuisance has become increasingly dependent upon proof of fault there have been arguments for a more developed form of strict liability in respect of damage to a variety of interests. Recently, for example, the EC-proposed Directive on Civil Liability for Damage Caused by Waste[1] proposed strict liability for damage to persons or property or to the wider environment caused by modifications to the physical or biological condition of water, soil and/or air. Although a factual burden of proof would lie on a plaintiff, 'no fault' would not be a defence for a defendant. See also the Comprehensive Environmental Response Compensation Liability Act 1980 (the 'Superfund' legislation) in the USA which, inter alia, imposes strict liabilities in respect of clean-up measures for affected land, and the Council of Europe's Convention on Civil Liability 1993, under which a system of liabilities could arise in respect of certain 'dangerous activities', for example those involving dangerous substances, ie those having properties which constitute a significant risk to humans, the environment or property.

Courts in the UK, however, have been wary of developing notions of strict liability, but to that general statement there are, of course, exceptions.

4.6.1 The rule in *Rylands v Fletcher*

In *Rylands v Fletcher*,[2] Blackburn J and Lord Cairns gave expression to a statement of the law which can be expressed as: persons who:

(a) for their own purposes;
(b) bring, keep and collect on;
(c) their land;
(d) anything likely to do mischief if it escapes;
(e) keep that material at their own risk;
(f) are answerable for all the damage which is the natural consequence of its escape, provided
(g) the defendant's use of the land for this purpose is non-natural.

Each of these statements requires explanation.

Generally, liability is tied to the concept that it is the defendant who should be made liable because it is his 'collection', for his own benefit, which has led to the infliction of loss on another. However, on occasions, occupiers of land who have allowed others to accumulate material on their land have been made responsible for escapes causing damage; so, for example, a company operating sewers, which is statutorily required to permit the discharge of other sewers

1 COM(89) 28L.
2 (1866) LR 1 Ex 265.

into those sewers, may be responsible for escapes of the resulting accumulated material.[1]

There must be an accumulation of material by the artificial bringing, keeping and collecting of material onto a person's land or premises. There is no liability in respect of material naturally on land or naturally accumulating there.[2] A *deliberate* release of material which has collected on land as a result of natural processes, coupled with pre-existing human activity, may be an exception to this principle (see *Whalley v Lancashire and Yorkshire Railway Co*,[3] where flood waters which had arisen naturally and were penned against a railway embankment were released through it onto the plaintiff's land by the defendants in order to reduce pressure on the embankment). The interest of the defendant in the land may be no more than a licence, and it is also possible for liability to arise in respect of accumulations within the strata of land.[4] Indeed, there have been suggestions that liability should be imposed in respect of escapes from something on the highway over which a person has control.[5]

The material must be likely to do injury or cause damage if it escapes. Anything may fall into this conceptual classification in particular circumstances, and certainly liability is not limited to things which are considered 'dangerous' per se.[6] Liability may be avoided, however, where the defendant shows that the material is not likely to do harm.[7]

There must be an escape from the place of accumulation to a place outside the defendant's control,[8] although what 'escapes' need not be the actual material accumulated but rather the consequences of that accumulation, for example material blasted off site by explosives gathered on it.[9]

The accumulation must be a 'non-natural' use of the land, ie some kind of special use which brings with it increased dangers to other persons, and which is not merely an ordinary use of land, nor one which is proper for the general benefit of the community.[10] This issue has been one of the most controversial features of the rule. The great 'high point' of liability under *Rylands v Fletcher* was the period between the First and Second World Wars, when liability was imposed for 'escapes' as varied and bizarre as flagpoles,[11] and chairoplanes in fairgrounds.[12] Since 1945, however, one has to comb with care the law reports

1 *Smeaton v Ilford Corporation* [1954] Ch 450.
2 *Pontardawe Rural District Council v Moore-Gwyn* [1929] 1 Ch 656; *Giles v Walker* (1890) 24 QBD 656.
3 (1884) 13 QBD 131.
4 *Charing Cross West End and City Electricity Supply Co v London Hydraulic Power Ltd* [1914] 3 KB 772.
5 *Rigby v Chief Constable of Northamptonshire* [1985] 2 All ER 985.
6 *Sullivan v Creed* [1904] 21 R 317.
7 *West v Bristol Tramway Co* [1908] 2 KB 14.
8 *Read v Lyons and Co Ltd* [1947] AC 156.
9 *Miles v Forest Rock Granite Co (Leicestershire) Ltd* (1918) 34 TLR 500.
10 *Rickards v Lothian* [1913] AC 263.
11 *Shiffman v Venerable Order of St John of Jerusalem* [1936] 1 All ER 557.
12 *Hale v Jennings Brothers* [1938] 1 All ER 579.

to find reports of successful *Rylands v Fletcher* actions. Therefore, for example, it appears doubtful that there could be liability in respect of petrol vapour 'accumulated' in the tanks of motor coaches stored on waste land, as this is 'natural'.[1] More pertinently, it appears to follow from the decision in *British Celanese v AH Hunt Ltd*[2] that the use of premises for storing industrial components in an industrial estate was 'natural'. One could have been forgiven for believing that any use of land specifically consented by planning permission would be considered 'natural'. However, just as planning permission is not a license to commit nuisances, a grant of permission, or an established use right, will not make a particular activity 'natural'. In *Mason v Levy Auto Parts of England Ltd*,[3] it was held that storing large amounts of combustible material in premises was non-natural, bearing in mind the quantity stored, the mode of storage and the character of the neighbourhood. More recently, in *Cambridge Water Co v Eastern Counties Leather plc*,[4] the House of Lords considered that the storage and use of chemicals in substantial quantities on an industrial site in a village where industries were well-established was an 'almost classic' case of non-natural use.

It is impossible to draw up a catalogue of natural and non-natural uses; instead, the concept should be used analytically to distinguish unusual from everyday situations. Thus, to provide heat and power to a business park from a common service network of pipes in the ground may be argued to be an everyday general community benefit which is nowadays accepted as a 'natural use' of that land. On the other hand, where an abnormal or extraordinary risk is created, such as where chemical or combustible material is stored in quantity, then the use of land is non-natural, even where the storage leads to indirect community benefit by creating employment.

Where an incident satisfies the foregoing requirements prima facie liability is strict, provided, following the *Cambridge Water* case, the damage suffered is of a foreseeable type – a restrictive notion which indicates the unwillingness of UK courts to create a general rule of liability in respect of injury arising from ultra-hazardous activities. However, there may be other circumstances which lead to a denial of liability.

4.6.2 Damage suffered is not of a type contemplated by the rule

It is doubtful whether there can be recovery for pure economic loss, ie loss of a money-making opportunity.[5] The 'pure economic loss' exemption does not extend to cases where economic loss results from physical damage to a person or property, and that 'damage' may be a simple physical change in the person/property in question. More controversially, it has been suggested in Australia

1 *Perry v Kendricks Transport Ltd* [1956] 1 WLR 85, although that case was decided on another issue.
2 [1969] 2 All ER 1252.
3 [1967] 2 QB 530.
4 [1994] 2 AC 264.
5 *Weller & Co v Foot and Mouth Disease Institute* [1966] 1 QB 569.

that liability may extend to a person who suffers economic loss as a result of purchasing or possessing property which has already been damaged by pollution, and that extends to cases where the property in question is/was an animal and where that animal has been purchased either alive or dead (eg in the form of meat).[1]

It is also debatable whether there can be recovery for personal injuries. During the 'high water' years of liability under *Rylands v Fletcher*, it was argued as being beyond doubt that recovery for personal injuries was possible, and there was authority to that effect.[2] However, the House of Lords doubted whether recovery was possible in *Read v J Lyons and Co Ltd*,[3] and the point was specifically left open in *Dunne v North Western Gas Board*[4] and in the *Cambridge Water* case (above). On the argument that liability in *Rylands v Fletcher* is merely a subspecies of nuisance, it can further be argued that liability for personal injury may be confined to injuries suffered by those who are in legal possession of land, or have some recognised interest therein. Thus, *Hale v Jennings Brothers*,[5] where a fairground concessionaire was injured by an 'escaping chairoplane' from a roundabout, would still be good law.

A concomitant issue is whether a person needs an interest of some sort in land to be able to sue at all under *Rylands v Fletcher*. *Charing Cross Electricity Supply Co v Hydraulic Power Co*[6] was a case where a licensee recovered damages. In addition, damages were recovered for atmospheric-borne smut damage to a car parked on the highway in *Halsey v Esso Petroleum Co Ltd*.[7] However, in this instance it is possible to argue that since an action in nuisance is available to a freeholder/leaseholder who holds an interest in land by virtue of possessing it and living there as his home (and, similarly, a licensee with exclusive occupation), recovery ought to be allowed in respect of damage to chattels where this is suffered as a necessary incident of that occupation of the home. Thus, where a householder's car is damaged in the street outside that person's home by an escape of noxious vapours from a local chemical plant, recovery in respect of the damage to the car is necessarily incidental to occupation of the dwelling – particularly where the dwelling has also been affected by the escape. However, in the case of an occupant of a dwelling who has no legally recognised interest in the property by way of freehold or leasehold possession etc, it appears that liability may only arise by virtue of the rule in *Rylands v Fletcher* – and possibly not even then if that rule is merely a subspecies of nuisance and thus subject to all the restrictive requirements of that tort, as reiterated by the House of Lords in *Hunter v Canary Wharf Ltd*.[8]

1 *McMullin v ICI Australia Operations Pty Ltd* (unreported) 24 June 1997; see (1997) 38 *Environmental Law Bulletin* 39.
2 *Hale v Jennings Brothers* [1938] 1 All ER 579; *Shiffman v Venerable Order of St John of Jerusalem* [1936] 1 All ER 557.
3 [1947] AC 156.
4 [1964] 2 QB 806.
5 [1938] 1 All ER 579.
6 [1914] 3 KB 772.
7 [1961] 2 All ER 145.
8 [1997] 2 WLR 684.

4.6.3 Consent

Where a person expressly or impliedly consents to an accumulation there is no liability in the event of a subsequent escape.[1] Such consent can be implied from entering onto a property knowing that it is affected by an accumulation,[2] but, it appears, is not to be implied merely by living close to hazardous premises such as a chemical factory or a quarry.[3] Contributory negligence may also reduce the defendant's liabilities under the normal principles of the Law Reform (Contributory Negligence) Act 1945. Similarly, the normal principle of the law of nuisance applies: that there is no liability in respect of damage to specially sensitive operations or property.[4]

4.6.4 Common benefit

Where an accumulation is maintained for the common benefit of both parties there may be no liability in respect of an escape, and, arguably, this extends to accumulations etc maintained by utility undertakers for the supply of public services to the community as a whole.[5] Similarly, there will be no liability where the plaintiff's own act or default led to the escape.[6]

4.6.5 Act of a stranger

Perry v Kendricks Transport Ltd[7] is also authority for the proposition that a person is not liable where an act of a stranger, such as a trespasser, caused the escape, provided the defendant could not reasonably have contemplated that presence and had guarded against it. In this context 'a stranger' appears to be one over whom the defendant could exercise no real degree of control,[8] and, therefore, much depends on the facts of each case. If a person accumulates flammable material on land which is left unfenced and unguarded, and trespassers are regularly known to be present there meddling with the property, it may be argued, at least by analogy with criminal liabilities in other areas of environmental regulation, that the defendant is responsible and could not plead act of a stranger.[9] Similarly, much appears to depend on the character of the stranger's act. An occupier *may* not be liable for the deliberate wrongdoing of a third party,[10] but may be liable where a third party has been negligent, as such negligence may be foreseeable by the occupier.[11]

1 *Attorney-General v Cory Brothers and Co Ltd* [1921] 1 AC 521.
2 *Peters v Prince of Wales Theatre (Birmingham) Ltd* [1943] KB 73.
3 *Thomas v Lewis* [1937] 1 All ER 137.
4 *Eastern & South African Telegraph Co Ltd v Cape Town Tramways Companies Ltd* [1902] AC 381.
5 *Dunne v North Western Gas Board* [1964] 2 QB 806.
6 *Perry v Kendricks Transport Ltd* [1956] 1 All ER 154.
7 [1956] 1 All ER 154.
8 *H & N Emmanuel Ltd v Greater London Council* [1971] 2 All ER 835.
9 *National Rivers Authority v Wright Engineering Co Ltd* [1994] 4 All ER 281 (since overruled on other grounds).
10 *Box v Jubb* (1879) 4 ExD 76; *Rickards v Lothian* [1913] AC 263.
11 *North Western Utilities Ltd v London Guarantee & Accident Co Ltd* [1926] AC 108.

4.6.6 Act of God

This, most untheological, defence, arises when an escape occurs without human intervention as a result of natural phenomena in circumstances against which no human forethought could provide, and whose occurrence human prudence could not be expected to recognise as possible. It should be noted that a lack of foreseeability alone is not enough, and there will be very few circumstances which are likely to be categorised as acts of God. Thus, in the water pollution case of *Southern Water Authority v Pegrum*,[1] a fall of heavy rain in the south of England causing slurry lagoons to overflow and break their banks, with consequent pollution of a river, was held to be foreseeable and certainly no act of God.

4.6.7 Statutory authority

The principles applying under *Rylands v Fletcher* in relation to statutory authority are the same as for those in nuisance considered above.

4.6.8 Damage too remote

Following the decision in *Cambridge Water Co v Eastern Counties Leather plc*,[2] the principles for remoteness of damage under *Rylands v Fletcher* are the same as those for nuisance generally (see above). Indeed, the House of Lords in *Cambridge Water* indicated that *Rylands v Fletcher* is merely a subspecies of nuisance, and is a special application of general nuisance principles applying to situations of isolated escapes causing damage and leading to liability even where all reasonable care and skill has been used to prevent an escape.

4.7 STATUTORY LIABILITY

In the context of atmospheric pollution it is likely that relevant liabilities will arise in the form of malodourous releases, or other escapes of an airborne nature. The most relevant legislation is that relating to sewers and drains, gas and waste deposition. There is no single rule governing all releases and escapes; in each case the relevant legislation has to be examined to see whether it is possible to sue directly under the statute for breach of statutory duty, and, if so, whether liability is strict or dependent on proof of fault. In general, there may be liability for breach of a statutory duty where:

- the legislation provides for no other remedy or penalty;[3]
- the legislation creates obligations intended to be for the protection or benefit of particular individuals forming a class;[4]
- a general public right is created and where breach has led to particular damage being suffered by an individual.[5]

---

1 [1989] Crim LR 442.
2 [1994] 2 AC 264.
3 *Cutler v Wandsworth Stadium Ltd* [1949] AC 398.
4 *Lonrho Ltd v Shell Petroleum Co Ltd* [1981] 2 All ER 456.
5 *Ibid.*

What is clear is that there is no general principle that because a service is provided under statute by an undertaker there is a presumption in favour of liability should that service fail.[1]

Thus, where sewers and drains are constructed under statutory authority, the authorities indicate that any liability will be dependent on proof of negligence.[2] Similarly, British Gas, as a 'public supplier of gas', is generally only liable on proof of fault.[3] However, under the Gas Act 1965, s 14, public gas suppliers are 'absolutely liable' for loss of life, personal injury or property damage resulting from the underground storage of gas except where that damage results from the fault of the plaintiff, his servants or agents. There may also be liability for the illegal deposit of waste on land where an offence is committed under s 33(1) of EPA 1990 (see s 73(6)–(9) of that Act). Thus, where controlled waste is deposited on land, or where such waste is knowingly caused or knowingly permitted to be deposited in or on any land, unless a waste management licence authorising that deposit is in force *and* the deposit is in accordance with that licence, and damage is caused, the person responsible is liable for that damage. 'Damage', in this context, includes the death of, or injury to, any person, including affectation by disease and any impairment of physical or mental condition, and extends, inter alia, to loss governed by the Fatal Accidents Act 1976. There is, however, no liability where it can be proved that the damage suffered arose wholly due to the fault of the person who suffered it, or where the victim can be shown to have voluntarily accepted the risk of damage being caused. In addition, there will be no liability where the defendant can show:

- that all reasonable precautions were taken, and all due diligence was exercised in avoiding the commission of an offence;
- that he was acting under his employer's instructions and neither knew nor had reason to suppose that his acts constituted a contravention of the law;
- that the acts in question were done in an emergency to avoid danger to human health in a situation where the defendant took all such steps as were reasonably practicable in the circumstances to minimise pollution of the environment and harm to human health, and particulars of the acts were furnished to the Environment Agency as soon as reasonably practicable.

4.8 NEGLIGENCE LIABILITY

Despite its vast growth and development in the twentieth century, the tort of negligence appears to have had little impact with regard to environmental issues. The main problems appear to lie in establishing the first two 'ingredients' of the tort, namely duty and breach.

1 *Atkinson v Newcastle Waterworks Co* (1877) 2 ExD 441.
2 *Hesketh v Birmingham Corporation* [1924] 1 KB 260.
3 *Pearson v North Western Gas Board* [1968] 2 All ER 669.

4.8.1 Duty of care

Before there can be even potential liability, the situation must be one in which the defendant owes the plaintiff a duty of care. The basic undergraduate notion that this element can be determined simply by applying the 'neighbour' *dictum* of Lord Atkin in *Donoghue v Stevenson*,[1] so dearly cherished for many years, must now be seen as simplistic. Indeed, since *Murphy v Brentwood District Council*,[2] the courts appear to be wary of extending situations in which a duty of care exists. Indeed, even before that case the courts had been slow to impose duties of care in relation to harm of what may be called an environmental nature. Thus, in *Gunn v Wallsend Slipway and Engineering Co Ltd*,[3] there was held to be no duty owed by the defendants in respect of the death by mesothelioma of a woman who had inhaled asbestos dust from clothes worn by her husband as a result of his working in the defendants' shipyard. A similar conclusion was reached in *Hewett v Alf Brown's Transport*,[4] where the facts were similar to *Gunn*, except that the injury arose from working clothes thick with lead oxide. Indeed, it is only recently that plaintiffs have succeeded in obtaining judgments that there can be liability for injury caused by inhalation of asbestos, and then only in very particular circumstances involving gross exposure to the material at a time when it was known to be implicated in the onset of pulmonary complaints.[5]

It is sometimes alleged that a regulatory agency could be under a duty of care to warn of the presence of polluting material, but the better view of the law is that such liability arises only in respect of the supply of polluted material.[6] Indeed, the whole trend of the authorities is that a purely regulatory agency is not liable simply because a person suffers damage from pollution in respect of which a warning could have been given, but was not.[7]

The most recent cases confirm this trend.[8] These cases restate the historic position that civil liability will not arise for a failure to perform a statutory function. It does not appear possible to argue that a sufficient degree of proximity between parties to ground a duty of care arises simply because one has regulatory functions with regard to the other. Civil liability will arise only in limited cases. Thus, if a regulatory authority abuses its powers, as in *Welton v North Cornwall District Council*,[9] and, if in reliance on statements made by the authority or its officers in the course of their *ultra vires* actions, a plaintiff

1 [1932] AC 562.
2 [1991] 1 AC 398.
3 (1989) *The Times*, 23 January.
4 [1992] ICR 530.
5 *Hancock v J W Roberts Ltd, Margereson v The Same* [1996] 8 ELM 8; *Margereson v J W Roberts Ltd, Hancock v The Same* [1996] 8 ELM 118.
6 *Barnes v Irwell Water Board* [1939] 1 KB 21; *Scott-Whitehead v National Coal Board* (1987) 53 P & CR 263.
7 *Dear v Thames Water* 33 Con LR 43; *Ryeford Homes Ltd v Sevenoaks District Council* (1989) 46 BLR 34.
8 *Welton v North Cornwall District Council* [1997] 1 WLR 570; *Stovin v Wise* [1996] 3 All ER 801.
9 [1997] 1 WLR 570.

takes action which leads to loss being suffered, there may be liability under the principles laid down in *Hedley Byrne v Heller*.[1] Similarly, where an authority provides a benefit or service of a routine or uniform nature so that everyone knows what is provided, and it would be irrational to provide the service to one person and to refuse it to another, and there is a general expectation in the community that the authority will act, and there is some policy reason clearly grounded in the relevant legislation which confers a right to compensation, a civil claim may lie.[2] However, these are exceptional cases, and the normal understanding must be that no civil liability will generally arise for the exercise by a regulatory authority of its law-enforcing functions, nor in respect of the provision of advisory services by such an authority if that would otherwise impede the due performance of statutory functions. It is one thing to provide a service at public expense, but it is another to impose compensation requirements in the event that a failure to provide the service results in loss – both as regards the performance of statutory duties and the exercise of statutory powers. This was affirmed in Australia in *McMullin v ICI Australia Operation Pty Ltd*[3] where the Federal Court of Australia stated that the court must determine the nature of the task performed by the defendant which is alleged to have injured the plaintiff. There will be no liability where that task falls within the 'policy remit' of the decision-making body, no matter how foreseeable the deleterious consequences would be to a reasonable person if the task were badly performed. Pointers to whether a task lies in the 'policy remit' of an authority will include whether that authority, in exercising its functions, has to take into account social, financial and economic considerations and also environmental effects.[4] The position is, of course, otherwise where an agency or authority has both policy and operational functions – such as the *supply* of water – and the injury arises in the course of the negligent performance of an operational function.[5]

4.8.2 Breach of duty

Breach of duty of care is probably nowadays best thought of as the unreasonable failure to achieve the law's required standard of care. That standard will itself depend on many factors, such as: the magnitude of the risk created by the defendant's activities, ie its probable gravity, imminence and frequency of occurrence; the utility of the defendant's objectives, ie their social importance; and the burden of taking adequate precautions to obviate the risk. A defendant will, however, be generally taken to have achieved the requisite standard unless it is shown that he failed to act according to the general and approved practices of the particular sphere of activity in question. In this way,

1 [1964] AC 465.

2 *Invercargill County Council v Hamlyn* [1991] 3 NZLR 513.

3 (Unreported) 24 June 1997.

4 See, further, *Murphy v Brentwood District Council* [1991] 1 AC 398; and, for a similar attitude in Scotland, *Landcatch Ltd v Gilbert Gillies*, 1990 SLT 688.

5 For the most recent pronouncement on this matter, see *R v Lam and Brennan (t/a Namesakes of Torbay) and Torbay Borough Council* [1998] PLCR 30, *sub nom R v Lam* [1998] EHLR 111.

as best practice is approved and adhered to a general raising of required standards can be achieved. Even so, it remains a general defence to an allegation of negligence that the usual trade or professional practices were followed – except, of course, where these were obviously inherently risky – or that activities were carried on according to received professional wisdom. Such a defence is not defeated by proof that the defendant made an error of judgment within the ambit of the exercise of reasonable skill, nor where it is shown that he did not know of a risk beyond reasonable scientific appreciation. Much will clearly depend on the outcome of a court's consideration of (lengthy) arguments by (expensive) technical witnesses.

The problems of expense, lack of technological 'know-how' and clashes of expert evidence, already dealt with in relation to nuisance, are of at least equal significance with regard to negligence. For example, in *Pearson v North Western Gas Board*,[1] the plaintiff and her husband were injured and their home destroyed by a gas explosion following an escape from a gas main and an accumulation of this gas under the floorboards of their home. The gas main had been laid in 1878, approximately two feet, nine inches below the surface of the soil, and was of good quality metal expected to last for 120 years. Severe frost had fractured the main but the expert evidence showed that there were no reasonable steps which could have been taken to protect against the consequence of such an occurrence. The expert evidence rebutted the allegation of negligence made against the defendants.

As with the technical issues of conflicting scientific evidence examined above in relation to *Graham and Graham v Rechem International*,[2] plaintiffs are not aided where there is scientific dispute as to the acceptability of expert studies of phenomena. In the April 1997 issue of the *Journal of Epidemiology and Community Health* the results of research carried out at the University of Birmingham were published, arguing that studies of 22,400 children up to the age of 15 dying of leukaemia and other childhood cancers between 1953 and 1980, indicated a 20 per cent higher risk of developing such a condition among those born within five kilometres of certain industrial plants. The highest death tolls were found to occur near oil refineries, car factories, non-nuclear power stations, steelworks, cement works and crematoria, while key pollutants appeared to be petrol fumes and similar volatile organic compounds emitted by high temperature furnaces and kilns, and spraying plant. Similarly, near to motorways and railways (ie within four kilometres) there was an alleged incidence of cancer between 15 and 20 per cent higher than would be expected – with fewer deaths than would be expected beyond the distance of four kilometres. The authors of the report pointed to a possible link between illness, and petrol and diesel fumes. The research methodology was based on plotting the birthplace postcodes of those who had died, and comparing these with the locations of different types of industrial plant. The findings held true across a variety of regions, and followed earlier studies showing the likely occurrence

1 [1968] 2 All ER 669.
2 [1995] 7 ELM 175.

of deaths in small geographical clusters. The authors dismissed counter theories that these clusters may result from the building of new factories in particular areas which draw migration to them and so expose the local population to new viral risks of cancer, and argued that it was the exposure of pregnant women and young children to airborne pollutants which would be the most likely cause of affectation. Moreover, in addition to primary pollutants, the report alleged that recombinations of emissions to form secondary pollutants were also responsible for illness. Interestingly, no clustering of cancers was found near industries such as brewing, cotton-making, furniture-making or nuclear power stations – although, in the past, there have been repeated arguments in the scientific journals that cancer clusters near nuclear installations can be found.

However, this impressive statistical study was greeted with considerable initial scientific reserve. It was pointed out that there had been no 'control' study with which to compare the results, ie no study of comparable deaths in areas which were not close to the type of plant in question. Other questions were raised as to whether it is likely that a cancer cluster will develop near a motorway with fast-moving traffic, as opposed to an urban road with frequent jams and slow-moving traffic which will emit much more by way of pollution. The methodology was also attacked for its use of postcode areas on the basis that that gave no indication of the number of people researched in total. The study also took no account of other possible causes of cancer, such as genetic influences or diet.

Without taking an indefensibly non-scientifically qualified stand in such a debate, one can, nevertheless, justifiably conclude that where there is such deep division in the scientific community among those who study the issues, it would be very difficult for an individual who wishes to allege that a particular affectation resulted from emissions coming from a particular source to be able to succeed, even on the basis of the balance of probability.

The issue has, in any case, been fought out in relation to epidemiological evidence concerning alleged links between childhood leukaemia and closeness to nuclear installations. Where, for example, a major nuclear incident occurs on a site, and on-site workers are exposed to radiation and display symptoms of 'radiation sickness' thereafter, a causal link can be established. However, it is much more difficult to show a link between the siting of a nuclear facility, and the cancer a given person in its vicinity develops over a number of years. Epidemiological evidence here is inconclusive, and is open to the counter argument that in any given population a number of people will develop cancers of one sort of another, and that it is generally impossible to distinguish a case induced by radiation from one otherwise occurring. Thus, in *Reay v BNFL plc*[1] and *Hope v BNFL plc*,[2] cases where plaintiffs alleged exposure to radiation outside the Sellafield nuclear installation which had damaged children by affecting their mothers' ova (preconception), *and* by affecting their fathers'

1 [1992] 4 LMELR 195.
2 [1993] 5 ELM 178.

sperm (preconception) – both fathers having worked within the nuclear plant – 90 days of a civil hearing, with evidence from 30 scientific witnesses, failed to produce proof that, on the balance of probabilities, there had been causation of injury consequent on a breach of duty. Incidentally, the *Hope* and *Reay* litigation was the longest and most expensive civil litigation on record until *Graham and Graham*.

The twin issues of showing a failure to meet the required standard of the law *and*, furthermore, proof that it was that breach which caused the plaintiff's loss, are major constraints on the development of environmental liability, particularly as regards personal injury claims made in negligence. Thus, in *Budden v BP Oil Ltd*,[1] it was alleged that petrol companies were negligent in supplying petrol which was, at that time, partially composed of lead. The case ran for two years before being struck out on the basis that the composition of petrol was in compliance with regulations made under Parliamentary authority. Those regulations, it was presumed, reflected a consideration of all relevant factors, including, but not limited to, issues of health and safety nationally, and in particular localities. Where Parliament has sanctioned a general policy and its associated standards after such due enquiry, it is not negligent for a manufacturer to comply with that policy and standards. Furthermore, UK courts are unwilling to make decisions which might have the effect of requiring compliance with differing and inconsistent policies.

It is unlikely that there will be major developments in environmental liability in the UK without legislative intervention either by our Parliament or originating in European obligations. This makes it all the more important to have appropriate regulatory frameworks in place to prevent the occurrence of injury, and, in any case, it must be accepted that prevention is indeed better than cure.

1 (1980) 124 SJ 376.

CHAPTER 5

STATUTORY NUISANCES AND STUBBLE BURNING

5.1 INTRODUCTION

The law relating to statutory nuisances has its roots in the movement to protect public health, the origins of which can be traced to Edwin Chadwick's decision in 1838 to send Poor Law medical investigators into the slums of London, which led to Chadwick's *Report on an Enquiry into the Sanitary Condition of the Labouring Population of Great Britain* (1842). This, in turn, led to the passage of the Public Health Act 1848, although few of its provisions were mandatory, and throughout the 1850s and 1860s there was a considerable degree of legal confusion consequent on the overlapping jurisdictions of various types of local authority, and uncertainty as to the meaning and applicability of subsequent legislation passed after 1848. It was not until the great codification of the law in the Public Health Act 1875 that a truly cohesive legal foundation of the improvement of public health was laid – and that itself was the product of the 1868 Royal Sanitary Commission's consideration of all sanitary laws.

However, one basic concept from the early days of the public health movement survives, which is that certain conditions that are either prejudicial to health or a nuisance, ie an unacceptably unreasonable interference with an innocent party's land or the use and enjoyment thereof, should be prohibited by law and punishable as criminal offences. In this regard, 'statutory nuisance' as a concept derives clearly from both the law of tort (private nuisance) and the criminal law (public nuisance). It is a well-established principle of civil law that persons may not use their land in such a way as to injure the legal rights of others, while criminal law has long prohibited acts or omissions which materially affect the reasonable comfort and convenience of 'a class' of the Monarch's subjects – meaning, here, a definable section of the public in the area affected by the action or omission in question.[1] Thus, to operate a cesspit or to accumulate filth so that the health or habitability of a neighbourhood was affected could historically be dealt with by way of a public nuisance action (see, further, Chapter 4).

Statutory nuisance brings together elements from both the civil and the criminal law. The local authority (as opposed to the Attorney-General in the case of public nuisance) are given the power to bring prosecutions in relation to certain activities or conditions which are prejudicial to health, or which affect

---

1 See, generally, *Attorney-General v PYA Quarries Ltd* [1957] 2 QB 169.

the physical quality, or the use and enjoyment, of an innocent party's land; there is no need to show that a whole neighbourhood or class has been affected.

Established in the nineteenth century, the concept of statutory nuisance has remained part of the law of public health – and now of environmental protection – ever since, via the medium of the Public Health Acts 1936 and 1961, the Public Health (Recurring Nuisances) Act 1969, and now the Environmental Protection Act 1990 (EPA 1990), Part III.

5.2 THE CURRENT LAW

Section 79(1) of EPA 1990 principally defines those matters amounting to 'statutory nuisances' which, in the context of atmospheric pollution, are:

- smoke emitted from premises;
- fumes or gases emitted from premises;
- dust, steam, smell or other effluvia arising on industrial trade or business premises.

'Premises', under s 79(7), includes land, and is not confined to buildings or structures.

5.2.1 Exclusions

In each case the matter in question must be 'prejudicial to health' or 'a nuisance', while certain matters are specifically excluded from the definition of 'statutory nuisance' by EPA 1990 itself. Thus, under s 79(4), fumes and gases may only amount to a statutory nuisance where emitted from a private dwelling, while the provisions relating to the emission of steam do not apply to steam emitted from a railway locomotive engine (see s 79(5)). Similarly, the provisions relating to dust emissions do not apply to dust emitted from a chimney as an ingredient of smoke (although smoke otherwise includes soot, ash, grit and gritty particles emitted in smoke), (see s 79(7)). The reason for these exclusions is that there is other relevant legislation applying to such emissions. A similar explanation underlies the exclusion from the provisions on smoke nuisances of: smoke emitted from the chimney of a private dwelling in a smoke control area; dark smoke emitted from a chimney of a building or a chimney serving the furnace of a boiler or industrial plant attached to a building or for the time being fixed to, or installed on, any land; smoke emitted from a railway locomotive steam engine; and dark smoke otherwise emitted from industrial or trade premises, as these are all subject to control under the Clean Air Act 1993 (CAA 1993),[1] and s 79(3) of EPA 1990. For the definition of 'industrial or trade premises', see **5.2.2** below.

Further exclusions from the statutory nuisance provisions exist. Under s 42 of CAA 1993, the provisions do not apply to smoke, grit or dust arising from the combustion of refuse deposited from mines and quarries falling within the

1 See Chapter 8.

Mines and Quarries Act 1954, from where coal or shale has been, is being, or will be, mined. Similarly, under s 45, a local authority may exempt any chimney from the ambit of the statutory nuisance provisions where it is satisfied, on an application from a person 'interested' in the chimney, that exemption is expedient so that investigative research into air pollution problems can take place.

A much more comprehensive exclusion, however, is contained in s 79(10) which states that without the consent of the Secretary of State local authorities are not permitted to initiate summary statutory nuisance proceedings in respect of nuisances arising out of, inter alia, smoke emitted from premises, or dust, steam, smell or other effluvia arising on industrial, trade or business premises where proceedings could be instituted under Part I of EPA 1990, or under the Alkali etc Works Regulation Act 1906 (since repealed), or under s 5 of the Health and Safety at Work Act 1974. As a restriction, this is not clearly phrased, and it would have been preferable for the draftsman to say that where the issue in question falls within the jurisdiction of enforcing authorities under Part I of EPA 1990 as a matter of integrated pollution control (IPC) or local authority air pollution control (LAAPC), summary statutory nuisance proceedings are not to be initiated. The restriction does not, however, apply to any proceedings commenced by, for example, a private citizen as a 'person aggrieved'. Although the obvious import of this provision is to prevent overlapping jurisdictions between the statutory nuisance and IPC and LAAPC regimes,[1] as is pointed out by the learned commentator in *The Encyclopaedia of Environmental Law*,[2] at p D589, controls under the IPC and LAAPC regimes would embrace matters of public health, such as offensive smells, where these arise in respect of prescribed processes and substances.

5.2.2 The realm of statutory nuisances

It may be surmised that there is very little which may be dealt with by means of the statutory nuisance provisions in respect of atmospheric emissions, given the exclusions outlined above. This is not the case, however. A smoky bonfire on someone's garden or allotment could fall to be dealt with under EPA 1990, s 79(1)(b). In *Crump v Lambert*,[3] it was considered that smoke unaccompanied by noise or vapour and *not* injurious to health could still constitute a nuisance. Fumes (ie 'airborne solid matter smaller than dust') and gas (which includes 'vapour and moisture precipitated from vapour' – see s 79(7)), resulting, for example, from the over-zealous amateur experiments of a private chemist at home, could be dealt with under s 79(1)(c); while, more importantly, dust arising from the handling of agricultural products outside situations otherwise controlled by the IPC and LAAPC regimes, could be dealt with under s 79(1)(d), provided the handling occurs on industrial, trade or business premises.[4] In this context 'industrial trade or business premises' is defined by

1 See Chapters 6 and 7.
2 Sweet & Maxwell, 1993.
3 (1867) LR 3 Eq 409.
4 *Wivenhoe Port v Colchester Borough Council* [1985] JPL 175.

s 79(7) as premises used for any industrial, trade or business purposes, or premises not so used on which matter is burnt in connection with any industrial, trade or business purposes, while premises are 'used for industrial purposes' where used for the purpose of any treatment or process, as well as for the purpose of manufacturing. The authorities appear to establish that 'trade or business' uses cover virtually all occupational and/or profit-oriented activities, but not domestic and recreational activities, nor 'one-off' transactions not intended to be repeated.[1] Arguably, on this wide understanding of 'trade or business' premises, farm premises could fall within control where activities there give rise to excessive amounts of dust.

However, proceedings may be instituted only where the matter in question can be shown to be 'prejudicial to health' or 'a nuisance'. Section 79(7) of EPA 1990 defines 'prejudicial to health' as 'injurious or likely to cause injury, to health', but does not define 'health'. Following *dicta* in *Coventry City Council v Cartwright*,[2] however, 'health' appears to be confined to physical well-being, and may not include mental health, although it appears enough to initiate action where conditions are such as to make someone already ill worse.[3] The question, however, whether a matter is 'prejudicial to health' will turn largely upon expert testimony. The court must pay due heed to this and not advance a lay assessment of facts over those of expert witnesses.[4] As far as matters which constitute alleged nuisances are concerned, it is necessary to show that these fall within the concept of public or private nuisance at common law (ie matters arising on the premises of one person and then proceeding to affect those of another),[5] although a single instance of a deleterious action may be sufficient to ground an action for a statutory nuisance.[6] Furthermore, there is a tradition of respectable antiquity that not every nuisance can be dealt with as a statutory nuisance, but only those matters which, in some way, can be shown to have a relevance to health.[7] In *Wivenhoe Port v Colchester Borough Council*,[8] Butler J distinguished nuisances arising as a result of inconvenience in the use of property, such as where dust falls on vehicles or plants, from those where persons are physically affected by, for example, dust getting in their hair or eyes.[9] The key concept is whether a condition is likely to make someone ill, as opposed to being unsafe.[10]

---

1 See, generally, *Aviation and Shipping Co v Murray* [1961] 1 WLR 974; *Rolls v Miller* (1894) 27 ChD 71 at 88; *R v Breeze* [1973] 1 WLR 994; *Town Investments v Department of the Environment* [1976] 3 All ER 147; and *Re Griffin ex parte Board of Trade* (1890) 60 LJQB 235 at 237.

2 [1975] 1 WLR 845.

3 *Malton Board of Health v Malton Manure Co* (1879) 4 ExD 302 at 305, per Kelly CB.

4 *Patel v Mehtab* (1989) 5 HLR 78.

5 *National Coal Board v Neath Borough Council* [1976] 2 All ER 478.

6 *East Northamptonshire District Council v Foster* [1994] Env LR 388.

7 *Bishop Auckland Local Board v Bishop Auckland Iron and Steel Co* (1882) 1 QBD 138 at 140–141.

8 [1985] JPL 175.

9 See also *Malton Board of Health v Malton Manure Co* (1879) 4 ExD 302; *Great Western Railway Co v Bishop* (1872) LR 7 QB 550.

10 *R v Bristol City Council, ex parte Everett* (1998) *The Times*, 27 May.

5.3 PROCEDURE

5.3.1 Local authority procedures: Environmental Protection Act 1990

Section 80 of EPA 1990 provides that where a local authority (ie generally, in England, a district council, London borough council, unitary authority, and, in Wales, the relevant county council or county borough council) is 'satisfied' that a statutory nuisance exists, or that one is likely to occur or recur, they must serve an 'abatement notice' which may impose all or any of the following:

- a requirement that the nuisance is abated, or a prohibition or restriction on its occurrence or recurrence;
- the execution of such works and the taking of such other steps as may be necessary for the foregoing purposes.

The notice must specify the time or times within which its requirements are to be complied with.

There is some debate on whether s 80 imposes a mandatory duty to act. Where an authority have a real choice of statutory provisions under which to act, it is unlikely that the court will order the authority to choose one in preference to the other.[1] Otherwise, where a nuisance clearly exists it is not enough for an authority merely to resolve that it is inappropriate to take action because some other agency is interested in the matter and may take action.[2]

Section 233 of the Local Government Act 1972 provides the procedure for the service of notice, which, while it does not have to be in a particular form, must at least comply with s 80(3) of, and Sch 3, para 6 to, EPA 1990 in informing recipients of their rights of appeal to the magistrates' court within 21 days of the date of service of the notice. More generally, the notice must identify what constitutes the nuisance in question and instruct the recipient clearly on what has to be done – in other words, the notice must be clear and certain.[3] However, it does not appear necessary to state in the abatement notice whether the matter in question is a statutory nuisance in consequence of its being 'prejudicial to health', or a nuisance otherwise actionable at common law.[4] What is necessary is that a clear statement be issued showing what must be done by way of abatement action, and works should be specified if there is a possibility of doubt. This was the law under the former public health legislation.[5] It is clear that this requirement continues under EPA 1990.[6] Where abatement can take place without any works or actions being needed, then no

1 *Nottingham City Council v Newton* [1974] 1 WLR 923; *R v Kerrier District Council ex parte Guppy's (Bridport) Ltd* (1975) 30 P & CR 194.

2 *R v Carrick District Council ex parte Shelley* (1996) *The Times*, 15 April.

3 *R v Secretary of State for the Environment ex parte Watney Mann (Midlands) Ltd* [1976] JPL 368.

4 *Lowe v South Somerset District Council* [1997] EGCS 113.

5 *R v Wheatley* (1885) 16 QB 34; *Millard v Wastell* [1898] 1 QB 342.

6 *Sterling Homes (Midlands) Ltd v Birmingham City Council* [1996] Env LR 121; and *Kirklees Metropolitan Borough Council v Field* (1997) *The Times*, 26 November.

such works or actions need be specified.[1] Where works or actions are required, however, the notice should be (as stated) sufficiently particular to make it clear what remedies are required in one 'package' of action.[2] However, over-particularity may not be needed where it is clear from the notice and the surrounding circumstances what has gone wrong and what is needed to put it right.[3] The period of time that must be specified for compliance must be reasonable in all the circumstances of the case,[4] but, in an appropriate case, depending, inter alia, on the nature of the nuisance in question and the equipment causing it, what is reasonable may only be a short time. For example, it may be reasonable to require at short notice some equipment not to be used until it is modified in some way,[5] but, nevertheless, the notice should still be practicable and easily understood by the recipient. It is more doubtful, however, whether it is possible for notices to direct the recipients in the day-to-day operation of their business, where, for example, an authority wished to pursue the implementation of certain handling measures so as to reduce emissions of dust.[6] Where a notice forbids the recurrence of a nuisance, that prohibition is apparently indefinite, and comes into immediate effect.[7] Where, however, a notice requires the abatement of an existing nuisance, it is necessary in subsequent proceedings for the court to consider whether the nuisance has continued to exist in order to decide whether there has been compliance, and this requires evidence from the prosecution that the nuisance continues. If a notice requires only the taking of specified steps, evidence of continuing nuisance does not appear to be required, because such steps may relate to preventing the recurrence of a nuisance.[8]

5.3.2 Local authority procedures: abatement notices

Abatement notices are, in general, served on the person responsible for the nuisance. Where a nuisance arises from a defect of a structural character the notice is served on the owner of the premises, while in cases where the 'person responsible' cannot be found, or where the notice anticipates and is to prevent a nuisance, it may be served on the owner *or* the occupier of the premises (EPA 1990, s 80(2)). Under s 79(7) the 'person responsible' is that person whose action, defaults or sufferances result in the nuisance, so that a person could be considered 'responsible' for allowing another to create a nuisance on his land.[9] It is clear, however, that the combined effect of s 160 of EPA 1990 and s 233 of the Local Government Act 1972 require an abatement notice to be served directly on the 'person responsible', ie, in general, the individual or company

1 *R v Wheatley* (1885) 16 QB 34; *McGillivray v Stephenson* [1950] 1 All ER 942.
2 *Network Housing Association v Westminster City Council* (1994) 27 HLR 189.
3 *Myatt v Teignbridge District Council* [1994] Env LR D18.
4 *Bristol Corporation v Sinnott* [1918] 1 Ch 52.
5 *Strathclyde Regional Council v Tudhope* [1983] JPL 536.
6 *Wivenhoe Port v Colchester Borough Council* [1985] JPL 175.
7 *R v Birmingham Justices ex parte Guppy* (1988) 152 JP 159; *R v Tunbridge Wells JJ ex parte Tunbridge Wells Borough Council* [1996] Env LR 88.
8 *AMEC Building Limited v London Borough of Camden* [1997] Env LR 330.
9 *Clayton v Sale Urban District Council* [1926] 1 KB 415.

responsible for the nuisance, and not, for example, an associated company of the relevant company, even where they both share the same registered office.[1] The expression 'owner' is not defined for present purposes in EPA 1990, but reference to the case-law under the previous legislation (the Public Health Act 1936) indicates a wide range of persons who can be classified as 'owners', including agents, receivers and mortgagees.[2]

5.3.3 Local authority procedures: grounds for appeal

As stated above, the recipient of a notice may appeal to the magistrates' court under EPA 1990, s 80(3). Currently, the Statutory Nuisance (Appeals) Regulations 1995, SI 1995/2644, provide the following grounds of appeal:

- the abatement notice was unnecessary;
- there is an informality, defect or error in, or in connection with, the notice;
- the authority unreasonably refused to accept compliance with alternative requirements;
- the notice's requirements are unreasonable in character or extent, or are unnecessary;
- reasonable amounts of time have not been specified for compliance;
- the recipient is able to avail himself of the 'best practicable means' defence (see further below);
- the notice should have been served on someone else as the 'person responsible' or, in appropriate cases, as the owner/occupier of the premises;
- the notice could lawfully have been served on someone else as an occupier of the relevant premises, or as their owner, and it is equitable for the notice to be so served, or on someone else in addition to the recipient as a 'person responsible' (or owner or occupier where relevant).

Where the recipient of a notice believes that a notice has been served incorrectly, for example because of factual circumstances which are not known to the local authority, it is important that he should utilise the right of appeal, rather than try to defend any charges which may be brought subsequently for non-compliance. This is because an authority is entitled to serve notice whenever it appears to them that certain factual situations appear to exist.[3]

Where appeals are made on the basis of alleged informalities, defects or errors in the notice, the court is required to dismiss such appeals unless it is satisfied that the informality etc in question is material. Otherwise, the court has a wide discretion to quash or vary the notice (but only in the appellant's favour) or to dismiss the appeal. Thus, the court may consider that an error etc is immaterial if it is clear that, despite the mistake (eg a slight misdescription of premises), it is clearly understood by both sides what the facts are. An error of this sort

1 *AMEC Building Limited v London Borough of Camden* [1997] Env LR 330.
2 *St Helen's Corporation v Kirkham* (1885) 16 QBD 403; *Bacup Corporation v Smith* (1890) 44 ChD 395; *Blackburn Corporation v Micklethwaite* (1886) 54 LT 539.
3 *Wiltshire Construction (London) Ltd v Westminster City Council* [1997] Env LR 321.

would, however, become material if the defendant was led to believe that a notice related to a site other than, or smaller than, the site actually in question.[1] It should also be remembered that it is not (apparently) necessary to state in a notice whether the nuisance in question is one which arises by virtue of a condition being either 'prejudicial to health' or 'a nuisance' at common law.[2] The court may make orders with regard to persons by whom works are to be executed or who are required to contribute towards works, and, in doing so, is to take into account the terms of any tenancy between the owner and the occupier of premises. In cases where the ground of appeal is that the notice might lawfully have been served on some person other than the recipient (or in addition to the recipient), the court should take into account whether that other person has received a copy of the notice of appeal, as is required under the Statutory Nuisance (Appeals) Regulations 1995.

Once an appeal is made, if compliance with the abatement notice would involve any person in expense by virtue of carrying out works before the appeal is heard, the making of the appeal has the effect of suspending the notice until the appeal has either been abandoned or decided. Where, however, the nuisance in question is one which is either injurious to health or is likely to be of limited duration, so that the efficacy of the notice would be negated by suspension, or where the expenditure referred to above would not be out of proportion to the benefit to the public expected by virtue of compliance pending the determination of the appeal, such suspension may be avoided. To avoid suspending the order, the local authority must include an appropriate statement, for example that the nuisance is one injurious to health. That statement must be specific as to the ground on which it is based, and has the effect of preventing suspension in the event of an appeal. On the making of an appeal, however, the court has a wide discretion under s 64 of the Magistrates' Courts Act 1980 to make orders as to costs.[3]

Where a local authority wish to challenge the findings of the magistrates' court, the better view of the law is that they should appeal on factual issues to the Crown Court, a request for the magistrates to state a case for the decision of the High Court should occur only where there are disputes over points of law or other special or unusual circumstances.[4]

5.3.4 Defences and offences

Where a person on whom an abatement notice is served fails to comply with any requirement or prohibition in the notice, or otherwise contravenes it, that person, unless there is a 'reasonable excuse', commits an offence and is generally liable to a fine not exceeding level 5 on the standard scale, together with a further fine of an amount equal to one-tenth of level 5 for each day on

1 Ibid – a noise case.

2 *Lowe v South Somerset District Council* [1997] EGCS 113 – a noise case.

3 *R v Southend Stipendiary Magistrates ex parte Rochford District Council* [1995] Env LR 1.

4 *R v North West Suffolk (Mildenhall) Magistrates' Court, ex parte Forest Heath District Council* [1998] Env LR 9 (CA).

which the offence continues after conviction. Where the offence is committed on industrial, trade or business premises, the guilty person is liable on summary conviction to a fine not exceeding £20,000 (see EPA 1990, s 80(4), (5) and (6)). However, the justices do have a discretion in setting the level of fines, both with regard to the initial and the continuing daily offence. Under s 34 of the Magistrates' Courts Act 1980, save where it is expressly otherwise provided, a court may sentence an offender to a punishment less than that specified in a statute.[1] In *Surrey Free Inns plc v Gosport Borough Council*,[2] the Divisional Court held that the correct date for examining the justification for and the validity of a s 80 notice is the date on which the local authority serves that notice. Mance J pointed out that in proceedings brought under s 80(4) the issue is whether the requirements of the notice have been complied with. An offence is committed under s 80(4) where service of the notice under s 80(2) is followed without reasonable excuse, by contravention of, or a failure to comply with, any requirement or prohibition imposed by the notice. Where there is an appeal against a notice under s 80(3), logic dictates that the court, whether the magistrates' court or the Crown Court, should consider the issues of justification and validity as at the time of service, not at the date of hearing. In this, Mance J followed *Northern Ireland Trailers Ltd v Preston Corporation*[3] and *Lambeth Borough Council v Stubbs*,[4] and doubted the correctness of *Johnson News of London v Ealing Borough Council*.[5]

The proceedings in respect of a statutory nuisance are clearly criminal in nature and, as such, the criminal burden of proof applies.[6] Various defences may be relied on.

'Best practicable means'

Under ss 80(7) and 79(9) of EPA 1990, there is the defence that the 'best practicable means' were used to prevent or counteract the effect of the nuisance. 'Practicable' in this context means reasonably practicable having regard, inter alia, to local conditions and circumstances, the current state of technical knowledge and financial implications. 'Means' is defined to include the design, installation, maintenance and manner and periods of operation of plant and machinery, and the design, construction and maintenance of buildings and structures. The defence is to be applied only so far as it is compatible with any other duty imposed by law, and so far as it is compatible with safety and safe working conditions, and the exigencies of any emergency or unforeseeable circumstances. This defence allows the issues of costs to be raised by the accused, and it is up to him to prove a claim that a particular act of abatement is impracticable. It is not enough to show that action required

1 *Canterbury City Council v Ferris* (1996) *The Independent*, 11 November.
2 (1998) *The Times*, 13 January – a noise case.
3 [1972] 1 WLR 203.
4 (1980) 255 EG 789.
5 (1990) 154 JP 33.
6 See, on the predecessor provisions under the Public Health Act 1936, *R v Oxted JJ ex parte Franklin* [1976] 1 WLR 420; and, more recently, on EPA 1990, *Lewisham London Borough Council v Fenner* (1995) 248 *ENDS Report* 44 (Crown Court).

will result in increased expenditure, or that an operation may be unprofitable.[1] It should, however, be noted that the defence of 'best practicable means' cannot be raised in respect of smoke or dust, steam, smell or effluvia nuisances, except where the nuisances arises on industrial, trade or business premises, and in the case of smoke nuisances there is a further restriction that the defence is not available except where the smoke is emitted from a chimney (see s 80(8)). Further illustrations of the best practical means defence are the cases of *Armitage Ltd v Nicholson*[2] and *Drummond and Sons Ltd v Nicholson*.[3]

'Reasonable excuse'

The accused may plead a defence of 'reasonable excuse'. Lack of finance is not a 'reasonable excuse'.[4] The phrase appears to contemplate some excuse which a reasonable person would consider consistent with a reasonable standard of conduct, and may then extend only to cases where there are special difficulties inherent in complying with the notice, for example where the accused is incapacitated through sickness.[5] However, a failed but genuine attempt to comply with a notice may be evidence of a 'reasonable excuse'.[6] It appears that simply reducing emission levels on request is not a 'reasonable excuse', although it may be a mitigating factor in sentencing, and a sufficiently great reduction may negate the existence of a nuisance at all.[7] No comprehensive definition of what may or may not constitute a 'reasonable excuse' can be given. It would appear that the personal circumstances of the defendant, such as serious personal ill-health or the ill-health or death of a close relative, may be enough, but each case must be carefully considered on its facts.[8] Where, however, under s 80(4) and (6) of EPA 1990 a defendant raises the defence of reasonable excuse and lays the evidential basis for that contention, it is for the prosecution to satisfy the court, using the criminal standard of proof, that the excuse is not 'reasonable'.[9]

No lawful requirement?

It remains uncertain whether there is a defence of 'no lawful requirement' in the abatement notice following a failure by the recipient to appeal it. In England and Wales there is some authority for such a proposition in *Sterling Homes (Midlands) Ltd v Birmingham City Council*,[10] but in Scotland it has been held, on parallel provisions, that a failure to appeal against an abatement

1 See *Wivenhoe Port v Colchester Borough Council* [1985] JPL 175; and dicta in *Polychronakis v Richards and Jerrom Ltd* (1997) *The Times*, 19 November that the burden of proving the defence in s 80(7) and (8) is on the defence.

2 (1913) 108 LT 993.

3 (1915) 84 LJKB 2190.

4 *Saddleworth Urban District Council v Aggregate and Sand* (1970) 114 SJ 931.

5 *A Lambert Flat Management v Lomas* [1981] 1 WLR 898.

6 *Sterling Homes (Midlands) Ltd v Birmingham City Council* [1996] Env LR 121.

7 *Wellingborough Borough Council v Gordon* (1990) 155 JP 494 – a noise case.

8 *Hope Butuyuyu v London Borough of Hammersmith and Fulham* [1997] Env LR D13 – a noise case.

9 *Polychronakis v Richards and Jerrom Ltd* (1997) *The Times*, 19 November.

10 [1996] Env LR 121.

notice deprives an accused of the ability to challenge the terms of the notice by way of defence at a subsequent trial.[1]

5.3.5 Supplementary provisions

Section 81(1) of EPA 1990 provides that where more than one person is responsible for a statutory nuisance, s 80 applies to each of them, whether or not the act for which any one of them is responsible would, by itself, amount to a statutory nuisance. Section 81(2) provides that where a nuisance which exists or has existed within a local authority's area, or which has affected any part of that area, appears to the authority to be wholly or partly caused by some act or default committed or taking place outside their area, the authority may still act under s 80 as if the act etc had been committed in their area, except that any appeal is to be dealt with by the magistrates' court for the area where the act etc is alleged to have taken place. Section 81(3) provides that in a case of non-compliance the local authority, whether or not they take criminal proceedings (they are not bound to take such action) under s 81(2), may themselves abate the nuisance and do whatever is necessary to execute the abatement notice. Section 81(4) further provides that authorities may recover costs incurred under s 81(3) in abating or preventing the recurrence of a nuisance from the person responsible for the nuisance, and where that person was the owner of the premises at the time of the nuisance the expenses may be recovered from any person who is for the time being their owner. Where more than one person is responsible for a nuisance the court has power to apportion the authority's costs between them. Section 81A supplements this power by providing that where expenses are recoverable under s 81(4) from the owner of premises, and the local authority serves on that person a notice under s 81A, the expenses will carry interest, at a reasonable rate to be determined by the authority, from the date of service of the notice until the amount is paid in full, and that the expenses and any interest accrued will be a charge on the premises. A s 81A notice must specify the amount of expenses alleged to be recoverable, state its statutory effect and the rate of interest, and the consequences for the property of the charging on the premises of the sum owed, together with the right of the recipient of the notice under s 81A(6) to appeal against it to the county court within a period of 21 days beginning with the date of service. The court has a wide discretion on such an appeal to confirm, vary or discharge the notice. A copy of the notice must also, under s 81A(3), be served on every other person known to the authority to have an interest in the property capable of being affected by the charge, while under s 81A(8) the local authority has the powers available to mortgagees under the Law of Property Act 1925 for the purpose of enforcing a charge. Section 81B then further supplements these provisions by enabling the local authority to declare that the expenses and interest due charged on the premises are to be paid by instalments within a specified period of up to 30 years from the date of the notice under s 81A. Instalments may be recovered from the owner or occupier for the time being of

1 *Stagecoach Ltd v McPhail* 1988 SCCR 289 – a noise case.

the premises, except that a person who is only an occupier may not be required to pay at any one time any sum greater than the aggregate of:

- the amount due from him by way of rent at the date the local authority served a demand for the money (together with a notice requiring that occupier not to pay rent to the landlord without having first deducted the sum demanded); and
- the amount that has become due from the occupier on account of rent since the date of the authority's demand.

5.3.6 Proceedings in the High Court

Where a local authority are of the opinion that proceedings in the magistrates' court would afford an inadequate remedy, they may take proceedings in the High Court in respect of a statutory nuisance to secure its abatement, prohibition or restriction, irrespective of whether they have suffered any damage (see s 81(5) of EPA 1990). Only rarely will resort be had to this provision, because it must be shown by the authority that they are satisfied on objective grounds that the normal procedure would not afford them an adequate remedy. However, on occasions authorities have used this power to obtain injunctive relief, usually in relation to noise nuisances. Thus, in *Hammersmith London Borough Council v Magnum Automated Forecourts*,[1] it was held that in a proper case injunctive relief may be granted irrespective of whether summary remedies have been exhausted. Authorities may also attempt to rely on their general powers under s 222 of the Local Government Act 1972 to seek injunctive relief and, in *City of London Corporation v Bovis Construction Ltd*,[2] the court indicated that such a remedy was appropriate: (1) where it was necessary to prevent damage not preventable by summary proceedings or in respect of which criminal remedies are not otherwise sufficient or are technically deficient in some way; or (2) where it is clear that an unlawful activity will continue unless restrained by an injunction. However, to rely on s 222, it is necessary to show that there is a threat to the proper exercise of an authority's statutory responsibilities. Where, therefore, an authority are acting in a law enforcement capacity, they may not be required to give a cross-undertaking in damages where an injunction is sought on an interlocutory basis. However, the matter is one for the discretion of the court at the application stage, and should be raised then. It is unlikely that on the discharge of interlocutory orders an inquiry into damages will be ordered where, at that stage, the court concludes that the authority were acting in a law enforcement capacity and that the court at the application stage could properly have exercised its discretion not to require an undertaking in damages.[3]

The courts have often stated in cases on s 222 of the Local Government Act 1972 and on decisions under s 100 of the Public Health Act 1936 (the

---

1 [1978] 1 WLR 50.

2 (1988) 86 LGR 600.

3 *Kirklees Metropolitan Borough Council v Wickes Building Supplies* [1993] AC 227; *Coventry City Council v Finnie* (1996) 29 HLR 658.

predecessor to s 81(5) of EPA 1990) that action taken must be expedient for the promotion or protection of the inhabitants of an authority's area. In *Warwick Rural District Council v Miller-Mead*[1] and *Stoke-on-Trent City Council v B&Q Retail Ltd*,[2] the court stressed that injunctive relief will not be made available to restrain mere infractions of the criminal law. Thus, generally authorities are expected to rely on criminal proceedings, but may seek injunctive relief where, for example, it is clear that a wrongdoer will not be deterred by fines, or where delay in seeking an end to particular acts of behaviour or the slowness of prosecution may encourage others to indulge in widespread breaches of the law.[3] There is no need, however, to show that a respondent is deliberately and flagrantly flouting the law, but the court will act with discretion and caution, and will need to be convinced that the respondent's behaviour is putting the proper exercise of the authority's statutory responsibilities at risk.[4]

These issues were recently examined in *Vale of White Horse District Council v DC & RJ Allen*[5] where the trend of the previous case-law was confirmed and elucidated. In the early 1980s the defendants, under what were then permitted development rights in planning law, had built two major pig units close to residential accommodation. In 1993 they applied for planning permission for more units, and this aroused considerable local opposition. Acting under their statutory nuisance powers the local authority concluded that there was a nuisance by virtue of smell, and served an abatement notice requiring remedial steps. The defendants complied with the notice, but complaints about the smell continued, although, by agreement with the defendants, one year was allowed to elapse to see how matters developed. At the end of the year the Chief Environmental Health Officer considered that the smells amounted to a statutory nuisance and that the only effective abatement would be the pigs' removal or a considerable reduction in their numbers. However, action by the local authority might have been met by a claim that the 'best practicable means' had been taken to prevent the nuisance; hence, the authority decided to seek injunctive relief, the proceedings for which were opposed by the defendants on the basis that the authority were not entitled to seek this relief. The case raised the issue of the relationship between s 81(5) of EPA 1990 and s 222 of the Local Government Act 1972: the former gives a power to seek injunctive relief where an authority is satisfied that ordinary proceedings would not give an adequate remedy; the latter allows proceedings to be taken where this is expedient to promote or protect the interests of the inhabitants of an area, for example to restrain a public nuisance.

In the High Court, Bell J developed the pre-existing law, considering that s 222 does not give an authority an extra power to seek an injunction in addition to

---

1 [1961] Ch 590.
2 [1984] Ch 1.
3 *Runnymede Borough Council v Ball* (1985) 135 NLJ 889.
4 *Camden London Borough Council v Alpenoak Ltd* (1985) *Surveyor*, 5 December, p 17 – a noise case.
5 (1997) 264 *ENDS Report* 43 – a smell case.

the statutory nuisance provisions which are a self-contained, preclusive code. Thus, an injunction can be sought only if the conditions laid down in s 81(5) are met, ie there must be a clear opinion on the part of the authority that proceedings for an offence would provide an inadequate remedy. Such an opinion could not be found; instead, it appeared that the authority had concluded that it would be more convenient to take proceedings in the High Court.

However, on the basis that s 222 might provide an independent remedy, Bell J concluded that the authority had still mistaken the extent of their powers. There was no doubt that the authority considered the use of s 222 proceedings to be 'expedient', but there were other matters they had ignored. These were whether, first, the defendants might have responded favourably to either a prosecution under the original abatement notice or the service of a new one and, secondly, whether this was a case where the High Court could grant injunctive relief in the absence of an immediate, urgent situation or the deliberate and flagrant flouting of the law.

It is unlikely that an injunction will be granted under s 222 unless such factors are present, and most unlikely where the prospective injunctee has taken steps to comply with abatement proceedings and the decision to seek an injunction is based on a desire for a flexible form of procedure. A more appropriate situation for seeking an injunction is where it is clear the wrongdoer is intent on continuing his misconduct and is using legal procedural devices, for example applications for adjournments, to evade other forms of court proceedings. Even on the basis that s 81(5) does provide a preclusive code for taking injunctive proceedings, the remarks made earlier in relation to cross-undertakings in respect of damages would still, it appears, apply.

5.3.7 Procedures available to private citizens

Section 82 of EPA 1990 enables a magistrates' court to act on a complaint of the existence of a statutory nuisance made by a 'person aggrieved'. Where the court is satisfied that such a nuisance exists, or that, although abated, it is likely to recur on the same premises, the court may make an order:

- requiring the defendant to abate the nuisance within a specified time, and to execute any works necessary for that purpose;
- prohibiting a recurrence of the nuisance and requiring the defendant to execute, within a specified time, works necessary to prevent a recurrence.

The court may also impose a fine on the defendant not exceeding level 5 on the standard scale.

As with local authority proceedings, the general rule is that such proceedings are to be brought against the person responsible for the nuisance, but may be brought against an owner where the nuisance arises from a defect in premises of a structural character, or against the owner or occupier where the 'person responsible' cannot be found. Similarly, where more than one person is responsible for a nuisance, proceedings may be taken against all of them whether or not the act for which any one of them is responsible would not, by itself, amount to a nuisance. The defence of best practicable means is available (so far as atmospheric nuisances are concerned) in effectively the same circumstances that apply to local authority proceedings (see above, and s 82(1), (2), (4), (5), (9) and (10) of EPA 1990). Just as with local authority proceedings, action taken under s 82 is criminal in nature and the criminal burden of proof applies.[1] The court has power under s 35 of the Powers of Criminal Courts Act 1973 to make a compensation order, up to a £5,000 limit, although this power is likely to be used only in a clearly appropriate case where the sum of compensation involved will not be great and where there is no other, or no other easily obtainable, civil remedy for the complainant. In *Herbert v Lambeth London Borough Council*,[2] the court indicated that a compensation order is not an appropriate remedy for an award of substantial sums in respect of personal injuries suffered where a civil action is also available. A compensation order may be additional to or in substitution for a fine; all will depend upon whether the compensation payable is in itself enough to have a punitive effect.[3]

Limits on the efficacy of compensation orders were revealed in *R v Liverpool Crown Court ex parte Cooke*.[4] Here Ms Cooke gave notice under s 82(6) of EPA 1990 of the alleged existence of a statutory nuisance – in this case the condition of her council-owned home. The council failed to comply with the notice. Ms Cooke took criminal proceedings in which the council was convicted and, in addition, ordered to pay £3,000 compensation by the justices. The council appealed against this order to the Crown Court, which reduced the sum to £250. Ms Cooke sought judicial review of this decision. In the Divisional Court it was pointed out that the summons in respect of the alleged nuisance had only alleged its existence on the date of its issue, ie 17 November 1994. It did not allege, as it could have done, the existence of the nuisance up to six months earlier. Ms Cooke sought to argue that the court was entitled to consider the whole period during which a nuisance had subsisted in fixing compensation, but Leggatt LJ could find no warrant for this in relevant legislation. The court held that compensation for statutory nuisance is for loss, injury or damage arising from a nuisance existing *at* the date of the hearing. That date must not be before whichever is the *later* of: (a) the date of expiry of the statutory notice served under s 82(6); or (b) a date of more than six months before the making of the complaint. No jurisdiction exists to make a compensation order in respect of any period prior to the expiry of the s 82(6) notice. In addition to compensation, costs have to be awarded; however, s 82(12) provides that where, on the hearing of proceedings under s 82(2), it is proved that the nuisance existed at the time of making the complaint, the court

---

1 *Bottross v Hammersmith and Fulham London Borough Council* (1994) 27 HLR 179; *Davenport v Walsall Metropolitan Borough Council* (1995) 28 HLR 754.

2 (1991) 24 HLR 299.

3 *R v Liverpool Crown Court ex parte Cooke* (1997) 29 HLR 249; *R v Crown Court at Inner London ex parte Bentham* [1989] 1 WLR 408; *R v Horseferry Road Magistrates ex parte Prophet* [1995] Env LR 104.

4 (1997) 29 HLR 249.

must order the defendant to pay to the person bringing the proceedings such amount as it considers reasonable to compensate the complainant for expenses properly incurred in bringing the proceedings. This was held to be a mandatory obligation in *Hollis v Dudley Metropolitan Borough Council*.[1] However, complainants should give advance notice of claims to costs under s 82(12), while respondents should indicate, again in advance, whether they accept either the claim or state the basis on which they challenge it.[2] The costs recoverable include those incurred in establishing that a nuisance existed prior to bringing the proceedings, although no expenses can be recovered if the nuisance is abated before proceedings are instituted. However, the magistrates have a discretion to disallow any expenses not 'properly incurred', ie which need not have been incurred.

5.3.8 'Person aggrieved'

To rely on s 82 of EPA 1990 a person must be a 'person aggrieved'. Ever since *Attorney-General (Gambia) v N'Jie*,[3] this phrase has been liberally construed. However, a mere busybody would not be able to take action; nor would someone whose interests were not in some way affected by the nuisance, even though they lived close to it.[4] The issue of whether a trespasser can take action was left open in *Coventry City Council v Cartwright*.[5] Otherwise, it appears that anyone whose health has been injured, or anyone with a legal interest in, or legal occupation of, property affected by a nuisance is within the definition.[6]

Before instituting proceedings, s 82(6) of EPA 1990 requires the 'person aggrieved' to give the person against whom the proceedings are to be taken a notice specifying the matter complained of, and, under s 82(7), that notice must be of not less than 21 days' duration. Only thereafter may the 'person aggrieved' proceed to lay the complaint, which must contain the details of why the complaint is made, the capacity in which the defendant is being made subject to action, and the steps alleged to be necessary to abate the nuisance.[7] Where, on the hearing of the proceedings, it is proved that the alleged nuisance existed at the date of the making of the complaint then, whether or not it still exists or is likely to recur at the date of the hearing, the court must order the defendant to pay to the complainant such compensation as the court considers reasonably sufficient to recompense the expenses properly incurred in the proceedings (see s 82(12)).

As with proceedings taken by a local authority, a person who, without reasonable excuse, contravenes any requirements or prohibitions imposed by virtue of the magistrates' order, is guilty of an offence and liable on summary

---

1 (1997) *The Times*, 12 December; *sub nom R v Dudley Magistrates' Court ex parte Hollis* [1998] EHLR 42.

2 *Taylor v Walsall and District Property and Investment Co Ltd* (1998) *The Times*, 5 February.

3 [1961] 1 All ER 504.

4 *Birmingham District Council v McMahon* (1987) 19 HLR 452.

5 [1975] 1 WLR 845.

6 See, generally, *Sandwell Metropolitan Borough Council v Bujok* [1990] 3 All ER 385.

7 See, on the predecessor provision, *Warner v Lambeth Borough Council* (1984) 15 HLR 42.

conviction to a fine not exceeding level 5 on the standard scale, with a further fine of one-tenth of the level 5 fine for each day on which the offence continues after conviction (s 82(8)). However, s 82(11) provides that where a person is convicted of such an offence the magistrates may, after giving the relevant local authority an opportunity of being heard, direct them to do anything which the convicted person was required to do by the initial order. Furthermore, as a final 'residual' provision, s 82(13) provides that where it appears to the magistrates that neither the person responsible for a nuisance, nor the owner or occupier of the premises in question can be found, they may, again after having given the relevant local authority (ie the authority in whose area the nuisance has occurred) a chance of being heard, direct them to do anything the magistrates might otherwise require the 'person responsible' etc to do.

5.3.9 Content of magistrates' orders

It is clear that although magistrates have little discretion but to make an order once satisfied that a nuisance exists or is likely to recur, they do have a very considerable discretion as to the terms of orders made.[1] The magistrates should, however, consider all the facts of the case, including the gravity of any health risks, and may require work to be carried out in phases, allowing for essential work to be done first.

5.4 STUBBLE BURNING

Throughout the 1980s, there was considerable public outcry over the burning of stubble residues in fields – particularly straw, where some 14 million tonnes were being produced annually, half of it being burnt on site. Various control provisions were available, but each was limited.

Section 161(2) of the Highways Act 1980 originally made provision in respect of fires lit near highways. This was replaced by s 161A (as inserted by the Highways Amendment Act 1986), which provides that it is an offence punishable by a fine not exceeding level 5 on the standard scale:

- to light a fire on any land off a highway; or
- to direct or permit the lighting of fires on any such land,

where, in consequence, a highway user is injured, interrupted or endangered by smoke from that fire, or from fires caused by that fire. Under the former law, liability extended only to fires lit within 50 feet of the highway, but the law now also imposes liability in respect of smoke arising from fire spread. It is a defence, however, for the accused to show that when the fire was lit he had reasonable grounds to be satisfied that it was unlikely that circumstances giving rise to an offence would occur, *and* that once the fire was lit, reasonable steps

1 *Nottingham Corporation v Newton* [1974] 1 WLR 923; *Salford City Council v McNally* [1976] AC 379; *Coventry City Council v Doyle* [1981] 1 WLR 1325 – all housing cases.

were taken to prevent such circumstances occurring, *or* that there was a reasonable excuse for not doing so.

In 1984, the Home Office issued model byelaws for local authorities to adopt which sought to impose bans on straw burning at weekends, bank holidays and at night (ie one hour before sunset until sunrise), and, further, to require the creation of firebreaks in particular circumstances, for example to protect houses, standing crops, hedgerows and telegraphs poles. Similarly, limits could be imposed by byelaws on the size of areas to be burnt – no more than 10 hectares – while each area had to be surrounded by a cleared, cultivated or ploughed strip of land at least 5 metres wide, with a further requirement that blocks of stubble simultaneously burnt were to be at least 150 metres apart. The byelaws also provided for requirements as to the supervision of burning, the provision of fire-fighting equipment, and for the giving of notice of an intention to burn to the local fire authority. Some 148 local authorities adopted the byelaws in 1984, and it was hoped that the byelaws, together with compliance with the voluntary National Farmers' Union Code on stubble burning, would solve the problem. It was, at that point, central policy not to introduce a ban on stubble burning, but to rely largely on voluntary restraint, backed up by the byelaws, largely because farmers argued that burning was the most effective and economic way of dealing with stubble.

The problem of stubble burning, although somewhat alleviated, did not disappear and a growing body of public opinion was opposed to the practice. This led to legislative change in the form of s 152 of EPA 1990 which empowers ministers to issue regulations to ban the burning of stubble and crop residues. An interim prohibition was introduced in July 1991 by the Crop Residues (Restrictions on Burning) (No 2) Regulations 1991, SI 1991/1590, which applied to specified crop residues such as linseed and oil seed rape, cereal straw and stubble, imposed restrictions on burning times, and required the prevention of fire spread and the supervision of burning. The requirements previously in the byelaws as to giving notice to relevant fire and environmental health authorities were continued in the Regulations, and were extended to the occupiers of adjacent premises. However, the law remained deficient in that its coverage was partial – not all crop residues were covered, and there were no requirements preventing crop burning when winds reached certain levels. Nevertheless, the Regulations added to the considerable reduction in stubble burning between 1989 and 1991.

5.4.1 The current law

The Crop Residues (Burning) Regulations 1993, SI 1993/1366, currently prohibit the burning on agricultural land of a longer list of crop residues (cereal straw and stubble, the residues of oil seed rape, field beans and peas), although there are minor exemptions for certain educational and research purposes. Where linseed residues are to be burnt, particular restrictions and requirements are imposed, for example as to the timing and extent of burning. It is an offence to burn residues in contravention of the Regulations, punishable on summary conviction with a fine up to level 5 on the standard scale. In actuality, the problem of stubble burning seems now to have disappeared – an example, perhaps, of public pressure overcoming government inertia and farming resistance, although the latter may have been weakened by the development of new techniques to deal with crop residues, and to find economic end uses for them.

CHAPTER 6

INTEGRATED POLLUTION CONTROL

6.1 INTRODUCTION

In accounting for the development of the concept of integrated pollution control, which culminated in its enactment in Part I of EPA 1990, it is necessary to acknowledge the significant debt owed by Parliament to the Royal Commission on Environmental Pollution. Since its establishment in February 1970, with the remit: 'to advise on matters, both national and international, concerning the pollution of the environment; on the adequacy of research in this field; and the future possibilities of danger to the environment',[1] the Royal Commission has examined and reported on various aspects and manifestations of environmental pollution. On 12 June 1974, the Royal Commission was invited by the Secretary of State for the Environment:

> 'To review the efficacy of the methods of control of air pollution from domestic and industrial sources, to consider the relationship between the relevant authorities and to make recommendations.'

The review itself was undertaken against the background of public concern, criticism of the Alkali and Clean Air Inspectorate, and the division of functions between the Inspectorate and local authorities. In the Royal Commission's Fifth Report, *Air Pollution Control: An Integrated Approach*,[2] which followed the review, the Commission acknowledged that it had found it increasingly difficult to limit its thinking to the remit which had been specified for it. Thus, rather than address the issue of air pollution control in a vacuum, the Royal Commission extended its field of vision to pollution control generally for the reason that:

> '... pollution of the air cannot be looked at in isolation from pollution of land or water. The reduction of emissions to the atmosphere can lead to an increase in wastes to be disposed of on land or discharged to water, and vice versa. If the optimum environmental solutions are to be found the controlling authority must be able to look comprehensively at all forms of pollution arising from industrial processes where difficult control problems exist.' (para 13)

This realisation that the best way of achieving effective pollution control was by adopting an integrated approach led to a further important recommendation by the Royal Commission: that a unified pollution inspectorate should be established to perform the task of IPC. It was envisaged that the new

1 *Air Pollution Control: An Integrated Approach* Cmnd 6371 (1976).

2 Cmnd 6371 (1976).

Inspectorate would be based on the Alkali and Clean Air Inspectorate and would be known as Her Majesty's Pollution Inspectorate (HMPI). However, in *Air Pollution Control*,[1] the Government's tardy response to the Royal Commission's Fifth Report, the related recommendations of a system of IPC and a unified body to enforce that system were separated by the Government in order that it could embrace one, while, at the same time, reject the other. The recommendation that a broad approach be taken to the control of pollution was regarded by the Government as the Royal Commission's 'most important contribution in this report', since the logic of such an approach was 'unassailable'. Nevertheless, the Government's acceptance of IPC was qualified. The principle was clearly attractive, but in spite of several examples identified by the Royal Commission in its report whereby pollution control had not occurred due to a failure to appreciate that to control discharges to one environmental medium may actually increase those to other such media, the Government considered that it was not easy to assess the real benefits that might accrue from the application of a system of IPC. Indeed, in a negative tone, the Government's response argued that:

> '... there is probably not a large number of situations in which major choices exist in practice regarding the forms in which pollution arises; and there is little evidence that the present system is seriously failing in terms of achieving a sensible balance in the control of pollution in different forms.' (para 5)

The Government considered that the creation of HMPI to administer the system of IPC would have a 'profound effect' upon the pollution control organisation that existed at the time. In essence, the Government was concerned that the effect of the Royal Commission's proposal would be to give rise to: 'a substantial increase in operational complexity by establishing another level in the control machinery', with the result that the existing pollution control authorities would tend to see that their position in relation to industry was being undermined. Accordingly, the creation of HMPI was, for the time being, rejected by the Government, although the door was left open for a change in policy if subsequent experience showed that this was necessary. As it turned out, the need for a central inspectorate achieved an irresistible momentum, and Her Majesty's Inspectorate of Pollution (HMIP) was accordingly established on 1 April 1987.

The next important stage in the chronology of events leading to the creation of a system of IPC was the publication by the DoE of a consultation paper on this subject in 1988, in which it was argued by the Government that there was a need to introduce an IPC system which would:

- introduce an effective cross-media approach to pollution control leading to a real and lasting overall reduction in pollution;
- fully accord with the UK's EC and international commitments;
- build upon the existing UK approach to pollution control in recognising the need to balance the application and cost of technology with effective

1 Pollution Paper No 18 (1982).

protection of the environment in terms of, for example, environment quality objectives (EQOs) and standards;

- be clear and transparent in operation;
- not impose excessive costs or delays upon industry;
- be practicable and cost-effective to implement;
- be adaptable to future developments in both science and technology.

6.1.1 Environmental Protection Act 1990

These objectives were, to a large extent, reflected subsequently in the provisions of Part I of the Environmental Protection Bill. The Bill itself was an absolute necessity in view of the radical overhaul being proposed for the UK system of pollution control. Such changes could be effected only by way of primary legislation. Nevertheless, it would be wrong to view the Environmental Protection Act 1990 (EPA 1990) as simply the vehicle for the establishment of IPC in the UK. This extensive piece of legislation also dealt with a wide variety of other environmental issues, such as waste on land, statutory nuisances, litter, genetically modified organisms, the creation of new conservation councils for England, Wales and Scotland, as well as other more idiosyncratic measures, such as abandoned shopping trolleys. The wide-ranging and eclectic nature of its provisions, which broadly fall under the theme of environmental protection, was not, however, welcomed by all. In the debate on the second reading of the Environmental Protection Bill in the House of Commons, the then 'shadow' Secretary of State for the Environment, Bryan Gould MP, dismissed the measure in the following terms:[1]

> 'The Bill is disappointing because it is little more than a rag-bag of measures drawn from disparate sources, many of which have been dusted down and brought to life again simply to be cobbled together to give it a lick of green paint and the impression of action and cohesion.'

Further criticisms were made of the Bill during the course of its parliamentary stages. In some instances, these criticisms centred as much upon what the Bill did not contain, such as a stated commitment to the principles of the EC Fourth Environmental Action Programme, or the creation of a new Environmental Protection Agency, as they did on the contents of the Bill itself. Nevertheless, its individual parts were closely scrutinised both on the floor of the two Houses of Parliament and in the Committee Room where the Bill was considered by Standing Committee H from 23 January to 20 March 1990. Certain Parts of the Bill, such as Part VII, which creates separate nature conservation councils for England, Wales and Scotland, were the favoured topics of a number of those who spoke in the parliamentary debates. It is worth noting, however, that the IPC provisions were the subject of broad parliamentary approval even if Bryan Gould MP described them as being 'long overdue' and generally deficient in that they would actually fail to prevent pollution. A more whole-hearted welcome for Part I of the Bill was received from Sir Hugh Rossi MP, the then Chairman of the House of

1 HC Deb, vol 165, col 50 (15 January 1990).

Commons Environment Select Committee. During the course of the second reading debate, he declared that:[1]

> 'I welcome Part I because of the integrated pollution control regime that it introduces. As has been said on previous occasions, it is impossible to separate the interrelationship between land, water and air and the effect that emissions into one has upon all the others. Environmentalists outside the House have generally recognised that Part I will introduce the most stringent form of pollution control to be found in Europe. That is something to be proud of, not to be thrown away lightly or for party political reasons.'

6.2 PRESCRIBED PROCESSES AND PRESCRIBED SUBSTANCES

Section 2 of EPA 1990 is concerned with the prescription of processes and substances by the Secretary of State by way of delegated legislation. The power to make regulations in this respect has been exercised on a number of occasions since this provision came into force (see the Environmental Protection (Prescribed Processes and Substances) Regulations 1991, SI 1991/472 (the 1991 Regulations), as amended by SI 1991/836, SI 1992/614, SI 1993/1749, SI 1993/2405, SI 1994/1271, SI 1994/1329, and SI 1996/2678). For the purposes of Part I of EPA 1990, 'process' is defined as being 'any activities carried on in Great Britain, whether on premises or by means of mobile plant, which are capable of causing pollution of the environment' (s 1(5)). A 'prescribed process' is a process which has been prescribed under s 2(1). 'Substance' includes electricity or heat (s 1(3)) and 'prescribed substance' means a substance prescribed under s 2(5) or (6) respectively.

The IPC regime is concerned with the regulation of the most complex industrial processes, and their emissions into all environmental media, whereas the local authority air pollution control (LAAPC) regime is concerned with the less complex industrial processes, and their emissions into the atmosphere alone. The 1991 Regulations seek to distinguish those processes designated for central control from those designated for local control by adopting a classification based on two lists, 'A' and 'B'. Part 'A' list processes fall under the jurisdiction of the Environment Agency and will thus be further considered in this chapter. Part 'B' list processes are generally subject to local authority control where they give rise to emissions to air, but in respect of discharges to land and water, such processes remain subject to the control of the Environment Agency. Accordingly, they will be considered in Chapter 7.

6.2.1 Part 'A' list processes

Schedule 1 to the 1991 Regulations is concerned with the description of Part 'A' and Part 'B' list processes. These processes are divided into six broad categories which appear as separate chapters in the Regulations. The chapters

1 HC Deb, vol 165, col 59 (15 January 1990).

are, in turn, subdivided into a number of sections. Part 'A' list processes are therefore as follows:

Chapter 1

Fuel production and combustion: gasification and associated processes (s 1.1), eg reforming or refining natural gas, odorising natural gas or liquefied petroleum gas or producing gas from coal; carbonisation and associated processes (s 1.2), eg pyrolysis, carbonisation, distillation, liquefaction, partial oxidation or other heat treatment of coal; combustion processes (s 1.3), eg burning any fuel in a boiler or furnace with a net rated thermal input of 50 megawatts or more, or in gas turbines or compression ignition engines of like capacity; petroleum processes (s 1.4), eg the loading, unloading or other handling of, the storage of, or the physical, chemical or thermal treatment of crude oil, stabilised crude petroleum or crude shale oil.

Chapter 2

Metal production and processing: iron and steel production (s 2.1), eg crushing, grading, grinding, screening, washing or drying iron ore or making, melting or refining iron, steel or any ferrous alloy or desulphurising iron, steel or any ferrous alloy produced by a Part A process or heating iron, steel or any ferrous alloy in order to remove grease, oil or any other non-metallic contaminant where this is related to other Part A iron and steel processes; non-ferrous metal processes (s 2.2), eg the mining of zinc or tin where the process may result in the release into water of cadmium or any compound of cadmium or the refining of any non-ferrous metal or non-ferrous metal alloy except where the process falls within specified paragraphs in Part B of s 2.2.

Chapter 3

Mineral industries: cement and lime manufacture and associated processes (s 3.1), eg making or grinding cement clinker or heating calcium carbonate or calcium magnesium carbonate for the purpose of making lime; processes involving asbestos (s 3.2), eg producing raw asbestos by extraction from the ore, the manufacture and industrial finishing of products such as asbestos cement, asbestos filters, asbestos floor coverings and asbestos textiles, or destroying a railway vehicle by burning if asbestos has been incorporated in, or sprayed onto, its structure; other mineral fibres (s 3.3), manufacturing glass fibre or any fibre from any mineral other than asbestos; glass manufacture and production (s 3.5), manufacturing glass or enamel frit and its use in any process where that process is related to its manufacture; ceramic production (s 3.6), firing heavy clay goods or refractory material in a kiln where a reducing atmosphere is used for a purpose other than coloration.

Chapter 4

Chemical industries: petrochemical processes (s 4.1), eg any process for the manufacture or polymerisation or co-polymerisation of unsaturated hydrocarbons; the manufacture and use of organic chemicals (s 4.2), eg the manufacture of styrene, vinyl chloride, acetylene, any aldehyde, amine, isocyanate, nitrile, any carboxylic acid or any anhydride of carboxylic acid or any organic sulphur compound or any phenol where the process may result in the release of any such substance into the air; acid processes (s 4.3), eg any process for the manufacture, recovery, concentration or distillation of sulphuric acid or oleum or any process for the manufacture or recovery of nitric acid or the manufacture or purification of phosphoric acid; processes involving halogens (s 4.4), eg any process for the manufacture of fluorine, chlorine, bromine, iodine, or hydrogen fluoride/chloride/bromide/iodide or any of their acids, or any process for the manufacture of chemicals which may result in the release into the air of any of the four last mentioned compounds; inorganic chemical processes (s 4.5), eg the manufacture of hydrogen cyanide or hydrogen sulphide other than in the course of fumigation, or the production of any compound containing antimony, arsenic, beryllium, gallium, indium, lead, palladium, platinum, selenium, tellurium or thallium where the process may result in the release into the air of any of these elements or compounds or the release into water of any substance prescribed in Sch 5 to the 1991 Regulations; chemical fertiliser production (s 4.6), eg the manufacture of chemical fertilisers or their conversion into granules; pesticide production (s 4.7), where the manufacture or formulation of chemical pesticides may result in the release into water of any substance prescribed in Sch 5; pharmaceutical production (s 4.8), where the manufacture or formulation of a medicinal product may result in the release into water of any substance prescribed in Sch 5.

Chapter 5

Waste disposal and recycling: incineration (s 5.1), eg the destruction by burning in an incinerator of any waste chemicals or waste plastics arising from the manufacture of a chemical or plastic, or compounds or elements including bromine, cadmium, lead, mercury, sulphur or zinc, or animal remains; recovery processes (s 5.2), eg the recovery by distillation of any oil or organic solvent; production of fuel from waste (s 5.3), eg making solid fuel from waste by any process involving the use of heat other than making charcoal.

Chapter 6

Other industries: paper and pulp manufacturing processes (s 6.1), eg the making of paper pulp where the capacity for production is more than 25,000 tonnes per annum; di-isocyanate processes (s 6.2), eg any process for the manufacture of any di-isocyanate or a partly polymerised di-isocyanate; tar and bitumen processes (s 6.3), eg the distillation of tar or bitumen in connection with any other process of manufacture; coating processes and printing (s 6.5), eg the application or removal of a coating material containing one or more tributyltin compounds or triphenyltin compounds at a ship or boatyard with the capacity to build, maintain or repair vessels in excess of 25 metres in length; manufacture of dyestuffs, printing ink and coating materials (s 6.6), any process for the manufacture of dyestuffs if the process involves the use of hexachlorobenzene; timber processes (s 6.7), the curing or chemical treatment as part of a manufacturing process of timber or wooden or mainly wooden products with any substance prescribed in Sch 5; treatment and processing of animal or vegetable matter (s 6.9), eg processing, storing or drying of any dead animal or plant matter if the process may result in the release into water of a substance prescribed in Sch 5.

6.2.2 Interpretation of Sch 1 to the Environmental Protection (Prescribed Processes and Substances) Regulations 1991

Schedule 1 to the 1991 Regulations thus distinguishes between a wide variety of industrial processes and determines, on the basis of their complexity, whether they are subject to central or local control. Where one particular process is carried on at a site to the exclusion of all other processes, designation as a Part A or Part B list process ought to be a relatively straightforward task. However, it may often be the case that a number of different but related processes are carried on at the same site, or that a site has unrelated processes taking place within its confines. In these circumstances, designating processes as either Part A or Part B list processes may give rise to difficulties, especially where the relevant process or part of a process does not necessarily fall within the chapters and sections of Sch 1. Some assistance in respect of this matter is provided by Sch 2 to the 1991 Regulations. This Schedule lays down a number of rules for the interpretation of Sch 1, although they do not override any specific provision in that Schedule. Rule 2, for example, states that all descriptions of processes in Sch 1 include any other process carried on at the same location by the same person as part of that process. Thus, to use an example which appears in the DoE publication *Integrated Pollution Control: A Practical Guide* (1991), three blast cupolas (Part B) and an iron and steel refinery (Part A) operated by the same person at the same location would constitute one iron and steel process for IPC control and would, therefore, require one authorisation. It is apparent from this example that if the processes involved are described in both Part A and Part B of the same section, they are to be regarded as part of a Part A process and should therefore be subject to central control (rule 3).

Where, however, the relevant processes fall within different sections of Sch 1, even though they are operated by the same person at the same site, they would constitute two processes and would thus require two authorisations. Finally, in this context, it is worth noting that where a process falls within more than one of the descriptions in Sch 1, that process is to be regarded as only falling within the most apt description. If, however, the descriptions are equally apt and are in different sections in Chapter 4 (the chemical industry), rule 4 provides for an order of priority for determining the description.

6.2.3 Exceptions

Regulation 4 of the 1991 Regulations exempts certain categories of process from the need to obtain an authorisation before they can lawfully be carried on. Thus, for example, a process is not to be taken to be a Part A process if it cannot result in the release into the air, water or land of a prescribed substance (as defined in Sch 4, 5 or 6 respectively), or that, if it does, the quantity of the prescribed substance is no greater than the background concentration in water, is incapable of causing harm, or has an insignificant capacity to cause harm where it is present in the air or on land. Exemptions are also provided for working museums, school displays, the running of an engine to power aircraft, hovercraft, road vehicles, railway locomotives and ships or other vessels, and processes which are carried on as a domestic activity in connection with a private dwelling. A fume cupboard is also an exempt process, provided it is used in a laboratory for research or testing and does not amount to an industrial and continuous production process enclosure or a cupboard in which substances or materials are manufactured. Where a defendant seeks to rely upon an exemption in reg 4, the burden of proof lies with him. The Divisional Court so held in *Tandridge District Council v P & S Civil Engineering Ltd*[1] in accordance with the terms of s 101 of the Magistrates' Courts Act 1980. It would seem to follow from this that in the context of a dispute between a process operator and an enforcing authority as to whether an application for an authorisation should be submitted, it will be for the operator to show that the process is exempted from this requirement by reg 4, rather than for the enforcing authority to show that it is not.

6.2.4 Prescribed substances

The control which Part I of EPA 1990 exerts over potentially polluting industrial activity is primarily concerned with the regulation of processes rather than substances. Generally speaking, the release of substances will be controlled as a consequence of the process authorisation requirement. However, for some substances, more specific provision is made in that they are prescribed substances, the release of which into the air is subject to control under ss 6 and 7 of EPA 1990. Whereas industrial processes are prescribed according to the nature of the process, substances are prescribed according to the environmental medium into which they are released. Schedules 4, 5 and 6 to the 1991 Regulations deal respectively with prescribed substances released into air, water and land. For present purposes, it is the prescribed substances in respect of a release into air with which we are concerned. Schedule 4 lists these substances as follows:

- oxides of sulphur and other sulphur compounds;
- oxides of nitrogen and other nitrogen compounds;
- oxides of carbon;
- organic compounds and partial oxidation products;
- metals, metalloids and their compounds;
- asbestos (suspended particulate matter and fibres), glass fibres and mineral fibres;
- halogens and their compounds;
- phosphorous and its compounds;
- particulate matter.

These substances, which largely mirror those to be found in Directive 84/360/EEC on air pollution from industrial plants, are subject to specific

1 [1995] Env LR 67.

requirements to ensure that the best available techniques not entailing excessive cost (BATNEEC) are used to prevent their release into the air. If this is not practicable, BATNEEC are used to minimise such releases.

6.3 AUTHORISATIONS

Sections 6 to 12 of EPA 1990 represent the means by which the Environment Agency and local authorities can exert some measure of control over atmospheric discharges by prescribed industrial processes. Essentially this has been achieved by stipulating in s 6(1) of the Act that:

> 'No person shall carry on a prescribed process after the date prescribed or determined for that description of process by or under regulations under section 2(1)... except under an authorisation granted by the enforcing authority and in accordance with the conditions to which it is subject.'

The key feature of this provision is that in order for a prescribed process to be carried on, it is necessary that it has first been authorised by the appropriate enforcing authority. If a process operator were to attempt to carry on that process without first having sought and obtained the relevant authorisation, then that person would be guilty of an offence under s 23(1)(a) of EPA 1990, and would be liable, on summary conviction, to a fine not exceeding £20,000, or, if convicted on indictment, to a fine or to imprisonment for a term not exceeding two years, or both. Clearly, therefore, there is a considerable incentive to comply with the terms of s 6(1).

6.3.1 Applying for an authorisation

The actual mechanics of applying for an authorisation are dealt with in Part I of Sch I to EPA 1990, and the Environmental Protection (Applications, Appeals and Registers) Regulations 1991, SI 1991/507 made pursuant thereto. Regulation 2 of the Regulations requires that an application for an authorisation shall be made in writing and that it shall contain the name of the applicant and his telephone number and address. If the address to which any correspondence relating to the application is to be sent is different from that given by the applicant, then the second address should also be stated, as should the address of its registered or principal office where the applicant is a body corporate. Regulation 2 distinguishes between applications where the prescribed process is to be carried on by means of mobile plant from those where this is not the intention. In the case of the former, it is necessary that the application includes the name of the local authority in whose area the applicant has his principal place of business and the address of that place of business. However, where the application relates to a prescribed process which will not be carried on by means of mobile plant, it must contain the following information:

- the name of any local authority in whose area the prescribed process will be carried on;

- the address of the premises where the prescribed process will be carried on;
- a map or plan showing the location of those premises; and
- if only part of those premises will be used for carrying on the process, a plan or other means of identifying that part.

All applications for authorisations, whether they relate to mobile or non-mobile plant and whether they are made to the Environment Agency or a local authority, must include information relating to the prescribed process itself. Thus, it is necessary to provide a description of the prescribed process, and a list of prescribed substances and any other substances which might cause harm if released into the environment which will be used in connection with, or which will result from, the carrying on of that process. Where the application for authorisation is made to a local authority, it is necessary to list, in addition to prescribed substances, only those other substances which might cause harm if released into the air. Further detailed information required by reg 2 takes the form of the following:

- a description of the techniques to be used for preventing the release into any environmental medium (or, in the case of LAAPC control, to air alone) of prescribed and environmentally harmful substances, for reducing the release of such substances to a minimum and for rendering harmless any substances which are released;
- details of any proposed release of prescribed and environmentally harmful substances into any environmental medium (or, in the case of LAAPC control, to air alone) and an assessment of the environmental consequences;
- proposals for monitoring any release of such substances, the environmental consequences of any such release and the use of any techniques to prevent release already described in the application;
- the matters on which the applicant relies to establish that the objectives in s 7(2) of EPA 1990 (including, in the case of IPC control, the objective referred to in s 7(7)) will be achieved and that he will be able to comply with the general condition implied by s 7(4).

In addition to all the above information, an applicant is entitled to include in his application such further information as he wishes the enforcing authority to take into account in considering his application. The picture which thus emerges is that the decision on whether or not to grant an authorisation is made on the basis of detailed information provided by the applicant in accordance with the requirements of the Regulations. However, if the relevant enforcing authority takes the view that it requires some further information for the purpose of determining the application, it may require, by notice in writing, that the applicant provides the information that has been requested within a specified time period (EPA 1990, Sch 1, Part I, para 1(3)).

Generally speaking, applications for process authorisations will be determined by the appropriate enforcing authority, ie the Environment Agency in respect of Part A processes, and local authorities in respect of Part B processes. However, by virtue of Sch 1, Part I, para 3 to EPA 1990, the Secretary of State may issue a direction to the enforcing authority stating that he is to determine a particular application or class of applications. In other words, he may 'call-in' applications for his own determination in the same way that he may 'call-in' applications for planning permission in accordance with his power under s 177 of the Town and Country Planning Act 1990. Where an application for an authorisation has been transmitted to the Secretary of State, the enforcing authority must notify the applicant of this. The power to 'call-in' an application is likely to be exercised only in limited circumstances where, for example, the application has aroused considerable public concern or where it relates to a sensitive or controversial process. In order to assist the determination process, the Secretary of State may cause a local inquiry to be held, or afford the applicant and the relevant enforcing authority the opportunity to appear before a person appointed by him. Where a local inquiry is held in England or Wales, s 250(2)–(5) of the Local Government Act 1972 governs the procedure to be followed. Once an application has been determined by the Secretary of State, he shall issue directions to the relevant enforcing authority on whether or not to grant the application and, if so, on the conditions to be attached to the authorisation. An identical 'call-in' power, which is subject to the same requirements, also exists in respect of applications for the variation of an authorisation (EPA 1990, Sch 1, Part II, para 8).

Concerns have been expressed about the length of time it may take to secure a process authorisation, and the amount of work involved for the operator. In the case of one company, BASF plc, it has been contended that: 'at least 60 man days were tied up in obtaining a relatively simple authorisation for a large combustion process'.[1] Figures which appeared in the HMIP Annual Report for 1993/94 revealed that approximately 59.6 per cent of all processes authorised during this period had their applications determined within the four-month time-limit laid down in EPA 1990. While this was still less than satisfactory, it did represent a considerable improvement on the figures for 1991/92 and 1992/93, which stood at 22 per cent and 16 per cent respectively. Nevertheless, for seven per cent of all the cases, the determination period was in excess of 12 months. In the same report, it was stated that:

> 'HMIP is acutely aware that its prime duty is to protect the environment, and is committed to delivering authorisations and the environmental improvements which they are intended to secure within the minimum possible time in order that powers can be exercised under EPA 90. Nevertheless, extra time spent on a particular case can pay dividends in terms of reaching a better understanding of the issues, and thus devising a more closely targeted authorisation.' (p 5)

Further difficulties were initially experienced in relation to the filling out of authorisation application forms. It was felt by some that the guidance note on the application procedure was not helpful, with the result that large numbers of the earlier applications were rejected. Indeed, HMIP noted in its 1993/94 Annual Report that the IPC applications for 1991 and 1992 were 'generally of a

1 Drake (ed), *Integrated Pollution Control* (Cambridge: Royal Society of Chemistry, no 152, 1994).

very poor standard'. Greater emphasis was therefore placed on providing individual guidance for applicants, with the result that, by 1994, the regulator confidently asserted that: 'Applications are now of a far better quality and can be determined more efficiently'.[1]

6.3.2 Granting an authorisation

Section 7 of EPA 1990 is the central regulatory provision in Part I of the Act since it is concerned with the conditions which will be attached to process authorisations granted by the Environment Agency. The prospect of an unconditional authorisation does not arise, therefore, under the IPC regime or, for that matter, under the LAAPC regime. All Part A authorisations are subject to: such specific conditions as the Agency considers appropriate; such conditions as are specified by the Secretary of State; and an implied general condition in s 7(4) which requires that, in carrying on an IPC process, the operator must use BATNEEC to prevent the release of prescribed substances into any environmental medium for which they have been prescribed, or, where that is not practicable, to reduce such substances to a minimum and for rendering them harmless and, in the case of any other substances which might cause harm to the environment if released, to render them harmless (see further below). Where the Agency decides to impose specific conditions, it will do so for the purposes of achieving the objectives laid down in s 7(2) of the Act. The relevant objectives are:

- ensuring that BATNEEC is used when carrying on a process;
- compliance with any directions made by the Secretary of State for the purposes of implementing any of the UK's EC or international law obligations in respect of environmental protection;
- compliance with any limits or requirements, and achievement of any quality standards or quality objectives prescribed by the Secretary of State under any of the following enactments: s 2 of the Clean Air Act 1968; s 2 of the European Communities Act 1972; Part I of the Health and Safety at Work etc Act 1974; Parts II, III or IV of the Control of Pollution Act 1974; the Water Resources Act 1991; s 3 of EPA 1990; and, s 87 of the Environment Act 1995;
- compliance with any requirements applicable to the grant of authorisations specified by or under a plan made by the Secretary of State under s 3(5) of EPA 1990.

With regard to the issue of directions in order to give effect to an EC obligation, the Secretary of State has used the power provided by s 7(2) on several occasions, most notably when making the Municipal Waste Incineration Directions 1991 and the Large Combustion Plant (New Plant) Directions 1995. These Directions implement, respectively, Directive 89/369/EEC and Directive 89/429/EEC (on new and existing municipal waste incineration plants) and Directive 88/609/EEC, as amended by Directive 94/66/EEC (on large combustion plant).

1 HMIP, Annual Report 1993/94.

Since all process authorisations that are granted will contain conditions, it is necessary that there is a mechanism by which such conditions can be reviewed in order to ensure that they remain relevant and appropriate and that they continue to comply with BATNEEC (see **6.4**). By virtue of s 6(6) of EPA, the Agency is under a duty to carry out a review of the conditions of each individual IPC authorisation which has been granted at least once in every four years. In practice, however, the Agency has had difficulty in complying with its statutory duty (see **6.25**). Where a review reveals that there is a need to alter or amend a condition or conditions attached to an authorisation, this may be achieved by serving a variation notice on the process operator (see **6.10**).

6.4 BATNEEC

Despite the importance of BATNEEC to the regulation of the IPC processes, the term is not defined by EPA 1990. The statute does, however, provide some assistance by declaring in s 7(10) that:

> 'References to the best available techniques not entailing excessive cost, in relation to a process, include (in addition to references to any technical means and technology) references to the number, qualifications, training and supervision of persons employed in the process and the design, construction, lay-out and maintenance of the buildings in which it is carried on'.

Thus, for the purposes of Part I of EPA 1990, BATNEEC is a wider concept than it was in its original form in the EC Framework Directive 84/360/EEC on industrial air pollution, where it required preventative measures and the use of best available technology not entailing excessive cost. Further clarification of the meaning of BATNEEC has been provided in the DoE publication, *Integrated Pollution Control: A Practical Guide* (1997). The terms are accordingly defined as follows:

- '*best*': the techniques which are most effective in preventing, minimising or rendering harmless polluting releases. It is noted that there may be more than one set of 'best' techniques;
- '*available*': the technique must be procurable by the process operator. This means, therefore, that it must be a generally accessible technique, although it need not be in general use, and, accordingly, it may include a technique which has been developed or proven at a pilot scale and can be applied with business confidence. A technique does not cease to be available if its source is outside the UK, nor does the fact that there is a monopoly supplier necessarily make it unavailable;
- '*techniques*': some assistance is provided by s 7(10) (see above). Essentially, the term embraces both the plant in which the process is carried on, and how the process is actually operated in practice. The concept and components of the plant are therefore considered together with the numbers and qualifications of the staff, working methods, training and supervision, and the design, construction, maintenance and lay-out of the relevant buildings.

The second part of the BATNEEC concept, 'not entailing excessive cost' (NEEC), clearly imports an economic element into the process of determining the best available techniques (BAT) for a particular process. Where the benefits of employing particular techniques outweigh the cost of applying BAT, they do not entail excessive cost. In this context, the benefits are primarily the prevention of environmental harm. Clearly, therefore, the determination of BATNEEC involves striking a balance between the need to ensure environmental protection while, at the same time, acknowledging that there are economic restrictions on how this can be achieved in practice. Generally speaking, however, it would seem that the greater the environmental harm that may result from a process, the greater the costs of BAT that can be required of the operator before those costs can be said to have become excessive.

6.4.1 New processes

In the case of new processes, costs can be taken into account where the cost of BAT would be excessive having regard to the particular industry in question and the degree of protection which would be achieved as a result. Thus, there may be circumstances where to require an operator to make a modification to a process or to install particular abatement technology may entail costs which are excessive on the basis that they will only result in a very marginal increase in environmental protection. For example, if a process could have its emissions reduced by 95 per cent on the basis of an expenditure of £20,000, and by 96 per cent if £120,000 were spent, it would seem likely that the first option could be justified on the basis of BATNEEC. Although the latter option actually ensures a greater degree of environmental protection, the difference is so marginal that it would be unlikely to justify additional costs of £100,000. Nevertheless, it should be noted that the profitability of an individual operator will never be a justification for the relaxation of BATNEEC standards since, were this to happen, it would be clear that the interests of environmental protection had been subordinated to questions of cost. It is possible that even after BATNEEC requirements have been met, serious harm to the environment may still be the likely result of operating a particular process. If the Environment Agency forms this opinion in respect of a process, it is obliged to refuse an authorisation for that process, and it would be an offence if the operator were subsequently to carry it on (s 23(1)(a)). In any proceedings for an offence under s 23(1)(a) which consists of a failure to comply with the general BATNEEC condition contained in s 7(4), the onus of proof as regards techniques and evidence is on the accused. In other words, by virtue of s 25 of EPA 1990, the accused is required to prove that there was no better technique not entailing excessive cost than that which was, in fact, used to satisfy the s 7(4) condition.

6.4.2 Existing processes

Where the Environment Agency is dealing with existing processes, NEEC justifies requiring the phased replacement of plant in accordance with an established timescale. In other words, it is likely that a demand made of an operator immediately to upgrade its plant to the very latest standards would fall foul of the NEEC criteria. In determining NEEC, the Agency would be entitled to take into account a variety of factors, such as the technical characteristics of the existing plant, its rate of use and predicated life, the nature and volume of emissions, the economic condition of processors in the same industry sector, and further developments in techniques which have occurred since the construction of the plant. Nevertheless, as with new plant, it would be wrong to take into account a firm's inability to afford to reduce releases to the required level when assessing BATNEEC for existing plant.

6.5 BPEO

Where a prescribed process is subject to control by the Environment Agency and is likely to involve the release of substances into more than one environmental medium, s 7(7) of EPA 1990 adds a further objective to those general objectives specified in s 7(2). Accordingly, a process operator must endeavour to ensure that BATNEEC will be used for minimising the pollution which may be caused to the environment taken as a whole by the release of substances, having regard to the best practicable environmental option (BPEO) available in respect of the substances which may be released. Put more simply, BATNEEC has to be applied in order to achieve BPEO. The discussion which follows will therefore focus upon the origins of and background to the statutory recognition of the concept of BPEO, its meaning, and the way in which it may be calculated in practice.

6.5.1 Origins and background

The term 'best practicable environmental option' first appeared in the Royal Commission on Environmental Pollution's Fifth Report, *Air Pollution Control: An Integrated Approach.*[1] In this report, which advocated, inter alia, the establishment of a unified inspectorate to perform the task of pollution control, the Royal Commission argued for 'an expansion of the concept of "best practicable means" into an overall "best practicable environmental option"' as a control mechanism for dealing with difficult industrial pollution problems at source. The term 'best practicable means' had long been a feature of the legislation relating to the regulation of the alkali industry where it had been used as a standard for the control of industrial emissions. However, it was to become the antecedent of a concept which would have a more general application than it had itself enjoyed.

Despite the Government's subsequent rejection of the idea of a unified inspectorate (see **6.1** above), it did, as has already been noted, find certain aspects of the Fifth Report with which it was in agreement. Of these, the Government considered that the Royal Commission's 'most important contribution' in the report was the identification of 'the need for a broad approach to the control of pollution, and for pollution control authorities to

1 Cmnd 6371 (1976).

achieve the "best practicable environmental option'". However, while the Government believed BPEO to be a concept of 'considerable power and utility', it did not rush to breathe statutory life into it. In the meantime, the Royal Commission returned to the concept in its Tenth Report, *Tackling Pollution – Experience and Prospects*[1] and its Eleventh Report, *Managing Waste: The Duty of Care*,[2] and in its Twelfth Report, *Best Practicable Environmental Option*[3] it addressed the matter head-on, as the title of the report implies. In this report, concern was expressed at 'the indiscriminate use of the term to describe almost any course of action which takes some account of environmental factors', but this failing is, perhaps, not very surprising when it is borne in mind that a satisfactory definition of the concept did not exist. Indeed, it has been argued by Susan Owens[4] that:

> '... the term "BPEO" had crept into the vocabulary of environmental management. It was frequently cited, government and other organisations claimed to apply it, and it was even described as "the foundation of the waste management policy". Everyone, it seems, expressed BPEO, but few could really define it.'

6.5.2 Meaning

Precisely what is meant by BPEO is clearly of some importance to the operation of the IPC regime. Nevertheless, the concept is not actually defined in EPA 1990 and, therefore, it becomes necessary to consider non-statutory sources in the quest for a definition. In its Twelfth Report (see above), the Royal Commission stated that:

> 'A BPEO is the outcome of a systematic consultative and decision-making procedure which emphasises the protection and conservation of the environment across land, air and water. The BPEO procedure establishes, for a given set of objectives, the option that provides the most benefit or least damage to the environment as a whole, at acceptable cost, in the long term as well as in the short term.' (para 2.1)

This definition is of some assistance in that it emphasises the need for BPEO to emerge from a systematic and reasoned decision-making process in which full weight is given to the effect of the process in question on the environment as a whole, rather than on one of its individual parts only. There are a number of similarities between the Royal Commission's chosen form of words and the working definition that the Environment Agency has adopted for the purposes of IPC. In Technical Guidance Note E1 *Best Practicable Environmental Option Assessments for Integrated Pollution Control*, the Agency defines BPEO as:

---

1 Cmnd 9149 (1984).
2 Cmnd 9675 (1985).
3 Cmnd 310 (1988).
4 The Unified Pollution Inspectorate and Best Practicable Environmental Option in the United Kingdom, in Haigh and Irwin (eds) *Integrated Pollution Control in Europe and North America* (The Conservation Foundation, 1990) p 171.

> 'The option which in the context of releases from a prescribed process, provides the most benefit or least damage to the environment as a whole, at acceptable cost, in the long term as well as the short term.' (para 3.5.1)

It will be noted that the key distinction between the two definitions is that the latter makes express reference to the fact that the BPEO relates to 'releases from a prescribed process', whereas the former does not. By so doing, the Agency's definition excludes other environmental effects which arise from the carrying-on of the process, such as the production and delivery of raw materials for use in the process, and thus accords with the specific reference in s 7(7) to 'the substances which may be released'. Despite this adaptation of its original definition, the Royal Commission's Twelfth Report remains a useful source of information and discussion on BPEO. One area in which it is particularly helpful concerns the meanings that should be ascribed to the words 'best', 'practicable', 'environmental' and 'option'.

Taking these words in reverse order, the report stressed that 'the procedure for selecting a BPEO should include a diligent and imaginative search for alternative ways of achieving the desired result' (para 2.3). In other words, care should be taken to consider all the options open to the process operator before making a decision. The environmental effects of these options should, the Royal Commission felt, be considered at an early stage in the decision-making process, since it is 'often more cost effective' to do so than 'to apply remedies later' (para 2.4). Moreover, the report emphasised the need to consider both the local, remote and short- and long-term effects of a process on all environmental media. Turning to the question of what is meant in the present context by the word 'practicable', the Royal Commission noted that it was unaware of any judicial interpretation of that term as it appeared in the Alkali Industry Acts in the formulation 'best practicable means'. Accordingly, by adapting a definition of 'best practicable means' to be found in an HMIP guidance note of the time, the Royal Commission concluded that, for the purposes of BPEO, '"practicable" implies that the option must be in accordance with current technical knowledge and must not have disproportionate financial implications'. Finally, the Royal Commission considered what is meant by the term 'best' in the concept of BPEO. It concluded that 'it is doubtful that there ever is an absolute best' and that any 'best' practicable environmental option that was chosen was 'unlikely to be the best choice for all time' (para 2.9). For this reason, therefore, the Royal Commission recommended that it was necessary to keep BPEO under review.

6.5.3 Determining BPEO

Guidance on the determination of BPEO for IPC processes is now provided by the Environment Agency in the form of Technical Guidance Note E1, which was published in 1997 (see **6.5.2** above). The guidance itself represents the culmination of a relatively long and detailed process of discussion and consultation with a number of organisations and bodies, such as the Confederation of British Industry and the Chemical Industries Association, which recognised the need for guidance from the regulatory agency in this area.

In addition, the need for guidance has become apparent following criticism of the Agency by, for example, the House of Commons Environment Select Committee, for not being sufficiently rigorous about the BPEO requirement, and for failing to apply a consistent methodology in the determination of BPEO. Volume I of the guidance therefore sets out the principles and methodology which can be used for BPEO assessments of IPC processes. Volume II, which is a consultative draft, contains the data which the Agency has put together to support the methodology. The Agency envisages that the methodology will be widely used. Indeed, the Agency is heartened by the fact that a number of applications for IPC authorisations have already based their submissions on the methodology. However, it is important to note that the methodology is neither compulsory nor prescriptive. A process operator is not obliged to comply with it, and it may be the case that a modified methodology or a different approach is more appropriate in respect of an operator's own particular process. In essence, the methodology is illustrative of how a BPEO appraisal *could* be carried out in practice. Since it is claimed in the guidance that it amounts to 'a first step in an evolving approach to environmental assessment of IPC processes' it follows that further refinements are likely to be made to the methodology in the light of practical experience. Nevertheless, in the opinion of the Agency:

> 'The application of the methodology should ensure that sufficient information is provided by an operator to enable the environmental effects of releases to be properly assessed. It should ensure that the process or abatement option chosen represents the "BATNEEC" to minimise pollution to the environment as a whole having regard to the "BPEO". In this regard, application of the guidance will assist the Agency in fulfilling its vision to "protect and improve the environment as a whole by effective regulation, by our own actions and by working with and influencing others".' (para 1.15)

Turning to the actual determination of BPEO, the guidance envisages that this process entails six stages which are similar to those advocated by the Royal Commission on Environmental Pollution in its Twelfth Report. The methodology therefore involves: defining the objective; generating options for achieving the objective; assessing the options; summarising and presenting the assessment; identifying BPEO; and reviewing BPEO. The discussion which follows seeks to explain a little more fully what is to happen at each of these various stages.

6.5.4 Defining the objective of the BPEO

A BPEO assessment will necessarily commence with a definition of the objective of the IPC process which is subject to the assessment. The guidance states, for example, that the objective for a new IPC process might be 'to produce a product or provide a service and operate the process in accordance with the aims of Integrated Pollution Control'. The question 'what are the aims of IPC?' is answered by the DoE publication, *Integrated Pollution Control: A Practical Guide* (1997). Thus, the aims of IPC include the following:

- to prevent or minimise the release of prescribed substances and to render harmless all substances which are released;
- to develop an approach to pollution control that considers releases from industrial processes to all media in the environment as a whole;
- to improve the effectiveness and efficiency of pollution controls on industry;
- to provide the appropriate framework to encourage cleaner technologies and the minimisation of waste;
- to maintain public confidence in the regulatory system through a clear and transparent system that is accessible and easy to understand, and is clear and simple in operation.

6.5.5 Generating options for achieving the objective of BPEO

At this relatively early stage in the determination of BPEO it is necessary to conduct a fundamental examination of the whole process. Ideally, the guidance suggests that all practicable options should be assessed in detail but, in practice, this seems unlikely since the benefits which may accrue from such an approach may be outweighed by the costs incurred by an applicant in carrying out environmental assessments for several options. Accordingly, the guidance advocates identifying a preferred option at an early stage, followed by an identification and quantification of those substances which will be released from this option, whether or not prescribed. In terms of the actual quantification of releases, it is suggested that an operator should supply information on: the concentration of substances in the release; the proposed release rate, ie quantity per unit of time; and an estimate of the total annual load released. This information is required in respect of peak releases, the proposed normal operating conditions and fugitive releases.

While all substances which may be released from the preferred option ought to be identified, it appears to be unnecessary to take what the guidance terms 'insignificant releases' through the rest of the assessment. In the present context, 'insignificant' means that the release in question has insignificant environmental effects. Insignificance can be determined by estimating the environmental concentration that would result from a release, the process contribution (PC), and comparing this with the environmental assessment level (EAL). Although insignificance has not been ascribed a fixed percentage of EAL in the guidance, the Environment Agency has proposed that, as a rule of thumb, insignificant substances are those for which:

- the long-term PC in air is less than 0.2 per cent of the long-term EAL for air;
- the long-term PC in water is less than 0.2 per cent of the long-term EAL for water;
- the deposition rate on land is less than 0.2 per cent of the maximum deposition rate for land;
- the short-term PC in air is less than 0.2 per cent of the short-term EAL for air; or

- the short-term PC in water is less than 0.2 per cent of the short-term EAL for water.

In order to minimise pollution to the environment as a whole having regard to BPEO, the guidance stresses the need for attention to be focused during option generation on priorities from the perspective of environmental effects. Substances released from the preferred option can be prioritised in terms of their environmental effects in a number of different ways. The guidance suggests that this may be done by: comparison with IPC guidance notes; chimney height determination; comparison of predicted environmental concentration with EAL; determination of compliance with environmental quality standards; consideration of sensitive receptors; and consideration of other environmental effects from the process.

Chimney height determination is clearly of importance in terms of releases to air. The guidance emphasises the need for operators to show that the current chimney height provides adequate dispersion for those pollutants produced by the process. Guidance on the assessment of chimney heights is currently to be found in Technical Guidance Note (Dispersion) D1, *Guidelines on Discharge Stack Heights for Polluting Emissions* (June 1993). In the event that the calculations show that the chimney height is inadequate, further calculations will need to be undertaken in order to identify the level of control which will be required to ensure adequate dispersion through the existing stack. Where it is practicable to do so, the guidance states that vents should be combined into a single release point and analysis on the basis of Technical Guidance Note D1 or some other technique should be used to determine the vent release height. The normal expectation is that a vent will be at least three metres above the building or structure.

6.5.6 Assessing the options of BPEO

This third stage in the determination of BPEO involves the assessment of the environmental effects of each option. These environmental effects include: long-term effects in air, water and land; short-term effects (particularly in air and water); global warming; ozone creation; waste arisings; and other environmental effects such as odour, visible plumes, critical loads and stratospheric ozone-depletion potential. The first step in this stage entails the identification and quantification of all the substances released from an option, whether or not prescribed, in order that the environmental effects of each option can be assessed and then compared. For the purposes of assessing the overall long-term effects of releases, the Agency proposes to use EALs, which will be the statutory environmental quality standard (EQS) where such a standard exists. Where no such standard exists, the Agency has derived provisional EALs from various data, which are to be used as indicators of environmental quality and assist in the prioritisation of the substances released and option selection. Volume II of the guidance contains these provisional EALs for the release of particular substances into the three environmental media. Thus, for example, the long-term EAL for the release of ammonia into the air is 170 micrograms per cubic metre, whereas, for chlorine, the long-term

EAL is 15 micrograms per cubic metre for release into the same environmental medium. However, the guidance notes that such values should be approached with caution in view of the fact that there are differences of opinion on how EALs should be derived. Accordingly, a working party is to be set up to advise on methods for determining EALs, and to recommend alternatives if it is felt appropriate to do so.

An environmental quotient (EQ) for each substance released to air from a preferred option can be calculated by dividing the PC by the relevant long-term EAL. The total EQ for air can then be calculated by adding together the EQs for each particular substance. Moreover, an integrated environmental index (IEI), in which the overall environmental effect of the option is obtained, can be calculated by adding together the EQ for each medium. Where the assessment is concerned with the identification of the photochemical ozone creation potential (POCP) for each option, this can be achieved by adding together the POCPs of each substance released by that option. The POCP for each substance is itself calculated by the product of the mass of the substance (in tonnes) released by the process over a unit of time and the individual POCP value for the gas concerned. The average POCP for a range of different compounds appears in volume II of the guidance. This volume also contains information regarding odour detection thresholds (ODTs), ie the concentration of an odorous compound at which the human nose detects the presence of an odour, and odour recognition thresholds (ORTs).

Where an operator proposes a process option on the basis that an environmentally superior option entails excessive costs, it will be necessary to apply a cost-estimation methodology. This entails estimating for each component technique of the option, the capital costs of purchasing and installation, the annual operating and maintenance costs for a typical year, and the operating life, expressed in years. From this information, it will be possible to determine a net present value (NPV) for each option, together with an annual cost, so that they may be compared.

6.5.7 Summarising and presenting the assessment of BPEO

The results of the assessment of the options are to be presented in a 'transparent and consistent manner' so as to enable the Agency and other interested parties to review and audit the proposals. With regard to cost data, the guidance emphasises the importance of having quantitative measures of the economic costs and environmental consequences of the releases involved. Operators are required to provide information on the costs of feasible abatement options based on a 'standard financial appraisal methodology'. This should show the costs to the operator of the option in question by making a comparison between the cash flow for the preferred option and for the other options.

6.5.8 Identifying BPEO

Identifying BPEO for a particular site will involve making a judgement on the basis of the information obtained during the course of the preceding four stages of the assessment. The guidance notes that operators should form a view as to which of the potential options represents the site-specific BPEO by considering the trade-off between the respective costs of options and the extra benefits of pollution reduction and prevention. This can be achieved by using techniques which involve: annual cost comparison; incremental costs compared to incremental environmental effects; and incremental costs over and above the option with greatest environmental effects. In the case of actual cost comparison, the best option may be the one for which the value of the incremental environmental benefits is broadly equivalent to the incremental cost of pollution control. Where an operator uses the second technique (incremental costs compared to incremental environmental effects), the guidance notes that the information will highlight any significant 'break point' beyond which reductions in pollution can only be achieved at a far greater incremental cost. Finally, the third technique will help to establish the magnitude of the incremental costs and environmental effects between each option and the option with greatest environmental effects.

In terms of the justification of BPEO, the guidance notes that this should be accomplished by clearly setting out the environmental factors that were most important, and demonstrating how the final ranking of the options and the choice of BPEO was made. Since the objective for the methodology is that set out in s 7(7) of EPA 1990, BPEO will be the option which provides the most benefit or least damage to the environment as a whole, in both the long and short term, at a cost that is not excessive. The Agency believes that by reference to this methodology and by the application of professional judgment, operators should be able to identify and justify BPEO. Nevertheless, the process that is ultimately authorised should meet all the objectives specified in s 7 of EPA 1990, especially those objectives which appear in s 7(2).

6.5.9 Reviewing BPEO

Once a conclusion has been reached on BPEO, the guidance stresses the need for an operator to review the data that has been used, together with the information obtained and the decisions taken. Indeed, it is stated that some benefit may be gained from carrying out a sensitivity analysis to see if the final decision would be altered by changes to any of the data. This entails varying the values of the parameters used in the assessment within reasonably expected bounds and determining how alternative assumptions could change the results of the assessment. The importance of sensitivity analysis lies in its ability to explore the uncertainties which may exist in respect of many of the assumptions made throughout the assessment. Accordingly, the guidance indicates that the technique may need to be used at various stages of the assessment.

Throughout all the stages in an assessment it is necessary to keep an audit trail. The value of an audit trail was highlighted by the Royal Commission on Environmental Pollution in its Twelfth Report, and the guidance clearly favours such an approach since it states, without further comment, the following words of the Commission:

> 'The presentation of information, opinions and conclusions reached at different stages of the BPEO study is clearly important. The decision maker, and other persons, should be able to see separately the data or score relating to each aspect of the decision for each option.'

BPEO assessment will be reviewed by the Agency, which may ask for further information in order to assist it in this task. Moreover, members of the public will be able to consult the public register containing BPEO assessments. Therefore, in the words of the guidance, it is 'in the operator's own interests to have a justified case which has taken into account all the relevant information'.

6.5.10 BATNEEC and BPEO in practice

In *R v The Environment Agency and Redland Aggregates Ltd, ex parte Gibson, R v The Environment Agency and Redland Aggregates Ltd, ex parte Leam* and *R v The Environment Agency, ex parte Sellers and Petty*,[1] the High Court was required to consider a number of issues in these three applications for judicial review, including whether or not the Environment Agency had complied with its statutory duty under s 7 of EPA when granting variations of the respondents' IPC authorisations. It was argued on behalf of the various applicants that prior to varying the respondents authorisations' so that they were able to use a combination of substitute liquid fuels and petcoke or coal to fire kilns in the manufacture of lime and cement respectively, the Agency ought to have carried out an assessment of all the practicable options and techniques relating to the process as a whole, rather than simply concluding that the variation should be granted because the proposed new fuel regime was a better environmental option than the existing regime. It was submitted that the Agency's failure to carry out a BATNEEC/BPEO exercise of this nature rendered the decisions legally unsafe and meant, therefore, that they should be quashed. In finding in favour of the respondents, Harrison J observed that what the Agency has to do to fulfil its s 7 duty is a matter of fact and degree in each case having regard to the particular circumstances of the case. In his opinion, it was not right that the Agency should, as a matter of course, be required to carry out a BATNEEC/BPEO exercise every time that it received an application for a variation under s 11 of EPA (see **6.10**). In some instances, a full-scale examination of the process may be necessary before a decision is made. However, in the present case, this was unnecessary because the Agency was entitled to treat the proposed improvements by the use of substitute liquid fuels as a continuation of the existing BATNEEC/BPEO position. Accordingly, the Agency had not failed to fulfil its duty under s 7 of EPA.

From a practical point of view, therefore, the decision on this issue must come as a considerable relief to the Environment Agency. Had Harrison J accepted the applicants' contention that, as a general rule, every time the Agency receives a s 11 application it must carry out a BATNEEC/BPEO exercise where discharges to more than one environmental medium are involved, the increase in its workload may have proved to be quite considerable. In effect, as

1 CO/3598/96, CO/2104/96, CO/3796/97, Queen's Bench Division, High Court, 8 May 1998.

counsel for the Agency argued in the present case, it would have meant that the Agency would have been required to treat every s 11 variation application as if it was an application for an authorisation made under s 6 of EPA. Moreover, this in turn may have deterred process operators from applying for a variation. Instead, however, no such general rule exists. Rather, whether or not an application for a variation requires a BATNEEC/BPEO assessment will depend upon the particular circumstances of the case. That will be a decision for the Environment Agency to make, subject to the supervisory jurisdiction of the High Court.

6.6 GUIDANCE

In order to assist HMIP (now the Environment Agency) and local authorities in the performance of their functions under Part I of EPA 1990, guidance of a statutory and non-statutory nature has been issued by the Chief Inspector of HMIP and the Secretary of State for the Environment respectively. Such guidance is clearly important in terms of the operation of the IPC and LAAPC regimes and, therefore, it is necessary briefly to explain the various forms it may take. Guidance for local authorities in respect of Part B processes has been issued by the Secretary of State and will, accordingly, be considered in Chapter 7 (see **7.7**). For present purposes, it is necessary to consider IPC guidance which falls into three main categories: industry sector guidance notes (IPR1 to IPR5); process-specific guidance notes (IPR 1/1, 2/1, 3/1, 4/1 etc); and technical guidance (TG) notes.

6.6.1 Industry sector guidance notes

Five guidance notes (IPR1 to IPR5) were issued by the Chief Inspector of the former HMIP in order to assist inspectors in the task of administering the IPC regime. As such, they do not constitute statutory guidance since they were not made under s 7(11) of EPA 1990. The guidance notes relate to the five main industry sectors for Part A processes, namely: fuel and power industry sector (IPR1); metal industry sector (IPR2); mineral industry sector (IPR3); chemical industry sector (IPR4); and waste disposal industry sector (IPR5). As the editors of the *Encyclopaedia of Environmental Law*[1] note, these five notes have a common format which includes, inter alia, details of those scheduled processes within the sector, a list of relevant EC Directives, other forms of international guidance, and details of abatement technologies and techniques.

6.6.2 Process-specific guidance notes

This form of guidance was formerly put out by HMIP as Chief Inspector's guidance notes but currently, as a consequence of an ongoing process of revision by the Environment Agency, such notes are appearing in their revised

1 Sweet & Maxwell, 1993.

form as IPC guidance notes. Thus, for example, with regard to gasification processes, IPR 1/11 on the gasification of solid and liquid feedstocks has been superseded by S2 1.08. These non-statutory notes have been issued and will continue to be issued to assist inspectors and their successors in their assessment of applications for authorisations and in the variation of existing authorisations, and to help applicants and others understand the criteria against which their applications and variations will be determined. The notes are particularly concerned with process-specific matters, and their very existence helps to ensure a consistent approach to the task of regulation. Process-specific guidance is drawn up on the basis of information obtained at a national and international level. Current industrial practices are described by the guidance, and attention is focused on preventing or minimising releases to the three environmental media of substances which have the potential to cause harm to the environment. In the case of releases to air, a specific section in the guidance will focus on this media and will state, inter alia, detailed requirements for emissions of smoke, sulphur dioxides and other such substances.

6.6.3 Technical guidance notes

As with industry sector guidance notes and process-specific guidance notes, technical guidance notes are non-statutory in that they have been issued by HMIP and its successor, the Environment Agency. As their name suggests, their purpose is to provide inspectors with technical guidance on particular matters, such as effluent techniques. In the context of atmospheric pollution, TGN D1 is entitled *Guidelines on Discharge Stack Heights for Polluting Emissions*. More generally, the recently published TGN (Environmental) E1 provides guidelines on the methodology for establishing BPEO assessments for IPC (see **6.5.2** to **6.5.5**).

6.7 MONITORING

The granting of an IPC authorisation and the imposition of conditions on that authorisation is clearly a central task of the Environment Agency under Part I of EPA 1990. However, in order to ensure that the terms of an authorisation are properly complied with, it is necessary for the relevant process to be monitored regularly. The most widespread and regular form of monitoring is carried out by the operator himself. Where an IPC authorisation is granted, it will usually be subject to conditions requiring the operator to monitor the relevant process in order to ensure that the discharges and emissions from that process do not contravene any of the other conditions in the authorisation relating to such matters. In the event of a contravention of an emission or discharge condition, the operator will be expected to inform the Agency, and where a condition to this effect has been included in the authorisation, as is often the case, a failure to do so would amount to an offence (s 23(1)(a)).

In addition to self-monitoring, HMIP also commissioned independent monitoring as a means of checking the accuracy of results submitted by operators. This form of monitoring essentially took three forms: routine monitoring; ad hoc or reactive monitoring; and site surveys and investigations. The work was carried out by contractors on behalf of HMIP and the results were reported to the regulator. In the present context, it is worth noting, for example, that ad hoc or reactive monitoring of stack emissions was undertaken for HMIP by CRE Group Ltd in the Midlands, the south-west and north of England, and in Wales, and by Laing Technology/Austrian Energy Joint Venture in East Anglia and southern England.

6.8 AUTHORISATION APPLICATION FEES

In addition to meeting the information requirements prescribed in the Environmental Protection (Applications, Appeals and Registers) Regulations 1991 (see **6.3.1**), an application for a prescribed process authorisation must be accompanied by the appropriate fee (s 6(2) of EPA 1990). It was formerly the case that the level of IPC fees was determined in accordance with a charging scheme made under s 8 of the Act. Now, however, as a consequence of an amendment to s 6(2) by Sch 22, para 48 to the Environment Act 1995, the Agency is required to levy in respect of 'environmental licences' such charges and fees as may from time to time be prescribed in the form of a charging scheme made under s 41 of the 1995 Act. 'Environmental licences' are accorded a wide definition by s 56 of the 1995 Act so as to include, for example, waste management licences under Part II of EPA 1990. However, in the present context, the important point to note is that an environmental licence can be 'an authorisation under Part I of the 1990 Act, other than any such authorisation granted by a local enforcing authority' (s 56(1)). Thus, by virtue of s 41(2)(a) of the 1995 Act, a charge may be prescribed in respect of, for example, an application for an IPC authorisation.

There are three main categories of charge in respect of IPC. The first of these, an application fee, is a one-off payment which accompanies the application. IPC processes are divided into a series of components for the purposes of charging, thus reflecting the degree of complexity of the process and the amount of work involved in its proper regulation. For 1996/97, the application fee was £3,860 per component. A reduced rate of £2,570 was payable where the process had transferred from pre-IPC controls. A subsistence charge is also payable annually in respect of each component in order to reflect the costs incurred by the Agency in the day-to-day administering of the IPC regime. For 1996/97, the subsistence charge was £1,730 per component. Finally, a variation fee is payable where the substances released from an authorised process have changed. This fee reflects the extra work involved for the Agency and, in 1996/97, was set at £1,290. The levels of these fees are subject to an annual review which usually results in an increase for the next financial year. IPC fees are much higher than those charged for LAAPC where the cost of regulating less complex industrial processes is not as great (see **7.6**). In addition to the three main categories of charge already referred to, a site-specific charge designed to cover the costs of independent monitoring has been levied since its introduction in 1994/95.

Where an operator has failed to pay a subsistence charge for an environmental licence, the Agency may, in accordance with the appropriate procedure, suspend or revoke the licence (Environment Act 1995, s 41(6)). The power to suspend the licence in these circumstances is an additional power of the Agency. The only power available to local authorities for the non-payment of a subsistence charge is the revocation of the authorisation (s 8(8) of EPA 1990 (see **7.6**)).

Changes may be made to the present charging system in the light of the feedback the Agency receives in respect of a consultation process it has set in motion. It has been reported that the current system has been subject to criticism on several grounds, which include the fact that the fees charged are too excessive and that firms are receiving no encouragement or incentive to improve their compliance with environmental standards and objectives.[1] With regard to the former criticism, firms operating IPC processes will be disappointed to learn that the Agency's corporate plan envisages a five per cent increase in fee levels above the rate of inflation for 1998/99. Several options are outlined in the consultation paper, and the Agency is keen to receive views and opinions on those options, which include defining components separately for the purposes of calculating subsistence charges or making use of operator and pollution risk appraisal (OPRA) ratings for the setting of these charges. OPRA is a scheme originally formulated by HMIP as a means of rating the competence of process operators and assessing pollution hazards posed by the particular process.

Version 2 of OPRA, which was launched by the Agency on 15 August 1997, illustrates that the competence of operators and pollution hazards can be determined by taking a number of factors into account. Thus, an operator's performance can be assessed on the basis of: recording and use of information; knowledge and implementation of authorisation; plant maintenance; management and training; process operation; incidents, complaints and non-compliance events; and recognised environmental management systems. Pollution hazard appraisal involves considering: the presence of hazardous substances; the scale of hazardous operations; the frequency and nature of hazardous operations; technologies for hazard prevention/minimisation; technologies for hazard abatement; location of process; and offensive characteristics. In the present context, OPRA would serve as a means by which processes could be banded for the purposes of charging, so that those operators which achieved a lower rating would be rewarded for their efforts with a lower subsistence charge. A further option mooted by the Agency is a fee for authorisation or variation applications based on the amount of time the regulator spends on dealing with the application. A similar suggestion in respect of subsistence charges has been dismissed by the Agency on the ground that it would be too unpredictable.

---

1 See (1997) 272 *ENDS Report* 37.

Two options have, however, been ruled out by the Agency: emission-based charges and a charge per unit of output. In the case of the former, while it is regarded as giving effect to the 'polluter pays principle' it has nevertheless been rejected on the ground that data on actual process releases does not have the necessary level of reliability. In the case of the latter, this is seen as unsuitable due to the difficulties involved in comparing outputs from different industries and then determining their contribution to environmental harm or their effect on the regulatory process. Whatever changes are made to the charging system, whether they reflect one or more of the options referred to above or none of them, the time-scale for implementation will be at least two years, and perhaps three. For the time being, therefore, the present charging scheme will remain in place.

6.9 TRANSFER OF AUTHORISATIONS

In addition to providing for the grant of prescribed process authorisations, Part I of EPA 1990 also provides for the transfer of authorisations from the current holder (the transferor) to a person who proposes to carry on the process in the holder's place (the transferee). It is apparent from the wording of s 9 that the transfer of the authorisation precedes the transfer of the control of the prescribed process itself. This must be the case since, otherwise, if there were some delay in the transfer of the authorisation, the new operator would be committing an offence contrary to s 23(1)(a) of EPA 1990 by carrying on the process in the absence of an authorisation. There is no mention in the statute as to how a transfer is actually to be effected and, therefore, while it could, in theory, be transferred verbally, in practice it is likely to be effected in writing. There are several advantages to be gained from a written transfer, not least of which is that it guards against any future uncertainty on this point. Moreover, a written transfer serves to reinforce the importance of the IPC regime, and can leave the new process operator in no doubt that the authorisation and any conditions attached to it apply as much to him as they did to its previous holder (s 9(3)).

While the Environment Agency plays a direct role in the actual grant of an authorisation, its role in respect of the transfer of an authorisation is more limited. The EPA 1990 does not require that the permission of the Agency must be sought before a transfer can properly take place. Instead, all that is required is that the transferee gives the Agency written notice of the transfer within 21 days of the date on which the transfer occurred. Failure to give the notice required by s 9(2) amounts to an offence contrary to s 23(1)(b). In the event that the Environment Agency is unhappy with a transfer, for example, because the transferee is unlikely to carry on the prescribed process in the authorised manner, it is unable to intervene to stop the transfer or to appeal against its taking place. The powers which the Agency does have available to it – to vary the authorisation (s 12) or to serve an enforcement, prohibition or revocation notice – could, however, be exercised subject to the limitations imposed upon it by the statute itself. One possibility, therefore, is that an enforcement notice issued in accordance with s 13 of EPA 1990 (see further below) could be served on a transferee following the completion of an authorisation transfer, especially where it has become apparent that there is an actual rather than a likely contravention of a condition attached to that authorisation. In these circumstances, the transferee would have the right to appeal against the notice in accordance with s 15(2) (see **6.15**), although prior to and during the course of any such appeal, the terms of the notice would have to be complied with.

6.10 VARIATION NOTICES

Variation notices may be served on a process operator by the Environment Agency either where the Agency has taken the initiative (s 10 of EPA 1990) or, alternatively, where the holder of an authorisation (the authorisee) has applied for a variation of the conditions attached to that authorisation. Although these provisions are classified as enforcement provisions by EPA 1990, their task is to make an authorisation reflect the changes that may have occurred in respect of BATNEEC for that process. In this sense, therefore, they are concerned with the regulation of ongoing processes which are complying with the provisions of Part I of the Act, rather than dealing with transgressions of these provisions, which is the task of enforcement notices.

Section 10 of EPA 1990 confers a *power* on the Agency to vary an authorisation at any time, but it also imposes a *duty* on the Agency where the requirements of s 7 dictate that conditions different to those currently attached to the authorisation ought to be included. 'Vary', therefore, in the context of existing conditions or other provisions of an authorisation, means 'adding to them or varying or rescinding any of them' (s 10(8)). In the event that the Agency decides to vary an authorisation, it is required to notify the authorisee of its decision by serving a variation notice on him. This notice will specify the variations to the authorisation, together with the date or dates on which such variations will take effect, which will apply unless the notice is itself varied or withdrawn. In addition, a variation notice served on an authorisee will require that person to notify the Agency, within a specified time, of the action he proposes to take to ensure that the process is carried on in accordance with the authorisation as varied by the notice (s 10(4)). A charge may be imposed by the Agency in respect of the process of variation, as determined by a charging scheme under s 41 of the Environment Act 1995. In circumstances where the Agency wishes to add to, vary or rescind a variation notice, it may also do so by serving on the authorisee a further notice specifying the variations to the variation notice and the date or dates on which they are to take effect (s 10(3A)).

Where the Agency is of the opinion that action taken by the authorisee in consequence of a variation notice is such as to entail a 'substantial change' in the manner in which the process is being carried on, it is required to notify the holder of its opinion (s 10(5)). In these circumstances, Sch 1, Part II to the Act applies, and a process of advertisement and consultation is set in motion which is not dissimilar to that in respect of an initial application for an authorisation. For the purposes of ss 10 and 11, 'substantial change' to a process means a substantial change in the substances released from the process or in the amount or any other characteristic of any substance so released. Whether or not a change to a process is 'substantial' will be a question of fact to be determined according to the circumstances of the particular case. The Secretary of State retains a residual power under s 10(6) to direct the Agency either to use or not to use its powers under ss 10 and 11.

Section 11 of the Act provides regulated operators with several different means by which they can bring about the variation of the conditions of an authorisation, or, for that matter, provisions other than conditions which are contained in an authorisation. The first of these arises where the authorisee wishes to make a relevant change in the process and, accordingly, notifies the Agency of that fact and requests that it determine the following matters:

- whether the proposed change would involve a breach of any condition of the authorisation;
- if it would not involve such a breach, whether the Agency would be likely to vary the conditions of the authorisation as a result of the change;
- if it would involve such a breach, whether the Agency would consider varying the conditions of the authorisation so that the change may be made; and
- whether the change would involve a substantial change in the manner in which the process is being carried on.

The Agency is required to notify the authorisee of its determination of these matters. Importantly, there is no right of appeal under s 15 in respect of such a determination. For the purposes of s 11, a 'relevant change' in a prescribed process is a change in the manner of carrying on the process which is 'capable of altering the substances released from the process or of affecting the amount or any other characteristic of any substance so released' (s 11(11)). Where the Agency has determined that the proposed change will not involve a substantial change, but will require the variation of the conditions of the authorisation, it is required to notify the authorisee of the variations which it is likely to consider making. The authorisee can then apply for the variations in order to make the proposed change (s 11(3)). If, however, the Agency has determined that the proposed change involves a substantial change which requires the variation of the conditions of the authorisation, in addition to the procedural requirements found in s 11(2), an application for variation must also be advertised and consulted upon in accordance with Sch I, Part II, para 7 to the Act.

An alternative to the foregoing requirements is where an authorisee, who is carrying on a process under an authorisation and who wishes to make a relevant change in that process, is aware that the change will require the variation of the authorisation's conditions. In these circumstances, the determination by the Agency of those matters referred to above is not required and, accordingly, the authorisee may apply to the Agency for the variation of the conditions of the authorisation referred to in the application (s 11(6)). Finally, where an authorisee does not wish to make a relevant change in the process, but wants the conditions of his authorisation to be varied, he may apply to the Agency requesting that it varies the conditions. In any case where an application for the variation of conditions has been made, the applicant is required to provide the Agency with any prescribed information and with such other information as the Agency may require. He may also be required to pay a fee in respect of his application which has been set under a charging scheme in accordance with s 41 of the Environment Act 1995. In making a decision on an application, the Agency has several possibilities available to it: it may refuse the application, in which case the authorisee may appeal against that decision by virtue of EPA 1990, s 15(1)(c); alternatively, it may, subject to the requirements of s 7 of EPA 1990, vary the conditions of the authorisation, in which case it is required to serve a variation notice on the authorisee. Where an application has been made in accordance with s 11(6), the Agency has the discretion to treat the application as if it were a request for a determination.

6.11 REVOCATION NOTICES

Section 12 of EPA 1990 confers a discretionary power on the Environment Agency to revoke a prescribed process authorisation by serving a notice in writing on the authorisee. Guidance as to when it may be appropriate to exercise this general power is provided by EPA 1990, s 12(2). Thus, a revocation notice is likely to be served when the Environment Agency has reason to believe that a prescribed process has not been carried on at all, or where it has not been carried on for a period of 12 months. However, if, for example, a mistake has been made in this respect, the Agency may withdraw a revocation notice before the date on which it was to have taken effect or, alternatively, vary the date specified in the notice (s 12(4)). As with many of the other provisions in Part I of EPA 1990, the Secretary of State retains a residual discretionary power to give the Environment Agency directions as to whether it should revoke an authorisation under s 12. Where an authorisation is revoked under s 12, the revocation has effect from the date specified in the notice, although this must be at least 28 days later than the date on which the notice was served. Thus, within this 28-day period, a process operator upon whom a revocation notice has been served may exercise his right of appeal under s 15(1)(d) of EPA 1990.

6.12 ENFORCEMENT NOTICES

The Environment Agency may, by virtue of s 13 of EPA 1990, serve an enforcement notice on a person carrying on a prescribed process under an authorisation where it is of the opinion that any condition of the authorisation is being contravened or that any such condition is *likely* to be contravened (s 13(1)). Thus, enforcement notices may be served in respect of apprehended as well as actual contraventions of authorisation conditions and, as such, represent an important preventive power available to the Agency. Whether or not the Agency serves an enforcement notice is a matter for its own discretion, although judicial review may be available in respect of the exercise of that discretion. Prior to taking enforcement action, however, the Agency must comply with the requirements of the Deregulation (Model Appeal Provisions) Order 1996, SI 1996/1678.

Chapter II of the 1996 Order establishes a procedure which must be followed before enforcement action is taken. It would seem from the definition of 'enforcement action' by s 5(6) of the Deregulation and Contracting Out Act 1994 that enforcement under EPA 1990 falls within the scope of the provision. Accordingly, under the 1996 Order, before enforcement action is taken the enforcing officer must give a notice (a 'minded to' notice) to the person against whom he proposes to take the enforcement action, stating that the officer is considering taking action, and why, and that the person may, within a specified period, make written representations to the officer or, if so requested, make oral presentations to the officer in the presence of a senior officer of the authority. The enforcing officer is required to consider any representations so made and if, after considering them, he nevertheless decides to take enforcement action, the officer must give the person a further written notice stating the reasons for his decision. The 1996 Order does not rule out the possibility of immediate enforcement action where the officer believes it to be necessary; however, in such circumstances the officer must, as soon as is practicable, give the person a written notice explaining why he believed it to be necessary.

Where enforcement action has been taken and there is a right of appeal (as under s 15 of EPA 1990 – see below), the enforcing officer must, as soon as is practicable, give a written notice to the person explaining how, where, within what period and on what grounds an appeal may be brought. Moreover, where an enforcing officer takes or considers taking enforcement action, he must take reasonable steps to identify any person who may be required to meet all or a significant part of the costs of compliance. In addition, the enforcing officer must give to that person a copy of any notice relating to the making of an appeal, and that person may then make representations which must be taken into account, unless they are withdrawn.

In the event that the Agency decides to serve an enforcement notice, s 13(2) of EPA 1990 requires that the notice:

- state that the Agency is of the opinion that there has been a contravention of a condition of an authorisation or that there is likely to be such a contravention;
- specify the matters constituting the contravention or the matters making it likely that the contravention will arise;
- specify the steps that must be taken to remedy the contravention or to remedy the matters making it likely that the contravention will arise; and
- specify the period within which those steps must be taken.

These steps are mandatory, and an enforcement notice which fails to comply with the requirements of s 13(2) will be a nullity. In a leading case on planning enforcement notices, *Miller-Mead v Minister of Housing and Local Government*,[1] Upjohn LJ observed that an enforcement notice would be a nullity where:

> '... on its true construction the notice was hopelessly ambiguous and uncertain so that the owner or occupier could not tell in what respect it was alleged that he had developed the land without permission or in what respect it was alleged that he had failed to comply with a condition, or, again, that he could not tell with reasonable certainty what steps he had to take to remedy the alleged breaches.'[2]

In its Annual Report for 1994/95, HMIP stated that during that period it served 92 enforcement notices on process operators who had breached conditions in authorisations This figure fell in 1995/96 to 77 notices, although it is worth noting that both totals reflect the number of enforcement notices served under EPA 1990 and the Radioactive Substances Act 1993. Table A5 in Appendix A to the 1995/96 Report reveals that the actual number of enforcement notices served on operators under EPA 1990 for that period was 59. Where a process operator fails to comply with, or contravenes, an enforcement notice, he commits an offence contrary to s 23(1)(c) of EPA 1990 for which he may be liable, on summary conviction, to a fine not exceeding £20,000, or to imprisonment for a term not exceeding three months, or both. In the event that the conviction is on indictment, the operator may be liable to a fine or to imprisonment for a term not exceeding two years, or both. Prosecutions for failure to comply with enforcement notices may, therefore, entail significant penalties on conviction. Alternatively, by virtue of s 24 of EPA 1990, where an enforcing authority is of the opinion that criminal proceedings for an offence under s 23(1)(c) would afford an 'ineffectual remedy', the authority is entitled to take proceedings in the High Court for the purpose of securing compliance with the notice (see **6.22**).

6.12.1 Questioning the validity of an enforcement notice

Assuming that a prosecution for an offence under s 23(1)(c) is instigated, an important issue is whether or not a process operator can seek to challenge the validity of the enforcement notice as a defence in those proceedings. In other words, can the operator escape conviction by demonstrating, during the course of criminal proceedings, that the enforcement notice was invalid, or does that operator have to challenge the *vires* of the notice by way of judicial review?

In *Bugg v DPP*,[3] which concerned a prosecution for an offence contrary to a byelaw made under the Military Lands Act 1892, the defendant sought to rely on the alleged *ultra vires* of the byelaw as a defence. In delivering the judgment of the court, Woolf LJ drew a distinction between substantive and procedural invalidity and concluded that a criminal court was in a position to hear

1 [1963] 1 All ER 459.
2 Ibid at p 470.
3 [1993] 2 All ER 815.

argument as to substantive invalidity only where it involved a question of law. Where it was alleged that a byelaw was procedurally invalid because, for example, a requirement to consult a particular party before making the byelaw had not been complied with, such an allegation would need to be supported by evidence, which would not be available to the court (ie the testimony of the party which made the byelaw). However, doubt has recently been cast upon the decision in *Bugg* by the House of Lords in *R v Wicks*.[1] Since the case was concerned with the question whether the defendant was entitled to challenge the validity of an enforcement notice issued under s 87 of the Town and Country Planning Act 1971 (now s 172 of the Town and Country Planning Act 1990) in criminal proceedings for a failure to comply with that notice, it is patently of interest in the context of the present discussion.

In an apparent rejection of the approach adopted in *Bugg*, the House of Lords concluded in *R v Wicks* that whether or not a defendant charged with a failure to comply with an order made under statutory powers could raise the alleged unlawfulness of that order as a defence in criminal proceedings depended upon the construction of the relevant statute. In the present case, an examination of Part VII of the Town and Country Planning Act 1990, together with the scheme of enforcement of planning control and the history of its provisions, led Lord Hoffmann to conclude that: '"enforcement notice" means a notice issued by the planning authority which is formally valid and has not been quashed'. It followed from this, therefore, that a defendant prosecuted under s 179(1) of the Town and Country Planning Act 1990 was not entitled, as a matter of right, to rely on the alleged invalidity of an enforcement notice as a defence in proceedings for having failed to comply with its terms. Moreover, in answering an additional point certified by the Court of Appeal to be of general public importance, Lord Hoffmann asserted that there are no exceptions to this rule, even where it is contended that the invalidity has arisen as a result of *mala fides* on the part of the authority issuing the enforcement notice. Such 'residual grounds of challenge', which may also include bias or whether the decision to issue the notice was based on irrelevant or improper grounds, were, the House of Lords felt: 'quite unsuitable for decision by a planning inspector' and, for that matter, lay justices who 'would not find it easy to apply the distinction ... between the legality of an administrative act and its substantive merits'. Accordingly, such matters ought to be raised before the Divisional Court by way of an application for judicial review.

The similarities between the enforcement provisions under the Town and Country Planning Acts and EPA 1990 are such that the principle which emerges from *R v Wicks* may be applied equally to enforcement notices under EPA 1990. The recent decision of the Secretary of State for the Environment, Transport and the Regions to delegate his power to take decisions on appeals by firms operating IPC and LAAPC processes to the Planning Inspectorate is a further example of the common ground between the planning and environmental protection regimes (see **6.15.5** below). However, whether a court would

1 [1997] 2 All ER 801.

conclude, if asked, that the validity of a s 13 notice could be challenged only by way of judicial review rather than during the course of criminal proceedings for its contravention would depend upon the construction placed upon the relevant provisions of Part I of EPA 1990.

6.13 PROHIBITION NOTICES

In addition to the service of enforcement notices, Part I of EPA 1990 requires the Agency to serve a prohibition notice where it is of the opinion that the carrying on of a prescribed process, or the carrying on of that process in a particular manner, involves 'an imminent risk of serious pollution of the environment'. The phrase 'pollution of the environment' which triggers the operation of s 14 is defined in s 1(3) of the Act as meaning 'pollution of the environment due to the release (into any environmental medium) from any process of substances which are capable of causing harm to man or any other living organisms supported by the environment'. 'Harm', for its part, is defined by s 1(4) as 'harm to the health of living organisms or other interference with the ecological systems of which they form part, and in the case of man, includes offence caused to any of his senses or harm to his property'. A prohibition notice will be served only under s 14, however, where the pollution of the environment which it is designed to prevent is 'serious' in nature. What amounts to 'serious pollution of the environment' is a matter for inspectors depending upon the particular circumstances, but clearly it will be something more than trivial environmental pollution. A process operator upon whom a prohibition notice has been served may disagree with the Environment Agency on this point and, accordingly, exercise his right of appeal to the Secretary of State under s 15(2) of EPA 1990 (see **6.15**).

Unlike enforcement notices, which are served as a consequence of the contravention or likely contravention of a condition attached to a process authorisation, prohibition notices are served irrespective of whether such a condition has or is likely to be contravened. Moreover, a prohibition notice may relate to any aspect of the prescribed process, whether or not regulated by a condition (s 14(2)). In practice, therefore, an enforcement notice will be served to preclude a process operator's wrongful conduct, whereas a prohibition notice will be served on an operator even though he may have committed no wrong under the Act. This distinction between enforcement and prohibition notices was further elaborated upon by Lord Reay during the course of a House of Lords debate on the Environment Protection Bill. In his speech, Lord Reay observed that prohibition notices:[1]

> '... are not designed primarily to be served when an operator is breaching or is likely to breach the conditions of an authorisation. They are designed to cover circumstances in which a process is being operated in a perfectly reasonable manner and within the conditions of the authorisation but where some event external to the process requires quick and decisive action. For example, an accident

---

1 *Hansard*, HL Deb, vol 520, col 897 (19 June, 1990).

> at one process could release substances which could react with those normally allowed to be released by a nearby process, so causing serious pollution. In those circumstances it would be right to close down temporarily the second process even though it was operating within its authorisation.'

The exceptional nature of the circumstances in which a prohibition notice would be used was also referred to by the then Minister for the Environment and Countryside, David Trippier MP, during the eighth sitting of the House of Commons Standing Committee H on the Environmental Protection Bill. These circumstances were likely to be 'outwith the operator's control' but, in addition to taking action to prevent a local disaster due to a combination of pollutants as envisaged by Lord Reay, the Minister was of the opinion that a prohibition notice 'would be invoked if an accident at one factory were to cast doubts about the safety of similar or identical techniques employed at other sites in other parts of the country'. Moreover, in a subsequent consideration by the Standing Committee of the appeals provision in Part I of the Bill, Mr Trippier was of the view that a prohibition notice would also serve as a useful contingency where it was clear that a company was deliberately manipulating the appeals procedure in order to delay the proper enforcement of the pollution provisions.

As with enforcement notices, EPA 1990 prescribes those matters which must, at the very least, be dealt with in a prohibition notice. Accordingly, by virtue of s 14(3), a prohibition notice is required to:

- state the authority's opinion;
- specify the risk involved in the carrying-on of the prescribed process;
- specify the steps which must be taken to remove the risk, and the period within which such measures must be taken; and
- direct that the authorisation shall, until the notice is withdrawn, wholly or to the extent specified in the notice cease to have effect to authorise the carrying on of the process.

The mandatory nature of this provision ensures that if a prohibition notice fails to comply with the terms of s 14(3), it will be rendered a nullity. In the event that a direction applies only to part of the authorised process, it may impose conditions in respect of that part which are to be observed while it is carried on. The impetus for the service of a prohibition notice is likely to come from the Environment Agency, but, as a consequence of s 14(4), the Secretary of State retains the power to give directions to the Agency on whether it should perform its duties under s 14. Moreover, if a prohibition notice is to be served on a process operator, the Secretary of State may give the Agency directions on the matters specified in the notice. Where a notice has been served, s 14(5) requires the Agency to withdraw it by giving written notification to the person on whom it was served when it is satisfied that the steps required by the prohibition notice have been taken.

Statistics contained in various HMIP annual reports reveal that the numbers of prohibition notices served under Part I of EPA 1990 have been relatively low since it came into force. In 1992–93, only one notice was served, and this figure had risen to three in 1994–95. During the last year of its existence (1995–96), 11 prohibition notices were served. These figures highlight the limited nature of the circumstances in which it might be appropriate to issue a prohibition notice in respect of IPC. The position with regard to LAAPC has been similar in that very few notices have been refused by local authorities (see **7.12**).

The statutory provisions relating to enforcement and prohibition notices discussed above reveal that these two methods of enforcement have much in common. A key distinction which can be made, however, relates to the freedom or otherwise which the Agency has to act. While the Agency has a discretion as to whether or not to serve an enforcement notice under s 13, even where a condition of an authorisation is being contravened, the imperative nature of the language used in s 14(1) ensures that it must serve a prohibition notice if the carrying-on of the process involves 'an imminent risk of serious pollution of the environment'. The effect of the service of an enforcement notice on a process authorisation is also different to the effect of a prohibition notice. While it is an offence to fail to comply with or contravene any requirement or prohibition of either notice (s 23(1)(c)), an enforcement notice does not affect a process authorisation: the authorisation remains extant. However, the service of a prohibition notice will cause a process authorisation to cease to have effect completely, in which case it would be unlawful for the operator to attempt to carry on that process.

6.14 GENERAL ENFORCEMENT ISSUES

HMIP's use of the enforcement powers under Part I of EPA 1990 was by no means excessive, as the figures already stated indicate. Collectively, these figures suggest a cautious, non-confrontational approach to the task of regulating industrial processes subject to IPC. The number of prosecutions initiated by HMIP remained relatively constant throughout its stewardship of the more complex industrial processes. In 1994–95 and 1995–96, 15 prosecutions were brought, and in one, Coalite Products Ltd was fined £150,000 for its operation of an incinerator which had contributed to the increased levels of dioxins found in herbage and milk in the Bolsover area.[1]

Now that the Environment Agency has taken over the responsibilities of regulator in this field, it remains to be seen whether there will be a noticeable difference in the numbers of enforcement and prohibition notices served on process operators, and the frequency with which prosecutions are brought. An insight into how the Agency proposes to approach the task of enforcement has been provided by the publication of an enforcement policy statement in April 1996. While this document is expressly stated not to be a comprehensive prosecution policy, it does, nevertheless, contain a statement of general principles upon which enforcement decisions will be taken. These principles are: proportionality in applying the law and securing compliance; consistency

1 See [1996] 8 ELM 108.

of approach; targeting of enforcement action; and transparency as to how the regulator operates and what the regulated may expect. Of these four principles, perhaps the most interesting is the transparency principle which, if applied properly, may reduce the need for formal enforcement action to be taken. The provision for 'minded to' notices to be issued by the Agency in accordance with the terms of Chapter II of the Deregulation (Model Appeal Provisions) Order 1996 (see **6.12** above) may go some way towards achieving a degree of transparency in the regulatory process.

Where the Agency is deciding whether or not to take formal enforcement action, the policy statement considers that this course of action may be justified in the following circumstances: where it is appropriate in order to 'draw general attention to the need for compliance with the law', and, hence, deter others from committing similar offences; where there is potential for 'considerable environmental harm' if a breach of the law occurs; and where the offence in question is of a serious nature and the general record and approach of the offender justifies a prosecution. In reality, these considerations are also taken into account regularly by bodies outwith the realm of environmental protection which have responsibility for bringing prosecutions. Nevertheless, it is clearly appropriate and, as such, in conformity with the principle of transparency, for the Agency to issue such a statement.

Some indication of the direction in which the Agency wishes to proceed in respect of its enforcement powers has been provided by a recent prosecution in which a director of a company which had operated a drum incinerator became the first person to be prosecuted for an IPC offence.[1] The director, who was prosecuted under s 157 of EPA on the basis that the offences charged were committed with his consent or connivance or attributable to his neglect, pleaded guilty to five charges of contravening authorisation conditions, contrary to s 6(1) of EPA. However, since the company had gone into liquidation and the director therefore had no assets, Bradford Crown Court rejected a fine or a custodial sentence as an appropriate punishment and instead ordered that he should do 60 hours' community service.

6.15 APPEALS

Section 15 of EPA 1990, together with the Environmental Protection (Applications, Appeals and Registers) Regulations 1991, SI 1991/507 (the 1991 Regulations) and the Environmental Protection (Applications, Appeals and Registers) (Amendment) Regulations 1996, SI 1996/667, is concerned with appeals arising under Part I of the Act. Essentially, these entail two categories of appeal: those in relation to authorisations, and those in respect of variation, enforcement and prohibition notices. With regard to process authorisations, any person who has been refused the grant of an authorisation may appeal to the Secretary of State, as may those persons who have been refused a variation

1 See (1998) 281 *ENDS Report* 50.

of an authorisation or who have had an authorisation revoked (s 15(1)(a), (c) and (d)). Additionally, any person aggrieved by the conditions attached to an authorisation has the right of appeal (s 15(1)(b)), although in each of these four cases, an appeal to the Secretary of State against a decision of an enforcing authority is not permissible where that decision was made to implement a direction made to the authority by the Secretary of State himself. Furthermore, rights of appeal are accorded to all those upon whom a variation notice, enforcement notice or prohibition notice has been served although, once again, there is no right of appeal to the Secretary of State where the notice was served to implement a direction of his (s 15(2)). Before appealing, however, *Guidance Note Number 1: section 15 Appeals* stresses the need for operators to enter into a dialogue with the Agency, especially where the dispute concerns the conditions in an authorisation, since to do so may resolve the problem and therefore make an appeal unnecessary. Appeals, the guidance contends, 'should be treated as a last resort'.

Any person who wishes to exercise a right of appeal under s 15 is required to give the Secretary of State written notice of the appeal in accordance with reg 9 of the 1991 Regulations. There is no appeal form as such, nor is there a charge for lodging an appeal. The appellant must also ensure that the written notice is accompanied by those documents specified in reg 9(2), and that copies of both the notice and the documents are sent to the enforcing authority whose decision is the subject of the appeal. The relevant documents are:

- a statement of the grounds of appeal;
- a copy of any relevant application;
- a copy of any relevant authorisation;
- a copy of any relevant correspondence between the appellant and the enforcing authority;
- a copy of any decision or notice which is the subject matter of the appeal; and
- a statement indicating whether the appellant wishes the appeal to be in the form of a hearing or to be disposed of on the basis of written representations.

In addition to prescribing that the above documents must accompany a written notice of appeal, the 1991 Regulations stipulate that an appellant must bring his appeal within a certain time-limit (reg 10). For persons who have been refused the grant of an authorisation or who are deemed to have had their application refused, persons aggrieved by conditions attached to an authorisation or persons who have been refused a variation of an authorisation, any appeal against such a decision must be brought within a period of six months from the date of the decision or the date of the deemed refusal. Where an enforcing authority has decided to revoke an authorisation, a notice of appeal against that decision must be submitted before the date on which the revocation takes effect. Finally, in the present context, those persons upon whom either a variation notice, enforcement notice or prohibition notice has been served have two months from the date on which the relevant notice was served to appeal against it (reg 10(1)(d)). Where an appeal is made outside the time-limits specified above it will not normally be accepted.

On being informed that an appeal has been lodged, reg 9 of the Regulations states that the Agency has 14 days within which to notify those parties which it considers are likely to be interested in the subject matter of the appeal. The enforcing authority is required to give written notice of the appeal to any person who made representations to it in respect of the grant or variation of an authorisation, and to any statutory consultee in respect of an application for such a grant or variation. Regulation 11 provides that a written notice of an enforcing authority must:

- state that the appeal has been lodged;
- give the name of the appellant and either (i) the address of the premises where the prescribed process will be carried on if the process is not to be carried on by mobile plant, or (ii) the address of the principal place of business where the prescribed process is to be carried on by means of mobile plant;
- describe the application or authorisation to which the appeal relates;
- state that representations in respect of the appeal may be made to the Planning Inspectorate by the recipient within 21 days of receipt of the notice and require that copies of such representations will be furnished to both the appellant and the enforcing authority;
- explain that such representations will be entered in a public register unless the person making them requests in writing that this should not be so in which case a statement will be made in the register indicating that representations have been made which are the subject of such a request; and
- state that in the event that a hearing is to be held wholly or partly in public, those persons who have been notified of the appeal as interested parties and who have made representations in respect of the appeal, or the prescribed consultees so notified, will be notified of the date of the hearing.

Regulation 11 requires the enforcing authority to perform two further tasks in connection with its receipt of a copy of the notice of appeal. First, it is required to notify the Planning Inspectorate of all those persons to whom a written notice of appeal has been sent, and the date on which such notice was sent, within 14 days of sending the written notice to the relevant persons. Secondly, in the event that the appeal has been withdrawn, the enforcing authority is required to notify in writing all those persons who were originally sent a written notice of appeal. Assuming that an appeal has not been withdrawn, the form the appeal will take is discussed below. First, however, mention must be made of an important practical issue: the status of an appealed decision.

6.15.1 Status of an appealed decision

Once an appeal under s 15 of EPA 1990 has been determined, the status of the authorisation, or the variation, enforcement or prohibition notice, becomes clear. However, prior to such a determination, the question which must be considered is the effect the act of bringing an appeal will have upon the authorisation or notice. The EPA 1990 provides some guidance here. A refusal to grant an authorisation is unaffected by an appeal. Thus, since there is no extant authorisation, an appellant would not be entitled to carry on the prescribed process in the hope that his appeal will succeed. To do so would clearly contravene s 6(1) of the Act, which amounts to an offence under s 23(1)(a). A person who is aggrieved by the conditions attached to an authorisation must, nevertheless, comply with them up to and during the course of the appeal, since such conditions are not suspended by the act of bringing an appeal. Similarly, a person who has been refused a variation of his authorisation is required to carry on the prescribed process subject to the terms of the original authorisation, at least until the appeal has been determined. However, in the case of a person whose authorisation has been revoked in accordance with s 12, s 15(8) of the Act provides that the revocation will not take effect pending the final determination or withdrawal of the appeal. Thus, an appeal against the revocation of an authorisation has the effect of suspending the operation of that revocation for the duration of the appeal, with the consequence that the prescribed process could continue to be lawfully carried on.

The position is different, however, in relation to appeals brought against variation, enforcement and prohibition notices. By virtue of s 15(9) of the Act, an appeal does not have the effect of suspending the operation of the relevant notice: the notice remains in force and, accordingly, must be complied with up to and during the course of an appeal. In the words of the then Minister for the Environment and Countryside, David Trippier MP, if such notices did not bite during an appeal, 'the first recourse of any unscrupulous operator [would be] to appeal so that he can avoid the cost of complying with the notice'.[1] A failure to comply with either an enforcement or a prohibition notice amounts to an offence contrary to s 23(1)(c) of EPA 1990.

6.15.2 The appeal process

Two principal modes of appeal are provided for by the legislation: written representations, or a hearing held either in public or private. It will be remembered that when an appellant gives the Planning Inspectorate written notice of appeal, such notice is required to be accompanied by a number of documents specified in reg 9 of the Regulations (see **6.15** above), including a statement by the appellant on how he wishes the appeal to be dealt with. Either party to the appeal may request that it is determined in the form of a hearing, in which case the Secretary of State is required by s 15(5)(a) of EPA 1990 to give effect to such a request. However, the person actually hearing the appeal

1 Standing Committee H, eighth sitting, 6 February 1990, at col 257.

retains a discretion over the extent to which the appeal is heard in private. By virtue of s 15(5)(b), the Secretary of State also has the power to cause a local inquiry to be held.

6.15.3 Written representations

Where an appellant has informed the Planning Inspectorate that he wishes the appeal to be disposed of by way of written representations, reg 12 of the 1991 Regulations lays down the procedure to be followed. The enforcing authority has 28 days from its receipt of the appellant's statement of the grounds of appeal and notification of the chosen mode of appeal within which to submit any written representations to the Inspectorate. Following this, the appellant has a further 17 days within which to make any additional representations to the Inspectorate in reply to those made by the enforcing authority. At the completion of this stage of the procedure, the Inspectorate will be in possession of written submissions from both parties, and any representations which have been made by interested parties and statutory consultees in respect of the appeal. It is incumbent upon the Inspectorate to send copies of any representations to both parties to the appeal and to give them a period of not less than 14 days within which to make comment. Both parties, for their part, will be in possession of the same information, since any representations which either makes to the Inspectorate must also be sent to the other party. Two final points of substance concerning the written representations procedure relate to the time limits within which the procedure is to be completed and the exchange of representations between the parties. The time limits referred to above will generally apply, but they are not absolute. Instead, the Inspectorate has a discretion to extend the time-limit prescribed in reg 12 in a particular case where it is felt appropriate to do so. Moreover, it may require further exchanges of representations between the parties in addition to those described above.

6.15.4 Hearings

Where an appeal against any of the decisions referred to in s 15 of EPA 1990 is to be disposed of by way of a hearing, reg 13 of the 1991 Regulations requires the appointed inspector to give the appellant and the enforcing authority at least 28 days' written notice of the date, time and place fixed for the holding of the hearing. Alternatively, he may give the parties such shorter period of notice as they have agreed upon. A copy of the written notice is also to be served upon all those interested parties who made written representations to the Inspectorate in respect of the notice of appeal, and to the statutory consultees. Despite these provisions, the inspector retains the power to vary either the date, the time or the place of the hearing. Although the Regulations expressly require the inspector only to 'give such notice of any such variation as appears to him to be reasonable' in respect of a variation of the time or place of the hearing, it can be presumed that reasonable notification will also be given to the parties where the intention is to vary the date of the hearing. In the event that the hearing is to be held wholly or partly in public, reg 13(2) requires the inspector to publish a copy of the notice relating to the date, time and place of the appeal in a newspaper, either, in the case of a non-mobile plant, in the locality where the prescribed process will be carried on, or, in the case of mobile plant, in the locality where the prescribed process was carried on prior to the revocation of its authorisation or the serving of a variation notice, enforcement notice or prohibition notice.

In terms of the actual hearing itself, reg 13(6) confers a right to be heard upon the appellant, the enforcing authority and the statutory consultees who include, in respect of an IPC authorisation, the Health & Safety Executive, the relevant local authority and the Ministry of Agriculture, Fisheries and Food. In addition, the person appointed to conduct the hearing has a discretion to permit any other person to be heard and, in exercising such a discretion, should ensure that permission is not unreasonably withheld. With regard to the manner in which the hearing is conducted, much emphasis appears to be placed on the need for a relatively informal, non-legal procedure in which the inspector enjoys a wide measure of discretion over how best to hear the appeal. In guidance on this matter provided by the DoE (GG5(91)), it is stated that:

> '... the procedure at a hearing will be left to the Appeals Inspector. He may hear the parties in whatever order he thinks most suitable for the clarification of issues. He may, for instance, review the case based on the papers already provided and then outline what he considers to be the main issues and indicate those matters which require further explanation or clarification. This will not preclude the appellant or the enforcing authority from referring to other aspects which they consider to be relevant. The approach that will be encouraged will be one of informality, for example, hearings may often take the form of a round table discussion, rather than a formal presentation of evidence.' (para 21)

In some hearings, it may be necessary for an assessor to be appointed by the Planning Inspectorate on behalf of the Secretary of State to advise the inspector on specific technical matters. In such circumstances, the assessor will attend the hearing and will sit alongside the inspector during the course of the proceedings. He will consider the representations made, and will usually write a report to the inspector, the contents of which will be made public save where they relate to matters of commercial confidentiality. Those who are entitled to attend the inquiry will be informed of the assessor's name and the matters on which he will be advising the inspector.

6.15.5 Determination of an appeal

On completion of the appeal process, whether it was conducted by way of written representations or a hearing, it formerly fell to the Secretary of State to determine the matter. However, in order to help speed up the appeals process, it has recently been announced that as from 1 September 1997 the Secretary of State for the Environment, Transport and the Regions has delegated his powers to take decisions on appeals by firms operating IPC and LAAPC processes to the Planning Inspectorate. Thus, rather than an appeal involving an inspector's report followed by a separate and not necessarily concurring decision by the Secretary of State which has been the practice to date, a more streamlined approach has been adopted for the determination of s 15 appeals. Planning inspectors will therefore determine the majority of appeals, although the Secretary of State has retained the right to 'recover' certain types of case for his own determination. The criteria for recovery appear at Annex A to *Guidance Note Number 1: section 15 Appeals*, and are as follows:

- cases involving processes or sites of major importance;
- cases giving rise to significant public controversy;
- cases which raise significant legal difficulties;
- cases which can be decided only in conjunction with other cases over which inspectors have no jurisdiction;
- cases which raise major or novel issues of industrial pollution which could set a policy precedent, for example cases involving the use of new techniques; and
- other cases which, exceptionally, merit recovery because of the particular circumstances.

Where a case has been 'recovered', the parties will be notified of this fact. In such cases, the inspector will make a report to the Secretary of State rather than determine the matter by way of a decision letter.

In terms of the actual disposition of the appeal, s 15 of EPA 1990 accords the Secretary of State/inspector a wide measure of discretion. With regard to the refusal of a grant of authorisation, the imposition of conditions on the authorisation, the refusal of a variation of an authorisation, or the revocation of an authorisation, the Secretary of State/inspector may conclude that the enforcing authority, ie the Environment Agency in respect of IPC, made the correct decision, in which case he will affirm such a decision. However, where he concludes otherwise (as he may do in the case of a refusal to grant an authorisation, since such a decision goes against the official approach to the control of prescribed processes), he may direct the enforcing authority to grant the authorisation and, additionally, give directions on the conditions to be attached to the authorisation. Similarly, where the enforcing authority has refused a variation of an authorisation, the Secretary of State/inspector may direct that the authorisation be varied and, additionally, give directions on the conditions to be attached to the varied authorisation. Where the appellant succeeds in an appeal against the conditions attached to an authorisation, or the revocation of an authorisation, a power to quash either all or any of the conditions, or the decision to revoke the authorisation, is vested in the Secretary of State/inspector. Once again, the Secretary of State/inspector may make directions in respect of the conditions to be attached to the authorisation.

Where an appeal relates to a variation notice, enforcement notice or prohibition notice, the Secretary of State/inspector may determine the appeal in one of two ways: either he may quash the notice; or, alternatively, he may affirm it, in which case, he has the discretion to affirm the notice in its original form, or with such modifications as he thinks fit in the circumstances.

6.15.6 Appeals: a critique

Decisions made by the enforcing authority in respect of authorisations under Part I of EPA 1990 can have a significant impact upon the manner in which that prescribed process is carried on subsequently. Attaching a number of very strict conditions to an authorisation may, for example, result in the process operator being put to considerable expense by having to purchase new machinery or substantially modify existing machinery in order to comply. Accordingly, s 15 of EPA 1990 rightly entitles an operator to appeal where he is aggrieved by a decision which may, in the more extreme cases, severely threaten the viability of an operation. The appeal provisions provide a further opportunity to look at the impugned decision, and to assess whether or not it was correct in the circumstances. However, while the appeal system can be praised for what it achieves, it can, nevertheless, be criticised for what it fails to do. No doubt a vast majority of the appeals lodged are entirely genuine and deserve a substantive hearing. However, since there is no provision in EPA 1990 to render an appellant liable for costs where the appeal has been unreasonably brought, the wily operator may lodge an appeal against an authorisation revocation which he knows will be lost in order to carry on the prescribed process in the meantime. The threat of costs for such an abuse of the appeal system may act as a disincentive for those minded to act in this way.

The second failing of the appeal system is that while it enables an impugned decision to be reconsidered, it gives the Secretary of State/inspector the right finally to determine the matter. There is no mechanism in s 15 by which an appellant can challenge the Secretary of State's decision in court; however, if there were a right to challenge an appeal decision on a point of law for a limited period only, as is the case in planning law matters, appeal decisions could escape from becoming the subject of judicial review proceedings. The need to be granted leave to apply for judicial review under RSC Ord 53 is a means by which unmeritorious claims can be prevented from proceeding any further, but if the disgruntled s 15 appellant successfully negotiates this hurdle, he may have a strong defence to any prosecution under s 23 of the Act where those judicial review proceedings are pending.

This absence of a right of appeal to the High Court against the decision of the Secretary of State/inspector may be such as to raise doubts over whether the remedy available to the appellant satisfies the requirements of Art 6(1) of the European Convention on Human Rights and Fundamental Freedoms. The material part of Art 6(1) provides that:

> 'In the determination of his civil rights and obligations ... everyone is entitled to a fair and public hearing ... by an independent and impartial tribunal ...'

In *Bryan v United Kingdom*[1] the European Court of Human Rights held unanimously that there had been no violation of Article 6(1) where the applicant had been able to challenge a planning enforcement notice served on him under the Town and Country Planning Act 1990 both before a planning

1 (1996) 21 EHRR 342.

inspector and the High Court. The important part of the judgment in the present context is not, however, the overall finding of the court, but its view as to whether the inspector was sufficiently independent and impartial for the purposes of Art 6(1). In the opinion of the court, although the inspector was required to decide the applicant's planning appeal in a quasi-judicial manner, the ability of the Secretary of State to revoke the power of the inspector to decide the appeal, even where proceedings were in progress, was 'enough to deprive the inspector of the requisite appearance of independence', even if such revocations rarely occurred in practice. Therefore, the review by the inspector did not, of itself, satisfy the requirements of Art 6(1) of the Convention. It was only as a consequence of the right of appeal to the High Court on points of law that Art 6(1) could be said to have been complied with. The absence of a similar right of appeal in respect of enforcement and other notices issued under Part I of EPA 1990 is, therefore, a curious anomaly which should, perhaps, be looked at in the interests of fairness and for the purposes of ensuring compliance with the UK's Convention obligations.

6.16 GENERAL POWERS OF ENTRY

In ss 16 to 18 of EPA 1990, as originally enacted, provision was made for the appointment of inspectors, and the various powers that inspectors were entitled to exercise in respect of premises on which prescribed processes were being or had been carried on. These provisions have now been repealed by s 120(3) of, and Sch 24 to, the Environment Act 1995, and replaced by broadly similar provisions in that Act. While ss 108 and 109 of the 1995 Act largely restate the terms of their predecessors, their application is wider than the earlier EPA 1990 provisions. Powers may now be exercised in relation to any of the pollution control functions of the Environment Agency as defined in s 108(15), and as such, are not restricted to the enforcement of the IPC regime alone. The bringing together of these powers amounts to a rationalisation which was a necessary corollary of the creation of a unified Environment Agency exercising many different pollution control functions. For the purposes of determining whether Part I of EPA 1990 is being or has been complied with, or determine whether, and if so how, to perform such functions, 'suitable' persons authorised in writing by the Agency may exercise any of the powers contained in s 108(4) of the 1995 Act. Such powers enable the authorised person to:

- enter any premises which he reasonably believes it is necessary for him to enter at any reasonable time or, in an emergency, at any time;
- enter premises accompanied by a duly authorised person or equipment or materials, or, where there is reasonable cause to believe that a serious obstruction will occur, a constable;
- carry out necessary examinations and investigations;
- direct that premises that he may enter, or any part of them or anything in them, shall be left undisturbed for the purposes of examination and investigation;

- take measurements, photographs and recordings which are necessary for the purposes of examination and investigation;
- take samples of any articles or substances in or on the premises and of the air, water or land in, on or in the vicinity of the premises;
- dismantle or cause to be tested any article or substance found in or on the premises for which there is reason to believe that it has caused or is likely to cause pollution of the environment or harm to human health;
- take possession of and detain any such article or substance for as long as necessary to examine it, to ensure that it is not tampered with prior to the completion of an examination, or to make it available as evidence in any proceedings for a pollution offence;
- require persons to answer questions and to sign a declaration attesting to the truth of the answers given;
- require information to be given, including extracts from computerised records;
- require such assistance and facilities from any person as are necessary to enable the performance of any of the s 108 powers;
- carry out test borings or other works on the premises and to install, keep or maintain monitoring equipment and other apparatus there.

6.16.1 Limitations to powers of entry

With the exception of entry in an emergency, the power to enter premises under s 108 is conditonal upon giving at least seven days' written notice of the proposed entry. Even then, an entry may take place only with the consent of a person in occupation of the premises, or with the authority of a warrant issued in accordance with Sch 18 to the Environment Act 1995. Moreover, save in an emergency, where entry has been or is likely to be refused and there are grounds for believing that force may be necessary to effect an entry, such an entry must be authorised by a warrant under Sch 18.

The powers accorded to Environment Agency officers under s 108 are wide in their scope, but there are generally recognised limits on what the occupier of premises can be compelled to do. Thus, for example, s 108 cannot require the handing over of documents to which legal professional privilege would attach (s 108(13)). In addition, answers in reply to questions cannot be used as evidence against that person in any proceedings whatsoever (s 108(12)). The protection afforded by s 108(12) appears only to apply to oral answers given by individuals and, thus, does not extend to documents obtained by the Agency. In *Re Green Environmental Industries Ltd and Another*,[1] the Court of Appeal held, inter alia, that the protection given by an identical provision in EPA 1990, the now repealed s 69(8), was not against answering the question at all – it merely extended to the use to which that answer was put in evidence.

1 (1997) *The Times*, 9 October.

6.16.2 Powers of seizure

Where an authorised person has reasonable cause to believe that any article or substance found by him on premises is a cause of imminent danger of serious pollution to the environment or serious harm to human health, s 109 of the 1995 Act empowers him to seize the article or substance and render it harmless. In order to exercise this power, it is necessary for the authorised person to produce a written report detailing the circumstances of the case. A signed copy of the report must be given to a responsible person at the premises, and the owner of the premises where that person is not the responsible person.

Under s 110 of the Environment Act 1995 it is an offence for a person intentionally to obstruct an authorised person in the exercise or performance of his powers or duties. Where the obstruction has occurred in respect of the exercise of s 109 powers, a person convicted on indictment may be subjected to a fine or to a maximum of two years' imprisonment, or both. Where, however, there is a summary conviction, the penalty is a fine not exceeding the statutory maximum. Obstructions in respect of the exercise of s 108 powers or those exercisable by virtue of a Sch 18 warrant result in, on summary conviction, a fine not exceeding level 5 on the standard scale. In addition to these offences, s 110 creates further offences, such as falsely pretending to be an authorised person (s 110(3)). Furthermore, it is an offence for a person, without reasonable excuse, to: fail to comply with any requirement imposed under s 109; fail or refuse to provide facilities or assistance or any information or to permit any inspection reasonably required by virtue of s 108; or prevent another from appearing before an authorised person or answering questions asked by that person in accordance with s 108(4).

6.17 OBTAINING INFORMATION

Section 19 of EPA 1990 entitles the Secretary of State for the Environment to require, by notice in writing, that the Environment Agency provide him with such information in respect of the discharge of its functions as he wishes to receive (see also s 51 of the Environment Act 1995). A similar provision entitles the Agency to require, by written notice, that a person provides such information as the Agency reasonably considers that it needs. A failure, without reasonable excuse, to comply with this requirement is an offence under s 23(1)(g) of EPA 1990. In *JB and M Motor Haulage Ltd v London Waste Regulation Authority*,[1] the Divisional Court held, in the context of a request to furnish information under s 93 of the Control of Pollution Act 1974, that the authority had been unable to establish that it had reasonably considered the need for the information. This conclusion could be drawn from the fact that the authority had failed to offer any evidence linking the appellants with the offences in respect of which it was exercising its s 93 power. Accordingly, the appellants' convictions for offences contrary to s 3 of that Act

---

1 [1993] Env LR 243.

were quashed. It follows from this case, therefore, that the reasonableness of the Agency's belief when acting in accordance with s 19 may be open to challenge before a court, and it is unlikely to be established in the absence of prima facie evidence.

A further point of interest in respect of s 19 also emerges from a case in which an almost identical statutory provision was interpreted by the courts. In giving judgment in *Re Green Environmental Industries Ltd and Another,*[1] the Court of Appeal held that the fact that information requested under s 71 of EPA 1990 might assist the waste regulation authority in establishing a criminal offence against the provider of the information was not a reasonable excuse for failing to provide it. Applying this reasoning to s 19, it follows that the danger of self-incrimination will not amount to a reasonable excuse for failing to comply with a request made under this section.

6.18 ENVIRONMENTAL INFORMATION – PUBLICITY

In order to ensure that the environment is properly managed, and that the processes and activities which harm it are effectively controlled, it is important that the decisions made to attain these objectives are based on good quality, accurate information. Furthermore, for the purposes of involving the general public in the process of environmental protection, such information must be made available to the public in an accessible format. However, the British culture of secrecy is at odds with the concept of publicity. Despite the fact that EC Directive 90/313/EEC on access to environmental information has been implemented in UK law by way of the Environmental Information Regulations 1992, SI 1992/3240, public access to environmental information is not, perhaps, what it ought to be. Difficulties have arisen over such fundamental issues as who or what is a 'relevant person' for the purposes of supplying information under the Regulations, with some bodies, such as water companies, regarding themselves as not bound by the obligation to allow access to environmental information. Nevertheless, in the context of the IPC and LAAPC regimes, the general right of access to environmental information is less significant, since the Regulations exclude from their ambit information contained in records which are required by statute to be available for public inspection, ie information on public registers. While this information is more limited in its scope than general environmental information, it is still important.

1 (1997) *The Times*, 9 October.

6.19 PUBLIC REGISTERS OF INFORMATION

In its Tenth Report, *Tackling Pollution – Experience and Prospects*,[1] the Royal Commission on Environmental Pollution recommended, inter alia, that there should be 'a presumption in favour of unrestricted access for the public to information which pollution control authorities obtain or receive by virtue of their statutory powers, with provision for secrecy only in those circumstances where a genuine case for it can be substantiated'. To an extent, this recommendation has been given effect subsequently in environmental statutes by the inclusion of a requirement to keep public registers of information. Thus, for example, the Environment Agency is required by s 190 of the Water Resources Act 1991 to maintain a pollution control register containing information relating to, inter alia, applications for discharge consents and, where consents have been granted, information on the conditions to which they are subject. Moreover, by virtue of s 196 of the Water Industry Act 1991 sewerage undertakers are required to keep trade effluent registers, and waste regulation authorities (now the Environment Agency) are required to maintain public registers in accordance with s 64 of EPA 1990. The picture which therefore emerges is of the widespread application of the public register concept, and, as such, it is not surprising that air pollution control under Part I of EPA 1990 also entails the maintenance of a public register of information. The advantages of a register approach were summarised by the DoE in a consultation paper entitled *Integrated Pollution Control and Local Authority Air Pollution Controls: Public Access to Information* (1989), where it was stated that:

> 'It fulfils in a transparent and administratively practical way the objective of giving the public a right of access to the information supplied to, and decisions taken by, the enforcing authorities. The approach is transparent because members of the public can see clearly and precisely what information is available, and because the information is readily available in a well-presented form. The public are not faced with the difficult task of having to find out what information is available before they can exercise their right of access. The register approach is administratively practical because the burden placed on the enforcing authorities is kept within finite bounds. The task of maintaining registers and making them available to the public represents a known and fixed burden on the authorities, in terms of workload and financial resources. They are not required to respond to ad hoc and possibly ill-defined requests for information which may not be readily available.' (para 9)

6.19.1 Type of information to be recorded on register

In the case of IPC, s 20 of EPA 1990 imposes a duty on the Environment Agency, in respect of prescribed processes for which it is the enforcing authority, to maintain a register containing information relating to:

- applications for authorisations made to the Agency;

1 Cmnd 9149 (1984).

- authorisations which have been granted by the Agency or in respect of which the Agency has functions under Part I of EPA 1990;
- variation notices, enforcement notices and prohibition notices issued by the Agency;
- revocations of authorisations effected by the Agency;
- appeals under s 15 of EPA 1990;
- convictions for such offences under s 23(1) of the Act as may be prescribed;
- matters concerned with the pursuance of the conditions of authorisations or under any provision of Part I of the Act;
- directions given to the Agency under any provision of Part I of the Act by the Secretary of State; and
- such other matters relating to the carrying-on of prescribed processes or any pollution of the environment caused thereby as may be prescribed.

Further clarification on the information which must be contained in the register is provided by reg 15 of the Environmental Protection (Applications, Appeals and Registers) Regulations 1991, as amended. The prescribed particulars which appear in the 1991 Regulations are many and various, but the importance of the registers demands that they are listed here in full. Thus, under reg 15, a register must contain:

- all particulars of any application for an authorisation, or for a variation of the conditions of an authorisation, which has been made to the Agency;
- all particulars of any advertisement published pursuant to reg 5 of the 1991 Regulations;
- all particulars of any notice to the applicant by the Agency under para 1(3) of Sch 1 to EPA 1990, and of any information furnished in response to such a notice;
- all particulars of any representations made by any person in response to an advertisement published pursuant to reg 5 of the Regulations, with the exception of those representations where the person who made them requested that they should not be placed on the register;
- in a case where such a request has led to the omission of representations from the register, a statement by the Agency on the register to this effect, although such a statement must not identify the person who made the representations;
- all particulars of any authorisation granted by the Agency;
- all particulars of any written notice of the transfer of an authorisation given to the Agency in accordance with s 9(2) of EPA 1990;
- all particulars of any notification given to the holder of an authorisation by the Agency under s 10(5) of the Act;
- all particulars of any revocation of an authorisation by the Agency;
- all particulars of any variation notice, enforcement notice or prohibition notice issued by the Agency;
- all particulars of any notice issued by the Agency withdrawing an enforcement notice or a prohibition notice;
- all particulars of any notice of appeal under s 15 of the Act, together with the documents relating to the appeal referred to in reg 9(2)(a), (d) and (e)

of the 1991 Regulations, any written notification of the Secretary of State's determination of the appeal, and any report accompanying such written notification;

- details of any conviction of any person for an offence under s 23(1) of the Act relating to the carrying-on of a prescribed process under an authorisation granted by the Agency, or of carrying on a prescribed process without an authorisation contrary to s 6(1) of the Act, such details to include the name of the offender, the date of the conviction, the penalty imposed and the name of the court;
- all particulars of any monitoring information in respect of a prescribed process which the Agency has authorised and which has been obtained either through its own efforts or has been furnished to it in writing by virtue of a condition of the authorisation or s 19(2) of the Act;
- in a case where any such monitoring information has been omitted from the register by virtue of s 22 of the Act, a statement by the Agency based on the monitoring information obtained or received by it, indicating whether or not there has been compliance with any relevant condition of the authorisation;
- all particulars of any other information furnished to the Agency on or after 1 April 1996 in compliance with a condition of the authorisation, a variation notice, enforcement notice or prohibition notice, or s 19(2) of the Act;
- all particulars of any report published by the Agency relating to an assessment of the environmental consequences of the carrying-on of a prescribed process in the locality of premises where the prescribed process is carried on under an authorisation granted by the Agency; and
- all particulars of any direction, with the exception of a direction under s 21(2) of the Act, given to the Agency by the Secretary of State under any provision of Part I of the Act.

6.19.2 Removal of information

Section 20 of EPA 1990 and reg 15 of the 1991 Regulations, as amended, thus provide a comprehensive answer to the question, 'What type of information relating to prescribed processes is to appear on the public register?' It must be noted, however, that by virtue of s 20(6) the Secretary of State may issue directions to the Agency requiring the removal of any information from the register that has not been prescribed or which should have been excluded from the register in accordance with either s 21 or s 22 of EPA 1990. A related question concerns the length of time for which such information will remain on the register. Under reg 17 the Agency is not required to retain monitoring information relating to a particular process on a register for any more than four years after that information was entered in the register. The same time limit applies where information relating to a particular process has been superseded by other information relating to that same process, so that the original information need no longer appear on the register. Bearing in mind the nature and quantity of information which may appear on a s 20 register, the practical effect of reg 17 is that it provides the Agency with an opportunity periodically to review the register, and to remove information which falls within the scope of the regulation and which is no longer of any use or significance. The four-year time period ensures that information will not be removed hastily from the register and, in any case, the Agency may opt to leave information on it even where the prerequisites in reg 17 are satisfied. An exception to reg 17 relates to any aggregated monitoring data on overall emissions of any substance or class of substances from prescribed processes generally, or from any class of prescribed process, since this information must remain on the register.

6.19.3 Public accessibility

Registers produced in accordance with s 20 may, in fact, be kept in any form, and, as such, the Agency has a measure of discretion over how the information is presented. The publicity aspect of the registers of information is dealt with by s 20(7) of EPA 1990. The Agency is under a duty to ensure that all the registers it maintains under s 20 are available for inspection by the public at all reasonable times, free of charge. A further duty exists on the Agency to afford members of the public facilities for obtaining copies of entries on the registers, on payment of reasonable charges. The Secretary of State has the power to prescribe places at which registers or facilities for obtaining copies are to be available to the public. Maintaining public registers clearly has resource implications for the relevant enforcing authorities, and the costs incurred will not be recovered by the payment of 'reasonable charges' alone. Indeed, such charges are unlikely to amount to very much and, therefore, as the DoE consultation paper on public access to information (see above) noted, the costs of maintaining public registers 'will be reflected in the proposed system of charging operators for authorisations' (para 25).

6.20 INFORMATION EXCLUDED FROM REGISTERS

The general principle reflected in s 20 of EPA 1990 is that the public should have access to information obtained in respect of the control of prescribed processes under Part I of the Act. However, two categories of information are expressly excluded from the ambit of this principle by the Act itself: information affecting national security; and information which is of a commercially confidential nature.

6.20.1 Information affecting national security

Section 21 of EPA 1990 provides that no information shall be included in a s 20 register which, in the opinion of the Secretary of State, would be contrary to the interests of national security if it were included. The decision on what information affects national security, therefore, falls to be determined by the Secretary of State, who may issue directions to enforcing authorities either specifying information or descriptions of information to be excluded from their registers, or specifying descriptions of information to be referred to him for his determination. Information excluded from the register under s 21 will remain so excluded for as long as the Secretary of State considers that its inclusion would be contrary to the interests of national security. A person (who will generally be a process operator) may give notice to the Secretary of State that he believes that specified information falls within the scope of s 21, and he is required to notify the Environment Agency in the case of IPC that this has been done. However, the determination of the matter remains with the Secretary of State, and any information notified to him in the above manner is not to be included in a register until he has determined that it should be included (s 21(4)(b)).

A determination made by the Secretary of State in the context of s 21 is subject to the supervisory jurisdiction of the Queen's Bench Division of the High Court. However, if judicial review of the Secretary of State's decision were sought, and assuming that the enforcing authority or other interested party was granted leave to do so, it is unlikely that the application would be upheld and the appropriate relief granted because of the approach taken by the judiciary in the past where arguments relating to national security have arisen. An applicant for judicial review who is met by the respondent's claim that a particular act or decision was taken in the interests of national security has a difficult task ahead of him. This is largely due to the judiciary's adherence to what has become known as the *Zamora* principle. In *The Zamora*,[1] which concerned the requisitioning of a neutral vessel with a cargo of copper in the custody of the Prize Court, Lord Parker observed that 'Those who are responsible for the national security must be the sole judges of what the national security requires'. Despite the plain meaning of these words, which appear to suggest that the courts will take a deferential view in respect of arguments of national security, the mere assertion that judicial review should be precluded on these grounds is not, by itself, enough to oust the jurisdiction of the court. Instead, the court will require cogent evidence of potential damage to national security before it accepts that the relevant executive act or decision was justified on this basis.[2]

6.20.2 Commercially confidential information

The second category of information which may be excluded from an EPA 1990, s 20 register is information which is of a commercially confidential nature. For the purposes of s 22, information is to be treated as commercially confidential 'if its being contained in the register would prejudice to an unreasonable degree the commercial interests' of the party seeking its exclusion. However, it is important to note that information is not deemed to be commercially confidential under the statutory regime simply because a process operator has asserted that this is the case. The process operator, when

1 [1918] 2 AC 77.

2 See *Council for the Civil Service Union v Minister for the Civil Service* [1985] AC 374 (the *GCHQ* case); and *R v Secretary of State for the Home Department ex parte Ruddock* [1987] 2 All ER 518.

furnishing information to the Environment Agency in respect of an application for an authorisation, or the variation of an authorisation, or in complying with a condition of an authorisation or pursuant to a statutory requisition under s 19(2) of EPA 1990, may apply for the information to be excluded from the register on the ground that it is commercially confidential. The Agency, for its part, will then determine whether it is indeed so. Thus, a clear distinction emerges between ss 21 and 22 of EPA 1990 since, in the case of the latter, the enforcing authority has no role to play in the determination of information affecting national security. The Agency has 14 days beginning from the date of the application to determine the matter, and if it fails to make a determination within that period, it shall be treated as having determined that the information is commercially confidential (s 22(3)). The Secretary of State may, by order, extend or contract this 14-day time period where he considers it appropriate to do so (s 22(10)).

The question of the commercial confidentiality of information may also arise where information has been obtained by the Agency in circumstances other than those already described above. Where information has been so obtained, and it appears to the Agency that it may be commercially confidential, the Agency is required to notify the relevant person or business and give such a person a reasonable opportunity to object to the inclusion of the information on the register and make representations in support of the objection (s 22(4)). In the event that the Agency determines that information obtained either under subss (2) or (4) is not commercially confidential, it shall refrain from entering the information on the register until 21 days from the date of its determination of the issue (s 22(5)). Accordingly, during this period an appeal may be brought against the Agency's determination, which will be heard by the Secretary of State since there has been no delegation of the decision-making power to the Planning Inspectorate in respect of s 22 appeals. Such an appeal must be held in private, but the documents accompanying the notice of appeal are the same as those in respect of other appeals under Part I of EPA 1990 as specified in reg 9 of the Environmental Protection (Applications, Appeals and Registers) Regulations 1991, SI 1991/507 (see **6.15**). Where an appeal is brought, s 22(5) provides that the information to which the appeal relates shall not be entered on the register pending the final determination or withdrawal of the appeal. In the draft guidance on commercial confidentiality, which accompanied DoE News Release No 56 (30 January, 1990), it was stated that:

> 'If the Secretary of State receives an appeal against a decision by an enforcing authority not to withhold information from the IPC register, he will require cogent and specific evidence to substantiate the claim that disclosure would prejudice to an unreasonable degree some person's commercial interests. This would need to demonstrate that disclosure of information would negate or significantly diminish the commercial advantage that one operator has over another. This might for instance relate to preserving the secrecy of a new process technology, or of a particular process material or catalyst, or of the capacity of the process, or of some other specific feature which if known to competitors might diminish a legitimate commercial advantage. Arguments based on general claims, for instance, that disclosure might damage the reputation of the operator and hence

his commercial competitiveness, are unlikely to be given weight. Where information is withheld from the register, the register will indicate that there has been an omission. The authority will periodically include a statement indicating whether the operator has complied with terms and conditions of the authorisation which are withheld from the register.'

The confidentiality exemption in s 22 may be overridden by a direction from the Secretary of State where it is in the public interest that the relevant information should be on the public register (s 22(7)). Moreover, since what is commercially confidential information at one point in time will not necessarily be so at some time in the future, EPA 1990 declares that the confidentiality exemption lasts for four years from the date of the original determination (s 22(8)). If a process operator believes that the effect of this provision would be to bring into the public domain information which he believes is still commercially confidential, he may apply to the enforcing authority for it to remain excluded. A right of appeal to the Secretary of State also exists in respect of this further determination (s 22(9)).

The concept of a public register of information was originally greeted with concern by those industries for which innovation and inventiveness were vital to their success. HMIP's Annual Report for 1994/95 noted, for example, that it had been in receipt of a number of requests from operators in the pharmaceutical industry not to put information on the register because it was commercially confidential. An earlier report[1] revealed that for the relevant period, HMIP had received 67 requests from operators not to enter information on the register. Two such requests, from PowerGen and National Power, resulted in appeals to the Secretary of State under s 22. The former, which was unsuccessful, concerned PowerGen's objection to information relating to future emissions being placed on the register, whereas the latter, which did succeed, related to information about future fuel consumption. In the opinion of the Secretary of State, National Power was right to think that information relating to future power supplies had no direct relevance to its application for an authorisation. Subsequent HMIP annual reports contained no statistics on commercial confidentiality determinations, but in its latest report, prior to the establishment of the Environment Agency, HMIP stressed that it sought to ensure that excluded information was kept to a minimum and that it 'strongly resists attempts by operators to regard details of releases to the environment as confidential'.

6.21 CHEMICAL RELEASE INVENTORY

The Chemical Release Inventory (CRI) is an alternative to the public registers of information on the releases of substances to the environment. Originally, it was intended to be published in 1993, but, in fact, the first inventory did not appear until 1994. The catalyst for its establishment was the US Toxics Release

1 1991/92.

Inventory (TRI) which was set up in 1987 and which required companies of a particular size to report releases of over 300 substances which appeared on a common list. The success of the US TRI lies in the fact that it has served as a means of publicly exposing those companies which have failed to use clean technologies and which consequently occupy high positions in the polluters league tables.

The British experience to date has not, however, been anything like as successful. The CRI has been described as being 'moribund',[1] which explains why the Environment Agency has proposed that it should be overhauled. The failings of the current CRI appear to be serious. It is compiled annually on the basis of the data submitted in respect of IPC authorisations and monitoring requirements, which also appear on the public registers. The CRI details the release of substances from particular industrial and process types to all environmental media on a country (England and Wales), county and regional basis. However, the very fact that it is limited to IPC-authorised processes alone is seen as a failing. Information received in respect of, for example, LAAPC or the discharge consent system under the Water Resources Act 1991, may be of equal importance where significant pollution is involved, and yet it does not appear on the CRI. Moreover, as the *ENDS Report* notes, the reporting requirements have frequently given rise to anomalies in that they are based on limits set for IPC authorisation, where the objective is process control rather than environmental significance. This has resulted in only 60 per cent of incinerators being required to report dioxin emissions. Such failings are compounded by the chronic lack of resources being applied to the CRI. According to the *ENDS Report*, the CRI is the responsibility of one full-time Agency official, whereas its US counterpart, the TRI, has an annual budget of $40 million and a staff of approximately 40.

The Environment Agency's proposals for reform of the CRI seek to create an inventory which has been compiled on the basis of reporting which is substance, as opposed to process, based. It is hoped that IPC-authorised operators will report against a priority list of substances in respect of each of the environmental media. In the case of air, the Agency has drawn up a proposed priority list which states the identity of the reported substance, together with the minimum reporting level. Thus, for carbon dioxide the minimum reporting level is 10,000 tonnes, whereas for benzene the proposed reporting level is 1 kg. Other substances which will need to be reported once the relevant reporting threshold has been reached are as follows: nitrogen oxides (10 tonnes); sulphur dioxide (10 tonnes); methane (10 tonnes); carbon monoxide (10 tonnes); particulates (10 tonnes); PM10 (1 tonne); hydrogen chloride (1 tonne); 1, 3-butadiene (1 kg); ozone (to be established); VOCs (100 kg); polycyclic aromatic hydrocarbons (PAHs) (100g); metals (1g to 100 kg, depending on metal); and dioxins/furans (0.01g TEQ). As the *ENDS Report*

1 See (1997) 269 *ENDS Report* 19.

notes, this priority list has been drawn up with local authorities' responsibilities in respect of the national air quality strategy firmly in mind.[1]

Reform of the CRI is currently on the Agency's agenda and, for many, especially the environmental pressure groups, it is long overdue. It remains to be seen whether the proposals will be accepted by these groups and industry alike, although the initial signs do not appear to be too discouraging. One weakness of the old scheme, which has not been directly addressed by the proposals, is the absence of data on LAAPC sources. Since it appears that the Agency intends to consult widely on these proposals, it may be that this matter is revisited during the consultation process

6.22 ENFORCEMENT BY THE HIGH COURT AND OTHER COURTS

Where the Environment Agency is of the opinion that proceedings for the offence of failing to comply with or contravening the terms of an enforcement or prohibition notice would afford 'an ineffectual remedy', s 24 of EPA 1990 entitles the Agency to take proceedings in the High Court in order to secure compliance with the relevant notice. Invoking the civil jurisdiction of the court to grant an injunction represents a means by which the Agency can ensure that the relevant notice is complied with swiftly. In this respect, therefore, it is a particularly useful alternative remedy for dealing with recalcitrant operators. On the basis of the decision in *City of London Corporation v Bovis Construction Ltd*,[2] it would seem that where an injunction is sought to enforce the criminal law, such a jurisdiction will be exercised exceptionally, and only then with great care. In this case, which concerned the grant of an injunctive relief to enforce a notice issued under s 60 of the Control of Pollution Act 1974 to control construction site noise, the Court of Appeal took the view that there had to be more than a mere infringement of the law before the assistance of civil proceedings could be sought. In effect, an injunction would not be granted solely on the basis that the operator was deliberately and flagrantly flouting the law; instead, it was necessary to show that the defendant's unlawful operations would continue unless and until they were restrained by the law, and that the only effective way to achieve such a restraint was by way of an injunction.

The High Court and the lower courts have an additional power under s 26 of EPA 1990 Act to order that the matters in respect of which a defendant has been convicted must be remedied where that person has been convicted for operating a process without an authorisation, or in contravention of a condition, enforcement notice, or prohibition notice. The power arises where the court is of the view that the convicted person has it in his power to remedy matters, and it may be exercised instead of or in addition to the imposition of

1 See Chapter 10.
2 [1989] JPL 263.

any punishment. The order itself will specify the steps which the convicted person must take to remedy matters, and will also stipulate the time within which this is to be done. The time-limit may be extended by order of the court following an application to this effect. Where a person fails to comply with an order under s 26, he commits an offence contrary to s 23(1)(l). If the time-limit for carrying out the remedial measures has been extended, the offence of non-compliance with the order will arise only following the expiry of the revised time-limit (s 26(3)).

6.23 POWER OF THE AGENCY TO REMEDY HARM

Where any of the offences which activate the power to make a s 26 order have been committed and they have caused harm which it is possible to remedy, the Environment Agency may, under s 27 of EPA 1990, arrange for any reasonable steps to be taken towards remedying the harm and recover the costs from the person convicted of the offence. This power is only exercisable in the event of harm having actually occurred. It does not confer upon the Agency the right to take steps in order to prevent such harm. Furthermore, it may be exercised only with the written approval of the Secretary of State and, in any case where it would involve going on to land occupied by a person other than the person on whose land the prescribed process is being carried on, the Agency must first obtain the permission of that person. The wording of s 27 is such that the power may be exercised only by the Environment Agency, or, in Scotland, by the Scottish Environmental Protection Agency. There is no mention in the statute of the possibility of the s 27 power being exercised by local authorities as part of its enforcement machinery. However, since it arises in respect of offences under s 23 of EPA 1990 which can be committed by operators subject either to IPC or LAAPC, it may be possible for the Agency to exercise the power even where the harm has been caused by an LAAPC process.

6.24 IPC/PLANNING INTERFACE

An interesting and important issue arises where an activity is subject to the dual control of the Town and Country Planning Act 1990 and the IPC provisions under Part I of EPA 1990. In such circumstances, it becomes necessary to determine the correct approach for the Secretary of State to adopt where there is, in effect, an overlap between these two statutory regimes. This was the task faced by the Court of Appeal in *Gateshead Metropolitan Borough Council v Secretary of State for the Environment*.[1]

The facts of this case were as follows. The Northumbrian Water Group plc (NWG) wished to construct and operate an incinerator for the disposal of clinical waste on a site approximately nine acres in size. In order to do so, it was first necessary for the company to obtain planning permission under the

1 [1995] JPL 432.

Town and Country Planning Act 1990. The proposed incinerator constituted a process within the meaning of s 2 of EPA 1990, and Sch 1 to the Environmental Protection (Prescribed Processes and Substances) Regulations 1991, SI 1991/472, as amended. Accordingly, an authorisation to carry on the process of incineration was required by virtue of s 6 of EPA 1990. NWG applied to the local planning authority for planning permission on two separate occasions. The second of these applications, which gave rise to the present proceedings, was rejected for a variety of reasons, which included the planning authority's belief that the proposal was contrary to the provisions of the approved development plan and that the applicants had failed to demonstrate that the overall effects on the environment, particularly in relation to health risk, had been fully investigated and taken account of. NWG appealed against this refusal to the Secretary of State and, accordingly, an inquiry was held. At the time the inquiry took place, an application had been made to HMIP for an IPC authorisation, but this had not been determined. Despite the inspector's recommendation that planning permission be refused, primarily on the basis of concerns over the impact of the development on air quality and the general public disquiet over environmental pollution, the Secretary of State allowed the appeal and granted outline planning permission subject to conditions. Gateshead MBC exercised its right under s 288 of the Town and Country Planning Act 1990 and applied to the High Court for an order that the Secretary of State's decision be quashed. The application was dismissed, and Gateshead subsequently appealed to the Court of Appeal.

The appeal was argued on two grounds: first, that the Secretary of State had not given proper or adequate reasons for rejecting the inspector's recommendations; and, secondly, that once planning permission had been granted, it was in practice very unlikely that HMIP would use its powers to refuse to authorise the operation of the plant. Neither of these arguments was accepted by the Court of Appeal. In his decision letter, the Secretary of State had considered the inspector's concerns over the environmental impact of the proposed development, but had taken the view that:

> 'Whilst it is necessary to take account of the impact of potential emissions on neighbouring land uses when considering whether or not to grant planning permission, control of those emissions should be regulated by HMIP under the Environmental Protection Act 1990. The controls available under Part I of the Environmental Protection Act 1990 are adequate to deal with emissions from the proposed plant and the risk of harm to human health.' (para 20)

In the opinion of the Court of Appeal, the Secretary of State's words were a correct statement of the true position: the controls under EPA 1990 were adequate to deal with the concerns expressed by the inspector and the assessor, and it was appropriate for HMIP to determine the matter. If it had been apparent during the inquiry that some of the discharges from the proposed development would have been such that HMIP were obliged to refuse to grant an authorisation, then planning permission ought to have been refused. However, the evidence in the present case relating to air quality was not strong enough to support such an approach.

The decision in *Gateshead* highlights how controls under the planning legislation and EPA 1990 may, in practice, overlap, even though the former is concerned with the use of land, whereas the latter is concerned, at least in the present context, with protecting the environment from the damaging effects of industrial processes.[1] Although the Court of Appeal agreed that the extent to which discharges from a proposed plant would necessarily or probably pollute the atmosphere and/or create an unacceptable risk to human health was a material consideration to be taken into account when deciding whether or not to grant planning permission, it would seem that in the light of *Gateshead* a local planning authority would be well advised not to refuse permission on pollution grounds alone unless its view is well supported by the available evidence. If planning permission for a new plant is refused, the grant or otherwise of a process authorisation ceases to be a matter of importance. However, if planning permission is granted, it does not necessarily follow that a Part I authorisation will be granted. The Environment Agency retains a discretion under s 6(3) of EPA 1990 to refuse to grant an authorisation and, provided it considered this to be the appropriate course of action, it would be entitled to do so, subject to the applicant's right of appeal under s 15.

Guidance on the relevance of pollution controls to the exercise of planning functions by local planning authorities has been provided by the DoE in the form of PPG 23, *Planning and Pollution Control*. The aim of this document, which claims to follow the Court of Appeal's decision in *Gateshead*, is 'to encourage close consultation and prevent unnecessary duplication and conflict of interest between planning and pollution control authorities' (para 1.4). Further clarification in respect of this aim is provided by para 1.34, which states that:

> 'Planning authorities will need to consult pollution control authorities in order that they can take account of the scope and requirements of the relevant pollution controls. Planning authorities should work on the assumption that the pollution control regimes will be properly applied and enforced. They should not seek to substitute their own judgement on pollution control issues for that of the bodies with the relevant expertise and the statutory responsibility for that control.'

The need for consultation between the planning authorities and the Environment Agency is clearly important in respect of potentially polluting developments which are subject to the IPC regime. The advantages of such consultation are that it ensures that conflicting requirements are not imposed on developers under the planning and pollution control regimes, and seeks to avoid the duplication of pollution control regimes through the planning system. Moreover, early consultation between the two parties may serve as a means of alerting the Agency to the likelihood of an application being made for an IPC authorisation if it has not already received such an application. This by-product of consultation may be of particular assistance to the Agency since, as the advice notes, an applicant may not have sufficient information to make an

---

1 For a further decision involving a consideration of the IPC/Planning interface, see *R v Bolton Metropolitan Council, see parte Kirkman* [1998] JPL 787.

application for an IPC authorisation at the same time as his planning application is submitted.

6.25 IPC IN PRACTICE

In January 1994, Environmental Data Services (ENDS) published a review of how IPC was actually working in practice. The review listed a number of factors about the regime which can be assigned either to the debit or the credit column. On the debit side, it was apparent that the preparation of process applications was a costly and time-consuming process involving between 100 and 500 man hours, and costing £29,000 to £150,000. In some cases, these upper figures were far exceeded. Despite the importance of the regime, the review found that many operators were still largely ignorant of the basic requirements of IPC, and there were a number of failures to comply with official guidance. This lack of compliance was exacerbated by HMIP's enforcement policy, which regarded formal enforcement action as a last resort. On the issue of the variation of existing authorisations the review identified that the proper procedure was by no means always being applied, with the result that some variations were being granted 'off the record' and, as such, details were absent from the public register. This had the knock-on effect that the accuracy and value of the registers were diminished. Finally, and, perhaps, most disappointingly of all, the review found that many companies subject to IPC were concerned only with the use of technology sufficient to stop emissions 'at the pipe's end'; in other words, little emphasis was being placed on the need to establish efficient, waste-free processes from the outset, which is contrary to the spirit of the preventative principle and IPC itself.

The credit column, by comparison, contains fewer entries. The review noted that, in practice, there have been relatively few applications for exclusion from the public register on the ground of commercial confidentiality, save for those referred to above (see **6.20.2**). Moreover, it would seem that IPC has brought about significant improvements in terms of investment by companies in environmental protection. However, even this positive result is qualified by the further observation that such investments have been undertaken primarily by those companies which had already exhibited a commitment to the environment prior to the enactment of EPA 1990. The issue of expenditure on pollution control technologies is, of course, important in any consideration of the success or otherwise of IPC in practice. In the recent study 'Environmental Protection Expenditure by Industry', carried out by Ecotec for the DoE in June 1996, it was claimed that 'clean technology' investment represents just under 25 per cent of industrial capital expenditure. Moreover, the study found that, in 1994, industry spent £2,340 million on enhanced pollution control technologies, which is comparable with that spent in other major European nations, even though the figure in fact represents only 0.4 per cent of Gross Domestic Product. It would seem that EPA 1990 has been the main catalyst for capital spending, with processes subject to IPC receiving the greatest sums of money. By contrast, processes subject to LAAPC have received fractional amounts of capital expenditure. Nevertheless, the study confirmed an impression that is widely held, namely that industry has been slow to realise that expenditure on cleaner technologies can ultimately result in the saving of money. Accordingly, IPC and, for that matter, LAAPC requirements have tended to be regarded as impositions rather than as opportunities for technological and environmental improvement.

In order to ensure that IPC authorisations properly reflect any technological improvements which may have occurred since they were originally granted, s 6(6) of EPA imposes a duty on the Agency to review the conditions of an authorisation at least once every four years. It has recently been reported, however, that the Agency has fallen behind with its review programme and that progress has been slow in trying to clear up the backlog which has resulted.[1] This is apparently due to a combination of factors which include, inter alia, disruption which resulted from the establishment of the Agency in April 1996 and inspectors' involvement in risk assessments which have arisen out of the BSE crisis. The concern is that, by prioritising clearing-up the backlog, other areas of the Agency's work may be affected, such as site inspections. Clearly, the prospect of less frequent inspections plays into the hands of any operator willing to take the chance of carrying on a process outside the scope of an authorisation.

One further recent development which may have serious consequences for the operation of the IPC regime concerns the regulation of processes which have ceased operating and have subsequently been restarted. It has been reported that legal advice obtained by the Environment Agency suggests that amendments made to the Environmental Protection (Prescribed Processes and Substances) Regulations 1991 are such that an 'existing process' is now defined as a process which was operated at any time in the 12 months to 8 January 1996.[2] It follows from this that old polluting industrial plants which were operational sometime during the course of 1995, and which have since been shut down, may now be returned to use having more or less escaped the need to comply with environmental improvements demanded by IPC. The dilemma faced by the Agency has been highlighted by the case of the coal producer, Celtic Energy, which has applied for an IPC authorisation to recommission a 40-year-old power station, Uskmouth B in South Wales, as an existing process, even though it is said to have 'a low thermal efficiency and crude emission control system'. The *ENDS Report* notes that both the DoE and the Environment Agency are examining ways in which this loophole can be closed before it is abused by operators.

1 See (1998) 281 *ENDS Report* 5.
2 See (1997) 269 *ENDS Report* 10.

6.26 THE FUTURE OF IPC

As with other areas of environmental law, the control of atmospheric pollution has been subject to developments and innovations which have taken place at the European level. Further proof, if such proof were needed, of the importance of European policy in this context has been provided by the coming into force on 30 October 1996 of the Integrated Pollution Prevention and Control Directive 96/61/EC. The purpose of this Directive, which was made in accordance with Article 130S of the Treaty of Rome (1957), is 'to achieve integrated prevention and control of pollution' arising from a whole host of industrial activities listed in Annex 1 to the Directive. It applies, therefore, to energy production, metal processing, mineral production, chemicals, waste management and, what the Directive terms, 'other activities', which include plants involved in the production of pulp and paper, textiles, tanning, food production and intensive poultry and pig rearing. From October 1999 onwards, an operator of a new plant proposing to carry on any of these activities will be able to do so only where it is in possession of a permit granted by a 'competent authority'. For existing plant, the Directive's provisions will apply from the year 2007.

6.26.1 Scope of the IPPC Directive

The IPPC Directive is based, in part, on the current IPC regime operated in the UK. However, in a number of important respects it goes further than the domestic regime. For example, the definition of 'pollution' in the Directive is wider than that which applies in respect of IPC (EPA 1990, s 1) since it includes vibrations and noise. Integrated pollution prevention and control (IPPC) uses the linked concepts of 'best available techniques' (see further below) and the achievement of a high level of protection for the environment as a whole, whereas the IPC regime operates in terms of BATNEEC and BPEO. Interestingly, in the context of the earlier discussion relating to the IPC/planning interface in UK law (see **6.24**), the Directive seeks to establish a link between an environmental assessment and the IPPC system, which does not currently exist domestically. Thus, any relevant information which emerges from the assessment may be taken into account for the purposes of granting a permit.

It is apparent that IPPC will apply to a much wider range of installations than are currently regulated under IPC. Figures provided by the Environment Agency, DoE and the Ministry of Agriculture, Fisheries and Food (MAFF) suggest that approximately 8,000 installations in England and Wales will fall within the scope of IPPC, whereas the number of IPC installations currently stands at approximately 2,000. The additional installations will include some 3,000 landfill sites, approximately 1,000 pig and poultry rearing units, in excess of 1,000 metal industry installations which are currently subject to LAAPC, and more than 400 installations in the food and drink industry. As the Minister for the Environment, Michael Meacher MP, noted in a speech in July 1997, 'For many of these installations, it is the first time they will have been brought under a permitting regime based on the concept of Best Available Techniques'.

Nevertheless, it does not follow from this that all the current IPC processes will necessarily be regulated under IPPC. It has been noted by Dr David Slater, the Director of Environmental Protection for the Environment Agency, that certain IPC sectors, such as research installations and the tar distillation industry, will be excluded from the mandatory coverage of IPPC. If the Directive were to be implemented in what he terms a 'minimalist' manner, the result would be the existence of two systems, IPPC and an IPC 'rump' consisting of those processes not falling within the terms of the Directive. This would be a confusing state of affairs for both the regulators and the regulated alike and, accordingly, the Agency has suggested that all IPC processes should be brought under IPPC.

6.26.2 Meaning of a 'permit'

For the purposes of the IPPC system, a permit will be a part or the whole of a written decision or decisions which grants the authorisation to operate all or part of the relevant installation, subject to the conditions guaranteeing that the installation complies with the terms of the Directive. The main requirement in the Directive is that the relevant installation will operate in accordance with the 'best available techniques' (BAT), a term defined in a broadly similar way to its UK counterpart. However, in determining the BAT, the Directive requires that special consideration should be given to employing low-waste technology, using less hazardous substances, promoting the recovery and recycling of substances generated by the process, reducing raw materials, and the need to promote energy efficiency. Where an installation is permitted to carry on a relevant activity, Article 3 of the Directive requires that it shall operate in such a way that: the appropriate preventive measures are taken against pollution; no significant pollution is caused; waste production is avoided, or, where it is produced, that it is either recovered or disposed of without detriment to the environment; energy is used efficiently; accidents are prevented; and clean-up takes place on the cessation of industrial activity.

6.26.3 Obtaining a permit

A permit must be obtained by making an application to the competent authority. The application must include a description of: the installation and its activities; the materials used; the energy used or generated; the sources of emissions; the conditions of the site; the nature and quantities of foreseeable emissions and the identification of their significant environmental effects; the abatement technology and prevention techniques to be used; the measures for waste prevention and recovery; and the measures planned to monitor emissions into the environment. Much of this information will be of a technical nature and, as such, the Directive requires that an application for a permit must also include a non-technical summary of the above details.

In making a decision on the application, a competent authority has the same measure of discretion as it does over applications for IPC or LAAPC authorisations. It may either grant a permit containing conditions guaranteeing the installation's compliance with the Directive or, alternatively, refuse to grant the permit. Where more than one competent authority is involved in this process, they must perform their roles in an integrated and fully co-ordinated manner. All permits which are granted must contain details of the arrangements made for the protection of the three environmental media. Article 9 of the Directive requires that the conditions of the permit must include emission limit values for pollutants likely to be emitted from the installation in significant quantities. In the case of emissions to air, the following substances, which are specified in Annex III to the Directive, are to be taken into account if they are relevant for fixing emission limit values: sulphur dioxide and other sulphur compounds; oxides of nitrogen and other nitrogen compounds; carbon monoxide; volatile organic compounds; metals and their compounds; dust; asbestos (suspended particulates, fibres); chlorine and its compounds; fluorine and its compounds; arsenic and its compounds; cyanides; substances and preparations which have been proved to possess carcinogenic or mutagenic properties or properties which may affect reproduction via the air; and polychlorinated dibenzodioxins and dibenzofurans. Long-distance and transboundary pollution must be minimised by conditions in permits, and a high level of environmental protection must be sought. Permit conditions will also impose release monitoring requirements, the results of which must be supplied to the competent authority by the operator for the purposes of determining compliance with the permit.

The IPPC Directive requires that permit conditions are to be reviewed, but, unlike the four-yearly review period specified in s 6(6) of EPA 1990, the Directive does not specify the frequency at which IPPC permits will be reviewed. In a consultation paper on the implementation of the Directive in the UK published in July 1997, the Government sought views on an appropriate period between reviews of permits. In the light of responses it received, the Government has proposed, in a second consultation paper published in January 1998,[1] that, rather than setting a fixed maximum period which applies to all industrial sectors, it prefers instead to create a power to specify different maximum permit review periods for different industrial sectors. The actual periods will be prescribed at a later date, but would depend upon factors such as: the expected rate of technological advance of a sector; the likelihood of sector operators making improvements on their own initiative; the risk and level of environmental impacts associated with a sector; the cost of undertaking the reviews; and, continuing the practical theme of the last factor, the need to ensure that a combination of different periods for different sectors fit together so as to avoid insurmountable peaks in the review workload.

6.26.4 Conclusions

IPPC represents a significant expansion on the present system in that it involves taking a far wider array of environmental considerations into account in the decision-making process. In the words of Dr David Slater, it 'is not just

1 UK Implementation of EC Directive 96/61 on Integrated Pollution Prevention and Control (1998) Second Consultation Paper.

"IPC with trimmings"'.[1] The Directive is concerned with 'installations' rather than 'processes' as in IPC, and, therefore, in many cases, two or more IPC processes will form the parts of a single installation. Far greater emphasis is placed on the need to achieve waste minimisation and recovery and the efficient use of energy than has been the case with IPC. Such factors are to be taken into account in determining 'best available techniques' and setting permit conditions, which is in line with current thinking on the need to ensure sustainable development. IPPC demands a more holistic way of thinking, since it is concerned with the minimisation of damage to the environment taken as a whole. If such a philosophy is enshrined in legislation, it ought to encourage a more cost-effective environmental performance by permit holders than has been the case to date. In practice, the tasks of monitoring, inspection and enforcement will become even more rigorous and testing than they have been to date. In order for the competent authorities properly to discharge these functions, it is imperative that they are allocated the necessary resources. Consideration will, therefore, have to be given to:

- drawing up a new charging regime to take account of the new range of activities to be regulated and the changed nature of the system;
- integrating and extending the various publicity and information regimes that apply to the activities currently regulated;
- ensuring that the need for sustainability is met by activities requiring permits;
- providing a genuinely coherent regulatory framework which takes account of the fact that 'permitting' will involve a number of different bodies, and also developing, where possible, a 'one-stop-shop' approach in order to avoid the duplication of effort and needless use of staff resources which could be better employed on enforcement;
- ensuring that regulation at all levels is consistent, targeted and proportionate;
- providing for the creation and dissemination of best practice guidelines to those who are regulated.

Clearly, the introduction of IPPC will result in fundamental changes for the regulators and the regulated alike. It has been described by the European Commission's Director-General of Environmental Protection as 'a gateway to the new Millennium', thus emphasising its importance as a mechanism by which to tackle the grave environmental concerns which have arisen at the end of this millennium. Nevertheless, as Dr David Slater notes, unless we move forward by seizing the opportunity provided, 'we may find that when we reach the "gateway to the new Millennium" – our entry point to a sustainable future – we do not have the key'.[2]

---

1 *Environment Action Newsletter* Issue 9, August/September 1997.

2 Environment Agency's Response to the Government Consultation Paper, UK Implementation of EC Directive 96/61 on Integrated Pollution Prevention and Control.

CHAPTER 7

LOCAL AUTHORITY AIR POLLUTION CONTROL

7.1 INTRODUCTION

The Environmental Protection Bill, which established the local authority air pollution control (LAAPC) system, was the subject of a number of criticisms during the course of its parliamentary stages. As was noted in Chapter 6, such criticisms often related as much to the Bill's omissions as they did to its actual contents. However, it is worth noting that the LAAPC provisions were broadly welcomed on both sides of the House of Commons as being a sensible and appropriate response to the need to control pollution, just as the integrated pollution control (IPC) provisions had also been the subject of parliamentary approval. In his speech, in which he moved that the Bill should be read a second time, the then Secretary of State for the Environment, Chris Patten MP, summarised the effect of these uncontroversial provisions in the following manner:[1]

> 'Part I establishes two innovatory pollution control systems, integrated pollution control and local authority air pollution control. Simpler, less polluting processes will be designated under Part I for local authority air pollution control. Up to now, local authorities have had to rely on cumbersome controls after the event. They are costly to local authorities, to the environment and to industry. The new regime strengthens the local authorities' role and gives them the means of tackling air pollution before it occurs. Their powers will cover a range of processes such as smaller power plants, glass works and municipal and hospital incinerators.'

7.1.1 Royal Commission on Environmental Pollution

The creation of a system of IPC undeniably represents an innovation in the fight against pollution, but, as was noted in Chapter 6, the Royal Commission on Environmental Pollution had came out strongly in favour of such an approach as long ago as 1976, when its Fifth Report, *Air Pollution Control: An Integrated Approach*,[2] was published. A system of air pollution control in which there was both a central and a local input was not, however, a new development. Local authorities had been involved in the process of dealing with emissions from industrial and domestic sources since the middle of the nineteenth century. At the time the Royal Commission's Fifth Report was

1 HC Deb, vol 165, col 34, 15 January 1990.
2 Cmnd 6371 (1976).

published, it was noted by its authors that there were some 459 authorities in England and Wales with responsibility for controlling the emissions from some 300,000 industrial premises. Of these 300,000 premises, the Royal Commission expressed the view that 'probably about 30–50,000 may cause significant air pollution' (para 100). With these statistics in mind, it is interesting to take account of the Royal Commission's assessment of the efficacy of LAAPC at the time its report was published.

A number of the observations made by the Royal Commission in this context could, perhaps, have been predicted before the publication of the report. For example, the report noted that there was a considerable variation in the extent and occurrence of air pollution in different local authority areas, and that this had a direct impact on the skill and expertise of those whose responsibility it was to deal with this matter. For example, the report remarked that since air pollution was less likely to occur in more rural areas, it followed that a rural local authority would not expect to employ staff with expertise in air pollution control. Moreover, irrespective of its quality, the Royal Commission stressed that local authority control of air pollution was far more susceptible to the influence of local pressures than the central control administered by the predecessor of HMIP, the Alkali Inspectorate. However, the report was anxious to stress that this by no means ensured that air pollution was dealt with more effectively at the local level. Indeed, it was considered to be possible that considerations such as the need to attract and retain industry in the locality as an important source of employment and rate revenue may encourage a local authority to be less than vigorous in its enforcement of air pollution controls. Conversely, the report noted that there was evidence to support the theory that some local authorities saw rigorous enforcement of such controls as a positive step which could be taken to attract cleaner industry to their area.

Thus, the picture which emerged from the Royal Commission's report was that the quality of local authority air control was decidedly variable and that it was subject to the vagaries of public opinion. At para 136 of the report, the Royal Commission described such local control as 'patchy', and opined that it was likely to remain so. However, its authors did not advocate bringing this approach to air pollution control to an end. Instead, the report stated that there were strong grounds for maintaining a system in which emissions were controlled both centrally and at the local level, with the division of responsibility between the two being determined by the technological complexities of the relevant process. Thus, a central body would be responsible for controlling the technologically complex processes, whereas local authority control would be confined to processes which fell within their technical competence. Interestingly, the Royal Commission noted a marked contrast between the views of some local authorities on this matter and those of environmental health officers (EHOs) who were the human face of LAAPC. While some authorities were anxious that the responsibilities of the Alkali Inspectorate should be transferred to them, the EHOs 'often conceded that they would not consider themselves equipped to take responsibility for control of the more difficult industries' (para 159).

In *Air Pollution Control*,[1] the response to the Royal Commission's Fifth Report, the Government welcomed the conclusion that the status quo should be preserved, ie that air pollution control should continue to be shared between local authorities and a central inspectorate. Central control was the appropriate approach where clear advantages were to be gained but, in the opinion of the Government, 'local authorities should continue to control the majority of processes'. This desire to see local authority control apply to the majority of processes has, in fact, been achieved in practice by the prescription of such processes as either Part 'A' or Part 'B' processes under the Environmental Protection (Prescribed Processes and Substances) Regulations 1991, SI 1991/472, as amended (see **6.2** and further below). Currently, some 12,000 industrial plants are regulated by local authorities in respect of their emissions to air, whereas 2,000 industrial plants are subject to the IPC regime and, hence, Environment Agency control.

Despite the difference in the identities of the enforcing authorities, the functions of a local authority in relation to air pollution are essentially the same as those of the Agency in respect of IPC. Accordingly, a local authority has a vital role to play in terms of the authorisation and enforcement of air pollution control under Part I of the Environmental Protection Act 1990 (EPA 1990). It has the power to grant authorisations for the carrying-on of a prescribed process, or it may refuse to grant such an authorisation (s 1 and Sch 1). Moreover, it is required to attach to any authorisation such conditions as it considers to be appropriate, in addition to a general condition which is implied in every authorisation (s 7). Where an authorisation has been granted, the local authority is the body to which any prescribed fees shall be paid (s 8) and, if the holder of an authorisation has transferred that authorisation to another, the local authority must be informed of this occurrence by the transferee (s 9). Finally, the local authority also has the power to vary or revoke authorisations, or to vary the conditions attached to them (s 11).

In addition to the various powers a local authority possesses for the authorisation of air pollution, Part I of EPA 1990 also confers upon it powers to enforce air pollution control. Where a local authority is of the opinion that a condition attached to an authorisation is being contravened, it may serve an 'enforcement notice' on the holder of the authorisation requiring that person to bring the contravention to an end (s 13). Furthermore, if the local authority takes the view that the carrying-on of an authorised prescribed process involves, what the statute terms, 'an imminent risk of serious pollution of the environment', it is required to serve on the holder of the authorisation a 'prohibition notice' prohibiting the continuation of the prescribed process (s 14). A local authority also has general powers of entry to premises for the purposes of carrying out its regulatory functions under s 108 of the Environment Act 1995, and, by virtue of s 109 of that Act, an authorised person is entitled to seize an article or substance found on the premises where

1 Pollution Paper No 18 (1982).

it is reasonably believed that it is a cause of imminent danger of serious pollution of the environment or serious harm to human health.

The foregoing represents a brief summary of some of the provisions which are contained in Part I of EPA 1990. In the remainder of this chapter, the various powers and obligations of a local authority in respect of air pollution will be considered more fully, including the requirement of publicity in respect of authorisations for prescribed processes, which is dealt with by ss 20–22 of the Act. Where appropriate, consideration will be given to the manner in which the statutory provisions have been interpreted by the Secretary of State and the courts. Moreover, in order to get some sense of how these provisions have operated in practice, it will be necessary to refer to the recent DoE publication, *Local Air Pollution Control in England and Wales: Five Year Report 1991–1996*,[1] in which the experiences of the 379 district and borough councils, and unitary authorities, and the 53 port health authorities charged with the responsibility of administering LAAPC, are detailed.

7.2 PRESCRIBED PROCESSES AND PRESCRIBED SUBSTANCES

Whether or not a process is subject to central or local control in respect of its emissions into the air is dependent upon whether that process is a Part 'A' or Part 'B' process according to the Environmental Protection (Prescribed Processes and Substances) Regulations 1991, SI 1991/472, as amended. These Regulations, which were made under the power conferred by s 2 of EPA 1990, are therefore very important in understanding the LAAPC system. It was seen in Chapter 6 that Part 'A' processes are complex and are, therefore, subject to the control of the Environment Agency. By contrast, Part 'B' processes are controlled by local authorities due to their less complex nature.

7.2.1 Part 'B' list processes

Part 'B' list processes are described in Sch 1 to the 1991 Regulations as follows:

Chapter 1

Fuel production and combustion: gasification and associated processes (s 1.1), eg odorising natural gas or liquefied petroleum gas, except where that process is related to a Part A process or blending odorant for use with natural gas or liquefied petroleum gas; combustion processes (s 1.3), eg burning any fuel in a boiler or furnace with a net rated thermal input of not less than 20 megawatts but less than 50 megawatts, or burning any fuel in a gas turbine or compression engine with a net rated thermal input within the same capacity limits; petroleum processes (s 1.4), eg the storage of petrol in stationary storage tanks at a terminal, or the loading or unloading of petrol into or from road tankers, rail tankers or inland waterway vessels at a terminal, or the unloading of petrol into stationary storage tanks at a service

1 Department of the Environment, December 1996.

station where the total quantity of the petrol unloaded is equal to or greater than $100m^3$ in a 12-month period.

Chapter 2

Metal production and processing: iron and steel production (s 2.1), eg making, melting or refining iron, steel or any ferrous alloy in an electric arc furnace with a holding capacity of less than 7 tonnes, or a cupola, crucible furnace, reverbatory furnace, rotary furnace, induction furnace or resistance furnace, or the desulphurisation of iron, steel or any other ferrous alloy if the process is not a Part A process; non-ferrous metal processes (s 2.2), eg the making or melting of any non-ferrous metal or non-ferrous metal alloy in any furnace, bath or holding vessel with a holding capacity of less than 5 tonnes, or the separation of copper, aluminium, magnesium or zinc from mixed scrap by differential melting, or melting zinc or a zinc alloy in conjunction with a galvanising process.

Chapter 3

Mineral industries: cement and lime manufacture and associated processes (s 3.1), eg storing, loading or unloading cement or cement clinker in bulk prior to further transformation in bulk, or blending or using cement in bulk other than at a construction site where none of these processes is related to a Part A process under this section; processes involving asbestos (s 3.2), the industrial finishing of asbestos products such as asbestos cement, asbestos filters, asbestos floor coverings, and asbestos textiles where that process is not related to the manufacture of the product; other mineral processes (s 3.4), eg the crushing, grinding or other size reduction, with machinery designed for that purpose, of bricks, tiles or concrete, or coating roadstone with tar or bitumen; glass manufacture and production (s 3.5), eg the manufacture of glass at any location which has the capacity to make 5,000 tonnes or more of glass in any 12-month period, or the manufacture of glass where the use of lead or any lead compound is involved, or the polishing or etching of glass or glass products in the course of any manufacturing process if hydrofluoric acid is used, or hydrogen fluoride may be released into the air; ceramic production (s 3.6), eg firing heavy clay goods or refractory material in a kiln where the process is not a Part A process under this section.

Chapter 4

Chemical industries: petrochemical processes (s 4.1), any process for the polymerisation or co-polymerisation of any pre-formulated resin or pre-formulated gel coat which contains any unsaturated hydrocarbons which is likely to involve, in any 12-month period, the polymerisation or co-polymerisation of 100 tonnes or more of unsaturated hydrocarbons, unless the process is related to and carried on as part of a Part A process under this section; the manufacture and the use of organic chemicals (s 4.2), any process for the polymerisation or co-polymerisation of any pre-formulated resin or pre-formulated gel coat which contains any styrene which is likely to involve, in any 12-month period, the polymerisation or co-polymerisation of 100 tonnes or more of styrene, unless the process is related to and carried on as part of a Part A process under this section; acid processes (s 4.3), any process for the surface treatment of metal which is likely to result in the release into the air of any acid-forming oxide of nitrogen and which does not fall within a description in ss 2.1 or 2.2 of Sch 1 and is not treated as so falling by virtue of the rule in Sch 2; the storage of chemicals in bulk (s 4.9), the storage in a tank or tanks, other than as part of a Part A process, and other than in a tank forming part of a powered vehicle, of any one or more designated acrylates, acrylonitrile, toluene di-isocyanate or vinyl chloride monomer where the total capacity of the tanks is more than 20 tonnes, or in the case of anhydrous hydrogen fluoride, anhydrous ammonia or ethylene, where the minimum storage capacities are 1 tonne, 100 tonnes and 8,000 tonnes respectively.

Chapter 5

Waste disposal and recycling: incineration (s 5.1), the destruction by burning in an incinerator other than an exempt incinerator of any waste, including animal remains, except where related to a Part A process, or the cremation of human remains.

Chapter 6

Other industries: di-isocyanate processes (s 6.2), eg any process not falling within any other description in Sch 1 where the carrying on of the process is likely to involve the use of 5 tonnes or more of any di-isocyanate or of any partly polymerised di-isocyanate in any 12-month period, or the hot wire cutting of polyurethane foams or elastomers, except where this process is related to any other Part A process; tar and bitumen processes (s 6.3), any process which is not a Part A process under this section and which involves the heating of tar or bitumen in connection with any process of manufacture, or the oxidation of bitumen by blowing air through it, to the extent that 5 tonnes or more of tar or bitumen are used in any 12-month period; coating processes and printing (s 6.5), eg any process, other than the repainting or respraying of or of parts of aircraft, road or railway vehicles, for the application to a substance of, or the drying or curing after such an application of, printing ink or paint or any other coating material as, or in the course of, a manufacturing process where the process may result in the release into the air of particulate matter or of any volatile organic compound, and the process is likely to involve the use of, during a 12-month period, at least 20 tonnes of printing ink, paint or other coating material, or the same quantity of metal coatings which are sprayed on in molten form, or at least 25 tonnes of organic solvents in respect of certain printing processes, or 5 tonnes of such solvents in respect of any other process; the manufacture of dyestuffs, printing ink and coating materials (s 6.6), eg any process for the manufacture or formulation of printing ink or any other coating material containing or involving the use of organic solvent, where the carrying-on of the process is likely to involve the use of at least 100 tonnes of organic solvents in any 12-month period; timber processes (s 6.7), the manufacture of wholly or partly wooden products where the process involves sawing, drilling, sanding, shaping, turning, planing, curing or chemical treatment of wood, and the throughput in any 12-month period is likely to exceed 10,000 cubic metres at works where wood is only sawed, and 1,000 cubic metres in any other case involving relevant processes; processes involving rubber (s 6.8), eg the mixing, milling or blending of natural rubber or synthetic organic elastomers if carbon black is used; the treatment and processing of animal or vegetable matter (s 6.9), eg breeding maggots in any case where more than 5kg of animal or vegetable matter or an aggregate of both is introduced into the process in any week.

7.2.2 Interpretation of Sch 1 to the Environmental Protection (Prescribed Processes and Substances) Regulations 1991

For the avoidance of any doubt which may arise as to whether a process is a Part A or a Part B process, especially where a number of different but related operations are carried on at the same location, Sch 2 to the 1991 Regulations lays down a number of rules for the interpretation of Sch 1. It should be noted, however, that Sch 1 takes precedence in the event of a conflict between one of its own provisions and a rule of interpretation. Perhaps the most important rule in the present context is Rule 3, which determines that where a Part A and a Part B process under the same section of Sch 1 are carried on at the same location, they are to be treated as requiring authorisation as a single process and shall be regarded as part of a Part A process. In other words, Part B processes will be subject to central rather than local control in the circumstances described by Rule 3. The precedence of Part A processes over Part B processes is also apparent where different processes are carried on at different times using the same plant or machinery. Where those processes include one or more Part A processes, Rule 7(1) requires that any other processes shall be regarded as within the descriptions of the Part A processes. Rule 2C provides for the situation where the same person carries on at the same location two or more Part B processes. In these circumstances, where those processes fall within certain prescribed sections of Sch 1, they are to be treated as requiring authorisation as a single Part B process falling within the first mentioned section. Thus, for example, where an operator carries on at the same location the refining of steel in a cupola (s 2.1) and the separation of zinc from mixed scrap by differential melting (s 2.2), they will require authorisation as a single s 2.1 Part B process.

7.2.3 Exceptions

Under reg 4 of the 1991 Regulations, certain processes are exempted from the need to obtain an authorisation before they can lawfully be carried on. A number of these exempted processes have already been referred to in Chapter 6, to which reference should be made (see **6.2.3**). For present purposes, it is enough to observe that a process will not be taken to be a Part B process unless it will, or there is a likelihood that it will, result in the release into the air of any of the prescribed substances in Sch 4 to the Regulations. Even where the process does give rise to such a release, it will still not be a Part B process where the quantity of the substance released is so trivial that it is incapable of causing harm, or its capacity to cause harm is insignificant. Guidance on the meaning of 'triviality' has been provided in the AQ Notes series (see **7.7.4**).

7.3 DEREGULATION

The DoE publication, *This Common Inheritance: The Second Year Report*,[1] stated that: 'It is important that processes with a potentially significant impact on air quality and local amenity are controlled. But the regulatory burden on small and medium enterprise must be kept to the necessary minimum'.[2] The effect of the previous Government's deregulation initiative on LAAPC led to a Deregulation Task Force, which made a number of recommendations in respect of the system. Foremost among these was the contention that certain categories of industrial activity should be completely exempted from LAAPC where it has been shown that they have low pollution potential. This recommendation has subsequently been acted upon, with the result that some processes have been removed from LAAPC by making amendments to the Environment Protection (Prescribed Processes and Substances) Regulations 1991. Thus, for example, by virtue of the Environmental Protection (Prescribed Processes and Substances) (Amendment) Regulations 1994, SI 1994/1271, processes such as small metal decontamination processes, stone cutting, small timber processes and knackers yards were removed from LAAPC.

7.3.1 Prescribed substances

For the purposes of Part I of EPA 1990, 'prescribed substance' means any substance which has been prescribed in regulations made by the Secretary of State. It follows from the act of prescription that the release of a prescribed substance is subject to control under ss 6 and 7 of the Act. 'Substance' is not exhaustively defined by the Act. However, by virtue of s 1(13), the term is stated to include electricity or heat. Prescribed substances for release into the air are to be found in Sch 4 to the 1991 Regulations. These have already been listed in Chapter 6, to which the reader is referred (see **6.2.4**).

7.4 AUTHORISATIONS

In order to carry out a Part B prescribed process an operator must first obtain an authorisation from the relevant local authority. This requirement is laid down in s 6(1) of EPA 1990, which states that:

> 'No person shall carry on a prescribed process after the date prescribed or determined for that description of process by or under regulations under section 2(1) ... except under an authorisation granted by the enforcing authority and in accordance with the conditions to which it is subject.'

Where an operator fails to comply with the terms of s 6(1) he commits an offence contrary to s 23(1)(a) of the Act, for which the penalties are a maximum fine of £20,000 in the event of a summary conviction, or a fine or two years'

1 Cm 2068 (1992).
2 At para 11.10, p 100.

imprisonment or both where he is convicted on indictment. Section 23 of the Act in fact creates a number of separate offences in respect of Part I. It is apparent from *Local Air Pollution Control in England and Wales* that up until the end of March 1995, there were approximately 60 prosecutions under s 23, with the vast majority of these, 52, relating to s 23(1)(a) where a prescribed process had been operated without an authorisation or in contravention of an authorisation condition. Of the 60 prosecutions, 37 were successfully completed at the relevant time, and a further 12 cases were pending. The performance review notes that all the successful prosecutions resulted in the imposition of fines rather than custodial sentence. The level of fines ranged from £200 to £15,000.

Process authorisations are actually obtained by way of an application submitted to the local authority. The procedure to be followed is laid down in Part I of Sch 1 to EPA 1990, and the Environmental Protection (Applications, Appeals and Registers) Regulations 1991, SI 1991/507 made pursuant thereto. The various requirements relating to the information which must accompany an application apply generally, irrespective of whether the application is made to the Environment Agency or a local authority. Accordingly, the reader is referred to that part of Chapter 6 which deals with this (see **6.3.1**). An exception, however, to the general nature of these provisions is provided for in the Regulations in respect of applications made to a local authority for the carrying-on of a prescribed process involving the burning of 'waste oil', which is defined as being any mineral-based lubricating or industrial oil no longer used for the purposes for which it was intended, in an appliance with a net rated thermal input of less than 0.4 megawatts. In such circumstances, the application is subject to broadly different information requirements from those referred to in Chapter 6. These include, inter alia, the name and number of the appliance (if any) and the name of its manufacturer, the net rated thermal input of the appliance, details of the type of fuel to be used in the burning process, and details of the height and location of any chimney through which waste gases produced by the appliance would be carried away (reg 2(3)).

In the first four years of operating LAAPC, local authorities received 14,816 applications for the authorisation of existing processes or new processes, or for substantial changes to be made to existing processes. By far the majority of these (13,671) were made for the purposes of securing an authorisation for an existing process. Part II of Sch 3 to the Environmental Protection (Prescribed Processes and Substances) Regulations 1991 prescribed a series of dates from which an application for a process authorisation could be made for the carrying-on of an existing process. In addition, the Schedule prescribed dates beyond which an application should not be made. The processes falling within the LAAPC regime were divided into three groups, and each group was allotted a six-month time-frame within which an application had to be made. The three relevant periods were: 1 April 1991 to 30 September 1991; 1 October 1991 to 31 March 1992; and 1 April 1992 to 30 September 1992. For the purposes of Part II, an 'existing process' was a process which either: was being carried on at some time in the 12 months immediately preceding the earliest date for which an authorisation application could be made in respect of that description of process; or was to be carried on at a works, plant or factory or by means of mobile plant which was under construction or in the course of manufacture or commission at the relevant earlier date, or the construction or supply of which was the subject of a contract entered into before that date.

The figures for the number of applications received by local authorities indicate that the majority were received between 1 July 1991 and 31 December 1992. During this period, peaks occurred in January/March 1992 and, not surprisingly, July/September 1992. Perhaps more important, however, are the figures contained in the performance review relating to the number of authorisations which were *decided* in the period 1991/95, and the length of time that it took to determine applications for existing processes. These figures indicate, for example, that in the first year of LAAPC to 31 March 1992, local authorities received more than 2,500 applications, and made just over 700 decisions. In each of the two following years, more than 5,000 applications were decided. The industrial sectors with by far the largest numbers of decisions made in respect of existing processes and, for that matter, new processes and substantial changes, were waste oil burners with a net rated thermal input of less than 0.4 megawatts, cement and lime, coating application and other mineral processes. Collectively, therefore, it is the regulation of these Part B processes which forms the bulk of the work for local authorities under Part I of EPA 1990.

In determining applications for authorisation, para 5(1) of Sch 1 to EPA 1990 imposes a four-month time-limit. However, by virtue of para 5(3) the Secretary of State was given the power to substitute for this period such time as he felt appropriate, and to make different provision in respect of different classes of application. This power has since been exercised by the making of the Environmental Protection (Authorisation of Processes) (Determination Periods) Order 1991, SI 1991/513, under which applications for authorisation of existing Part B processes are to be determined within a period of 12 months from the date on which the application was received, or such longer period as the local authority may agree with the applicant. Exceptions exist in respect of certain processes which have transferred from Part A to Part B, under the Environmental Protection (Prescribed Processes and Substances) (Amendment) Regulations 1994, in which case the period for determination is nine months. Where the process involves a small waste oil burner with a net rated thermal input of less than 0.4 megawatts, the relevant period is 18 months. The deadline for determinations in respect of new plant therefore remains at four months, as stated in para 5(1) of Sch 1 to EPA 1990.

The figures in the performance review suggest that, with the exclusion of small waste oil burners, 66 per cent of the applications relating to existing processes received between 1991 and 1995 were decided within a 12-month period. Nevertheless, this still means that one-third of the applications received in this period were decided outside the specified period. In later years, most notably 1993/94 and 1994/95, the proportion of applications not decided within 12 months actually stood at 48 per cent and 68 per cent respectively.

7.4.1 Applications for authorisation: the local authority decision

Where an application for a prescribed process authorisation has been made to a local authority, that authority may deal with the application in one of two ways (EPA 1990, s 6(3)): it may grant the authorisation subject to the conditions required by s 7 of EPA 1990 (see further below); or it may refuse to grant the authorisation. The local authority cannot grant a prescribed process authorisation unconditionally. Thus, in performing the task of controlling air pollution under Part I of EPA 1990, a local authority is subject to greater constraints than if it were, for example, exercising control over the building development in its area in its guise as a local planning authority. Under the Town and Country Planning Act 1990 a planning authority has three courses of action available to it when deciding upon an application for planning permission: it may grant the application unconditionally; it may grant the application subject to such conditions as it thinks fit; or it may refuse the application (s 70(1)).

A further constraint imposed by EPA 1990 on a local authority's decision-making power in relation to authorising applications is the ability of the applicant to carry on the prescribed process in compliance with the conditions imposed on the authorisation. Section 6(4) of the Act states that:

> 'An application shall not be granted unless the enforcing authority considers that the applicant will be able to carry on the process so as to comply with the conditions which would be included in the authorisation.'

7.4.2 The *Compton* decision

The precise meaning of this provision was referred to *obiter* in the judgment of Mr Malcolm Spence QC, sitting as a Deputy Judge in *R v Secretary of State for the Environment and NC Compton T/A RJ Compton and Sons ex parte West Wiltshire District Council.*[1] This appears to have been the first consideration of s 6(4) of EPA 1990 in the High Court, and, as such, merits some discussion.

The case concerned an application for judicial review by the district council of a decision made by the Secretary of State to grant the second respondents an authorisation under EPA 1990. The second respondents had operated a piggery and animal by-product rendering business for many years, but their application for a process authorisation was refused by the district council in its capacity as enforcing authority under EPA 1990. The second respondents accordingly appealed to the Secretary of State under s 15 of the Act, but, following a subsequent hearing, the inspector concluded that the authorisation should not be granted. However, the Secretary of State took a different view of the matter and granted the authorisation subject to numerous conditions. Before Mr Malcolm Spence QC, it was contended on behalf of the district council that the first respondent, the Secretary of State, had misdirected himself in law as to the meaning of s 6(4) and that, as a consequence of this misdirection, he had failed

1 [1996] Env LR 312.

to have regard to relevant considerations such as the extent to which the second respondents had, in the past, been able to comply with the relevant conditions.

In order to set the *Compton* case in its appropriate context, it is worth noting that both the district council and the inspector had refused the application for an authorisation because of the perceived inadequacies in the way the second respondents managed, operated and maintained their business. In the inspector's report, a number of findings of fact were made which had clearly influenced the decision not to grant the authorisation. It was noted, for example, that the business had not been run well over the years and that the site and its processes had been, and continued to be, a source of offence to the local population. The odours given off by the process had deterred tourism and business in the town, and fugitive emissions had occurred due to a lack of maintenance of the buildings. The general level of maintenance at the site was found to be unsatisfactory by the inspector, as was the treatment of liquid effluent, the storage of waste products and the cleaning and housekeeping generally. In the report which accompanied his decision, the inspector concluded that:

> 'I consider that a clear and detailed set of costed upgrading proposals, backed by cogent evidence that the BATNEEC standard is likely to be achieved, is essential for authorisation to be granted. However, such detailed proposals are lacking; there are indications that the plant design will not facilitate observance of the objectives in section 7(2) of the Act; the plant is not complying with the BPM standard; there is an acknowledged history of problems with the management of this plant; no proposals are available to demonstrate a likelihood that these management and design shortcomings will be overcome, and this is a vulnerable and sensitive locality. I therefore conclude that the company is unlikely to be able to carry on the process in plant nos 1 and 2 so as to comply with the requirements of the Act.'

In his decision letter, which effectively overturned the inspector's finding, the Secretary of State considered that s 6(4) gave rise to two connected questions which should both be answered in the affirmative before an authorisation could be granted. The first entailed identifying what conditions would be included if the authorisation were to be granted, and the second addressed the issue whether it would be possible for the applicant to carry on the process in compliance with those conditions. Mr Malcolm Spence QC held that in interpreting the section in this manner the Secretary of State had not actually misconstrued s 6(4), but that he had, nevertheless, failed to apply the section properly. Unlike the district council and the inspector, who had both clearly considered the likelihood of the second respondents being *able* to comply with the conditions laid down in an authorisation, and had concluded that they would not be able to do so, the Secretary of State had failed to do likewise. Instead, he had considered whether it would be *possible* for the applicant to carry on the process in compliance with the conditions. Patently, as Mr Malcolm Spence QC observed, '"will be possible" is not necessarily synonymous with "will be able"' when considering whether an applicant would comply with the conditions imposed in an authorisation. Whether or not it will be *possible* for an applicant to comply with authorisation conditions is a question more likely to be answered in the affirmative than the question whether an applicant is *able* to comply with such conditions. Accordingly, if the wider interpretation accorded to s 6(4) by the Secretary of State were, in fact, the correct interpretation, it would mean that the provision would cease to have any real significance. Virtually every application for authorisation would be granted if the enforcing authority needed only to satisfy itself that it would be *possible* for the applicant to carry on the process in compliance with the conditions attached.

A further point of interest which emerged from the *Compton* case related to the question whether, in coming to a decision as to the applicant's ability to comply with the conditions included in the authorisation, the past history of the operator is a relevant factor that can be taken into account. In the present case, the second respondents' extremely poor management record prior to the time of their application for authorisation clearly cast doubt on their ability to comply with the conditions attached to any authorisation. One aspect of this poor record was what the inspector described as 'a cycle of improvement and deterioration' whereby an improvement was observed at the site following enforcement action only for there to be a subsequent deterioration with the effluxion of time from the date of the enforcement action. In his decision letter, the Secretary of State had observed that a range of enforcement actions were available to the relevant authority under EPA 1990 in the event that authorisation conditions had been breached.

It can be concluded from the Secretary of State's decision letter that the refusal of an authorisation was regarded in official circles as being very much a last resort. Indeed, it has been reported that even post-*Compton* the official line remained that an applicant's past record is 'usually far from being sufficient evidence in itself to justify taking away someone's livelihood'.[1] Further proof of this was seen in a case involving a decision by North Kesteven District Council to refuse to grant A Hughes & Son an authorisation for their rendering and maggot-breeding business. The Secretary of State declared in a decision letter in favour of the grant of an authorisation that:

> 'The test to be applied is whether the appellant is able to comply, rather than whether in practice he would comply. The council's argument is effectively that because the appellant has run the process in an environmentally unacceptable way to date, he is unable to do so. The Secretary of State considers this to be a *non sequitur*'.[2]

However, despite such sentiments, it is arguable whether in the light of their previous record, Compton had not already demonstrated that enforcement action was capable only of achieving a temporary respite from the problems of odour nuisance emanating from their premises. In circumstances such as these, it has to be questioned whether it is appropriate to grant process authorisations, even where such authorisations are subject to conditions that can be enforced by way of prosecutions.

1 (1996) 263 *ENDS Report* 25.
2 (1996) 259 *ENDS Report* 10.

7.4.3 Recent developments

The recent change of government appears to have had a potentially significant impact on the approach which the new Department of the Environment, Transport and the Regions (DETR) proposes to take in respect of the *Compton* case. As a consequence of the ruling of Mr Malcolm Spence QC, the predecessor of the current Secretary of State was required to redetermine the appeal, although initial indications were that Compton's process authorisation would still be granted. However, the new Secretary of State is reported to have taken a different view on the matter in that he has indicated to the company that he is 'minded to dismiss the appeal'.[1] Apparently, he considers that Compton will not be able to comply with the conditions attached to their authorisation in respect of the day-to-day management and maintenance of the process. Provided the Secretary of State remains firm in his resolve on this matter, his intended course of action marks a shift in policy from that adopted by his predecessor. It would seem, therefore, that an operator's past pollution record may now be an appropriate ground on which to refuse to grant a process authorisation. Nevertheless, in view of the fact that the argument and counter-argument in the *Compton* case has been going on for more than five years, it is by no means certain that the company will refrain from seeking redress in the courts if the Secretary of State opts subsequently to endorse his provisional decision.

The emission of offensive odours from an animal by-product rendering process was also at issue in *R v Secretary of State for the Environment and Peninsular Proteins Ltd ex parte Torridge District Council*,[2] where the Secretary of State's decision to allow an appeal against the council's refusal of an authorisation was quashed by the High Court in judicial review proceedings. In the opinion of the council, the only course open to it had been to reject Peninsular Proteins' application to carry on its existing activities because the council did not believe that the renderer could prevent emissions migrating beyond the plant boundary. However, when, subsequently, the Secretary of State directed that an authorisation be granted subject to conditions under s 7 of EPA 1990, he failed to include a condition previously agreed between the council and the renderer to the effect that all emissions to air would be free of odour outside the plant boundary. The council considered that such a condition, which was the same as a specimen condition contained in Guidance Note PG6/1(91), *Animal by-product rendering*, was both necessary and appropriate; but the Secretary of State took an opposing view, namely that such a condition was unenforceable and inappropriate according to his own general rule on the need for exceptional circumstances to justify a condition of this nature.

The Secretary of State's view was rejected by the High Court. Although it would have been inappropriate to include an unenforceable condition in an authorisation, the Secretary of State had failed to have regard to relevant considerations in respect of the condition, such as the height of the emission,

1 (1997) 272 *ENDS Report* 14.
2 [1997] Env LR 557.

the prevailing wind, the lie of the land, the density and distribution of the population affected, and the offensiveness of the smell or the frequency of its occurrence. Since he had confined his considerations to the proximity of the plant to nearby residents when deciding whether or not there were exceptional circumstances justifying the imposition of the condition, the Secretary of State had acted unlawfully. This was further apparent in the failure to give the council an opportunity to make representations in respect of his decision. Had such an opportunity been afforded to the council, McCullough J considered that 'it could ... have argued, with a not unrealistic prospect of success, that proximity was not the only material consideration' (at p 571).

It is apparent, therefore, from the foregoing discussion, that the regulation of the rendering industry in particular has caused some difficulties for both local authorities and the Secretary of State alike, with a consensus not always being reached between these two parties in relation to a particular application, or the conditions to be attached to an authorisation. The Government has expressed the view that difficulties raised by s 6(4) may be overcome by modifying the provision. In the second consultation paper on the UK's implementation of EC Directive 96/61/EC on integrated pollution prevention and control (for further details, see **6.26.1** to **6.26.4** and **7.19** to **7.20**) it proposes to replace s 6(4) with a provision which would enable or even require the regulator to withhold an authorisation where it is satisfied that the applicant *would not* be able to comply with the conditions of the authorisation. In the Government's opinion, this approach would enable regulators to refuse an authorisation to those applicants with poor track records, but would not require regulators to look into the matter where no evidence of such a record has been put before them.

A further difficulty inherent in the present system is that a process operator can become embroiled in extensive and protracted legal proceedings to determine the question of its authorisation, while, at the same time, continuing to operate in breach of conditions attached to that authorisation. Nowhere has this been more apparent than in the case of Smith Brothers (Hyde) Ltd whose lengthy battles with both Tameside Metropolitan Borough Council and the Secretary of State have appeared regularly in the pages of the *ENDS Report*.[1] It has been reported, for example, that the company received the largest fine yet imposed under the LAAPC system when, in December 1996, Dukinfield magistrates fined it £216,000 for committing 11 offences contrary to s 23(1) of EPA 1990.[2] It was also reported at the time that the company had appealed on the dual basis that the magistrates erred in law and that the fines imposed were excessive, but this appeal was dropped in July 1997. Nevertheless, it appears that Smith Brothers is facing the prospect of further legal action by the local authority since the operation of its works is still giving rise to foul odours and, as such, many complaints by local residents.[3]

1 See, for example, (1996) 253 *ENDS Report* 8; (1996) 254 *ENDS Report* 7; (1996) 257 *ENDS Report* 7; (1996) 264 *ENDS Report* 45.

2 (1996) 264 *ENDS Report* 45.

3 (1997) 272 *ENDS Report* 14.

7.5 BATNEEC AND BPEO

Where a prescribed process authorisation is granted by a local authority under Part I of EPA 1990, that authorisation will be subject to such conditions as the local authority considers appropriate, and such other conditions as are specified in directions given by the Secretary of State (s 7(1)). In addition, all authorisations granted by a local authority will have an implied condition whereby the operator will be required to carry on the relevant process using the best available techniques not entailing excessive cost (BATNEEC). The BATNEEC standard is to be adopted in respect of LAAPC so as to prevent the release into the air of any of those substances prescribed in Sch 4 to the Environmental Protection (Prescribed Processes and Substances) Regulations 1991 (see **6.2.4** above) or, where that is not practicable, to reduce the release of any such substances to a minimum and for rendering harmless any such substances which are released (EPA 1990, s 7(4)(a)). Moreover, BATNEEC also requires an operator to render harmless any other substances which might cause harm if released into any environmental medium (s 7(4)(b)).

The meaning of the BATNEEC standard was discussed in Chapter 6, to which the reader is referred (see **6.4** to **6.4.2**). For present purposes, it is worth noting that, when setting conditions, a local authority is required to achieve the objectives specified in s 7(2) of EPA 1990, which include, inter alia, compliance with any directions issued by the Secretary of State for the purposes of ensuring the UK's compliance with EC or international law obligations in respect of environmental protection, and compliance with any limits or requirements and achievement of any quality standards or quality objectives prescribed by the Secretary of State under a relevant Act. In the case of an IPC process, a further objective is that BATNEEC will be used 'for minimising the pollution which may be caused to the environment taken as a whole by the releases having regard to the best practicable environmental option available as respects the substances which may be released' (s 7(7)). However, local authorities do not need to achieve this objective when setting conditions. They are not required to have regard to the best practicable environmental option (BPEO) because they perform a regulatory function only in respect of releases to air.

7.6 FEES AND CHARGES FOR LAAPC AUTHORISATIONS

Where an application for a prescribed process authorisation is made to a local authority, it must be accompanied by a fee which has been prescribed in a scheme made by the Secretary of State with the approval of the Treasury (s 8(2) of EPA 1990). Such a scheme may also prescribe fees in respect of the variation of existing authorisations, or applications for such variations, and annual subsistence charges. If an application is unaccompanied by a fee, it has not been duly made and, accordingly, the local authority is under no obligation to determine it (s 6(2),(3)). The Secretary of State has the power to revise any charging scheme but, in either case, he is required to lay before both Houses of Parliament a copy of the scheme, or a copy of the alterations that have been made to the scheme, or, if he considers it more appropriate, a copy of the revised scheme (s 8(3)). Prior to its repeal by Sch 22, para 50 to the Environment Act 1995, s 8(4) entitled the Secretary of State to make separate schemes for different descriptions of enforcing authorities. However, with the advent of the Environment Agency as enforcing authority for IPC authorisations with the power to make charging schemes in accordance with s 41 of the 1995 Act (see Chapter 6), subject to approval by the Secretary of State, such a provision ceased to be necessary.

In exercising the power to make a scheme under s 8(2), the Secretary of State is accorded some measure of discretion by the legislation so that he may, for example, make different provision in relation to different persons, circumstances or localities (s 8(5)(a)). There is also scope to allow for reduced fees or charges where the same person carries on a number of prescribed processes. Furthermore, a scheme made under s 8(2) may make provision for the times when, and the manner in which, the payments required under the scheme are to be made. Perhaps the most interesting aspect of s 8 is the requirement in s 8(6) that the Secretary of State 'shall, so far as practicable, secure that the fees and charges payable under the scheme are sufficient, taking one financial year with another, to cover the relevant expenditure attributable to authorisations'. Thus, it was envisaged at the time of the enactment of EPA 1990 that the enforcing authorities, namely HMIP in respect of IPC and the local authorities in respect of LAAPC, would have the costs of administering the authorisations process covered by the fees and charges imposed on process operators. The concept of a cost-recovery scheme in respect of IPC was mooted in a consultation paper jointly issued by the DoE and the Welsh Office in April 1989. In a subsequent consultation paper, *Pollution Regulation: Cost Recovery Charges* (1990), the Government set out its proposals for cost-recovery charging schemes under what was then the Environmental Protection Bill. The statement in the 1989 consultation paper that the Government intended to introduce a comparable charging scheme for LAAPC was thus expanded upon, although a majority of the respondents to that paper appear not to have commented specifically on this proposal.

In terms of the basic structure of the local authority charging scheme, the 1990 consultation paper noted that it was the intention to adopt the same charging structure as for IPC. Thus, there would be an application fee in order to cover the costs of determining applications, and an annual charge in respect of compliance monitoring and enforcement costs, including costs relating to the sampling and analysis of emissions. However, the consultation paper outlined a clear distinction between IPC and LAAPC charging schemes, which was to take the form of a subdivision of IPC prescribed processes into components. This subdivision, which was considered more fully in Chapter 6, was considered necessary by the Government in order to take account of the considerable differences which may exist between IPC processes in terms of their size and complexity, and the corresponding effect which this would have on the level of resources the enforcing authority would need to devote to their control. However, it was considered that the less-varied nature of LAAPC processes, and the fact that they would generally be conducted on a smaller scale and involve less-technical complexity, rendered their subdivision into components unnecessary. The only exception to this approach envisaged in the consultation paper related to small appliances with a net rated thermal output of less than 0.4 megawatts which, because of their size, could be distinguished from all other processes under LAAPC and should, therefore, be subject to a lower level of charge.

In accordance with s 8 of EPA 1990, the Secretary of State made a scheme of fees and charges on 8 March 1991. The scheme, which appeared in General Guidance Note 1, originally envisaged that an application fee of £800 for authorisations, and an annual charge of £500 per process, would be enough to cover a local authority's costs of performing its Part I function. The fees and charges under the scheme are regularly reviewed and updated. As from 1 April 1997, the standard application fee for an authorisation was set at £1,040, and the annual subsistence charge was £640. Where an operator has failed to pay a subsistence charge, the local authority may, by notice in writing, revoke the process authorisation (s 8(8)). In addition to fees for applications and annual subsistence charges, s 8 entitles the Secretary of State to prescribe fees for the variation of existing authorisations as a part of the charging scheme. The 1990 consultation paper proposed that where an application was made for a substantial change to an existing authorised process, a prescribed fee of two-thirds of the standard application fee should be charged. This proposal is reflected in the April 1997 charges, which set the fee for an authorisation variation at £665 (just under two-thirds of the standard application fee). In the case of a process involving one or more waste oil burning appliances with a net rated thermal input of less than 0.4 megawatts, the application fee and subsistence charge is £100, with an application for substantial change cost of £65.

The level of income received by local authorities as a consequence of these fees and charges is detailed in *Local Authority Air Pollution Control in England and Wales*, which indicates the following: income received from application fees initially far outweighing income from annual subsistence charges, although, with the passage of time, the position is reversed and it is the annual subsistence charge which provides most income. Thus, in 1991/92 the income received by all authorities in respect of application fees stood at £3,691,920, whereas for annual subsistence charges the figure was £238,302. By 1994/95, however, application fee income was £739,312, whereas annual subsistence charge income for that year was £5,414,839. For the first four years of the LAAPC regime, total income for all charges and fees was £20.9 million. Viewed in isolation, however, these figures are not very informative and tell us nothing about the cost of administering LAAPC, which is really what the fee income ought to be judged against. In the Chartered Institute of Environmental Health's annual report for 1995/96, which deals with the day-to-day work of local authority environmental health departments in areas such as noise pollution, odour pollution and industrial air pollution, 195 of the 267 departments which provided questionnaire responses gave information on the income they had received from LAAPC fees. During 1995/96 the 195 departments received £3.49 million income, but the collective figure for operating LAAPC stood at £3.85 million. Slightly less than half of the departments were able to cover their costs from the charges that were imposed.[1]

In 1993, consultants looked into the possibility of replacing the flat rate subsistence charge with a banded scheme. They concluded that a three-banded charging scheme was a possibility, although they were of the opinion that banding by size alone would be inequitable since it would not necessarily follow that the bigger the plant, the more regulatory work would be required. Options for revising the charging scheme are currently reviewed annually. The Industry Forum, a body created by the DoE in 1993 to discuss the implementation of LAAPC from the industry perspective, has concluded that the scheme should remain unchanged for 1997/98.

7.7 GUIDANCE

Guidance has been issued to local authorities by the Secretary of State for the Environment in order to assist them in the performance of their functions under Part I of EPA 1990 in respect of Part B list processes. Since it has been issued by the Secretary of State in accordance with s 7(11) of EPA 1990, the guidance is statutory and, therefore, differs from the guidance issued in respect of IPC which is, generally speaking, non-statutory in nature (see **6.6**). LAAPC guidance takes four forms: process guidance notes; general guidance notes; upgrading guidance notes; and additional guidance notes.

7.7.1 Process guidance notes

Process guidance (PG) notes, as their name implies, relate to particular Part B list processes for which local authorities are responsible The notes were originally drawn up by a team of three environmental health officers experienced in the control of industrial air pollution who were seconded to the DoE from the Institute of Environmental Health Officers (now the Chartered Institute of Environmental Health). The drafting process itself took place against the backcloth of consultation, with working parties comprised of relevant trade associations, companies, local authorities and any other interested parties. Draft notes were circulated by the DoE and the Welsh Office to the working parties and other interests for final comment before their publication. This process of consultation did not, however, escape teething problems. For example, the British Aggregates Construction Materials Industries has expressed the opinion that the original PG notes relating to the aggregates industry 'contained a number of grey areas which had led to

1 (1997) 272 *ENDS Report* 12.

differing interpretations of objectives and requirements'. In its opinion, the reason for this may have been the 'speed with which they were drafted and discussed'.[1] These problems were resolved subsequently in restructured revisions of the relevant PG notes. With such practical experience of the system of guidance in mind, the five-year report on the LAAPC system has, nevertheless, opined that: 'The notably low level of doubts raised about the balance, realism and practicality of the guidance appears largely a reflection of the experience of the seconded EHOs and the close involvement of process operators'.[2]

Process guidance notes contain guidance in respect of new and existing processes, although the information they contain is technically less complex than that which appears in IPC guidance notes. As with IPC notes, however, a number of the PG notes which have been issued to date share common features. The most notable of these is the specification of requirements relating, inter alia, to emissions free from visible smoke in normal operation and chimney height and efflux velocity. A great number of PG notes have been issued by the DoE since Part I of EPA 1990 came into force. The Blue Pages of the *Environment Business Directory 1997/98*[3] list 87 PG notes which have been issued, revised, amended or cancelled in the relevant period. They are referred to with regard to the description of the process to which they relate, the number of the note and the year in which they were made, which appears in brackets. Thus, the process guidance note for hot and cold blast cupolas is cited as PG2/5 (96) since the process falls within Chapter 2 of the Environmental Protection (Prescribed Processes and Substances) Regulations 1991, as amended, and the revised note was published in 1996.

7.7.2 General guidance notes

Five general guidance (GG) notes have been issued by the DoE to date. They are generally concerned with the broad issues arising from Part I of EPA 1990 for local authorities such as authorisations (GG2(91)), applications and registers (GG3(91)), and appeals (GG5(91)). GG1(91) provides an introduction to the substantive provisions of Part I of the Act and other related issues, while GG4(91) is of practical value to those actually enforcing LAAPC since it is concerned with the interpretation of terms used in process guidance notes. Importantly, GG notes do not, generally speaking, amount to statutory guidance and so they differ from PG notes in this respect. Several of the GG notes expressly declare themselves not to be statutory guidance. For example, GG5(91) on appeals declares in its introduction that: 'It does not constitute guidance to local authorities from the Secretary of State in exercise of his powers under section 7(11) of the Act'. The introduction continues, 'It should also not be taken as an authoritative interpretation of that Act or of any subordinate or related legislation referred to in the Note'. Less clear, however,

1 *Local Air Pollution Control in England and Wales: Five Year Report 1991–1996* (DoE, 1996) para 3.49, p 27.
2 Ibid, para 3.8, p 16.
3 Published in conjunction with Environment Business by Information for Industry Ltd (1997).

is the status of a GG note which does not contain such a declaration. GG4(91) falls into this category but, as the editors of the *Encyclopaedia of Environmental Law*[1] note, since it is concerned with the interpretation of PG notes which are statutory guidance, it may be inferred that it also constitutes statutory guidance.

7.7.3 Upgrading guidance notes

Upgrading guidance (UG) notes are designed to effect revisions and additions to existing PG and GG notes, as well as giving additional general guidance. To date, only one UG note has been issued by the Secretary of State. The relationship between a UG note and a PG note is not clear. It may be that a UG note serves as a means by which revisions may be made to a number of PG notes and that this represents a stopgap until the relevant PG notes are revised individually. Alternatively, where the revisions in question are of no great consequence, it may be that a UG note is a more effective way of making changes than the revision and subsequent republication of the affected PG notes. Whatever the rationale for UG notes, the experience to date demonstrates no great enthusiasm on the part of the Secretary of State to issue them. Greater potential for the UG note may lie in its capacity to act as an alternative source of additional guidance note, which it can reproduce in a collected and therefore more accessible form.

7.7.4 Additional guidance notes

Additional guidance (AQ) notes are, like the other three forms of LAAPC guidance, issued by the DoE. They are non-statutory and tend to be issued in response to difficulties and problems which may have been encountered during the course of administering the LAAPC regime. In this respect, therefore, as guidance on how to overcome such practical difficulties, AQ notes have some similarities with the previous inspectors' technical notes which were issued by HMIP 'to provide a rapid means of issuing advice on techniques and standards to inspectors where a query has been raised by an inspector, where a request for advice is made by an Industry Sector Group, or where there is a need for such advice'.[2] To date, AQ notes have been issued in respect of a wide array of matters, such as the interpretation of 'triviality' for specific industrial sectors, what is meant by the phrase 'existing process', and whether charging income is subject to VAT. In this world of advancing technology, it is worth noting that the DoE provides information on recently published additional guidance, and other matters relating to LAAPC, on the Internet.

1 Sweet & Maxwell, 1993.

2 *HMIP* Annual Report, 1994/95, p 21.

7.8 TRANSFER OF AUTHORISATIONS

Where an authorisation has been granted for the carrying on of a Part B prescribed process, that authorisation may subsequently be transferred from the holder to another person who proposes to carry on the process in the holder's place (EPA 1990, s 9(1)). This process of transfer is not conditional upon an application being made to the relevant local authority. It would seem from the statute's silence on this point that the transfer may be effected either verbally or in writing, although, in practice, it is likely that it will be a written transfer (the advantages of such an approach were discussed at **6.9**). Where a transfer does take place, the party now in possession of the authorisation (the transferee), is required to inform the relevant local authority of this in writing within 21 days of the date of the transfer (s 9(2)). The authorisation and the conditions attached to it will apply to the transferee in the same way that they applied to the former holder, the transferor (s 9(3)).

7.9 VARIATION NOTICES

Section 10 of EPA 1990 empowers local authorities to serve variation notices on the holder of an authorisation in order to ensure that the conditions of that authorisation properly reflect any changes that have been made to the best available techniques in respect of the process since the original authorisation was granted. In other words, the ability to vary an authorisation is a necessary corollary of the local authority's duty to keep authorisations under review in accordance with s 6(6) of EPA 1990. Section 11, by contrast, entitles the authorisee to request a variation by the local authority by submitting an application to this effect.

The nature and scope of these two provisions has been considered in Chapter 6, to which the reader is referred (see **6.10**). In the context of LAAPC, several points not discussed in Chapter 6 are worthy of mention. First, any fee charged in respect of a variation notice or an application for a variation will, of course, be that which has been set by a charging scheme under s 8 of EPA 1990 (see above), rather than under s 41 of the Environment Act 1995. Secondly, in the first four years of the operation of LAAPC, 69 per cent of the total of 2,968 notices (variation, enforcement, prohibition or revocation) served on operators were variation notices. The vast majority of these, 1,733, were s 10 variation notices, whereas, during the same period, 318 s 11 notices were served.

7.10 REVOCATION NOTICES

Under EPA 1990, s 12, local authorities have a general power to revoke a process authorisation by serving a notice in writing to that effect on the holder of the authorisation. Whether or not an authority will exercise the s 12 power will depend upon a number of factors and considerations of which it will be the judge, subject to the holder's right of appeal under s 15(1)(d) of the Act and the

Secretary of State's residual power to direct the authority to revoke an authorisation (s 12(5)). One circumstance in which a local authority may decide to revoke an authorisation is where it has reason to believe that the relevant process has not been carried on for a period of 12 months (s 12(2)). Where an authorisation holder appeals against a revocation, it is important to note that this has the effect of suspending the effect of a s 12 notice for the duration of the appeal. Therefore, unlike variation, enforcement or prohibition notices, which must be complied with even where they are the subject of an appeal, a process authorisation in respect of which a revocation notice has been served remains extant in similar circumstances, and the process may be carried on without the commission of an offence. It would, however, be an offence to carry on the process if the authorisation had been revoked and an appeal had been unsuccessful (s 6(1) and s 23(1)(a)).

The figures in *Local Air Pollution Control in England and Wales* indicate that between 1991 and 1995, 510 revocation notices were issued, although the figures do not distinguish between notices issued under s 8(8) of EPA 1990 for non-payment of subsistence charges, and those issued under s 12. The review draws attention to the fact that information received in respect of other matters serves to suggest that the figure of 510 may, in fact, be a conservative estimate of the number of revocation notices actually issued. Moreover, on the basis of what the review terms 'anecdotal evidence', it would seem that many of the revocation notices were served as a consequence of the circumstances envisaged in s 12(2), ie due to process closures.

7.11 ENFORCEMENT NOTICES

Section 13 of EPA 1990 provides for the service of an enforcement notice upon a process operator which the local authority believes has contravened a condition of the authorisation or is likely to contravene such a condition. The necessary ingredients of an enforcement notice were detailed in the corresponding section in Chapter 6 (see **6.12**). For present purposes, it is worth noting that the number of enforcement notices served by local authorities increased dramatically in the first five years of the operation of the LAAPC regime. Thus, in 1991–92 only one notice was served, although this must be due in part to the infancy of the regime. However, in 1992–93, 35 notices were served, and for the periods 1993–94 and 1994–95, 125 and 240 notices were served respectively. Collectively, these figures reveal that for the period 1991–95, 401 enforcement notices were served by local authorities in England and Wales.

Where an enforcement notice has been served, it is an offence either to fail to comply with it or to contravene any requirement of the notice (s 23(1)(c)). In *Local Air Pollution Control in England and Wales: Five Year Report 1991–1996* (from which the enforcement notice statistics referred to above were obtained), the DoE states that up to the end of March 1995, 60 prosecutions were instigated in respect of the 12 separate offences under s 23. While the vast majority of these prosecutions were for offences under s 23(1)(a), four prosecutions related to the contravention of an enforcement or prohibition notice. The report does not specify whether or not these prosecutions were successful, but it could be argued that, on the basis of these statistics alone, the enforcement notice system is working well at local level – four prosecutions is a very small number when compared with the number of enforcement notices served by local authorities during the relevant period, even allowing for the fact that subsequent prosecutions may have occurred in respect of s 13 notices issued towards the end of that period.

7.12 PROHIBITION NOTICES

An additional weapon in local authorities' arsenal for enforcing LAAPC is the prohibition notice. By virtue of s 14 of EPA 1990, a prohibition notice must be served on the operator of an authorised process where the continued carrying-on of that process or the continued carrying-on of that process in a particular manner 'involves an imminent risk of serious pollution of the environment'. The meaning of this expression, together with other features of the prohibition notice, such as the statutory requirements as to its content, have already been considered in Chapter 6 (see **6.13**). One facet of the prohibition notice which deserves further consideration, however, is its service. While there are a number of common features shared by enforcement and prohibition notices, the essential difference is that in the case of the former, the local authority has a discretion over whether or not to serve, whereas, in the case of the latter, there is no such discretion. Where the trigger of an 'imminent risk of serious pollution of the environment' is present, the local authority *must* issue a prohibition notice.

In the discussion on prohibition notices in Chapter 6, attention was drawn to the fact that, during the passage of the Environmental Protection Bill, ministerial statements were made to the effect that prohibition notices were likely to be issued only in exceptional circumstances; in other words, it was anticipated that they would be issued with far less frequency then enforcement notices. The first five years of operating LAAPC have demonstrated that, in practice, this has proved to be the case. In 1992–93, only one notice was issued and, although the figure for 1994–95 was four, it is still negligible when compared with the 240 enforcement notices issued in the same period.

7.13 APPEALS

Appeals against a decision of the local authority in respect of a process authorisation are made in accordance with s 15 of EPA 1990 and the Environmental Protection (Applications, Appeals and Registers) Regulations 1991, SI 1991/507, as amended by the Environmental Protection (Applications, Appeals and Registers) (Amendment) Regulations 1996, SI 1996/667. The detail of these provisions was considered in Chapter 6 and, accordingly, the reader is referred to the relevant section since the provisions apply in the same manner to LAAPC authorisations as they do to IPC authorisations (see **6.15**). The following discussion is therefore primarily concerned with the guidance issued by the Secretary of State to local authorities on the subject of the appeal system.

General Guidance note 5 of 1991 (GG5(91)) is one of a series of guidance notes issued by the Secretary of State in order to help local authorities with the discharge of their functions under Part I of EPA 1990. It should be borne in mind that the guidance does not have the status of statutory guidance since it was not made in the exercise of powers under s 7(11) of EPA 1990; nor does it amount to an authoritative interpretation of the Act. Nevertheless, paras 20 to 27 of the guidance are stated to constitute a code of practice which is 'important for the smooth and efficient running of the appeals system'. In order for the hearing procedure to operate effectively, the guidance stresses the need for the appeals inspector to be made fully aware of the various issues and arguments likely to arise at the appeal so that he may lead the discussion. Accordingly, he will receive, via the DoE or Welsh Office, a written statement from each of the parties in which is stated the cases they will make at the hearing. The time-scale for the submission of the statement is within six weeks from the date of the appeal being lodged, or at least 21 days before the hearing, whichever is first.

The procedure to be followed at a hearing is very much left to the discretion of the appeals inspector, although emphasis is placed on the desirability of an informal approach. Despite the absence of formal procedural rules applying to the hearing, the guidance stresses that the rules of natural justice will apply. Therefore, the appeals inspector is required to ensure that all those interested parties who wish to give evidence at the hearing have a fair opportunity to do so, but he retains the right to 'refuse to hear evidence which is irrelevant or repetitious and is therefore wasting time' (para 22). If the parties so wish, they may be professionally represented, although the guidance observes that representation 'will not normally be necessary in order to gain an effective hearing'. It would seem, however, that professional representation is more likely where the hearing is concerned with complex issues. In order to avoid the adjournment of a hearing, the parties are encouraged to refrain from introducing new material at the hearing. However, an appeals inspector has the power to adjourn a hearing to such time, place and on such terms as he thinks fit.

The procedures described in the guidance will generally be suitable for the majority of appeals heard under s 15 of EPA 1990. If an appeal is concerned with matters of complexity or controversy, the guidance recognises that a more formal procedure may be more appropriate. In such circumstances, it is envisaged that the hearing would be akin to a public inquiry, in which case the relevant parts of the Town and Country Planning (Inquiries Procedure) Rules 1988, SI 1988/944 may be applied.

Where an appeal is dealt with in accordance with the written representations procedure, the guidance notes that it will require substantially less organisation than a hearing and that, as such, a determination is likely to be reached more quickly. In particular, it is stated that this procedure will normally be the most appropriate means of dealing with appeals relating to the issue of commercial confidentiality. The procedure itself is the same as that in respect of IPC appeals (see **6.15.2**), although, of course, in terms of the parties involved, the DoE is dealing with the appellant and the local authority, rather than the appellant and the Environment Agency. In complex cases, it may be necessary for further exchanges of information to take place in addition to those required by the Environmental Protection (Applications, Appeals and Registers) Regulations 1991. Moreover, if a site visit is to take place, the parties will receive prior notification of this fact. If at any stage during the written procedure it becomes apparent that insufficient progress is being made with the appeal, either party or the Secretary of State may suggest that the matter be determined by a hearing. Where new evidence comes to light after the conclusion of a hearing or following a consideration of the exchange of written representations, but before the final determination of the appeal, it will be referred to the parties for their comments if it is material to the decision. In some cases, it may be necessary to reopen a hearing in order to ensure the proper investigation of the new evidence.

The DoE publication *Local Air Pollution Control in England and Wales* indicates that by the end of September 1996, 63 out of a total of 70 appeals (the remaining seven appeals having been made under s 22 of EPA 1990) had been made under s 15. Of the combined figure of 70, 21 appeals were outstanding, 22 had been determined, 25 had been withdrawn, and two were made out of time. Of the 22 appeals that had been determined, 14 were allowed, six were split decisions and two were dismissed. Clearly, therefore, the continued need for an appeal system is evidenced by the high percentage of appeals which actually succeed where a determination is made.

7.14 GENERAL POWERS OF ENTRY

In order to assist local authorities in the manifold tasks associated with the control of air pollution under Part I of EPA 1990, ss 108 and 109 of the Environment Act 1995 create various powers which may be exercised by 'suitable' persons authorised in writing by the local authority. These powers have been described in detail in Chapter 6 (see **6.16**), and, in essence, amount to powers of entry, examination, investigation, seizure and questioning in relation to the relevant premises, and any article or substances on those premises or persons on those premises. In the case of s 109, a specific power to seize an article or substance found on the premises is activated where the officer has reasonable cause to believe that it is a cause of imminent danger of serious pollution of the environment or serious harm to human health. Where such a power is exercised, certain reporting requirements laid down in s 109 must be complied with, which include, inter alia, producing a written report explaining the circumstances of the case which merited the use of the s 109 power. It is an offence contrary to s 110 of the 1995 Act intentionally to obstruct an authorised person who is exercising powers conferred under either s 108 or

109, and further offences are created by s 110, such as refusing to permit any inspection reasonably required by virtue of s 108.

7.15 OBTAINING INFORMATION

Under s 19 of EPA 1990, the Secretary of State has the power to obtain such information as he may require from local authorities in respect of the discharge of their functions under Part I of the Act. Moreover, this provision also entitles local authorities to obtain, from any person, information which it reasonably considers it needs for the discharge of its LAAPC functions (s 19(2)). It is an offence to fail, without reasonable excuse, to comply with a requirement of s 19(2), for which a person may be liable, on summary conviction, to a fine not exceeding the statutory maximum or, on conviction on indictment, to a fine or a maximum of two years' imprisonment, or both (s 23(1)(g)). During the first four years of LAAPC, three out of a total of 60 prosecutions for offences contrary to s 23 of the Act related to a failure to comply with a notice under s 19.

7.16 PUBLIC REGISTERS OF INFORMATION

The duty under s 20 of EPA 1990 to maintain a public register of information in respect of prescribed processes under its control applies to a local authority in the same way as to the Environment Agency (for a description of the type of information which is to be entered on the register, see **6.19**). As with IPC registers, information judged to be commercially confidential or deemed to have national security implications may be excluded from the register in accordance with ss 21 and 22 of EPA 1990.

One important and distinct point to note about a local authority's duty under s 20 is that, in addition to the maintenance of a register in respect of its own functions under Part I of the Act, it is also required by virtue of s 20(2) to include in that register information relating to the carrying-on in its area of Part A prescribed processes under the control of the Environment Agency.

In *Local Air Pollution Control in England and Wales*, one of the three objectives of the system was stated to be 'to allow the public greater access to information about their local environment'. This objective was to be achieved by the public consultation and public register provisions of Part I of EPA 1990, which would 'enable members of the public not only to comment on applications to operate a process, but also to see the conditions under which it is required to operate, and observe compliance with the conditions through the availability of monitoring data'. In other words, the effect of the statutory provisions would be to 'strengthen the accountability of firms to those who live and work around them'.

In practice, the performance review found that local authorities complied with their obligation to provide access to the registers, and that for those who were unfamiliar with the registers, environmental health officers were willing to provide assistance. The opportunities for the general public were advertised by the DoE in a leaflet entitled 'The Environmental Protection Act 1990, Part I AND YOU'. Apparently, approximately 100,000 copies of this leaflet were printed and despatched to local authorities and Citizens Advisory Bureaux. Nevertheless, even with such an initiative, the performance review notes that 'current evidence is that take-up is at present modest'. Speaking at a symposium organised by the North East Region Committee of the Industrial Division of the Royal Society of Chemistry, held in Harrogate on 28 and 29 September 1993, one contributor observed that:[1]

> 'Fortunately the public registers have been something of a non-event so far. The author's own experience recently in an audit of the local public register showed a surge of complete indifference. A total of only 11 other members of the public had taken the trouble to inspect the register. They were an investigative journalist, a few students and the inevitable environmental consultants.'

If the general public are *choosing* not to consult the public registers then their 'complete indifference' is their own affair. If, however, the current, modest take-up is because of a lack of public awareness, it may be that further methods of increasing awareness of the existence of registers need to be found.

7.17 JUDICIAL ENFORCEMENT

Sections 24 and 26 of EPA 1990 provide for alternative remedies in respect of certain offences committed under s 23 of the Act. Where a local authority is of the opinion that proceedings for the offence of contravening an enforcement or prohibition notice would provide an 'ineffectual remedy', it can, by virtue of s 24, seek an injunction from the High Court to ensure compliance with the relevant notice. Where, however, s 23 proceedings are considered to be an effectual remedy, and a person is convicted of the aforementioned offence, or of having carried on a process without an authorisation or in contravention of a condition, the court may, if it believes that the convicted person has it within his powers to remedy matters, order that he shall do so either instead of, or in addition to, the imposition of any punishment. A failure to comply with a s 26 order is an offence (s 23(1)(l)). Up to the end of March 1995, only one prosecution had been brought for this offence, out of a total of 60. Of more interest, however, is the fact that of the 37 successful prosecutions under s 23 during the relevant period, three resulted in magistrates making an order for remedial action under s 26 rather than imposing a fine.

1 Drake (ed), *Integrated Pollution Control* (Cambridge: Royal Society of Chemistry, no 152, 1994), p 55.

7.18 LAAPC IN PRACTICE

So far, this chapter has focused on the powers and duties placed upon local authorities under Part I of EPA 1990. Where appropriate, statistics have been included in the text to demonstrate the frequency with which certain powers have been exercised and whether successful outcomes have been achieved in terms of controlling atmospheric pollution from Part B processes. However, the figures do not convey the whole story, providing only a partial answer to the question 'How have local authorities responded to the challenge of administering LAAPC?' The answer the figures provide tends to be negative in that it focuses on instances where operators have failed to do what they are required to do by the statute. In order to obtain a fuller answer, and to see the LAAPC system in the round, it is necessary to consider the positive aspects of the LAAPC system. In other words, it is necessary to ask the question 'What initiatives have local authorities and others adopted in order to ensure the more effective regulation of Part B processes?'

Part 3 of *Local Air Pollution Control in England and Wales* contains a section entitled 'Views from the front-line' which, as its name implies, is concerned with the views of both the regulators and the regulated alike on how the LAAPC system has operated in practice. One of the contributors to this section, Yorkshire and Humberside Pollution Advisory Council (YHPAC), is an advisory body made up of 35 local authorities in the Yorkshire, Humberside and Lincolnshire region. During the first five to six years of LAAPC, the YHPAC has apparently been the focal point for meetings between local authorities, industry and central government in respect of various matters and issues relating to LAAPC. Workshops and seminars have been held, and the council has established a database of all Part B processes in the region as a means of ensuring that local authorities are aware of what is happening elsewhere. The implication seems to be that local authority groupings such as the YHAPC have had to be created, if they did not exist already, to provide a means of disseminating guidance and training among themselves in order to respond to the demands of LAAPC. The claim that there is great inconsistency between local authorities in respect of matters such as the interpretation of guidance notes is not infrequently made by the regulated. Therefore, any initiative such as the establishment of advisory councils, which helps to ensure a more consistent approach by local authorities to the task of regulation, ought to be welcomed.

Further initiatives designed to achieve the same objective have included the publication by the Chartered Institute of Environmental Health of a number of issues of its *Environmental Protection Bulletin*, which contain information relating to LAAPC procedural matters and, equally as importantly, the names of environmental health officers with expertise in respect of particular industrial sectors. The spread of information has been increased by harnessing up-to-date technology so that, for example, the Institute has its own website, an electronic e-mail facility, and a database inquiry system. The DoE publication *Local Air Pollution Control in England and Wales* notes that half of the UK's local authorities are connected to this ECnet system. For its part, the Association of District Councils has contributed to the spirit of co-operation and co-ordination between local authorities in this field by bringing together authorities with a common interest in certain categories of process by way of 'link authorities'. Under this scheme, which was officially launched on 1 January 1996, one of the local authorities involved takes on a lead role for the purposes of promoting networking between the other authorities.

Collectively, such initiatives demonstrate that a positive approach has been taken to the task of regulating Part B processes. However, it would appear that not everybody is happy with the way in which local authorities have responded to the challenge. In addition to the obvious cases concerning disgruntled operators who believe that they have been treated unfairly, criticism has been levelled at local authorities by another, often overlooked, party, the suppliers of abatement equipment. In a survey of some of its members which specialise in the supply of air pollution control, the Environmental Industries Commission (EIC) has come to the conclusion that the ineffective regulation of Part B processes by local authorities is having an adverse effect upon its members' interests. For example, of the 30 EIC members which participated in the survey, three-quarters claimed that the introduction of the LAAPC regime has had no effect upon the demand for their equipment. Moreover, 31 per cent of the respondents took the view that 'relaxed enforcement practices' by local authorities were the principal reason for poor sales of their equipment, whereas 23 per cent felt that this was due to the inconsistent way in which processes were regulated. As is noted in (1997) 274 *ENDS Report* 9, however, the Chartered Institute of Environmental Health has responded to these claims with a degree of scepticism. It points out, for example, that the EIC survey is based on a small sample of members and, more importantly, that investment in new technology should not be used as the sole criteria to determine the effectiveness of LAAPC.

7.19 LAAPC/PLANNING INTERFACE

The difficulties which may arise in respect of the duality of controls under the IPC and planning regimes (see **6.24**) should not arise in respect of the LAAPC/planning interface. This is because, while there are still two sets of powers available in the present context, the local authority is able to exercise both as the air pollution control authority and the planning authority for its own particular area. Nevertheless, in some cases it may be too much to assume that departments within local authorities are in regular contact with one another, or that, if they are, it is for the purposes of adopting a co-ordinated approach in respect of their particular functions.

7.20 THE FUTURE FOR LAAPC

The system of LAAPC is, according to *Local Air Pollution Control in England and Wales*, now 'firmly established and operating effectively'. Nevertheless, the future for LAAPC is one in which a number of challenges will have to be met. For example, in order to ensure that the system remains effective and achieves the objectives which it has set for itself, it will be necessary to keep it under regular review both in terms of actual performance and the guidance under which it operates. In part, this can be achieved by the statutory obligation on local authorities to review authorisations every four years, which helps to ensure that the regulated processes reflect the current thinking on what constitutes BATNEEC for that particular process.

7.20.1 NAQS and LAAPC

A further challenge facing local authorities is the need to carry out periodic reviews of air quality in their areas following the setting-up of a National Air Quality Strategy under Part IV of the Environment Act 1995.[1] In the event that the strategy's prescribed standards or objectives are unlikely to be met, it is incumbent on a local authority to designate an air quality management area (AQMA) under s 83 of the 1995 Act. Further obligations then arise in respect of the AQMA which include, inter alia, causing an assessment to be made of the air quality in the area for the time being, and the likely future quality of the air. This, in turn, will lead to the drawing-up of an action plan consisting of a number of measures designed to bring about the achievement of air quality standards and objectives in the designated area. The benefits derived from this process are clearly significant for LAAPC. A better understanding of local air quality will help to ensure the more effective regulation of Part B list processes under Part I of EPA 1990. Indeed, since local authorities are required to impose conditions on authorisations which meet the objectives stated in s 7(2) of the Act, which include, inter alia, any quality standards or objectives prescribed by the Secretary of State, it follows that such conditions may be stricter than might otherwise have been the case if they were set on the basis of information gained from the local air quality review.

7.20.2 IPC and LAAPC

In Chapter 6, discussion of the future for IPC centred upon the Integrated Pollution Prevention and Control Directive 96/61/EC which will, in effect, ultimately take the place of the current IPC system. Such a measure clearly has implications for the LAAPC system, especially since it has been estimated by the DoE that approximately 1,600 of the 12,000 processes currently regulated under Part I of EPA 1990 will fall within the scope of the Directive. One issue which is of particular interest, bearing in mind the existence of central and local control under the Act, is who will regulate those installations which require permits under IPPC. The Directive itself envisages that the need for an integrated approach to the prevention and control of pollution will also extend to the issuing of permits and the setting of permit conditions. Thus, Art 7 requires that where more than one 'competent authority' is involved in these tasks, the Member State must ensure that they are carried out in a 'fully co-

1 See Chapter 10.

ordinated' manner so as 'to guarantee an effective integrated approach by all the authorities'. In its first consultation paper on the implementation of the Directive published in July 1997,[1] the Government took the view that this meant 'more than simple administrative co-ordination of permits issued by different regulators'. Accordingly, it felt that the option of 'co-ordinated pollution control' needed to be considered further.

7.20.3 CPC and LAAPC

For some processes not currently subject to IPC but, nevertheless, within the scope of the Directive, the co-ordinated pollution control (CPC) approach may be a viable alternative to the present arrangements. This may be the case especially with regard to installations currently regulated by way of a combination of LAAPC, trade effluent consents and/or water discharge consents. The consultation paper notes that if CPC were adopted, there may also be grounds for applying it to some of the less-complex industrial processes currently regulated under IPC. In terms of the practicalities of CPC, it is believed that a fully co-ordinated approach would have to be taken in respect of matters such as the sharing of information, consultation and the resolution of any disagreements arising between the regulators. Nevertheless, one regulator would be designated the 'lead regulator' for the purposes of co-ordinating the procedures and, as such, it may serve as the single point of entry into the system. Therefore, an operator would submit a single application for a permit, with copies being sent to the other designated regulators. Any permit or permits issued subsequently, and any conditions to which it or they were subject, would be the product of the collective input of the regulators. This may be achieved by the lead regulator issuing a single permit covering all integrated pollution prevention and control (IPPC) matters or, alternatively, the issue of separate permits, with the lead regulator acting as the procedural co-ordinator, and resolver of conflicts. Whether the lead regulator could also co-ordinate inspection would be a matter on which a decision would have to be reached.

7.20.4 The consultation paper

The consultation paper takes the view that the lead regulator should be either the local authorities or the Environment Agency, and views were sought on this as well as other matters, such as the various features of the CPC approach. Indeed, the detail of CPC will need to be determined only if it is accepted, as a matter of principle, that it should replace IPC as a mechanism for implementing the Directive in respect of certain installations. Accordingly, opinion was sought by the consultation paper on this fundamental question.

In its response to the consultation paper, the Environment Agency has indicated, inter alia, that it is opposed in principle to CPC. Its reasons for this are that it considers that CPC would be less effective than a sole regulator in

1 UK Implementation of EC Directive 96/61 on Integrated Pollution Prevention and Control (1997) First Consultation Paper.

achieving the aim of holistic control. CPC would, in its opinion, result in a 'fragmentation of control, loss of the integrated, "one-stop shop" approach, and burdensome resource requirements and charging arrangements'. Nevertheless, if CPC is introduced, the Agency takes the view that it has the necessary qualifications to act as 'lead regulator', although for some installations it recognises that there are arguments for other bodies to exercise control. It may be that a contracting agreement between the Agency and local authorities is the appropriate approach to the question of control in respect of some installations and, accordingly, the Agency has welcomed the possibility of discussing this idea further with the Government and local authorities.

In a second consultation paper on the implementation of the IPPC Directive published by the DETR in January 1998,[1] the Government notes that there were 'sharply polarised' views on the principle of CPC from those who responded to the first consultation paper. Local authorities and some of the industrial respondents were in favour of the principle, whereas most environment groups, the Environment Agency (see above) and the other industrial respondents were opposed. Concerns were expressed over the workability of CPC, which was seen by a significant number of the respondents to be 'bureaucratic and overly complicated'. The Government shares these concerns, and has suggested, therefore, that other options in addition to CPC ought to be considered. The four options which it suggests for the involvement of local authorities in IPPC are as follows:

(1) designation of the Environment Agency as the sole regulator for all IPPC installations in England and Wales, with local authorities acting as statutory consultees;
(2) as a variant on the first option, the Environment Agency might delegate some functions to local authorities, such as permitting certain installations, in addition to some inspection and enforcement functions;
(3) a division of regulatory responsibility, with the Environment Agency responsible for some installations and local authorities responsible for others; or
(4) CPC.

Views are sought on all four options, although several interesting points emerge from the consultation paper. The first is that option one is considered to have 'certain attractions' in that a sole regulator: would ensure greater consistency in the administering of the IPPC system; ensure a more straightforward system for collating data required by the Directive; and lead to economies of scale. With regard to the second option, which would involve local authorities acting as subcontractors for the Agency in respect of less-polluting installations, the consultation paper refers to the Government's concern that this option would render uncertain the extent of local authorities' responsibilities and make them dependent upon contractual arrangements with the Agency. The third option, which entails a division of regulatory

1 UK Implementation of EC Directive 96/61 on Integrated Pollution Prevention and Control (1998) Second Consultation Paper.

responsibility between the Agency and local authorities, is, in effect, the present system under Part I of EPA 1990. If this were the preferred option it would be necessary, following further consultation, to draw up criteria for determining which installations were to come under Agency or local authority control. At this initial stage, the Government's tentative suggestions on the appropriate criteria reflect the status quo. In other words, it considers that the Agency ought to regulate the large, complex installations from which multi-media discharges take place, all waste management installations, and installations with discharges to controlled waters or discharges of special category effluent or other prescribed substances to sewers. Turning to the fourth option, CPC, the consultation paper comments that while this option did attain a level of support in the first consultation exercise, those who favoured it tended not to offer any firm views as to how it would operate in practice. Accordingly, the Government seeks views on this matter.

Finally in this discussion of IPPC, it ought to be noted that the Government has taken the view that none of the above options involving local authorities as regulators could take immediate effect from the time of the transposition of the Directive. This is because the guidance which is deemed necessary to support local authorities in their role could not be produced in time. It is therefore proposed by the Government that transitional arrangements should apply without prejudice to any eventual decision in respect of the above options. Under these arrangements the Environment Agency would be the sole regulator in England and Wales for the issue of all new IPPC permits (ie from late 1999 onwards), with existing IPPC installations which are currently regulated by local authorities remaining under their control (unless such installations undergo substantial change) at least until the deadline for compliance with the new system had expired (30 October 2007).

CHAPTER 8

CLEAN AIR LEGISLATION

8.1 HISTORY[1]

Attempts to control emission of smoke by some form of general public regulation have a long history, dating back to 1307. In the reign of Queen Elizabeth I, at least one proclamation was made to forbid the burning of 'sea-coal' in London during parliamentary sessions. The Sanitary Act 1866 and the Public Health Act 1875 contained provisions dealing with statutory smoke nuisances, while *St Helens Smelting Co v Tipping*[2] and *Salvin v North Brancepeth Coal Co*[3] among other cases, established that a claim could lie in nuisance for the emission of noxious fumes. However, these attempts by the legislature and judiciary did nothing to curb the growing problem of low-level atmospheric pollution caused by the burning of coal. Coal was coked in municipal and commercial plants to produce gas for heating and lighting, and coke for domestic and industrial use. Coal was burned in locally based electric power stations to produce electricity, by the railways and in domestic homes. As is so often the case with environmental degradation, it was people's lifestyles that caused the problem: the common law, for instance, could hardly make it an actionable nuisance for everyone to burn coal domestically; such an activity was part of the 'give and take' of everyday life.

8.1.1 The great smog and its aftermath

A further legislative attempt to control domestic smoke emissions by the Public Health (Smoke Abatement) Act 1926 continued the saga of ineffective legislative intervention. In December 1952, a unique set of climatic conditions in the Thames Valley gave rise to a heavy, dense, persistent, cold fog. Industry, commerce and homes increased their consumption of coal in the cold weather and the resulting emissions combined with the fog to produce 'smog' – an acrid, pea-soup coloured, ground-level cloud. This smog was claimed to have resulted in 4,000 deaths over a period of two weeks – a major environmental disaster. In response to this the Government set up the Beaver Committee in 1953 to examine air pollution problems and the efficacy of the law, to consider further preventive measures and to make recommendations. The final report of that Committee[4] led to the Clean Air Act 1956, which was completely in force

1 In this chapter, unless otherwise stated, statutory references are to the Clean Air Act 1993, which consolidated the Clean Air Acts 1956 and 1968 together with some provisions of the Control of Pollution Act 1974.

2 (1865) 11 HLC 642.

3 (1874) LR 9 Ch 705.

4 Cmnd 9322 (November 1954).

by June 1958. Further amending legislation was passed in 1968, and the legislation was consolidated in 1993.

8.2 PROHIBITION OF DARK SMOKE EMISSIONS

'Dark smoke', under s 3(1), is smoke which, if compared with a 'Ringelmann Chart', would appear to be as dark as, or darker than, shade 2 on the chart. A Ringelmann Chart has five squares, each of 101 mm^2. One square is 'white', while the others are progressively 'darker' by virtue of the drawing of thicker, cross-hatched lines. From a distance, the lines merge with the background to produce the effect that each square appears 20 per cent 'darker' than its predecessor. In practice (and it should be noted that there is no obligation to use a Ringelmann Chart – see s 3(2)) other charts and observational methods may be used, such as that provided under BS 2742. Dark smoke may not, under s 1(1), be emitted from the chimney of any building, and, where it is, the occupier is guilty of an offence. Similarly, under s 1(2) dark smoke may not be emitted on any day (ie a period of 24 hours commencing at midnight – see s 64(1)) from a chimney serving the furnace of any fixed boiler or industrial plant, and, where it is, the person possessing the boiler or plant is guilty of an offence. Thus, an emission commencing at 10.55 pm on one day and continuing until 1.05 am on the next day constitutes two offences. A person guilty of an offence is liable under s 1(5) on summary conviction to a fine on the standard scale not exceeding level 3 in the case of smoke emitted from the chimney of a domestic building, and in any other case to a fine not exceeding level 5. Whether apparatus is in a 'fixed boiler or industrial plant' will initially depend upon whether it is attached to a building, or is being fixed or installed on land. This will be a question of fact in each case, and some degree of fixation – although not permanent fixation – is necessary. It is a defence in proceedings to prove under s 1(4) that:

- the alleged emission was due solely to lighting up a furnace which was cold and that all practicable steps had been taken to prevent or minimise the emission of dark smoke; or
- the alleged emission was due solely to some failure of a furnace or its associated equipment, and that the failure could not have been reasonably foreseen, *or*, if it could have been foreseen, could not have been reasonably provided against, *and* the emission could not reasonably have been prevented by action taken after the failure occurred; or
- the alleged emission was due solely to the use of unsuitable fuel, and that suitable fuel was not available while the least non-suitable available fuel was used, *and* all practicable steps had been taken to prevent or minimise the emission of dark smoke as a result of the use of that fuel;
- the alleged emission arose from a combination of any of the foregoing circumstances, subject to the preconditions for their applicability being satisfied.

Defences relied on need not be notified to the prosecuting authority. In order to succeed, the defence need only be proved on the basis of the balance of probabilities.[1] The requirements of s 51 (see **8.2.2**) must also be noted.

8.2.1 Definitions

Section 64(1) defines 'chimney' to include structures and openings of any kind from or through which smoke, grit, dust or fumes may be emitted. The definition includes flues, and further extends to chimneys serving the whole or part of a building, but which are structurally separate. 'Industrial plant' (which must be attached to a building or fixed on land) includes stills, melting pots or other plant used for any trade or industrial purpose, and incinerators; fixed boilers include those attached to buildings or fixed to land. Relevant 'owners' are those who receive the rack rent of premises (ie the maximum rent legally obtainable) whether on their own account or as agent for others, or who would receive such a rent if the premises were let. Where a building is occupied by more than one person or company, the person who has control over the relevant portion of the building is responsible under the legislation. 'Control' in this context will be a matter of fact and degree in each case, but a licensee of part of a building could have sufficient degree of 'control'.[2] 'Practicable' means reasonably practicable having regard to, inter alia, local conditions and circumstances, financial implications, and the current state of technical knowledge, while 'practicable means' includes the provision, maintenance and proper use of plant. 'Smoke' is defined to include soot, ash, grit, and gritty particles. 'Building' would appear to include any structure of appreciable size, intended for use and with a degree of permanency. By analogy with the law of town and country planning, 'building' would also appear to include anything which forms part of the land and which changes its character,[3] although such a structure may require a roof to be classified as a 'building'.[4]

The Secretary of State has power under s 1(3) to exempt certain emissions from the general s 1(1) prohibition. The Dark Smoke (Permitted Periods) Regulations 1958, SI 1958/498, provide that emissions of dark smoke for no longer than any aggregate period of 10 minutes in any eight-hour period are not to be taken into account, and, similarly, while soot blowing is carried out, for not longer than 14 minutes in each eight-hour period. Proportionate increases in emission times are allowed where a chimney serves more than one furnace: where a chimney serves two furnaces the periods are 18 and 25 minutes; where three furnaces are served the periods are 24 and 34 minutes; and where four furnaces are served, the periods are 29 and 41 minutes. Where, in one boiler or item of plant, there are multiple furnaces discharging into the same chimney, they are deemed to be only one furnace. However, nothing in the Regulations authorises either the continuous emission of dark smoke (otherwise than as caused by soot blowing) for a period exceeding four minutes, or the emission

1 *R v Hudson* [1966] 1 QB 448.
2 *Stevens v London Borough of Bromley* [1972] Ch 400.
3 *Cheshire County Council v Woodward* [1962] 2 AC 126.
4 *Moir v Williams* [1892] 1 QB 264.

of black smoke (ie smoke as dark or darker than shade 4 on a Ringelmann Chart) for more than two minutes in aggregate in any period of 30 minutes.

8.2.2 Trade premises

Section 2(1) prohibits the emission of dark smoke from any industrial or trade premises, and where, on any day, such smoke is emitted, the occupier, together with any other person who causes or permits the emission, is guilty of an offence. In this context, proof that a person 'causes' requires no proof of an element of intention or recklessness on the part of the accused. There is ample authority, for example in relation to water pollution offences, to show that the accused need only have had operational control of, or otherwise 'set up' the situation leading to the commission of an offence.[1] It is possible, however, to defeat a charge of 'causing' pollution by showing that the emission in question was the result of either an act of God, or the extraordinary intervening act of a third party such as a terrorist.[2] To 'permit', on the other hand, requires: (a) knowledge of a situation; plus (b) a failure to prevent it when one had the right and power to do so.[3] However, this provision does not apply to any chimney falling within s 1, nor to emissions of dark smoke caused by burning any material prescribed in regulations, in which connection see the Clean Air (Emission of Dark Smoke) (Exemption) Regulations 1969, SI 1969/1263, which exempt, subject to certain conditions (see below), the following materials:

- timber and waste resulting from building demolition or site clearance in connection with building operations or work of engineering constructions (conditions A, B and C apply);
- explosives within the Explosives Act 1975 which are waste, or matter contaminated by explosives (conditions A and C apply);
- matter burnt in connection with research into the causes and control of fire, or in the course of fire training (condition C applies);
- tar, pitch, asphalt and other matter burnt in connection with preparing and laying surfaces, or which is burnt off a surface in connection with resurfacing (condition C applies);
- carcasses of animals/poultry which have died as a result of disease, or have been slaughtered, or have been required to be slaughtered because of disease (conditions A and C apply);
- containers contaminated by pesticides or toxic substances used for veterinary or agricultural purposes, including sacks, boxes or receptacles (conditions A, B and C apply).

The conditions referred to above are as follows: condition A requires that there should be no other reasonable, safe and practicable way of disposing of the matter; condition B requires that the burning is carried out so as to minimise

1 *Alphacell v Woodward* [1972] AC 824; *FJH Wrothwell Ltd v Yorkshire Water Authority Services Ltd* [1984] Crim LR 43.

2 See *Southern Water Authority v Pegrum* [1989] 2 All ER 357 and *Empress Car Company (Abertillery) Ltd v National Rivers Authority* [1998] 1 All ER 481, [1998] EHLR 3, (1998) *The Times*, February 9.

3 *McLeod v Buchanan* [1940] 2 All ER 179; *Price v Cromack* [1975] 1 WLR 988.

the emission of dark smoke; and condition C requires that the burning is carried out under the direct and continuous supervision of the occupier of the premises, or of some person authorised to act on his behalf.

Where material is burned on industrial or trade premises in circumstances such that the burning is likely to give rise to emissions of dark smoke, in any proceedings there is taken to have been an emission unless the occupier or any person who caused or permitted the burning shows that no dark smoke was emitted (s 2(3)). Careful note should be taken of this reversal of the normal burden of proof. The provision is designed to deal with burning at night, where it might otherwise be hard to show that dark smoke was emitted. Those who are convicted of offences under s 2(5) are liable on summary conviction to a fine not exceeding £20,000. It is, however, a defence to proceedings under s 2(4) to prove that an alleged emission was inadvertent and that all practicable steps had been taken to prevent or minimise the emission of dark smoke; otherwise, the normal principles applicable to regulatory offences would appear to apply, and neither 'causing' nor 'permitting' the emission of dark smoke requires proof of intention or recklessness. The requirements of s 51(1) in relation to the charging of offences should also be noted.

Industrial or trade premises are those used for any industrial or trade purposes, or any premises on which matter is burnt in connection with any industrial or trade purpose (s 2(6)) and, in this connection, note *Sheffield City Council v ADH Demolition Ltd*,[1] where it was held that demolition was a 'trade process', so that a bonfire lit on a site to burn rubbish resulting from demolition fell within the control of the Act. Note also that for an emission to take place there does not have to be a transgression of site boundaries.[2]

Offences under both ss 1 and 2 are subject to s 51. Under that section if, in the opinion of an authorised officer of the local authority, an offence is being or has been committed he must, unless he has reason to believe that due notice has already been given by or on behalf of the authority, notify the appropriate person, ie the occupier of the premises, or the person having possession of the boiler or plant, as the case may be. If that notification is not in writing it must be confirmed in writing within four days following the day on which the officer became aware of the offence. It is then a defence to show that these requirements have not been complied with. However, to lighten the administrative burden on authorities, s 3(2) states that where proceedings are being taken under ss 1 or 2, the court may be satisfied that any smoke is 'dark' using a 'Ringelmann style' comparison. This enables environmental health officers to rely on their professional skill and judgment. The Secretary of State is empowered by s 3(3) to prescribe methods of ascertaining whether or not smoke is dark, and s 3(3) makes subsequent provision for any such evidence to be accepted conclusively by the courts.

1 (1983) 82 LGR 177.
2 *O'Fee v Copeland Borough Council* [1995] 7 ELM 129.

8.3 SMOKE, GRIT, DUST AND FUMES

The following provisions apply generally to emissions of smoke, grit and dust from furnaces, but are excluded in certain cases – for example, where a process falls under Part I of the Environmental Protection Act 1990 (see Chapter 6, and s 41), or where the discharge is from mine or quarry waste (s 42), from a locomotive (s 43(5)), or from a vessel (ss 44(6) and 46(4)). The material in question is 'smoke', which includes, under s 64(1), soot, ash, grit and gritty particles in smoke. 'Grit', under the Clean Air (Emission of Grit and Dust from Furnaces) Regulations 1971, SI 1971/162, is defined as particles more than 76 microns in diameter. 'Fumes' are defined under s 64(1) as airborne solid matter smaller than dust. Finally, 'dust' is defined by BS 3405 as solid particles between 1 and 75 microns in diameter.

8.3.1 Installation of furnaces

Under s 4(2), the installation of furnaces (except 'domestic furnaces', for which see below) in any building, and in any fixed boiler or industrial plant, is forbidden without notice of the proposed installation being given to the local authority, ie the district, metropolitan, London borough or unitary authority as the case may be. Furthermore, under s 4(2) no installation may take place unless the furnace is, so far as practicable, capable of being operated continuously without emitting smoke when burning fuel of the type for which it was designed. A furnace which is installed in accordance with plans and specifications submitted to and approved by the local authority is treated as complying with the foregoing requirements. It is, however, an offence to install or to instruct the installation of a furnace in contravention of the requirements. Contravention of s 4(1) is punishable by a fine up to level 3 on the standard scale, and contravention of s 4(2) up to level 5. The provisions apply additionally to attaching a boiler or industrial plant which already contains a furnace to a building, and to the fixing or installation of any such boiler or plant on any land. This extends to cover resiting existing plant. 'Furnace' appears to refer to the whole structure of the equipment in question, not just its combustion parts,[1] but also appears to extend to cremation ovens and incinerators. There appears to be no need for the equipment in question to be physically attached to the land; the test is instead whether the equipment can be used for the purposes of the premises in which they are installed.[2] The provisions do *not* apply to installing 'domestic furnaces', ie furnaces designed solely or mainly for domestic purposes and used for heating a boiler, with a maximum heating capacity of less than 16.12 kilowatts. A boiler may be used 'domestically' even in non-residential premises, provided it is being used to supply hot water for a purpose for which people normally require it in their homes – for example, the provision of central heating, provided the heating

1 *British Steel Corporation v Pittock* (1970) 16 RRC 374.
2 *Tyne Boiler Works Co v Overseers of Long Benton* (1886) 18 QBD 81.

capacity limits are not transgressed.[1] Finally, it should be noted that installation under and in accordance with s 4 would not serve as a defence to a charge of emitting dark smoke under s 1.

8.3.2 Grit and dust controls

In relation to non-domestic furnaces (see above), s 5 gives the Secretary of State power to make regulations to prescribe limits on the rate of emission of grit and dust from furnace chimneys, and, where these limits are transgressed, the occupier of any building containing the offending furnace is guilty of an offence punishable by a fine up to level 5. It is, however, a defence to show that the 'best practicable means' had been used for minimising the alleged emission (see **8.2.1** for comment on 'best practicable means' under s 64(1)). Where a building contains a non-domestic furnace in relation to which no limits have been set by the Secretary of State, an offence, punishable as above, is committed if the occupier of the building fails to use any practicable means for minimising emissions of grit or dust. It is, of course, a defence to show that practicable means for avoiding emissions were used. The detailed requirements are laid down in the Clean Air (Emission of Grit and Dust from Furnaces) Regulations 1971, SI 1971/162. These apply to two types of furnace, specified in Schs 1 and 2 of the Regulations. Schedule 1 covers boiler furnaces, eg those for boiling or heating liquids or for generating steam, and indirect heating appliances wherein the material heated is gas or liquid. Schedule 2 covers indirect heating appliances not falling within Sch 1, and those in which combustion gases are in contact with material being heated, but where that material makes no contribution to grit and dust in the combustion gases. Schedule 1 furnaces are further defined by relation to their heat output, so that the higher the maximum continuous rating in pounds of steam per hour (from and at 100°C) or in thousands of British thermal units (BTU) per hour, the higher the maximum permitted quantity of grit and dust in pounds per hour – although the permitted quantities are lower where a furnace burns liquid as opposed to solid matter. Further, where solid matter is burnt, there is a limit of 20 per cent on the proportion of particles that can be produced in excess of 76 microns diameter, rising to 33 per cent where the maximum continuous rating does not exceed 16,800 pounds per hour (16,800,000 BTU). Schedule 2 furnaces are further designated by heat input, and, again, the greater the input in millions of BTU per hour the higher the maximum permitted quantities of grit or dust per hour, with lower limits applying to furnaces burning liquid matter, and limits similar to those applied to Sch 1 furnaces in respect of the emission of particles exceeding 76 microns diameter. Incinerators, ie appliances designed to burn solid or liquid waste, are not covered by the Regulations, even where their heat is used for a purpose. Where a relevant chimney serves more than one furnace using multiflues, each flue counts as a separate chimney serving a separate furnace, while in other cases the chimney is to be taken as a single

1 See, further, *Smith v Miller* [1894] 1 QB 192; and *Re an arbitration between the Mayor, Alderman, and Burgesses of the Borough of Willesden and Municipal Mutual Insurance* [1944] 2 All ER 600 on the meaning of 'domestic'.

chimney serving a single furnace with a heat input/output equal to the aggregate of the furnaces involved (reg 4(2)). The Regulations apply to furnaces during any period of standard operation, ie when a furnace is operating at or close to its normal loading *and* at any time when the furnace is operated at a higher loading, provided this is done regularly for a limited time (reg 5).

8.3.3 Arrestment plant for non-domestic furnaces over specified sizes

Under s 6, non-domestic furnaces may not be used in a building to burn pulverised fuel, nor to burn at a rate of 45.4 kilograms or more per hour any other solid matter, nor to burn at a rate of 366.4 kilowatts per hour any liquid or gaseous matter, unless provided with grit and dust-arresting plant approved by the local authority, or which has been installed in accordance with plans and specifications approved by the local authority. In all cases the plant must also be properly maintained and used. The prescribed figures for burning rates may, however, be altered by regulations made by the Secretary of State under s 6(3) with the approval of Parliament, although any reduction in the permitted rate of output does not apply to furnaces which have been installed or part installed, or which are subject to installation agreements made, before the date any regulations come into force. From the requirements of s 6(1) *et seq* the Secretary of State may, by regulations, provide exceptions in respect of any class of furnaces under s 7 so that where a building's occupier applies to the local authority and they are satisfied that the emission of grit or dust from any chimney serving as a furnace in the building will not be prejudicial to health or a nuisance if the chimney is used for a particular purpose not in compliance with s 6, they may exempt the chimney from control while it is used for that purpose. Such applications must be determined in writing within eight weeks of the receipt of the application or such longer period as is agreed in writing, otherwise the application is deemed to be granted (s 7(3)). If, however, the local authority decide not to grant an exemption, they must give written notice supported by reasons, and, thereafter, the applicant has 28 days in which to appeal to the Secretary of State, who may confirm the decision, grant the exemption, or vary the purpose for which the furnace in question may be used without complying with s 6(1). The Secretary of State's decision must be reasoned and in writing – see below for procedural requirements. Where, on any day, such an exempted furnace is used for a purpose other than a prescribed purpose or one for which an exemption has been given, the occupier of the building is guilty of an offence punishable by a fine up to level 5. For the exemptions, see the Clean Air (Arrestment Plant) (Exemption) Regulations 1969, SI 1969/1262. Exempted furnaces are those under Sch 1 of the Regulations, which are mobile or transportable heat and power sources providing temporary sources of heat etc during building or engineering construction works, or for investigative or research purposes, or for agricultural purposes as defined in s 109(5) of the Agriculture Act 1947, or which are small-scale burners which, in general, burn material at a rate of not more than 25 pounds per hour for each square foot of grate area, where the matter being heated does not contribute to the emission of grit and dust and where the purpose in question is *not* the incineration of refuse. These exemptions do not apply where a furnace is designed to burn solid material at a rate of one ton or more per hour. Otherwise, however, the exemptions apply to hand-fired, magazine gravity fed, underfeed stoker furnaces, chain grate stoker furnaces, and cooling stoker furnaces. The 1969 Regulations, which were originally made under the Clean Air Act 1968 and are now, in common with other pre-1993 Regulations, continued in force under the 1993 Act, also provide, in Schs 2 and 3, the procedures and forms for exemption applications to local authorities made under s 7(2). Applicants must give certain information about themselves, their grounds for claiming an exemption, and details of the type and description of their furnaces, such as maximum ratings, the fuel burnt, rates of consumption, methods of firing, draughting, grit and dust production, and patterns of operation.

8.3.4 Arrestment plant for specified types of domestic furnace

Domestic furnaces may not be used in buildings to burn pulverised fuel, or solid fuel in dry form, or solid waste at a rate of 1.02 tonnes per hour, unless grit and dust-arrestment equipment is provided as approved by the local authority, or which has been installed in accordance with approved plans and specifications, and which is properly maintained and used; otherwise, an offence is committed punishable by a fine up to level 5 (s 8). (On the meaning of 'domestic', see s 64(1), and **8.3.1**.)

8.3.5 Appeals

Section 9 provides the appeal mechanism in respect of refusals of approvals by local authorities under ss 6 and 8. Where approval is not given it must be supported by written reasons. The disappointed applicant or any person interested in a building to which such an application refers may, if dissatisfied, appeal within 27 days to the Secretary of State, who may give any approval which was capable of being given by the local authority.

8.3.6 Measurement of grit and dust

Under s 10, where a furnace in a building is used to burn pulverised fuel, or other solid matter, at a rate of 45.4 kilograms or more per hour, or to burn any liquid or gaseous material at a rate of 366.4 kilowatts or more per hour (ie larger plants), the local authority may, by notices served on the occupier of the building, require that person to comply with stipulated measures: to make and record, from time to time, measurement of grit, dust and fumes emitted from the furnace; to make adaptations to the furnace chimney for measurement purposes; to provide and maintain measuring equipment; and to inform the authority of the results, or to make the results available to the authority. Thus, measurement requirements etc can be imposed as either the occasion arises or as the local authority reasonably considers it appropriate.[1] A notice applying directions under s 10 must further inform the occupier of the buildings of the terms of s 11(1) to (3) (see below). The measurements in question are those provided for under regulations made by the Secretary of State.[2] These measurements must be undertaken either by the relevant occupier or on his behalf. Subject to a minimum period of compliance of six weeks, adaptations must be made and appropriate measuring equipment provided, and thereafter maintained, according to the scheme under BS 3405 (1961), within such a period as is specified in the notice. Thereafter, on receipt of 28 days' notice in writing, the occupier must make and keep measurements of grit and dust emitted from the furnace in question over a specified period, and must give the authority 48 hours' notice in writing of the commencement of measurements. Measurements may be required either on a time-to-time basis, or at stated periods, but are, in general, to be required only once in any given period of three months. Measurements made are to be transmitted to the authority within 14 days, and must state the date of their making, the numbers of furnaces which discharged into the chimney on the date in question, and amounts of grit and dust emitted, including the percentage of grit in solids emitted. It is an offence to fail to comply with such requirements, punishable by a fine up to level 5. Furthermore, where an obligation to make measurements exists there is, under s 10(5), a further obligation to allow a local authority representative to be present during measurements. Where an authority direct that any relevant furnace is subject to requirements, they may revoke that direction and may substitute another. Once a duty to comply with requirements under s 10 is in place, in relation to any furnace which is used to burn solid matter other than pulverised fuel at a rate of less than 1.02 tonnes per hour, or to burn liquid or gaseous matter at a rate of less than 8.21 megawatts, the occupier of the building in which the furnace is situated may, under s 11(1) to (3), request the local authority to make the required measurements. Thereafter, the duty to record grit, fumes and dust is on the authority, and the occupier is generally freed of burdens, save that of making any necessary structural adaptations to a chimney to enable measurements to be made.

8.3.7 Information on furnaces

To enable authorities to perform their functions under ss 5 to 11, they may require the occupiers of buildings by written notice to furnish them within 14 days (or such longer time as may be allowed) with reasonably required information as to furnaces in the building and the fuel and waste burned therein. It is an offence to fail to comply with such a notice in time or to give a false response, punishable with a fine up to level 5 (s 12). Although it is for the

1 *Halliday v Wakefield Corporation* (1887) 57 LT 559.

2 See the Clean Air (Measurement of Grit and Dust from Furnaces) Regulations 1971, SI 1971/161.

prosecution to prove that any information given was 'false', information may be tainted with falsity where its giver has clearly ignored what is obvious, and this probably extends to situations where a person has deliberately chosen not to seek out the truth,[1] although simple neglectful ignorance would not be sufficient to ground liability. Finally, s 13 generally applies ss 5 to 12 to outdoor fixed boilers and industrial plants as they do to furnaces in buildings, with the possessor of the boiler being substituted where appropriate for the occupier of the building for the purposes of liability.

8.4 HEIGHT OF CHIMNEYS

8.4.1 Furnace chimneys

A building occupier must not knowingly cause or permit any furnace served by a chimney to be used in a building to burn pulverised fuel, or any other solid matter at a rate of 45.4 kilograms per hour, or any liquid or gaseous matter at a rate of 366.4 kilowatts per hour, unless the height of the relevant chimney has been approved and any conditions of approval have been complied with (s 14(1) and (2)). A failure to comply constitutes an offence. Similarly, persons in possession of any fixed boilers or industrial plant must not knowingly cause or permit furnaces of such boilers or plant to be used to burn fuels of the above descriptions at the above rates, unless the heights of the chimneys serving those boilers etc have been approved and any conditions in the approval have been complied with. Again, non-compliance constitutes an offence (s 14(4) and (5)). However, certain boilers and plants may be exempted from this provision if they are used wholly for purposes specified in regulations made by the Secretary of State under s 14(7), and their chimney heights have been otherwise centrally or locally approved (see the Clean Air (Height of Chimneys) (Exemption) Regulations 1969, SI 1969/411). The exemptions apply to chimneys serving new or enlarged furnaces in connection with boilers or plant:

- where these temporarily replace other boilers etc which are under inspection, repair or maintenance, in the course of being rebuilt, or in the course of being replaced by other permanent boiler/plant;
- where they temporarily provide sources of heat or power during building works or those of engineering construction, or for the purposes of investigation or research; or
- where they provide heat or power for agricultural purposes within the meaning of s 109(3) of the Agriculture Act 1947.

8.4.2 Obtaining approval

Section 15 provides the approval mechanisms. Application for approval is generally made to local authorities which may not, under s 15(2), grant

1 *James and Son Ltd v Smee* [1955] 1 QB 78; *Taylors Central Garages (Exeter) Ltd v Roger* (1951) 115 JP 445.

approval unless satisfied that the height of the chimney will be sufficient to prevent (so far as practicable) smoke, dust, grit, gases or fumes emitted from the chimney from becoming prejudicial to health or a nuisance having regard to the chimney's purpose, the position and description of buildings near it, the levels of neighbouring ground, and any other relevant circumstances. Approval may be given without qualification or subject to conditions as to the rate or quality, or the rate and quality of emissions. Thus, conditions may relate to rate *and* quality, or rate *or* quality. Applications must be determined within four weeks, or such longer period as both sides agree, and, if not so determined, are deemed approved (s 15(4)). Refusals or conditions imposed must be supported by written statements of reasons. Where approval is refused, the authority must specify the lowest height, if any, of chimney they would approve without qualification, or the lowest height they are prepared to approve subject to conditions, or both. A disappointed applicant has the right to appeal to the Secretary of State in writing within 28 days of receipt of an authority's decision (s 16(6)). The Secretary of State, on appeal, may approve the height of the chimney with or without conditions as to emissions, or may cancel and/or substitute conditions imposed. The Secretary of State's decision must be given in a form similar to that required for local authority decisions.

Guidance to authorities on reaching decisions under s 15 was given by the DoE in Circular 25/81, *Third Memorandum on Chimney Heights* (1981). Authorities are to have regard not just to the height of a chimney, but also its effect on local topography, and also existing pollution levels in an area. To this end, areas are categorised as:

A – undeveloped land where further development is not likely;
B – partially developed land with scattered residences;
C – built-up residential area;
D – mixed urban developed areas; and
E – large urban areas of mixed heavy industrial and dense residential development.

In areas A and B, a chimney having a given rate of flue gas discharge should be required to be proportionately lower than equivalent chimneys in areas D and E. The guidance furthermore applies only to furnaces with a gross heat output of 0.15 to 150 megawatts; smaller furnaces fall outside the requirement for approval under s 14. The methodology in the guidance does not apply to any directly fired heating system which discharges into the space to be heated, nor to gas turbines or incinerators. However, in general, authorities are counselled to determine a minimum height sufficient to ensure adequate dispersal of sulphur dioxide and other normal products of combustion, using formulae laid down in the guidance. The height of a chimney may have to be increased to take account of other adjacent buildings and chimneys, and should ensure an efflux velocity sufficient to prevent the plume of emissions from flowing down the outside of the chimney. In the case of a works having a number of adjacent fuel burning plants, the normal requirement should be for one, common, multiflued chimney which will produce a sufficient efflux velocity, taking into account the aggregation of the maximum emissions of sulphur dioxide from each furnace. In addition, chimneys should rise at least three metres above the level of any other generally accessible area or feature, should never be less than the calculated, uncorrected chimney height, nor less than the height of any attached building within a distance of five uncorrected chimney heights. Furthermore, final calculations should be rounded up to the nearest metre, while the height of the chimney may also be a relevant consideration with regard to the making of any necessary grant of planning permission.

The guidance does not apply to the following: emissions of grit or dust; excessive concentrations of carbon monoxide where a very low sulphur (VLS) fuel is used and is insufficiently combusted; where a chimney discharges on a roof with a complicated structure; where there are particular local topographical problems; or where there are a number of chimneys closely adjacent. In such circumstances authorities are counselled to seek further specialist advice in coming to their decision. Finally, it should be remembered that although the guidance is detailed (very detailed in some places), so as to reduce local authority discretion, nevertheless, it remains only guidance. Authorities must continue to exercise their discretion generally according to the law: ie reasonably; for the purpose for which the discretion has been granted; and without fettering their discretion.

8.4.3 Other chimneys

Under s 16, where there are plans for erecting or extending a building outside Greater London or in an outer London borough, and these are in accordance with building regulations deposited with the local authority and show proposals to construct a chimney, other than one serving a furnace, for carrying smoke, grit, dust or gases from the building, the authority must reject those plans unless satisfied that the height of the chimney as shown will be sufficient to prevent, so far as practicable, the smoke etc from becoming prejudicial to health, or a nuisance, having regard to the chimney's purpose, the positioning and description of buildings near it, the neighbouring ground levels, and other relevant circumstances. Where plans are rejected, appropriate notice must be given under s 16(6) of the Building Act 1984, and the disappointed applicant may appeal to the Secretary of State, who may confirm or cancel the rejections.

This provision does not, however, apply to plans for buildings to be used as residences, shops or offices. Indeed, while such buildings may fall within the area smoke control provisions of the Clean Air Act 1993 (see **8.5** *et seq* below), supplementary controls are also found in s 73 of the Building Act 1984 to deal with smoke dispersal problems etc. Section 73 provides that where persons erect buildings to heights greater than those of adjoining buildings, and the chimneys or flues of any such adjoining buildings are in party walls between those buildings, or are six feet or less from the nearest part of the taller building, the local authority may, by notice, require those creating the taller buildings within a specified time to increase the height of those other relevant chimneys and flues, where this is reasonably practicable, so that their tops will be the same height as those of the chimneys of the taller buildings, or the top of those buildings, whichever is higher. The local authority may further require the owners/occupiers of the adjacent buildings to allow those erecting taller buildings to enter the existing buildings to carry out such work as the authority, by notice, require, although owners or occupiers may elect to do such work themselves, and have 14 days to elect to do so from receipt of service of notice by serving counter-notices on the authority and the persons proposing to erect taller buildings, in which case the owners'/occupiers' expenses may be recovered from those erecting the taller buildings. There is a right of appeal to the justices against notices, while authorities also have default powers where there is non-compliance; such non-compliance is also an offence.

Control under the Building Regulations 1991, SI 1991/2768, also requires that *all* chimneys must be installed so as to receive sufficient air to enable proper combustion of fuel and effective flue operation, be capable of normal operation without their combustion products constituting health hazards, and be capable of normal operation without damaging the fabric of their parent building by heat or fire.

The foregoing provisions reflect the pollution abatement philosophy of the 1950s and 1960s that dispersal equals disposal. They are designed to ensure that chimneys are of a sufficient height to enable exhaust velocities of emissions to be such as to prevent material falling back to produce localised, ground-level nuisances, bearing in mind, in particular, local conditions such as ground levels and other buildings etc in the vicinity.

'Dispersal equals disposal' made apparent sense. The most obvious problem at that time was low-level nuisance caused by factories and power plants burning coal in towns. It thus appeared sensible to try to curb such nuisances by a combination of legal measures and, with particular regard to power production, by resiting power generation in a reduced number of larger plants situated well away from towns and cities. In addition, the increased efficiency of modern furnaces reduced smoke output, because smoke ('suspended particular matter') is largely the product of inefficiently and incompletely combusted fuel. What was not realised, however, was the problem caused by the almost invisible emission of, for example, sulphur dioxide (SO_2) from the large combustion plants which replaced older 'smoker stack' installations. The clean air legislation may well have been successful in eliminating local nuisances, but it did little to prepare the nation for the more insidious and intractable problems of acidification and traffic-induced smog. It is for that reason, at least in part, that the further legislative measures, considered in Chapters 6, 7 and 10 had to be undertaken.

8.5 SMOKE CONTROL AREAS

8.5.1 Declaration by local authorities

Section 18 empowers a local authority (ie a district, London borough or unitary authority) to declare the whole or any part of its district to be a smoke control area by means of a 'smoke control order'. Different provisions may be made for different parts of a smoke control area, and an order may apply prohibition on smoke emissions to specified classes of buildings in an area, and may, furthermore, exempt certain buildings or classes of buildings, or classes of fireplace, from control, subject to specified conditions. The powers also extend to fixed boilers or industrial plant within an area. Once made, an order may be revoked or varied by a subsequent order.

The procedure for making an order is laid down in Sch 1, and follows the usual pattern of prior advertisement of the proposal for an order by the local authority in the local press and the *London Gazette* for two successive weeks, stating the intention to make the order, specifying a place in the district where the order can be inspected, and publicising the right of those affected by the order to object within the two-week period. This period will begin on the day after the last publication of the notice.[1] Local postings of the relevant notices must also be posted in the affected locality. Where objections are made and not withdrawn the order cannot be made until those objections have been considered, but, subject thereto, an order comes into force some months after it is made. Where, however, under s 18(6), before an order comes into operation the local authority resolve to postpone its operation, and give the same amount of newspaper coverage to that decision as to the initial making of the order, the order will only come into force on the date contained in the authority's resolution. Part III of Sch 5 contains publicity requirements in respect of confirming and the coming into operation of smoke control orders once they have been made. Newspaper publicity is required for two weeks, stating the making of an order and its effect, and naming a place where the order can be inspected at reasonable times, free of charge, for a period of six weeks. Notices to a similar effect must also be posted in affected areas. Those affected by the making of the order must be informed of their right to object to the confirmation of the order to the Secretary of State, who may not confirm the order if any objection is made and not withdrawn without holding a local inquiry or hearing into the objection(s). Section 250(2) to (5) of the Local Government Act 1972 will apply to that inquiry with regard to summoning witnesses and producing documents, and also with regard to costs incurred. The Secretary of State may confirm the order with or without modification after the conclusion of the inquiry or hearing, or where no objection has been duly made, or where every objection duly made has been withdrawn, and, generally, the order will come into effect six months after confirmation, although the local authority concerned may postpone that date for up to 12 months, or longer with the Secretary of State's consent.

Section 19 further empowers the Secretary of State to direct an authority to prepare and submit to him within a minimum period of some months proposals for implementing smoke control in the local authority's area. However, before doing so he must be satisfied, after a consultation with the authority, that it is expedient to abate smoke pollution in the area, and that the

1 See *R v Turner* [1910] KB 346.

authority have not exercised their s 18 powers, or have exercised them incorrectly. Proposals submitted may be varied subsequently within permitted periods of time; the Secretary of State is not bound to accept proposals, but may approve, reject or modify them. Furthermore, the Secretary of State has default powers to direct an authority to behave in a specified fashion should they fail to submit required proposals or submit proposals rejected in whole or part.

8.5.2 Prohibitions in smoke control areas

Section 20 prohibits the emission of smoke from the chimney of any building within a smoke control area, and from a chimney serving the furnace of any fixed boiler or industrial plant. In the first instance the occupier of the building and, in the second instance, the possessor of the boiler are liable on summary conviction to a fine not exceeding level 3 on the standard scale. However, under s 20(4) in any such proceedings it is a defence to prove that the alleged emission was not caused by the use of any fuel other than an authorised fuel, ie a fuel declared authorised by regulations made by the Secretary of State – see the Smoke Control Areas (Authorised Fuels) Regulations 1991, SI 1991/1282, as amended by SI 1997/2658. 'Authorised fuels' fall into two categories. The first comprises fuels which are naturally smokeless, for example gas (thus covering 'coal effect' fires), and other solid fuels with low-volatile steam control. The second group are specifically created solid fuels, and those 'authorised' are listed by their name, the identity of their manufacturer, their constituent raw materials, and manufacturing process. This provision has effect subject to any exemptions in force under s 18 (see above) or ss 21 or 22 (see below), and is also subject to the requirements of s 51 that there must be prior notification to an occupier that an offence is being committed. Where such notification is not given, the occupier thereby has a defence.

Section 21 empowers the Secretary of State to exempt certain fireplaces from the ambit of s 20 where he is satisfied that they can burn fuel other than authorised fuel without producing smoke or a substantial quantity of smoke.[1] Inter alia, the regulations exempt fireplaces designed to burn oil, wood and wood waste in addition to coal, subject generally to specific treatment. However, the exemptions apply only where a fireplace is used to burn its design fuel, and is installed and used according to design instructions. Section 22 further empowers the Secretary of State, where it appears to him to be necessary or expedient, to suspend or relax the operation of s 20 in relation to the whole or part of a smoke control area, but before doing so he must consult with the relevant local authority unless satisfied that the matter is one of urgency and that consultation is impracticable. Once such an order is made, it is for the authority, as soon as practicable, to take suitable steps to bring the

1 See the Smoke Control Areas (Exempted Fireplaces) Orders 1970, SI 1970/615, and SIs 1970/1667, 1971/1265, 1972/438, 1972/955, 1973/2166, 1975/1001, 1975/1111, 1978/1609, 1982/448, 1982/1615, 1983/277, 1983/426, 1983/1018, 1984/1649, 1984/1805, 1985/315, 1986/638, 1987/383, 1988/2282, 1989/1769, 1990/345, 1990/2457, 1991/2892, 1992/2811, 1993/2277 and 1997/3009.

change to the notice of those affected by it. The consensus view of commentators is that the s 22 power is to be used only in emergencies, eg where there are shortages of authorised fuels.[1]

8.5.3 Unauthorised fuel

Any person who acquires unauthorised solid fuel for use in a building in a smoke control area (other than for an exempted building or fireplace) or who acquires any unauthorised solid fuel for use in any fixed boiler or plant in such an area (other than an exempted boiler), or who sells by retail any unauthorised solid fuel to a building in such an area or to premises in such an area where there is a fixed boiler or industrial plant, is guilty of an offence under s 23(1), and is liable on summary conviction to a fine not exceeding level 3. 'Retailing' is generally given a wide meaning in law to cover sales in a shop or market, or sales by post, sale for cash, on credit or by way of part exchange, but excludes sales subject to highly restrictive conditions which limit the range of potential customers.[2] However, for a person charged with retailing an unauthorised fuel a defence exists under s 25(5). This arises where the accused can show that there are objective grounds for reasonably believing that the building in question was exempted from the smoke control provision of s 20, or that the fuel was being acquired for use in some exempt fireplace, boiler or plant. The Secretary of State's suspensory powers under s 22 extend to suspending or relaxing the operation of s 23(1) (s 23(4)).

8.5.4 Adapting fireplaces

Local authorities have powers under s 24(1) to require, by notice in writing, occupiers and owners of private dwellings which are in smoke control areas to adapt fireplaces so that the prohibition in s 20 on the emission of dark smoke is not contravened. An appeal against such a notice is allowed under Part XII of the Public Health Act 1936. What constitutes a 'private dwelling' is a question of fact in each case, but is largely determined by the mode of user of the building.[3] It is not declared in the Act, however, which obligations should be imposed on owners, and which on occupiers. Leeson[4] argues convincingly that where works required affect the structure of a building, the obligation should lie on the owner, while occupiers' responsibilities should be restricted to matters of moveable fittings only, as a general rule. Works of adaptation include, under s 27, adapting and converting fireplaces, replacing fireplaces, and altering chimneys.

Grant aid is available in respect of adaptation (provided, under s 27, it is reasonably necessary and does not go beyond what is reasonably necessary) under s 25 and Sch 2, but only in respect of 'old private dwellings', ie those

1 See also Leeson, *Environmental Law* (Pitman, 1995), Ch 10, to which indebtedness throughout this chapter is generally acknowledged.
2 See, generally, *Chappell & Co Ltd v Nestle Co Ltd* [1958] 2 All ER 155.
3 *McNair v Baker* [1904] 1 KB 208.
4 Leeson, *Environmental Law* (Pitman, 1995), p 277.

erected before 15 August 1964, or which were produced after that date by the conversion of other premises. What constitutes 'reasonably necessary' expenditure will be a question of fact in each case, bearing in mind the availability of fuel needed in consequence of works of adaptation. However, s 64(5) precludes consideration of the cost of a fuel which is available only at a very high price. Section 28 provides that the cost of fixed heating or cooking appliances can be considered, even though these constitute moveable items. Section 27(3), however, enables authorities to ignore the cost of works which are not reasonably necessary for the purposes of smoke control when calculating grants (see further below). Grant aid in respect of 'relevant expenditure' can be given where expense is incurred *before* a smoke control order comes into force, provided the local authority approve, or the expense is reasonably incurred in carrying out the requirements of a s 24 notice. If satisfied with the work done, the authority must refund seven-tenths of the costs, and *may* refund the whole sum. 'Relevant expenditure' for the foregoing purposes is further defined by Sch 2, para 1(2) as that which is spent on adapting or, in connection with an 'old' private dwelling, which *either* is incurred before the smoke control order comes into force (with approval of the local authority specifically given for the purpose), *or* is reasonably incurred in carrying out works required by a notice under s 24(1). Schedule 2, para 1(5) gives a further discretion to an authority to approve expenditure *after* it has been incurred. Grant aid is not available in respect of the installation of heating appliances which have been designated by an authority as 'unsuitable' for their area by virtue of their fuel consumption characteristics, and a similar prohibition applies in respect of appliances designated as 'unsuitable' by the Secretary of State. Exchequer assistance may be given in respect of such grant aid.

Section 26 empowers authorities to make grants towards the adaptation of fireplaces in churches, chapels, and in buildings occupied by charities where it is necessary to meet the requirements imposed under s 20. It must be remembered that assistance is not generally available to meet expense incurred other than that which is reasonably incurred. Where such expense is incurred in doing works, the excess expenditure is not to be taken into account, although this prohibition does not apply in respect of works actually required by the local authorities under s 24 (s 27(3)).

8.6 ASSESSMENT OF THE EFFECTS OF THE CLEAN AIR ACT PROVISIONS

According to the Royal Commission on Environmental Pollution's Tenth Report,[1] the average urban concentration of smoke index with regard to coal combustion declined from almost two million tonnes in 1960, to less than 0.5 million tonnes in 1980. However, much of this reduction could be attributed to changing patterns of domestic heating, as gas and oil-fuelled central heating

1 Cmnd 9149 (1984).

replaced coal fires. Enhanced technologies for consuming fuel more efficiently and the reduction in 'smoke stack industries' also account for some of the decline. Indeed, it is possible to argue, as the Government did when it took powers under the Deregulation and Contracting Out Act 1994, that the 1993 Act's powers are now largely redundant in that its purposes with regard to smoke control have largely been achieved. Local authorities, however, argued against repeal, emphasising their ability under the legislation to take *preventive* action in respect of smoke – a power they prize.

8.7 SPECIAL CASES

8.7.1 Relationship of the 1993 Act powers with those under the Environmental Protection Act 1990

Section 41 provides that the foregoing provisions do not apply to 'prescribed processes' under the Environmental Protection Act 1990 (EPA 1990). However, note that under s 33 a person who burns insulation from cable with a view to metal recovery is guilty of an offence punishable on summary conviction not exceeding level 5 *unless* the burning is part of a process subject to Part 1 of EPA 1990 – for which see Chapters 6 and 7. It should be noted, however, that the Environmental Protection (Prescribed Processes and Substances) Regulations 1991, SI 1991/472, as amended, apply, inter alia, to processes for recovering certain metals by heat, including certain non-ferrous metals. Thus, the conditions in an authorisation under EPA 1990 should be framed so as to control substances emitted during the burning of cables.

8.7.2 Colliery spoil banks

Under s 42, the owners of coal or shale mines must employ all practicable means to prevent the combustion of refuse deposited from their mines and quarries, and to prevent or minimise the emission of smoke and fumes from such refuse, on pain of committing an offence punishable on summary conviction by a fine not exceeding level 5 on the standard scale, and by a cumulative penalty in respect of repeated or continued offences (see further on s 50 below). Section 42 is a preclusive code which applies to spoil banks to the exclusion of the other provisions in Parts I to III of the Act and also those under Part III of EPA 1990.[1]

8.7.3 Railway engines

Under s 43(1), the prohibition on emission of dark smoke applies to railway engines, the obligation being laid on the owners of the locomotive in question. It should be remembered that diesel locomotives on the main rail network can emit smoke although, perhaps, not as obviously as steam locomotives on 'preserved' railway lines. Any relevant owner is required to use 'any' practicable means for minimising the emission of smoke from the chimney

1 See Chapter 5.

of the engine. 'Chimney' includes any opening, eg a grill, through which smoke is passed (s 64). If the owner fails to do so, and smoke is emitted, he is guilty of an offence punishable on summary conviction by a fine not exceeding level 5, while, again, the cumulative penalty provisions also apply. This provision explains the notices often seen posted on 'preserved' lines, reminding drivers and firemen to use all means to prevent the escape of smoke. Where, however, a steam locomotive is properly fired, draughted and maintained, its emissions of smoke should be minimal, with what escapes from its chimney being primarily exhaust steam. Parts I to III of the 1993 Act are otherwise excluded from applying to railway locomotives.

8.7.4 Vessels

A vessel is any ship within the meaning of the Merchant Shipping Act 1995. Section 44 applies the prohibition on the emission of dark smoke to vessels in certain waters, making their owners, masters and other officers in charge responsible for discharging the obligations imposed, with the usual level 5 fine, being the penalty for non-compliance. However, under s 45(3) the Secretary of State has power to make regulations exempting certain emissions of dark smoke from the foregoing prohibition.[1] These are broadly similar in object and content to the regulations applying to chimneys on land (see **8.4** above). Thus, vessels are banded in classes according to their boiler type, and each type is granted specific exemptions. Emissions of dark smoke from forced draught oil-fired boilers or oil engines are allowed for 10 minutes in aggregate in any period of two hours; emissions from natural draught oil-fired boiler furnaces are generally allowed for 10 minutes in aggregate in any one-hour period (see, however, below); emissions from a coal-fired boiler furnace when a vessel is under way are allowed for 20 minutes in aggregate in any one-hour period, while when the vessel is anchored, made fast or aground, the permitted period is 10 minutes in aggregate in any one-hour period. However, certain special cases exist. Whether a vessel has a natural draught oil-fired boiler furnace or a coal-fired boiler furnace, if its funnels are shortened to enable it to navigate the Manchester Ship Canal, if it is a tug not under way but preparing to get under way or otherwise supplying power to other vessels or shore installations, or if it is a vessel not under way but using its main power for dredging, lifting, pumping or some other special purpose for which it was designed, the permitted period is 20 minutes in aggregate in any one-hour period. As far as emissions from any other source on a vessel are concerned, the permitted period is five minutes in aggregate in any one-hour period.

Section 44 applies to vessels in all waters not navigable by sea-going ships, and all vessels which are within the seaward limits of UK territorial waters and which are also contained within any port, harbour, river, estuary, haven, dock, canal or other place so long as a person or body empowered by statute may make charges in respect of vessels entering or using the facilities of the port etc. Where waters are not within the district of a local authority, they are deemed

1 See the Dark Smoke (Permitted Periods) (Vessels) Regulations 1958, SI 1958/878.

to be in the area of the authority whose district includes the point on land which is nearest to the spot where the vessel is situated. Parts I to III of the 1993 Act in relation to smoke, grit or dust are otherwise generally excluded in relation to vessels (ss 44(6) and 46(4)).

8.7.5 Crown premises and ships

Under s 46, where it appears proper to do so local authorities are to report to the responsible minister any cases of:

- emission of dark smoke, grit or dust from any premises under the control of any government department and occupied for the public service of the Crown or for any departmental purpose;
- emissions of any smoke from any such premises in a smoke control area;
- emissions of any smoke from such premises which appear to be a nuisance to the inhabitants of the area;
- emissions of dark smoke from any of Her Majesty's ships or any government ship in the service of the Secretary of State while employed for Royal Naval purposes which appear to constitute a nuisance to the inhabitants of the neighbourhood.

On receipt of such a report, the minister must make an inquiry and, if a cause for complaint is revealed, he must employ all practicable means for preventing or minimising the emission or for abating the nuisance or its recurrence. This provision also applies to premises occupied on behalf of the Duchies of Lancaster and Cornwall. Section 46(4) also applies s 44 to vessels owned by the Crown, but excluding Royal Naval ships and government ships on Royal Naval business, eg fleet auxiliaries. Section 46(5) also applies the Act generally to premises occupied by visiting forces as if they were premises occupied for the public service of the Crown.

8.7.6 Exemptions

Under s 45, where a local authority are satisfied on the application of any 'person interested' that it is expedient, for the purpose of enabling investigations or research into atmospheric pollution to be carried out, without rendering that applicant liable under certain provisions of the Act, or under Part III of EPA 1990 (ie statutory nuisances – see Chapter 5), it may, by written notice, exempt that person wholly or in part from certain requirements relating to:

- any chimney with regard to ss 1, 5, 20 and 43 of the 1993 Act, and Part III of EPA 1990;
- any furnace, boiler or industrial plant with regard to s 4(2);
- any premises with regard to s 2;
- any furnace with regard to ss 6, 8 and 10;
- the acquiring for sale of fuel with regard to s 23.

The exemption may be conditional and may be for a specified period of time. A person refused exemption may appeal to the Secretary of State under s 45(2), who may, in writing, give the exemption on such terms as the authority could have done.

8.7.7 Fumes and gases

Section 47 empowers the Secretary of State to make regulations to apply all or any of the provisions of ss 5, 6, 7, 42(4), 43(5), 44(6) and 46(1) to fumes or particular gases or both in the same way that they apply to grit and dust. Similarly, the provisions of s 4 may be applied to fumes or particular gases, while s 11 may be applied to prescribed gases. Any regulations made may contain such exceptions and modifications as the Secretary of State considers expedient, although the regulations must be approved by Parliament. It should be noted that 'gas' is defined to include vapour and moisture precipitated from vapour. No regulations have been made under this provision, which has almost certainly been rendered otiose by the introduction of the IPC and LAAPC systems under EPA 1990.

8.8 ADMINISTRATION AND ENFORCEMENT

Under s 49, it is an offence for any person to disclose information relating to a trade secret used in carrying on any particular undertaking given to, or obtained (actively by normal investigations, or passively) by him by notice of the Act. On summary conviction a fine up to level 5 may be imposed. No offence is committed where a disclosure is made in the performance of a duty, or with the consent of a person having the right to disclose the information, or by virtue of s 34(1)(b) which relates to the disclosure of certain atmospheric pollution research information.[1]

8.8.1 Cumulative penalties

Under s 50, where a person is convicted of an offence which is subject to cumulative penalties on continuation *and* it is shown to the satisfaction of the court that the offence was substantially a repetition or confirmation of an earlier offence by him after a previous conviction for that offence, on summary conviction the person shall be liable to a fine up to level 5, *or* £50 for every day on which the earlier offence has been repeated or continued within the period of three months following the earlier conviction, whichever is the greater. Section 50(3) further provides that where an offence is subject to cumulative penalties, the court by which a person is convicted of the original offence may fix a reasonable period following conviction within which the defendant is to comply with any direction from the court, in which case the daily penalty referred to above is recoverable only once the compliance period has expired.

1 See further Chapter 10.

8.8.2 Notifications to occupiers

Under s 51, where an authorised officer (ie one authorised in writing, generally or specially, to act in relation to specified matters) considers that an offence is being, or has been, committed under s 1, s 2 or s 20, he must, unless he reasonably believes that prior notice has already been given by the local authority, notify 'the appropriate person' (ie the occupier of premises, the owner of the boiler or plant, the owner of the railway locomotive, or the owner or master of the vessel in question), as soon as he can. Where that notification is not in writing it must be confirmed in writing within four days of the date on which the officer became aware of the offence. Where proceedings are taken it is a defence to show that appropriate notification was not given.

8.8.3 Offences by companies

Section 52 provides that where an offence has been committed by a body corporate, and it is proved that this was done with the consent or connivance of, or was attributable to any neglect on the part of, any director, manager, secretary, or other similar officer of the company, or of any person purporting to act in such a capacity, that person is guilty along with the company, and may be proceeded against. In this context, 'consent' may be found to have existed where a person has knowledge of a particular act or course of action, and has agreed to it.[1] 'Connivance' may be evidenced by passively standing by while wrong acts are committed which could be prevented, or by wilfully 'turning a blind eye' to their occurrence. Where the members of a company manage its affairs, acts or defaults committed by a member in connection with a management function are treated as if they were those of a director. Those who are the directors and secretaries of companies are determined by law, but whether any given person is or is not a manager of a company is a question of fact in each case. The court will ask whether, in any case, an individual was a person of real authority within a company, ie someone who was part of its 'controlling mind' and who had the power and responsibility to decide upon corporate policy and strategy.[2] Liability will not usually extend to junior managerial staff, although they may commit wrongful acts for which, of course, their company employer is liable.[3] Similarly, under s 53, where the commission of an offence by any person was due to the act or default of some other person, that other person is guilty of the offence, and may be charged and convicted of the offence whether or not proceedings in respect of the offence are taken against any other persons.

8.8.4 Authorisation of works

Where works are reasonably necessary in connection with a building to enable it to be used without contravening the Act, its occupier may, under s 54, apply

---

1 *Huckerby v Elliot* [1970] 1 All ER 189.
2 *R v Boal* [1992] 3 All ER 177; *Woodhouse v Walsall Metropolitan Borough Council* [1994] Env LR 30.
3 *NRA v Alfred McAlpine Homes South Ltd* [1994] 4 All ER 286.

to the county court for an order to enable works to be carried out where there are restrictions on his interest in the building which render him incapable of carrying out those works without the consent of the building's owner or of some other person and that consent cannot be obtained. Similarly, an order can be applied for where the occupier considers that the whole or part of the cost of carrying out works should be borne by some other person. The court may make such orders as it considers just.

8.8.5 General enforcement functions

Local authorities, ie district councils, London boroughs, metropolitan boroughs and unitary authorities, are to enforce Parts I to III (ie ss 1 to 29), together with s 33 (cable burning) and Part VI (ss 41 to 46). In the case of smoke affecting any part of an authority's district, where the smoke comes from a chimney or premises outside their district they may take proceedings under s 1 or s 2 as if the offence was committed in their district.

Local authorities may authorise any person to enter, at any reasonable time, any land or vessel in order to perform any relevant statutory function, to determine whether, and in what way, such a function should be performed, to determine whether there is compliance with the Act, and to carry out relevant inspections, measurements and tests on the land or vessel or any articles on it, and to take away appropriate samples (s 56(1)). This does not generally apply with regard to private dwellings, although it may apply where an adaptation to a dwelling in a smoke control area is in question. Furthermore, under s 56(3) a justice of the peace may authorise entry by warrant if he is satisfied on sworn information in writing that: admission to relevant land or vessels has been refused; a refusal is apprehended; the land or vessel is unoccupied; the occupier is temporarily absent; the case is one of emergency; or an application to enter would defeat the object of the exercise. However, before doing this the justice must be satisfied that:

- admission has been sought in an emergency and had been refused; or
- the land or vessel is unoccupied; or
- an application for admission would defeat the object of the exercise.

'Emergency' in the current context is defined as meaning a situation where there is reasonable cause to believe that circumstances exist which may endanger life or health, and that immediate entry to the land/vessel is necessary to verify the existence of such circumstances, to ascertain their cause, or to effect a remedy (s 57(7)).

Persons authorised to enter under s 56 must, by virtue of s 57(1), produce evidence of their authority to do so if required. They may take with them any other persons or necessary equipment. However, admission to any land or vessel used residentially, or admission to any other land or vessel with heavy equipment cannot be demanded as of right under s 56(1) unless prior notice has been served on the occupier seven days beforehand. This restriction does not apply in cases of emergency or where the land or vessel is unoccupied (s 57(3)). Where entry is made on land or vessels which are unoccupied, or from which the occupier is temporarily absent, the land etc must be left as effectually secured against trespass as it was found to be. Furthermore, where damage is caused by the exercise of any of the foregoing powers the local authority is liable to pay full compensation to the person suffering the loss, save where the damage is attributable to the default of the person sustaining it. Disputes over compensation are to be settled by arbitration (s 57(5)).

Wilful obstruction of powers of entry is an offence punishable on summary conviction to a fine up to level 3 (s 57(6)).

Section 61 empowers local authorities to combine together for the purpose of declaring an area a smoke control area. Such an area may be the whole or any part of their districts, but, generally, each authority must exercise their smoke control functions solely within that part of the smoke control area affecting their district. Similarly, where premises extend across district boundaries the relevant authorities may agree that the premises are to be treated as wholly within the district of one of them. It should, finally, be noted that s 62 extends certain powers of Part XII of the Public Health Act 1936 to authorities exercising clear air functions, as follows:

- s 275 – the power to execute works;
- s 276 – the power to sell materials;
- s 278 – compensation for individuals damaged by the exercise of any powers;
- s 283 – form of notices;
- s 284 – authorisation of documents;
- s 285 – service of notices;
- s 289 – the power to require an occupier to permit an owner to undertake works;
- s 291 – recovery of expenses by way of charge;
- s 293 – recovery of expenses generally;
- s 294 – limitation of liability;
- s 299 – aggregation of several sums in one complaint;
- s 305 – exclusion of members' and officers' personal liability.

8.9 FUNCTIONS OF THE SECRETARY OF STATE – DEFAULT AND OTHER POWERS

Section 59 enables the Secretary of State to hold public inquiries into the operation of any provision of the Act, or in relation to the prevention of, or method of dealing with, air pollution at any place. Such an inquiry will fall within the terms of the Tribunals and Inquiries Act 1992.

Under s 60, where the Secretary of State is satisfied that a local authority have defaulted in performing any clean air functions, he may make an order which declares the authority to be in default, and direct them to perform specified functions. Directions may also be given as to the manner and timing of the performance of functions. Where a defaulting authority fail to comply with any such directions, the Secretary may either pursue his common law powers and seek an order of *mandamus* in court or, under s 60(2), may make a further order transferring specified functions to himself, although the cost of performing these functions will be owed by the authority to the Secretary of State (s 60(3), (4)(a) and (b)). A transfer order may further, under s 60(5), provide for the transfer to the Secretary of State of such property, rights, liabilities and obligations of the authority as he considers appropriate. Orders, once made, can be varied or revoked subsequently. However, under s 60(7) the default powers do not apply to a failure by a local authority to discharge their functions under s 18 (declaration of smoke control areas) or under s 19(1) (power of the Secretary of State to require the creation of a smoke control area). Section 59 empowers the Secretary of State to hold an inquiry in any situation where he considers it appropriate in connection with the Act's provisions, or with a view to preventing or dealing with pollution at any place. Section 250(2) to (5) of the Local Government Act 1972 applies to any such inquiry held. Finally, under s 63, wherever the Secretary of State has powers to make delegated legislation under the Act different provision may be made to deal with different circumstances, while such incidental, transitional and other supplemental provisions may be included as the Secretary of State considers appropriate. In general, such legislation is to be made in the form of a statutory instrument (except where it is made under ss 19(4) and 60, and Sch 3, para 3), and any such instrument is subject to annulment by resolution of either House of Parliament, except where it is made under s 6(3), s 10(5) or s 47(2) where approval by Parliament for draft regulations is required. Under s 63(3), any statutory instrument containing an order under s 21 or s 22 (exemption provisions relating to smoke control areas) is subject to annulment in pursuance of a resolution by either House of Parliament.

8.10 CLEAN AIR LEGISLATION AND UK EUROPEAN OBLIGATIONS

Directive 80/779/EEC on air quality limit values and guide values for sulphur dioxide and suspended particulates (smoke) lays down, inter alia, ground level concentration limits for sulphur dioxide and smoke, to be met over a period between 1983 and 1993. Member States are due to move towards stricter guide values laid down in Annex II of the Directive. The limit values work on a 'trade off' basis. For each year, and each winter in each year, there is an absolute fixed smoke limit, and the amount of sulphur dioxide present is allowed to rise or fall depending on how much smoke is present below that absolute limit. Thus, in any year, the limit value for smoke taken as the median of daily values is 80 micrograms per cubic metre; for sulphur dioxide the limit is 120 micrograms per cubic metre where smoke is less than 40 micrograms; and 80 micrograms per cubic metre where smoke is more than 40 micrograms.[1]

---

1 For further details, see Haigh, *Manual of Environmental Policy: The EC and Britain* (Cartermill) to which indebtedness is acknowledged.

Initially, the UK Government sought to meet its obligations by relying primarily on the clean air legislation, arguing that co-ordination of existing measures would largely eradicate smoke, and that areas not meeting EC limit values by the earliest compliance date of 1983 would meet the requirements by the last date in 1993. The Commission, however, considered that mere administrative means for co-ordinating existing measures were not a sufficient performance of directive obligations, and issued a reasoned opinion to that effect in January 1988. The UK Government, accordingly, introduced the Air Quality Standards Regulations 1989, SI 1989/317[1] and, subsequently, reinforced these Regulations by enacting Part I of EPA 1990.[2] The clean air legislation did not, therefore, prove to be an effective instrument to meet UK European obligations because of the overall lack of a quality standard under that legislation. The power given to the Secretary of State to direct local authorities to create smoke control areas was an insufficient provision in this context. It is, therefore, necessary to look elsewhere in UK law for a more modern approach to air quality standards.[3]

1 See Chapter 10.
2 See Chapter 6.
3 See Chapter 10.

CHAPTER 9

ATMOSPHERIC POLLUTION AND MOTOR VEHICLES

9.1 INTRODUCTION

A system of effective pollution control should be based on the three principles of compensation, mitigation and prevention. Most legal systems have provisions to allow persons injured by polluting emissions to recover, at least in certain circumstances, compensation for their injuries. Many legal systems also have provisions which attempt to mitigate the effects of emissions by requiring their minimisation or reduction to a particular level. However, prevention of pollution is less frequently encountered because, for instance, no adequate preventive technology exists, and because the polluting activity in question is so popular or widespread that there could be considerable resistance to attempts to curtail it. These statements have a degree of truth in the UK with regard to vehicle emissions. Standards exist for reducing vehicle emissions, but only recently has the possibility of preventing emissions by, for example, restricting vehicle use in particular situations, been considered, and the popularity of the private motor car is unlikely to be reduced for some time to come. Furthermore, there is no system for allowing civil recovery of damages by persons claiming to have been adversely affected by vehicle emissions – not least because it would not be possible to show that a given vehicle operator was at fault in relation to a given sufferer for the emission of fumes which caused the injury in question.[1]

Even where standards for requiring reductions in vehicle emissions exist, controversy surrounds their development and application. Emission standards can be variously set according to: whether they are measured with engines running at constant or varying speeds, or idling; which gear ratios are selected; and whether they have been based on tests carried out in rigs designed to reproduce certain test results which enable an indication of high-speed emissions to be obtained. Further variables which may be taken into account in setting emission standards include whether the emission in question is able to colour a particular filter, and the opacity and volume of exhausts. The use of varying test parameters can thus lead to different standard requirements. Historically, for example, tests in the European Community were based on a model in which the maximum speed was 50 km per hour, with an average speed of 18.7 km per hour, starting with a 'cold' engine. This was a good set of parameters for measuring emissions of carbon monoxide and hydrocarbons, but less effective with regard to nitrogen oxides, which emissions increase at

1 See also **4.8.2** on negligence liability in respect of the composition of vehicle fuel.

higher speeds. In most US States, however, the test parameters took into account main road speeds up to 91.2 km per hour, with an average speed of 34.3 km per hour, whilst California based its tests on a speed up to 96.4 km per hour, with an average speed of 77.4 km per hour. In addition, any given set of standards *may* allow a certain amount of tolerance, so that production line vehicles do not all have to meet the standards.

It is against this background that the following discussion must be understood, and it must also be remembered that UK law is now effectively the national application of common EC standards. Interestingly, there is little room for Member States to manoeuvre in relation to these standards, partly because of their extremely specific nature and partly because the car builders of Europe exist on such a multinational basis that it would make no sense for different standards to be applied to what are essentially identical cars produced in various Member States, frequently on a kit-of-parts basis, with components from a variety of sources – even assuming that was legally possible according to EC rules.

9.2 THE PROBLEM AND ITS CAUSES

We are a transport-based society. People tend to live long distances from their work, children are driven to school, and cars are used for shopping and leisure. This is partly the consequence of a planning system which sought consciously, after 1948, to separate people's homes from their places of work (much along the lines of US models), with the laudable object of ensuring that people were removed from localised smoke nuisances coming from factories. It was not realised for many years that there would be consequential disbenefits as more and more workers gave up public transport for the freedom provided by increasingly affordable private motoring. However, by the 1970s, it was clear that vehicle emissions were becoming a major problem. In 1977, for example, 849,000 tonnes of nitrogen oxides were released, which rose to 1,031,000 tonnes in 1987, with 40 per cent of that coming from vehicles. Vehicle carbon monoxide emissions rose in the same period from 3.70 million tonnes to 4.47 million tonnes. By the end of the 1980s an average family car, clocking up 13,000 miles per annum, produced 78 pounds of hydrocarbons, 50 pounds of nitrogen oxides and 1,056 pounds of carbon monoxide. By 1992 the DoE *Digest of Environmental Protection and Water Statistics*, No 15 indicated that of all major atmospheric pollutants, road traffic contributed 36 per cent of hydrocarbons, 51 per cent of nitrogen oxides, 89 per cent of carbon monoxide, 70 per cent of lead, 42 per cent of black smoke and 19 per cent of carbon dioxide. In weight terms, the Royal Commission on Environmental Pollution, in its report *Transport and the Environment*,[1] revealed that road traffic emitted 6,029,000 tonnes of carbon monoxide, 1,398,000 tonnes of nitrogen oxides, 949,000 tonnes of volatile organic compounds, 215,000 tonnes of particulates (smoke) and 62,000 tonnes of sulphur dioxide – far in excess of rail, air and

1 Cm 2674 (1994).

shipping emissions put together. Most of these emissions came from motor vehicles, which produce them by combusting their fuel – a mixture of hydrocarbon material, together with additives such as lead, and contaminants such as sulphur – in air, which is a mixture of nitrogen and oxygen. Where that fuel is completely combusted it produces nitrogen, carbon dioxide and water vapour (the 'cleanest' outcome), but complete combustion is not always achieved, and incomplete combustion produces carbon monoxide, unburnt fuel (hydrocarbons) and partially burnt fuels (as volatile organic compounds – VOCs – and smoke). In either case there will also be combustion by-products, such as oxides of nitrogen, together with sulphur dioxide, and the emission of substances such as lead compounds where lead additives have been utilised. The fitting of catalytic converters can largely eliminate carbon monoxide, hydrocarbons, VOCs, nitrogen oxides and sulphur dioxide – although not completely; and other emissions such as hydrogen sulphide are still produced. More importantly, as is pointed out in the DoH *Handbook on Air Pollution and Health* (1997), para 1.9, no vehicle that burns fossil fuels can be pollution free; even with a catalytic converter a car produces the greenhouse gas carbon dioxide.

Vehicle emissions can be dealt with from a legal point of view by regulating the way in which vehicle engine and exhaust systems are constructed, by regulating the composition of vehicle fuels, by fiscal means, and by road traffic regulation under the 'banner' of air quality management. The first two techniques are historically the best developed in UK law and practice. As far as fiscal measures are concerned, tax differentials between leaded and unleaded petrol exist to promote the sale of the latter, but, as yet, there is no scheme of tax concessions to encourage the use of 'cleaner' cars as, for example, in Germany, Greece and The Netherlands. Such measures may, however, form part of the implementation of the National Air Quality Strategy[1] which also contains measures on road traffic regulation. The remainder of this chapter will concentrate on relevant vehicle construction and use, fuel composition and storage standards, but it must be remembered that these are largely palliatives, not cures, for the vehicle exhaust emission problems.

9.3 FUEL COMPOSITION STANDARDS

Section 30 of the Clean Air Act 1993 (CAA 1993) empowers the Secretary of State to make regulations for the purpose of limiting or reducing air pollution, to impose requirements on the composition and content of motor vehicle fuels, and, where such requirements are in force, to prevent or restrict the production, treatment, distribution, transport, sale or use of non-complying fuels. Before making such regulations the Secretary of State must consult with such representative motor manufacturers, fuel manufacturers, representative users of vehicles and fuel, and representative atmospheric pollution experts, as he considers appropriate. Any regulations made may refer to standards,

1 See further Chapter 10.

specifications, descriptions and tests laid down in other documents, and may further require that information as to the composition of fuel is displayed at its point of supply. Local weights and measures authorities (ie in general, county, metropolitan and London borough councils under s 201 of the Local Government Act 1972) are, by s 30(4) of CAA 1993, the enforcing bodies for such regulations and have supplementary powers under the Trade Descriptions Act 1968 to make test purchases, to enter premises and seize goods and documents, to deal with obstruction of their authorised officers, and to give notice of tests to be carried out. It is an offence to fail to comply with regulations (s 32), punishable on conviction by a fine.

9.4 REGULATIONS

The Motor Fuel (Composition and Content) Regulations 1994, SI 1994/2295, were made under the powers of CAA 1993 and apply generally to 'motor fuel', ie diesel or petrol, the latter being defined by s 23 of the Petroleum Spirit (Consolidation) Act 1928 as 'of a kind used as fuel in motor vehicles' while the former refers to fuel used in diesel engines of which not more than 65 per cent by volume is distilled at a temperature of 350°C according to British Standards Specification BS7392 (1990). These Regulations replaced the previous provisions on the lead content of motor fuel, based on British Standards Specifications BS4040 (1988), BSEN 228 (1993), BS7800 (1992) and BSEN 590 (1993), and further embrace the requirements of Directives 85/210/EEC and 93/12/EEC on the lead content of fuel. The Regulations specify that petrol must comply at stated periods throughout the year with British Standards criteria for unleaded petrol, and, accordingly, restrictions are placed on the distribution and sale of non-complying petrol. Exemptions from these restrictions are granted only in respect of:

- tests and experiments in connection with the composition or content of motor fuel;
- tests etc in connection with the design or performance of articles using motor fuel, or any component or lubricant of such an article in circumstances where the composition or content of the fuel is relevant to design or performance;
- distribution or sale of fuel for use in aircraft (other than hovercraft);
- distribution or sale or use in vehicles constructed or adapted solely for competitions or trials;
- distribution or sale of fuel which is in the course of being manufactured or blended.

Similarly, it is not unlawful for a person to distribute or sell non-compliant fuel if the failure to comply is due to a mistake or to reliance on information supplied to him, or to the act or default of another person, or to an accident or some other cause beyond his control, *and* that person has taken all reasonable precautions and exercised all due diligence to avoid such a failure by himself or by those under his control. The cumulative nature of these requirements must be noted. The Secretary of State is empowered to grant further exemptions from the prohibitions under the Regulations.

The Regulations implement European obligations. Initially, the Community set limits on lead in petrol by Directive 78/611/EEC, both to reduce lead pollution of the atmosphere and to prevent barriers to car trade being set by different national systems. This Directive set upper and lower parameters for the lead content of petrol of 0.40 grams per litre (g/l) and 0.15 g/l. Under Directive 85/210/EEC, the Community required unleaded petrol to be widely available and promoted for use. Directive 87/416/EEC furthered these policies by enabling prohibitions to be placed on the sale of regular leaded petrol, ie 'two star'. Directive 85/210/EEC also required Member States to reduce the maximum lead content in petrol to 0.15 g/l as soon as appropriate. Similarly, the benzene content of both leaded and unleaded petrol may not exceed five per cent by volume since 1 October 1989. Oil companies in the UK in the 1970s were already decreasing the lead content of petrol, but the powers to impose mandatory requirements, now found in CAA 1993, were included as s 75 of the Control of Pollution Act 1974, at least partly in contemplation of anticipated Community legislation. Thereafter, a number of regulations were made, eg SI 1976/1866, as amended by SI 1979/1, which introduced the upper parameter for the lead content of petrol of 0.40 g/l by 1 January 1981, and SI 1981/1523 which introduced the upper limit of 0.15 g/l by 31 December 1985.

In parallel with the progressive reduction of the maximum permitted lead content of petrol, and its increasingly wide availability throughout the 1980s, requirements were made that all new models of car over two litres should be capable of running on 'lead-free' petrol, with the same requirement applying to all new models from 1 October 1989, and all new registrations from 1 October 1990. Fiscal measures were also introduced to promote the use of unleaded petrol by budget measures in 1987 and 1988, the latter giving unleaded petrol a specific price advantage over leaded so that, for example, by 1991, unleaded petrol was 14p per gallon cheaper than leaded. Thus, while in early 1988, only 3.5 per cent of petrol outlets retailed unleaded petrol, by June 1989 the figure was 50 per cent, and by January 1991, 98 per cent. Similarly, in April 1989, unleaded petrol sales constituted 15 per cent of the market, rising to 28.3 per cent in December 1989, 37.3 per cent in December 1990, and, in January 1991, 70 per cent of cars on UK roads could run on lead-free petrol.[1] Under the EC 1996 'Auto/Oil Programme', it has been agreed that a Directive should be made to phase out general sales of leaded petrol by 1 January 2000.

1 Those wishing to know more of the history of this issue and the various arguments over the need to reduce lead in petrol are referred to Haigh, *Manual of Environmental Policy: The EC and Britain* (Cartermill), Section 6.7, to which indebtedness is acknowledged.

9.4.1 Sulphur content of gas oil

'Gas oil' refers to certain medium distillates of petroleum used as fuel, and includes 'diesel fuel' which is used in 'compression ignition' vehicles (as opposed to the more common spark ignition). Particular limits are set under EC law for the sulphur content of gas fuel. The European Community first took action on this issue in 1973 as part of a programme to remove barriers to trade experienced by oil manufacturers in complying with different national standards. In 1975, Directive 75/716/EEC allowed the use of type A gas oil with a sulphur content by weight of 0.5 per cent, and type B with a content of 0.8 per cent. Type A oil could be used anywhere in the European Community, but type B could be used only in designated areas. The content limits were to last until October 1980, when they were to be lowered to 0.3 per cent and 0.5 per cent respectively. Directive 87/219/EEC removed the distinction between type A and type B oil, setting a maximum sulphur content of 0.3 per cent, with a permissive lower limit of 0.2 per cent. A number of States took this permissive option and, by 1991, the option applied in Belgium, Denmark, Germany, Luxembourg and The Netherlands, with Directive 92/13/EEC applying a Community-wide limit of 0.2 per cent.[1]

Legislation to implement these requirements existed in the UK initially under ss 75 to 77 of the Control of Pollution Act 1974, but is now enacted by s 30 of CAA 1993. To meet the requirements of Directive 93/12/EEC, the current regulations are the Marketing of Gas Oil (Sulphur Content) Regulations 1994, SI 1994/2249, and the Motor Fuel (Composition and Content) Regulations 1994, referred to above. These replaced earlier regulations as from 1 October 1994. The Regulations prohibit the marketing of 'gas oil' whose sulphur content exceeds 0.2 per cent by weight, with the enforcement of sampling etc entrusted to local authorities. The 1994 Regulations further reduced the 0.2 per cent limit on sulphur content in diesel fuel set in 1994 to 0.05 per cent from 1996. As a financial incentive to boost the use of even lower sulphur diesel oils, in November 1996 the Government announced an intention to introduce a 1p per litre duty differential for diesel fuel with a sulphur content up to 0.005 per cent. Such ultra low' sulphur fuels may lead to reductions in emissions of particulates by between 15 and 30 per cent. The scheme received EC approval in June 1997 and was introduced under s 7 of the Finance Act 1997.[2]

9.5 VEHICLE CONSTRUCTION STANDARDS

UK law mirrors EC requirements which, over the years, and by somewhat tortuous paths, have generally imposed stricter emission limits on motor vehicles. Initially, Directives on vehicle exhausts were introduced in order to

1 See also Directive 93/12/EEC.

2 See Haigh, *Manual of Environmental Policy: The EC and Britain* (Cartermill), to which indebtedness is acknowledged, see also SI 1997/1960.

promote the harmonisation of trade, and Directives issued between 1970 and 1988 were 'permissive' or 'optional' in the sense that no Member State had to introduce their terms as mandatory national requirements. However, vehicles complying with the terms of these Directives could not be refused 'type approval' (see further below) or the opportunity of being marketed in Member States. The development of those Directives was further guided by non-binding regulations used by the United Nations Economic Commission for Europe (UNECE), which generally applied to all States in Europe, not just those of the European Community.

9.6 DEVELOPMENT OF EC REQUIREMENTS

Under Directive 70/220/EEC, limits were set on emissions of carbon monoxide (CO) and unburnt hydrocarbons (HC) in respect of petrol engined vehicles, with the exception of tractors and public works vehicles. These limits were then made more strict by Directive 74/290/EEC, while Directive 77/102/EEC introduced a limit for nitrogen oxide (NO*x*) emissions. The limits for all these emissions were further reduced by Directive 78/665/EEC. By the early 1980s, however, developing concern over the acidification of Europe's forests led to mounting pressure for even stricter vehicle emission rules, a pressure which was more potent following the Single European Act 1986 which introduced qualified majority voting in Community decision-making on environmental issues. Germany, with its powerful Green Party, led the call for 'clean' cars, and was supported in its calls for the fitting of three-way catalytic converters by Denmark and The Netherlands, although opposed by the UK, France and Italy, whose 'small car' industries argued that the fitting of catalytic converters would be so prohibitively expensive that they favoured the introduction of 'lean burn' engines. While this debate continued, however, Directive 83/351/EEC introduced generally stricter emission standards in respect of CO, HC and NO*x*, and limits on emissions of these pollutants from diesel engines.

Under Directive 88/76/EEC, a move was made away from setting emission limits according to vehicle weight or 'reference mass', which had previously characterised EC practice. Instead, bands were introduced based on engine size: above two litres, 1.4 to two litres, and under 1.4 litres. This reflected the differing views of Member States above. Three-way catalytic converters were introduced by Directive 88/76/EEC for cars of two litres or more – the Directive itself being made under the qualified majority voting system. However, a 'second-stage' reduction was needed, and, following tough negotiation and the intervention of the European Parliament under powers obtained by virtue of the Single European Act 1986, even stricter emission limits for small cars were introduced by virtue of Directive 89/458/EEC, which were also in line with standards introduced in the USA and Japan. There then followed a further restriction on emissions for medium and large cars in order that all new models should meet what were then the current US emission standards, by 31 July 1992. These limits were continued in Directive 91/441/

EEC, which was furthermore notable in applying, for the first time since 1985, uniform limits on all sizes of vehicles. The requirements under the Directive are mandatory and must be translated into the laws of Member States. Thus, all new model cars from July 1992 have had to be fitted with three-way catalytic converters, while a similar requirement has applied to all new registrations from 1 December 1992. The Directive applies not only to emissions of CO, HC and NO*x*, but also to CO emissions from idling engines, crankcase gases, VOC emissions, and the durability of anti-pollution devices. The Directive also improved test procedures for emissions standards by introducing an extra-urban driving cycle, while the Type II test of idling engines specifies that CO must not exceed 3.5 per cent of total exhaust emissions in the test overall; the Type III test requires that there should be no emissions from the crankcases of petrol engined cars; and the Type IV test requires a maximum of 2 g/test of HC evaporative emissions from petrol engined cars.

The emissions limits for cars (both petrol and diesel powered) set under Directive 91/441/EEC were, as stated, to come into force on 1 July 1992 for new models and 31 December 1992 for all new cars registered. However, further tightening of standards was required by Directive 94/12/EC, which applies both to petrol and diesel engined cars, and which covers new models from 1 January 1996 and all new registrations from 1 January 1997: this Directive also introduced a new method of checking to ensure that production line vehicles meet standards, which require vehicles to which they apply (motor vehicles with at least four wheels used to carry passengers) to have emissions (in grams per kilometre) of 2.2 (CO) and 0.5 (HC and NO*x*). For diesel vehicles with indirect injection, the figures are 1.0 (CO), 0.7 (HC and NO*x*) together with a particulate limit of 0.08. For diesel vehicles with direct injection, the figures are 1.0 (CO), 0.9 (HC and NO*x*) and 0.10 (particulates). Separate emission limits for commercial and light commercial vehicles applied under Directives 91/542/EEC and 93/59/EC. Directive 96/69/EC amends the vehicle exhaust legislation further to harmonise the requirements for 'Class II and III vehicles' (ie light commercial vehicles) with those previously applicable to cars. In addition Article 3 of this Directive continues to allow Member States to apply tax incentives to facilitate attaining the new emission limits, although they must inform the Commission of the introduction of, or any changes to, such incentives. Article 4 required the Commission to propose further emission limits by 30 June 1996, with these to be agreed by Member States by 31 December 1997, and in force from 2000. Any such limits must form part of an integrated and multi-directional approach to the vehicle exhaust problem, embracing all measures for reducing pollution. This provision indicated that over time the European Community will move not just in the direction of 'cleaner' vehicles, but also 'cleaner' fuels – and the costs of developments will fall not just on vehicle makers but also on the petroleum industry. However, in June 1996 under the 'Auto/Oil programme' the Commission's initial proposals related primarily to vehicles, with further limits to be imposed on both light commercial and heavy duty vehicles, and tighter rules in relation to vehicle inspection and maintenance. These measures were designed to reduce CO, VOCs and urban particulate emissions by 30 per cent on 1996 levels by 2010, with a 65 per cent reduction in NO*x*. The limits were to be in force for new vehicle types from 2000, and for all new vehicles from 2001. Test procedures were also to be modified to include the first 40 seconds from ignition, when emissions are greatest. Petrol engined cars with catalytic converters would have to be equipped with on-board diagnostic equipment to indicate converter failure, and 'in use compliance control' to verify an appropriate repair. Further 'indicative' emission limits were proposed for 2005 which would depend on developing 'de-NO*x*', catalytic converters for diesel engined vehicles, and 'pre-heat' converters for conventional cars. These proposals were not popular with vehicle makers who considered that too much of the emission-reduction burden would fall on them.

On 29 June 1998, it was announced that agreement had been reached between the Council of Ministers and the European Parliament under the conciliation process on new Directives for cars and light vans and new better quality motor fuels. Under these proposals, steps will be taken:

- to reduce exhaust emissions from cars and vans in two stages: the first stage, between 1 January 2000 and 1 January 2002 (depending on vehicle type), requiring 30–40 per cent reductions in emissions from petrol engined cars and of up to 50 per cent from diesel engined cars; the second stage, from 1 January 2005, to aim for a further 50 per cent reduction in emissions, with proposals for this to be submitted by the Commission by December 1999;
- to introduce and require on-board diagnostics systems for petrol cars and small vans from 1 January 2000, for diesels from 1 January 2003, and heavier vehicles will have to have such systems from 2005;
- to modify test procedures in respect of evaporative emissions;
- to introduce a new low temperature, 'cold start' (−7 per cent) emission test for petrol cars and smaller vans;
- to amend fuel specifications used in emission type approval tests;
- to introduce new in-service checks for vehicle emissions;
- to reduce from 1 January 2000 the maximum allowable sulphur content of petrol by 70 per cent to 150 ppm and of diesel by 30 per cent to 350 ppm, with further reductions from 2005 of 66 per cent and 71 per cent (ie 50 ppm) respectively;
- to allow Member States to offer from 2000 tax incentives on fuels meeting the 2005 standards;
- to require all vehicles in-use to meet agreed standards after 100,000 km or five years;
- to reduce the benzene content of petrol by 80 per cent.

For the future a further 'Auto/Oil II programme' is due to be completed in 1999. However, certain new technologies needed for the completion of the above 'package' still remain to be developed, for example, 'de-NO*x*' diesel catalysts.

For the moment, however, EC requirements apply a stringent set of uniform emission limits on all sizes of car. The UK meets these requirements generally under the terms of the Road Traffic Act 1988, and the Road Vehicles

(Construction and Use) Regulations 1986, SI 1986/1078, as amended by SI 1990/1131 implementing the requirements of Directives 88/77/EEC and 88/436/EEC, SI 1992/2137 implementing Directives 91/441/EEC and 91/542/EEC, SI 1993/2199 implementing Directive 93/59/EEC, SI 1996/2329 implementing Directives 91/542/EEC and 96/1/EC, SI 1995/2210 implementing Directive 94/12/EC, and SI 1997/1544 implementing Directive 96/69/EC. A more detailed examination of these measures is undertaken below.

9.7 VOLATILE ORGANIC COMPOUNDS

Volatile organic compounds (VOCs) is a generic term referring to compound materials given off from organic substances into the atmosphere in a volatile form. The term, of course, includes various fuels, as these are carbon based. More particularly in the present context the term refers to emissions from petrol being stored and distributed, as these are implicated in transboundary air pollution incidents. The 1991 VOC Protocol to the UNECE Convention on Long-Range Transboundary Pollution 1984 (the Geneva Convention) requires signatories to reduce their annual VOC emissions by 30 per cent between 1988 and 1999, a target accepted by the UK. The European Community, under the Fifth Environmental Action Programme, set VOC reduction targets of 10 per cent by 1996 and 30 per cent by 1999 relative to 1990 levels. While a comprehensive VOC reduction programme of Directives is still awaited, in 1994 legislation was put in place to deal with 500,000 tonnes of VOCs – approximately five per cent of total emissions – released from petrol storage and distribution. Directive 94/63/EC sets mandatory limits in respect of mobile petrol containers, and base limits – which Member States may exceed in national legislation in order, inter alia, to protect human health or the environment – in respect of storage installations at terminals, equipment for loading/unloading mobile containers at terminals, and loading into storage at service stations. The Directive lays down highly prescriptive rules to ensure that petrol vapours either are not given off, or are otherwise recovered so as not to pollute the atmosphere, with a 'target reference value' of reducing annual petrol losses consequent on loading and storage.

Thus, for storage and installation facilities at terminals the 'target' is 0.01 per cent of 'throughput weight', and to achieve this the storage tanks in question must be fitted with vapour recovery units or with extra external or internal roofs with specified seals; those not fitted with recovery units must be painted in specified colours to ensure reflection of heat of 70 per cent or more to prevent volatility. The 'target reference value' for loading and unloading mobile petrol containers at terminals is 0.005 per cent of 'throughput weight', with relevant equipment being fitted with vapour recovery units in order that petrol vapour may be regenerated. The equipment must be regularly monitored, and must be shut down where a leak is detected. The maximum vapour concentration in exhaust from a vapour recovery unit is 35 grams per cubic metre as an hourly average, although in the UK a higher limit of 50 grams per cubic metre is permitted for units installed before 1 January 1993, and up to 31 December 2004. Mobile containers – which means petrol road tankers – must be so designed and operated that after unloading they retain any residual vapour; they must also retain any vapours from storage tanks at service stations or terminals. Equipment for loading into tanks at service stations has a 'target reference value' of 0.01 per cent of 'throughput weight'. To this end, relevant equipment must return vapours given off during petrol delivery to the mobile container delivering it.

The foregoing requirements were made mandatory for new installations, terminals, containers and service stations as from 31 December 1995. For existing facilities, the requirements will be introduced on a rolling programme, largely determined by 'throughput weights', between 31 December 1998 and 31 December 2004. The UK, however, missed the first date, although its requirements came into force on 1 December 1996 under the Environmental Protection (Prescribed Processes and Substances etc) (Amendment) (Petrol Vapour Recovery) Regulations 1996, SI 1996/2678.

It is now appropriate to examine in detail the UK legislation under which vehicle emission limits are set.

9.8 STATUTORY BASIS FOR VEHICLE EMISSION CONTROL

Section 41(1) of the Road Traffic Act 1988 empowers the Secretary of State to make regulations generally governing motor vehicles, their construction and equipment, and the conditions under which they may be used, and, in particular, under s 41(2) and (6) with regard to the emission or consumption of smoke, fumes or vapours, sparks, ashes or grit. This is a general regulatory power, and it appears that a breach of any regulations made under it does not give rise per se to a civil suit on the part of any injured individual.[1] However, under s 42 of the 1988 Act a person who fails to comply with any construction or use regulations made under s 41, or who uses on a road a non-compliant vehicle or causes or permits a motor vehicle to be so used, is guilty of an offence for which a fixed penalty applies under s 51 of, and Sch 3 to the Road Traffic Offences Act 1988. The statutory wording can apply to situations where a vehicle is stationary on a road while it is being loaded or unloaded,[2] or where a person controls, manages or operates a vehicle on a road, even extending to a person who hires out a vehicle and its driver.[3] 'Cause' or 'permit' bear their usual meanings in regulatory offences and predicate, in the

1 *Phillips v Britannia Hygienic Laundry Co Ltd* [1923] 2 KB 832; *Tan Chye Choo v Chong Kew Moi* [1970] 1 WLR 147.

2 *Andrews v HE Kershaw* [1922] 1 KB 70.

3 *Mickleborough v BRS (Contracts)* [1977] RTR 389.

case of 'cause', an element of dominating control over a vehicle, or some positive and express mandate in relation to it, while 'permit' connotes an act of giving a permission or licence with regard to a vehicle.[1] 'Permitting' a use further connotes some state of mind, eg knowledge of a relevant defect, although that knowledge may constructively exist where a person shuts his eyes to what is obvious,[2] so that failure to supervise a vehicle may amount to such a state of mind.[3] A merely negligent omission may not, however, amount to such a failure to supervise.[4] The relevant regulations for the purposes of s 41 are the Road Vehicles (Construction and Use) Regulations 1986, SI 1986/1078 (see further **9.9**).

9.8.1 Regular testing of vehicles

Under s 45(1) of the Road Traffic Act 1988, motor vehicles other than goods vehicles are subject to tests on whether they satisfactorily comply with construction and use regulations – the MOT test. Section 45(2) empowers the Secretary of State to make test regulations and to provide for vehicle examinations, while s 46 makes further provision, inter alia, as to the manner in which, and the conditions under which, tests are to be carried out. These regulations are the Motor Vehicles (Test) Regulations 1981, SI 1981/1694, as amended.

A person who uses a motor vehicle on a road at any time, or who causes or permits a motor vehicle to be so used, where that vehicle is not a goods vehicle but otherwise falls within the vehicle registration requirements of the vehicles (excise) legislation (ie the Vehicles (Excise) Acts 1949, 1962 and 1971, and the Roads Act 1920) is required generally to have a test certificate under s 47(1) of the 1988 Act to indicate compliance with vehicle testing regulations. The certificate is required normally when a vehicle has been registered for three years. However, where a vehicle is used for the carriage of passengers and has more than eight seats, excluding the driver's seat, or it is a taxi, ie a vehicle licensed to ply for hire under s 64(3) of the Transport Act 1980, or an ambulance, ie a vehicle constructed or adapted and primarily used to carry persons to or from a place where they will receive medical or dental treatment and is readily identifiable as such, the test certificate will be required one year after registration. It is an offence to fail to have the required test certificate. In this connection, s 192(1) states that a 'road' in relation to England and Wales means any highway and any other road to which the public have access, including road bridges. Thus, 'road' includes public highways, ie those ways over which there is a public right of passage, and those ways to which the public at large have access, which is expressly or impliedly allowed by the owner of the way in question, for example an access way to a farm,[5] or a cul de

1 *Howton v Buchanan* [1940] 2 All ER 179.
2 *Wilson v Bird* [1963] Crim LR 57.
3 *Brown v Burns Tractors Ltd* 1986 SCCR 146.
4 *Robinson v DPP* [1991] RTR 315.
5 *Harrison v Hall* 1932 JC 13.

sac between houses.[1] However, it will depend on the facts in each case whether any given area of land can constitute a 'road' in this connection.

9.8.2 Provisions with regard to goods vehicles

Section 49 of the Road Traffic Act 1988 empowers the Secretary of State, inter alia, to make regulations to enable goods vehicles to be examined to determine whether or not they comply with construction and use requirements. A 'goods vehicle' is defined by s 192(1) of the Act as a 'motor vehicle constructed or adapted for use for the carriage of goods, or a trailer so constructed or adapted'. This provision enables a comprehensive system of testing to be created, with special reference to goods vehicles, and, in particular, powers exist (see further below) to prohibit the driving of non-compliant vehicles. The specific regulations are found in the Goods Vehicles (Plating and Testing) Regulations 1988, SI 1988/1478. As the requirements are specific and comprehensive, s 50 of the 1988 Act allows for an appeal to be made by a person aggrieved by a test determination to the Secretary of State, who must then cause the vehicle in question to be re-tested and make a further determination of the matter. In particular, the Testing Regulations may, under s 51, provide for regular testing of goods vehicles at periodic intervals, and provide for the manner and mode of testing. As with non-goods vehicles, it is an offence to use, or cause or permit to be used, on a road a goods vehicle falling within the Testing Regulations without appropriate certification or 'plating'.

9.8.3 Type approval

Section 54 of the Road Traffic Act 1988 empowers the creation by the Secretary of State of a 'type approval' system for vehicles and vehicle parts in respect of design and construction requirements. 'Type approval requirements' ensure that new models of vehicles comply with certain standards before they may go into production, with each production model having to comply with the required standard. These requirements are in addition to any others which apply to the everyday operation of vehicles. Type approval has applied to all passenger motor vehicles manufactured after 1 October 1977, and those first used after 1 August 1978, although there are a few exempted vehicles such as ambulances, motorised caravans and vehicles temporarily in the UK from abroad. Type approval also applies, of course, to goods vehicles as well as passenger vehicles, and to diesel as well as petrol engined vehicles. The emission requirements with which type approval vehicles must conform are those set under EC Directives applicable at the date of their introduction.

Under s 55(1) of the 1988 Act, where the Secretary of State is satisfied (on an application made by the manufacturers of a vehicle falling within a class subject to regulations made under s 54) that the vehicle, after examination, complies with relevant type approval requirements, and that adequate arrangements have been made to secure that other vehicles purporting to conform with that

1 *Bass v Boynton* [1960] Crim LR 497.

test vehicle will, in fact, conform, the test vehicle may be approved as a 'type', and, under s 55(2), a 'type approval certificate' must then be issued. Type approval certificates may, under s 56, be issued subject to conditions providing for inspections by authorised officers of vehicles, parts and equipment which purport to conform with the approval. Officers have rights of entry to relevant manufacturing premises to carry out inspections. Conditions may also require manufacturers to notify any design or construction differences which could affect the approval requirements. Once a type approval certificate is issued, the manufacturer may proceed to issue other vehicles (or components) which conform to the approved type, provided a manufacturer's certificate is issued along with the vehicle component stating conformity (s 57).

In addition where, under s 58, the Secretary of State is satisfied after examination (following an application made to him by any person in respect of a vehicle of a class falling within regulations made under s 54) that the vehicle, inter alia, complies with relevant type approval requirements, he may issue a 'minister's approval certificate', which states that the vehicle complies with type approval requirements. This provision applies to goods vehicles. The manufacturer's certificate in relation to type approved goods vehicles must also, in addition to general requirements under s 57, state the 'plated weight' of the vehicle, ie under s 40(7) its weight as required to be stated on a fixed plate pursuant to construction regulations. Again, because the type approval requirements are so detailed and crucial to the marketing of classes of vehicles (eg a new type of car), where a person is aggrieved by a determination made on behalf of the Secretary of State in respect of a type approval certificate, or a minister's approval certificate, he may appeal to the Secretary of State within a prescribed time and in a prescribed manner. The Secretary of State must then redetermine the issue and may hold inquiries and appoint assessors in connection with assisting him with the appeal or holding the inquiry (s 60). Section 61 then further empowers the making of regulations for the purposes of ss 54 to 60, and the relevant provisions (as amended) are the Motor Vehicles (Type Approval for Goods Vehicles) (Great Britain) Regulations 1982, SI 1982/1271; the Motor Vehicles (Type Approval) (Great Britain) Regulations 1984, SI 1984/981; the Motor Vehicles (EC Type Approval) Regulations 1992, SI 1992/3107; and the Motor Vehicles (Type Approval and Approved Marks) (Fees) Regulations 1996, SI 1996/958.[1] The Regulations contain requirements in respect of vehicle emissions.

9.8.4 Other supplementary provisions

Section 62 of the Road Traffic Act 1988 not only empowers the Secretary of State to provide and maintain vehicle testing stations for the purposes of ss 54 to 61 and regulations made thereunder, but also to extend the type approval system to cover vehicles manufactured in other countries which have type approval systems recognised by the UK Government. This power is obviously

1 For the current detailed position, it is always essential to check, inter alia, the *Encyclopaedia of Road Traffic Law and Practice* (Sweet & Maxwell, 1996).

essential in respect of vehicles made by the UK's partner EC nations, and for this purpose ministers have issued the Motor Vehicles (Type Approval) (EEC Manufacturers) Regulations 1981, SI 1981/493, as amended. Section 63(1) makes it an offence for any person at any time after a date specified in regulations to use, or cause or permit to be used, on a road a vehicle of any prescribed class, or a vehicle having a part from a prescribed class of parts, where it does not appear from certificates issued under ss 54 to 58 that the vehicle or part in question complies with relevant type approval requirements.

However, under s 63(1(A)) a vehicle is taken to comply with all relevant type approval requirements if an EC Certificate of Conformity has effect with respect to the vehicle. Similarly, under s 65, it is an offence either to sell or supply a vehicle, or a part for a vehicle, where that vehicle or that part is subject to type approval requirements, without the requisite certification showing that the necessary approval has been given under ss 54 to 58. In this context, 'supply' includes selling, offering to sell or supply, and exposing for sale (s 65(2)). A similar offence exists in respect of the sale or supply of 'light passenger vehicles' which, under s 85, are defined as vehicles with at least four wheels, equipped with an internal combustion engine, constructed or adapted for the carriage of passengers, having no more than eight seats in addition to the driver's, and a maximum design speed exceeding 25 kilometres per hour. An EC Certificate of Conformity means any certificate of conformity issued by a manufacturer under reg 4 of the Motor Vehicles (EC Type Approval) Regulations 1992, SI 1992/3107, or under any provision or law of an EC Member State giving effect to the requirements of Council Directive 70/156/EEC on light passenger vehicle type approvals, as amended.

9.8.5 Vehicle examination

Vehicle examiners appointed by the Secretary of State under s 66A of the Road Traffic Act 1988 may, under s 67(1), test any motor vehicle on the road for the purpose, inter alia, of ascertaining whether it complies with construction and use requirements. This power may also be exercised by duly authorised constables or other persons appointed by the police authority for a given area, although, with the exception of constables, only on production of authority to act (s 67(4) and (5)). This provision thus authorises the carrying-out of roadside checks to ascertain whether emission limits are being complied with. Under s 67(9), it is an offence to obstruct an examiner while he is discharging his duties under the Act.

In addition, a vehicle examiner appointed under s 66A may at any time inspect goods vehicles, public service vehicles and motor vehicles which are not public service vehicles but which are adapted to carry more than eight passengers, or at any reasonable time enter any premises for test purposes, where he has reason to believe such a vehicle is being kept. An examiner may be required to produce his authority to act, but it is an offence intentionally to obstruct an examiner in the execution of his duties (s 68(1) and (3)).

Vehicle examiners and constables in uniform may, under s 68(4), at any time require any person in charge of a goods or public service vehicle etc, where that vehicle is stationary on a road, to proceed with that vehicle, for the purpose of having it inspected, to any place, within five miles of where the requirement is imposed, where such an inspection can suitably be made. Vehicles found to be unfit for service, or likely to become unfit for service, on any inspection under ss 41, 45, 49, 61, 67, 68 or 77 of the 1988 Act, may, under s 69(1), be made subject to a prohibition on their being driven, either absolutely or in relation to specified purposes. This power is entrusted to vehicle examiners. Such prohibitions generally come into force at a specified time not later than 10 days from the date of the inspection – the date to be fixed by the examiner having regard to all the circumstances (s 69(4)).

Under s 69(3), a prohibition may have immediate force where driving the vehicle would involve a danger of injury to any person. Prohibitions, once in force, continue until lifted under s 72, which occurs only when the vehicle has been officially tested and found to be fit (s 69(5)). However, where a prohibition is imposed, s 69(6) requires the person imposing the prohibition to give to the person in charge of the vehicle a written notice which specifies the defects occasioning the prohibition, the nature and extent of the prohibition, and the time at which it will come into effect. Such notices may subsequently be varied or even suspended once in force by an endorsement by any vehicle examiner or an authorised constable (s 69(8)). Such a prohibition on the driving of an unfit vehicle may, under s 69A, be made irremovable unless and until the vehicle in question has been inspected at a public service vehicle testing station or an official testing station provided under s 72A in respect of goods vehicle tests, or a vehicle testing station. It is an offence to drive a vehicle in contravention of a prohibition under s 69 (s 71). Section 72 sets out the requirements in respect of the removal of prohibition orders, the basic requirement under s 72(1) being that the vehicle examiner or authorised constable must be satisfied that the vehicle is fit for service. However, in respect of prohibitions imposed, coupled with directions under s 69A, the vehicle must in general be tested as directed before the prohibition may be removed. Where the examiner or constable in question refuses to remove a prohibition a person aggrieved may appeal to the Secretary of State, who then has a wide discretion to determine the issue (see further the Road Vehicles (Prohibition) Regulations 1992, SI 1992/1285).

9.8.6 Miscellaneous

Section 74(1) of the Road Traffic Act 1988 empowers the Secretary of State to make regulations to require goods vehicle operators to ensure that regular inspection of their vehicles takes place to ensure, inter alia, compliance with prescribed construction and use requirements. Under s 75(1), it is an offence to supply, sell or offer to sell or supply, or to expose for sale, any motor vehicle in an 'unroadworthy condition' – a term including, under s 75(3), any vehicle in such a condition that its use on the road would be unlawful under, inter alia, the Road Vehicles (Construction and Use) Regulations 1986 and s 41. Similarly, it is an offence under s 75(4) and (5) to alter a motor vehicle or to supply an altered vehicle, where its condition is such that it would contravene the 1986 Regulations. The offence under s 75(1) is one of strict liability.[1] Similar prohibitions apply to the fitting of parts to a vehicle so that its use on a road would, inter alia, constitute a contravention of the 1986 Regulations (s 76(1)).

9.9 THE DETAILED REGULATORY FRAMEWORK

The Road Vehicles (Construction and Use) Regulations 1986, as amended, provide the detailed general framework for limits on vehicle emissions, while type approval requirements generally are contained in the Motor Vehicles (EC Type Approval) Regulations 1992, although see also the Motor Vehicles (Type Approval) (Great Britain) Regulations 1984, SI 1984/981, as amended, and, for goods vehicles, the Motor Vehicles (Type Approval for Goods Vehicles) (Great Britain) Regulations 1982, SI 1982/1271, as amended.[2]

The general requirement of reg 61(1) of the 1986 Regulations is that vehicles must be so constructed and maintained as not to emit any avoidable smoke or avoidable visible vapour. This very vague and general requirement is, however, effectively superseded by reg 61(3B), which provides that vehicles may comply with the terms of 'relevant instruments', which is, of course, a reference to EC Directives (reg 61(4)). Regulation 61(5) and (6) further requires, inter alia, that no person may use, or cause or permit to be used, any motor vehicle on a road where any smoke, visible vapour, grit, sparks, ashes, cinders or oily substances are emitted if such an emission causes or is likely to cause damage to property or injury or damage to persons who may reasonably be expected to be on the road. Neither may petrol driven vehicles first used on or after 1 January 1972 be so used unless there is equipment fitted (and maintained in good working order) to ensure that while the engine is running any vapours or gases in the engine crankcase are prevented from escaping into the atmosphere otherwise than through the engine's combustion chamber. In general, a vehicle may not be used or be caused or permitted to be used on a road in contravention of relevant emission requirements for production models of that type of vehicle according to EC requirements, unless the failure to meet such requirements does not result from an alteration to the vehicle's propulsion unit or exhaust system, nor to a lack of normal maintenance work, nor from the failure of any device to control emissions of CO, HC, NO*x* or particulates by being other than in good and efficient working order (reg 61(7)). The various EC requirements, the dates from which they apply, and the vehicles to which they apply, are contained in Table II of reg 61. The substance of this is produced in Figure 1, with explanatory editorial comments given in italics.

1 *Sandford Motor Sales Ltd v Habgood* [1962] Crim LR 487.

2 To keep up with amendments, reference should be made to the *Encyclopaedia of Road Traffic Law and Practice* (Sweet & Maxwell, 1996).

Figure 1

(1) Item	(2) Class of Vehicle	(3) Date of First Use	(4) Design, Construction and Equipment Requirements (a) Instrument	(b) Place in Instrument where Requirements are Stated	(5) Vehicles Exempted from Requirement	(6) Emitted Substances
1	Vehicles propelled by spark ignition engine (*ie petrol driven vehicles such as cars*).	1 October 1982	Community Directive 78/665. (*The terms of EC Directives mirror those adapted by the UN Economic Commission for Europe (UNECE); hence, as an alternative to compliance with Directives it is generally acceptable for a vehicle to comply with relevant UNECE regulations.*)	Annex I, paragraphs 3 and 5 Paragraphs 5, 8 and 11	(a) A vehicle whose maximum gross weight exceeds 3,500 kg; (b) A vehicle which complies with the requirements of item 2, 4, 5, 8, 11 or 12; (c) A vehicle whose maximum speed is less than 50 km/h; (d) An exempt vehicle. (*'Exempt vehicle' where it appears means those with fewer than four wheels, or with a gross weight of less than 400 kg, or a maximum speed of less than 25 km/h, or an agricultural motor vehicle.*)	Carbon monoxide, hydrocarbons and oxides of nitrogen
2	All vehicles.	1 April 1991	Community Directive 83/351	Annex I, paragraphs 5, 7 and 8 Paragraphs 5, 8 and 12	(a) A vehicle propelled by a compression ignition engine and whose maximum gross weight exceeds 3,500 kg; (b) A vehicle which complies with the requirements of item 4, 5 8, 11 and 12; (c) A vehicle within the meaning given by Article 1 of Community Directive 88/77 and which complies with the requirements of item 6, 9 or 10; (*Directive 88/77 applies to diesel engines in commercial vehicles over 3.5 tonnes and sets its own limits in respect of CO, HC and NOx*) (d) An industrial tractor, works truck or engineering plant; (e) A vehicle whose maximum speed is less than 50 km/h; (f) An exempt vehicle.	Carbon monoxide, hydrocarbons and oxides of nitrogen
3	Industrial tractors, works trucks and engineering plant propelled in each case by a compression ignition engine (*ie diesel*).	1 April 1993	UNECE Regulation 49	Paragraphs 5 and 7	A vehicle which complies with the requirements of item 6, 9, 10, 11 and 12.	Carbon monoxide, hydrocarbons and oxides of nitrogen

(1) Item	(2) Class of Vehicle	(3) Date of First Use	(4) Design, Construction and Equipment Requirements (a) Instrument	 (b) Place in Instrument where Requirements are Stated	(5) Vehicles Exempted from Requirement	(6) Emitted Substances
4	Passenger vehicles which – (a) are constructed or adapted to carry not more than 5 passengers excluding the driver; and (b) have a maximum gross weight of not more than 2,500 kg, not being off-road vehicles.	1 April 1991	Community Directive 88/76 or Community Directive 89/458	Annex I, paragraphs 5, 7 and 8 Annex I, paragraphs 5, 7 and 8 Paragraphs 5, 8 and 13	(a) A vehicle which complies with the requirement of item 2, 8, 11 or 12; (b) A vehicle whose maximum speed is less than 50 km/h; (c) An exempt vehicle.	Carbon monoxide, hydrocarbons and oxides of nitrogen
5	Vehicles which are not of a description specified in this column in item 4 but which – (a) are propelled by a spark ignition engine and have a maximum gross weight of not more than 2,000 kg; or (b) are propelled by a compression ignition engine and have a maximum gross weight of more than 3,500 kg.	 1 April 1992 1 April 1991	Community Directive 88/76	Annex I, paragraphs 5, 7 and 8 Paragraphs 5, 8 and 13	(a) A vehicle within the meaning given by Article 1 of Community Directive 88/77 and which complies with the requirements of item 6, 9, 10, 11 or 12; (b) An industrial tractor, works truck or engineering plant; (c) A vehicle whose maximum speed is less than 50 km/h; (d) A vehicle which complies with the requirements of item 8; (e) An exempt vehicle.	Carbon monoxide, hydrocarbons and oxides of nitrogen
6	All vehicles propelled by compression ignition engines.	1 April 1991	Community Directive 88/77	Annex I, paragraphs 6, 7 and 8	(a) A vehicle whose maximum gross weight is less than 3,500 kg and which complies with the requirements of item 2; (b) A vehicle which complies with the requirements of item 4, 5, 8, 9, 10, 11 or 12; (c) A fire appliance which is first used before 1 October 1992; (d) An industrial tractor, works truck or engineering plant; (e) An exempt vehicle.	Carbon monoxide, hydrocarbons and oxides of nitrogen

(1) Item	(2) Class of Vehicle	(3) Date of First Use	(4) Design, Construction and Equipment Requirements (a) Instrument	(4) (b) Place in Instrument where Requirements are Stated	(5) Vehicles Exempted from Requirement	(6) Emitted Substances
7	Passenger vehicles which – (a) are constructed or adapted to carry not more than 5 passengers excluding the driver; (b) have a maximum gross weight of not more than 2,500 kg; and (c) are propelled by a compression ignition engine of the indirect injection type. (*Indirect injection refers to a fuel injection system utilising injection as a subsidiary part of a divided combustion chamber, as opposed to direct injection where there is an open combustion chamber or where fuel is injected directly into the main part of a divided chamber.*)	1 April 1991	Community Directive 88/436	Annex I, paragraphs 5, 7 and 8, as far as they relate to particular emissions	(a) A vehicle which complies with the requirements of item 8, 11 or 12; (b) A vehicle whose maximum speed is less than 50 km/h; (c) An off-road vehicle; (d) An exempt vehicle.	Particulates
8	All vehicles.	31 December 1992	Community Directive 91/441	Annex I, paragraphs 5, 7 and 8 Paragraphs 5, 8 and 13	(a) A vehicle within the meaning given by Article 1 of Community Directive 88/77 and which – (i) complies with the requirements of item 6 and is first used before 1 October 1993, or (ii) complies with the requirements of item 9, 10, 11 or 12; (b) An industrial tractor, works truck or engineering plant; (c) A vehicle whose maximum speed is less than 50 km/h; (d) An exempt vehicle.	Carbon monoxide, hydrocarbons, oxides of nitrogen and particulates
9	All vehicles propelled by a compression ignition engine.	1 October 1993	Community Directive 91/542	Annex I, paragraphs 6, 7 and 8 (excluding line B in the Tables in sub-paragraphs 6.2.1 and 8.3.1.1) Paragraphs 5, 6 and 7 (excluding line B in the Tables in sub-paragraphs 5.2.1 and 7.4.2.1)	(a) A vehicle which complies with the requirements of item 8, 10, 11 or 12; (b) An industrial tractor, works truck or engineering plant; (c) An exempt vehicle.	Carbon monoxide, hydrocarbons, oxides of nitrogen and particulates

(1) Item	(2) Class of Vehicle	(3) Date of First Use	(4) Design, Construction and Equipment Requirements (a) Instrument	(b) Place in Instrument where Requirements are Stated	(5) Vehicles Exempted from Requirement	(6) Emitted Substances
10	All vehicles propelled by a compression ignition engine.	1 October 1996	Community Directive 91/542	Annex I, paragraphs 6, 7 and 8 Paragraphs 5, 6 and 7	(a) A vehicle which complies with the requirements of item 8, 11 or 12; (b) An industrial tractor, works truck or engineering plant; (c) An exempt vehicle.	Carbon monoxide, hydrocarbons, oxides of nitrogen, and particulates
11	All vehicles.	1 October 1994	Community Directive 93/59	Annex I, paragraphs 5, 7 and 8	(a) A vehicle within the meaning given by Article 1 of Community Directive 88/77 and which complies with the requirements of item 9, 10 or 12; (b) An industrial tractor, works truck or engineering plant; (c) Vehicles whose maximum speed is less than 50 km/h; (d) An exempt vehicle.	Carbon monoxide, hydrocarbons, oxides of nitrogen, and particulates
12	All vehicles.	1 January 1997	Community Directive 94/12	Annex I, paragraphs 5, 7 and 8	(a) A vehicle within the meaning given by Article 1 of Community Directive 88/77 and which complies with the requirements of item 9, 10 or 11; (b) An industrial tractor, works truck or engineering plant; (c) Vehicles whose maximum speed is less than 50 km/h; (d) An exempt vehicle.	Carbon monoxide, hydrocarbons, oxides of nitrogen and particulates
13	All vehicles.	1 October 1997	Community Directive 96/97	Annex I, paragraphs 5, 7 and 8	(a) A vehicle within the meaning given by Article 1 of Community Directive 88/77 and which complies with the requirements of item 9, 10 or 12; (b) A vehicle as defined in column 2 of item 14; (c) An industrial tractor, works truck or engineering plant; (d) Vehicles whose maximum speed is less than 50 km/h; (e) An exempt vehicle.	Carbon monoxide, hydrocarbons, oxides of nitrogen and particulates

(1) Item	(2) Class of Vehicle	(3) Date of First Use	(4) Design, Construction and Equipment Requirements		(5) Vehicles Exempted from Requirement	(6) Emitted Substances
			(a) Instrument	(b) Place in Instrument where Requirements are Stated		
14	Vehicles falling within – (a) Class II or III as specified in the Annex to Community Directive 96/69, of Category N1; or (b) Category M and specified in footnote (2) of that Annex. (*This means light commercial vehicles.*)	1 October 1998	Community Directive 96/69	Annex I, paragraphs 5, 7 and 8	(*There are no exemptions as this item is meant to end a particular exemption for light commercial vehicles.*)	Carbon monoxide, hydrocarbons, oxides of nitrogen and particulates

9.9.1 Type approval regulations

The principal current type approval regulations are the Motor Vehicle (EC Type Approval) Regulations 1992, SI 1992/3107, which implement Directive 92/53/EEC and effectively replace much of the earlier legislation as far as light passenger vehicles (eg motor cars) are concerned. Under the Directive, Member States may not register, or permit the sale or entry into service of vehicles not accompanied by a valid EC Certificate of Conformity: equally, vehicles with such a certificate may not be refused sale or entry into service. The Directive also has a general applicability to certain motor vehicle parts. The Regulations came into force on dates between 1 January 1993 and 1 January 1996.

Under reg 3(1) to (3), applications for EC type approval or for amendment of an approval must be made to the Secretary of State, and must be made in writing accompanied by documentation as required under the Directive. Where approval is given or amended an appropriate certificate must be issued in a form conforming to Directive requirements; similarly, approvals may be given to components etc. A refusal of certification, which must be accompanied by a notice to the applicant, may be decided upon if the Secretary of State considers that the applicant has not made adequate arrangements to comply with the requirements of reg 4(2), 5 or 6 (see below). There is also a general power under reg 3(10) to refuse a certificate where there are no adequate arrangements to ensure that production vehicles conform to the EC approved type.

Under reg 4(2), holders of EC vehicle type approvals must, for 10 years, keep records of each certificate of conformity issued by them in respect of the certificate's serial number, the identity number of the vehicle to which the certificate relates and the reference numbers of the Directives with which the vehicle conforms. Regulation 5 requires certificate holders to give to the Secretary of State undertakings that they will carry out tests and checks at specified intervals to verify conformity of production, and to keep records of such tests etc for 10 years. There is also a general obligation on holders under reg 6 to co-operate with the Secretary of State in the performance of his functions under the Directive.

Where the Secretary of State, after an examination has been carried out on his behalf on two or more type approved light passenger vehicles (or components as the case may be), is satisfied that there is a failure of conformity he may, by notice to the holder, withdraw the EC type approval (reg 8(2)). Alternatively, approval may be suspended under reg 8(3) where the Secretary of State is satisfied that there is a failure to comply with the requirements of reg 4(2), reg 5, reg 6 or reg 7 (which applies to components), or that there are inadequate arrangements for ensuring production line conformity with type approval. Notice of the proposed withdrawal or suspension must be given to the holder under reg 8(4) together with supporting reasons, and giving the holder 28 days' grace to make representations, which must be taken into account before the decision is finalised. Suspensions may be revoked by the Secretary of State. Any certificates of conformity issued during a suspension are invalid (reg 8(6) and (7)).

Part III of the 1992 Regulations provides that a first licence or registration of a light passenger vehicle may not take place generally after 1 January 1996 unless it has either an EC Certificate of Conformity or a minister's approval certificate under s 58(1) of the Road Traffic Act 1988 (see **9.8.3**). However, under reg 9 the Secretary of State may direct that all EC Certificates of Conformity shall be invalid for a specified period of not more than six months if he considers that the relevant vehicles are a serious risk to road safety.

Regulation 11 makes it an offence to forge, alter or use with intent to deceive an EC type approval certificate, and this applies to anyone who lends or allows to be used such documents, or who makes or possesses any documentation which so closely resembles a type approval certificate as to be calculated to deceive. Similarly, it is an offence to make false statements intentionally or recklessly in supplying information or documents for the purposes of EC type approval, or intentionally or recklessly to produce, provide, send or make use of documents which are false in material particulars.

Regulations 12 and 13 lay down the detailed framework for review of notices given by the Secretary of State. 'Relevant notices' are, inter alia, those under reg 3(4) (refusal of type approval), reg 8(2) (withdrawal of approval), reg 8(3) (suspension of approval), and reg 10(10) (refusal of first registration of a vehicle). Regulation 12(1) requires the notice to specify the reason for the decision, and to state the recipient's right to request a review of the decision, and the time-limits for that request. Regulation 13(1) to (3) provides as follows:

> '(1) Where the Secretary of State has given a relevant notice to a person, that person may by notice request the Secretary of State to review the decision to which the relevant notice relates.
>
> (2) Such a request must be made by the person within 28 days from the date that he receives the relevant notice.

(3) On any review under this regulation the Secretary of State may –
(a) hold an inquiry in connection with it, and
(b) appoint an assessor for the purpose of assisting him with the review or any such inquiry.'

Regulation 14 (as amended) further provides:

'(1) Any document required or authorised by virtue of these Regulations to be given to any person by the Secretary of State may be given –
(a) by delivering it to him or by leaving it at his proper address or by sending it by post to him at that address, or
(b) if the person is a body corporate, by serving it in accordance with sub-paragraph (a) on the secretary or clerk of that body, or
(c) if the person is a partnership, by serving it in accordance with sub-paragraph (a) on a partner or a person having the control or management of the partnership business.

(2) For the purposes of this regulation and section 7 of the Interpretation Act 1978 (which relates to the service of documents by post) in its application to this regulation, the proper address of any person on whom a document is to be served shall be his last known address, except that –
(a) in the case of service on a body corporate or its secretary or clerk, it shall be the address of the registered or principal office of the body.
(b) in the case of service on a partnership or a partner or a person having the control or management of a partnership business, it shall be the address of the principal office of the partnership,
and for the purposes of this paragraph the principal office of a company registered outside the United Kingdom, or a partnership carrying on business outside the United Kingdom is its principal office within the United Kingdom.

(3) If a person to be served by virtue of these Regulations with any document by the Secretary of State has specified to the Secretary of State an address within the United Kingdom other than his proper address (as determined in pursuance of paragraph (2)) as the one at which he or someone on his behalf will accept documents of the same description as that document, that address shall also be treated as his proper address for the purposes of this regulation and for the purposes of the said section 7 in its application to this regulation.'

Regulation 15 empowers the Secretary of State to provide testing stations where relevant vehicles and components may be tested.

9.9.2 Stopping engines of stationary vehicles

Although it is entitled a 'control of noise' provision, reg 98 of the Road Vehicles (Construction and Use) Regulations 1982 lays down requirements that have particular relevance for air quality.[1] Drivers of stationary vehicles are required to stop the action of any machinery, including the engine, attached to or forming part of the vehicle, as necessary, for the prevention of noise. This requirement does not, however, apply: (a) where the vehicle is stopped in traffic; (b) so as to prevent the examination or working of the machinery in question where such examination is made necessary by any failure or

1 See further Chapter 10.

derangement of the machinery, or where the machinery must be worked for a purpose other than driving the vehicle (eg a mobile concrete-mixer lorry delivering on site); or (c) in respect of vehicles propelled by on-board gas producer plant.

CHAPTER 10

AIR QUALITY

10.1 INTRODUCTION

In Chapter 8, it was stated that the clean air legislation had not proved capable of dealing with forms of atmospheric pollution other than smoke. As 'smoke stack' industries declined throughout the second half of the twentieth century, it became apparent that while the visible pollution of smoke was largely disappearing, the less visible pollutants from industry and transport, such as sulphur dioxide, nitrogen oxides, carbon monoxide, benzene, etc, also needed to be tackled. Insofar as controls exist over emissions from industry they are to be found in the integrated pollution control (IPC) and local authority air pollution control (LAAPC) systems under the Environmental Protection Act 1990 (EPA 1990)).[1] Specific controls over the construction of motor vehicles and the fuels they use are considered in Chapter 9. There is, however, a broader issue of air quality which cuts across the neat boundaries of individual Acts of Parliament. This arises partly as a result of the UK's European obligations, which have forced us to develop a specific policy for the quality of the medium of air (as opposed to the traditional, British method of controlling individual polluting sources), and partly because of a growing perception that air quality is a major issue in itself.

10.1.1 The air we breathe and our health

The August 1997 issue of *Occupational and Environmental Medicine* contained a correlation of some 400,000 hospital admissions in London in the 1980s and 1990s with the levels of five key pollutants produced mainly by traffic. There were strong indications that daily heart and circulatory disease admissions were linked to episodes of poor air quality on the previous day. In particular, heart attacks rose in line with the previous daily levels of carbon monoxide, nitrogen dioxide, sulphur dioxide and particulate material. The linkage occurred during the months of October to March, when cold air trapped over London prevented traffic fumes from dispersing. It was argued that traffic emissions trigger blood circulation disorders, and, further, that one in 50 heart attack victims in London hospitals were there as a consequence of poor air quality. It was concluded that some 6,000 heart attacks arise each year from this cause, although there may well be other contributory factors. This evidence graphically highlighted the fact that it is the *use* of the motor car, not just its construction and fuel, which may need to be curbed.

---

1 See Chapters 6 and 7.

Further research by the Committee on the Medical Effects of Air Pollutants, *Quantification of the Effects of Air Pollution on Health in the UK*, published in 1998, indicated that atmospheric pollution, particularly urban smog, leads to up to 24,000 hospital admissions each year, and hastens the deaths of between 12,000 and 24,000 otherwise vulnerable people, eg those already seriously ill with respiratory diseases. This compares with cold spells between October and March each year, which hasten some 30,000 deaths. Other research[1] shows that peak levels of low-level ozone caused by reactions largely occurring between volatile organic compounds and nitrogen oxides in the presence of sunlight have decreased by 20 per cent since 1987 – but average levels are still increasing. In summer, levels of ozone frequently exceed thresholds for damaging effects on crops, vegetation and human health, particularly on uplands and in the south of England. Even average ozone levels can damage rubber and plastics.

10.1.2 The legislative basis for a National Air Quality Strategy

The Environment Act 1995, which will be considered at length below, contains the legislative basis for a National Air Quality Strategy, although much of the Strategy will be achieved under other legislation. Under the Strategy, moves may be made to tackle 'lifestyle issues' such as car use, but probably only to a limited extent. However, local authorities, for example, will be able to impose spot fines on motorists whose vehicles fail to meet emission controls (see further below). Whether authorities may be encouraged to go further and introduce bans on vehicle use is another issue. The Road Traffic Regulation Act 1984 grants powers to regulate traffic, inter alia, to preserve or improve the amenities of areas through which roads run – 'amenity' here meaning the pleasantness and enjoyability of an area.[2] In relation to trunk roads, the appropriate authority is the Secretary of State; otherwise, under s 1 of the 1984 Act, the matter rests with the county council, metropolitan district or unitary authority as the case may be, and, in Greater London, with the London boroughs under s 6.

Traffic regulation orders may provide for the prohibition, restriction or other regulation of vehicular traffic, either specifically or in general terms. Under s 122 of the 1984 Act, authorities are, however, generally required to secure the expeditious, convenient and safe *movement* of traffic, having had regard, inter alia, to the amenities of affected localities. While the Environment Act 1995 amends the 1984 Act to provide that relevant authorities may make orders to achieve the purposes of the National Air Quality Strategy, and are to take the Strategy into account in exercising road traffic regulation functions, it remains unclear how far an authority may go in restricting the flow of traffic in episodes of traffic-induced atmospheric pollution. It has been pointed out in court that there is no point making an order if its only effect is to create more

1 *Ozone in the United Kingdom 1997* (Photochemical Oxidants Review Group).
2 *Cartwright v Post Office* [1968] 2 All ER 646.

congestion and pollution elsewhere as drivers seek to use roads not affected by an order.[1] The ministerial view under the Conservative Government was that it would be wrong to use the 1984 Act's powers on a temporary or ad hoc basis where no advance notice is given of restrictions. Ministers did, however, consider that the power to restrict traffic could be used on environmental grounds to provide for contingency orders which, on a planned, publicised basis, regulate traffic movement and which come into effect by the unveiling of restriction signs when particular pollution levels are reached.

Further guidance on the use of these powers was given in *Air Quality and Traffic Management*.[2] A traffic regulation order (TRO) may be made to pursue air quality objectives; this can be pursued in London without restriction, but in other areas a TRO made for the purposes of such objectives cannot restrict access for more than eight hours in any 24 hours to premises on, or adjacent to, restricted roads. In all cases where a TRO is used it must be carefully planned, with full and accurate signing, and preferably with alternative routes which should be signalled well in advance of the restriction. Attention should also be paid to whether restricted routes will need an enforcement presence and/or some form of physical restriction. A TRO may be permanent, periodic or applicable only at particular times; it should be employed only after consideration has been given to minimising the loss of overall accessibility to an area, particularly for delivery or disabled drivers. In general, authorities are warned against making TROs which come into force only when particular pollution levels are reached because of the problems of giving sufficient advance warning to drivers and the need to make arrangements for enforcement and diversion of traffic. The guidance further repeats the general policy that ad hoc responses to particular pollution episodes are unlikely to be effective. Where low emission vehicle types exist or are developed it may be appropriate to apply TROs to particular types of vehicles which do not meet emission standards in order to ban them from areas of concern. Alternatively, authorities may consider the use of systems found in some European mainland cities where TROs are used to restrict access to an area to all except residents, essential vehicles and badge holders. Roads could then be closed by barriers which can be opened only by use of, eg smart card technology. TROs may also be used to reallocate highway space by the introduction of bus or cycle lanes. In principle, it is also possible to use a TRO a create a high occupancy vehicle lane available only to vehicles carrying more than a specified number of persons.

Powers to regulate parking also exist under the 1984 Act with regard to the location, availability and cost of parking, and with regard to on-street and municipal off-street facilities. Authorities may then withdraw public parking spaces, or so price parking that it favours, inter alia, park and ride schemes or vehicles with more than one passenger. With regard to the regulation of privately owned public parking, conditions may be imposed under the 1984

1 *R v Greenwich London Borough ex parte Jack Williams* (1995) 253 *ENDS Report* 49.

2 LAQMG3(97), paras 5.06 et seq.

Act stipulating the number of places available, quotas of long-term, short-term, regular and casual parking, and tariff scales and opening hours, although little use has been made of these in the past because of the ability of car park owners to claim compensation for reduced income. Controls may also be imposed on the provision of private parking associated with new developments under planning controls.

10.1.3 Road traffic reduction legislation

The Road Traffic Reduction Act 1997 entrusts local traffic authorities to prepare reports on the level of road traffic in their areas. Under s 2(1) of that Act, the Secretary of State may direct such authorities from time to time to make reports assessing local road traffic levels in their areas and forecasting the growth of those levels. It is the duty of authorities then to prepare such reports. In particular, s 2(2) requires that targets should be specified in those reports for reducing local road traffic levels and their rate of growth. Such targets need not be specified (s 2(5)) where an authority consider it inappropriate, although in such cases they must say why, and give reasons. Under s 2(4), reports may specify different reduction targets for different parts of an authority's area, or for different classes of local traffic, and may variously specify target reductions with regard to both areas and classes. Section 2(6) empowers the Secretary of State to issue guidance to authorities on the preparation and content of reports, and on consultation in connection with preparing a report, and that guidance has to be considered by authorities. Finally, under s 2(7) and (8), where a report is made a copy must be sent by the preparing authority to the Secretary of State, who must lay it before each House of Parliament. The authority must also generally publish the report as they consider appropriate. The Act does not, however, apply to national or 'trunk' and 'special' roads (motorways) for which the Secretary of State is the highway authority.

The Road Traffic Reduction Act 1997, which reached the statute book unexpectedly in the last days of the Conservative Government, has (at the middle of 1998) yet to be brought into force. Guidance on its implementation was promised by LAQMG3(97), and it has been superseded by the Road Traffic Reduction (National Targets) Act 1998 (which received Royal Assent on 2 July 1998). This Act makes provision for nationally created programmes of reduction targets. The legislation is a further indication that vehicle use may come to be increasingly restricted, particularly in urban areas, and especially as the National Air Quality Strategy is implemented. However, before that is examined, regard must be had to generally relevant European obligations, and the long-standing provisions relating to information on air pollution found in the Clean Air Act 1993.

10.2 EUROPEAN AIR QUALITY ISSUES

The European Community developed a stance on air quality comparatively late in its growth, largely in response to pressures from Member States, such as Germany, which were suffering from transboundary pollution. Among other measures, the European Community then developed a range of air quality limit values (AQLVs), which prescribe legal maxima for the presence of given pollutants in ambient air over particular time periods, the idea being to set a particular 'limit' value for the exposure of human beings which is considered to be safely below likely lethal or damaging exposure limits. In addition, the European Community adopted a 'standstill' principle so that deterioration of air quality under the various standards set does not occur. There are therefore AQLVs for sulphur dioxide and suspended particulates (smoke) under Directive 80/779/EEC, for lead under Directive 82/884/EEC, for nitrogen dioxide under Directive 85/203/EEC, and for ozone under Directive 92/72/EEC. In addition, measuring and sampling procedures for the various pollutants are laid down. To meet its obligations under the first three Directives, the UK introduced the Air Quality Standards Regulations 1989, SI 1989/317, as amended by the Air Quality Standards (Amendment) Regulations 1995, SI 1995/3146, which, however, effect no more than minor, aesthetic amendments to the principal Regulations.

The limit values are as follows:

Figure 2. Sulphur dioxide and suspended particulates (smoke)

Reference Period	*Smoke*	*Sulphur Dioxide*
All year (median of daily values)	80 micrograms per cubic metre (pcm)	120 micrograms pcm if smoke is less than 40 micrograms pcm 80 micrograms pcm if smoke is more than 40 micrograms pcm
Winter (median of winter values) – 1 October to 31 March	130 micrograms pcm	180 micrograms pcm if smoke is less than 60 micrograms pcm 130 micrograms pcm if smoke is more than 60 micrograms pcm
Year (peak) 98 per cent of daily values	250 micrograms pcm	350 micrograms pcm if smoke is less than 150 micrograms pcm 250 micrograms pcm if smoke is more than 150 micrograms pcm

The UK has largely achieved these values by action taken under the clean air legislation in respect of smoke, although not until the beginning of the 1990s was there compliance in all areas with smoke control provisions. 'Suspended particulates' can also include dust, however, and with regard to quarrying and opencast mining operations it is also now the practice of the DETR to consider dust-generation issues if there is an appeal against a refusal of a mining/quarrying planning permission application, to ensure that EC limits are not broken. The sulphur standards are met by action taken under EPA 1990 with regard to IPC and LAAPC authorisations.[1]

The Air Quality Standards Regulations 1989 (reg 4) require the Secretary of State, in relation to lead in ambient air, to take:

> '... necessary measures to ensure that the mean annual value of concentration of lead in air [measured by sampling stations installed at sites where individuals may be exposed to lead in air continually for a long period and where on the opinion of the Secretary of State the limit value is likely to be exceeded] does not exceed the limit value of 2 micrograms of lead per cubic metre expressed as an annual mean concentration.'

The obligation has been met by the creation of a network of monitoring sites nationwide since 1985, and by the introduction of unleaded petrol for motor vehicles.[2] UK ambient air local levels are now well below the limit values, and continue to fall.

Limits for nitrogen dioxide are set by reg 6 of the 1989 Regulations (see Figure 3).

Figure 3

	Reference period	*Nitrogen dioxide*
Limit value (mandatory)	One year (98th percentile of one-hour means, ie the 98th percentile of mean values per hour recorded throughout a year)	200 micrograms pcm
Guide value (to be pursued)	One year (50th percentile of one-hour means)	50 micrograms pcm
	One year (98th percentile of one-hour means)	135 micrograms pcm

For an explanation of percentile terms, see **10.10.4**.

The UK meets these obligations in practice by monitoring its air at a network of monitoring sites at 'high risk' locations in areas with high traffic concentrations and industrial sites initially created in Central and West London, Manchester, Glasgow, Billingham and Walsall, but since much expanded. After an unimpressive start (to the requirement that the Secretary of State should take the necessary measures to ensure limit values are not breached when it was revealed in 1984 that in 18 out of 65 of the London monitoring sites the limit values were being broken), the Commission took warning action against the UK under Art 169 of the Treaty of Rome. However, with the increasing introduction of catalytic converters fitted in cars, the official figures indicated no exceedences of limit values in 1995, although the guide values are still exceeded in a number of locations. Meeting the guide

1 See Chapters 6 and 7.

2 See Chapter 9.

values will be undertaken as part of the National Air Quality Strategy (see further **10.8** et seq).

Ozone (O_3) results from reactions between volatile organic compounds (VOCs) and nitrogen oxides (NO*x*) released into the air. It is thus a 'secondary' pollutant which, in high concentrations, may adversely affect human and plant life, and damage buildings. In 1992, the European Community took action to further Community-wide understanding of ozone by requiring the creation of monitoring networks and the sharing of information obtained with a view to develop further measures in future. Provision was also made for public warnings to be given of ozone levels which exceed stated thresholds, with the purpose of enabling individuals to take preventive and protective action. These threshold limits are set out in Figure 4.

Figure 4

Health protection	8-hour mean	110 micro-grams pcm	55 parts per billion
Vegetation protection	One-hour mean	200 micrograms pcm	100 parts per billion
	24-hour mean	65 micrograms pcm	32.5 parts per billion
Population information	One-hour mean	180 micrograms pcm	90 parts per billion
Population warning	One-hour mean	360 micrograms pcm	180 parts per billion

Transgression of the last two thresholds leads to requirements for information to be widely disseminated via the press and broadcasting networks as soon as possible, to enable individuals to react appropriately. Member States are also required to submit annual reports for each of their monitoring stations to the Commission as from 1995. In the UK these obligations were implemented under the Ozone Monitoring and Information Regulations 1994, SI 1994/440, which impose the requirements to warn the public and create the necessary monitoring network on the Secretary of State. In practice, the UK has relied on developing its national ozone monitoring network created in 1987 with 17 sites around large cities, into a national scheme of 53 sites. Ozone-warning systems have also been in place since 1990, and these have been revised to comply with EC requirements; air quality bulletins are available hourly on Ceefax and Teletext, via the Internet and by Freephone services. Many have argued that these are not a sufficient system of warning, and that news bulletins should also be used for this purpose. Recent modifications have been made to change the reporting system in general (see **10.6.2**). Further action on ozone will be undertaken under the National Air Quality Strategy (see also further **10.10.3**).

10.3 EUROPE – THE FUTURE

As a move towards a general revision and upgrading of air quality standards, the European Community adopted the Air Quality Framework Directive 96/

62/EC in 1996. This framework Directive sets out the principles of ambient air quality monitoring, with 'daughter' Directives used to create objectives for specific pollutants. In practice, however, there has been some slippage in the programme of agreeing the daughter Directives. Thus, the target date for Directives on sulphur dioxide, nitrogen dioxide, fine particulate matter, eg soot, suspended particulate matter (smoke) and lead was 31 December 1996 – a date which was not met. Indeed, by May 1997 there was still no agreement, although draft standards were emerging. Some of these, however, fell below the standards proposed for the UK's National Air Quality Strategy (see below). The proposals, on which the Council reached a common position in June 1998, were initially as follows:

Sulphur dioxide – Hourly limit values of 350 micrograms pcm, with 24 permitted exceedences per annum. A margin of tolerance of a further 150 micrograms pcm would apply for five years, with the standard in general to be met by 2005. This is less stringent than the UK limit of 262 micrograms pcm on a 15-minute average, but provision is proposed under the draft Directive to allow the UK to retain its standard.

Nitrogen dioxide – 200 micrograms pcm to be achieved at the 99.9th percentile by 2010. This is stricter than the proposed UK standard, which would have to be revised.

Fine particulates – 50 micrograms pcm to be achieved at the 98th percentile by 2010, slightly laxer than the proposed UK standard. However, there would be a stricter annual mean level of 20 micrograms pcm.

Lead – 0.5 micrograms pcm as an annual mean limit.

Standards for benzene and carbon monoxide *were* due to be set by 31 December 1997, and for poly-aromatic hydrocarbons, cadmium, arsenic, nickel and mercury by 31 December 1999. There must be doubt, however, that even these later targets will be met.

In addition to setting limit values, the daughter Directives are to contain higher 'alert threshold' values, while further action on ozone is due under Directive 92/72/EEC by 1 March 1998. Other pollutant standards may be fixed under the framework Directive where these are found necessary to protect human health or the environment. Monitoring requirements are also imposed on Member States in respect of the particular pollutants, and these will 'bite' once the daughter Directives are in place. Mandatory monitoring will be required, inter alia, in areas with populations in excess of 250,000. There will also be obligations to comply with limit values where: (a) there are risks of exceedence from time to time; (b) pollution levels generally exceed limits; and (c) levels are lower than limit values. With regard to (a), there will be requirements for action plans to provide for short-term ameliorative action, including, as one option, the suspension of vehicular traffic. With regard to (b), Member States will be required to identify offending areas and to draw up plans to meet limit values within specified periods. These plans must be publicly available and will be scrutinised by the Commission as they are implemented. Integrated plans will be required for areas where two or more pollutants exceed limits. With regard to (c), Member States are to list such areas and maintain their quality.

In June 1998, a common position was, however, reached on a 'daughter' Directive on the Sulphur Content of Liquid Fuels, whereunder, from 2003, the sulphur content of heavy fuel oil used in power stations, and some industrial boilers and furnaces, will be reduced to 1 per cent, while the sulphur content of gas oil (used in smaller industrial and domestic boilers) will fall to 0.1 per cent from 0.2 per cent by 2008.

The UK is expected to meet its obligations via the National Air Quality Strategy and the terms of the Environment Act 1995 (see below). First, attention will be given to the legal structure of air quality information in the UK.

10.4 INFORMATION ON AIR POLLUTION

10.4.1 The general research and publicity power

Part V of the Clean Air Act 1993 (CAA 1993) contains a number of provisions on local authority powers and obligations in respect of air pollution information. Thus, s 34(1) gives authorities broad general powers to:

- undertake investigations or conduct research relevant to air pollution problems, or contribute towards the cost of such studies;
- arrange for publication of information on air pollution;
- arrange for lectures and addresses to be delivered, and for discussions to be held relating to air pollution problems;
- arrange for the display of pictures, films or models, or the holding of exhibitions concerned with air pollution; and
- prepare, or join in, or contribute to the cost of preparation of such pictures, films, models and exhibitions.

However, where relevant information is published, authorities must ensure, under s 34(2), that the material is presented in such a way that no information relating to a trade secret is disclosed, except with the written consent of a person authorised to disclose that information. If an authority contravene this requirement, they may be sued under s 34(3). In any civil or criminal proceedings brought against an authority, or any of their members or officers, on the ground that information has been published, it is a defence to show compliance with the requirements of s 34(1) and (2) (s 34(4)).

The purpose of this general provision is to allow authorities to amass and disseminate information on air pollution issues. Public awareness of problems may need to be stimulated if there is to be a climate of opinion which is broadly supportive of the regulatory powers of authorities, either generally or in relation to emissions of particular pollutants or from particular sources.

10.4.2 Supplementary powers

To supplement the general power contained in s 34, s 35 of CAA 1993 enables authorities to obtain information on emissions of pollutants and other substances into the air by:

- issuing notices under s 36 (see **10.4.3**);
- measuring and recording relevant emissions and, to that end, to enter premises by agreement or by use of powers contained in s 56 (the power to enter and inspect; see also Chapter 8); and
- entering into arrangements with the occupiers of premises whereby they measure and record emissions on behalf of authorities.

The second and third powers above may not be exercised in respect of private dwellings or caravans. Furthermore, under s 35(2), the power to enter premises to measure and record emissions may not be exercised unless the authority has given the occupier 21 days' written notice (which must expire before the entry is made) specifying the kind of emissions in question, and the steps proposed to be taken on the premises in order to measure and record relevant emissions, and further stating that the authority propose to exercise that power for their stated purpose unless the occupier requests, by notice served on the authority, that notice is alternatively served under s 36. If such a request notice is served at any time during the 21-day period, the authority may not proceed under s 35.

Section 35(3) further provides that authorities are not authorised under s 35 to investigate emissions from processes subject to Part I of EPA 1990 otherwise than by means of notices under s 36 or by exercising their general research and investigation powers under s 34(1) *without* entering relevant premises.

Where authorities exercise powers under s 35, they must, under s 35(4), (5) and (6), carry out appropriate consultations with persons carrying on trades and businesses within their areas (or with representative organisations of such trades and businesses) and with persons conversant with air pollution problems, or interested in local amenity. The purpose of the consultations, which must take place as often as authorities think necessary, but not less than twice in each financial year, is to consider the ways in which powers under ss 35 and 36 are being exercised, and the extent to which and the manner in which information collected under such powers should be made publicly available.

10.4.3 Requiring information

Section 36(1) and (2) of CAA 1993 enables authorities to require, by notice, the occupier of any premises in their areas (other than insofar as the premises consist of a private dwelling or a caravan) to furnish specified estimates or specified or described information concerning the emission of pollutants and other substances into the air from the premises. Such a notice must be in writing, and may require information to be supplied either by way of periodical returns or by other means. Where, however, a notice relates to a process subject to Part I of EPA 1990, for example, a process subject to IPC regulations, the person on whom it is served is not obliged to supply any information which is certified by an inspector appointed under the 1990 Act, as not being of a kind which is being supplied to that inspector for the purposes of the 1990 Act. Thus, an authority can only require the supply of information already suppliable to the Environment Agency (see s 36(3)).

Where a notice under s 36 is served, its recipient must comply with it within six weeks of the date of service, or such longer period as the authority may, by notice, allow (s 36(4)), and a person who fails without reasonable excuse to comply with a s 36 notice, or who, in furnishing any estimate or information required, makes a statement which he knows to be false in a material particular (or who makes such a false statement recklessly) commits an offence under s 36(8) and is liable on summary conviction to a fine up to level 5 on the standard scale. On a conviction, the limitations in s 35(2) on exercising powers of entry (see above) are lifted to enable the authority to enter the premises to obtain the requisite information.

Notices under s 36 may not require returns at intervals of less than three months, and no single notice, whether or not it requires periodical returns, can call for information concerning more than a 12-month period (s 36(5)). However, the s 36 power extends generally to Crown premises and Crown servants except insofar as they are excluded by regulations made by the Secretary of State (s 36(6)), although this does not entitle authorities to exercise powers of entry and to obtain information under ss 56 to 58 of the Act in relation to such premises and servants (s 36(7)).

10.4.4 Appeals

Section 37(1) of CAA 1993 provides for appeals against s 36 notices to the Secretary of State by any person served with a notice, or by any other person having an interest in relevant premises. The appeal may be made on the basis that:

- the giving to the authority of all or any part of the requisite information, or its public disclosure, would either prejudice to an unreasonable degree a private interest in consequence of disclosure of information on trade secrets, or would otherwise be contrary to the public interest; or
- the information required is not immediately available and cannot readily be collected or obtained without the recipient of the notice incurring undue expenditure.

Where an appeal is allowed, the Secretary of State may, under s 37(2), direct the authority to withdraw or modify the notice, or to take such other specified steps to ensure that prejudicial information is not disclosed to the public, and it is the authority's duty to comply with such a direction. Appeals under s 37 are governed by regulations made under s 37(3) which, inter alia, enables regulations to make provision as to the time allowed for bringing appeals and the circumstances in which all or any part of the appellant's case is to be withheld from the respondent. Before regulations are made or replaced, s 37(4) requires the Secretary of State to consult with such representative bodies and persons in respect of local authorities and industry, together with experts on air pollution, as he considers appropriate. The current regulations are the Control of Atmospheric Pollution (Appeals) Regulations 1977, SI 1977/17, and the Control of Atmospheric Pollution (Research and Publicity) Regulations 1977, SI 1977/19, which, inter alia, require certain information relating to appeals to be entered on a public register (see further below).

10.4.5 Further powers and duties of the Secretary of State

Section 38(1) of CAA 1993 requires the Secretary of State to make regulations to prescribe the manner in which, and the methods by which, local authorities are to perform their functions under ss 34(1), 35 and 36 (see above). Consultation with such representatives of local authorities, industry and air pollution experts as the Secretary of State considers appropriate, must take place before any regulations are made or replaced. Particular power is given to make provision in regulations for:

- prescribing the types of emissions to which a s 36 notice may relate;
- prescribing the type of information which may be required by a s 36 notice;
- prescribing the manner in which any such notice is to be given, and the evidence which is to be sufficient evidence of its having been given, and of its contents and authenticity;
- requiring all authorities to maintain in prescribed form a register containing such information as they obtain by virtue of s 35(1), except information on which a direction under s 38(2) provides for non-disclosure, and any other information as the Secretary of State may determine, or as may be determined by or under regulations with respect to any appeal under s 37 which the Secretary of State did not dismiss;
- specifying circumstances in which authorities may enter into arrangements with owners and occupiers of premises under which they will record and measure emissions on behalf of authorities;
- specifying the kinds of apparatus which authorities are to have power to provide and use for measuring and recording emissions and other purposes.

Regulations may also, in particular, require returns as to:

- the total volume of gases, whether or not pollutants, discharged from relevant premises, over any period;
- pollutant concentrations in gases discharged;
- heights at which discharges take place;
- hours during which discharges take place;
- ground-level pollutant concentrations.

Where an authority maintain a register pursuant to the requirements of regulations, this must be open to public inspection at the authority's principal office, free of charge and at all reasonable hours, and facilities must be afforded for the public to obtain copies of entries at a reasonable charge.

The current regulations are the Control of Atmospheric Pollution (Research and Publicity) Regulations 1977[1] which provide (reg 4) that emissions which may be the subject of a local authority notice are:

- sulphur dioxide and particulate matter deriving from combustion processes where the matter heated makes no contribution to the emission;
- any gas or particulate matter deriving from combustion processes where the matter heated does contribute to the emission;
- any gas or particulate matter derived from non-combustion processes or similar industrial activities (reg 3).

Regulation 4 further provides that the type of information that may be required is that which relates to:

- sulphur dioxide emissions during specified periods – in particular, the aggregate duration of all discharges, emissions from specified chimneys, flues and outlets, and their temperatures, efflux velocities, volume flow rates and above-ground levels of discharge, aggregate quantities of sulphur dioxide emissions ascertained either from calculations of the quantities of fuel burnt and its sulphur content or, subject to agreement between the authority and the occupier, by direct measurement;
- total emissions of particulate matter during specified periods – in particular, the aggregate duration of all discharges, discharges from specified chimneys, flues and outlets and their temperatures, efflux velocities, volume flow rates and above-ground levels of discharge, the average concentration of particulates discharged measured in grams per cubic metre at 15°C and one bar barometric pressure, and the aggregate quantity of particulate discharges during the specified period;
- emission of gases other than sulphur dioxide or any specified particulate matter – in particular, their aggregate discharge durations, discharges from specified chimneys, flues and outlets, their efflux velocities, volume flow rates and above-ground levels of discharge, and the aggregate quantities of specified pollutants discharged during the specified period.

However, under reg 4(2), information on past emissions can be required by a notice only where the occupier of the relevant premises is already in possession of that information, or has it immediately available to him.

The Secretary of State, under s 39, may also, for the purpose of obtaining information on air pollution, direct local authorities to make specified arrangements to provide, install, operate and maintain appropriate measuring and recording equipment, and to transmit information obtained to the Secretary of State. Directions may be made to authorities on an individual basis, and, before any such direction is issued, consultation with the authority concerned must take place. It is the duty of authorities to comply with directions given, but where an authority are required to provide apparatus, the Secretary of State must meet the whole capital cost of providing and installing it.

---

1 SI 1977/19.

10.5 MISCELLANEOUS ISSUES

Section 40 of CAA 1993 provides that where a reference is made in the foregoing provisions to emissions of substances to the atmosphere, it extends to substances in a gaseous, liquid or solid state, or any combination of those states, while references to measurements include the taking of samples.

It should further be noted that local authorities have considerable powers under ss 10 to 13 of CAA 1993 to obtain information on furnaces and atmospheric emissions, and these powers extend in certain cases to making requirements on the provision and operation of monitoring apparatus by occupiers.[1] Furthermore, s 58(1) empowers an authority to serve on any person a notice requiring him to furnish them, within a specified period or from time to time, and in a specified form, with specified information which they reasonably consider that they need for the purposes of, inter alia, their Part V functions. The Secretary of State may, under s 58(2), make regulations to restrict the information and the forms in which it may be required. However, it is, in general, an offence for any person to fail, without reasonable excuse, to comply with a s 58 notice, or to furnish information known to be false, or recklessly to make a statement which is false in a material particular. On summary conviction, a fine up to level 5 on the standard scale may be imposed. However, in general under CAA 1993, s 49 will apply to 'information' obtained under Part V so that its disclosure by any person who has obtained it by virtue of the Act is punishable on summary conviction by a fine up to level 5. It is, of course, no offence to disclose any such information in the performance of duties, or under s 34(1)(b) (publication of certain information, see above) or with the consent of a person having the right to disclose it. Note that the 'information' in question is either that obtained by a person under the Act, or given to such a person, and this would seem to include information which has been given to that person voluntarily, as well as information obtained by virtue of statutory notices.

10.6 INFORMATION ABOUT AIR POLLUTION – THE PRACTICE

The quality of the atmosphere is monitored not only by local authorities under the powers of CAA 1993, but also by central government at 14 sites. As from 25 March 1996, 27 local authorities in the provinces integrated their air quality monitoring sites into the DoE's network, along with 16 London borough sites, to give a national total of over 100 sites providing instantaneous measurements of air pollution levels available via Ceefax, Teletext, Freephone and the Internet. The sites chosen for integration vary in type, from roadside locations to urban background, suburban and rural, while the pollutants measured include nitrogen oxides, carbon monoxide, ozone, sulphur dioxide and

1 See further Chapter 8.

particulate matter of less than 10 microns diameter (PM_{10}); however, only some sites monitor all these pollutants, while some monitor only one or two. Nevertheless, the sites chosen reflect the need to monitor pollution in areas of high population, where elevated levels of air pollutants may occur. The network also enhances the spatial distribution of monitoring sites to enable better tracking of air pollution episodes and forecasting.

10.6.1 Emissions inventories

On 14 November 1996 the first comprehensive inventory of urban atmospheric emissions was published by the DoE covering the West Midlands, and identifying the major polluting sources and amounts of pollutants emitted: not surprisingly, road traffic was identified as the major source of pollution in the area. The pollutants measured included sulphur dioxide, nitrogen oxides, carbon monoxide, methane, non-methane volatile organic compounds, carbon dioxide, benzene, 1,3-butadiene, total suspended particulates, PM_{10}, and black smoke. This inventory supplemented existing national surveys, and was to be followed over the two years to November 1998 with further publications relating, inter alia, to Bristol, Portsmouth/Southampton, Glasgow, Liverpool/Manchester, Swansea/Neath/Port Talbot and Sheffield. The principle behind such inventories is to ensure a sufficient flow of information to support advisory guidelines issued by central government on steps everyone can take to prevent atmospheric pollution, particularly the incidence of smog in wintertime, and on how to avoid its ill-effects, such as reducing the use of road vehicles, and reducing the use of energy at home by turning down central heating thermostats. However, in September 1997 Friends of the Earth argued that air pollution levels in Britain reach levels harmful to health once every five days on average. This conclusion was reached on the basis of figures taken from official monitoring statistics, and highlighted particular pollution blackspots which were not all in urban areas – the worst ozone levels were recorded at Lullington Heath in East Sussex, and Somerton in Somerset. Particulate emissions were, however, worst in urban areas such as Leeds city centre and Port Talbot. On 19 November 1997 ministers announced a new system of public information on air pollution, designed to ensure a flow of accurate, comprehensive and timely information on air quality, and to influence individuals in their decision-taking, so that, for example, journeys by car could be avoided on days when pollution levels were high; the overfilling of petrol tanks leading to spillages which evaporate releasing hydrocarbons, a precursor of ozone, can be avoided; the burning of solid fuels could be minimised; and the use of water-based paints, glues and varnishes could be promoted.

10.6.2 Pollution forecasts

The present information system relates to 'air pollution', not air 'quality' as before – a more understandable concept. It is based on health effects, and bands pollutant levels as 'low', 'moderate', 'high' or 'very high' (see below), as determined by the Committee on Medical Effects of Air Pollutants. Hourly information and daily forecasts on sulphur dioxide, nitrogen dioxide, ozone, carbon monoxide and PM_{10} (airborne particles) will be given in the form of overall summaries followed by pollutant-specific information. Hourly bulletins will be available on Ceefax, Teletext, the Internet and via a Freephone number. Daily pollution forecasts will be sent by fax or e-mail to environmental groups, local authorities, regional and national newspapers, television and radio stations and international organisations. Advice can also be given to vulnerable groups on how to avoid the ill-effects of air pollution. The previous system of rating air quality as 'very good', 'good', 'poor' and 'very poor' was not, apparently, well understood, and it is hoped that the new system will achieve more public trust. Broadly, the new levels are:

- 'low' – effects are unlikely to be noticed, even by sensitive individuals;
- 'moderate' – sensitive individuals may notice effects but will not need to take action;
- 'high' – sensitive individuals may notice effects and should take action, such as spending less time outdoors;
- 'very high' – sensitive individuals will find that effects may worsen, and even non-sensitive individuals may notice conditions such as eye irritation, coughing and pain on breathing deeply.

Forecasts will be given on a precautionary basis, so that a higher band warning will be advised where it is considered likely or possible. The forecasts will, however, be given on a general environmental level, and cannot predict particularly unusual local conditions (see, further, **10.9.1**).

However, such a voluntary approach to reducing pollution has been realised for some years to be ineffective. Information and persuasion alone are not enough to counter the problems experienced, particularly where these arise not primarily from identifiable sites but from the collective impact of the lifestyle decisions of large numbers of individuals, eg decisions on car use and maintenance, or on central heating levels. A much more strategic approach has long been needed, and that task was principally entrusted to local authorities under the overall 'banner' of the National Air Quality Strategy by virtue of the Environment Act 1995.

10.7 THE NATIONAL AIR QUALITY STRATEGY

As with the introduction of smoke control under the Clean Air Act 1956 (see Chapter 8), various pollution incidents led to the enactment of Part IV of the Environment Act 1995 on air quality. In particular, concern has centred on the problem of 'smog' – an atmospheric condition caused by the interaction at a low level of certain pollutants in particular climatic conditions, and also the incidence of low-level ozone (O_3). Especial concern has arisen over the increasing incidence of asthma among young children, which has been attributed primarily to increasing emissions from the ever-growing volume of road traffic. Smog episodes in December 1991 were investigated by the DoH, and further health fears were raised by the recurrence of such episodes in the summer of 1994, by which time the Government had already published a consultation paper, *Improving Air Quality*[1] which was followed in January 1995 by legislative proposals, in *Air Quality: Meeting The Challenge*.

10.7.1 EPAQS and COMEAP recommendations

In fact, public concern paralleled Government action. Following publication of the Environment White Paper, *This Common Inheritance*,[2] in 1990, the Government set up the Expert Panel on Air Quality Standards (EPAQS), which worked alongside the Committee on the Medical Aspects of Air Pollutants (COMEAP). These bodies took into account the work being carried out within the European Community on setting limit values for particular pollutants under the Air Quality Management Framework Directive of June 1995, and the revision of air quality guidelines by the World Health Organisation (WHO). By late 1995 the advice from these bodies led the Government to accept that 'fine' particulate matter, in particular that less than 10 microns in diameter (PM_{10}) emitted from road vehicles, domestic and commercial heating, industrial combustion and dust from soil, and resulting also from materials handling, construction work and quarrying, is consistently associated with measures of ill health. While the average level of PM_{10} by 1995 was approximately 20–30 $\mu g/m^3$ (micrograms per cubic metre), the recommended daily standard was being exceeded for 10 per cent of the year at most of the UK's urban measurement sites, for example rising at some sites to 100 $\mu g/m^3$ during winter smog episodes; other evidence suggested that in parts of London levels could be as high at times as 200 $\mu g/m^3$. The principal source of PM_{10} is road traffic; by 1993 vehicle emissions accounted for 26 per cent of such emissions nationwide, with high concentrations in urban areas – 86 per cent in Greater London. During periods of cold, still weather in winter, emissions from urban traffic are unable to disperse and go towards creating smog. In summertime, the process of smog creation is more complex, being a combination of the action of sunlight on emissions of sulphur and nitrogen compounds from Europe as a whole to produce ozone and what is known as 'secondary aerosol', and emissions from road vehicles.

Reductions in PM_{10} over a 10-year period to 2005, were expected to result from the following:

- the introduction of European particulate limits for new diesel cars in 1992, new diesel lorries and buses in 1993, and new diesel vans in 1994;
- the subsequent tightening of those limits for new diesel lorries and buses in 1996 and for new diesel cars in 1997;
- the reduction of sulphur levels in diesel fuel from 0.3 to 0.2 per cent in 1994, and a further reduction to 0.05 per cent in 1996;
- proposals to tighten particulate limits for new diesel vans under 2.5 tonnes in 1997;

1 March 1994.
2 Cm 1200 (1990).

- tightening UK diesel in-use smoke standards in 1995;
- continuing implementation of international agreements to reduce SO_2 emissions, with a reduction in UK emissions of 70 per cent by 2005 and 80 per cent by 2010 relative to a 1980 baseline;
- continuing implementation of the Large Combustion Plant Directive 88/609/EEC;
- tighter atmospheric controls introduced under the IPC and LAAPC systems consequent on EPA 1990;
- final completion of smoke control programmes under CAA 1993.

Nevertheless, further action on PM_{10} was considered essential, as part of a wider package of reduction of pollution by carbon monoxide, benzene, 1,3-butadiene, ozone and sulphur dioxide by 2005, especially as PM_{10} is the pollutant with the greatest potential impact on health.

10.7.2 The Government's response

In its preliminary response of 8 November 1995 the Government:

- accepted EPAQS' recommendation that annual average levels of PM_{10} in the UK should continue progressively to be reduced;
- accepted its conclusion that $50\,\mu g/m^3$ as a running 24-hour average represents a level at which a large majority of individuals should be unaffected, and adopted this level as a relevant benchmark for policy; and
- announced that it would, as quickly as possible, consider whether such a level should also be adopted as a target for policy in line with the Air Quality Strategy then being prepared under the Environment Act 1995.

The Government also concluded that the further development of its strategy for tackling particles should have the following key elements:

- the reduction of winter and summer peak levels of PM_{10} as a priority;
- in wintertime, when peaks are highest, the reduction of vehicle emissions is crucial. The central element of any strategy would concentrate on technology-based measures to secure further long-term abatement of vehicle emissions, particularly from diesel vehicles. The Government would therefore press for positive further improvements in emission performance and technology which would offer wide environmental benefits;
- the Government recognised that such standards would take some time to have effect. It intended, therefore, to take early action to reduce emissions from vehicles in urban centres. The Government accordingly set out further short-term measures in the transport sector to reduce the current impact of emissions, and to yield shorter-term benefits, beyond those currently in prospect, in the years up to 2000, to be included in the Air Quality Strategy under the 1995 Act (see below);
- the most important elements in summer smogs are secondary sources of particles. European action will be needed to tackle them successfully. The Government therefore committed itself to taking an active part in

negotiations at the UN Economic Commission for Europe (UNECE) for further reductions in secondary particles;

- given the expert conclusion that any reduction in background levels would have a beneficial effect on health, and the possibility of local exceedences from specific sources, the Government also concluded that it would be right to continue to seek reductions in emissions from all other relevant sources, including industry, quarrying, construction and domestic coal burning. It therefore undertook to ensure that targets for reducing particle emissions from such sources, which take account of the reports of the two committees, would be built into existing air pollution control regulatory systems.

The need for action was highlighted by evidence published in the *British Medical Journal*, 16 March 1996, that the death rate for heart and respiratory diseases increases by up to 5.4 per cent on days when suspended particulates, ozone, SO_2 and NOx are at their highest concentrations. That evidence indicated that while vehicle emissions in London are below WHO guidelines, both ozone and black smoke (despite the latter now being at an historically low level) are present in quantities having an adverse effect on human beings, and are sufficient to cause the death of those in the population who are vulnerable. A further DoE report of 13 May 1996 from the Quality of Urban Air Review Group confirmed that:

- the best information indicates that the major sources of primary particles (emitted directly from the source into the air) are road transport (25 per cent), non-combustion processes, such as construction, mining and quarrying, and industrial processes (24 per cent), industrial combustion plants and processes with combustion (17 per cent), commercial and residential combustion plants (16 per cent) and public power generation (15 per cent);
- within urban areas generally the influence of road traffic is marked: in Greater London it is estimated that 86 per cent of PM_{10} emissions in 1990 arose from this source;
- industrial sources and domestic coal burning may lead to locally elevated levels of particles;
- in summer, secondary particles (formed by the action of sunlight on emissions of sulphur and nitrogen compounds) appear to be the main cause of episodes of high PM_{10} concentration, although the contribution from re-suspended road dust is also important. Numerical models predict that agreed controls on emissions of sulphur and nitrogen oxides across Western Europe will deliver an improvement of about 40 per cent in average concentrations of secondary particles across the UK by the year 2010. This alone is unlikely to be sufficient to bring summer concentrations in line with EPAQS recommendations (see above);
- in the winter, the major contributor to episodes of high PM_{10} concentration is exhaust emissions from road transport. A reduction of about two-thirds in emissions from this source would lead to achieving the air quality standard recommended by EPAQS at background sites in most UK urban areas;

- control of roadside concentrations and pollution episodes to meet the EPAQS recommendation would require further emission reductions. Current official projections indicate that a cut is needed in road transport emissions of about 52 per cent by 2010.

10.8 THE LEGISLATIVE SKELETON OF THE NATIONAL AIR QUALITY STRATEGY

Under Part IV of the Environment Act 1995, provision is made both for central government and local government action on air quality. The prime central government duty is the creation of a National Air Quality Strategy with standards and targets for the main pollutants and timetables for achieving these, while local government is charged with the duty of regularly assessing local air quality and the creation of air quality management areas in those places where action is required to meet national targets. As at the middle of 1997, the following provisions relating to air quality were in force: s 80 (1 February 1996 under SI 1996/186); s 81 (1 April 1996 under SI 1996/186); ss 87 to 89 (1 February 1996 under SI 1996/186); s 90 and Sch 11, partially (1 February 1996 under SI 1996/186). This should, of course, be borne in mind when reading the rest of this chapter, and regular reference should be made to literature on appointed day orders for other commencements.

10.8.1 Duties of the Secretary of State, the Environment Agency and the Scottish Environmental Protection Agency

Section 80(1) and (2) of the Environment Act 1995 require the Secretary of State to prepare and publish a National Air Quality Strategy (NAQS) containing policies for implementing UK obligations in respect of European and other international legal commitments. Under s 80(3), the NAQS must include either a single statement relating to the whole of Great Britain, or a number of statements which collectively do so. The NAQS under s 80(4) must be kept under review and may be modified from time to time. In particular, s 80(5) requires the inclusion in the NAQS of statements on air quality standards and objectives for restricting the levels at which particular substances may occur in air, together with measures to be implemented by local authorities, and other persons, to achieve those objectives. In preparing and monitoring the NAQS, the Secretary of State is required by s 80(6) to consult with the Environment Agency in England and Wales and the Scottish Environmental Protection Agency (SEPA) in Scotland, together with representative local government bodies and such other persons or bodies considered 'appropriate' by the Secretary of State. Section 80(7) further requires the publication of the NAQS in a draft form for public consultation, and further obligates the Secretary of State to take into account any representations received before promulgating the NAQS. A similar obligation applies to any future modification of the strategy. Section 81 obligates the Environment Agency and SEPA to have regard to the NAQS in discharging their pollution control functions, for example with regard to operating the IPC system, thus attempting to ensure a co-ordinated approach to the overall issue of air quality.

10.8.2 Obligations of local authorities

Section 82(1) and (2) of the Environment Act 1995 require local authorities (ie under s 91, in England and Wales, unitary and district authorities, the Common Council of the City of London, and the Sub Treasurer of the Inner Temple and Under Treasurer of the Middle Temple and, in Scotland, areas constituted under s 2 of the Local Government etc (Scotland) Act 1994) to review, from time to time, the current and likely future quality of the air within their areas, and also to assess whether air quality standards and objectives as set under the NAQS are being or are likely to be achieved within their areas within the 'relevant period', ie a period to be prescribed by the Secretary of State. Where that assessment indicates a current or likely future failure to meet standards, relevant authorities must, under s 82(3), identify those parts of their areas where the failure arises, or is likely to arise. Section 83 then requires authorities to designate, by order, as air quality management areas (AQMAs) those failing parts of their districts. Such orders may be varied or revoked where a subsequent air quality review concludes that air quality standards and objectives are being met, and are likely to be met within periods prescribed by the Secretary of State. Once an area has been designated under s 83, s 84(1) requires the designating authority to supplement the information it already has about the area with an assessment of the current and likely future quality, within the prescribed period, of air within the area and the respects, if any, in which it appears that air quality standards and objectives are either not currently reached or are not likely to be reached. Section 84(2) further obligates the authority to prepare, within 12 months of the coming into effect of the designation, a report of the results of the assessment and a written 'action plan' for the exercise by the authority of its powers to achieve air quality standards and objectives. That action plan, under s 84(3), must include a statement of the time or times by or within which the authority proposes to implement each measure comprised in the plan, although, under s 84(4), a plan, once made, may be revised from time to time.

Sections 84(5) and 86 make particular provision with regard to district councils within county council areas – thus excluding, for example, metropolitan districts and London boroughs. Where the county council disagrees with a constituent district about either the content of a proposed action plan or the revision of such a plan, s 84(5) enables either council to refer the matter to the Secretary of State, who may then confirm the plan or its revision, with or without modifications (either his own or the county council's), or he may reject the plan, and the district council may not finally determine the content of the action plan or its revision save in accordance with the Secretary of State's decision, or in accordance with directions given by him under s 85. County councils may also, under s 86(2), make recommendations to any of their constituent districts with regard to carrying out any particular air quality review, or any particular assessment under s 82 or s 84, or the preparation or review of an action plan. District councils are required to take such recommendations into account. In addition, where a district council is preparing an action plan the county council must, within a period prescribed by the Secretary of State, submit to the district council proposals for the exercise by the county council of any powers exercisable by them (for example as a highway authority) in order to pursue achieving air quality standards and objectives (s 86(3)). Section 86(4) further requires a county council in such situations to submit a statement of the time or times by or within which they propose to implement their proposals. Action plans must then include a statement of proposals made under s 86(3) and (4) (s 86(5)). Under s 86(6), where it appears that air quality standards or objectives are not being achieved or are not likely to be achieved within a prescribed period within a district council's area, or that the county council has failed to discharge their duties under Part IV of the Environment Act 1995, or that the actions or proposed actions of a county council under Part IV are inappropriate, or that developments in science or technology, or material changes in circumstances have rendered action or proposed action inappropriate, the Secretary of State may give the county council directions requiring them to take specified steps. In particular, a direction under s 86(7) may require the submission of proposals under s 86(3) or statements under s 86(4), the modification of any such proposals or statements, the submission of such modified proposals or statements to relevant district councils, and require the implementation, in a specified fashion, of any measures contained in an action plan. Section 86(8) empowers the Secretary of State to direct county councils to take specified steps in order to implement relevant European and other international legal obligations. Directions given must be published in such manner as the Secretary of State considers appropriate in order to bring the matter to the attention of those likely to be affected, but copies of directions must be publicly available and must be included in the *London Gazette* (s 86(9)).

The clear object of s 86 is to ensure that, within a county area, district councils neither ignore the views of the county council, nor pursue their own policies in an unco-ordinated fashion.

10.8.3 Local authority functions – supplementary provisions

Schedule 11, para 1 to the Environment Act 1995 provides that where authorities carry out air quality reviews, or assessments under ss 82 and 84, or prepare or revise any action plan, they must carry out prescribed consultations with the Secretary of State, the Environment Agency (in Scotland, SEPA), the appropriate highway authority, any other local authority whose area is contiguous with the area of the authority taking action, any county council in whose area the authority wholly or partly lies, any national park authority within whose area the authority taking action wholly or partly lies, any other public authority exercising functions in the area in question as the authority taking action considers appropriate, such representatives of business within its area as the authority considers appropriate, and any other body or person considered appropriate. Schedule 11, para 2 applies in areas where there are both county and district councils to provide districts with all such information as they may reasonably request to enable them to carry out their air quality functions, and vice versa, although each tier of local government requesting information may require, subject to a requirement of reasonableness, information to be provided in a particular manner and form. An authority supplying information may recoup their reasonable costs from a requesting authority, while a requesting authority may ask for information not in the possession of a supplying authority, provided it is reasonable for that authority to obtain it. Under Sch 11, para 3, the Secretary of State (in Scotland, SEPA) may issue directions requiring two or more authorities to exercise their functions jointly, or requiring an authority not to exercise powers, or not to exercise them in a specified manner. Where joint arrangements have been made by authorities they may also be required subsequently to revoke or modify them in accordance with directions given. Finally, Sch 11, para 4 obligates every local authority to make available for free public inspection at all reasonable times, certain information, and to enable the public to obtain copies at reasonable cost. That information is: reports of any air quality reviews carried out by the authority; reports of assessments made under ss 82 and 84; orders made under s 83; any action plan prepared; any proposals or statements submitted pursuant to s 86(3) and (4); and any directions given to the local authority or, where appropriate, the county council.

10.8.4 Supplementary powers of the Secretary of State

The Secretary of State (in Scotland, SEPA, acting with the approval of the Secretary of State) has power under s 85(2) to conduct or make, or cause to occur: reviews of current and likely future air quality in a prescribed period, and within the area of any local authority; assessments on whether air quality standards and objectives are being achieved, or are likely to be achieved, within such an area in a prescribed period; the identification of any parts of an authority's area where standards and objectives are not likely to be achieved; assessments of any respects in which it appears that air quality standards and objectives are not being achieved or are not likely to be achieved in a prescribed period within an authority's area or within a designated area. Where it appears that standards and objectives are not being met, or are not likely to be met, or that the relevant local authority has failed in its obligations under the 1995 Act, or that the actions, current and future, of an authority in discharging those obligations are inappropriate, or that developments in science and technology, or changes in circumstances, have rendered an authority's current or proposed action inappropriate, the Secretary of State (in Scotland, SEPA) may, under s 85(3), give directions requiring specified action, and such directions must be complied with under s 85(7). In particular, under s 85(4), an authority may be required: to conduct or re-conduct an air quality review, in whole or part, or in a specified manner; to designate an area under s 83 as an AQMA, or to revoke or modify any such plan; and to implement any measures in an action plan. The Secretary of State may also, under s 85(5), give directions to authorities to take specified steps to meet the European or other international legal obligations of the UK relating to air quality. Where a direction is given it must be published in such form as is appropriate to bring it to the attention of persons likely to be affected, while copies must also be publicly available, and appropriate notices of the giving of the direction and how copies may be obtained must be published in the *London Gazette* (in Scotland, the *Edinburgh Gazette*).

10.8.5 Powers to make regulations

Section 87 of the Environment Act 1995 gives ministers considerable powers to make regulations to implement the UK Air Quality Strategy, to meet European and international legal obligations, and to provide for the assessment of air quality. In particular, regulations may provide for:

- air quality standards;
- objectives for restricting the levels at which particular substances are present in air;
- conferring powers and duties on local authorities;
- authorising authorities to exercise functions on behalf of ministers;
- directing the concurrent performance of ministerial functions with local authorities;
- transferring ministerial functions to local authorities;
- prohibiting or restricting the carrying-on of prescribed activities, or the access of prescribed vehicles or mobile equipment to prescribed areas, either generally or in particular circumstances;
- designation of AQMAs by authorities in certain prescribed circumstances not falling within s 83, and for applying, with or without modifications, the provisions of the Act to such areas with regard to air quality reviews, assessments, designating AQMAs and action plans;
- prescribing measures which authorities and other persons are to adopt in pursuing air quality standards and objectives;
- communicating to the public information on the current or likely future quality of the air;
- enabling local authorities to obtain from any person information they reasonably need in the discharge of air quality functions;
- imposing fines up to level 5 on the standard scale on those guilty of offences under regulations, or for fixed penalty offences;
- holding appeals against determinations made under the regulations.

More particularly, s 87(3) enables regulations to lay down the scope or forms of reviews, assessments and action plans, the times and periods of reviews and assessments and the preparation of plans, and the methods to be employed in carrying out reviews and assessments and in monitoring the effectiveness of plans. Similarly, regulations may lay down factors to be taken into account in preparing plans, and the actions to be taken by authorities and other persons in consequence of reviews, assessments and plans. Provision may also be made for consultation, publicising copies of reports, reviews, assessments and plans, and for requiring such information to be sent to the Secretary of State or the Environment Agency (in Scotland, SEPA). Further provision may be made under s 87(4) for ministerial directions to bind those making determinations on appeals arising in respect of reviews etc. Section 87(5) provides for regulations to lay down requirements as to who may determine appeals, and the procedures to be followed, although in this connection different provision may be made for different cases, areas and localities. Section 87(6) precludes the making of regulations which enable anyone other than a uniformed constable from stopping a vehicle on the road.

The power to make regulations prescribing the performance of air quality functions is, it will be noted, extremely wide, concentrating considerable discretion in ministerial hands. To ensure some form of accountability in relation to such matters, s 87(7) imposes an obligation on the Secretary of State before making regulations to consult with the Environment Agency (in Scotland, SEPA), such local government representative bodies and bodies representative of industry as he considers appropriate, together with any other bodies or persons. Section 87(8) also provides that regulations have to be made in the form of a statutory instrument laid in draft before Parliament and receiving the positive approval of each House.

10.8.6 Fixed penalty offences

Schedule 11 to the Environment Act 1995 contains further detail on the fixed penalty offences which may be introduced by regulations made under s 87. Provision may be made in relation to the qualifications, appointment and authorisation of persons who may issue fixed penalty notices; for determining offences for which a fixed penalty may apply, and the manner in which such a penalty notice may be issued; for giving a period of grace for payment of a fixed penalty during which other proceedings in respect of the offence may not be commenced; and for prohibiting a conviction for the offence where a fixed penalty is paid within a prescribed time. Provision may also be made for a person subject to a fixed penalty to request a hearing in respect of the offence; for a fixed penalty to be increased in amount where it is not paid on time and no hearing has been requested; and for the recovery of fixed penalties by way of civil debt procedure, although provision may also be made in connection with the enforcement of unpaid fixed penalties by prescribed persons. Provision may also be made for rendering fixed penalty notices etc nugatory in certain cases where statutory declarations are made; the extension of periods for complying with fixed penalties; the withdrawal of a fixed penalty notice; repayment of sums pre-paid where a notice is withdrawn; and prohibiting the subsequent commencement or continuation of proceedings following withdrawal of such a notice. A whole range of other matters may be dealt with, including the disposition of sums received as fixed penalties, and certification of payment or non-payment as the case may be. Regulations may also specify that fixed penalty notices must contain specified information about the offence in question, the amount of the fixed penalty, the place at which and the person to whom payment is to be made, and to whom relevant correspondence may be sent, the method of payment, the period for payment, and the consequences of non-payment.

Even though, as has been seen, the Secretary of State has more than ample powers to control the exercise of local air quality functions under the above provisions, s 88 finally empowers him to issue guidance to authorities in connection with those air quality functions, and those authorities are required to take any such guidance into account in discharging their functions. This obligation is, of course, a lesser one than that to 'act in accordance' with central guidance which is found in relation to dealing with contaminated land under the provisions of the Environment Act 1995 and EPA 1990.

10.8.7 Subsequent development of air quality policy in practice

The Secretary of State announced on 8 February 1997 that some 80 local authorities, including all those in London, had been selected to carry out preparatory trials to ensure the subsequent smooth introduction of the new statutory obligations. The authorities, chosen by the Air Quality Management Working Group (a joint central/local government body), included both urban and rural areas, and certain counties and unitary authorities in an attempt to ensure a good geographical spread of areas. Special funding from central government was made available for this purpose. Contemporaneously, the then Department of Transport announced consultation on new regulations to allow local authorities to fine drivers, or ban their vehicles, if they failed roadside emission tests, although, as with the air quality powers considered above, there was no proposal to allow anyone other than a uniformed constable to require a vehicle to stop for testing. The proposals were particularly aimed at discouraging the wasteful and polluting practice of keeping the engine of a vehicle running while it is parked and, as with the air quality proposals, it was envisaged that trials in pilot areas would precede new regulations.

However, some time before the foregoing proposals, work had commenced on a preparatory National Air Quality Strategy (NAQS). Initially, air quality standards were proposed based on the work of the EPAQS and the WHO with regard to specified pollutants: benzene, 1,2-butadiene, carbon monoxide, lead, nitrogen dioxide, ozone, PM_{10} and sulphur dioxide, and a target date of 2005 for fulfilling targets was set in June 1996, although a built-in review for NAQS was set for 1999 to enable further modifications to take place following its proposed launch in 1997 and for account to be taken of further European and international legal obligations. One proposal rejected in 1996 was for tradeable sulphur emission permits whereby all relevant operators would be given a 'quota' of permitted emissions; plants that could more easily meet their sulphur dioxide emission targets would be able to transfer their excess permits to other, less well-placed operators, with the power for a regulatory agency to intervene from time to time to 'call back' unused permit quotas and thus, over time reduce the total emission of a particular pollutant. No mention was made of such a scheme in the consultative document *Proposals for a National Sulphur Strategy*;[1] the Government apparently concluding that sulphur reduction targets can be met with 'room to spare' without introducing such a scheme.

Other features of the draft NAQS were as follows:

---

1 June 1996.

- the use of percentile standards so that, in any given year and at any given place, a number of exceedences of standards could take place;
- no requirement that air quality targets should be met everywhere, but, instead, an emphasis that targets be met in places where people are likely to be exposed over particular periods of time – an indication, perhaps, of a public health protection bias in the proposals, as opposed to a wider environmental protection position;
- AQMAs to be the exception rather than the norm, with authorities being counselled to concentrate activity on isolated areas where localised air quality is, and is likely to remain, a problem;
- AQMAs to be concentrated in parts of local authorities to deal with pollution 'hot spots' rather than blanketing whole districts or even groups of districts, although the influence of an AQMA in an area would be reflected in wider air quality improvement action in its surroundings;
- control over industrial emissions to be exercised primarily by the IPC and LAAPC systems under EPA 1990 as opposed to the Environment Act 1995;
- caution to be exercised in closing roads in episodes of high pollution, although some seasonal restrictions could occur with regard to wintertime smog occurring between October and February;
- no sectoral targets for polluting emissions to be set, eg nothing specific to be achieved in relation to vehicle emissions, the hope being that reductions would occur in consequence of better planning (reducing the need for travel) and better emission-control technology.

The Labour Party in opposition broadly supported the draft strategy, while indicating that it might, when in power, allow individual local authorities to set local standards which were stricter than those set nationally, place greater reliance on planning powers in respect of particular developments in AQMAs, and adopt an integrated approach whereby reduction of travel was a feature of all planning guidance. Formal consultation on the draft NAQS was launched on 21 August 1996.

10.8.8 Responses to the draft NAQS

Campaigners for cleaner air and others in the wider environmental movement were critical of the draft NAQS, arguing that too much reliance was placed on technical improvements in vehicle construction and petroleum products, and that too many potentially false assumptions had been made on how many technical improvements could be made. There was also criticism of the exceedences permitted by the draft standards, and concern that on the promised review of NAQS in 1999 there would be a relaxation of standards. Commentators pointed out that in 1996 the proposed standards for nitrogen dioxide were exceeded on 12 days in Manchester, and on 10 days in Sheffield, the proposed ozone limit was exceeded in Cardiff on 29 days and in Birmingham on 26 days, and the PM_{10} limit was exceeded in London on 43 days, in Liverpool on 51 days, and in Belfast on 40 days. However, the Government reaffirmed its belief in the ability of stricter vehicle emission standards to be introduced under European obligations (see Chapter 9) to reduce atmospheric pollution, for example by fitting enhanced catalytic converters which commenced operation within five seconds of ignition, rather than the two-minute starting time which existed in 1996 – eight per cent of pollution from cars being emitted in those two minutes. However, such improvements would add £180 to the cost of a small family car, and add £1,330 to the cost of a heavy goods vehicle. Estimates from road hauliers indicated that compliance with new air pollution targets could add between £85 to £90 million per annum to road freight costs, whilst British oil refiners might have to expend £1 billion on upgrading plant to produce cleaner fuels.

However, the Government pressed ahead with developing its strategy, and on 29 November 1996 the DoE issued a number of papers to local authorities: *General Principles of Reviewing and Assessing Air Quality*; *The Review of Local Authority Powers*; and *Draft Air Quality Regulations*, which were designed, inter alia, to give an indication of the likely relationship between the Environment Act 1995 and other legislation, regulations made under the 1995 Act, and non-statutory guidance.

10.8.9 Existing legislation

The paper *The Review of Local Authority Powers* was issued on a consultative basis, but made a point of reminding authorities that the 1995 Act provided only some of the legislative means at their disposal for furthering the NAQS, and, again, stressed that an AQMA should be designated only where there was a particular local problem which could not be solved by the application of general national measures, and then only after an assessment of whether the various legislative and other options open to an authority would not be sufficient, according to the criteria of local 'action plans', to deal with particular 'hot spots'. The document further stressed the need for fostering local voluntary solutions to pollution problems on a flexible and innovative basis. Thus, a local authority should seek additional powers under an AQMA designation only where:

- it could be demonstrated that despite the use and existence of general powers the achievement of national air quality objectives remained at risk;
- effective existing or proposed mechanisms for dealing with a problem area were absent;
- action could be justified on the balance of costs and benefits.

The consultation paper stressed that many air pollution problems would be obviated by measures other than those under the 1995 Act. Thus, sulphur dioxide emissions by 1996 had decreased by more than 60 per cent since 1970, and by more than 45 per cent since 1980. Changes in fuel burning away from coal should continue to bring about further reductions, and most polluting sources would be further controlled under the national plan on sulphur existing under EPA 1990. This might leave a large number of small unregulated sources in respect of which local action may be justified. In relation to nitrogen dioxide and other oxides of nitrogen, the consultation papers reiterated reliance on new vehicle emission and fuel standards negotiated within Europe, with further support for reducing emissions coming from the control of sources under the IPC and LAAPC programmes. Ozone levels were only likely to be controlled by action taken at national and international levels, with local initiatives being of limited significance. It can be easily appreciated that the consultation paper left few options open to authorities to pursue vigorous independent action in respect of local air quality, with the one area where some local leeway was recognised as needed being in relation to reducing PM_{10} in congested urban areas.

Overall, the paper stressed use of existing powers to achieve NAQS at the local level rather than introducing new regulatory provisions (eg use of LAAPC powers to achieve NAQS standards and objectives) as, for example, under s 7(1) and (2)(c) of the 1990 Act, which requires LAAPC authorisations to lay down conditions to achieve compliance with the requirement of any quality standards or objectives prescribed by the Secretary of State (see further Chapters 6 and 7).

In general, therefore, the consultation exercise envisaged only limited needs for new regulatory powers for local authorities. Possible extensions of regulation were, however, identified as:

- controls over small combustion plant boilers of 20 to 50 megawatts, and waste combustion plant below 3 megawatts net rated thermal input which currently fall outside the controls under EPA 1990;
- a review of the guidance on chimney heights (see Chapter 8);
- a ban on 'over-the-counter' sales of unauthorised fuels in smoke control areas;
- a limit on the sulphur content of solid fuel for domestic use; and
- enhanced monitoring by local authorities of road vehicle emissions, with powers to control drivers who leave vehicle engines running unnecessarily, and stricter enforcement of emissions in respect of those vehicles licensed annually by local authorities, such as taxis and private hire vehicles.

The paper *General Principles of Reviewing and Assessing Air Quality* was not issued on a consultative basis, but was released to give a summary of the proposed package of guidance, and to enable authorities to make budgetary provision for implementing their 'share' of NAQS. The guidance, it was stated, would take the form of a circular on air quality and land use planning (in Scotland, a planning advice note), a circular on air quality and traffic management, and guidance on developing local air quality action plans and strategies. Once again, however, it was stressed that authorities should pay particular heed to identifying those localities where national plans and policies in themselves would be unlikely to deliver national air quality standards. It was also recognised that there will be a number of 'residual' hot spots of pollution caused by localised factors such as traffic density, geography or topography where national targets will not be met over the initial period of the NAQS up to the year 2005. It is in those areas where local action will be needed and justified. However, the paper stressed that an AQMA should be declared only where it was the most efficient and cost-effective way of securing excellent air quality, and, furthermore, only where it was clear that air quality was currently poor and would continue to be so in 2005.

10.8.10 Approaches to local implementation

As far as the general principles of reviewing and assessing air quality on a local basis are concerned, the paper indicated that the Government expects authorities to carry out their tasks within a consistent framework, according to a consistent time-scale and in a systematic way, while allowing authorities a degree of freedom to deal with particular local problems affecting their areas. It was stated that some authorities, however, would generally be able to rely on existing atmospheric data, both national and local, produced by the National Air Quality Archive which is a national database of information set up by the Government on 21 August 1996. Further guidance was, however, promised to indicate those areas where a greater sophistication of modelling and monitoring of air quality would be required. In general, however, the key elements of local implementation were identified as follows:

A phased approach

There should be an initial screening of industrial, transport and other significant pollution sources in an area, which should, however, bear in mind the reductions in polluting emissions which are likely to be achieved by national measures. Some areas at this stage will have pollution levels below national air quality objectives and which are likely to remain so; no further investigation of those areas should be necessary. Detailed and accurate air quality reviews should be undertaken only in relation to those areas where it is predicted that pollution levels will not meet relevant air quality objectives in 2005, although an absolutely accurate forecast review cannot be expected.

A step-by-step approach

Authorities will be counselled to identify potential pollutant sources in their areas according to criteria indicating whether a source is likely to give rise to elevated levels of particular pollutants. Sources include roads reaching certain levels of use or congestion, processes falling within IPC control or LAAPC control, other significant pollution sources, and any future planned developments likely to affect air quality. Where, according to guidance criteria, no significant sources exist, there will be no need for further action. Where, however, a source exists, and there is potential for consequential public exposure to pollution, a 'second stage assessment' should take place. This should only occur in areas where there is a potential risk of elevated levels of a pollutant. Authorities will estimate ground level concentrations at various locations – roadside, industrial and urban background – in order to predict the highest potential pollution concentrations, using a variety of methodologies which will be the subject of future guidance. The object will be to see whether concentrations of pollutants are likely to exceed the relevant air quality standard making it unlikely that air quality objectives will be achieved. Estimates will take place on a limited, precautionary basis to the extent that if there is a significant risk that an objective will not be achieved, and it appears that by 2005 relevant standards will either be approached or exceeded, authorities will proceed to the next stage. The third stage will involve authorities in more sophisticated modelling and monitoring techniques, and will require them to predict whether an exceedence of an air quality standard is likely to indicate a failure to meet an air quality objective by 2005. If the answer is affirmative, that will trigger the designation of an AQMA. These principles have been incorporated in official guidance (see **10.13** to **10.14**).

A timed approach

Despite the fact that in November 1996 the Government was unwilling to set a statutory deadline for the completion of reviews and assessments, it was expected that most authorities would make speedy progress once the Environment Act 1995 was fully implemented – with the Secretary of State's reserve powers being available to deal with any failing to act. Approximately 90 authorities had already begun phase 1 of their reviews and, in general, it was expected that authorities should complete a review of air quality in their areas by early 1999, with a further review and assessment before 2005.

A flexible approach

AQMAs need to have boundaries, which should be fixed on a flexible, evaluative basis, taking into account factors relevant to particular pollutant sources – for example, in relation to traffic-generated pollution, travel-to-work patterns and the existence of national and local traffic routes will have to be considered. Furthermore, an authority's action plan cannot be limited simply to an AQMA, but will, by necessity, relate to a wider area. However, all such plans must have as their key focus and priority the need to secure national air quality objectives within the AQMA. AQMAs should, therefore, be broadly yet reasonably defined; it would not, in general, be reasonable therefore to designate the whole of an authority's area as an AQMA on the basis that air quality objectives will not be achieved in only one part of that area. It would, however, appear sensible to designate an AQMA otherwise by reference to easily recognised physical and geographical boundaries. Where a particular air pollution problem traverses local authority boundaries, each authority involved should apply consistent criteria in designating land within their areas as an AQMA.

10.8.11 Duties once the AQMA is designated

Once an AQMA is designated, s 4(1) of the Environment Act 1995 requires the relevant authority to carry out a further assessment of air quality. This is a supplementary review as most information will already be to hand as a result of the review leading to designation, and will relate only to the area within the AQMA. The object of this exercise is to determine pollutant sources within the area, and to consider the relevant contributions of industry, transport and other sectors on achieving action plan objectives (which themselves must be cost-effective and proportionate). The action plan drawn up after the review must state the time-scale within which the authority propose to implement plan provisions. While there is no statutory date by which an action plan has to be prepared, the 1996 guidance indicated that a plan should be completed within one year of the completion of the further assessment of air quality within an AQMA under s 84.

In addition, while the legislation contains no specific requirement on the submission to ministers of completed reviews and assessment of air quality, the guidance *General Principles of Reviewing and Assessing Air Quality* (see **10.8.8**) indicated that use would be made of Sch 11 to the Environment Act 1995 which requires consultation with Ministers, the Environment Agency (in Scotland, SEPA), highway authorities, all neighbouring authorities, the relevant county council (if any), the relevant national park authority, and other relevant public and representative bodies. It was made clear that such consultation should take place in relation to air quality reviews, air quality assessments, further assessments within AQMAs and the preparation and revision of action plans, and should extend beyond statutory consultees to relevant community and environmental groups, as well as involving the general public by means of displays and meetings etc in order to foster local 'ownership' of plans and policies. Consultation should take place on the basis of certain information being supplied to consultees; for example, in relation to an air quality review, the information should include the proposed start date, the time-scale for completing the review, and the broad plan of approach, including arrangements for including consultees in discussion and steering groups and arrangements for co-operation with other local authorities. Any consultative exercise should enable consultees to make their general views known, and should identify areas of concern. It should also enable authorities to notify relevant interest groups of the need to exchange information and to invite their involvement in the review process. Where a review is completed, there should then be further consultation on the assessment of air quality, with consultees being able to comment both on data collected and its interpretation.

The review procedure, its assessment methodologies, and the rationale for its conclusions should be accessible to consultees. Consultative reports should also indicate what stage in reviewing air quality an authority has reached, and should be made publicly available in good time to enable comment to be made.

Where an AQMA is designated, consultation should take place at the end of the further assessment of air quality within the AQMA, with reports being made of the data collected, methodologies used and conclusions drawn. Such reports should be made publicly available. The consultative views thus received should be fed into the action plan for the AQMA, which itself should be the subject of further consultative exercises at the draft stage, in order that it can then be finalised.

Where a plan contains broad general proposals, further consultation should take place where these are revised during the course of execution. In particular, where consultation takes place it should relate, inter alia, to the pollutants to be addressed, with indications of their source, the boundaries of any proposed action plan, the involvement of other local authorities in securing plan objectives, any proposals from the relevant county council, time-scale for implementing proposed measures, an indication of any action required by other persons and agencies to secure a plan's objectives, and the arrangements proposed to ensure co-operation between the parties involved. No consultative exercise should be less than six weeks in length.

10.8.12 The special role of county councils

While s 86(2) of the Environment Act 1995 specifies that a district council must take into account county council recommendations in relation to air quality reviews and assessments, the 1996 general principles guidance (see **10.8.8**) was more explicit in indicating the need for the tiers of local government to work closely together, particularly as county councils are road traffic regulation authorities. The general principles guidance envisages that county councils would be involved in reviewing air quality through the review process, and that district and county councils should agree the scope and format of any air quality review at its inception. In addition to the need under the legislation for district and county councils to exchange information (see **10.8.2** above), and the requirement that county councils should inform district councils of action they propose to take with regard to its inclusion in an action plan (s 86(3)), the general principles guidance further advises district councils to make special arrangements with county councils to ensure that the most comprehensive action plan is produced – which requires consultation at a stage before any action plan is even drafted.

The general principles guidance further advises, with regard to action plans, that preparing authorities should liaise with any other relevant agencies, eg the Environment Agency, and that steering groups should be created to supervise the plan preparation process to include representatives of the Environment Agency (in Scotland, SEPA), local business representatives, and community groups etc. In relation to the requirements to inform the general public, the guidance reminds authorities of their obligations to make available AQMA designation orders, any action plans made and any proposals put forward by a county council for inclusion in an action plan. There is no obligation on an authority to make available all material collected in the course of a review and assessment of air quality, and although a report has to be issued, the scope, format, circulation and distribution of the report is at the discretion of the authorities. The general tenor of the guidance was, however, that because wide public 'ownership' of policies is required, wide publication of reports could be justified. In any case, air quality information held by an authority would fall within the scope of the Environmental Information Regulations 1992, SI 1992/3240, and so might have to be made available on any request from a member of the public.

10.8.13 The draft air quality regulations

The final document in the November 1996 guidance (see **10.8.8**) was on draft regulations, but only in relation to a limited number of matters.

'The relevant period'

At a number of places in the legislation, authorities are required to complete or undertake action within a 'relevant period', ie a time to be prescribed by the Secretary of State. This period was proposed as follows:

(a) for the purposes of s 86(3) of the Environment Act 1995, ie the period within which a county council has to submit proposals to a district council which is preparing an action plan (a situation which can arise only in parts of England, as county councils are part of a two-tier system of local government) the time should be nine months beginning with the date on which the district council first consults the county council under Sch 11, para 1(2)(e) to the Act;

(b) for all other purposes, the relevant period is the period between the coming into force of s 82 of the Act and ending with 31 December 2005.

Air quality objectives

A number of specific air quality objectives were set out in the document, derived from the terms of the NAQS. The only exclusion at a local level was that no quality objective was set for ozone, it being the Government's view that this pollutant can be dealt with only by action taken at national and international level. Otherwise, a number of quality objectives for local air quality were set out on the understanding that in certain parts of Britain local action will be required to achieve such objectives by virtue of localised pollution 'hot spots', and, in such places where objectives are not likely to be attained by 2005, local action should be taken.

Figure 5. Air quality objectives (as initially proposed)

Substance	*Air quality objective levels*
Benzene	5 ppb or less, when expressed as a running annual mean
1,3-butadiene	1 ppb or less, when expressed as a running annual mean
Carbon monoxide	10 ppm or less, when expressed as a running 8-hour mean
Lead	0.5 micrograms per cubic metre or less, when expressed as an annual mean
Nitrogen dioxide	104.6 ppb or less, when expressed as the 99.9th percentile of hourly means, and 20 ppb or less, when expressed as an annual mean [based on WHO figures]
PM_{10}	50 micrograms per cubic metre or less, when expressed as the 99th percentile of daily maximum running 24-hour means
Sulphur dioxide	100 ppb or less, when expressed as the 99.9th percentile of 15 minute-means

ppm = parts per million; ppb = parts per billion; PM_{10} = particles of less than 10 microns in size. For the meaning of percentile terms, see **10.10.4.**

As will be seen below (see **10.10.3**), these proposals were largely, although not entirely, retained by the Labour Government in 1997.

10.9 AN INTERIM ASSESSMENT

The air quality provisions of the Environment Act 1995 at first sight promised a great deal – in particular appearing to confer very wide discretionary powers on local authorities. However, as is the case with so much modern environmental legislation, the law in practice is narrowed down by delegated legislation and the influence of extensive ministerial 'guidance', which has a potent quasi-legislative effect. Thus, the draft air quality regulations 1996 made it clear that legal action on air quality should be taken only in a limited range of circumstances by local authorities, and only where certain air quality objectives are not likely to be met by 2005. The whole tenor of the 1996 guidance (see **10.8.8**) was that the prime initiatives lie with central government, that local government's role is secondary and limited, and that an over-enthusiastic use of air quality powers by local authorities would be unwelcome and should be discouraged. Furthermore, it was made clear that the national air quality standards, set out in the Government's strategy, would not, at least initially, be made regulatory, but would remain advisory only, being benchmarks or reference points for the setting of air quality objectives, and tools for the making of national policy. Those standards would represent levels of air pollutants at which no risk, or only an extremely small risk, to human life could arise, but central policy was limited to getting, and keeping, air quality as close to those standards as would be considered reasonable and could be justified on a cost-benefit basis.

10.9.1 Subsequent developments

On 10 December 1996 the Government reiterated its policy that AQMAs should be declared only in those areas where air quality objectives are unlikely to be achieved by 2005, with much reliance being placed on administrative measures to ensure improvements in the quality of the air, eg by issuing advice in the form of circulars on air quality and traffic management which could take the form of restricting access to some areas, regulating speeds, smoothing out traffic flows, and promoting alternatives to the use of private cars. On 30 January 1997 the national air quality information service was revised to come into line with the final version of the NAQS. The object was to provide a consistent framework within which air quality could be described, both locally and nationally, and which reflected the national strategy. The information service does not carry with it any executive force, nor does it require the taking of any legal enforcement action, rather, it is designed to warn vulnerable people of the need to be aware. (See **10.6.2**.)

The interpretation of the categories as proposed by the Government was as follows:

- 'very good air quality' if the level of the pollutant is at or below the 'standard' threshold – based on the air quality standard proposed for inclusion in the NAQS. In this band, harmful effects are unlikely to occur, even in sensitive groups;

Figure 6. Thresholds and associated action for five air pollutants

Description of air quality	very good	'Standard Threshold'	generally satisfactory/moderate	'Information Threshold'	poor	'Alert Threshold'	very poor
Sulphur dioxide		100ppb/15 minute		200ppb/15 minute		400ppb/15 minute	
Ozone		50ppb/8-hour running		90ppb/hour		180ppb/hour	
Carbon monoxide		10ppm/8-hour running		15ppm/8-hour running		20ppm/8-hour running	
Nitrogen dioxide		150ppb/hourly		300 ppb/hourly		4000ppb/hourly	
Fine particles (PM_{10})		50μgm^3/24-hour running		75μgm^3/24-hour running		100μgm^3/24-hour running	
Effects	Harmful effects are unlikely to occur, even in sensitive groups.		There could be a small risk of effects in sensitive individuals, and/or disamenity may begin to occur.		Some adverse effects in sensitive groups may occur and disamenity would increasingly be experienced.		Risk of more serious adverse health effects may occur, not necessarily confined to sensitive groups. Serious disamenity may occur.
Action					Provision of relevant advice to those who may be affected.		Provision of advice more generally. Additional action may be necessary.

ppm=parts per million; ppb=parts per billion; $\mu g/m^3$ = micrograms per cubic metre; PM_{10} = particles of less than 10 microns in size.
* = these objectives were to be regarded as provisional

- 'moderate' or 'generally satisfactory air quality' if the level of the pollutant is above the 'standard' threshold but at or below the 'information' threshold – based on DoH recommendations or, for ozone, EC requirements. In this band, there could be a small risk of effects in sensitive individuals;
- 'poor air quality' if the level of the pollutant is above the 'information' threshold but at or below the 'alert' threshold – based on DoH recommendations or, for ozone, EC requirements. In this band, some adverse effects in sensitive groups may occur;
- 'very poor air quality' if the level of the pollutant is above the 'alert' threshold. In this band there would be a risk of more serious, adverse health effects, not necessarily confined to sensitive groups.

Where pollutants have the potential to affect people's health due to exposure over long periods of time (benzene and 1,3-butadiene), it was proposed that these should be described as either above or below the standard proposed for inclusion in the NAQS (ie 5ppb as a running annual mean for benzene, and 1ppb as a running annual mean for 1,3-butadiene). Both of these are known carcinogens where there is no absolutely safe level of exposure, and it has never been possible to describe their presence in 'good' or 'bad' terms, but only as 'low' or 'high', or gradations thereof.

10.10 RELEASE OF THE NAQS

The NAQS was finally released on 12 March 1997. It had not been changed greatly following consultation. Approximately 450 responses to the consultation exercise were received, 210 of which were from local authorities. Some respondents had called for air quality objectives to be even more tightly framed, while others had countered this by arguing that stricter controls would impose high costs on industry. It appears, however, that the majority of respondents endorsed the original draft objectives and the target date for achievement of 2005. The NAQS sets out the contribution which key sectors, ie industry, transport and local government, will need to make if the objectives are to be achieved. It relies heavily on the existing pollution control framework, ie EPA 1990 and the CAA 1993, stressing, yet again, that the system of local control introduced by the Environment Act 1995 is designed to complement existing legislation, dealing with individual pollution 'hot spots'. Even as launched, the NAQS contained some objectives which were stated to be 'provisional' (see further **10.10.3**) because of uncertainties over the exact reductions which are needed and achievable. The NAQS as a whole would also be subject to periodic review, beginning in 1999, so that its progress may be assessed, together with the relevance of the objectives and the cost-effectiveness of any proposed improvement measures.

10.10.1 Features of the NAQS

Although the NAQS exists under law, and has, as its background, a considerable panoply of powers and duties with the ability reserved to ministers of introducing a whole new range of regulatory measures, a reading of the Strategy gives rise to the following conclusions:

- regulatory activity will play, at most, a limited role in achieving policy objectives;
- the role of local authorities is limited – they are not encouraged to take radical action on air quality issues and are required to behave proportionately, taking into account cost–benefit issues;
- much will depend on the continuing implementation of measures under the CAA 1993 and EPA 1990, as opposed to the specific provisions of the Environment Act 1995;
- there is a touching reliance on voluntary activity, information and education leading to the making of 'environmentally friendly' choices by individuals, organisations and companies – in many cases, however, without the financial 'carrot and stick' approach which figures elsewhere in environmental protection legislation (eg with regard to countryside protection, where positive programmes of national grant aid to farmers encourage the voluntary adoption of particular practices);
- some use may increasingly be made of fiscal measures to assist in achieving policy implementation.

The content of the national strategy must be studied in some detail to appreciate these points in context.

10.10.2 Policy background

Air quality management in the UK is part of the wider commitment to sustainable development, with emphasis on developing strategic, objective-led techniques of managing environmental change. In particular, good air quality is essential to the promotion of good human health, although, in the UK, healthy individuals are unlikely to suffer acute problems in the sort of pollution episodes which may occur. Good air quality is also important for the good health of forests, lakes, crops, wildlife and buildings, and at a further level of abstraction the control of individual emissions which are the precursors of major pollutants (eg ozone) can have a 'knock-on' effect in relation to reducing global warming.

A framework for achieving good air quality nationally is emerging rapidly. The clean air legislation has largely curbed domestic smoke emissions, while EPA 1990 applies to manage and reduce industrial emissions. There is also a comprehensive approach, based on European obligations, to reducing vehicle emissions. Indeed, there is an emergent European framework for managing air quality for the next decade and beyond, while international treaties apply to control most transboundary pollutants. In particular, the NAQS refers to the EC's Ambient Air Quality Assessment and Management Directive (Directive 96/62/EC) – a 'framework' Directive, under which 'daughter' Directives will specify limit or guide values for particular pollutants to replace the existing air quality Directives. This will require monitoring of pollutants, and the preparation of plans to reduce them will increase where limit values are transgressed or are likely to be transgressed (see **10.2**). The UK will meet its obligations under the Environment Act 1995. Nevertheless, there remain certain ambient concentrations of pollutants at a local level arising from local sources which give rise to episodes of elevated pollution levels. The NAQS is particularly concerned with managing such sources and episodes, on a cost-effective and proportionate basis. The strategy does not therefore deal with 'interface issues' such as the contribution air quality may make to the eutrophication of water.

10.10.3 Standards and objectives

Currently, in both the UK and the European Community, the legislative approach to air quality is fragmented, with concepts and measures not easily related to one another, and consisting of a range of standards, objectives, targets, guide and limit values. The NAQS aims to introduce a more easily understood conceptual framework by introducing 'standards' and 'objectives':

- *Standards*: concentrations of pollutants in the air which broadly achieve a particular level of environmental quality based on an assessment of the effect of each pollutant on health.
- *Objectives*: policy targets indicating what central government believes should be achieved in the light of the standards, and generally expressed as an ambient concentration of a pollutant to be achieved within a given time-scale.

Overall national policy is directed to achieving the objectives, while the Environment Agency, SEPA and local authorities are further required to take account of the NAQS when exercising functions under EPA 1990. On their being given regulatory force under the Environment Act 1995, local authorities will be required to create AQMAs in places where the objectives are not likely to be met by national action alone, and particular local complementary action is needed. For the finalised NAQS standards and objectives proposals, see Figure 7.

The standards have been set solely on the basis of scientific and medical evidence relating to the effects of pollutants on health, and, in some cases, on the wider environment, and are defined in terms of zero or minimum risk levels. Objectives, which are the regulatory measures, do take into account cost–benefit issues. Standards cannot be taken to be free of a degree of evaluation, although they are based on the best available scientific evidence and understanding. Thus, for ozone, sulphur dioxide, carbon monoxide and nitrogen dioxide, concentrations below which effects are unlikely even for sensitive persons can be identified, but for the genotoxic carcinogens such as benzene and 1,3-butadiene, there is no such level because these are 'zero risk' and, as such, standards are set on a basis reflecting an exceedingly small risk to human health. Similarly, for particulate matter the standard reflects a minimum risk of health impact on the population.

The objectives have been designed to be achieved by 2005, although where improvements in air quality can be achieved before then on a practicable, cost-effective basis, they should be so achieved. Once an improvement is achieved it should be sustained. However, the aim is to secure a steady decrease in ambient pollutant levels by 2005. In some cases it is open to doubt whether the objectives are achievable, partly because much depends on the efficacy of measures taken under current and future European legislation. In relation to nitrogen dioxide and particulates, for example, a 10 per cent gap could arise between objective and performance – a gap affected by a range of variables such as the weather, the accuracy of emission-reduction predictions, the effects of individual local actions (eg traffic management plans), changes in consumer behaviour (eg driving patterns), and further scientific or medical understanding of the effects of pollutants. Thus, some objectives are set on a provisional basis, and may be changed as the NAQS is reviewed and modified, when the costs and benefits of various alternative measures and their relationship to the objectives will be considered. Furthermore, the objectives have a particular ambit in that they apply in non-occupational near ground level, outdoor locations where, over a relevant averaging period, a human being might reasonably expect to be exposed. Objectives do not, therefore, have to be met in every conceivable location, but only in those places where a particular pollutant could be reasonably taken to affect a 'target' person.

Figure 7. Standards and objectives

Pollutant	*Standard*		*Objective – to be achieved by 2005*
	concentration	*measured as*	
Benzene	5ppb	running annual mean	5ppb
1,3-butadiene	1ppb	running annual mean	1ppb
Carbon monoxide	10ppm	running 8-hour mean	10ppm
Lead	0.5 $\mu g/m^3$	annual mean	0.5 $\mu g/m^3$
Nitrogen dioxide	150ppb	one-hour mean	150ppb, hourly mean*
	21ppb	annual mean	21ppb, annual mean*
Ozone	50ppb	running 8-hour mean	50ppb, measured as the 97th percentile*
Fine particles (PM_{10})	50 $\mu g/m^3$	running 24-hour mean	50 $\mu g/m^3$, measured as the 99th percentile*
Sulphur dioxide	100ppb	15-minute mean	100ppb, measured as the 99th percentile*

ppm=parts per million; ppb=parts per billion; $\mu g/m^3$ =micrograms per cubic metre;
* = these objectives were initially regarded as provisional, but have since been given legal force by the Air Quality Regulations 1997, SI 1997/3043, see **10.13.3**.

10.10.4 Further explanation

The references to 'percentiles' are explained as follows. Where an objective is to be complied with to the 99.9th percentile, 99.9 per cent of all measurements at each point of measurement during the relevant period (eg one year) must be at or below the specified level. This allows for occasional exceedences and reflects acceptance of arguments that requiring 100 per cent compliance would impose disproportionate costs. Similarly, the values for nitrogen dioxide, lead, sulphur dioxide and particles reflect current EC requirements and, if and when these are changed, there will be a review to see whether UK national objectives need to be further revised.

10.10.5 A controversial issue

A controversial feature of the 'standards and objectives' is the nitrogen dioxide concentration. The draft strategy suggested a concentration standard of 104.6ppb as an hourly mean, and 20ppb as a yearly mean. The justification for this change was given in December 1996 when the EPAQS concluded that a 1976 study, which showed that a concentration of 100ppb of nitrogen dioxide could affect persons with asthma, was isolated and its findings had never been repeated. The EPAQS therefore concluded that the initial concentration figures, derived from WHO figures, were excessive, and that the 150ppb hourly average figure would be sufficient to secure a high level of health protection.

10.10.6 Possible future standards

The EPAQS has recommended a long-term benzene exposure standard of 1ppb, and the possibility of including that figure will be examined on review. Similarly, the EPAQS has recommended a review of the particulate standard in 2002, reconsideration of the nitrogen dioxide standard by 2000 and of the 1,3-butadiene standard within a period of five years at most. The Government undertook to address these issues in the review, which will also examine whether other pollutants should be brought within the scope of the NAQS, for example polycyclic aromatic hydrocarbons (PAHs), which may, by then, be subject to an international treaty on the control of persistent organic pollutants. The review will also address the issue of further integrating ecosystem protection into the strategy.

10.11 ACHIEVING THE OBJECTIVES: THE NATIONAL PATTERN

The NAQS declares that the Government will consider the full range of policy options open in order to achieve the objectives, including regulation and the use of economic instruments, pointing to the existence of the price differential between leaded and unleaded petrol, and the introduction in the 1996 budget of a lower duty rate on ultra low-sulphur diesel relative to ordinary diesel fuel.

The strategy then goes on to consider the general framework for achieving the objectives for individual pollutants.

10.11.1 Nitrogen dioxide and other nitrogen oxides

The principal means of achieving the objectives for nitrogen dioxide and other nitrogen oxides are vehicle emission and fuel quality standards, which exist within a European dimension and which should achieve a 42 per cent reduction in nitrogen oxide emissions from urban road transport relative to 1995 levels by 2020. An earlier reduction of 45 to 47 per cent could be achieved by 2005 if the EC Commission's auto-oil programme is implemented. In addition, the application of controls under the IPC and LAAPC programmes is essential where there are significant stationary pollution sources. Where local traffic conditions create pollution hot spots there may be a need for local traffic management programmes.

10.11.2 Ozone

Ozone damages crops, materials and, in some cases, human health. Discernible effects are observed at 80 to 100ppb, hence the objective standard of 50ppb over an eight-hour averaging period. The emission of precursors of ozone could be reduced by the UK, but, because of the transboundary nature of the pollutant, Europe-wide action is needed. However, by reducing nitrogen oxide emissions and those of volatile organic compounds (VOCs), both significant precursors of ozone, the UK can play a major part in that action. Upgrading of emission standards under IPC and LAAPC, and the introduction of new fuel composition standards, will, for example, reduce total VOC emissions by 40 per cent relative to 1988 levels by 2005. From time to time measures will need to be targeted at key pollutants, particularly at critical times at the onset of an ozone episode, but some of these could occur on a short-term voluntary basis. The Government, nevertheless, hoped that the combination of these measures would enable the UK to meet its objective by 2005 throughout the summer months in most areas, and in the south, where the problem of summer ozone smog is worst, for all but 10 days per annum or better on average – thus, the setting of an objective of achieving the ozone standard on a 97 percentile basis. To reinforce this the Government will: further seek an early agreement on and ratification of a UNECE protocol on multi-pollutant emissions; seek to ensure that a proposed EC Directive on solvents deals appropriately with those having a high photochemical ozone creation potential; improve co-ordination internationally in giving warning of potential ozone episodes; and discuss voluntary measures with industry and other groups on limiting emissions at the onset of photo oxident emissions. The benefits of reduced ozone could be reflected in fewer hospital admissions of living impairment function cases, and a reduction in the estimated £350 million bill for ozone damage to materials and buildings.

10.11.3 Particles

The objective is to reduce particles in urban areas so that they contribute less and less to wintertime smog and, thus, improve public health. Urban transport is the main target for the emission-reduction programme, and a reduction of 60 per cent in 1995 levels by 2005 is needed. This can, it is believed, be achieved by: a cost-effective package of vehicle and fuel standards from the European Community; giving guidance to local authorities on traffic management powers which they could implement under the Environment Act 1995; enhanced enforcement of vehicle emission standards; encouraging use of alternative fuels shown to be cost-effective means of improving air quality; reviewing the use of economic instruments as a means of encouraging environmentally friendly transport choices; the continued application of IPC and LAAPC in relevant situations; and the continued application of budgetary measures already encouraging the use of particular fuels. In themselves, these factors can reduce emissions by 50 to 55 per cent – some five to 10 per cent short of meeting the required 60 per cent reduction, particularly in some areas. It remains to be seen, therefore, whether the existing measures will be able to close that gap in a cost-effective manner.

10.11.4 Sulphur dioxide

National policy should achieve the overall objective, but this will leave local problems of two sorts: high background levels of sulphur dioxide during the winter months in those areas where there is still considerable domestic coal burning; and localised plume grounding – a phenomenon whereby the efflux from a chimney bends down to ground level rather than dispersing into the atmosphere – from certain local combustion sources still using coal or oil by 2005. These problems may be obviated by a continuing change from coal to other fuels for domestic heating, but if this does not appear to be the case by the time of the review of the NAQS, consideration should be given to the introduction of further regulatory powers or economic instruments aimed at reducing domestic fuel sulphur content. The plume grounding problem, which is largely associated with electricity production, should be obviated by the closure of, or reduction in, the operation of coal combustion power generation plants, and an 85 per cent reduction of sulphur emissions from such sources is predicted between 1997 and 2005. Conditions could be imposed under IPC authorisations on certain pollution sources that at such times when climatic conditions are likely to cause plume grounding, low sulphur fuels are burned. Such arrangements are already proposed for some power stations. A further problem is the existence of small combustion plants not covered by IPC/LAAPC regulations. These will be subject to further review, and a modification of the guidance on chimney heights under the CAA 1993 may be issued to ensure that such sources do not contribute to local sulphur dioxide concentrations. Such plant may also be subject to fuel composition controls and economic instruments influencing fuel use. As an indication of likely future policy, on 8 January 1998 the Environment Agency, taking into account the NAQS objectives for sulphur dioxide, began consultation on bringing forward the 84 per cent reduction in power station emissions in England and

Wales from 2005 to 2001. Changing technologies in power production, such as the use of gas fired stations, should reduce sulphur dioxide emissions from 2,340,000 tonnes per annum (1991 levels) to 500,000 tonnes in 2001. The Agency sought a further reduction to 365,000 tonnes. Station operators could be expected to extend the use of flue gas de-sulphurisation techniques, utilise more low-sulphur coal, inject neutralising limestone into furnaces, or decrease the use of older coal fired stations – most of which are due to be decommissioned by 2010 in any case.

10.12 ACHIEVING THE NAQS: SECTORAL CONTRIBUTIONS

In order to achieve the objectives of the NAQS, central government will need to work closely with business and industry, and take particular heed of the problems of air pollution arising from transport. Local authorities will have a special rôle to play, especially insofar as local initiatives will need to be accepted by local people. Indeed, at the national level a considerable amount of public education will be needed if the objectives are to be met, particularly where the strategy relies on voluntary acts by businesses, organisations and individuals.

10.12.1 Contribution of business and industry

While industry may reduce its emissions by developing new, cost-effective technologies and by taking voluntary action such as converting vehicles to run on alternative fuels or by promoting car-sharing among employees, the regulatory framework is likely to be of prime importance in achieving air quality objectives, particularly in relation to pollutants such as particles and sulphur dioxide where industrial emissions are, respectively, 59 per cent and 89 per cent of national totals. In exercising IPC/LAAPC powers, relevant authorisation bodies[1] are required by the Environment Act 1995 (see s 7(12)(g) of EPA 1990, inserted by the 1995 Act) to take the NAQS into account, and this will be reflected in upgrading the conditions in plant authorisations. In situations where a pollution hot spot is identified in a particular locality, even following tightened BATNEEC requirements under IPC/LAAPC powers, it is clear that before a local authority could take action under the 1995 Act the strategy would require them to ask whether eliminating the hot spot would bring about a proportionate benefit to the environment locally. It is further clear policy that a disproportionate burden should not fall on industry in the elimination of a hot spot, bearing in mind industry's share in responsibility for its existence relative to other sources, and the Government will ensure, either by using powers to give directions, eg to the Environment Agency, or, if necessary, via primary legislation, that this principle is observed. In cases where a number of sectors are responsible for the emission of a pollutant, a reduction overall should be sought on a marginal cost basis, ie by seeking reductions

1 See Chapters 6 and 7.

from sectors best able to reduce their emissions at lowest cost. Such an approach should preclude disproportionate costs being inflicted on industry. Indeed, as a general principle, pollution-reduction targets should be sought from the most cost-effective quarter. In any case in relation to IPC-regulated plant, the primary requirement of the EPA 1990 is that pollution control should follow the route of the best practicable environmental option (BPEO), ie to seek the best 'pollution route' for the environment as a whole, and the existence of the strategy does not mean that the atmosphere should be given a favoured status relative to land and water. Achieving the objectives, therefore, is just one factor to be taken into account in an IPC/LAAPC authorisation, along with BATNEEC requirements, site-specific issues and the fact that in some cases an authorisation may need to be framed so as best to deal with more than one pollutant. The principle of targeting reductions on those sectors best able to achieve them at the lowest cost should also apply to targeting reductions against different firms in the same industrial sector, and to targeting reductions as between different industrial sectors.

The strategy adds that overall policy is also to give individual operators flexibility so that they may choose emission measures which deliver the greatest reductions at the lowest cost. Furthermore, where an IPC or LAAPC authorisation is given its conditions should generally be expressed as site-specific emission limits, rather than as a requirement to institute a particular technology, and it will continue to be the general case that emission limits are set on a plant-by-plant basis, although in individual cases it may be more appropriate to prescribe a particular technology or technical measure, for example where a general emission limit might be difficult to enforce. The NAQS does, however, contain a warning for operators that air quality considerations are to be major factors in informing the judgment of regulatory bodies. Indeed, where *already existing* statutory air quality limits are likely to be exceeded, the law requires regulators to consider how industry could contribute to achieving the limits, which could be enough to justify stricter conditions on an individual plant authorised under the IPC provisions than would otherwise have been imposed solely on the BATNEEC and BPEO considerations. However, this latitude for regulators applies only in respect of plant subject to IPC control.

Clearly, the above issues could be very important for any business seeking to appeal against or otherwise challenge an IPC/LAAPC authorisation on the basis that its requirements imposed disproportionate obligations not imposed on similar operators, or, perhaps even more controversially, imposed obligations where the same pollution-reduction target within an area could have been achieved by taking measures aimed at other sectors. The relationship between IPC/LAAPC authorisations and the strategy may well, therefore, give rise to litigious opportunities.

In any case, it is policy that the authorisation requirements of the IPC and LAAPC processes should be upgraded, and this may lead to the replacement of older plant with new, thus bringing about reductions in emissions. The strategy document claims that there is a visible trend towards significant emission reductions consequent on the operation of the IPC system – a trend likely to be continued as authorisations become subject to four-yearly reviews. These claims are supported by the Government's *Digest of Environmental Statistics* (July 1997), which indicated the following:

- *nitrous oxides*: 1995 emissions were 95,000 tonnes – 21 per cent down on 1990, but with non-combustion processes contributing to 67 per cent of the total;
- *sulphur dioxide*: 1995 emissions were 2.4 million tonnes – 13 per cent down on 1994 figures, while total emissions were 4.9 million tonnes in 1980 and 6.4 million tonnes in 1970; coal fired power stations accounted for most of the emissions, and coal as a fuel type was the principal source of sulphur dioxide emissions overall;
- *particles and black smoke*: 1995 emissions of black smoke were 356,000 tonnes – 12 per cent down on 1994 figures, 50 per cent of emissions coming from road transport, while emissions from domestic users fell by 75 per cent between 1980 and 1995; PM_{10} emissions fell by 14 per cent between 1990 and 1995, and the 232,000 tonnes emitted in 1995 were 32 per cent down on 1980, some 50 per cent of PM_{10} emissions coming from road transport and non-combustion processes, eg construction, mining and quarrying;
- *nitrogen oxides*: 1995 emissions of 2.3 million tonnes – down five per cent on 1994 levels, 49 per cent of these coming from road traffic, but such emissions have reduced since 1989 following the introduction of catalytic converters for motor cars;
- *carbon monoxide*: 1995 emissions were 5.5 million tonnes – down eight per cent on 1994 levels, 75 per cent coming from road vehicles, although even here, a 28 per cent reduction has occurred since 1989;
- *lead*: 1995 emissions were some 1,000 tonnes – down 50 per cent on the 1990 figure;
- VOCs: 1995 emissions were 2.3 million tonnes – down four per cent on 1994 levels, use of solvents and road transport contributing 30 per cent each to local emissions.

The digest of figures also shows that: sulphur dioxide led to poor air quality being recorded at 50 per cent of monitoring sites at least once in 1995, with Belfast being the most affected centre; PM_{10} exceeded air standards at all urban monitoring sites in 1995 at least once, with Liverpool city centre and Bloomsbury in London being the most affected areas; nitrogen oxide exceedences of standards leading to poor air quality were recorded at least once in 1995 at 15 out of 29 national monitoring sites – all in urban areas. Ground level concentration of ozone led to poor quality recordings at 22 out of 32 monitoring sites at least once in 1995 – mostly in rural areas. Air quality would therefore appear to be improving overall, but with no room for complacency. Government claims for the efficiency of the IPC/LAAPC system in reducing emissions may also be justified, and further reductions in particular emissions may be achieved by considering regulation of certain small combustion plants currently outside LAAPC terms of reference, ie those of less than 20 megawatts rated thermal input. Consideration of this was promised in the NAQS, but the 1997 *Digest* figures point to transport, and, in particular, road transport, as the prime source of emissions.

10.12.2 Contribution of transport

The NAQS admits that transport emissions now match or exceed those of other sectors with regard to major pollutants, and in many urban areas transport is now the main pollution source due to increased traffic. Dealing with this problem demands a flexibility which allows the nation a modern transport system which is capable of supporting sustainable development with as little adverse environmental impact as possible, the promotion of personal safety and the preservation of freedom of choice (all at an acceptable cost). This is a difficult aim to achieve. Nevertheless, the strategy accepts that the progressive reduction of transport emissions from individuals, and reductions in the quality or growth of road transport, especially in vulnerable areas, must be central aims of policy on air quality, and this must be achieved against an increase in the number of cars on the road from 16 million to 20.5 million between 1984 and 1994, and further rapid growth predicted by 2025. Currently enhanced emission standards for new vehicles and the promotion of unleaded fuel appear able to contain the growth in emissions consequent on the increase in the number of vehicles, and emissions are expected overall to decline by 2010, but, thereafter, traffic growth could outstrip the ability of regulatory measures to contain emissions. Government policy must therefore:

- ensure that predicted reductions in emissions are realised, on an accelerated basis wherever possible, in order to meet objectives by 2005;
- sustain emission levels at objective levels once these have been achieved.

10.12.3 Achieving policy

It is not policy to set sectoral emission targets, and, as such, transport will not be made subject to a particular emissions limit. Nevertheless, it must be borne in mind that to achieve objectives in urban areas requires, inter alia, a reduction of 45 per cent to 60 per cent in nitrogen oxide emissions, and of 60 per cent in PM_{10}. How far the use of local measures and voluntary initiatives can go in achieving these reductions is uncertain, and this will be a matter returned to in the review of the NAQS. The task of central government is to seek:

- improvements in vehicle and fuel technology in order to reduce emissions;
- tighter controls over the management and operation of vehicles;
- promotion of a culture of environmental responsibility among vehicle fleet operators and the public at large;
- reduction in the need to travel by car by changes in planning and transport policy.

These aims must be pursued in a cost-effective manner. Moreover, no single aim is an 'instant fix' for the problem for the following reasons: vehicle technology improvements take up to five years to apply in practice; changing transport systems and traffic management priorities in urban areas could take five to 10 years; and changes in planning policies will only bear fruit sometime in the next century. Only improvements in vehicle inspection and maintenance, and changes in driver behaviour can deliver short-term gains, and thus, while all policies will be pursued, the first 'fruits' are likely to be tighter enforcement of vehicle emission standards, together with local action on traffic management and enhanced driver education on improved driving practices.

To reinforce good driving practice etc, in 1995 the former Department of Transport introduced, via its vehicle inspectorate, a programme of roadside emission compliance testing. The NAQS proposed a new, permanent legal framework for such testing, with roadside checks in urban areas implementing annual in-use tests, and enabling local authorities, with police assistance, to carry out their own roadside checks with enforcement powers utilising fixed penalties. A further regulatory power for authorities would be to issue fixed penalty notices to those who leave stationary vehicles with engines running unnecessarily. It will also be the case that post-2000 European vehicles standards will require vehicles to carry on-board emission diagnosis systems, so that drivers know when they are 'over the limit'.[1]

Public education is also requisite to promote responsible personal transport decisions. The Government can provide accurate information to the public on the problems of vehicle-generated pollutants, so that individuals may make informed choices; it can also encourage fleet owners to operate in an environmentally responsible way, and can work alongside local and voluntary bodies to promote responsible vehicle use. At a more strategic level the Standing Advisory Committee on Trunk Road Assessment (SACTRA) is now looking at links between traffic growth, transport investment and economic growth to see whether economic prosperity can be fostered with less-intensive vehicle use. Local traffic management and planning policies can also reduce vehicle use, but these are discussed further at **10.16** et seq.

10.12.4 Other transport sectors

Aircraft cause emission problems at high altitude where their nitrogen oxide emissions appear to be significant greenhouse gases and are also involved in a relationship with ozone. Only international action can deal with such problems, but the International Civil Aviation Organisation (ICAO) tightened nitrogen oxide emission standards by 20 per cent in 1993, and a further 16 per cent reduction is under consideration. Aviation fuel is currently tax exempt and action through the ICAO is possible to end this, thus making the fuel more expensive and, as such, helping to drive down its use – in theory at least.

Rail transport may be able to re-attract freight from the roads, which currently carry the bulk of freight. While rail transport is not emission-free, emissions from diesel engined trains account for less than one per cent of total UK emissions of pollutants. Furthermore, these should reduce even more as new or refurbished rolling stock comes on line. The new train companies are required by the Railways Act 1993 to have in place an environmental policy and must

1 See further Chapter 9.

take advice on environmental issues from the rail regulator. This, combined with control of diesel engined locomotives and trains in workplaces (eg while they are in stations, under the Health and Safety at Work Act 1974), is considered to be sufficient regulation of emissions from the railways.

10.12.5 Contribution of local authorities

Much of the implementation of the NAQS will fall to local authorities, particularly where cost-effective elimination of pollution hot spots by national measures is not possible. However, the strategy suggests that where it is appropriate for an authority to act, it should do so only in a cost-effective fashion. Where a local pollution hot spot is identified and national measures are insufficient to deal with it, it will be appropriate for the local authority to draw up a local plan under the Environment Act 1995 to tackle the issue. If authorities find, however, that their existing powers are insufficient for this task it will be for central government to determine whether further national or local powers are needed. Authorities are concerned not just with polluting emissions from particular sources, but should also use their planning and transport powers to further the national policy on air quality. Thus, the principles underpinning local authority action are:

- the need to operate in a cost-effective fashion, bearing in mind local environmental needs;
- the need to seek an appropriate balance in controlling emissions from domestic, industrial and transport sources;
- the need to avoid unnecessary regulation while observing principles of clarity, consistency and certainty;
- the need to bring together public, private and voluntary efforts.

Authorities will (as has become clear from the discussion earlier in this chapter) be subject to extensive guidance from central government on the development of local air quality strategies and action plans – all within the overall 'envelope' of developing local sustainable development strategies. It is clear that they are not expected to step outside the parameters set by this guidance – at least not so far as the previous Conservative Government was concerned. Thus, the local strategy should be achieved not just by particular initiatives on the air, but also as a result of transport planning, traffic management, land use planning, and energy and waste management functions. Authorities should also be prepared to work collaboratively with their neighbours to achieve their strategies, particularly in urban areas, and the local strategy should provide a framework for working with other authorities, the Environment Agency (in Scotland, SEPA), central government and transport agencies. Similarly, a partnership approach to achieving the implementation of policy with local industry is recommended, as is the educative function of authorities in furthering the central policy of providing the public with information about air quality, so that informed and responsible decisions may be made by individuals. This is particularly important where an AQMA exists, and members of the public need appropriate advice during high pollution episodes. The overall thrust of central strategic advice is that the public must be kept involved and informed if they are to 'own' certain local policies and to take appropriate action where needed. In this respect, authorities can also set good examples by minimising their own impact on air quality, for example by considering their use of vehicles of particular types.

10.12.6 Two inescapable principles for authorities

Two issues deserve highlighting: one is the central insistence on proportionate and cost-effective action by authorities; the second is the need to focus attention on problems recurring in particular locations. The task of authorities is to assess whether air quality objectives are likely to be met by 2005, using a variety of techniques variously appropriate to particular local circumstances; only these objectives can serve as 'triggers' for local action. An AQMA may, of course, be declared before 2005 where it is clearly needed, and all authorities should conclude their initial reviews and assessments of air quality by 1999, with at least one further review occurring before 2005. Some authorities have, since 1996, already commenced such a review and assessment on a voluntary basis and, in consequence of their experience, the rate support grant settlement for local authorities now provides some financial support for the new duties under the Environment Act 1995, as does a new supplementary credit approval scheme in England.

As part of the principle of 'proportionality', it is not envisaged that an AQMA, where designated, should blanket an authority's entire area, although, on a collaborative basis, an AQMA may cover parts of another authority's area. A flexible and responsive approach will be needed to tailor each AQMA to the needs of each area where one is needed. Within an AQMA, a further assessment of air quality is required within 12 months of designation, which should be subject to periodic review contemporaneously with, for example, a major revision of land use plans. The written action plan for improving air quality in an AQMA must be completed within two years of designation, and should lay down a time-scale for its implementation. As part of the cost-effective approach principle, it is clear that authorities will be given further regulatory powers only where it is clear that air quality cannot be improved by other (eg voluntary) means.

10.12.7 Relating local air quality powers to other functions

Planning

Air quality functions must be taken into account in the planning process as part of a more effective co-ordination of planning and environmental protection controls. To this end, central guidance to planning authorities will ensure that land use planning makes a contribution to achieving national air quality standards and objectives, and that air quality considerations are material factors in the planning process. Land planning policies will also have to be more effectively co-ordinated with the system for planning trunk roads, and regional planning guidance should be issued to provide for this.

Smoke controls
The clean air legislation has now been applied in most parts of England and Wales to introduce smoke controls, but in coalmining areas much coal is still burned domestically, leading to high levels of smoke and sulphur dioxide. If this problem cannot be dealt with under the CAA 1993, additional legislation may be needed.

Transport planning
It is the aspiration of central policy that improved transport planning can lead to achieving both local air quality policies and the Government's own climate change programme. The national strategy document is unfortunately vague, contenting itself with general statements as to the need to strike balances between improving air quality and maintaining the vitality and accessibility of urban centres. Local authorities are left with the task of developing local solutions to local problems. This is also true of particular measures of traffic management, whereby authorities may discourage the use of private transport and promote public transport, cycling or walking. The Environment Act 1995 must be taken into account where an authority is contemplating the use of powers under the Road Traffic Regulation Act 1984, and the Government has not ruled out the possibility of giving authorities additional permissive powers to control traffic – for example allowing for congestion charges to be introduced, or implementing area licences so that private car journeys into certain locations would have to be paid for. In addition, there are proposed powers for authorities to check emissions from vehicles at the kerbside, reinforced by fixed penalty charges (see **10.12.3**).

Urban environmental management
It is accepted that localised air quality problems are most likely to be encountered in urban areas, which may also experience other environmental problems such as litter, noise, accessibility problems and a lack of safety and security. Local programmes to enhance air quality should not exacerbate these problems, and authorities should produce local solutions which produce multi-benefits wherever possible, for example by introducing a combined heat and power scheme as a way of reducing atmospheric emissions, and upgrading local housing stock with an efficient source of affordable heat.

10.12.8 The role of individuals, commerce and industry

Transport emissions are nowadays generally the greatest polluting output from commerce and industry. Local authorities, in partnership with industry, should promote more effective vehicle fleet management to reduce emissions by introducing fuel-efficient vehicles and by seeking to reduce mileages by better route-planning. Employees could be encouraged to use trains and taxis, rather than cars, and thought should be given to phasing out fixed 'mileage allowances' which amount to a personal fuel subsidy. Industry and commerce may also be able to reduce their emissions by relocating their enterprises, and by more efficient fleet maintenance. Employees could be encouraged to become 'green commuters' according to a strategic framework which encourages reductions in car use, for example by providing incentives to buy public transport season tickets in the form of an easily repaid initial loan, giving out information on car-sharing and public transport, and encouraging the use of cycles via loan schemes and facilities for cycles to be stored safely. These schemes will not work, however, unless they have the clear support of both workers and management – hence the need for these schemes to be positively promoted. The public must be well-informed, both centrally and locally, about air quality and the choices available to individuals to 'do their bit', for example by avoiding short car journeys, adopting car-sharing, driving smoothly at moderate speed, and maintaining vehicles properly. It must be admitted, however, that the NAQS depends to a very considerable extent on the goodwill of the populace.

10.13 AFTER THE NAQS

The NAQS document appeared in the dying days of the outgoing Conservative Government in March 1997, but not before the Department of Trade and Industry had insisted on the inclusion of passages which stress the need for a proportional approach by local authorities. This was prompted by fear that industry could be saddled with heavy costs by some local authorities imposing emissions upgrading requirements over and above those required by IPC and LAAPC. The informed view now is that the working of the strategy will allow local controls above those existing under EPA 1990 only where an authority can make out a case that a particular operator or operators should accept a reasonable share of the additional cost of local anti-pollution measures under the Environment Act 1995. It is not thought that this will be likely to happen frequently once the new measures are fully operational. The most likely 'thrust' of the new strategy will be felt from a regulatory point of view with regard to traffic management, which will affect industry and individuals. The future may also bring enhanced fiscal measures favouring 'green' transport.

10.13.1 The Labour Government and the NAQS

The future will also bring implementation of, and modifications to, the NAQS. On 17 July 1997 ministers of the Labour Government announced that they would proceed to implement the strategy in full as a matter of urgency. Thus, the necessary air quality regulations were expected before the end of 1997, while the initial review promised for 1999 would commence in 1997, with proposals for modification to be brought forward by the end of 1998. The economic and scientific basis of the strategy will be examined along with a whole range of policy options taking account of all sources of pollution, but ensuring that disproportionate burdens do not fall on any one sector of society – thus preserving the previous Government's policy that no undue burdens fall on industry and commerce. The means to achieve this exist in legislative powers for ministers to give directions to authorising authorities in respect of IPC/LAAPC authorisations. If necessary, sections of EPA 1990 could be amended to further enhance the requirement in s 7(2)(c) of the Act that when authorisation conditions are imposed they should achieve compliance with any quality standards or objectives created by the Secretary of State, independently of the overall BATNEEC requirement. The NAQS will also take account of the EC Auto Oil Agreement of June 1997, under which Directives will be made to introduce stricter vehicle emission and fuel standards.[1]

In July 1997, 14 'first phase' areas were designated to test the draft air quality guidance on reviewing and assessing local air quality, including London where fears were immediately voiced that the various London boroughs do not keep corresponding records of traffic flows, thus making it difficult to reach conclusions on the contribution traffic makes to pollution. Furthermore, long-distance vehicles travelling through London may add considerably to local pollution problems. Approximately 90 authorities are involved overall in this exercise and, once their work is finished, more detailed guidance will be issued. In the meantime, further interim guidance was issued in August 1997, which recommends a three-stage approach to assessing local air quality:

- initially, 'significant' pollution sources should be screened (such sources to be defined in supplementary guidance);
- where this indicates a significant risk of non-compliance by 2005 with an air quality objective, 'homing in' should take place on locations having the highest likely concentrations of relevant pollutants, eg by monitoring ground level concentrations at industrial, urban and roadside locations;
- if this confirms a risk of significant non-compliance, further assessment will be required, perhaps requiring a detailed emission inventory of individual pollutants.

It appeared in mid-1997 that the full range of technical support information would not appear until December 1997 (eg national maps of background concentration of pollutants, historic air quality data, source maps of pollutants etc), with guidance on the selection and use of dispersion models for pollutants appearing in March 1998. It further appeared that the former Government's insistence that a local authority should not place blanket designation on their areas as AQMAs might be relaxed, and that it was accepted that there may be advantages in aligning AQMA boundaries with existing administrative or physical boundaries.

10.13.2 Green transport initiatives

The overall direction of the Labour Government's policy was made clearer in May 1997, when a series of 'green transport' initiatives was announced for the following month to draw attention to the dangers of air pollution, to encourage the use of bicycles for journeys to work, and to get children to walk to school, with a national 'car-free' day on 17 June 1997 - an event that was not a

1 See further Chapter 9.

conspicuous success. All these initiatives took place under a ministerially promoted 'Don't Choke Britain' campaign, as part of which ministers indicated that while no new additional public finance would be available, existing transport funding would be channelled increasingly towards local authorities putting forward schemes to improve public transport at the expense of the private car, such as integrated bus and train ticketing schemes and cycle lanes. This was the first step to redeem a Labour election manifesto pledge on integrated transport. On 6 June 1997 the Deputy Prime Minister, who is in overall control of the Department of the Environment, Transport and the Regions (DETR), promised a White Paper early in 1998 to put forward proposals to make public transport in towns more speedy, more reliable, more frequent and more efficient, while at the same time making private motoring more expensive by various taxing initiatives, and less convenient by 'squeezing' road space for cars consequent on the introduction of more bus lanes, possibly even permanently segregated. It was also made clear that the only way to meet the Government's pledge to reduce UK emissions of carbon dioxide by 20 per cent by 2010 would be for at least half the target to be met by restrictions on transport. The White Paper was preceded by a consultation exercise in autumn 1997.

The consultation exercise took initial account of arguments that despite improvements in vehicle technology, only reductions in the number of vehicles and their movements can, in the long term, reduce atmospheric pollutants. It is the declared policy of government now to increase use of public transport at the expense of the private car, and official predictions that traffic levels will increase by 36 to 57 per cent within 20 years, with approximately 10 million more cars on the roads by 2025, are unacceptable. A reduction in car use is also essential if the Government is to meet its target of reducing carbon dioxide emissions by 20 per cent by 2010. The consultation exercise thus invited comments on the extent to which the Government should restrain traffic, how far it should go in introducing traffic-reduction targets, the balance to be struck between the use of economic instruments and other forms of regulation, and how to improve public transport. The consultation paper made it clear, however, that hard public and private transport choices must be faced. Thus, taxes may be imposed on company parking spaces, and charges for public parking increased, while receipts may be channelled directly into enhanced public transport. Charging for road use by private vehicles may also enhance funding for public transport. There may be a reversal of the previous Government's deregulation of bus services which have led to unnecessary competition in some areas, while, overall, there has been a reduction in bus journeys since 1986 of 29 per cent, and an increase in local fare levels over the same time of 22 per cent in real terms. Stricter franchising controls over local public transport may be required to obligate transport companies to hold down fares and improve services. Further consultation on the role and use of trunk roads and motorways launched in July 1997 may lead to restricting local access to motorways, the setting of variable speed limits for different classes of traffic, and the giving of priority to certain classes over, for example, private cars.

10.13.3 Reiteration of the air quality objectives

Late in 1997 air quality regulations were laid in draft before Parliament by the Secretary of State, receiving parliamentary approval in December 1997 as the Air Quality Regulations 1997, SI 1997/3043, in force from 23 December 1997 and retaining the initial proposals considered at **10.8.13** above. The 'relevant period' for the purposes of s 86(3) of the Environment Act 1995 in relation to preparation of action plans is nine months, commencing when the district council first consults the relevant county council. For all other purposes the period is the time between the coming into force of the Regulations and 31 December 2005. The Regulations reiterate earlier proposed air quality objectives (see **10.10.3**) for listed substances:

- benzene – 5ppb or less, expressed as a running annual mean;
- 1,3-butadiene – 1ppb or less as a running annual mean;
- carbon monoxide – 10ppm or less expressed as a running eight-hour mean;
- lead – 0.5 micrograms per cubic metre or less, expressed as an annual mean;
- nitrogen dioxide – 150ppb or less when expressed as an hourly mean, and 21ppb or less expressed as an annual mean;
- PM_{10} – 50 micrograms per cubic metre or less when expressed as the 99th percentile of daily maximum running 24-hour means; and
- sulphur dioxide – 100ppb or less when expressed as the 99.9th percentile of 15-minute means.

For each of these substances the air quality objective is to restrict, by the end of the relevant period, the level at which the substance is present in air to that which is prescribed. For determining whether or not an objective is met, reference is to be made to the quality of air at locations which are outside buildings and other natural or man-made structures, above or below ground, and where members of the public are regularly present. Where, of course, any prescribed objective is not likely to be achieved in any part of an authority's area within the relevant period, they will have to designate that portion as an AQMA, and prepare an action plan stating how the various powers of the authority are to be used to meet the objectives. However, no objective has to be achieved before 2005.

10.13.4 Emission Factor Database

It was stressed by ministers on 18 December 1997 that authorities should commence a nationwide survey of air quality. The central government Emission Factor Database (EFD) was released on the Internet, containing information on the content and quality of emissions from transport and industry, to assist authorities in their task, along with four specific local emission inventories for Merseyside, Bristol, Southampton and Portsmouth, and Swansea and Port Talbot. The EFD, which is also available on CD-Rom, is accessible at http://www/environment.detr.gov.uk/airq/acinfo.htm. The four specific inventories are designed to show how the nature and extent of polluting activities can be mapped and analysed, together with the relative importance of different pollution sources (eg transport, industry etc) and their geographical distribution within regions. Further specific guidance for authorities exists in the form of:

- Environment Circular 15/97 (Welsh Office Circular 63/97);
- a framework for review and assessment of air quality;
- principal considerations in developing local air quality action plans and strategies;
- air quality and traffic management;
- air quality and land use planning.

Environment Circular 15/97 serves to summarise briefly the air quality functions of local authorities under the Environment Act 1995, to announce the publication of four general guidance documents, and to draw attention to the preparation of four further technical guidance notes on monitoring for air quality reviews and assessments, preparation and use of atmospheric emission inventories, selection and use of dispersion models, and pollutant-specific guidance for reviews and assessments. Both the general and specific guidance will be updated from time to time, and it is also intended to make them available on the Internet.

10.14 GENERAL GUIDANCE

The framework for review and assessment of air quality[1] lays down general principles for reviewing and assessing air quality, indicates the information local authorities should collect and collate for this purpose, and outlines the role of reviews and assessments in local air quality management. The initial objectives of reviews are stipulated as: first, identifying local areas where national measures appear to be unlikely to achieve national air quality objectives by the end of 2005; and, secondly, to ensure that air quality considerations are integrated into decisions on land use planning and traffic management. Authorities are further reminded that the air quality objectives provide the framework to determine the extent to which policies should aim at improving air quality, and provide a measure for each relevant pollutant whereby progress towards improved air quality can be assessed. Within this framework, authorities should concentrate activities only on priority areas where the objectives are unlikely to be met. To this end, all authorities should complete a first-stage review and assessment of air quality screening industry, transport and other sources of pollutants having significant impact within their districts. In any area where air pollution levels are below national air quality objectives, it will be unnecessary to undertake any more detailed investigation. Where, however, there is potential for elevated pollution levels, authorities should proceed to a second-stage review, estimating and modelling likely significant pollutants (eg from road transport). Only where this indicates a

1 LAQMG1(97). Specific technical guidance is also to be found in: LAQM.TG1(98) – monitoring for air quality reviews and assessments; LAQM.TG2(98) – preparation and use of atmospheric emissions inventories; LAQM.TG3(98) – selection and use of dispersion models.

failure to reach quality objective levels by 2005 should an authority progress to the third stage of making a detailed and accurate modelled review and assessment of relevant pollutants. There is no national blueprint for local reviews, but a general framework is available which all authorities should utilise. Thus, in areas likely only to need a first-stage review, existing air quality data and modelling techniques relying wholly or largely on existing national and local information will be adequate. It appears that in most localities existing national policy will achieve quality objectives for carbon monoxide, benzene, 1,3-butadiene and lead by 2005. Only authorities within whose areas there are plants or sources having the potential to result in elevated levels of these pollutants will need to undertake further review stages. In this context, 'potential' does not include the consequences of major industrial accidents. The fact, therefore, that, for example, the failure of an industrial storage tank in a given district could cause elevated pollution levels does not require the relevant authority to proceed to a further stage of assessment. It is with regard to SO_2, NO_x and PM_{10} emissions that local action is most likely, in areas where there is still considerable coal or oil combustion, or where there are major or highly congested roads.

10.14.1 The first stage – compilation of information

The first stage of the review will basically comprise:

- compilation and collation of existing/proposed significant sources of relevant pollutants of concern within each local authority's area, and those outside their areas which may lead to exceedences of objectives within them;
- collation of details of significant transport-related pollution sources, eg roads (existing or proposed);
- detailing industrial sources regulated under the IPC/LAAPC provisions of EPA 1990;
- detailing any other existing or proposed significant source of pollution, including, where appropriate, its location;
- describing sources of information used to compile the review and assessment;
- describing any surveys/investigations undertaken to compile the review and assessment;
- identifying all the foregoing existing and proposed activities having the potential, singly or together, to emit significant quantities of relevant pollutants and likely to be in existence/operation at the end of 2005, and in respect of which individuals in relevant locations are likely to be exposed.

There is no requirement at this stage to undertake monitoring of sources, construction of emission inventories or utilisation of air quality dispersion models, but the review should indicate that the authority in question have considered all sources of relevant pollutants which could have a significant impact within their area, have conducted a thorough search of existing information, have made reasonable attempts to obtain any missing information, and have used that information to come to a conclusion as to whether a second review stage is needed where there is/are a process/processes and/or activity/activities giving rise to emissions of a relevant pollutant/pollutants so that there is a more than negligible risk of failing to meet an air quality objective/objectives by the end of 2005.

10.14.2 The second stage – further screening

The purpose of the second stage of the review is to further screen pollutant concentrations identified at the first stage. While not requiring an estimation of every area of exceedence within the boundary of an authority for each relevant pollutant, this stage will involve authorities selecting a number of areas within their localities where the highest likely concentrations of relevant pollutants identified at the first stage are likely to occur in places where members of the public are likely to be exposed. In addition, any area highlighted at the first stage as containing uncharacterised pollutant sources which could be significant sources of relevant pollutants should be reviewed. Further review and assessment should be undertaken in all areas on whether there is a significant risk of an air quality objective not being met by 2005. This will entail estimating ground level concentrations of relevant pollutants at a combination of roadside, industrial and urban background locations, as appropriate, to predict potential pollution concentrations as at 1998 and 2005 levels. These estimates will take place according to technical guidance from the DETR. In selecting measurement locations, however, authorities should proceed on a precautionary basis.

Second-stage information will consist of the following:

- lists of pollutants requiring further examination as identified by stage 1;
- details of monitoring of these pollutants, including pollutant species measured, their concentrations and averaging times, monitoring periods, estimates of the accuracy of any resulting measurements, monitoring techniques and sampling systems employed, site details, quality-control measures, calibration of instruments, descriptions of data-processing techniques employed, and references to central technical guidance;
- details of modelling activities, including model outputs of predicted pollutant concentrations, details of model input data, estimations of the accuracy of models, descriptions of models, details of validation of models, and references to central technical guidance;
- details of reviews and assessments of methodologies used, including references to central technical guidance, estimated background concentrations used in assessments, and details of calculation methods.

This information may be collated and presented in a map format, while the second-stage report should indicate pollutants which require further investigation. This will result in a third-stage review where, in appropriate areas, stage 2 indicates that an air quality objective is not being achieved or, while being achieved, is at significant risk of being exceeded in future.

10.14.3 The third stage – the detailed review

More sophisticated modelling and monitoring techniques will be required at the third stage, but the crucial issue at this stage – and no earlier – is to determine whether a failure in a given area to achieve an air quality objective by the end of 2005 is likely, as this will trigger the need for an AQMA. Acting with the aid of central technical guidance, authorities will investigate areas where there is a likely failure to achieve objectives and a potential of exposure of individuals to relevant pollutants, on the basis of the magnitude and geographical extent of potential exceedences. This may require the compilation of a detailed emissions inventory for an area, and the use of sophisticated modelling dispersion techniques which must, however, be checked against and validated by actual monitoring of emissions. Monitoring should certainly occur in any area where pollutant concentrations are high, and where there is likely to be exposure of members of the public.

Third-stage information will consist of the following:

- a list of pollutants identified at stage 2;
- details of monitoring of these pollutants, including species measured, their concentrations and averaging times, monitoring periods, estimates of the accuracy of measurements, monitoring techniques employed, sampling systems used, site details, quality-control measures, descriptions of data processing techniques employed, and references to central technical guidance;
- details of construction of emission inventories, including pollutant species considered, the time period of the inventory and its spatial resolution and geographical boundary, sources of information used and methodological statements, including references to central technical guidance;
- details of modelling activities, including model outputs, details of model input data such as assumptions as to meteorology, emissions, traffic flows etc, estimates of the accuracy of predictions, references to validation of models, and references to central technical guidance;
- details of review methodologies, including references to central technical guidance, estimates of background concentrations used in assessments and details of estimation methods.

This information may be collated and presented in map format, and the third-stage report should conclude by listing pollutants reviewed and any areas to be designated as AQMAs. The various reviews should be concluded expeditiously, although the Secretary of State may, exceptionally, use his reserve powers under the Environment Act 1995 to order a review where an authority is not making sufficient progress. In general, authorities should undertake one complete review cycle within two years of Part IV of the 1995 Act coming into force (ie effectively by 2000), and one further cycle before the end of 2005.

10.14.4 Designating an AQMA

Although an AQMA should be designated only in areas where air quality objectives are not likely to be achieved, some latitude will be allowed in the drawing of boundaries because air quality in localities will vary on a spatial and temporal basis, thus making the designation of precise boundaries on the basis of the empirical evidence impossible. Authorities may configure AQMAs according to existing physical or administrative boundaries, provided that is defensible according to the data to hand. Authorities should also remember that air quality within an AQMA may be affected by factors arising outside it, for example, transport movements. Powers relevant to achieving AQMA objectives may therefore have to be exercised over a wider area than the AQMA itself. Once an AQMA is designated there must be, under s 84(1) of the Environment Act 1995, a 'further assessment' of existing and likely future air quality in the area to supplement information already to hand. All this information should be used to reassess existing and future air quality so that there is a sufficient information base for developing action plans. Further supplementary assessments of air quality may also be necessary. One particular task, however, is to identify the relative contribution of each pollutant source (identified in the review processes) to local air quality problems so as to allow an authority to identify sources over which they may exercise control or influence in the pursuit of the air quality objectives. Following completion of the s 84(1) assessment, an authority should be able to make a final determination of the extent to which air quality objectives are unlikely to be achieved by the end of 2005, and to make their action plan response. This should involve targeting responses to problems and ensuring that each sector's contribution to achieve plan objectives is proportionate and cost-effective.

10.14.5 The action plan

The action plan must include statements of the time-scales according to which its proposals are to be implemented, while the plan itself should, according to central policy, be completed within one year of the s 84(1) further assessment (see further **10.15** et seq on guidance on developing local air quality strategies and action plans).

10.14.6 Consultative requirements

Schedule 11 to the Environment Act 1995 requires consultation on the part of authorities in the air quality review and assessment process with the Secretary of State, the Environment Agency, the Highways Authority, neighbouring local authorities, the county council (where applicable), relevant national park authorities, other relevant public authorities and bodies representative of local business interests, and other bodies considered appropriate. This consultation refers to air quality reviews and assessments, the 'further review' once an AQMA is designated, and preparing and/or revising an action plan. Consultation is further counselled with, inter alia, relevant community and environmental groups, and the involvement of the general public via public meetings, use of the media and displays of information. The object is to secure local 'ownership' of action plans, although there is no legal obligation to make publicly available all material collected in the review and assessment process. However, information held by authorities is subject to the requirements of the Environmental Information Regulations 1992, SI 1992/3240, which impose particular disclosure obligations in respect of requests for information. Consultation should take place, inter alia, on the proposed starting date of an air quality review and assessment, its time-scale for completion, and the broad plan of approach. Consultees should be informed whether the review is being carried out on the basis of a grouping of authorities, and of the existence of other consultees or classes of consultees. The process should enable all concerned to make their views known and to highlight areas of concern. Consultees should also be able to comment on the full set of data collected during the review and assessment process, its interpretation and any conclusions drawn from it. The review methodology adopted should therefore be accessible, as should the reasoning which leads to the designation of an AQMA where this occurs. It should also be made clear to consultees what stage the overall review procedure has reached, and whether different stages apply to different areas within an authority's district. A report on the review should be made available for consultation, and the final report must take account of consultation responses during the entire process. There should also be consultation on the s 84(1) further assessment following designation of an AQMA, which will produce information on which the action plan will be based. A report of data relevant to the area in question collected in the review and assessment process should be released publicly at this stage. Further public consultation is required on the preparation of the action plan, and it is central policy that consultees should be entitled to state a preliminary view on the plan's contents at the same time as the s 84(1) further assessment is subject to consultation. There should also be consultation on the draft action plan, which should include: details of pollutants to be addressed and indications of their source(s); involvement of other local authorities in achieving plan objectives; any proposals from a relevant county council; the time-scale of implementation; and indications of where action by other persons or bodies is needed to secure implementation. In general, at least six weeks should be allowed for each consultation exercise.

Consultation with county councils

Guidance is given centrally on the consultation exercise required under s 86(2) and (3) of the Environment Act 1995 between, where appropriate, district and county councils. It is particularly stressed that this consultation should take place at the beginning of the action plan preparation process, and immediately after the designation of an AQMA. In addition, stress is laid on the development of voluntary information exchange systems involving relevant local authorities, the Environment Agency, business and community groups.

10.15 DEVELOPING LOCAL AIR QUALITY ACTION PLANS AND STRATEGIES

The Framework for review and assessment of air quality[1] lays down the principal considerations in relation to developing local air quality action plans and strategies. These include basic requirements that action to achieve air quality objectives may need to be carried out on a geographically wider base than an AQMA, while air quality strategies and plans must be updated regularly to take account of changes in air quality. Furthermore, any action taken may need to complement the plans and actions of other authorities – air quality is no respecter of administrative boundaries. Thus, the local strategies and plans of neighbouring authorities should be complementary and effective.

10.15.1 Local air quality strategies

The prime objective in relation to local air quality strategies is to integrate air quality considerations into local policy frameworks and to ensure that they complement other local strategies, irrespective of whether an authority needs to designate an AQMA. Furthermore, air quality must be taken into account in local decision-making, especially in the broader context of seeking to promote sustainable development. This has implications for the transport, planning, waste and other economic functions of authorities, and entails a multi-disciplinary teamwork approach. Furthermore, as air pollution is no respecter of administrative boundaries, inter-authority co-operation is essential, and may best be promoted by local strategic authority groupings. Strategies should also provide for liaison with outside bodies, such as the Environment Agency, central government departments, business interests and representatives of local communities (particularly the latter if local ownership of air quality improvement measures is to be achieved). In some cases, it may be appropriate to enter into partnership arrangements with local businesses, interests and communities to deliver air quality improvements. In addition, forums can be established in which all interested sectors can discuss their contributions to making improvements. Authorities should also utilise their educative and informative functions to raise public awareness of air quality issues generally, to improve local responses, and to ensure that the public has day-to-day information on air pollution issues utilising the pollution bandings adopted by central government in November 1997 – 'low', 'moderate', 'high' and 'very high' (see **10.6.2**). Finally, authorities should demonstrate their own local commitment to improving air quality by their practices, for example by encouraging cycling to work by their staff, using alternative fuels in vehicles, encouraging 'green' commuting, etc.

10.15.2 Action plans for AQMAs

Where an AQMA is designated and an action plan is required, authorities should:

---

1 LAQMG2(97).

- evaluate the options available in improving air quality;
- involve all relevant authority departments to ensure an integrated approach;
- use all available statutory powers (eg under clean air legislation) as part of that considered and integrated approach;
- ensure that the contributions of all sectors to improvements are cost-effective and proportionate;
- bear in mind central government work on reviewing the NAQS;
- identify local hot spots where action taken at a national level will not be enough to deliver air quality objectives;
- identify areas where local action alone will not be sufficient to deliver objectives (which may lead to further additional national action) to ensure that action is taken at the most appropriate level;
- adopt flexible co-operative arrangements where these are more appropriate than regulatory measures;
- identify matters which cannot be dealt with within the parameters of existing local powers, and indicate where achieving the objectives of an AQMA is dependent on action by other agencies and their involvement in plan production;
- where appropriate, act collaboratively with other tiers of local government according to the terms of the Environment Act 1995;
- ensure that all those likely to be affected by an AQMA designation are consulted and fully informed about the consequences of designation to ensure that they understand the purposes and objectives of the action plan.

10.16 AIR QUALITY AND TRAFFIC MANAGEMENT

The Framework for review and assessment of air quality[1] is designed to assist authorities in determining the role of traffic management in achieving a balanced approach to local air quality improvements. In particular, in drawing up an action plan for any AQMA the authority must consider local traffic's contribution to pollutant levels in their area, and whether local traffic management could play a part in achieving improvements, in which case the authority will still need to pursue a balanced and integrated approach so that the burdens falling on various sectors are proportionate and cost-effective. To this end, authorities should bear in mind that:

- it is necessary to consider traffic management and planning over a wide area as localised schemes may have little impact outside their immediate locality;
- reducing congestion and keeping traffic moving freely reduces emissions;
- reduced congestion, however, must be protected against increases in the overall number of vehicle movements;
- a package of complementary measures will probably be needed in most cases to reduce vehicular movement in critical areas.

1 LAQMG3(97).

10.16.1 Aims and objectives

The overall objective of air quality and traffic management should be to reduce emissions by reducing traffic congestion in sensitive areas. This may entail redistributing movements of traffic, although it is not appropriate to redirect traffic from arterial routes through residential areas. Measures should, wherever possible, be adopted to provide multiple benefits, such as reducing pollution and accident levels by reducing car journeys. It is also imperative that traffic management and local transport plans should be integrated with development planning, and this may entail, in certain areas, liaison between two tiers of local government. However, traffic is currently a major contributor to all relevant pollutants within the NAQS (except sulphur dioxide), and traffic management will assist in achieving objectives for carbon monoxide, benzene and 1,3-butadiene. Where NO*x* and particulates (PM_{10} etc) cause problems in areas where AQMAs are designated, local traffic management will be crucial in achieving objectives since national measures alone are unlikely to do so. Furthermore, while vehicles will become 'cleaner' due to improved technical specifications, emissions may, in the long term, increase due to the increase in numbers of vehicles coming onto the roads and in the number of short trips which are disproportionately polluting. To counter this potential problem authorities are expected to promote the UK National Cycling Strategy (July 1996) which aims to double the number of cycle trips by 2002 and to double that again by 2012. Authorities will also be expected to promote the National Walking Strategy to encourage walking as a mode of transport and as a link between other modes, for example by creating safe, convenient pedestrianised ways, and by promoting walking as an alternative to short car rides.

A traffic management strategy should aim to:

- reduce the growth in the number and length of motorised journeys;
- encourage alternative means of travel which have less environmental impact;
- reduce reliance on private cars;
- ensure that town centre and other facilities are accessible by a variety of transport modes, with new residential and commercial developments being channelled towards existing centres.

Similarly, a traffic management scheme must take account of the volume and make-up of traffic, times and frequencies of journeys, degrees of congestion, average speeds, driving styles and numbers of persons using each mode of transport. The impact of any scheme will be measured by the numbers of vehicles affected, its success or failure in reducing traffic levels, whether it redirects traffic to areas where fewer people will be exposed to emissions, whether smoother traffic flows are produced at relatively constant medium speeds, and whether advantages are produced for particular vehicular types.

10.16.2 Considerations and principal features

Considerations in drawing up strategies and schemes are as follows:

- the volume of local traffic;
- the make-up of local traffic – in particular, whether there are certain vehicle types with high emissions whose use should be discouraged, or whether permits could be used to encourage the use of low-emission types;
- the types of journeys made – in particular, whether there are many short journeys by car which are disproportionately polluting because pollution-abatement equipment works best once warmed up;
- the level of local traffic congestion;
- the average driving speeds and styles of driving – for example, whether there is a great deal of stopping and starting in slow-moving traffic queues which result in disproportionately high emissions. While the ideal driving speed is a constant speed between 25mph and 55mph, road safety must be borne in mind, as must the need to ensure that decongestion does not lead to an increase in traffic volume. Thus, if roads are decongested by parking restrictions, the space 'saved' should not then be occupied by moving cars, but instead be devoted to bus lanes etc;
- the relevant local geographical features, such as hills (emissions increase when vehicles drive uphill) and the location of sensitive places, such as schools, hospitals, homes for the aged and busy shopping streets (in order that they are protected against the build-up of heavy congestion).

The principal features of traffic management measures are as follows:

- road-building proposals should not bring traffic into congested centres;
- shifts away from private car use to public transport should be encouraged;
- measures should be included on demand management and traffic restraint;
- the environmental effects of traffic measures should be assessed;
- modes of transport other than the car should be encouraged;
- car use should be made less convenient and more expensive for certain types of journey;
- traffic flow should be smoothed, for example by improved traffic signal co-ordination using new technologies;
- industry, commerce and the public should be educated in the implications of transport policies and choices.

The first four items will be required features of any bid for local transport funding from central government.

10.17 AIR QUALITY AND LAND USE PLANNING

Framework for review and assessment of air quality[1] gives guidance on the links between air quality issues and the land planning process to ensure, in particular, that land planning makes an appropriate contribution to achieving air quality objectives, and that air quality issues are material considerations in the planning process. Authorities should therefore ensure that their air quality

1 LAQMG4(97).

reviews and assessments inform their land planning processes, with appropriate lines of communication at both member and officer levels. Particular implications for land planning arise in relation to:

- *development plans* – national air quality objectives must be taken into account in the preparation of development plans, while those plans should also have regard to, and refer to, any AQMA action plan (and vice versa), and it may also be appropriate for authorities to co-ordinate their air quality reviews with revisions of development plans which should, in any case, be appraised against their detailed assessments of air quality;
- *development control* – the impact of a development on air quality arising from its operational characteristics and any traffic generated will be material considerations in the development control process. A development having a significant impact in air quality terms, although only in relation to the use and amenity of land, could be refused planning permission or be made subject to appropriate conditions.

In overall planning terms, the demands of NAQS point towards promotion of mixed use development so as to reduce travel, for example between work and home, locating certain development types in existing urban centres, with a high density of development in such centres where appropriate, and directing polluting industries to sites where their impact is minimised. Planning decisions on car parking and other transport issues should also take into account air quality issues.

10.18 FURTHER DEVELOPMENTS IN LATE 1997

Further aspects of the NAQS emerged in late 1997. On 23 September, it was announced that, in a pilot scheme, seven local authorities would be given power early in 1998 to stop vehicles and impose fixed penalty fines on vehicles which failed emission tests. An engine which is running needlessly while a car is parked will also be a spot fixed-fine offence. This pilot scheme will test the powers given by the Environment Act 1995 and was proposed to operate in Birmingham, Glasgow, Bristol, Swansea, Middlesborough, Canterbury and Westminster. It appears that, if it is successful, the pilot scheme will be extended only to other authorities on an 'opt-in' adoptive basis. Tests carried out will include a test for soot in fumes for diesel engined vehicles, which will be equivalent to the MoT road-worthiness test. As only a uniformed constable may actually stop a vehicle on the road, some of the finance raised in fines for non-compliance may have to go to police forces to pay for the presence of officers. In the current testing programmes, one in 20 cars fails, while almost one in 10 taxis do not reach the standard of requirements.

10.18.1 Fixed penalty offences

The specific powers for fixed penalty offences are contained in the Road Traffic (Vehicle Emissions) (Fixed Penalty) Regulations 1997, SI 1997/3058 made under s 87(8) of the Environment Act 1995 on 19 December 1997, and utilising powers granted by s 87(1), (2) and (5) of, and Sch 11 to that Act (**10.8.5** to **10.8.6** above). Under reg 3, any of the seven 'participating authorities' may take such steps as are required to enforce the emission requirements of the Road Vehicles (Construction and Use) Regulations 1986, SI 1986/1078, as amended (see Chapter 9). Failure to comply with the requirements of regs 61 (construction) and 98 (stopping engines of stationary vehicles) of the 1986 Regulations, on the part of a vehicle, or the use of a non-compliant vehicle on a road, or causing or permitting such a use, becomes a 'fixed penalty offence' for the purposes of s 87(2) of the 1995 Act. Authorised officers of the participating authorities may require the drivers of vehicles to disclose their names, addresses and dates of birth, and failure to comply is itself an offence punishable with a fine on summary conviction up to level 5. Participating authorities may authorise their officers – and others who have successfully completed a ministerially approved emissions checking training course – to issue fixed penalty notices in respect of relevant offences. Such notices may be issued where, following a test of vehicle emissions, an authorised person considers that a relevant offence has been committed by the user of a vehicle under reg 61 of the 1986 Regulations. Where an offence under reg 98 has been committed, an authorised person may issue a notice to the driver of the vehicle as soon as practicable, and, in any case, less than 24 hours after commission of the relevant offence. The notice must give reasonable particulars of the alleged offence, but must state:

- the name and address of the person to whom the notice is issued (for example its owner);
- the registered number of the vehicle in question;
- the date of the offence;
- the monetary amount of the fixed penalty which may be paid;
- the person to whom, and the address at which, the penalty may be paid, and to whom any relevant correspondence may be sent;
- the person to whom, and the address at which, any request for a hearing may be sent;
- the method(s) by which payment of the penalty may be made;
- the period for payment; and
- the consequences of non-payment.

The reg 98 notice may be issued either to the person himself, or under a covering letter via pre-paid postage, and is taken to be issued either when given in person or when duly posted.

Where a notice is issued under reg 5 of the 1997 Regulations there is, under reg 6, a period of grace during which no proceedings are to be instituted before the expiry of the period for paying the penalty, nor may any person be convicted of a relevant offence if the fixed penalty is paid in due time. The penalty levels are fixed by reg 2 of the 1997 Regulations, and are £60 in the case of an offence under reg 61 of the 1986 Regulations, and £20 in the case of an offence under reg 98 of the 1986 Regulations. However, under reg 7 of the 1997 Regulations the recipient of the notice may request a hearing in respect of the alleged offence by a request in writing made to the person stated in the notice within 28 days, beginning with the day following the day on which the notice was issued. Where a hearing is so requested, the fixed penalty is not payable. Thereafter, under reg 8 the notice may be treated as an information for the purposes of a prosecution in connection with the relevant offence. If, however, no request for a hearing is made, and there is a failure to pay the penalty in due time, the amount of the penalty is increased to £90 in the case of a reg 61 offence, and £40 in the case of a reg 98 offence (reg 9 of the 1997 Regulations). A county court may, under regs 10 and 11 of the 1997 Regulations, order the recovery of unpaid fixed penalties once the period for payment has expired, by means of execution, and the matter shall be treated as a Part II debt falling within Article 2(1)(a) of the Enforcement of Road Traffic Debts Order 1993, SI 1993/2073, with the removal of the limitation in that Order of the normal requirement that a warrant of execution is not to be issued until the time for serving a statutory declaration has expired.

A notice may be withdrawn where an authorised person determines that it should not have been issued, or ought not to have been issued to the particular recipient in question, and if any amount has been paid under the notice it is to be refunded to the payer, while no proceedings are to be continued or instituted against the recipient in respect of the alleged offence (reg 12).

10.18.2 Further likely developments

By November 1997 there were reports that the Government may impose a ban on cars in certain city centres on days when atmospheric pollution levels are in excess of safe levels. In Leicester and Nottingham a pilot project, environmental monitoring in metropolitan areas (EMMA), has been carried out on an academic research basis, funded by the Government with some EC funding. The project consists of a number of sophisticated air quality sensors on main roads enabling the prediction of congestion and pollution problems up to 48 hours before they occur. To translate this information into traffic restrictions would require electronic tagging of vehicles (also on test in 1997 in Leicester). On 'high' pollution days, drivers could be warned by local radio and roadside signs that they will be charged a fee for entering a polluted area, which could be in addition to a general levy on vehicles for their use on roads, while a nationwide system of monitors could be linked to computers which could alter traffic flow systems or even close roads. Pollution fee levels over and above general road use levy levels would be designed to deter the use, in particular, of cars. In Leicester, predictions from the EMMA system were used in 1997 to alter traffic light sequences so that fewer cars could enter polluted parts of the city as build-ups of pollution were detected. The outcome of this exercise was due to be incorporated into the Government's promised 1998 White Paper on integrated transport policy. If the current trend of policy continues for a second term of Labour Government, significant changes may be predicted in the pattern of road use some time in the new millennium.

In 1997, it was, however, argued that producing a national road charging scheme could take up to 10 years while the necessary expensive infrastructure is put in place. Consequential issues were also raised that unless the use of all roads is charged for, congestion may simply move from 'charged' roads (eg motorways) to 'uncharged' roads. A further question is at what level the charge should be fixed, and according to what parameters – deterrence, harmfulness of pollutants released etc. Initial evidence from a trial scheme run for eight months in Leicester in 1997 led to the conclusion that a road price charge of £3 per day would lead to only a 15 per cent reduction in commuting by car, and that motorists generally would pay £4 a day to use their cars, with a fee of £6 a day being needed to reduce car use to any degree. Thus, by the end of 1997 ministers were receiving advice that road charging in city centres might be unworkable, while electronic tagging of vehicles appeared to have been abandoned, as technologically unproven, in favour of issuing permits on a 'pay-for' basis to individual motorists. However, even that raises considerable enforcement problems, together with fears that a scheme for levying charges on parking spaces could be attacked as merely an alternative means of taxation – a charge of £100 per annum per space could raise £1 billion a year in taxes, with charges rising to £400 in major cities and £1,000 in central London. The Government White Paper expected in July 1998, with legislation following possibly in 1999, may, nevertheless, concentrate on charging companies for parking places because: (a) some six out of 10 city centre parking spaces are workplace related; while (b) 1.7 million companies already pay a parking charge via the uniform business rate system which can place a value up to £1,000 on a parking space. Extending this existing system, which could be administratively simple for authorities, coupled with above-inflation increases on vehicle fuel duties, which is already policy, might lead to much less use of cars for commuting to work, and halving the number of workplace parking spaces might reduce central congestion by 20 per cent. Enhanced use of bus lanes or lanes reserved for heavy goods vehicles, even on motorways, may also be made, together with encouraging road-narrowing, pedestrianisation, free or subsidised use of public transport for particular categories of persons (eg children otherwise driven to school), enhanced park and ride schemes, use of car pools for residents in particular areas to discourage individual car ownership and use, and giving cycling subsidies to individuals able to cycle to work. All of these methods were examined in Edinburgh, York, Nottingham, Leicester, Southampton and Heathrow Airport in 1997.

10.19 THE PROBLEMS

The problems outlined above have not prevented other countries introducing road charging – Norway has had a road price scheme since 1992 and tolls will be introduced in The Netherlands in 2001. The way forward may be a combination of powers for local authorities to levy 'urban tolls' on roads in their areas, with taxes imposed centrally on 'non-residential' parking spaces provided for business users, thus reducing congestion in towns while raising a levy on the company car sector. The 'free' use of the roads may, therefore, come to an end.

INDEX

References are to paragraph numbers.

Abatement notice, *see* Statutory nuisance
Acid processes
  control of 6.2.1
Acid rain 2.3, 3.4.1, 3.4.2
  framework for tackling 3.4.1
  neutralisation 3.4.2
  northern hemisphere, problem of 3.5
Aeroplane 10.12.4
Air quality
  action plan 10.8.2, 10.8.5, 10.8.11, 10.8.12
    time for preparation 10.13.3
  Guidance, *see* Guidance (air quality)
  health, relation to 10.1.1
  information requirements 10.4, 10.5
  legislative provisions 10.8
  local authority obligations 10.8.2, 10.8.3
  monitoring 10.3–10.6
  objectives, *see* National Air Quality Strategy
  public information on 10.6.1
  reviews 10.8.2, 10.8.3
  standards, *see* Air quality standards
  strategy, *see* National Air Quality Strategy
  traffic regulation order 10.1.2, *see also* Traffic
Air quality management area, *see* Local authority
Air Quality Management Group 10.8.7
Air quality standards
  AQLVs 2.5, 8.10, 10.2
  alert thresholds 10.3, 10.6.2
  Expert Panel on 10.7.1, 10.10.6
  failure to meet, local authority obligation 10.8.2
  monitoring 10.3–10.6
  National strategy 10.8.5, 10.8.13, 10.9.1
    meaning for 10.10.3
    see also National Air Quality Strategy
  smoke control, insufficiency of 8.10, 10.1
  UK 10.2
    compliance with EC Directive 10.3
Airborne particles, *see* Fine particulates
Aircraft 10.12.4
Alkali and Clean Air Inspectorate 6.1
Animal matter processes 7.2.1, 7.4.2
  by-product rendering 7.4.3
Appeal
  see also Environment Agency; Local authority air pollution control (LAAPC)
  abatement notice, *see* Statutory nuisance
  pollution estimates notice 10.4.3
Asbestos 6.2.4
Authorisation
  Environment Agency (IPC), *see* Environment Agency
  local authority, *see* Local authority air pollution control (LAAPC)

BATNEEC 1.6.4, 2.3, 2.3.1, 2.4, 6.2.4
  application to achieve BPEO 6.5
  'available' 6.4
  'best' 6.4
  cost aspects 6.4, 6.4.1
  existing processes 6.4.2
  LAAPC, use for 7.5
  meaning 6.4
  new processes 6.4.1
  objectives 7.5
  'techniques' 6.4
  use of, ensuring 6.3.2
BPEO 6.5
  audit trail 6.5.9

BPEO – *cont*
  authorisation (IPC), and
    methodology for assessment 6.5.3, 6.5.8, 6.6.3
    variation application, Agency position on 6.5.10
  'best practicable environmental option' 6.5, 6.5.1
    meaning ascribed to words 6.5.2
  cost 6.5.6, 6.5.7, 6.5.8
  definition 6.5.2
  determination 6.5.8
    guidance 6.5.3 *et seq*
    stages, *see* 'stages for determining' below
  environmental quotient (EQ) 6.5.6
  'insignificant releases' 6.5.5
  integrated environmental index (IEI) 6.5.6
  LAAPC, no relevance for 7.5
  NAQS objectives, and 10.12.1
  objectives
    defining 6.5.4
    meeting 6.5.8
    option generation to achieve 6.5.5
  odour detection and recognition 6.5.6
  photochemical ozone creation potential (POCP) 6.5.6
  register of 6.5.9
  review 6.5.2, 6.5.3, 6.5.9
  stages for determining 6.5.3–6.5.9
    assessing options, criteria for 6.5.6
    defining the objective 6.5.4
    generating options 6.5.4
    identification of the BPEO 6.5.8
    summary and presentation of options 6.5.7
  standards (EALs) 6.5.6
Beaver Committee 8.1.1
Benzene
  reduction of levels 10.7.1
    NAQS objectives/thresholds 10.8.13, 10.9.1, 10.10.3, 10.10.6
  reporting level 6.21
Boiler
  see also Furnace
  emissions 8.2, 8.3.7, 8.4.1, 8.5.2
    ship 8.7.4
1,3-Butadiene
  NAQS objectives/thresholds 10.7.1, 10.8.13, 10.9.1, 10.10.3, 10.10.6
Bus
  deregulation of services 10.13.2
  lanes 10.1.12, 10.13.2, 10.18.2

CFCs 2.9.1, 3.5.3
Cable
  burning insulation for metal recovery 8.7.1
Cancer clusters
  negligence liability, and 4.8.2
Carbon dioxide emissions 3.6, 3.8
  mitigation schemes 3.8.2
  prescription 6.2.4
  reduction (NAQS) 10.13.2
Carbon monoxide
  limits 10.7.1
    NAQS objectives/thresholds 10.8.13, 10.9.1, 10.10.3
  monitoring of levels 10.6
  reporting of 6.21
  statistics 10.12.1
  vehicle emissions 9.2, 9.6
Chemical industries
  production process control 6.2.1, 6.6.1, 7.2.1
  Release Inventory (CRI) 6.21
    limitations 6.21
Chimney
  see also Smoke
  definition 8.2.1
  emissions
    dark smoke, prohibition 8.2
    grit, dust etc, height control 8.4
    statutory nuisance exclusion 5.2.1, 5.3.4
  furnace 8.3.2, 8.3.3
  height 8.4
    furnace 8.4–8.4.2
    guidance on 6.5.5, 8.4.2
    non-furnace 8.4.3
  installation, Building Regs 8.4.3
  railway locomotive 8.7.3
Clean air legislation 8.1 *et seq*, *see* Fumes; Smoke
  EC Directive compliance 8.19

Climate
  Global Climate Change Convention 3.6.1, 3.7, 3.8
    Conference of Parties 3.6.1, 3.8.2
  Kyoto Protocol, effect of 3.8.2
  precautionary measures 3.6.1
  reduction in greenhouse gases, agreement on 3.8
  threats to 3.6
Coal
  emissions 2.3.1, 5.2.1, 10.11.4
    clean air legislation, background 8.1
    see also Sulphur dioxide
  mine, combustion of refuse 8.7.2
  smoke index 8.6
Colliery spoil 8.7.2
Committee on the Medical Aspects of Air Pollutants 10.7.1
Common law remedies 4.1 *et seq*, *see also* Negligence; Private nuisance; Public nuisance; Statutory duty, breach of
Company
  officer liability, clean air legislation 8.8.3
Compensation
  EC law, under 1.12
  injury from polluting emission, for 9.1
  statutory nuisance, for 5.3.7
Confidentiality
  commercial, exclusion from register on grounds of 6.20.2, 6.25, 7.16
  trade secret 8.8, 10.4.1
Conventions 3.2.2, *see also* Climate; European Convention on Human Rights; Geneva Convention; Vienna Convention
Co-ordinated pollution control (CPC) 7.20.3, 7.20.4
Cost
  BATNEEC, and 6.4, 6.4.1
  BPEO, and 6.5.6, 6.5.7, 6.5.8
  industry's expense on pollution control 6.25
County Council
  consultation with 10.14.6
  information to 10.8.3
  obligations 10.8.2
  role in air quality strategy 10.8.12
Criminal proceedings
  authorisation condition contravention 6.14, 7.4.3
  enforcement notice contravention 6.12.1, 7.11
  public nuisance, for 4.2
  statutory nuisance, for 5.3.5, 5.3.7
Crown court
  abatement notice appeal 5.3.3
Crown premises
  dark smoke, grit, dust emissions 8.7.5
Customary law 3.2.3, 3.4
  evidence, scope, etc, of 3.2.3
  global issues, role in 3.5.1
  Treaty, in 3.2.2
Customs, *see* Smuggling

Damage
  leak, spill, etc, caused by, *see* Private nuisance
Dark smoke, *see* Smoke
Declarations 3.2.2
Demolition/site clearance
  dark smoke emissions 8.2.2
Diesel
  content 9.3, 9.4
  engine emissions 9.6
    tractors 2.7.2
  particulate limits 10.7.1
  sulphur content 2.5.1, 10.7.1
Di-isocynate processes 7.2.1
Director
  clean air legislation liability 8.8.3
District council
  co-operation with county council 10.8.12
  information to 10.8.3
  obligations 10.8.2
Dust 8.3, 8.3.2–8.3.4
  air quality limits 10.2
  measurement 8.3.6

Earth Summit 3.7
Emission
  see also specific substances; Dust; Fine particulates; Fumes
  area categories 2.6
  banking concept 3.8.1
  bubble concept 3.8.1

Emission – *cont*
carbon dioxide, *see* Carbon dioxide
Chemical Release Inventory 6.21
combustion plant/power station 2.3, 2.3.1, 10.11.4
compliance measures (UK) 2.3, 2.4.2, 2.5, 2.7, 2.10, 6.26
control in UK, *see* Air quality; Integrated Pollution Control; Local authority air pollution control (LAAPC); Vehicles
dark smoke 8.2, *see also* Smoke
furnace, from 8.3, *see also* Furnace
gases, liquids and solids 10.5
greenhouse gas 3.6.1, 3.7, 3.8, *see also* Climate
agreed reductions (Kyoto Protocol) 3.8
aircraft producing 10.12.4
guidance 10.13.4, 10.14–10.16
incinerators, from, *see* Incineration
industrial plant 2.3
information/notification duties 2.3, 2.5.2, 2.6, *see also* Information
integrated control, *see* Integrated pollution control
inventories 10.6.1, *see also* Monitoring of air pollution
lead 2.7, 10.2, *see also* Lead
limits 2.3–2.7, 10.7
alert thresholds 2.6
measuring and recording, local authority powers 10.4.2
mitigation schemes 3.8.2
monitoring of, *see* Monitoring air pollution
motor vehicles, from, *see* Traffic; Vehicles
nuisance liability, *see* Private nuisance; Public nuisance; Statutory nuisance
oil industries lobby 3.7
ozone, *see* Ozone
reduction programmes 2.3.1, 10.7
smoke control, *see* Smoke
standards
BATNEEC 1.6.4, 2.3, 2.3.1, 2.4, 6.2.4, 6.4
quality 2.5, 2.6, 2.7, 6.3.2
sulphur 2.5.1, 9.4.1, 10.7.1
sulphur dioxide, *see* Sulphur dioxide
trading 3.8.1
transboundary 3.2.4, 3.4, 3.5
Emission Factor Database 10.13.4
Emission permit trading 3.8.1
Employee
commuter, encouragement to be 'green' 10.12.8
statutory liability of employer 4.7
training and supervision 6.4
vicarious liability for 8.8.3
Enforcement
European Community legislation, *see* European Community
notice
Environment Agency 6.12, *see also* Environment Agency
local authority 7.11, *see also* Local authority air pollution control
Environment Agency
appeals 6.12, 6.15
commercial confidentiality question 6.20.2
determination 6.15.5
effect of 6.15.1
formalities and time-limits 6.15–6.15.5
hearing 6.15.2, 6.15.4
limitations of system 6.15.6
modes of 6.15.2
withdrawal 6.15
written representations to Planning Inspectorate 6.15, 6.15.2, 6.15.3
authorisation (IPC) 6.3, 10.12.1
see also BATNEEC; BPEO
application procedure 6.3.1
breach and enforcement 6.8–6.15
conditions 6.3.2, 6.4, 6.15, 6.15.1, 6.15.5, 6.15.6, 8.7.1
condition contravention, prosecution for 6.14
existing process, for 6.4.2, 6.25
fees for application 6.8
grant of 6.3.2
offence to operate without 6.3
processes 6.3.1
refusal, appeal against 6.15, 6.15.1, 6.15.5
review of conditions 6.3.2, 6.25
revocation, *see* 'revocation of authorisation' *below*
time for 6.3.1

Environment Agency – *cont*
authorisation (IPC) – *cont*
transfer 6.9
variation notice, *see* 'variation' *below*
charges 6.8, 6.10, 6.19.3
changes possible 6.8
distinguished from LAAPC scheme 7.6
consultation with 10.8.1, 10.14.6
control of atmospheric discharges 6.3 *et seq*
planning regime, interface with 6.23
enforcement notice 6.9, 6.12
appeal against 6.15, 6.15.1, 6.15.5
circumstances for 6.12
contravention 6.12, 6.15.1, 6.22
discretion as to 6.12, 6.13
formalities and procedure 6.12
prohibition notice distinguished 6.13
statistics 6.12, 6.14
validity 6.12, 6.12.1
enforcement policy statement 6.14
enforcing authority, as 6.3.1
entry and examination, etc, powers 6.16, 6.17, 6.23
emergencies 6.16.1
limits on 6.16.1
notice requirement 6.16.1
obstruction offence 6.16.2
self-incrimination, and 6.16.1, 6.17
'environmental licences' 6.8
Guidance 6.6, *see also* Integrated Pollution Control
High Court proceedings 6.22
information provisions 6.17, 6.18
injunction application 6.22
inspectors 6.16
lead regulator, as 7.20.4
monitoring 6.7
NAQS, taking account of 10.10.3
operator's duties 6.7
operator and pollution risk appraisal 6.8
processes, Part A and B list 6.2.1, 6.3.1
existing 6.4.2, 6.25
new 6.4.1
release into more than one media 6.5, *see also* BPEO
prohibition notice 6.9, 6.13
appeal against 6.15, 6.15.1, 6.15.5
circumstances and formalities 6.13
contravention of 6.15.1, 6.22
distinguished from enforcement notice 6.13
statistics 6.13, 6.14
registers to be kept 6.19.1
'commercially confidential' information 6.20.2, 6.25
exclusion of information 6.20
inspection by public 6.19.3
national security exclusion 6.20.1
removal of information from 6.19.2
Release Inventory, Chemicals (CRI) 6.21
release levels (EALs) 6.5.6
remedying harm, power to take steps 6.23
revocation of authorisation 6.8, 6.9
appeal 6.15, 6.15.1
notice 6.11
withdrawal 6.11
seizure powers 6.16.2
variation 6.5.10, 6.9, 6.10
appeal 6.15, 6.15.1, 6.15.5
application by authorisee for 6.10
notice 6.3.2, 6.10, 6.15.5
power and duty of Agency to give notice 6.10
Environment Industries Commission 7.18
Environmental Action Programmes 1.2, 1.4.4, 1.6
establishment of principles by 1.6–1.6.6
information and research 2.8
Environmental monitoring in metropolitan areas 10.18.2
Escapes, *see* Private nuisance; *Rylands v Fletcher*; Statutory duty, breach of
European Community
air quality 10.2, 10.3
background, post-war 1.1.1–1.1.3
Brundtland Report 1.6.1
COREPER (permanent committee) 1.8.4

European Community – *cont*
  Commission
    function of 1.8.1, 2.1
    power delegated to 1.8.2
    'reasoned opinion' 2.1.2
  compensation 1.12
  Council (of the EU) 1.8.1, 1.8.2
    back-up for 1.8.4
    confidentiality 2.8
    decision-making and voting 1.8.2
    function 1.8.2
  Court of First Instance 1.9, 1.9.1
  Decisions 1.5, 1.5.3
    nature of 1.5.3
  direct effect concept 1.4.4, 1.5.1, 1.5.2, 1.10
    development and meaning of 1.10
    'directly applicable' compared 1.10.1
    horizontal effect 1.10.2
    legal rights of natural/legal persons 1.10.1, 1.10.2
    'State', for 1.10.2
    vertical 1.10.2
  Directives 1.4, 1.5, 1.5.2
    atmosphere, relating to 2.2–2.10
    direct effect, *see* 'direct effect concept' above
    enforcement 2.1, *see also* 'enforcement' *below*
    implementation 1.5.2, 1.10.1, 1.11
    non-compliance 1.5.2, 1.10, 1.12, 2.1
    notification/publication 1.5.2, 1.10.1
  Directorate General on environment 1.8.1
  ECJ 1.9
    appeal from 1.9.1
    authority, development and parameters of 1.6
    domestic courts, relationship with 1.9
    function 1.9
    interpretative stance of 1.4.3, 1.4.4, 1.6, 1.9
    judicial review by 1.7, 1.9
    jurisprudence of Member States, use of 1.6
    principles emanating from 1.6
    reference to (Art 177) 1.9.2, 1.10
  ECSC 1.1.1, 1.1.2, 1.8
  enforcement 1.8.1, 1.8.2, 1.10.2, 1.12, 2.1
    Commission function 1.8.1, 2.1, 3.3
    defence by Member State 2.1.2
    environmental matters 1.10.2, 2.1.1
    fellow Member State, by 2.1.2
    financial penalties 2.1.1
    notice of infringement and response period 2.1.2
    reference by Commission to ECJ 2.1.2
  environmental regulation 2.2
  framework of 1.8
  general principles 1.6
  indirect effect 1.11, 1.12, 2.1.2
  information requirements 2.8
  integrated pollution control 2.10, 6.26.1
  international obligations 2.9, 3.3
    'competence' for 3.3
  intervention by 1.6.5
  Maastricht 1.1.3, 1.2, 1.4
  membership
    growth in 1.1.3
    reduction in influence of 1.8.2
    representation on Council 1.8.2
  national law, and 1.5.1, 1.9
    directions to give effect to obligation 6.3.2
    domestic court reference to ECJ 1.9.2
    obligation of interpretation 1.11
    primacy of EC law 1.10, 1.12
    State liability 1.12
  opinions 1.5.4
  Paris Summit 1.1.3, 1.2
  Parliament 1.8.5
    Assembly renamed as 1.8.5
    expanding power of 1.8.2
    members 1.8.5
  policy on environment 1.2
    Agency for (EEA) 1.3
    Belgian importation of waste case 1.4.4
    competence on environmental issues 1.1.3, 1.6.5
    Danish returnable bottles case 1.4.3

European Community – *cont*
policy on environment – *cont*
Environmental Action Programmes 1.2, 1.4.4, 1.6, 2.8
general powers 1.1.2, 1.1.3
implementation by Member State 1.4.4
integration and primacy of 1.4.2, 1.4.3
minimum standards 1.1.3, 1.4.3
objectives and principles (Title XVI) 1.4.2
'polluter pays' 1.4.3, 1.4.4, 1.6.2, 3.2.4
precautionary principle 1.6.3, 3.2.4
proportionality 1.6.6
rectification at source 1.6.4
subsidiarity 1.6.5
sustainable development 1.6.1, 3.2.4
Recommendations 1.5.4
Regulations 1.4, 1.5, 1.5.1, 2.9
directly applicable 1.5.1, 1.10.1
incorporation into domestic law 1.5.1
publication requirement 1.5.2, 1.10.1
use of 1.5.1
Treaty of Rome 1.1.2, 1.4.1, 1.6
authority on environment, amendments giving 1.1.3, 1.2, 1.4.1, 1.6
derogation for environmental protection 1.4.3
directly applicable 1.10.1
general authority of 1.1.3, 2.3
infringement, judicial review for 1.6, 1.7
objectives (Art 2) 1.1.2
obligations on Member Sates 1.8.1
principles 1.6
spirit of 1.4, 1.4.3, 1.9, 1.10
vehicles, type approval 9.8.3, 9.8.4, 9.9
certificate 9.8.4, 9.9.1
European Coal and Steel Community 1.1.1, 1.1.2, 1.8
European Convention on Human Rights
appeal limits on IPC control, and 6.15.6
European Council 1.8.3
European Environment Agency 1.3, 1.6.3, 2.1
information dissemination 2.8
reports 1.3
European Monitoring and Evaluation Programme 3.4.2
European Union
citizenship 1.4.1
Council of 1.8.2
objectives 1.4.1
Exhaust (vehicle)
emissions, *see* Vehicle
construction 9.5
Expert Panel on Air Quality Standards 10.7.1, 10.10.6

Fine particulates
effect on health 10.7.1
forecasts of pollutants 10.6.2
limits 10.7.1, 10.7.2
NAQS objectives/thresholds 10.8.13, 10.9.1, 10.10.3, 10.11.3
monitoring of levels 10.6
sources 10.7.1, 10.7.2
standards proposed 10.3
statistics 10.12.1
winter and summer, differences 10.7.1, 10.7.2
Fire
see also Fumes; Smoke; Stubble burning
highway, on 5.4
research, for, dark smoke exemption 8.7.6
Flue, *see* Chimney
Forecasts (pollution) 10.6.2
Forest
protection against atmospheric pollution 2.8.1
statistics of loss 3.7
Fuel
see also Chimney; Coal; Furnace; Power station
'authorised' (smokeless) 8.5.2
diesel, *see* Diesel
lead content (petrol) 2.7, 4.8.2, 9.3, 9.4, 10.11.1

Fuel – *cont*
lead content (petrol) – *cont*
phasing out 9.4
production process control 6.2.1, 6.6.1, 7.2.1
sulphur content 2.5.1, 8.10, 9.4.1
reduction, EC 10.3
very low sulphur 8.4.2
unauthorised 8.5.3
unleaded petrol 2.7.2, 9.4, 10.2
waste, making from, controls 6.2.1
Fumes 8.3
see also Emissions; Smoke
emission limits, local authority power 8.7.7
IPC requirements 6.6.2
nuisance liability 5.2, 5.2.2, 5.3.4, *see also* Private nuisance; Public nuisance; Statutory nuisance
Furnace
chimney height 8.4.1
approval 8.4.2
exemption, plant/boiler categories 8.4.1
Guidance 8.4.2
information as to 8.3.7
emissions, local authority power 10.5
smoke control area, in 8.5.2
smoke, grit etc, from, control of 8.3, 8.4.2
appeals 8.3.5
arrestment plant 8.3.3, 8.3.4
domestic 8.3.4
exemptions 8.3.3
grit and dust control 8.3.2–8.3.4
grit and dust measurement 8.3.6
installation control 8.3.1
non-domestic 8.3.1–8.3.3

Gas oil 2.5.1, 9.4.1
Gases 8.7.7, 10.5, *see also* specific gases; Fumes
Geneva Convention 3.4
see also Acid rain
aims, membership etc 3.4.1
Executive and Secretariat 3.4.1
Protocols 3.4.2
Global issues 3.1–3.5
see also International law
climate, *see* Climate
global warming 3.7, *see also* Ozone
scope of global environment 3.5.2
Greenhouse gases 3.6.1, 3.7, 3.8, 10.12.4
Grit 8.3, 8.3.2–8.3.4
measurement 8.3.6
Guidance (air quality)
'Framework for review and assessment of air quality' 10.14–10.16
action plan development 10.14.4–10.14.6, 10.15, 10.15.2
emissions inventory and other detailed reviews 10.14.3
further screening 10.14.2
information compilation 10.14.1
objectives of reviews 10.14
stages for local authority action 10.14.1–10.14.3
strategies 10.15.1
time for achievement 10.14.1, 10.14.3, 10.14.4
traffic management, on 10.16
'General Principles for Reviewing and Assessing' 10.8.9, 10.8.11, 10.8.12
Guidance (IPC/LAAPC) 6.6, 7.7

HBFCs 2.9.1
HCFCs 2.9.1, 3.5.2
HFCs 2.9.1, 3.8
Halogens 6.2.4
Hazardous waste
incineration of 2.4.2
Her Majesty's Pollution Inspectorate
Environment Agency, becoming 6.6
establishment 6.1
Guidance and monitoring 6.6, 6.7, *see also* Environment Agency; Integrated Pollution Control
High Court
enforcement by 6.22, 7.17
injunction application, *see* Injunction
statutory nuisance abatement
appeal against notice 5.3.3
proceedings 5.3.6
Highway, *see* Road
Hydrocarbons 9.6, 10.6.1
see also Ozone

Hydrocarbons – *cont*
polycyclic aromatic (PAHs) 10.10.6

Incineration
furnace
is incinerator 8.3.1
is not incinerator 8.3.2
see also Furnace
hazardous waste 2.4.2
municipal waste 2.4
compliance by UK 2.4.1
existing plant 2.4.1
meaning 2.4
waste chemical or plastics 6.2.1
Industrial processes
authorisation etc 2.3, 2.10
control, Part A list 6.2.1, 6.3, *see also* Environment Agency; Integrated pollution control
IPPC Directive list 6.26.3
processes within scope of Directive 7.20.2
control, Part B list 7.2.1, *see also* Local authority air pollution control (LAAPC)
dust from 5.2.2, 5.3.4, *see also* Statutory nuisance
NAQS objectives, and 10.12.1, 10.12.8
plant for 2.3
Information
air pollution 10.4, 10.5
chemical releases, on 6.21
Environment Agency powers 6.17
furnaces, on 8.3.7, 10.5
local authority powers and functions 7.15, 10.4–10.6, 10.8.3, 10.8.5
Guidance on compilation 10.14
public access to 2.8, 6.18, 6.19, 7.16, 10.8.3–10.8.5, 10.8.12
reciprocal exchange 2.8.2
registers 6.5.9, 6.19, 7.16
exclusion provisions 6.20
'relating to the environment' 2.8
Injunction
Environment Agency application 6.22
local authority application 7.17
nuisance, for
private 4.5.2
public 4.2
statutory 5.3.6
Integrated pollution control 2.3, 2.4.2, 2.10, 6.1 *et seq*
aims 6.5.4
authorisation, *see* Environment Agency
background to 6.1
charging scheme, *see* Environment Agency
competent authority 2.1
EC law compliance by UK 2.10, 6.26
consultation papers 7.20.4
IPPC Directive, scope of 6.26.1, 6.26.4, 7.20.2
permit 2.10, 6.26.2, 6.26.3
effectiveness 6.25
establishment 6.1.1
future of 6.26
Guidance on 6.6
industry sectors 6.6.1
non-statutory nature 6.6.1
process-specific 6.6.2
releases into air, requirements for emissions 6.6.2
technical notes 6.6.3
permits 2.10, 6.26.2, 6.26.3
planning authority, overlap with 6.24
authorisation for use, *see* Environment Agency
designation/interpretation rules 6.2.2, 7.2.2
exceptions from control 6.2.3
Part A list 6.2.1
Part B list, *see* Local authority air pollution control (LAAPC)
substances having specific provision 6.2.4
review by ENDS 6.25
International Court of Justice 3.2.1–3.2.6
disputes under Global Climate Change Convention 3.6.1
pronouncements of 3.2.6
International law 3.1 *et seq*
acid rain, *see* Acid rain
Agreements, Declarations etc 3.2.2
arbitration 3.2.6, 3.6.1
climate, protecting, *see* Climate
courts 3.2.6

International law – *cont*
custom 3.2.2, 3.2.3, 3.5.1
EC
adoption of obligations by 3.3
Regulations 2.9
general principles, adoption of 3.2.4
Geneva Convention 3.4.1, 3.4.2
judicial decisions 3.2.6
jurists' opinions 3.2.5
ozone layer, *see* Ozone
soft law 3.2.1
sources 3.2.1
sovereignty issue 3.1, 3.2.1
transboundary effects, *see* Transboundary pollution
Treaties
3.1, 3.2.2
categories 3.2.2
meaning 3.2.2
ratification 3.2.2
Treaty contracts 3.2.2

Judicial review
authorisation variation 6.5.10
EC law 1.6, 1.7, 19.1
authority, problems of 1.7
'direct and individual concern' 1.7.1
enforcement notice validity 6.12.1
exclusion from register, of determination on 6.20.1

Kyoto Protocol 3.6, 3.6.1, 3.8

Lead
air, levels in 2.7.1, 10.2
NAQS objectives/thresholds 10.8.13, 10.9.1, 10.10.3
proposed levels 10.3
petrol
content of 2.7, 2.7.2, 4.8.2, 9.4, 10.11.1
emission as by-product 9.2
unleaded 2.7.2, 9.4, 10.2
statistics 10.12.1
Lead regulator 7.20.3, 7.20.4
Local authority
see also Public authority
air pollution control, *see* Local authority air pollution control (LAAPC)
air pollution information powers
entry and inspection 10.4.2
information and research 10.4.1
information request 10.4.3, 10.4.4
measurement, records and consultation 10.4.2, 10.4.5
monitoring, *see* Monitoring air pollution
NAQS, taking account of 10.10.3, 10.12.5–10.12.7
notice 10.4.3–10.4.5, 10.5
Secretary of State's powers 10.4.4, 10.4.5
air quality management area 7.20.1, 10.8, 10.8.2, 10.12.6, 10.14.3, 10.14.6
action plan for 10.8.2, 10.8.5, 10.8.11, 10.8.12, 10.14.4–10.14.6, 10.15, 10.15.2
consultation 10.8.11, 10.14.6
defining area, criteria 10.8.10
designation of 7.20.1, 10.8.2, 10.8.5, 10.8.9, 10.8.10, 10.14.4
duties as to 10.8.11, 10.12.6
review and assessment 10.8.11, 10.12.6, 10.14
traffic management 10.16
air quality obligations 10.8
action plan 10.8.2, 10.8.5, 10.8.11
guidance on 10.13.4, 10.14–10.17, *see also* Guidance (air quality)
map, production of 10.14.3
other functions, relation to 10.12.7
review obligation 10.8.2, 10.8.3, 10.12.6, 10.14
strategies 10.15.1
supplementary 10.8.3
traffic management 10.16
trials 10.8.7
consultation 10.8.3, 10.14.6
planning 10.12.7, 10.17
Review of Local Authority Powers 10.8.9
smoke control 8.1 *et seq*
area designation 8.5.1
default, DoE powers on 8.9

Local authority – *cont*
  smoke control – *cont*
    entry and enforcement powers 8.8.5
  statutory nuisance procedure 5.3
Local authority air pollution control (LAAPC) 2.4.2, 2.10, 7.1 *et seq*
  appeal 7.4.3, 7.10, 7.13
    procedure and Guidance 7.13
    statistics 7.13
    written representations or hearing 7.13
  authorisation 7.4, 10.12.1
    application procedure 6.3.1, 7.4
    compliance with conditions, ability of applicant 7.4.2, 7.4.3
    conditions 7.4.1–7.4.3, 7.5, 7.9, 7.20.1
    contravention 7.17
    decision by local authority 7.4.1
    fees 7.6
    offence not to have 7.4
    refusal 7.4.1, 7.4.3
    review 7.20
    revocation 7.6, 7.10
    statistics 7.4
    time-limit for determination 7.4
    transfer 7.8
    variation notice 7.9
  BATNEEC and BPEO, adoption of 7.5
  capital expense on 6.25
  charges 7.6
    failure to pay 7.6
  co-ordinated pollution control, and 7.20.3, 7.20.4
  Deregulation Task Force 7.3
  effectiveness 7.18
  enforcement notice 7.11, 7.17
  enforcing authority, as 6.3.1
  entry, examination and inspection powers 7.14
  establishment and background 7.1
  'existing process' 7.4
  future of 7.20
  grouping of local authorities for training etc 7.18
  Guidance (DoE) 6.6, 7.7
    additional 7.7.4
    drafting 7.7.1
    general notes 7.7.2, 7.13
    process notes 7.7.1
    status of 7.7.2
    upgrading notes 7.7.3
  IPC, and 7.20.2
  IPPC Directive, options for involvement 7.20.4
  information 7.15
  lead regulator, as 7.20.4
  management and review of air quality 7.20.1
  planning authority, relation with 7.19
  prescribed processes/substances (Part B list) 6.2, 6.2.2, 7.1.1, 7.2
    exempted processes 7.2.3, 7.3
    interpretation rules 7.2.2
    list set out 7.2.1
    'prescribed substance' 7.3.1
    transfer from Part A 7.4
  prohibition notice 7.12, 7.17
  registers to be kept 7.16
    Part A processes in addition 7.16
  role of local authority 7.1.1
  seizure powers 7.14
  statutory nuisance, interaction with 5.2.2
  trivial quantities 7.2.3, 7.7.4

MOT test 9.8.1
Magistrates' court
  statutory nuisance
    abatement notice appeal 5.3.3
    order on private complaint 5.3.8, 5.3.9
    proceedings 5.3.1, 5.3.5, 5.3.7–5.3.9
Metal processing
  production process control 6.2.1, 6.6.1, 7.2.1
Metal recovery 8.7.1
Methane 3.8
  reporting level 6.21
Mines 8.7.2
Mineral industries
  see also Coal; Quarry
  dust generation 10.2
  production process control 6.2.1, 6.6.1, 7.2.1
Mobile plant
  prescribed process carried on at 6.3.1, 7.4

Monitoring air pollution 2.3.1, 2.5, 2.6, 2.8.3, 10.3–10.6
- *see also* National Air Quality Strategy
- EMMA 10.18.2
- forecasts 10.6.2
- integration of sites 10.6
- inventory of emissions 10.6.1, 10.14.3
- local authority obligation 10.8.2
- research and information powers 10.4–10.6

Montreal Protocol 3.5.3

National Air Quality Archive 10.8.10

National Air Quality Strategy 7.20.1, 9.2, 10.1.2, 10.3, 10.7, 10.8 *et seq*
- category interpretation 10.9.1
- county and district council obligations 10.8.2, 10.8.12
- creation 10.8
- draft 10.8.7, 10.8.8
  - consultation 10.10
  - responses to draft 10.8.8
- European etc obligations, meeting 10.8.4
- final version 10.9.1, 10.10
- Guidance, *see* Guidance (air quality)
- implementation 10.8.5, 10.8.10, 10.13.1
  - fiscal measures to help 10.10.1
- industry's contribution 10.12.1
- information service 10.9.1
- Labour Government, effect 10.13.1
- limits on key pollutants 10.8.5, 10.8.13, 10.9.1, 10.10.3
  - compliance to 'percentile' 10.10.4
- local authority obligations 10.8.2, 10.8.3
  - action plan 10.8.2, 10.8.5, 10.8.11, 10.8.12
  - air quality management areas, *see* Local authority
  - approach to 10.8.10
  - consultation 10.8.11, 10.8.12, 10.14.6
  - guidance 10.13.1, 10.14–10.16
  - legal action, circumstances for 10.9
  - phasing 10.8.10
  - proportional approach 10.13
  - 'relevant period' for action 10.8.13
  - Review of 10.8.9
  - review procedure 10.8.11, 10.12.6
  - role 10.12, 10.12.5–10.12.7
  - scope 10.10.1
  - stages 10.8.10
  - supplementary review 10.8.11
- local implementation 10.8.10
- modification of 10.8.1, 10.8.2
- need for 10.7
- objectives 10.8.13, 10.10, 10.13.3
  - achieving 10.11, 10.12
  - meaning 10.10.3
  - time for achieving 10.13.3
- offences and penalties 10.8.6
- preparation duty 10.8.1
- Regulations 10.13.3
  - draft 10.8.13, 10.9
  - power to make 10.8.5, 10.8.6
  - role of 10.10.1
- review and consultation 10.8.1–10.8.4, 10.8.11, 10.14.6
- Secretary of State powers 10.8.4–10.8.6
- 'standards' 10.10.3
- thresholds for pollutants 10.9.1
- trials 10.8.7
- vehicle emission and fuel standards 10.11, 10.12.3, 10.12.4
  - traffic, records, management etc 10.13.1, 10.13.2
- voluntary activities, reliance on 10.10.1

National security
- exclusion of information for 6.20.1, 7.16

National Walking Strategy 10.16.1

Negligence 4.8
- care, defendant's duty of 4.8.1
  - breach, proving 4.8.2
- causation issue 4.8.2
- environmental liability, constraints on 4.8.2
- foreseeability, relevance of 4.3.8, 4.8.2
- ingredients, establishing 4.8–4.8.2
- private nuisance, and
  - act done under statutory authority 4.4.2
  - contributory 4.6.3

Negligence – *cont*
regulatory agency, of 4.8.1
statutory duty breach, relevance to 4.7
Nitrogen dioxide
see also Nitrogen oxides; Nitrous oxide
air quality standards for 2.5.2, 10.2
NAQS objectives/thresholds 10.8.13, 10.9.1, 10.10.3, 10.10.5, 10.10.6
proposed levels (EC) 10.3
prescription of 6.2.4
reduction programmes (Geneva Convention) 3.4.2
Nitrogen oxides
aircraft emissions 10.12.4
reporting levels 6.21
statistics 10.12.1
vehicle emissions 9.2, 9.6
Nitrous oxide 3.8, 10.12.1
Noise 5.3.6, *see also* Private nuisance; Public nuisance; Statutory nuisance
Nuisance, *see* Private nuisance; Public nuisance; Statutory nuisance

Operator
authorisation for, *see* Environment Agency; Local authority air pollution control
Ozone
depletion 2.9.1, 3.5.3
protection of layer, Vienna Convention 3.5.2, 3.5.3
time-span for control 3.5.3
effects 10.11.2
photochemical ozone creation potential (POCP) 6.5.6
pollution 2.8.3, 10.1.1, 10.2
reduction 10.7.1, 10.11.2
threshold limits 10.2
warning system 10.2

PFCs 3.8
Pact 3.2.2
Paper and pulp manufacture
control of 6.2.1
Particulates, *see* Fine particulates
Permit (CPC) 7.20.3
Permit (IPPC) 2.10, 6.26.2, 6.26.3
review 6.26.3
Permit trading 3.8.1
Petrol
see also Fuel; Vehicle
composition standard regulation 9.3, 9.4
lead content, *see* Lead
storage tank design 2.9.2
VOCs, *see* Volatile organic compounds
vapour recovery 2.9.2
exceptions 2.9.2
Phosphorous 6.2.4
Photochemical ozone creation potential (POCP) 6.5.6
Planning authority
Environment Agency, interface with 6.24
local authority air pollution control, interface with 7.19
NAQS obligations, and 10.12.7, 10.17
Framework guidance 10.17
Planning Inspectorate
appeals on IPC authorisations, etc, powers 6.15–6.15.5
'Polluter pays' principle 1.4.3, 1.4.4, 1.6.2, 3.2.4
origins and status of 3.2.4
Pollution
definition (Geneva Convention) 3.4.1
Power station
see also Fuel
emission limits 2.3.1, 10.11.4
Precautionary principle 1.6.3, 3.2.4
Printing and coating processes 7.2.1
Private nuisance 4.3, 4.4
see also Rylands v Fletcher
adoption of nuisance, failure to abate, etc 4.3.6, 4.4.4
balance of interests 4.3.2
basis for action 4.3
continuing 'state of affairs' 4.3, 4.3.4
damage 4.3.8
caused prior to acquisition 4.3.5, 4.3.6
foreseeable losses 4.3.8
remoteness 4.3.8
showing 4.3.4, 4.3.8
damages 4.5.1, 4.5.2

Private nuisance – *cont*
defences 4.4
consent 4.4.4
planning permission, and changes to area 4.4.3, 4.4.4
prescriptive right 4.4.1
statutory authority, acting under 4.4.2
trespasser 4.3.6
defendant to action 4.3.6
intention of, relevance 4.3.3
non-delegable duties 4.3.6
injunction 4.5.2
forms of 4.5.2
suspension of 4.5.2
landlord, position of 4.3.7
meaning 4.3
negligence, *see* Negligence
one incident 4.3
plaintiff for action 4.3.5
proof 4.3.4
amassing evidence for 4.3.4
actual damage 4.3.5
'reasonable' use notion 4.3.2
remedial interference 4.3.1
self-help, circumstances for 4.5.3
strict liability 4.6, 4.6.1
development of 4.6
types 4.5.1
Process, prescribed, *see* Integrated Pollution Control (IPC); Local authority air pollution control (LAAPC)
Guidance notes 6.6, 7.7
smoke control exemption 8.7.1
Prohibition notice
Environment Agency 6.13
local authority 7.12
Public authority
information duty 2.8
legal right against under EC law 1.10.2
Public health law 5.1, *see also* Statutory nuisance
Public nuisance
criminal proceedings for 4.2
injunction to prevent 4.2
meaning 4.2
tort damages for 4.2

Quality standards (air) 2.5, 6.3.2, *see also* Air quality; BATNEEC
Quarry 8.7.2

Rail transport 10.12.4
emissions from engines 8.7.3, 8.8.2
Register 6.19, 7.16, 10.4.5, *see also* Information
Reporting levels
chemical emissions 6.21
Research 2.8
air pollution, local authority powers 10.4.1
forests 2.8.1
Geneva Convention, feature of 3.4.1
smoke control exemption 8.7.6
Revocation
IPC authorisation, of, *see* Environment Agency
LAAPC authorisation, of 7.6, 7.10
Ringelmann Chart 8.2
Rio Conference (UNCED) 3.2.4, 3.6.1, 3.7
Road
building, local management of 10.16.2
charging scheme 10.18.2, 10.19
highway 5.4
Authority 10.14.6
resurfacing 8.2.2
Royal Commission on Environmental Pollution 6.1, 7.1.1, 8.6
Rubber processes 7.2.1
Rylands v Fletcher 4.6.1–4.6.8
act of God 4.6.6
common benefit/act of plaintiff 4.6.4
consent of plaintiff 4.6.3
contributory negligence 4.6.3
damage 4.6, 4.6.1, 4.6.8
defences 4.6.2–4.6.8
economic loss 4.6.1
foreseeability 4.6.1, 4.6.5, 4.6.6
interest in land, whether necessary 4.6.2
natural and non-natural uses 4.6.1
'no fault' 4.6, 4.6.1
personal injury 4.6.2
plaintiff's own act 4.6.4
pure economic loss 4.6.2
rule 4.6.1

Rylands v Fletcher – cont
statutory authority, acting under 4.6.7
third party, act of 4.6.5

Scotland 10.8.1
Environmental Protection Agency (SEPA) 10.8.1, 10.8.4, 10.8.5, 10.8.12
consultation with, by Secretary of State 10.8.1
NAQS, account of 10.10.3, 10.12.5
Ship
dark smoke, grit, dust emissions 8.7.4, 8.7.5, 8.8.2, 8.8.5
vessel 8.7.4
Slaughtering 8.2.2
Smells
nuisance, as 5.2.1, *see also* Private nuisance; Statutory nuisance
odour detection threshold (ODT) 6.5.6
odour recognition threshold (ORT) 6.5.6
Smog 8.1.1, 10.1.1, 10.6.1
meaning and monitoring of 10.7
sources 8.4.3, 10.7.1, 10.7.2
summer 10.11.1
winter 10.11.2
Smoke
air quality limits 10.2
control areas 8.5, 10.12.7
adaptation of fireplaces and grants 8.5.4
administrative provisions 8.8
authorisation of court for building work 8.8.4
company officer liability 8.8.3
confirmation of, by DoE 8.5.1
DoE default powers 8.9
declaration procedure 8.5.1
enforcement and penalties 8.8
entry and inspection powers 8.8.5
exemption of fireplace 8.5.2
exemptions for research etc 8.7.6
local authority boundaries 8.8.5
objection procedure 8.5.1
powers extended to local authority 8.8.5
prescribed processes 8.7.1
prohibitions in 8.5.2
publicity requirements 8.5.1
smokeless (authorised) fuel 8.5.2
special cases 8.7
suspension 8.5.2
unauthorised fuel, use, supply etc 8.5.3
dark smoke emission inventory 10.6.1
dark smoke emission prohibition 8.2, 8.3.1, 8.5.4
defences 8.2, 8.2.2
definitions for 8.2.1
exemptions 8.2.1, 8.2.2
fixed boiler 8.2
industrial or trade premises 8.2.2
industrial plant 8.2, 8.2.1
furnaces, from 8.3
index, drop in 8.6
legislation to control 8.1 *et seq*
Ringelmann Chart 8.2
Smoke quality standards 2.5
Smuggling
banned substances 2.9.1, 3.5.3
Sodium dioxide 2.3.1, 3.4.2
Soot, *see* Fine particulates
Statutory duty, breach of 4.7
defences 4.7
negligence, relevance of 4.7
Statutory nuisance 5.1–5.3
abatement notice 5.3.1, 5.3.2
appeal, grounds and costs 5.3.3, 5.3.5
appeal, failure to make 5.3.4
'best practicable means' defence 5.3.4
copies 5.3.5
error in 5.3.3
failure to comply 5.3.4, 5.3.5, 5.3.6
offence 5.3.4
'reasonable excuse' defence 5.3.4
service 5.3.2
civil and criminal law elements 5.1
criminal proceedings 5.3.5, 5.3.7
compensation order 5.3.7
court for proceedings
High Court 5.3.6
magistrates' court 5.3.1, 5.3.5, 5.3.7–5.3.9
definition 5.2

Statutory nuisance – *cont*
definition – *cont*
exclusions 5.2.1
IPC/LAAPC, relation with 5.2.1
injunction, availability of 5.3.6
'nuisance' 5.2.2, 5.3.1, 5.3.3
origins of 5.1
'person aggrieved' 5.3.8
'person responsible' 5.3.2
more than one 5.3.5, 5.3.7
'prejudicial to health' 5.2.2, 5.3.1, 5.3.3
'premises' 5.2, 5.2.2
private complaint of 5.3.7, 5.3.8
contravention of order, offence 5.3.8
notice to defendant 5.3.8
order by magistrates 5.3.8, 5.3.9
procedure (local authority) 5.3.1–5.3.6
act outside own area 5.3.5
supplementary provisions 5.3.5
remedies 5.3.6
scope 5.2.2
Stubble burning 5.4
byelaws/Regulations 5.4
exemptions 5.4.1
NUF Code 5.4
offence 5.4, 5.4.1
Subsidiarity 1.6.5
Substance, prescribed, *see* Integrated Pollution Control (IPC); Local authority air pollution control (LAAPC)
Sulphur
content of fuels 2.5.1, 9.4.1, 10.7.1
oxides and compounds, prescribed substances 6.2.4
Sulphur dioxide
see also Smoke
air quality limits
EC 2.5, 8.10, 10.2
NAQS objectives/thresholds 10.8.13, 10.9.1, 10.10.3, 10.11.4
proposed (EC) 10.3
UK 10.2, 10.7.1
IPC requirements 6.6.2
monitoring of levels 10.6
prescription of 6.2.4
reporting levels 6.21
smoke from combustion plant, in 8.4.3
statistics 10.12.1
vehicle emissions 9.2, *see also* Vehicles
Sulphur hexafluoride 3.8, 6.2.4
Suspended particulate matter, *see* Smoke
Sustainable development principle 1.6.1, 3.2.4

Tar and bitumen processes 7.2.1
Thresholds for pollutants
alert thresholds 2.6, 10.3, 10.6.2
NAQS 10.9.1
Timber processes 7.2.1
Tort 4.2, 4.3, 4.8
Trade secret 8.8, 10.4.1
Traffic
see also Transport; Vehicles
bus/cycle lanes 10.1.2, 10.13.2, 10.18.2
management
Guidance 10.8.9, 10.9.1, 10.16
local programmes 10.11.1
monitoring and restrictions 10.18.2
parking 10.1.2, 10.18.2, 10.19
reduction targets 10.1.3
regulation order 10.1.2
smog creation 8.4.3, 10.7.1, 10.7.2
Training
employees 6.4
Transboundary pollution 3.2.4, 3.4, 3.5
local solutions, effect of 3.4
regional nature of sources 3.5
regulation of, range of 3.4
Transport 10.12.4, 10.12.7, 10.12.8
see also Vehicles
'green', encouragement of 10.12.8, 10.13.2, 10.16.1
public, use of 10.12.8, 10.16.2, 10.18.2
Treaty law 3.1, 3.2.2, *see also* International law
Treaty of Rome, *see* European Community
Trespasser 4.3.6
Type approval of vehicles 9.8.3, 9.8.4, 9.9
EC Certificate of Conformity 9.8.4, 9.9.1

UN Charter 3.2.2
UN Conference on Environment and Development, *see* Rio Conference
UN Environment Programme 3.5.2
USA
  emission trading 3.8.1
  position on environment 3.6, 3.7
  Toxics Release Inventory (TRI) 6.21
  vehicle emission test parameters 9.1

Urban environmental management 10.12.7

Variation
  authorisation (IPC), of, *see* Environment Agency
Vegetable matter processes 7.2.1, 7.4.2
Vehicle
  ban on 10.18.2
  catalytic converters 9.6
  charging scheme 10.18.2, 10.19
  commercial 2.7.2
  construction 9.5, 9.8, 9.9
  diesel 10.7.1, *see also* Diesel
  emissions 2.5.1, 2.5.2, 2.7, 3.7, 9.6–9.9
    cars and light vans, EC phased reduction 9.6
    categories of vehicle 2.7.2
    control difficulties 9.1
    damage or injury, causing 9.9
    EC standards apply 9.1
    limits 9.6 *et seq*
    monitoring, *see* Monitoring of air pollution
    NAQS, and 10.11, 10.12.2
    offences 10.18
    problem of 9.2
    smog induced by 8.4.3, 10.7.1, 10.11.3
    statistics 9.2
    Table of requirements 9.9
    UK legislation 9.8, 9.8.3, 9.8.5, 9.9
    VOCs, *see* Volatile organic compounds
  exhaust construction 9.5
  fuel composition 9.3, 9.4
    control powers of authorities 9.3
    EC obligations 2.7.2, 9.4
    lead content of petrol 2.7.2, 4.8.2
    NAQS, and 10.11.1
    regulation of 9.4
    sulphur content 2.5.1, 8.4.2, 8.10, 9.4.1, 10.3
  goods vehicles 9.8.2, 9.8.3, 9.8.5, 9.8.6, 9.9
  offences, non-compliant vehicle 9.8, 10.8.7, 10.18
    fixed penalty 10.8.6, 10.18.1
  passenger cabs 2.7.2
  regulatory powers
    general 9.8
    proposals 10.8.7
    traffic management 10.1.2, 10.13.2, 10.16
  stationary, requirements 9.9.2, 10.8.7, 10.18
  testing
    EC type approval, for 9.9.1
    fuel 9.3
    goods vehicles 9.8.2, 9.8.5
    MOT 9.8.1
    road-side, powers 9.8.5, 10.8.7, 10.12.3, 10.18
  tractors 2.7.2, 9.9
  type approval system 9.8.3, 9.8.4, 9.9
    EC Certificate of Conformity 9.8.4, 9.9.1
  'unroadworthy condition', in, sale etc 9.8.6
  use, curb needed 10.1.1, 10.6, 10.13.2
Vessel, *see* Ship
Vienna Convention 3.5.2, 3.5.3
  see also Ozone
  Montreal Protocol 3.5.3
Volatile organic compounds (VOCs) 2.9.2, 3.4.2
  see also Ozone
  inventory of emissions 10.6
  petrol storage and loading, limits 9.7
  reporting levels 6.21
  statistics 10.12.1
  vehicle emissions 9.2, 9.6, 9.7

Waste
disposal and recycling control 6.2.1, 6.6.1, 7.2.1
hazardous 2.4.2
incineration of, *see* Incineration
management systems 2.10
Waste derived fuels
use of 2.4
Waste oil
burning process 7.4
White Paper, 'This Common Inheritance' 10.7.1